The SANDERS PRICE GUIDE TO AUTOGRAPHS

4th Edition

THE WORLD'S LEADING AUTOGRAPH PRICING AUTHORITY

George Sanders, Helen Sanders, and Ralph Roberts

ALEXANDER Books

The Leading Autograph Reference Publisher ™

Publisher: Ralph Roberts
Vice-President/Publishing: Pat Hutchison Roberts

Cover Design: **WorldComm**®

Executive Editor: Vivian Terrell

Editors: Helen Sanders, George Sanders, Pat Roberts, Ralph Roberts, Vivian Terrell,
    Gayle Graham

Interior Design and Electronic Page Assembly: **WorldComm**®

Printed in the United States of America

10 9 8 7 6 5 4 3 2
Fourth Edition, Second Printing

ISBN 1-57090-032-9

Library of Congress Catalog Card Number: 96-078803

The authors and publisher have made every effort in the preparation of this book to ensure the accuracy of the information. However, the information in this book is sold without warranty, either express or implied. Neither the authors nor Alexander Books will be liable for any damages caused or alleged to be caused directly, indirectly, incidentally, or consequentially by the information in this book.

The opinions expressed in this book are solely those of the authors and are not necessarily those of Alexander Books.

Trademarks

Names of products mentioned in this book known to be or that are suspected of being trademarks or service marks are capitalized. Use of a product or service name in this book should not be regarded as affecting the validity of any trademark or service mark.

Alexander Books—a division of Creativity, Inc.—is a full-service publisher located at 65 Macedonia Road, Alexander NC 28701. Phone (704) 252-9515 or (704) 255-8719 fax or **ralph@abooks.com**. Dealer inquiries welcome.

Internet web sites: **http://www.autograph-book.com** and **http://www.abooks.com**

Contents

Section I: INFORMATION

1 THE FUTURE OF AUTOGRAPHS by Chuck McKeen 15

2 ADVENTURES IN AUTOGRAPH COLLECTING by Roy Deeley 25

3 DREAM AUTOGRAPHS by George Sanders and Ralph Roberts 39

4 AUTOGRAPHS OF THE OLD WEST by Michael Minor and Larry Vrazalik 43

5 PHILOGRAPHY JOINS PHILATELY by George Sanders 69

6 THE TOP 100! by George and Helen Sanders 155

7 THE WAR BETWEEN THE STATES by Michael J. Masters, M.D. 161

8 THE U.A.C.C. by Bob Erickson　　181

9 OLD VERSUS HISTORIC by Stuart Lutz and John Reznikoff　　183

10 P.A.D.A The Professional Autograph Dealers Association　　187

Section II: PRICES

11 HOW TO USE THIS PRICE GUIDE by Helen Sanders　　191

PRICES　　201

Section III: FACSIMILES

FACSIMILES   509

Section IV: BIBLIOGRAPHY

BIBLIOGRAPHY   563

Section V: DEALERS

DEALERS   567

A collector for almost 70 years, the late Charles Hamilton was acknowledged worldwide as the leading expert on autographs, their authenticity, and rarity. He was the author of over a dozen books, most of them concerning autographs. His impact on the autograph field has been immense and lasting. We are proud to respectfully salute his considerable accomplishments in the autograph world and regret his recent passing.

PREFACE

by Charles Hamilton

I said it for the third edition and I'll say it again. Throw out your other price guides on autographs! This one is the best. It is the most complete and the most accurate, nothing less than the philographic Baedeker. It is without equal. My own copy is almost worn out. *In* fact, if there is a prize for the most tatterdemalion copy, I herewith enter mine into the competition.

One of the most *intriguing* things about the Sanders price guide is that it casts light on the autographic values of people you never heard of and makes you *want* to look at their handwriting. But the best thing about it is that it's a great browsing book. A book to keep at your bedside. Better than Montaigne, and more illuminating. I never pick it up without adding to my fund of autographic knowledge.

If I had owned a book like this fifty years ago, it would have changed the course of my life. I would have wound up today not just older and wiser, but smarter and richer.

I am often asked by young collectors and dealers for my groat's worth of advice. Here it is: Read and study this book.

December 24, 1913—December 11, 1996

7

About This Price Guide

This is our fifth autograph price guide. The first two were published by the Wallace-Homestead Book Company of Radnor, Pennsylvania—owned by Capital Cities/ABC. These are **The Price Guide to Autographs** 1st and 2nd editions, and were released in 1988 and 1991 respectively. Our third price guide, **The 1994 Sanders Price Guide to Sports Autographs**, was published by Scott Publishing, the famous stamp guide people, in 1994. The fourth book (and the 3rd edition of this compendium of general prices) was **The 1994-95 Sanders Price Guide to Autographs**. Our fifth price guide you now hold in your hands, **The Sanders Price Guide to Autographs, 4th edition**.

The autograph field has grown dramatically in the last few years; just as our efforts in compiling the best price guides in the hobby have also expanded severalfold. This price guide reaches new heights of completeness with the most names and prices of any autograph price guide ever published. That's the good news.

The bad news is *this book*—even though it has more names and more prices than you've ever had in one convenient place before—*has no sports-related names or prices*. All sports material is now found in **The Sanders Price Guide to Sports Autographs**. We simply have too many names and prices to put everything into one volume any more. So, yes, you'll need both books, but these two volumes together give you over *eleven hundred* pages of the best information available in the world of autographs.

Acknowledgments

These are the splendid men and women (in alphabetical order) who have made the interesting hobby of auto-graph collecting one of the most rewarding experiences of our lives. They are, in varying degrees, responsible for the happi-ness and financial gains that make this never-ending pursuit such a truly exciting undertaking. In most cases this list includes personal friends, acquaintances, competitors, suppliers, mem-bers of the media, families members, and, most importantly, learned advisors. Not one forger or spin doctor is included.

Jon Allan
Bob Allen (*Antique Week*)
Allan Abrams (Toledo *Blade*)
Tim Anderson
Russell Atwood, *Arts & Entertainment*
Al Avalon, Hawaii
Jack L. Bacon
Edward Baig (*Business Week*)
Arbe Barais
Catherine Barnes
Robert F. Batchelder
Chris Bell, Midpoint
Mary A. Benjamin
Saimi Rote Bergmann (The Repository, Canton, OH)
Jim Berland
Barbara Bigham (*Autograph Times*, Phoenix, AZ)
Norman Boas
Warren Boroson (Hackensack *Sunday Record*)

Harvey Brandwein
Fremont Brown, Asheville
Brenda Burch (WLOS-TV, Asheville, NC)
Walter Burks
Carol Cain (Mobile Alabama *Register*)
Dr. Ronald R. Caldwell
Paul Carr, VP UACC
Dwight Chapin (San Fran-cisco *Examiner*)
John Crudele (New York *Post* Syndicate)
Duane Dancer (KLIF, Dallas)
Roy and Mies Deeley (England)
Suzanne Dolezal (Detroit *Free Press*)
Amy Dunkin (BusinessWeek)
Sophie Dupre (England)
Carla Eaton
Robert "Bob" Eaton

Tom Eisaman
Bob Erickson (Pres., UACC)
Nancy Fraser, Midpoint
    Trade Books
Clifford O. Feingold, D.D.S.
Phillip Fiorini (*USA Today*)
Cathy & Roger E. Gilchrist
Bud Glick
Anita Gold, syndicated
    columnist
Cy Gold, Ace Enterprises
Miegan & Chandler Gordon
Marilyn Greenwald (Boys
    Life magazine)
Gil and Karen Griggs
Jim Hagar
Diane Hamilton
Donn Harmon
Gary Hendershott
Stephen Hisler
Jeanne Hoyt
Jaime Hubbard, *Financial
    Post*, Toronto
A. Bruce Hunt III
Christopher C. Jaeckel
Betty, Susan & Greg
    Johnson
Eric Kampmann, Midpoint
    Trade Books
Eileen Keiter
Sandy Kenyon, KQNA,
    Arizona
Kristin & Michael Kern
    (Oregon)
Susan and Peter Kerville
    (Australia)
Carol King (Asheville,NC)
Stephen Koschal (Florida)
Pierce A. Koslosky, Jr.
    (Omaha,Neb.)
Gail Kump, Midpoint
Neale Lanigan
Maggie Lauterer (WLOS-
    TV,Asheville,N.C.)
John Laurence (Florida)

Kenneth R. Laurence
    (Florida)
Gary & Connie Lawrence (IL)
Alan Levi
Martin Levy
Stephen Levy
William Linehan
Jerry D. Litzel (Ames, Iowa)
James Lowe
David H. Lowenherz
George S. Lowry
Bill Luetge
Joe and Scott Lusk (TN)
Bill Maloney (Software
    Solutions, Asheville NC)
Cathy Marshall (CNN News)
J.L. Mashburn
Dr. Michael J. & Patrice
    Masters
Frank & Ruth Ann Matthews
Rebecca May *curiocity for
    kids*
Ann McCutchan (Gannett
    News Service)
Peggy & George McGill
Pam & Chuck McKeen
Beth McLeod (South Palm
    Beach *County Living*)
Harold P. Merry
C.J. Middendorf (San Diego,
    CA.)
Bonni J. Miller (Goldmine
    magazine)
George Robert Minkoff
Michael Minor
Gil Moody
Stuart J. Morrissey
Howard S. Mott
Matthew Mrowicki and the
    CACC
J.B. Muns
Harry Nadley, Phila.
Donn Noble
William J. Novick
Karen & James Oleson

Nancy Page
Basil "Bill" Panagopulos
Beverly Parkhurst, Dallas
Jerry E. Patterson
Louise Pennisi
Cordelia & Tom Platt
Robert L. Polk
Talmage Powell
Angelica Giesser & Udo
    Prager (Germany)
ProComm Studio Services
    (Arden, N.C.)
Stephen S. Raab
Larry Rafferty
Celeste & Ray Rast
Diana J. Rendell
Annette Reynolds, Baton
    Rouge *State-Times*
Tracy & John Reznikoff
Brian Riba
Stanley J. Richmond
Pat Roberts
Hinda Rose (England)
Sheila & Rhodes T. Rumsey
Bill Safka
Joseph R. Sakmyster
Rebecca & Stephen G.
    Sanders
Dana and George M.
    "Sandy" Sanders
Richard Saunders
Todd Savage, Chicago
    Tribune
Harris Schaller, UACC
David Schulson
Gemma Sica
Ann & Louis Sica, Jr.
Kaye & Merv Slotnick
James Smalldon
Dr. Leslie Smart
Pat & Jim Smith (Wells,
    Maine)
Dr. Lewis C. Sommerville
William W. Stanhope
Christophe Stickel

Jim Stinson
Gerard A.J. Stodolski
Georgia Terry
Bob Tollett
E.N. Treverton
Louis Trotter
Wallace Turner (New York
    Times)
Larry Vrzalik
Susan Sanders Wadopian
Joan, Erin & Lael Wadopian
Joel Sanders Wadopian
John Waggoner (*USA
    Today*)
Dewey Webb (Phoenix,
    Arizona *New Times*)
Daniel Weinberg
Bob Wieselman, UpTime
    Computers, Asheville
Michelle and Tom Williams
John Wilson (England)
Al Wittnebert (Treasurer,
    UACC)
Chris Wloszczyna (*USA
    Today*)
Jaye Wright (*Florida Today*)
Dr. Ellis "Bill" Zussman
    (Wisconsin)

A special thanks to all the members of our *country* friendly Enka, North Carolina Post Office (28728) including Postmistress Betty Joan Rice, lovely Cheryl Eakes, Cyndy Evans, and the phantom of our post office, seldom actually sighted, Ken Singleton. They haven't lost or misplaced a single treasured autograph (incoming or outgoing) or a copy of our various Price Guides in 20 years. Their courteous and efficient service to Autograph House encourages us to believe that the United States Postal Service is the finest of its kind in the world!

Above, George Sanders, author Pat Conroy, and bookmeister Chan Gordon at a book signing held in Chan's antiquarian book collector's haven, the Captain's Bookshelf in Asheville, North Carolina. Below, Helen Sanders is pictured with Conroy.

The SANDERS 4 4th Edition

PRICE GUIDE TO AUTOGRAPHS

THE WORLD'S LEADING AUTOGRAPH PRICING AUTHORITY

Section I:
INFORMATION

Doctor Benjamin Spock, famed pediatrician and author, signs for George Sanders.

THE FUTURE OF AUTOGRAPHS

by Chuck McKeen

The dawn of a new century hovers just ahead, and the growth that awaits this avocation of ours truly boggles the mind.

Autograph collecting is already the hobby of the 21st Century. There are millions and millions of us, each different in what we collect, each with different goals. Each made happier by the acquisitions which push our own particular buttons.

Just make no mistake: the numbers are really that impressive. Millions of autograph collectors are out there, as active as each cares to be, only a handful really aware of the fact that there is an "organized" hobby. Most couldn't care less about that aspect of autographs. They don't care to be embroiled in the endless controversies about who is a true "Philographer" and who isn't. They just want to have fun and collect what they enjoy.

What connects us all is that we are, for whatever reason, enchanted by those snippets of writing: "To Lou: My best wishes. Glynnis O'Connor" Lou's remembrance is on a torn piece of notebook paper. But he looks at it and recalls that gorgeous blonde actress, and it makes his day a little lighter.

Another buys a book on the life of Albert Einstein, finding

inside a browning 1930s business card with notes on the book, and signed "Albert Einstein. Berlin. 1931." It's a true story. It happened just that way, and now my friend who found that business card has a handsomely matted and framed autograph and photo of the great scientist hanging on his office wall. He is now an autograph collector. You couldn't get that signature away from him if you offered a thousand dollars. I know. I tried.

There are those who will say this man is not truly an autograph collector. Well, I don't know what else to call him. He likes that autograph. He admires that man. He enjoys telling the story of how he found the book and the card inside. And, if another autograph of another person he admires should come within his grasp—well, you can bet Albert will have a partner hanging nearby.

I have another friend who is retired and who collects autographed photos of actresses and models. Another who collects autographed magazine covers of sports figures, and one who collects signed business cards.

I turned the guy who purchased our house into an autograph collector. He has a beautiful selection of signed photos of San Francisco Giants and San Francisco 49ers. He loves them and they look very nice on the walls of the family room of their home.

I know an old Brooklyn Dodger fan who collects just that—BROOKLYN Dodger autographs. He couldn't care less about the Los Angeles Dodgers. He just wants those guys who competed with that beautiful "Brooklyn" attached to their records.

Of course there is also the collector friend who has been trying to find a Wyatt Earp for years. He wouldn't mind adding brothers Morgan and Virgil to his collection either. An Ike Clanton signature would probably mean a divorce in his

Pam and Chuck McKeen and their twin daughters Hayley and Marin with George Sanders during the author's 1990 visit in Oregon..

family because I'm sure the wife would not be able to bear so much of his financial affection going into a framed autograph.

It goes on and on. This hobby of ours is big business. That word "business" offends a lot of people who are involved in autographs. However, there is no way to have the hobby without having the business. There are a lot of dealers out there. There are a lot more collectors.

There's nothing wrong with the business side. There's nothing wrong with the collecting side. They each need the other. The fact is that most dealers are also collectors. That is the way virtually all of them got going, and most still collect.

What we all need to understand is that it's a big world, this field of autograph collecting... big and going to get one whole

lot bigger. There's room for each and every collector and their particular viewpoints and passions. The trick is to not get the hobby all messed up with the infighting, bickering, and back-stabbing that seems inevitable in any enterprise that grows as fast and as large as we've seen happen to autographs over the past 20 years.

Good Things Happening

There are, indeed, so many good things happening. We now have two monthly publications devoted solely to the entire autograph field.

The information available in *The Pen and Quill* and *Autograph Times* is so valuable to all of us. The fact that these exist is vivid testimony to just how far our hobby has come.

There are wonderful address lists available which direct hobbyists to potential contact with thousands upon thousands of celebrities in every field imaginable. True, there is not as much chance for legitimate response from celebrities through the mail today as there was 20 years ago. However, we now have addresses for 10 times as many celebrities as we could find 20 years ago. So there are a lot of people who can be contacted today and who will respond with legitimate autographs to a well-worded request.

The avenues for reaching celebrities and dealers have also multiplied with the advent over the past few years of really professionally done shows and antique sales. Some of the best of these take place on the west coast, but they are spreading to the East and Midwest.

Ray and Sharon Courts from Florida have set standards with their Hollywood Collector Shows that aren't easily matched by other promoters. They began this enterprise in the Beverly Garland Hotel in North Hollywood, California. It

took a lot of work and four shows a year but the Courts have put together a formula that has really worked.

The fact is the Courts's weekend event at the Beverly Garland is an autograph show. Each show features an incredible assortment of celebrities, most in the entertainment field. All are there to sign autographs, and most do so for a very reasonable price.

In addition there are all sorts of dealers of memorabilia around the Beverly Garland's sprawling facility. A good percentage of these specialize in autographs.

Ray and Sharon have also begun their highly successful shows in New Jersey and Chicago, and have both events following the same pattern as they set in North Hollywood.

Another avenue that has helped the growth of autographs has been the Antique Expo shows produced by Chris and Chuck Palmer of Portland, Oregon. Their ten and more shows a year are highly anticipated in Portland, San Francisco and Tacoma, Washington. Each draws a handful of autograph dealers and an ever-growing number of collectors.

The interest in autographs at the Palmer shows has been growing rapidly. Much of it has been from people who had no interest in the field before, but like most everyone they admire certain celebrities and have found autographs a pleasant way to express that admiration.

No one can ignore the success and growth of shows in the Florida area, either. Some of the most successful "autograph" shows that the hobby has ever seen take place there. Al Wittnebert and Stephen Koschal have been the men most associated with the top-notch efforts that have gone on in that state and dealers clamor to get tables, but there is more demand than tables available.

The more success events of this type have, the more

shows there will be... success draws imitators. If the new productions truly emulate the ones that already exist, it will mean many more availabilities for collectors and for dealers.

While on the subject of what's happening in this rapidly-growing hobby, here are thoughts on some other aspects of the game:

Inscriptions

One of the thorny areas of the hobby of autograph collecting comes in the form of inscriptions. You know: "To Mabel. God Bless You. Arthur Godfrey." Some people swear by them. Others swear at them.

We know collectors who don't care if an item is inscribed: some actually feel better about the item if it is made out to a particular individual.

Others, of course, vastly prefer that such sentiments not be involved in their signed items.

Like everything else in this hobby, it obviously is a matter of preference. However, in at least some situations that addition of an inscription has to be looked upon as a plus for most any autographed item.

In many cases an inscription adds credibility to the authenticity of the signature. And certainly an inscription made out to a prominent figure would add value and appeal to most any autograph. Among the highly-sought collections are those from players, crew, or officials involved in the entertainment industry.

These are people who were right there on the scene and obviously received their autographs right in person. There can be little better provenance provided than the fact that a particular collection was obtained by a co-worker of the stars.

And, in the end, there is the argument that if we collect

the handwriting of celebrities, then the more handwriting provided the more attractive the item should be.

Understand, this is not intended to convince anyone of the legitimacy of collecting inscribed autographs. Everyone should collect what they enjoy. However, it doesn't seem reasonable that inscriptions should receive that contempt that occurs from so many. Like anything else in the hobby, there are good points and bad points. You should weigh both.

To out of hand dismiss inscribed autographs can be a serious mistake. The fact is, they can be among the best bargains in the hobby and ignoring any autograph just because it is inscribed seems to be a serious mistake.

In-person Autographs

A legitimate autograph is just that—it was written by that person. It doesn't matter if it was gotten in person, or through the mail, or by someone who is unknown.

"In-person" is a wonderful title to affix to a particular autograph. However, it is only as meaningful as you determine it should be.

Its "in-person" status really shouldn't determine the value of an autograph. Whatever the item is, it has a price that should reflect the value... the value should reflect more than the circumstances under which the autograph was obtained.

At the same time, it has to be explained that virtually 100 percent of the autographs obtainable from the "hot" celebrities of today come only through in-person contact. So now we move from the area of "in-person" determining the value, to the old laws of supply and demand.

Only so many autographs are possible from the in-person sources. Celebrities are seen on a hit-and-miss basis. Some-

 **The Sanders Price Guide to Autographs**

times they are readily available for autographs. Other times they are not.

With this taken into consideration, "in-person" becomes more understandable as a description of autographs from these celebrities. However, the price is set more because autographs from these people are simply difficult to get, not because of the in-person factor. The two go together, but we sometimes get mixed up as to the true determining factors that result in price.

Entertainment and Sports Autographs

For whatever reason, a percentage of the "organized hobby" of autographs has always looked down on those who collect autographs from movie and TV stars, or from sports stars.

Oh, they have always allowed that you can collect Humphrey Bogart or Walt Disney. Elizabeth Taylor is a "legitimate" autograph to collect, many of these folk intone. Babe Ruth, of course, is allowable. So would be Lou Gehrig or Ty Cobb. Yes, there are names that are collectable, but they are few and far between.

Well, the fact is, there are way more people out there collecting in these areas than there are in any other auto-graph field. So, while these self-appointed powers that be attempt to limit the "legitimacy" of autograph collecting, one would be foolish to pay much attention to them.

Have fun. Collect what you wish. Enjoy your hobby. It is so vast that most of the fools out there trying to convince everyone that they know better than you what should be collected have no idea how many people are enthralled by this field.

Forget them. Don't listen to them. The legitimacy of collecting is decided by the collector. Not by self-titled, so-call *experts*.

As God directed man: go forth and multiply. That

directive certainly seems to be taken to heart by the autograph fraternity. We are multiplying rapidly, and there seems no end ahead to this incredible growth.

Unless we listen to the doomsayers and screw it up.

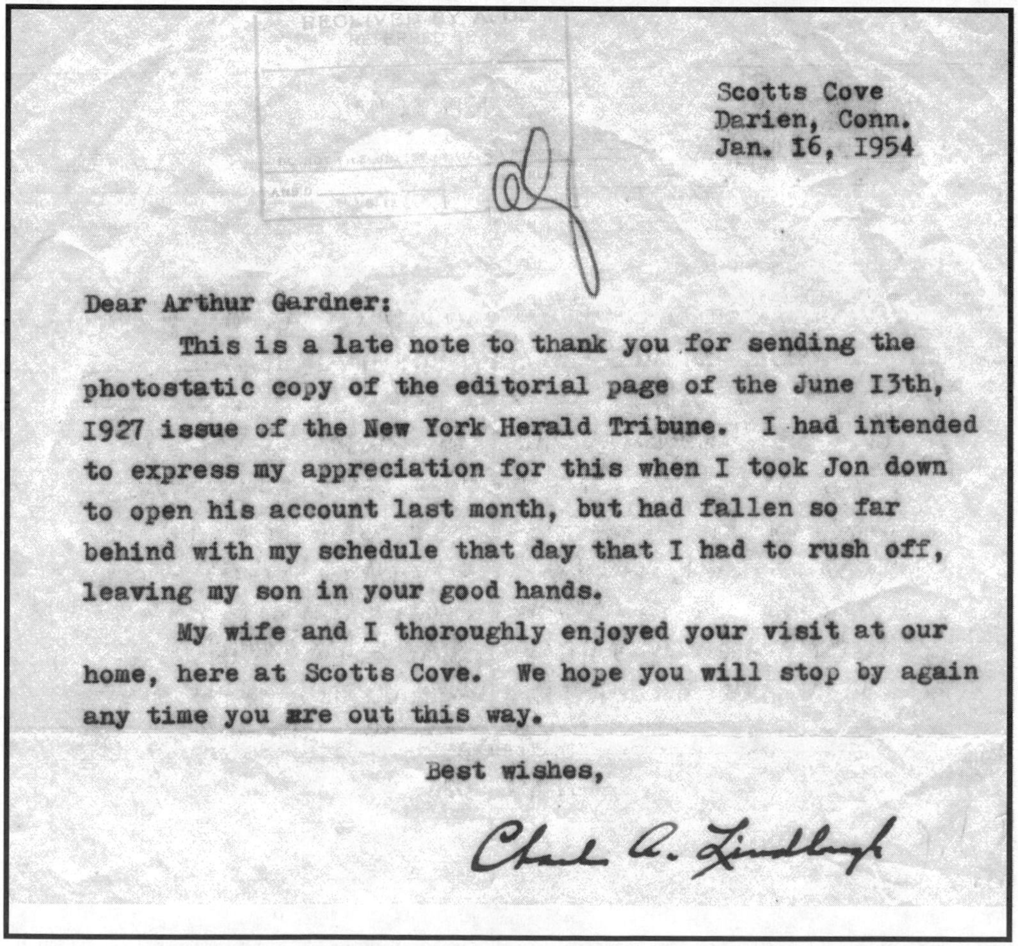

Scotts Cove
Darien, Conn.
Jan. 16, 1954

Dear Arthur Gardner:

This is a late note to thank you for sending the photostatic copy of the editorial page of the June 13th, 1927 issue of the New York Herald Tribune. I had intended to express my appreciation for this when I took Jon down to open his account last month, but had fallen so far behind with my schedule that day that I had to rush off, leaving my son in your good hands.

My wife and I thoroughly enjoyed your visit at our home, here at Scotts Cove. We hope you will stop by again any time you are out this way.

Best wishes,

Charles A. Lindbergh

Always look through those bundles of old letters. You might just find a true treasure like this letter signed by Colonel Charles A. Lindbergh ("Lucky Lindy"), the first man to fly solo across the Atlantic.

Long before actor Robert Stack (right) portrayed crimebuster Elliot Ness or hosted "Unsolved Mysteries," he was giving baseball advice to author George Sanders in Hollywood.

ADVENTURES IN AUTOGRAPH COLLECTING

The View From England by Roy Deeley

My first interest in collecting autographs, was not film stars or famous people. At the age of ten I was given a part in the great Pageant of Birmingham and played the part of a prehistoric boy. The pageant was a history of Britain from prehistoric times through to the Battle of Crecy, and on to the reign of Queen Victoria. The actors were just local people, but I remember looking at all the principles as stars and so had to have their autographs.

That whet my interest in collecting autographs in my first

Roy, the Prehistoric Boy, gets his first signature.

autograph book, which my father bought me. Later, the great cowboy, Tom Mix, came to appear on the Birmingham Hippodrome, and I stood at the stage door well before his show started. Seeing the stage doorkeeper's office unattended, I slipped by and went down some stairs, then across a darkened stage and came to the dressing rooms. There I saw the name *Tom Mix*, and I knocked on the door.

A voice said, "Yes, who's that?" I opened the door, and there was the great man sitting at his mirror. He just looked at me, and I said sheepishly, "please, can I have your autograph?"

"Sure," he said, and took my book. "What brought you here?" he asked. I told him I had slipped in from the stage door. He just looked at me, and at that moment I saw his gun holster on the back of his chair. I asked if I could see his gun, and I put my hand forward to the holster.

"Don't touch that son! It's loaded," he said, and he lifted it out to show me. I just thanked him and slipped back out of the stage door without giving the stage doorman a chance to ask me anything, and sped away as fast as I could with my treasure.

The only great disappointment was later when my autograph book was stolen and I lost the autograph I had personally gotten.

Stepping in Front of Royalty

The theft of my autograph book didn't deter me from collecting and so later the late Duke of Kent visited the Castle Bromwich Aircraft Company where they were making Spitfires and Lancaster Bombers.

I remember hiding in a doorway, and as he came past, I stepped out, and asked for his autograph. He paused for a moment, took my book, and signed it. Later that day I was

Roy Deeley, author George Sanders, and Mrs. Deeley together at the Deeley's lovely home in Guildford, England during the Sanders' 1995 tour of Europe.

hauled before the director and the police and was told quite firmly that you do not step in front of Royalty.

Later Winston Churchill visited the factory. This time I stood in the open in a line of workers eager to see him and as he passed me, I said, "Please can I have your autograph?"

This wonderful man stopped, looked down at me, and said, "I'm sorry, I can't." Those few words to me from this great man will be something I will treasure and always remember.

The Duke of Kent was killed in an air crash, and I sent the Duchess a photograph that had been taken at the works, which the works photographer had given me. She kindly wrote back thanking me for this photograph and sent one

that she said was the last photograph taken of him, and with it she enclosed a monogrammed card with her signature, signed *Marina*.

At this time I was around fourteen years old and was not scared of stepping in front of famous people to ask for an autograph. Eleanor Roosevelt visited the factory surrounded by the Press. I had the cheek to go into that pack and get close to Mrs. Roosevelt and ask for her signature. She was very annoyed with me and said, "No, I am talking to the press." Then all the pressmen grabbed me and threw me out. I later wrote her an apology and sent a photograph taken at the factory which she signed for me.

I found that Churchill's nurse lived quite near to me and went to see her. She sold me a fine photograph signed by him, one of his cigars, and a book of matches used by him. She also had a double pack of cards which were a gift to Churchill from Bernard Baruch, with his facsimile signature on them. Those I sold for her to members of the UACC.

Later I was working at a Pop concert where Paul McCartney came to collect an award. Luckily I was backstage, and Paul had a jug of beer in his hand. I offered him a few programmes to sign, and he said, "Hold my beer then." He took the programmes, signed them for me, then passed them to Linda to sign, and took back his drink. He really is a nice person to meet.

More Than Just Getting Signatures

Then came the moment when I realised there was more to collecting autographs than just getting signatures, and so I became interested in collecting more historical figures. Nelson has always been my hero, and I was determined to get something written by him. That is when I discovered my first dealer, Maggs Brothers. At that time there was quite a lot of his

material about because he was a prolific writer, like Napoleon, and this material could be gotten at reasonable prices.

Would you believe that I bought a Nelson letter with the signature cut off for just £5.00 from Maggs, but the content of the letter was wonderful? It was dated 1805, and at that time he was chasing the French fleet which led to the battle of Trafalgar.

Later I was to get a signature from that lovely lady, Winifred Myers, of Nelson to go with my letter. My collecting fever became stronger, and as the years went by, I bought letters and signed photographs of many great persons.

In those days, autograph collecting was not the frantic hobby it is now, and prices were affordable. With so many people getting into this hobby, you have to be a rich man these days to be able to buy historical letters. I've never been tempted to become a dealer because I think I would get letters and documents that I wouldn't want to part with. I do sometimes look through my collection and take things out that I don't feel I need any more, or perhaps I have gotten a better example of a particular person, and so enhance my collection.

Focus Your Collecting

Over the years I have made the mistake of collecting too widely. I would advise anyone first starting to pick two or three subjects that you want to collect. For instance, I like early English Royalty and also the period when Cromwell took the crown away from them. So I was pleased to be able to buy a document signed by Cromwell from an American dealer and felt pleased that I had brought it home to England where it belongs. I am now just Guardian of this document for the time that I live.

I have also an interest in Aviation, an interesting

subject, especially if you can get a relic to go with the autograph. I have an autograph of Louis Bleriot and a fragment of the covering of the plane in which he flew the channel. I also have the autograph of The Red Baron Richtofen and a fragment of the plane in which he was shot down. With the autograph of Graf Zeppelin I have a fragment of the Zeppelin bearing his name; so this makes collecting even more interesting and makes autographs look better framed together.

I have a water-stained photograph of Hitler taken out of the Berlin Bunker, but it has his clear handwriting and signature. It was signed to Hans Jung who married Traudl Jung the lady who was Hitler's secretary, and the secretary who typed Hitler's will. Hans Jung left the bunker soon after his marriage to go and serve at the front and soon after he was killed. He may have left this photo in the Bunker with his new wife when he left. It is in a poor state but a truly historic relic.

I admire Napoleon as much as I do Nelson, and so I have tried to make a collection of all his family, and then of all his marshals. The hardest to get was that of his mother, which I did eventually get and of his marshals. I am still looking for Marshal Lannes who was killed quite early, but since everything comes to he who waits, my set will be complete.

Fakes and Forgeries

As a true collector, I enjoy having my collection around me so that I can look at them from time to time. It is sad that some people go to auctions, buy great documents, and then hide them in a bank vault as an investment and they or no other person gets the pleasure of seeing them. It is also sad that many of the modern signatures are poor forgeries, and care needs to be taken when buying these signed photographs of today's

stars.

I was recently called to the British customs to look at about 200 photos of today's stars. They were all written with the same blue pen, even though these stars live miles apart. As I have little knowledge of these names or what their real signatures look like, I was not able to advise them, but my feeling was that they were all fakes. I later sent photocopies to reputable dealers, and they agreed with me.

These fakes seem to be flooding into the country from the USA, but it's good to know that the British Customs intend to put a stop to this. They will charge heavily, which will help to stop this trade of people ruining the autograph hobby. They hope to stop these fakes flowing into the country to be sold at film fairs to unsuspecting fans of the stars.

Content and Context

As you know it's not always the signature that is valuable, but also the content of a letter or document and their moment in history. I have the signatures of the Schneider trophy team, signed on the very day they won the trophy, but also on this page is the signature of the designer who was later to become more famous as the man who designed the Spitfire fighter plane, which was the plane that helped to win the Battle of Britain. His name R.J Mitchell, probably the rarest signature in aviation because I have never ever seen one in a catalogue or in an auction.

At the 50th Anniversary of that battle, I bid for a signed photograph of a Spitfire, which was supposed to be signed by all the battle of Britain pilots still surviving. I won this bid, and part of the prize was to be present at all these events and to be presented with the picture. So there I was, together with these men of history when the picture was presented. It had

just two signatures on it, and they apologised for not getting it fully signed. In my return speech, I said I was thrilled to get it and said when these great men have signed it, I would be so honoured because each one of them had given me a moment of their life. At that, Johnnie Johnson our great Air ace, got up, took me by the arm, led me to a table where I laid out the print, and he signed it. Then he called all of these other heroes to come and sign it for me. He then stood with me to have my photograph taken with him and called over the comedian Michael Bentine to join us. Bentine had served in the RAF in the war.

Great Moments

So these are the great moments of autograph collecting. When I look for content, I look at my Nelson letter which was written on the Victory 1805, when he was chasing the French fleet and read his words, "Grieved as I am by the information from General Breerton at St Lucia which deprived us of a battle...."

To actually hold the thoughts of a man as he sat writing in his cabin is really an exhilarating moment, which makes you want to know as much as you can about him.

I have a letter of the Duchess of Wellington where she was entertaining HM King George the fourth, and she talks of his bad manners at the table. She writes, "The eating and drinking of the king is perfectly monstrous, and two days ago he drank a very large jugful of Orangeade and not finding that to quench his thirst, which Orangeade never does, he drank a quart of Burton Ale right on top of it."

I have a short letter of Vaughan Williams, the composer, saying to the person who had written to him. "Sorry I do not give autographs." signed Vaughan Williams. What a joke!

When you read of Che Guevara, you would expect a large,

strong flowing hand. Instead his signature is minute. The letter I have he signed only "Che," so small—just not what you would expect.

You may wonder what this article is all about, well I am just trying to show that it's not just having great names, but the joy that can be had being a genuine collector.

I remember during the war reading an article about the young King Faisal the second, of Iraq. They called him the lonely king; so I wrote to him to ask if I could be his pen pal, and to my surprise he accepted, and we wrote several letters to each other right up to the time he was murdered. When he came to England I was invited to meet him at Grove Lodge, Winkfield in Berksire. I remember his coming into the room, and as he smiled, I noticed he had a brace on his top teeth. He sat and talked to me and then brought in his three Siamese cats, and we played on the floor with them. He told me that he was taking them back to Iraq, but he thought that the Gazelles at the bottom of his garden would kill them.

He asked me if I could find him a snowstorm paper-

S i r:

I refer to your letter of July 19 and regret to

inform you that my book '' La Guerra de Guerrillas ''

has only been published in Spanish.

Yours truly,

Com. Ernesto Che Guevara

Che Guevara's signature.

The Sanders Price Guide to Autographs

weight. I was able to find a very old victorian one, but the snow had slightly browned. I sent it to him when he returned to Iraq, and he wrote and told me that it reminded him of a sandstorm which they have in the desert there. Later he sent me packets of dates and a fine photograph which he had signed.

The famous car designer, Bentley, lived near me, and one day I found a lithograph of one of his cars. I thought I would knock on his door and ask him to sign it, which I did. The great man answered the door himself, and on getting my request invited me inside. He signed the print for me and spoke to me for quite a while. He was a really kindly man. The thing I noticed though, was that the pictures on his walls were not of cars, but all of aeroplanes, some lovely paintings of Air battles in World War One. So I must find his autobiography and find out his connection with aviation.

At the UACC fair I met the man who dropped the bomb on Hiroshima, Thomas Ferebee, and had the pleasure of taking him

A detail copy of the print signed by Bentley.

34 ADVENTURES IN AUTOGRAPH COLLECTING

to the restaurant for a cup of coffee. I asked him how the bomb was released, and he told me that he had two levers, one was labeled *Automatic* and the other *Manual*. He should have pulled the manual lever, but when the time came to release the bomb, he decided to pull both levers at once. So, he doesn't know whether he realeased the bomb or whether the plane did. I was grateful to have met this man, and I treasure a photograph he signed for me.

I also had the pleasure of taking Butterfly McQueen down to the restaurant. When the waitress came with the menu, I asked what she would like. She said, "Just give me a plate." I ordered something for myself, and when it arrived with a separate empty plate, she opened her bag and took out a pile of fruit, bananas and apples and proceeded to eat those. Again that was a moment I will remember. Later she signed a photograph for me.

When Joe Louis came to England to give some demonstration boxing at Earls Court, I waited outside the entrance to his booth. Eventually the door opened and out came this man wearing a camel coat with his hands in his pockets. When I asked for an autograph he just looked straight ahead and ignored me; so as he passed, I gave him a punch. I think it hurt me more than him, for all I felt was a rock hard body, and I don't think he felt anything.

Later Johnny Weismuller came in a show partnering Belita. For some reason I had to be backstage, and so arming myself with a programme, I just hoped I would see him. Sooner than I expected, I all of a sudden saw a man in a dressing gown coming towards me, and I looked at that lined face, and just held out my programme. He so nicely stopped, took my book, and signed his photo, and after a few words sauntered on to wherever he was going.

Yes autograph collecting can be so much fun, especially if you meet these people. But, alas, the greater names from the past all now dead, you must be content with their writing and

their thoughts.

Another situation I got into concerned Rudolph Hess. I wanted his autograph and wrote to his wife. She offered to sell me a cover from Spandau written by Hess, which I bought from her. I told her that I thought Hess, the last of the Nazis in Spandau, was being used as a political football by the Russians so that they could still have a foot hold in West Berlin and I felt he could be released because he was not convicted of any war crimes against people. I promised to write to the Prime Minister to ask for his release. I think she got the impression that I had some influence with the Prime Minister which, of course, I didn't have, but it led to a correspondence with her.

In one of her letters to me she said, "I know the man in Spandau is my husband." That was because a Dr. Thomas had written a book claiming that the man in Spandau was not Hess because when he examined Hess he could find no trace of a bullet wound Hess had received during the first World War. I spoke to Dr. Thomas on the phone, and he gave me several other reasons. I asked if he could send me samples of Hess's handwriting from all periods of his life. He agreed and got samples for me. With the recent sample I had from Spandau, I compared them and came to the conclusion that the man in Spandau was in fact Rudolph Hess. When I reported this to Dr Thomas he told me that he had asked three experts to compare the handwriting and two,including myself, said it was Hess and one said it wasn't Hess.

From the correspondence with Frau Hess, I was made a member of the Freedom for Hess movement, and so was invited to a meeting in Munich where I met his son, and on opening the meeting he announced that there was a supporter of the movement from England in the audience. Everyone rose and applauded me for coming. I was quite embarrassed being feted by what must have been many members of the Nazi party. At

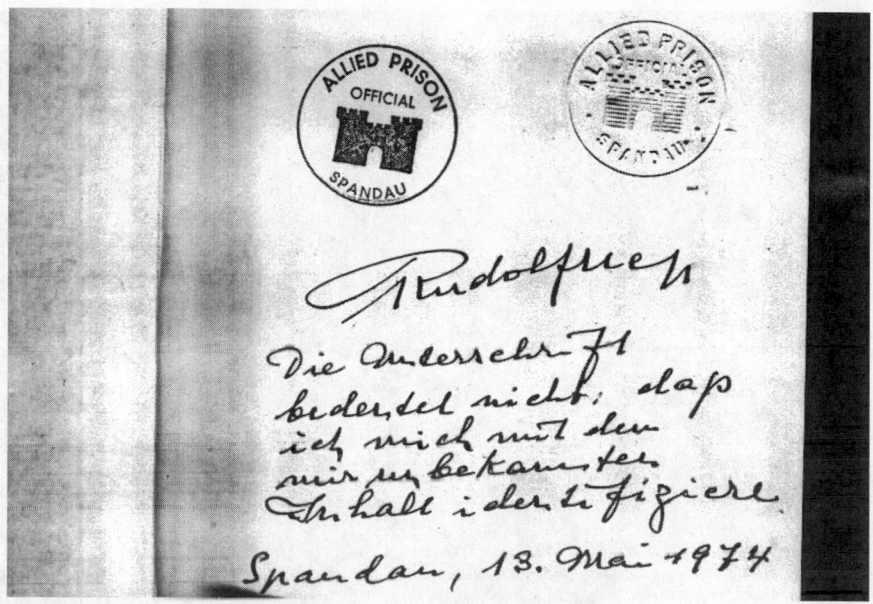

The autograph of Rudolph Hess, signed at Spandau prison in 1974.

the end of the meeting Hess allowed me to take some photos of him. He told me that when he visited his father, he was not allowed to touch him, and was surrounded by a Russian, a French, and an English officer. He was only allowed to ask simple questions and could not ask his father anything about his journey to Britain.

It was, for me, another adventure which brought me the autographs of Rudolph Hess, his son, and his wife. Later I was able to get a fine signature of Hess signed in Spandau with the Spandau Rubber stamp.

Collecting autographs can be a hobby of adventure, the sort of thing I enjoy doing, which makes the hobby so much more pleasurable.

The late actress Natalie Wood and her kid sister Lana Wood, who has become one of the bustier pin-up queens in the autograph world, joined George Sanders at Grauman's Chinese Theater for the world premiere of "Giant" in 1956.

Chapter 3

DREAM AUTOGRAPHS

by George Sanders and Ralph Roberts

We are often asked, "What is the *most* valuable autograph?" Our stock answer for the past ten years that we have been doing autograph price guides has consistently been, "Button Gwinnett"—that being the highest valued autograph outside of a museum that a private collector might reasonably hope to acquire. Gwinnett was a Signer of the Declaration of Independence and the first governor of Georgia. Gwinnett County, where a great deal of Atlanta lies, was named after him. He had a brief moment of glory, then promptly got himself killed in a duel. Hence, his very rare signature is valued at approximately $85,000.

The above answer, however, begs the question. Handwriting, after all, has been around something like 5,000 years. The authentic handwriting of truly great historic figures would certainly soar into the millions of dollars. The signature of Our Lord, Jesus Christ (with provenance) would be incalculable. Moses, Alexander the Great, Hamurabi, Socrates, Julius Caesar, Buddha, Cleopatra, Helen of Troy, a signed poem by Homer—all would grace any collection and be worth millions, even billions.

Well, dream on. No one has found a signed Julius Caesar in a yard sale yet. But, following are some you *might* find.

First, the bad news—no known signatures by famed persons of classic antiquity exist. The earliest attributable autographs (i.e. *handwriting* instead of actual signatures) belong to clerics during the early Middle Ages, literacy being pretty much their sole province in those generally illiterate times. It was mostly—says the *Encyclopedia Britannica*—"an age of anonymity rather than individuality and works such as chronicles are often of unknown authorship."

The earliest known "lay" autograph is that of the Spanish captain, The Cid, dating from the year 1096. (Remember Charlton Heston in the movie *El Cid*?—that's the guy!)

Early English kings usually signed with an "X." While Edward III (1327-77) was not the first literate English monarch, he is the first whose writing survives. And there are examples in museums of all following English kings and queens. So, yes, you could dream about finding one of those. Don't hold your breath, but at least those are not totally impossible.

Most of the big names of the Renaissance—Leonardo of *Mona Lisa* fame, Michaelangleo, and so forth—have their autographs preserved in national libraries. It is possible you *could* run across one out there somewhere but—remember—this chapter *is* entitled "Dream Autographs."

Still, just in case, following are some facsimiles of highly collectible names to dream about. Enjoy. And please let us know if you find any. And *where* you found them. Thanks.

Henry VIII (1491-1547) of England, whose marital problems put those of the current English royal family to shame.

Elizabeth I (1533-1603), queen of England and Ireland, only child of Henry VIII.

Charles I (1600-1649) was dethroned and beheaded by Oliver Cromwell.

John Calvin (1509-1564), one of the leaders of the Protestant Reformation.

Juan Ponce de Léon (c 1460-1521) Spanish explorer—discovered Florida.

Hernando de Soto (1500-1542), Spanish explorer and the first white man to cross the Mississippi River.

Sir Frances Drake (c 1540-1596) was the first Englishman to sail around the world.

Sir John Hawkins (1532-1595), first English slave trader and Elizabethian naval hero.

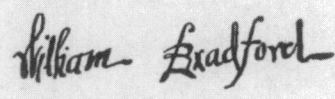

William Bradford (1590-1657), second governor of Plymouth Colony and author. Called "the father of American History."

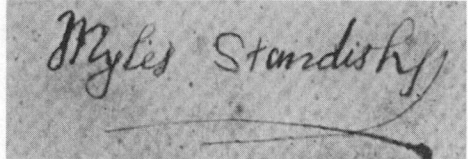

Myles (or Miles) Standish (1584?-1656), Pilgrim military hero and assistant governor of Plymouth Colony.

1951: Elizabeth Taylor presents a broadcasting award to George Sanders inHollywood.

Chapter 4

AUTOGRAPHS OF THE OLD WEST

by MichaelMinor and Larry Vrazalik

Western Americana autographs are among the most avidly sought of all autographs. They are also among the rarest, most expensive, and most frequently forged of all autographs because of their high price tags. Most of the major old west characters were semi-literate at best and many signed only with an "X". In the case of Geronimo, Sitting Bull, and Rain-In-The-Face, they were taught to crudely print or write their names only after they were taken captive; however, the letters of their names meant nothing to them.

Technically speaking, they drew their signatures. All three usually "signed" their names in pencil, making them a particularly easy target for forgers whose forte has become to add (usually) pencil signatures to old paper or photographs. While it is now possible to date ink both by its composition and when applied (determined by a Scanning Auger Microscope which measures how far the ink has migrated by capillarity from its point of application, thus determining how long the ink has been on the paper), there is no practical test for determining the age of penciled writing.

All Western Americana autographs should be approached

with the utmost caution and should only be purchased from dealers or auction houses who offer unconditional no time limit warranties of authenticity--and even then such material should be accompanied by impeccable provenance. While the field of Western Americana is a veritable mine field for the collector, the rewards outweigh the perils. And we can think of no better investment than old West autograph material.

THE TRAGIC STORY OF GERONIMO

GERONIMO (1829-1909). Indian name Goyathlay, i.e., "one who yawns." An American Apache chief, he was born at the present site of Clifton, Arizona. He was admitted to the Warrior's Council of the Chiricahua Apaches (1846); given nickname "Geronimo" (Jerome in English) by the Mexicans. He led a sensational campaign (1885-86) against the whites and was ultimately captured by General Crook but escaped and later surrendered to General Miles, who had relieved Crook.

Geronimo was a captive of the U. S. government for the rest of his life. After his capture he was initially taken to Florida, then Alabama, and, finally, in 1894, the government permanently moved the Apaches to Ft. Sill, Oklahoma. By then disease had taken its toll and less than 300 Apaches remained, mostly children born in captivity. Geronimo settled as a farmer near Ft. Sill, Oklahoma.

During his captivity he periodically worked at expositions where he was put on "exhibition" by the government. He was, however, allowed to sell his autographs and bows, arrows and other objects he made. He would also sell articles of his clothing, including the shirt off his back! While incarcerated in Alabama (1888-94) Geronimo was taught to print his name sometime between 1888-1890. Since Geronimo could not read and write, the individual letters in

his name meant nothing to him. In fact, according to contemporary accounts, he printed his name vertically, top to bottom, much like a totem or drawing, instead of writing horizontally, left to right.

Geronimo went on the warpath in the 1850s after the Mexicans killed his mother, wife and children. His tribe had camped outside a Mexican town and Geronimo and the men had gone into the town to trade. In their absence Mexican troops attacked their camp and killed and scalped all the women and children which included Geronimo's entire family.

At that time the Mexican government paid fifty dollars for a woman's scalp and twenty-five dollars for a child's. The scalps of Geronimo's family brought someone $175. Before Geronimo was finally captured he had extracted a terrible revenge on the Mexicans and whites in both blood and money.

In Geronimo's autobiography he stated: "In all the battles I thought of my murdered mother, wife and babies—of my vow of vengeance, and I fought with fury. Many fell by my hand, and constantly I led the advance...Still covered with the blood of my enemies, still holding my conquering weapon, still hot with the joy of battle, victory and vengeance, I was surrounded by the Apache braves and made war chief...then I gave orders for scalping the slain."

Geronimo has passed into history as the most notorious of all the Indian warriors, but when the Apaches: embarked on their long-continuing series of last stands, he was not feared so much by settlers as were some of the others, because until late in his fighting career Geronimo had concentrated on raiding the Mexicans, those despised people who had massacred his family.

As the flow of white settlers into Arizona increased and as

the U.S. government sought more and more to resist roaming Apaches and to regulate their lives, Geronimo's hatred expanded to include Americans along with Mexicans.

Apaches made the most fanatical last stands of all the Indians and their violence bloodied the southwestern United States and Sonora, Mexico for many years.

In fairness, however, it must be stated that the United States government broke every promise it made to the Apaches and violated every treaty. The conditions on the Indian reservations were squalid. Corrupt Indian agents stole the Indians' rations and supplies and many died of starvation or white man's diseases. The unconscionable mistreatment of the Indians by the United States government will forever remain a black page in our history.

By the time Geronimo and his people were transferred to Ft. Sill, Oklahoma in 1894, he had literally become a commercial property; an "exhibit" to insure the success of a celebration.

Geronimo's conduct on these occasions was a lasting demonstration of the code of courtesy and good breeding the Apaches had retained even as hunted outlaws. He appeared self-possessed, alert, and not unfriendly to the people who crowded around him. At the same time he was observing, learning, making note of everything with his active mind and curiosity. He used every opportunity to plead for a return to his homeland—and he constantly kept an eye open for business.

What is not generally known is that after his capture Geronimo became a capitalist, a Christian, a Sunday school teacher, and a farmer, not necessarily in that order; and his death, literally and figuratively, resulted from "falling off his wagon" in a drunken stupor!

The first major "exhibition" of Geronimo was in 1898 at

the Trans-Mississippi Exhibition at Omaha. Geronimo was the main attraction. His next public exposition was at the Pan-American Exposition at Buffalo in 1901, the Louisiana Purchase Exposition at St. Louis in 1904, and many more.

Sometime after Geronimo was taken captive, he discovered that his "souvenirs" had commercial value to the whites. He started making bows and arrows, quivers, canes, and other work in which he was skilled.

On the souvenir bows, arrows, and other items he made with his hands, Geronimo wrote his name in ink. He did so by sharpening a stick and dipping the point in ink and then printing his name; however, he almost always used a pencil to write his autograph, which he also started selling when he learned it had commercial value. Ink signatures of Geronimo are extremely rare.

Geronimo charged from ten cents to fifty cents for his autograph and from ten cents to two dollars for his photograph. He would sign his photograph usually on the back for an additional charge. In short, he sold his souvenirs and autographs for whatever the market would bear.

About his souvenir business at the St. Louis Exposition, Geronimo wrote in his autobiography: "I sold my photographs for twenty-five cents and was allowed to keep ten cents for myself. I also wrote my name for ten, fifteen, or twenty-five cents, as the case might be, and kept all of that money. I often made as much as two dollars a day, and when I returned I had plenty of money — more than I had ever had before."

At the same fair, Geronimo was given a ride on a Ferris wheel, about which he dictated this account in his autobiography: "One time the guards took me into a little house that had four windows. When we were seated the little house started to move along the ground. The guards called my

 **The Sanders Price Guide to Autographs**

attention to some curious things they had in their pockets. Finally they told me to look out, and when I did so I was scared, for our little house had gone high up in the air, and the people down in the Fair Grounds looked no larger than ants. The men laughed at me for being scared."

About a puppet show Geronimo said: "In front of us were some strange little people who came out on a platform. They did not seem to be in earnest about anything they did."

The Christian missionary work among the Ft. Sill Apaches was carried out by the Reformed Church in America, the successor to the Dutch Reformed Church, and was done by the gifted Choctaw Minister, Frank Hall Wright, and Dr. Walter C. Roe.

Initially, Geronimo said at a religious meeting: "I, Geronimo, and these others are now too old to travel your Jesus road. But our children are young and I and my brothers will be glad to have the children taught about the white man's God."

However, some eight months later, Geronimo himself professed his faith and belief and was baptised a week later. Amazingly, Geronimo even taught a Sunday School class for a short period of time. As with many American Indians, Geronimo still clung to his traditional beliefs and merely supplemented them with his new-found Christianity which became a source of inner conflict to him in his old age.

By the winter of 1908-09, Geronimo's rugged body began to show signs of breaking down. He was ill that fall and his sturdy figure had shrunk. His activity was slowing, and he became very absent minded. To the amusement of his young friends, he would search for his hat while it was on his head and would look for his knife while he was holding it in his hand.

On one occasion he asked his wife to help him find his

knife, but she refused (that was Azul, the last of his six wives), saying, "You're old enough to look for your own knife." He became angry and said to his friends, "Boys, you see how she is! I advise you not to marry!" Finally, he saw the knife in his hand, and, shocked, said: "Why, I'm nothing but a fool."

On a cold day in February, 1909, Geronimo rode to Lawton and sold some bows and arrows. While there, he asked Eugene Chihuahua to get him some whiskey. It was illegal to sell liquor to an Indian, but the method of obtaining it was easy. Eugene simply asked a soldier to go into the saloon and buy it for him.

The young man regretted his part in obtaining the whiskey for Geronimo to the end of his life. Geronimo became intoxicated, and in attempting to ride back home after dark, fell off the seat of his wagon (by some accounts a horse) and lay all night in the cold rain.

The next morning Geronimo was found lying partly in the water and partly on the ground. He contracted a severe cold which grew steadily worse. For three days, his family and friends cared for him, but finally, the post surgeon ordered him sent to the Apache post hospital. By this time Geronimo was critically ill with pneumonia.

During his final hours he relived the youthful tragedy of his first family's massacre and his violent hatred of Mexicans. He talked of the men who were with him on his first war trail.

Geronimo's rugged body finally gave way the third day of his hospitalization. He died at 6:15 a.m. on February 17, 1909. Christian funeral services were held for him, and he was buried in the Indian cemetery near Ft. Sill beside his wife Zi-Yeh.

Although Geronimo signed numerous autographs at

AUTOGRAPHS OF THE OLD WEST   49

various public exhibitions he attended, these autographs are today among the rarest and most eagerly sought and most costly of all Western Americana autographs.

GERONIMO'S AUTOGRAPH

Geronimo's signature was very crude, primitive, and childlike; however, inasmuch as he knew how to print his name for about twenty years, his signature, like anyone else's, changed. His earlier signatures seemed to be more ornately and laboriously written than his later signatures, with straight lines artistically drawn through the "G," "R," and "O's".

Because Geronimo invariably used a pencil to "sign his name" and because his signature was a child-like printing, his signatures, like Sitting Bull's, have been widely forged. We would urge the collector to be extremely wary of all Geronimo material and unless it has a well-documented provenance, not to purchase it. In fact, we would urge

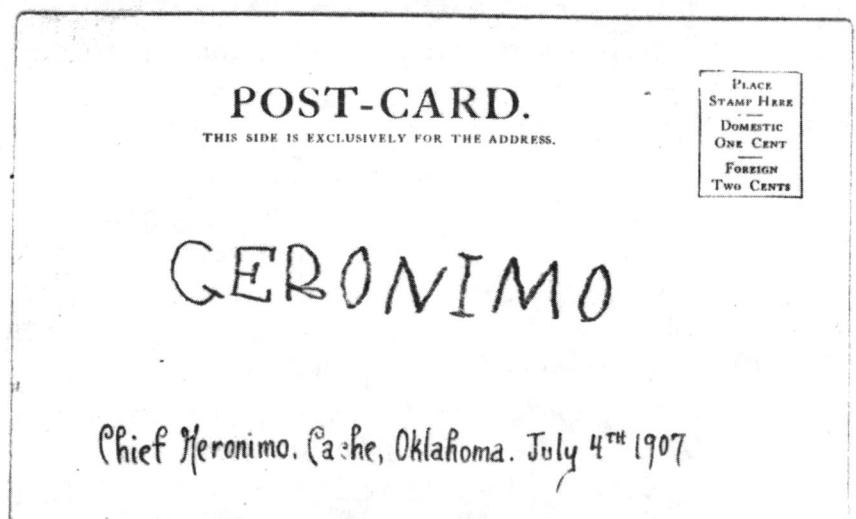

Authentic pencil signature of Geronimo, on verso of post card photograph of him (see top of next page), with provenance written in ink beneath his signature.

collectors to regard all Geronimo and Sitting Bull material as not being genuine unless and until proven otherwise.

There are very few signed photographs of Geronimo, and these in particular, because of their high price tags, must be closely scrutinized.

Because of their high prices and the great demand for them, Western Americana autographs have become a popular target for forgers. In one week during the recent past, e.g., we were offered an obviously forged Annie Oakley signature as well as a beautifully framed forged "ink" Geronimo signature!

We urge collectors to purchase all autographs only from reputable and established dealers and auction

GERONIMO (1829-1909). An authentic signed photograph.

Authentic pencil signature of Geronimo, circa 1905, with provenance (above).

Forged pencil signature of Geronimo (above, size reduced).

Authentic pencil signature of Geronimo, circa 1890, with provenance (size reduced).

houses who will provide an unequivocal, unconditional, no-time limit warranty of authenticity.

SITTING BULL

Sitting Bull (Tatanka Yotanka), Hunkpapa Sioux medicine man and chief, (Mar. 1834-Dec. 15, 1890). Born on the Grand River, South Dakota, he was, according to Hodge "a chief by inheritance" and according to Marquis "all of the Uncpapas...looked upon Sitting Bull as their principal chief." At the time of the Little Big Horn Battle, Sitting Bull was generally regarded by the Sioux as the most able chief of all those in the five Dakota tribes present, but he had no authority beyond the Uncpapas. Marquis added, "That he was a genuine chief is the testimony of all the old Indians of that time—and they know.

That he was a great chief... is shown by the high regard all of the plains Indians had for him." Vestal, Sitting Bull's principal biographer, (who believed he was born in 1831), regarded him as the leading chief, perhaps the head chief, of the Teton Sioux, although conceding that some elements of the Tetons did not recognize him as such. At any rate, the notion that Sitting Bull was a medicine man only, and not a chief or a true chief, is fiction, for indeed he was a chief by inheritance and by selection. The denigration of him to a subsidiary and less-reputable role was the work of James McLoughlin and whites who wished to subvert his intractability and work with more malleable leaders such as Gall, who might be persuaded to accept the white cause and blandishments.

As a boy Sitting Bull was known as Jumping Badger; he hunted buffalo calves at ten and at fourteen accompanied his father on the warpath against the Crows, counting coup on an enemy. On the return of the party his father, also named

Sitting Bull,(or Four Horns), gave a feast and announced that the boy was entitled to bear his name Four Horns, which was changed to Sitting Bull in 1857, when he first "made medicine."

Sitting Bull took an active part in the plains wars in the 1860's and led a raid against Fort Buford (December 24-25, 1866). Sitting Bull was on the war-path with his band from 1869 to 1876, espe-cially against the Crows, Shoshones, and others, and raided white posts and installations.

In 1876 he refused— or was ignorant of—the demand that he bring

Authentically signed cabinet photograph of Sitting Bull, signed in ink. Courtesy of Custer Battlefield Museum, Garryowen, Montana, Christopher Kortlander, President.

his people to a reservation, and this led to extended military operations against the Sioux, culminating in the Custer fight on the Little Big Horn June 25, 1876, in which Sioux and Cheyennes destroyed the bulk of Custer's command and decimated what was left.

During the engagement, Sitting Bull was in the hills "making medicine;" he took no part in the actual fighting. But his accurate predictions of the battle led him, according to McLaughlin, "to come out of the affair with higher honour

among his people than he possessed when he went into it."
After the fight, the great Indian encampment broke up
because it was impossible to gather enough food for so
many people.

Sitting Bull, in command of the western party, ravaged
the North Plains and harassed troop operations in Montana,
although never in a major confrontation. On October 21,
1876, Miles had an inconclusive conference with Sitting Bull,
the Indian stating that he would trade for ammunition but
wanted to live free, and Miles insisting that he come into an
agency and surrender. In an ensuing fight on Clear Creek, in
Montana, two soldiers were wounded and five Indians killed;
on October 27th 400 lodges, or about 2,000 Sioux, surrendered, while Sitting Bull, later joined by Gall and others,
escaped northward.

Sitting Bull hovered around the upper Missouri River and
its tributaries for some time, but eventually withdrew to
Canada. In 1881, under a pledge of amnesty, he returned to
Fort Buford, Dakota, and was held at Fort Randall, the
present Gregory County, South Dakota, until 1883. He
remained largely unreconciled, and refused to go along with
white demands. Sitting Bull had become one of the most
famous Indians, however, and on June 6, 1885, he signed a
contract to appear with Buffalo Bill's Wild West Show for four
months; the contract provided that he receive fifty dollars a
week, a bonus of $125, and the right to sell his photographs
and laboriously traced autographs. (See illustration in this
article).

He frequently drew hisses as a villain at appearances in
the United States, but was royally treated in Canada and
appeared to enjoy the attention and miss it when it was
lacking. He met President Cleveland and some of the army
officers against whom he had fought. It was Sitting Bull's

Authentic ink signature of Sitting Bull.

Forged ink signature of Sitting Bull, likely an Arthur Sutton forgery.

only season of show business, but there is no indication that he was dissatisfied.

Yet he continued to reject white overtures designed to persuade him to agree to the sale of Sioux lands and for that he was considered "unfriendly" at best, and a rascal at worst by white officials. It was through his influence that the Sioux in 1888 rejected a new offer to sell their lands. It was at his camp at Standing Rock Agency, and at his invitation, that Kicking Bear organized the first ghost dance on the reservation, although the extent to which Sitting Bull was influenced by the movement is unestablished. The attempt to arrest Sitting Bull, had nothing to do with the ghost dance, but the ghost dance was the pretext.

The real reason for Sitting Bull's arrest may have been that he was regarded by McLoughlin and others as an obstacle to management of the Sioux, largely because of his unwillingness to bend to their importunities. They could not control Sitting Bull. At any rate, he was shot and killed by

under continuous control of Road Management. for summer season of four months (1885) and if extended to be at same terms.

John M. Burke does also agree to pay all expenses of the party from Standing Rock, to the Show. and to pay all expenses of the party from the Show to Standing Rock - at expiration of this Contract.

James McLaughlin
Standing Rock Agency
Joseph Grimeau
Standing Rock agency

Witness

John M. Burke
Bus Manager Cody & Salsbury

Sitting Bull

P.S. Sitting Bull is to have sole right to sell his own Photographs and Autographs.

John M. Burke
Bus Manager Cody & Salsbury

Signature of Sitting Bull on final page of his contract with William F. "Buffalo Bill" Cody to appear in the famous Buffalo Bill's Wild West Show. This is the only known signed contract of Sitting Bull and contains his only known attested signature. This is the most important Sitting Bull item in existence. Courtesy of Custer Battlefield Museum, Garryowen, Montana, Christopher Kortlander, President.

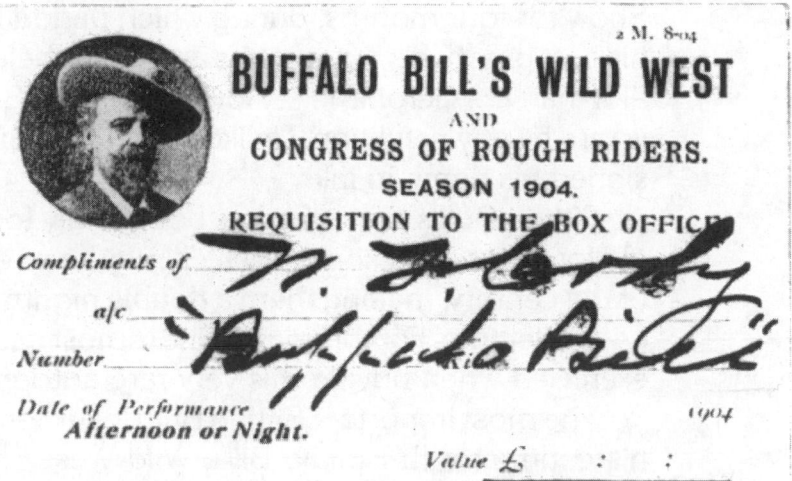

BUFFALO BILL'S WILD WEST
AND
CONGRESS OF ROUGH RIDERS.
SEASON 1904.
REQUISITION TO THE BOX OFFICE

Compliments of

a/c

Number

Date of Performance
Afternoon or Night.

1904

Value £ : :

Complementary pass to Buffalo Bill's Wild West and Congress of Rough Riders, 1904, signed with his double signature. Courtesy of the Senator Ralph Y. Yarborough collection.

Lieutenant Bullhead and Sergeant Red Tomahawk of the Indian police in the course of the arrest ordered by the military months after McLaughlin requested it. His son, Crow Foot, 17, and several others, including six of the Indian police, were also killed, Bullhead being mortally wounded.

Out of the ensuing turmoil developed the Wounded Knee affair, another debacle for the Sioux and another black page in our history. McLaughlin, in an obituary wrote, "The shot that killed (Sitting Bull) put a stop forever to the domination of the ancient regime among the Sioux of the Standing Rock Reservation," and that was the true reason for his slaying. Sitting Bull was married several times (one report states nine times) and fathered nine children.

According to a contemporary account, Sitting Bull laboriously and childishly wrote his signature by copying his name from a piece of paper on which someone had written his name. Although he was only with Buffalo Bill's Wild West

Show for four months, during which period of time he sold his autograph, his autographs are, nevertheless, more plentiful than are Geronimo's. However, Sitting Bull's autograph is rare by any definition. Unlike Geronimo, Sitting Bull often signed his name in ink.

Sitting Bull's signature has been avidly forged and many old forgeries exist, some of which may be as early as the turn of the century, making them a double nightmare for dealers and collectors. For this reason the utmost caution should be exercised when buying this very rare autograph.

The most important Sitting Bull document in existence is his contract with Buffalo Bill's Wild West Show which was recently acquired by Christopher Kortlander of Historical Rarities/Custer Battlefield Museum, which is illustrated in this article. It contains the only known attested signature of Sitting Bull.

RAIN IN THE FACE

The signature of the fierce Sioux chief, Rain-in-the-Face, is very rare, indeed. Rain-in-the-Face is reputed to have killed both General Custer and his brother, Captain Tom Custer at the battle of Little Big Horn, cutting out and eating Tom Custer's heart!

Rain-in-the-Face (Itiomagaju) was born 1835 near the forks of the Cheyenne River in North Dakota. He died circa1905. A noted and important Sioux Warrior and Chief of the Uncpapa tribe. Brother of Iron Horse. He received his

Rain in the face

Rare signature of Chief Rain-in-the-Face.

name after fighting all day in the rain. It had been his habit to paint his face half red and half black to represent the sun when covered by darkness. The rain caused his red and black paint to run and his face to become streaked.

Rain-In-The-Face went on the warpath many times, but his first important experience as a warrior was in the attack on Fort Phil Kearney, Wyoming, in December 1866, when Captain Fetterman and his command of eighty men were killed. After the discovery of gold in the Dakotas, which brought a steady stream of miners, settlers, and the railroad, the Indians were in an ugly and troublesome mood. They welcomed neither railroad nor men.

In 1873 an expedition of some seventeen hundred men under General Stanley was sent to the Dakotas. General George Armstrong Custer and the Seventh Cavalry formed a large part of the command. Custer's brother, Tom Custer, was in his command. On August 4, 1873, Custer's command engaged in a skirmish with a band of renegade Indians which included Rain-In-The-Face. The Indians unsuccessfully attempted to stampede the soldiers' horses. The only casualties that day were two civilians, Dr. Honzinger, the regiment veterinarian, and Mr. Baliran, the sutler. Both had wandered away from the troops and were killed by the Indians. Dr. Honzinger was killed by Rain-InThe-Face.

In 1874 the Seventh Cavalry was stationed at Fort Abraham Lincoln, near Bismarck. Word was brought to Custer by a scout that Rain-In-The-Face was at Standing Rock Agency, some twenty miles away, boasting that he had killed Dr. Honzinger. Rain-In-The-Face was already a renowned warrior of extraordinary courage. The very fact that he had left Sitting Bull and his hostiles to come to the agency denoted great courage. General Custer dispatched his brother, Captain Tom Custer, and Captain Yates, with one hundred

troops to the agency to arrest Rain-In-The-Face. Tom Custer overpowered and arrested Rain-In-The-Face by seizing him from the back in an iron grip. Rain-In-The-Face was taken to Fort Lincoln. He confessed that he had shot Baliran and Honzinger, who had fallen off his horse, whereupon he had crushed his head with stones.

Rain-In-The-Face was put in the guard house and held prisoner pending his trial for murder. He was kept imprisoned despite the effort of many prominent Indians to obtain his release. He was kept in the guard house with some civilians who had been arrested for stealing grain. One bitterly cold night, during a raging blizzard, the civilians, with some outside assistance, succeeded in making their escape. Rain-In-The-Face took advantage of this opportunity and also escaped.

He then joined the hostiles under Sitting Bull and sent word back to the Custers that he intended to have his revenge for the treatment he had received. Rain-In-The-Face later stated that, "I sent Little Hair (his name for Tom Custer) a picture, on a piece of buffalo skin, of a bloody heart. He knew I didn't forget my vow. The next time I saw Little Hair, ugh! (referring to the massacre at Little Big Horn). I got his heart. I have said all."

In a remarkable interview with W. Kent Thomas, Rain-In-The-Face (who was at Coney Island, N.Y. on August 12, 1894, where the "Custer Indians" were taken following the World's Fair) gave the following very remarkable account of the Battle of Little Big Horn, in part: (Thomas wrote the following in his diary). "Rain-In-The-Face hobbled into the tent tonight, as McFadden and I were discussing the events of the day. Seating himself, unbidden, and with true Indian stoicism, he grunted out that one word of all words so dear to a

Lakota, Minnewaukan!" which, literally translated, means "Water of God", but which by usage, has been interpreted as "fire water." Since the other Indians were away from camp on a visit to their friends, the Oglalas, at Buffalo Bill's Camp, I decided to yield for once to Rain's oft-repeated demand, which had been hitherto as regularly denied. He took my flask, and with a guttural "How" drained it at one gulp, without straining a muscle on his face. "Ugh! Good! Like Rain's heart," he remarked.

With respect to the Custer Massacre, McFadden and Thomas wanted to know the details thereof and how he took Tom Custer's heart. McFadden, who was quite an artist, made an imaginary sketch of "Custer's Last Charge." He handed it to Rain, saying: "Does this look anything like the fight?"

Rain studied it a long time and then burst out laughing. "No," he said, "this picture is a lie. These long legs have swords—they never fought us with swords, but with guns and revolvers. These men are on ponies—they fought us on foot, and every fourth man held the others' horses. That's always their way of fighting. We tie ourselves onto our ponies and fight in a circle.

"These people are not dressed as we dress in a fight. They look like agency Indians — we strip naked and have ourselves and our ponies painted. This picture gives us bows and arrows. We were better armed than the long swords. Their guns wouldn't shoot but once — the thing wouldn't throw out the empty cartridge shells. (In this he was historically correct, as dozens of guns were picked up on the battle-field by General Biggon's command two days later with the shells still sticking in them, showing that the ejector wouldn't work).

"When we found they could not shoot we saved our

bullets by knocking the long swords over with our war clubs—it was just like killing sheep. Some of them got on their knees and begged; we spared none — ugh! This picture is like all the white man's pictures of Indians, a lie. I will show you how it looked."

Then turning it over, he pulled out a stump of a lead pencil from his pouch and drew a map of the battle. Regarding the massacre, Rain said: "I had sung the war song, I had smelt the powder smoke. My heart was bad—I was like one that has no mind. I rushed in and took their flag; my pony fell dead as I took it. I cut the thong that bound me. I jumped up and brained the long sword flag man with my war club, and ran back to our line with the flag...The long sword's blood and brains splashed in my face. It felt hot, and blood ran in my mouth. I could taste it. I was mad. I got a fresh pony and rushed back, shooting, cutting, and slashing. The pony was shot, and I got another...This time I saw Little Hair (Tom Custer). I remembered my vow. I was crazy; I feared nothing. I knew nothing would hurt me, for I had my white weasel-tail charm on. (He wears the charm to this day). I don't know how many I killed trying to get at him. He knew me. I laughed at him and yelled at him. I saw his mouth move, but there was so much noise I couldn't hear his voice. He was afraid. When I got near enough I shot him with my revolver. My gun was gone, I don't know where.

"I leaped from my pony and cut out his heart and bit a piece of it and spit it in his face. I got back on my pony and rode off shaking it. I was satisfied and sick of fighting; I didn't scalp him." I didn't go back on the field after that. The squaws came up afterward and killed the wounded, cut their boot legs off for moccasin soles, and took their money, watches and rings. They cut their fingers off to get them quicker. They hunted for Long Yellow Hair to scalp him but

could not find him. He didn't wear his fort clothes (uniform), his hair had been cut off, and the Indians didn't know him."

(Notwithstanding his "white weaseltail charm," Rain-In-The-Face was wounded in this battle. A bullet pierced his right leg above the knee. Among the plunder which fell to him after the action was over was a razor taken from the person of some dead soldier. With this razor he cut deeply into the front of his leg, but failed to reach the bullet. Then he reached around to the back of his leg and chopped reck-lessly into the flesh from that quarter. He got the bullet, also several tendons, and narrowly missed cutting the artery and bleeding to death. (He was lame and had to walk on crutches all his life thereafter.)

At the time of the interview, 1894, "Rain-In-The-Face (Itiomagaju) is about sixty years of age now, and is the only chief that survives to tell the tale of the Custer fight. Gall and Sitting Bull have both gone to hunt the white buffalo long since. Rain can write his name in English. I taught him to do it at the World's Fair in order to sell Longfellow's poem, entitled 'The Revenge of Rain-In-The-Face.' He doesn't know the significance of it after he writes it.

"His knowledge of English is confined to about thirty words, but he can't say them so any one can understand him though he can understand almost anything that is said in English. Like all other Indians, his gratitude is for favours to come and not for favours already shown. He is utterly heartless and unprincipled, physically brave but morally a coward. His redeeming feature lies in the fact that you can depend upon any promise he makes, but it takes a world of patience to get him to promise anything.

"Even at the age of sixty he is still a Hercules. In form and face he is the most pronounced type of the ideal Fenimore Cooper, dime novel Indian in America." It was also claimed

that "Rain-In-The-Face" killed General Custer, which he would neither confirm nor deny.

The autograph of Rain-In-The-Face is one of the rarest of all Americana and Old West autographs. Like Geronimo and Sitting Bull, he only learned to sign his name later in life, for a fee, and few examples have survived. The signature of the fierce and legendary Rain-In-The-Face is much scarcer than that of Geronimo and Sitting Bull whose authentic material has now become virtually unobtainable and prohibitively expensive.

"LITTLE MISS SURE SHOT"—ANNIE OAKLEY

Annie Oakley (1860-1926) was born in Darke County, Ohio as Phoebe Anne Oakley Mozee. She was attracted to shooting at an early age and became locally famed as a markswoman, hunting game for the Cincinnati markets. Matched with side show marksman Frank E. Butler, she handily beat him; he later married her (1876). Butler incorporated her into his act and, when she became famous and universally popular, Butler took over as her manager.

They joined the Sells Brothers Circus and, in 1885, the Buffalo Bill Wild West Show, (1885-1902) where for seventeen years she was a star of the organisation. Some of her shooting feats were phenomenal; she was an especial success in Europe, performing before royalty. In 1901 she was badly injured in a railroad wreck but recovered to continue her career.

Notably religious, she supported numerous orphans, having been fatherless herself from the age of four. She died at Greenville, Ohio, in 1926 and was buried in Ohio, her husband dying three weeks later at Detroit and being buried beside Annie in the Brock Cemetery, Darke County, Ohio.

She was nicknamed "Little Miss Sure Shot" by Sitting

RECTO

VERSO

Rare Annie Oakley Target Card on which she has shot a hole through the heart and signed on both sides.

Bull, who, for a time, was part of the show. She once shot the lit end of a cigarette out of the Kaiser's mouth and, on another occasion, exhibited before five kings and four queens. She shot an apple off her husband's head over 8500 times in a fifteen year period. She frequently broke 100 straight targets with a shotgun and defeated some of the world's greatest marksmen on even terms.

Oakley had 4 3/4" x 2" cards printed with a small photo of herself on horseback with a 1" x 1" red heart on the right side of the card. As part of her act she would have her husband hold one of these cards in his hand at a great

distance, sometimes fifty paces, and unerringly shoot a hole through the heart.

Oakley would sometimes give these cards as souvenirs and, if asked, would autograph them. Few of these cards are known to exist or have ever come on the market. The example illustrated in this article has a small bullet hole she fired through the heart, beneath which she signed her distinctive signature. On the verve she again signed her name, beneath which she wrote her address: "Annie Oakley, c/o Evergreen Hall, Woodbury, New Jersey."

Oakley's signature is extremely rare in any form. In the recent past a number of forgeries, most written in brown ink, have come on the market. Oakley's authentic material is among the scarcest and most desirable of all Western Americana/Old West material.

BUFFALO BILL

William Frederick Cody, known as "Buffalo Bill," (1846-1917), American scout and showman. He was a rider for the Pony Express (1860), and a scout for the Kansas Cavalry against the Indians (1863). He served in the army (1863-1865) and furnished buffalo meat for the Union Pacific Construction crews (1867-1868). He served as scout for the 5th U. S. Cavalry (1868-1872, 1876). Cody was on stage as an actor or showman (1872-1883), at first in "Scouts of the Plains" by E. Z. C. Judson. He organized and managed Buffalo Bill's Wild West Show (from 1883) and toured the U. S. and Europe successfully (to 1916). He assembled one of the greatest shows of all time which included many legendary Old West figures including Sitting Bull and Annie Oakley.

The autographic material of William F. Cody is refreshingly obtainable albeit not plentiful. However, the brisk

Double signature autograph of W.F. Cody and "Buffalo Bill."

demand for Cody material has always kept the prices high. Handsome signed cabinet photographs showing him in his dramatic western regalia are obtainable as well as good content letters, on his colourful letterhead with his vignette, often mentioning his Wild West Show, or bookings or even possible locations to winter his livestock. Perhaps the most desirable form of his signature is his "double signature" which contains his usual signature and famous sobriquet. No Old West-collection is complete without an example of William F. "Buffalo Bill" Cody's signature.

George Sanders with Sir Alfred Hitchcock (he of the famous profile and *Psycho* fame).

Chapter 5

PHILOGRAPHY JOINS PHILATELY:

COLLECTING THE SIGNATURES
OF FAMOUS FACES DEPICTED
ON POSTAGE STAMPS

by George Sanders

In recent years it has become clear that a great many intellectual collectors are beginning to assimilate impressive assortments of valuable signatures of distinguished celebrities who appear on the postage stamps of the United States and other nations. Obviously, the list of collectible names grows each year and the hobby possibilities are nearly limitless. Thus, two hobbies, stamp collecting and the acquisition of autographs have rather peculiarly but wonderfully come together.

The U.S. postage officials are being most cooperative, and because it is a highly profitable pursuit for their financial coffers, the postage powers-that-be issue new faces on stamps nearly every month. From Marilyn Monroe, James Dean, Elvis Presley, and star-crossed Richard Nixon to popular American cartoonists, we collectors have a rainbow of colors, portraits, and themes to choose from.

It was about 35 years ago that we decided that such a combination of celebrities-on-stamps and signatures would become part of our own autograph collection. However, we had another angle that we thought might add some special interest to the famous people on postage theme.

Too often the faces on postage stamps become almost

UNreal. They seem unreachable partially because these tiny bits of adhesive paper are ultimately mutilated, cancelled, destroyed, or because the vast quantities that are issued make stamps things to be just taken for granted as an integral part of an international delivery service. Add to that, the U.S. Postal Service cannot celebrate a famed person until they have been dead for five years.

To my wife and to me, as former journalists, radio and TV interviewers, and friends of the rich and famous, the faces are REAL. They are valid and recognizable because we have either KNOWN the face on the stamp personally or because we possess some memento of such a person that proves that he or she was a worthwhile historic living human being and part of our own American heritage. In most cases they were overachievers who have made their marks as makers of history. Dead but not forgotten.

It has been particularly satisfying to assemble such an assortment including a very special, to us, autographed First Day Cover of a foreign land Down Under. On August 30, 1975, the New Zealand Postal Service created a special commemorative cachet celebrating the "50th Jubilee of New Zealand Radio (1925-1975)." The FDCs in our possession bear the signatures of Sir Keith Holyoake, who served as prime minister and later as governor general longer than any other Kiwi chief executive in their history, and Sir William E. Rowling who served as prime minister for probably less time than any of his predecessors. He was later a popular New Zealand ambassador to the United States for several years in the 1980s.

The other signatures on these rather rare First Day Covers include the then Minister of Broadcasting Sir Hugh Templeton, Sir Alister McIntosh (Chairman of the New Zealand Broadcasting Council), attorney Patrick Downey, who was chairman of Radio New Zealand, Geoffrey Whitehead who was an Assistant

Director General (later Director General of Australian Broadcasting) and an American named George Sanders was included as an Assistant Director General of Radio New Zealand from 1974 through 1977.

As a longtime stamp collector who specialized in First Day Covers, you cannot imagine what a thrill it was to affix my own signature on those limited issue envelopes bearing special salutes to an industry in which we had diligently served in the U.S. and New Zealand for over 50 years. Yes dear readers, we made our own entry into Detroit, Michigan radio in 1934 as a child actor, and into Los Angeles commercial television in 1948.

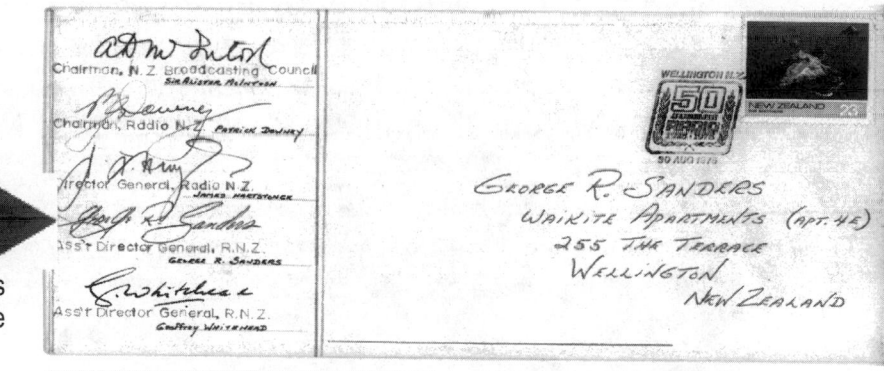

Sanders signature on FDC.

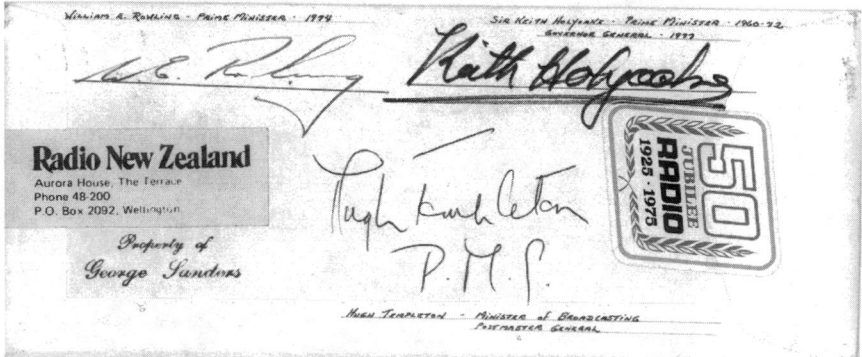

On August 30, 1975, the New Zealand Postal Service created a special commemorative cachet celebrating the "50th Jubilee of New Zealand Radio (1925-1975)." George Sanders, as Assistant Director General, is listed on the cover, thus fulfilling any FDC collector's ultimate dream of being part of that which he collects!

By 1960, we had decided to include photographs that had been taken with celebrities we had actually met plus at least one example of their respective autographs. For us, being in broadcasting, the possibilities seemed limitless. On the initial pages of our three-volume collection we have a very nice ANS of Bud Abbott & Lou Costello on one page with a pane of the U.S. 29-cent stamps dedicated to them on the opposite sheet. The comics are followed by similar arrangements set up for Secretary of State Dean Acheson, Emperor Akihito and Empress Machico of Japan, trumpeter Louis Armstrong, comedian Jack Benny, Nobel author Pearl S. Buck, United Nations Under-Secretary Ralph J. Bunche, country music's The Carter Family, the ill-fated Astronaut Roger B. Chaffee, baseball's immortal Ty Cobb, jazz musician Nat "King" Cole (on a Republic of Mali 130-

George Sanders with Sir Keith Holyoake, Prime Minister of New Zealand.

George with Sir William E. Rowlings, who also served as Prime Minister of New Zealand (1974-75) during George's tenure with New Zealand Radio.

franc stamp) as well as a U.S. commemorative, Academy Award-winning actors Gary Cooper and Bing Crosby, Radio's inventor Dr. Lee DeForest, New York Governor Thomas E. Dewey, Astronauts Charlie Duke and Ken Mattingly on Liberian, Togolaise and Khaima stamps. We've only reached the letter "D" in the alphabet. We have yet to name a celebrity whose autograph is not frequently available in affordable dealer catalogues. In other words, there are literally thousands of low-cost items readily purchasable for your own collection of famous people on stamps with their autographs.

Now, let's devote some space to those of you not in the least interested in contemporary celebrities. You probably prefer and can afford to invest in such people on stamps as

the very rare Sojourner Truth or George Washington or Abraham Lincoln. So be it.

Thanks to the availability of Linn's "Who's Who on U.S. Stamps" by the brilliant biographer Richard Louis Thomas and his second volume, "More Who's Who on U.S. Stamps," you will have little difficulty in targeting the signatures you'll need to accompany the equally available U.S. postage stamps that salute your heroes or heroines. You'll start searching for the autographs of Shadoo, chief of the Kiawah tribe; Belva Lockwood, an attorney who drafted a bill for equal pay for equal work by women; Dr. Crawford Long, one of the first to use ether during surgery; Dr. Paul Dudley White, a heart specialist on a bicycle; Moina Belle Michael, who gave us Poppy Day for war veterans; Thomas Carlyle, the Scottish essayist and biographer; Francis E. Stanley, who gave us the redoubtable Stanley Steamer; Charles Lindbergh, who gave us a 1927 flight to Paris never to be forgotten; Henry C. Stutz, whose car won early dirt races and on and on.

The aforementioned books give you concise and wonderful biographies to grace the pages of your autographs and stamps. As you surely know, every famous American is on stamps and every famous American, for a price, is available on autograph material including signatures, letters, manuscripts, documents, and if the celebrated signers are not too ancient, signed cabinet, *carte de visite* or photographs are usually available.

If you ultimately wish to include the postage stamps of foreign lands, you will find a limitless supply of world leaders, sports stars, film luminaries, artists, composers, architects, scientists, and others too numerous to mention. We personally choose to draw the line at acquiring hoof prints of champion horse-racing thoroughbreds shown on many European stamps. Our autograph collecting

knows some limitations and the latter heads the list, though we do have a genuine hoofprint of Roy Rogers' "Trigger" acquired long ago.

As we mentioned earlier, the U.S. Postal Service has always maintained a strict policy of never producing stamps representing living persons. A celebrated person must have been dead at least five years before being honored with the exception of assassinated presidents or the like of martyred Dr. Martin Luther King. The Post Office would like us to believe there are no exceptions—you have to be in a grave somewhere before your face makes it to philatelic glory. We've got autographic proof that they goofed.

Back in 1932 the Post Office Department issued a 2-cent red Arbor Day stamp picturing a boy and girl planting a tree. It is one of the few stamps with a design including readily identifiable living persons at that time.

The two children were Alvin Hall, Jr., and his sister Ruth, whose father, Alvin W. Hall, was director of the Bureau of Engraving and Printing. The tree also is identifiable. It is a maple still growing beside the Hall home at 1319 Kalmia Road, NW, Washington, D.C. We were delighted to acquire an original

The Hall children—Ruth and Alvin, Jr.— in the photograph that served as the basis for the famous Arbor Day stamp design.

Autograph of Alvin W. Hall, father of the children above and director of the Bureau of Engraving and Printing.

photograph of the Hall kids planting the now famous tree and have the autograph of their father as well. Just one more example of how much fun this wonderful hobby can be. We've proved that joining two great hobbies such as philography and philately offers another facet to collectible jewels.

In the following pages are some examples from our extensive collection in which philography has joined philately.

FDCs, Stamps, and Autographs

(Helpful definitions: FDC = First Day Cover, sig = signature.)

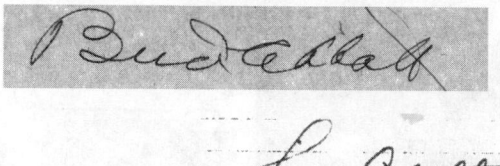

The classic comedy team of Abbott and Costello, stamp and autographs.

Jane Addams stamp and sig.

Horatio Alger, up by his bootstraps—sig above, FDC to left.

Below, author Louisa May Alcott—stamp & sig.

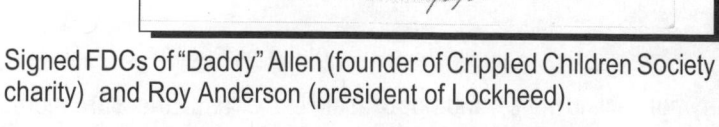

Signed FDCs of "Daddy" Allen (founder of Crippled Children Society charity) and Roy Anderson (president of Lockheed).

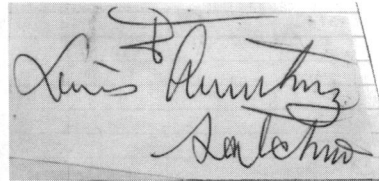

George with Louis Armstrong. Above, right—Armstrong sig, U.S. stamp, and foreign stamps.

Theda Bara, vamp of the silent screen.

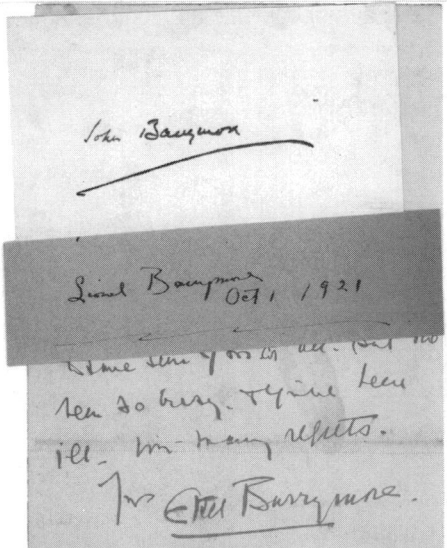
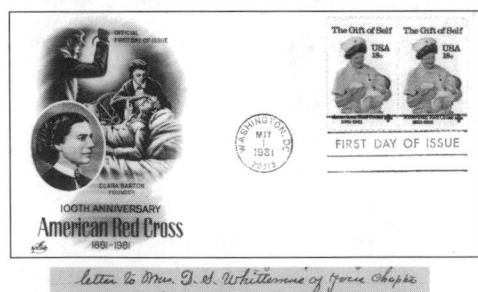

Clara Barton of the American Red Cross.

Above, FDC honoring the Barrymore acting family, and sigs of John, Lionel, and Ethel Barrymore.

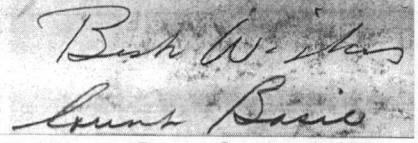

Right, young George Sanders (in 1938) with Count Basie. Above Count Basie U.S. stamp and autograph.

Above, Alexander Grahram Bell.

Jack Benny with George in Hollywood, his sig and U.S. stamp.

Ezra Taft Benson, served in Eisenhower's cabinet and as President of the Mormon church.

Thomas Hart Benton, artist.

Edgar Bergen, creator of Charlie McCarthy (and Candice Bergen's father). Sig and stamp.

Mary McLeod Bethune, American educator and founder of the Daytona Normal and Industrial School for Girls.

Supreme Court Justice Hugo L. Black, U.S. stamp and sig.

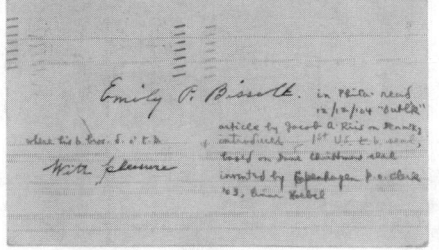

Emily Bissell, founder of the Christmas Seal campaign. FDC and sig.

Mongomery Blair, Abraham Lincoln's first Postmaster General. FDC and sig.

Jazz great, Eubie Blake on a U.S. stamp, and his autograph.

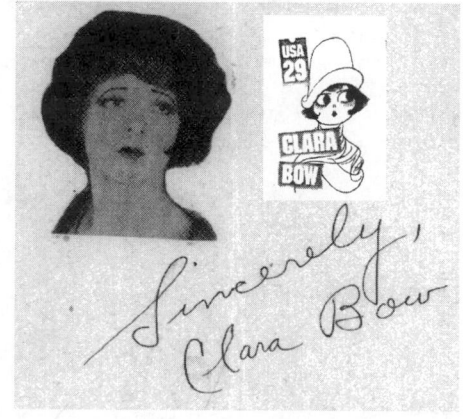

Silent film's "It girl," Clara Bow—stamp & sig.

PHILOGRAPHY JOINS PHILATELY   81

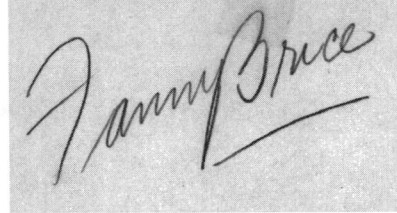

Silent movie funny lady, Fanny Brice.

Author Pearl S. Buck, George and Helen Sanders, the Buck stamp and her sig.

Plant wizard, Luther Burbank—sig and U.S. stamp.

APOLLO 11 ASTRONAUT EDWIN E. ALDRIN JR. WALKS ON MOON

Lunar astronaut Buzz Aldrin—stamp and signed photograph.

Left, Dr. Ralph Bunche of the United Nations stamp and sig. Above, Dr. Bunche with George Sanders.

Sincerely,

Admiral Richard E. Bryd, polar explorer.

Above, rare glossy 8x10 signed photograph with signatures of Gus Grissom, Edward White, and Roger Chaffee, who all three died in the first NASA rocket accident. Picture also has the sig of James McDivitt. Also shown are three Chaffee foreign stamps and photo of George with Chaffee.

Author Rachel Carson—sig and stamps.

Cartoonist Al Capp, creator of Li'l Abner.

Members of country music's legendary Carter family with George Sanders. That's Mother Maybelle to his left (your right) and June Carter Cash, wife of Johnny Cash, on his right. Also shown is June Carter Cash's sig and the Carter Family stamp.

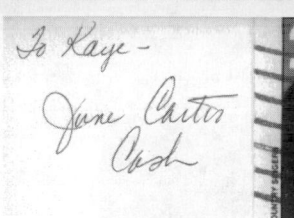

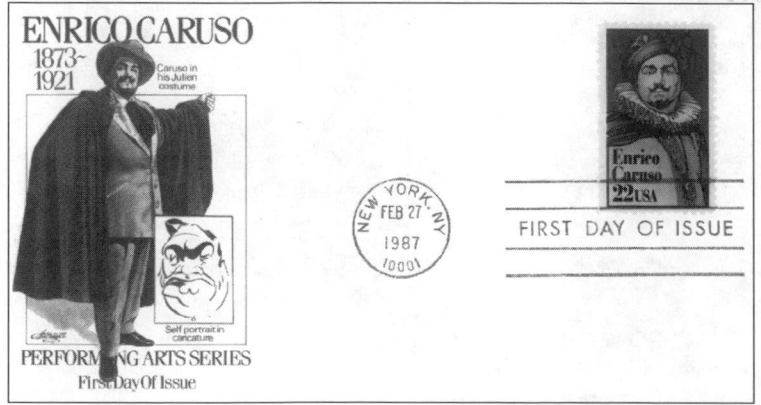

Opera singer of note, Enrico Caruso.

Author Willa Cather—FDC and sig.

Senator Dennis Chavez, U.S. stamp and SP.

Scientist George Washington Carver.

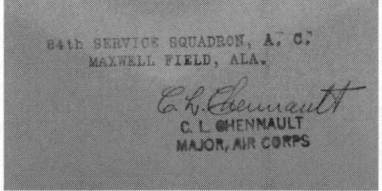

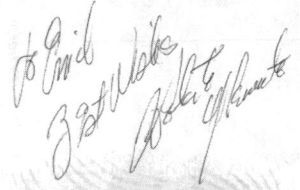

Baseball star Roberto Clemente—FDC and sig.

General Claire Chennault, commander of the legendary Flying Tigers in World War II.

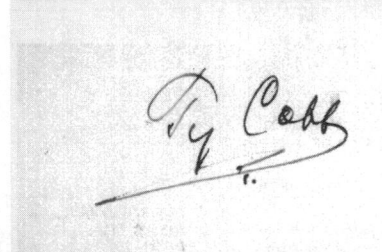

That's George kneeling in front of baseball legends (l to r) Ty Cobb, Fred Haney, and George Sisler. Above is a Ty Cobb sig and two stamps.

Composer George M. Cohan, FDC and sig.

Above, singer Nat King Cole stamp. Left, 1950's Hollywood charity baseball game photo—Cole is in front. On back row are George Sanders, Elizabeth Taylor, and Oscar-winning actress Shelley Winters.

President Calvin "Silent Cal" Coolidge—stamp and sig.

Top left of page, famed actor Gary Cooper with George Sanders. Lower left, a Cooper SP. Above are two Cooper stamps, one U.S. and one foreign.

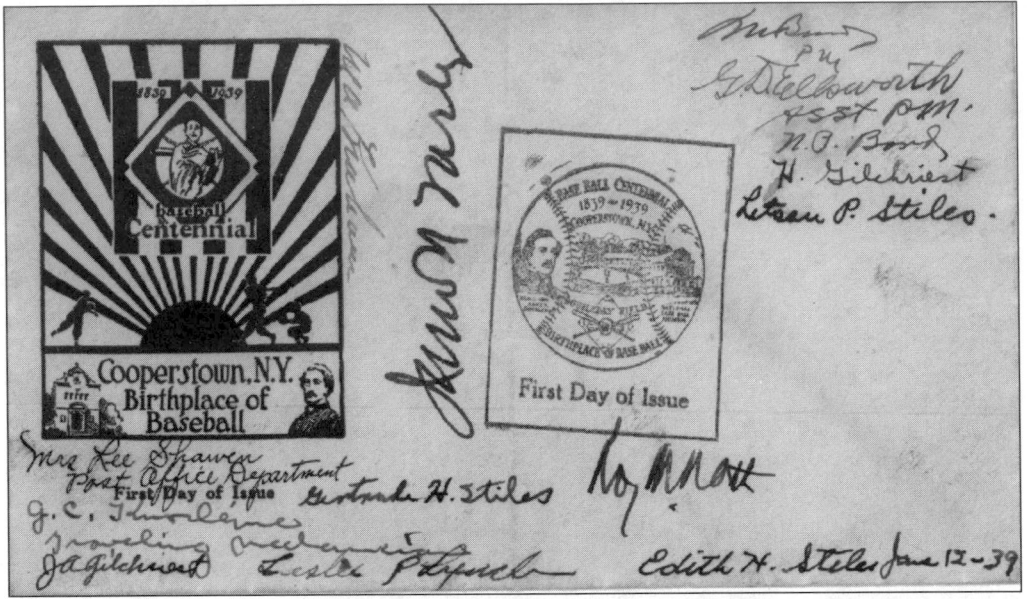

Front and back of FDC issued at Cooperstown, NY and honoring the baseball's centennial in 1939. Sigs are mostly of local notables of the time.

Singer Bing Crosby—sig, stamp, and photo with George.

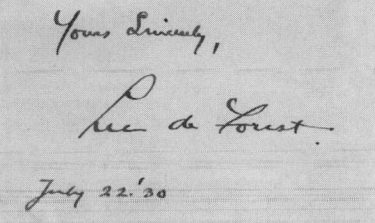

Aviation pioneer Glenn
Curtiss—stamp and sig.

Radio pioneer Lee de
Forest—FDC, sig and
photo (seated) with
George Sanders.

American statesman Dean
Acheson—sig and stamp.

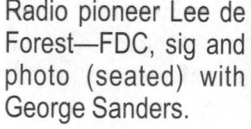

Rebel actor James Dean—stamp, sig,
and photo of George, Terry Moore
(Howard Hughes' wife), and Dean.

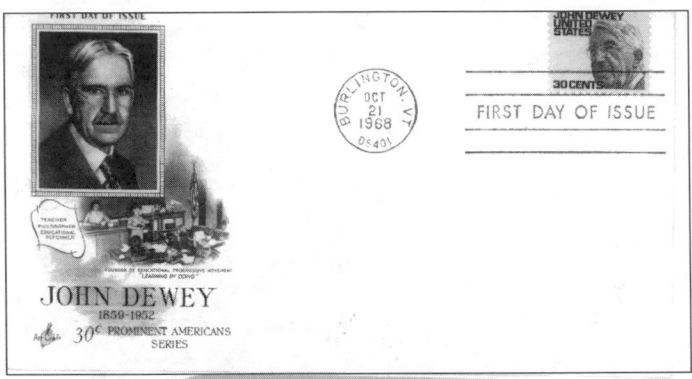

Philospher John Dewey—FDC and sig.

Inventor Henry Dearborn—stamp and sig.

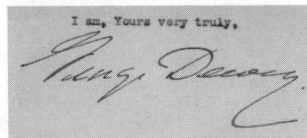

Stamp of Admiral George Dewey and two other heroes of the Spanish-American War, and a sig of Dewey.

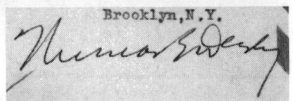

George with Thomas E. Dewey, presidential candidate. Sig to right.

Humanitarian Dorthea Dix—FDC and sig. She worked to relieve the suffering of the mentally ill.

Big band leaders, Tommy and Jimmy Dorsey—above top left stamp, left George with Jimmy Dorsey and Dorsey sig, right Tommy Dorsey signed photograph.

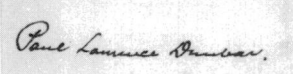

Famous African-Americans: Frederick Douglass—stamp & sig—and Poet Paul Dunbar—FDC & sig.

Top, Apollo 16 astronaut stamps. Pictured left Astronault Charlie Duke with George, right sigs of Charlie Duke and Ken Mattingly, and photo of Ken Mattingly with George

American statesman and Secretary of State, John Foster Dulles—FDC and signed photograph.

Top, President Dwight D. Eisenhower with George Sanders (in white circle), above various stamps, left Eisenhower sig.

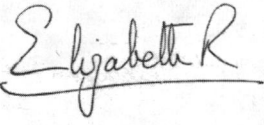 

Above, (in white circle) Roger Gilchrist of Auction House autograph auctions and author George Sanders watch Queen Elizabeth II during a 1970s visit to New Zealand. Also shown above—sig and stamp of Queen Elizabeth II.

And speaking of the nobility, here are stamps and the sig of jazz great Duke Ellington. The top photo is George with Duke in 1959, and the bottom photo is a younger George with him in 1939.

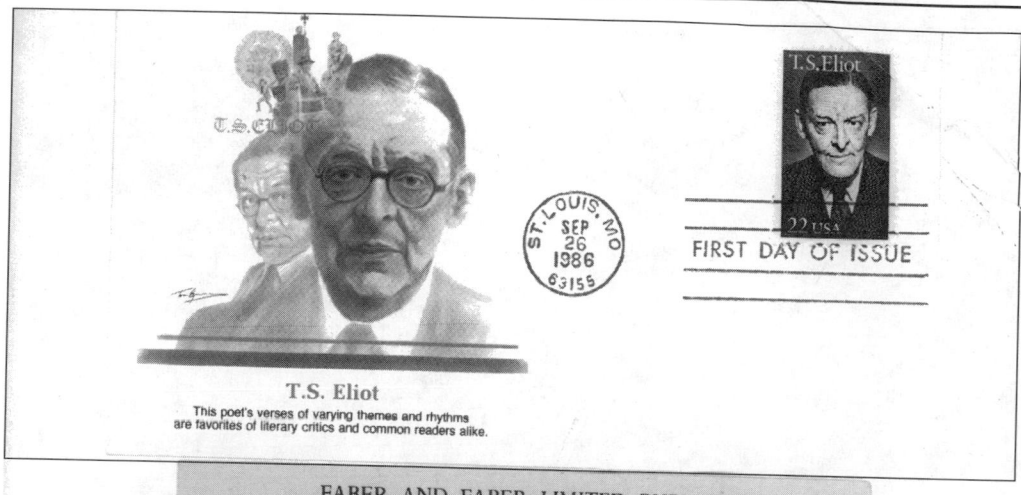

T.S. Eliot

This poet's verses of varying themes and rhythms
are favorites of literary critics and common readers alike.

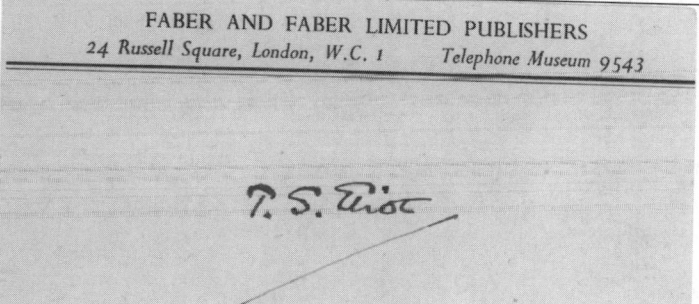

FABER AND FABER LIMITED PUBLISHERS
24 Russell Square, London, W.C. 1   Telephone Museum 9543

English poet T.S. Eliot—FDC and sig.

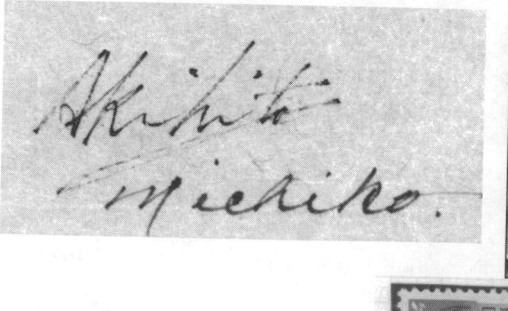

Above, sigs of Japanese Emperor
Akihito and Empress Michiko. Left,
a stamp with both, and a photo of
George Sanders during his
newsman days with the Empress
and Emperor in the background.

ENKA PARK BOARD — Newly elected members of the Enka Park Board of Commissioners are (L-R) Jack Duckett, George R. Sand- ers (chairman), Troy Lewis, Wilbur Davis and Tollie Roberts (secretary-treasurer). The board oversees the area's lighting and sewer systems.

Enka Couple Receives Citizen Of The Year Award From Lions

By Peggy Gastello

GEORGE AND HELEN SANDERS point proudly to the plaque which they received from the Enka Lions Club as Citizens of the Year.

Top left: signed cover honoring the small town of Enka, North Carolina. Enka is now the home of George and Helen Sanders, and of Autograph House. Above left: clipping from the Asheville *Citizen-Times* showing the Enka Park Board with George (2nd from left) it's newly elected chairman. Also shown (and also from the *Citizen-Times*) are clippings reporting Helen and George being named as Enka's Citizen of the Year.

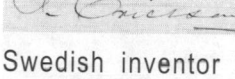

Swedish inventor John Ericsson— stamp and sig.

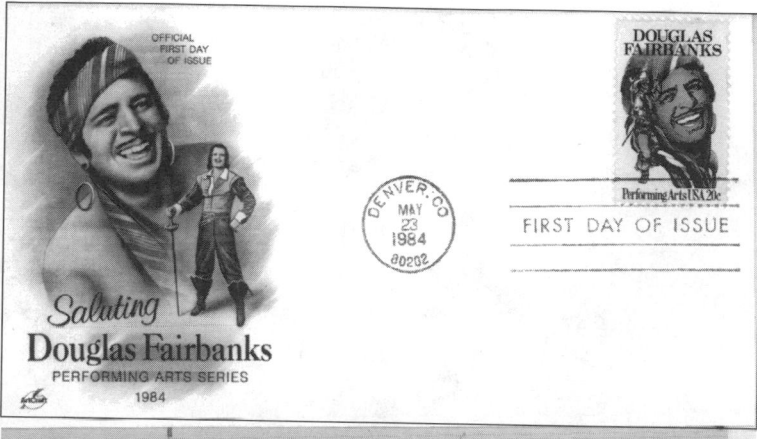

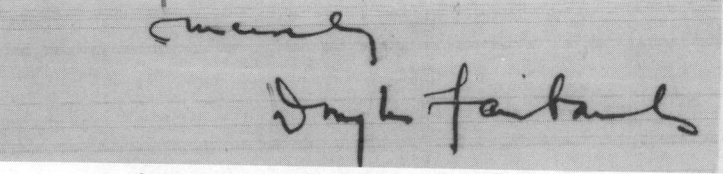

Actor Douglas Fairbanks, Sr.—FDC and sig.

American inventor Philo T. Farnsworth— FDC and sig.

Actor and comedian, W.C. Fields—FDC and sig.

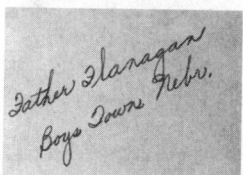

Left, Father Flanagan of Boys' Town fame—FDC and sig.

Above, George with figure skater Peggy Flemming—her sig and stamp.

Top, signed drawing of Prince Valiant by cartoonist creator Hal Foster. Directly above, the Prince Valiant stamp.

John Charles Fremont, American explorer, soldier, and political leader—stamp and sig.

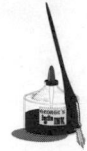

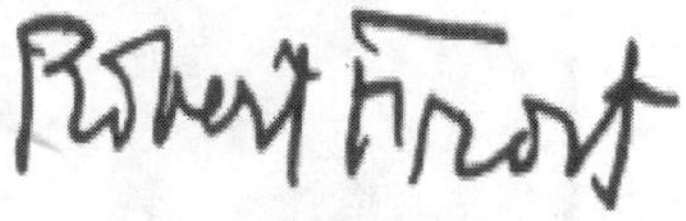

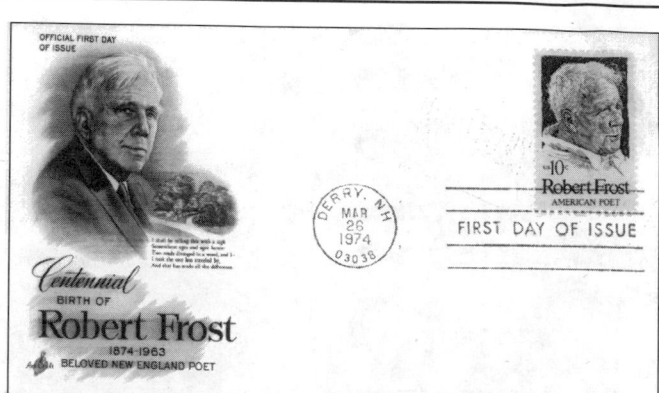

Notable American poet, Robert Frost—FDC and sig.

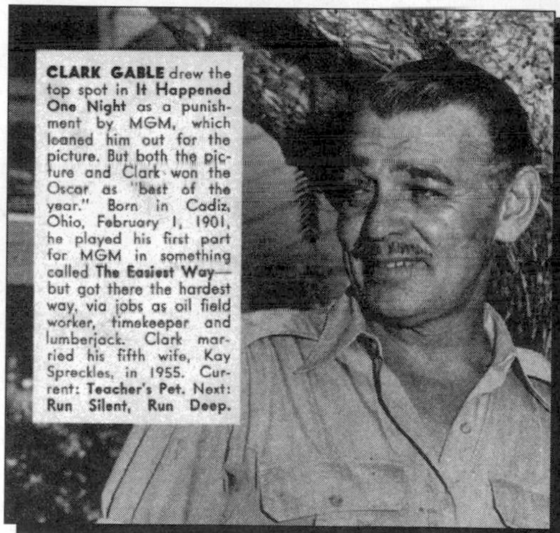

CLARK GABLE drew the top spot in **It Happened One Night** as a punishment by MGM, which loaned him out for the picture. But both the picture and Clark won the Oscar as "best of the year." Born in Cadiz, Ohio, February 1, 1901, he played his first part for MGM in something called **The Easiest Way**—but got there the hardest way, via jobs as oil field worker, timekeeper and lumberjack. Clark married his fifth wife, Kay Spreckles, in 1955. Current: **Teacher's Pet.** Next: **Run Silent, Run Deep.**

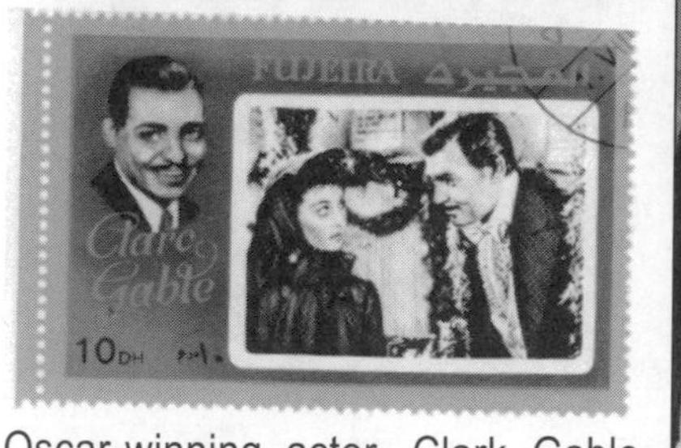

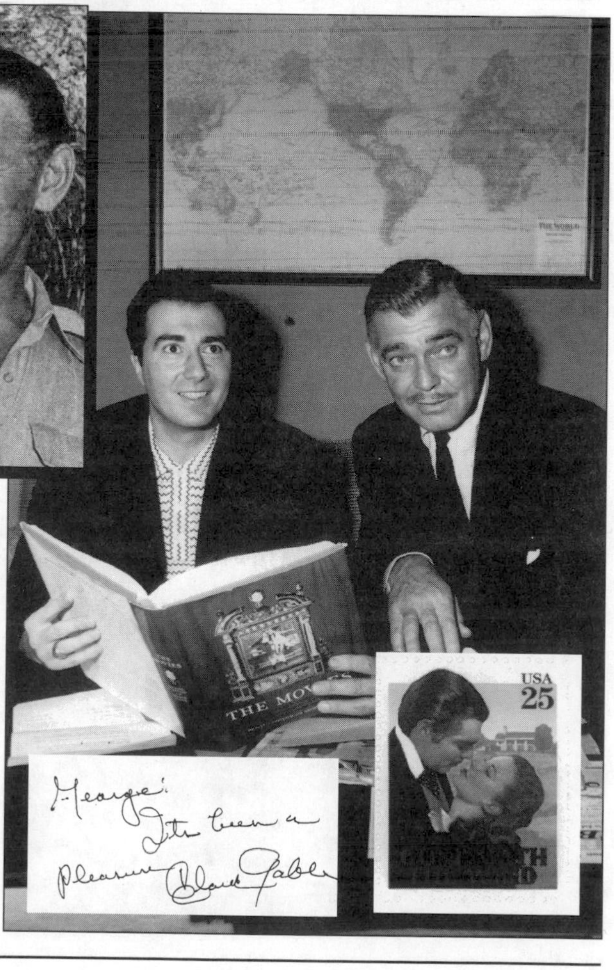

Oscar-winning actor, Clark Gable. Above, clipping from 1950s movie fan magazine, above stamp, left photo of George and Gable, Gable's sig, and U.S. stamp honoring Gable's part in the classic move, "Gone With the Wind."

India's champion of passive resistance, Mahatma Gandi—stamps and sig.

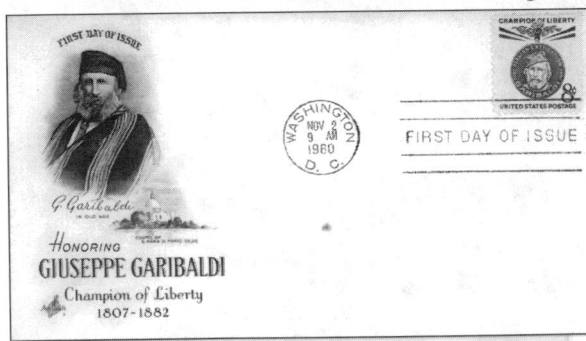

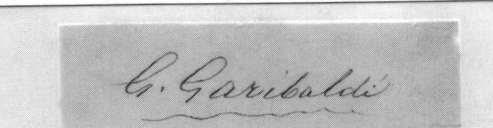

Red-shirted Italian fighter for freedom, Giuseppe Garibaldi—FDC and sig.

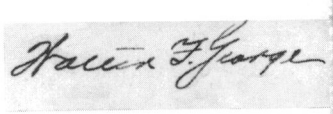

Senator Walter George— stamp and sig.

Actress Judy Garland in her most famous role—stamp and sig.

Baseball Hall of Famer Lou Gehrig—signed FDC and stamp.

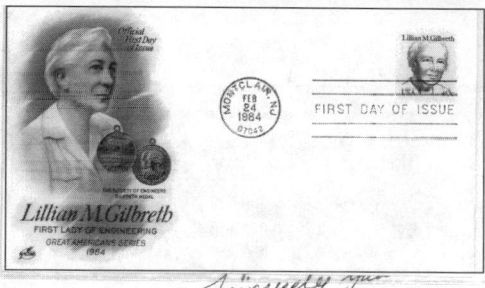

Lillian M. Gilbreth, the "First Lady of Engineering"—FDC and sig.

Cartoonist Rube Goldberg—signed drawing and stamp.

Jazz clarinetist and band leader Benny Goodman—stamp and sig.

PHILOGRAPHY JOINS PHILATELY   103

Astronaut and now Senator John Glenn (first U.S. astronaut to fully orbit the Earth)—signed photo, FDC, signed cover, and three foreign stamps.

Princess Grace of Monaco (actress Grace Kelly)—top right, rare instance of U.S. and foreign stamp being of the same design, top left Princess Grace with George Sanders, below photo signed stamp, other stamps.

Explorer Adolphus W. Greely—signed check and stamp.

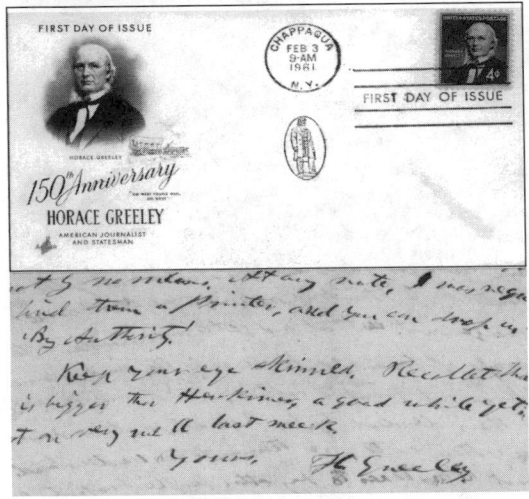

Horace Greeley, journalist—FDC and portion of signed letter.

Musician W.C. Handy—stamp and sig.

Above, rocker Bill Haley—signed photo and stamp.

Jazz saxophonist Coleman Hawkins—
sig and stamp.

Author and storyteller
Joel Chandler Harris—
stamp and signed note.

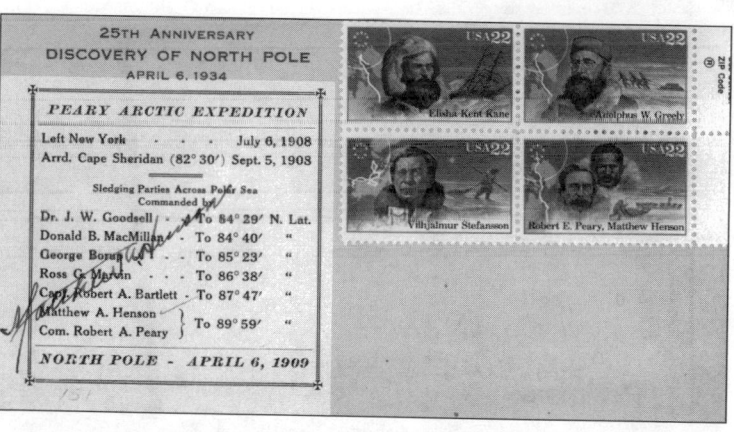

Above, author Bret
Harte—stamp and sig.

Right, two rare FDC
signed by Matthew
Henson, African-
American Arctic
explorer.

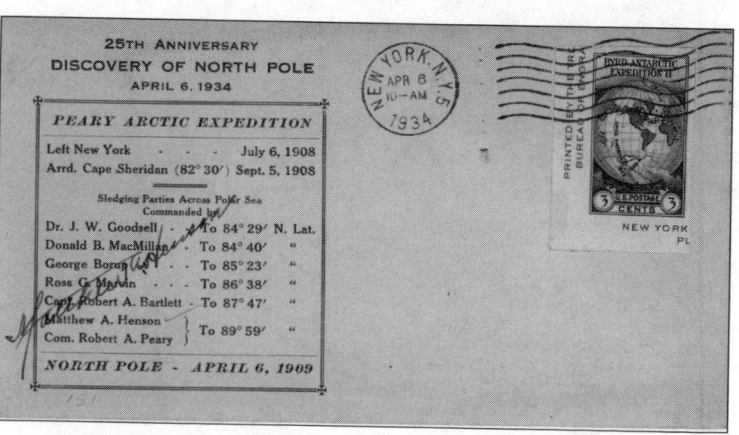

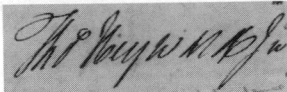

Thomas Heyward, Jr., Signer of the Declaration of Independence—stamp & sig.

William Hooper, Signer of the Declaration of Independence— stamp & sig.

Above, artist and stamp designer Hirschfeld—signed drawing and stamps.

American statesman Cordell Hull— stamp and sig.

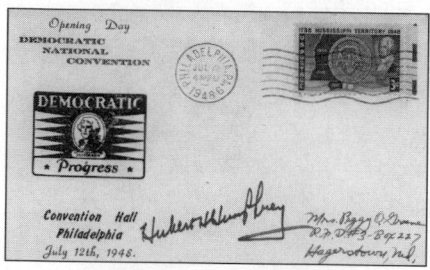

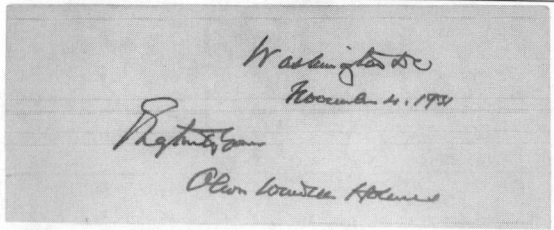

Supreme Court Justice Oliver Wendell Holmes— FDC and sig.

1968 Democratic Presidential nominee and former Vice President of the United States Hubert Humphrey was only one of thousands of celebrities interviewed by George Sanders during his long career as a journalist, and many of these celebrities are now honored by stamps. Above is a Humphrey signed FDC, stamps, and photo with George.

Artist Robert Indiana, designer of the "Love" stamp—signed FDC

Lou Jacobs, famous clown—signed FDC

UNITED STATES POSTAGE

3¢

IWO JIMA

John H. Bradley

Cpl. Rene A. Gagnon

Sgt. Michael Strank

Pfc. Ira H. Hayes

Pharmacist's Mate John H. Bradley

Pfc. Franklin R. Sousley

Pfc. Rene A. Gagnon

Cpl. Harlan H. Block

Joe Rosenthal

| SOUSLEY | HAYES | STRANK | BRADLEY | GAGNON |

Three survivors scattered around the country are Bradley, Hayes and Gagnon

Upper left, the very well-known photograph of the flag-raising on Iwo Jima during World War II with identifications of participants. Upper right, the Iwo Jima stamp. Below stamp, Joel Rosenthal (the photographer)—photo and sig. Just above caption, the five survivors of the war. The sigs of Bradley and Gagnon are superimposed on photo on top right of page.

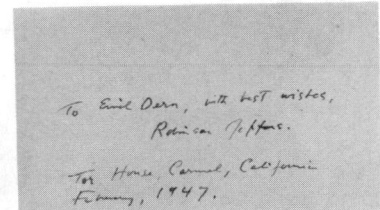

Robinson Jefferson, American poet—FDC and sig.

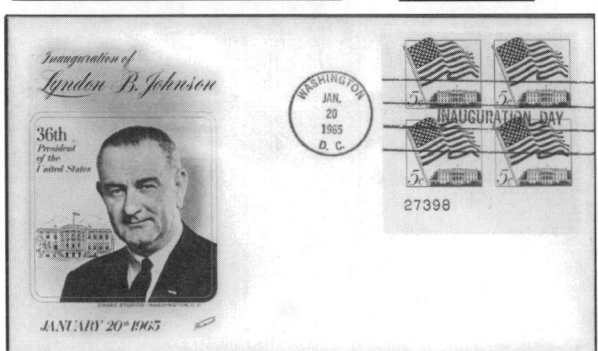

Lyndon B. Johnson. White House card signed

President Lyndon Baines Johnson. Top right, U.S. stamp, below that are some of the many foreign stamps honoring LBJ. Above, an FDC. Right, photo with George Sanders and sig.

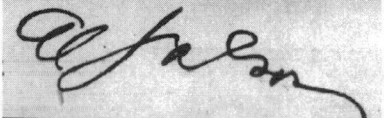

Jazz singer Al Jolson—stamp and sig.

Comic actor Buster Keaton—stamps and sig,
and photo with George.

Golfer Bobby Jones—
stamp and sig.

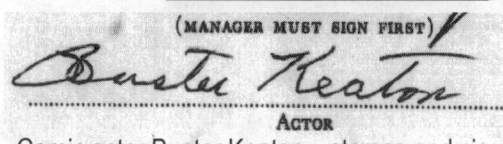

Blind writer and lecturer Helen Keller
and her famous teacher, Anne Sullivan
on a FDC. To the left are both sigs.

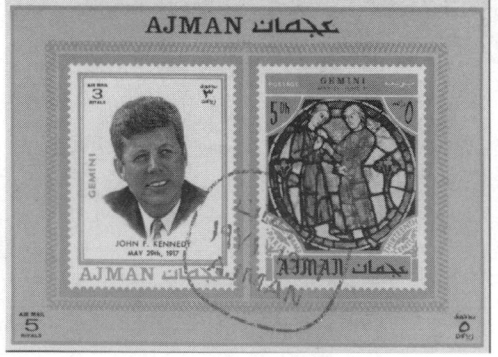

President John F. Kennedy has been the subject of many stamps around the world. Above he is shown with George Sanders. Superimposed on that photo is a JFK sig and a U.S. stamp honoring this slain president. Also shown are just a few of the myriad of foreign stamps whose subject has been President Kennedy.

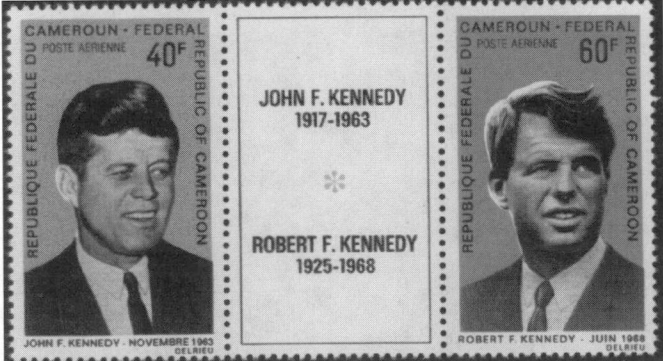

Robert F. Kennedy, former Attorney General, senator, presidential candidate, and victim of assassination as was his brother President John F. Kennedy. Top, photo of RFK interviewed by George Sanders the week before his death. Superimposed on photo are U.S. stamp and sig.

The silent screen's hilarious Keystone Kops—stamp and sigs of "kops" Edgar Kennedy, Charley Chase, and Billy Bletcher.

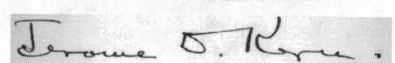

Composer/songwriter Jerome S. Kern—stamp and sig.

Civil rights leader Dr. Martin Luther King. Top, portion of signed *Time* cover. Left photo with George and U.S. stamp. Foreign stamps also shown.

Hungarian patriot Lajos Kossuth—
stamp and sig.

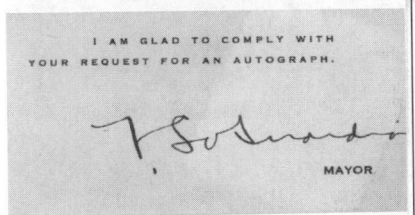

President of Brazil, Dr. Juscelino Kubischek. Above, photo with George and stamp. Left currency
and, directly above caption on right, sig.

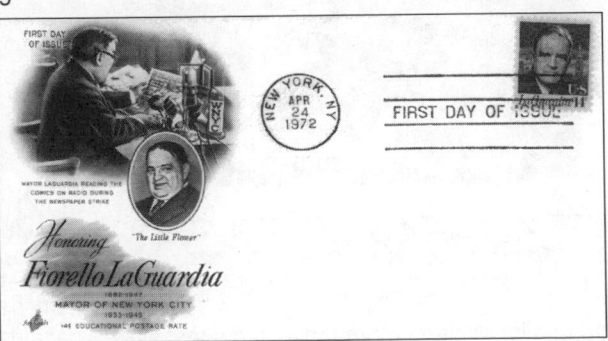

Mayor of New York City, Fiorello
LaGuardia ("the Little Flower")—sig
and stamp.

PHILOGRAPHY JOINS PHILATELY   117

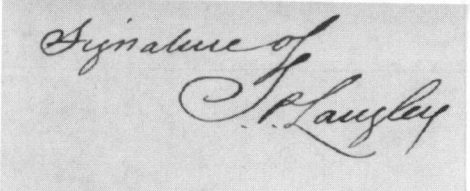

Inventor Samuel P. Langley—stamp and sig.

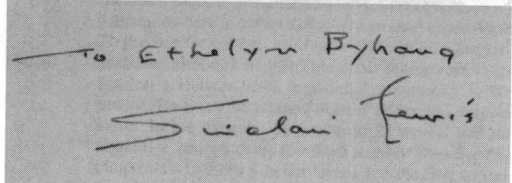

Author Sinclair Lewis—stamp and sig.

Journalist Walter Lippmann—stamp and sig.

Belva Ann Bennett Lockwood, first woman attorney and first woman presidential candidate—stamp and sig.

An unique piece, a check written and signed by silent film comedian Harold Lloyd to himself—front and back are shown along with the stamp honoring this clock-clinging classic funny guy.

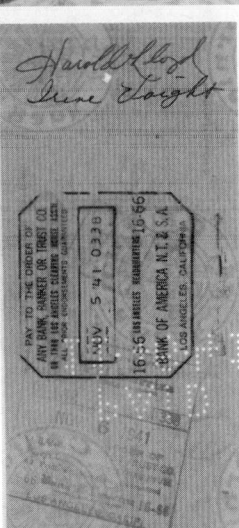

Joe Louis, the Brown Bomber, with George and George's son Sandy. Also sig and stamp (circa 1958).

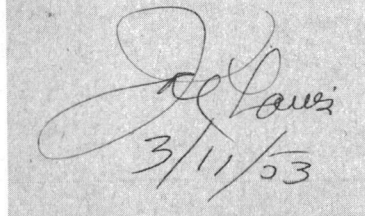

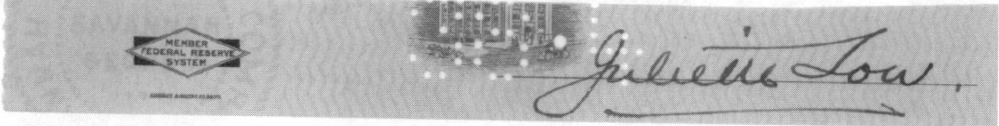

Juliette Low, founder of the Girl Scouts in America—FDC and sig.

Mary Lyon, educator and founder of Mount Holyoake Seminary—stamp and sig.

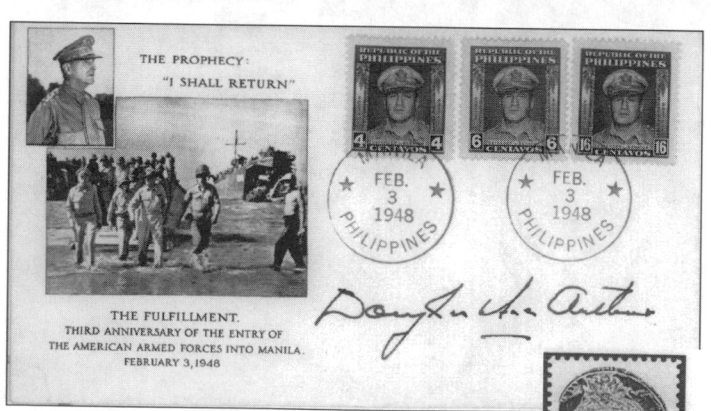

General Douglas MacArthur—signed FDC and stamp.

Ramon Magsaysay, president of the Philippine Republic—FDC, stamp, and signed photograph.

King Mahendra of Nepal (a Buddhist leader) sig on a Christmas FDC. Also shown, stamps, and a photograph with George.

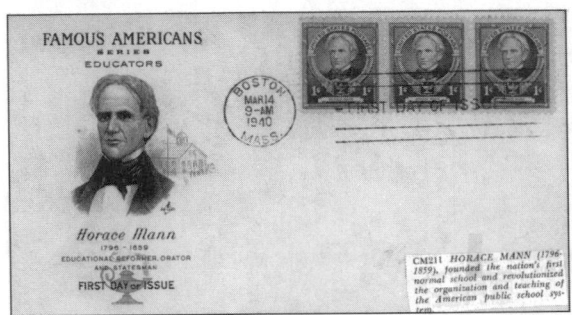

Horace Mann, American educator—FDC and stamp.

Air mail cover bearing stamps honoring Imelda Marcos
(famous for her many pairs of shoes) of the Philippines,
along with her sig.

Tomas Garrigue Masaryk,
Czechoslovakian patriot—SP
and stamp.

Luis Munoz Marin, governor of Puerto Rico. A signed
First Day Cover (FDC) and a U.S. stamp honoring this
significant Puerto Rican leader.

George "Lucky Dog" Sanders with Hollywood sex goddess Jayne Mansfield. with a stamp and sig.

WAR DEPARTMENT

THIS IS MY AUTOGRAPH.

CHIEF OF STAFF, U.S. ARMY.

General George C. Marshall—stamp and sig.

Designer Peter Max—signed FDC.

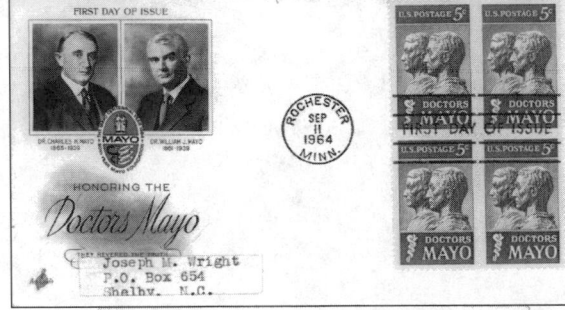

The famous doctor brothers Charles and William Mayo of the Mayo Clinic—FDC above and (left) sigs of both.

Poet Edgar Lee Masters—FDC and sig.

Olympic champion and Congressman Bob Mathias—above FDC, left with George and on foreign stamp.

Irish tenor John McCormack—FDC and sig.

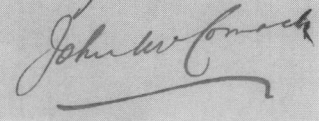

Cartoonist George McManus—stamp and drawing.

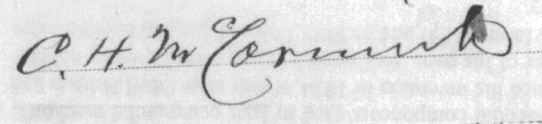

Inventor Cyrus McCormick—stamp and sig..

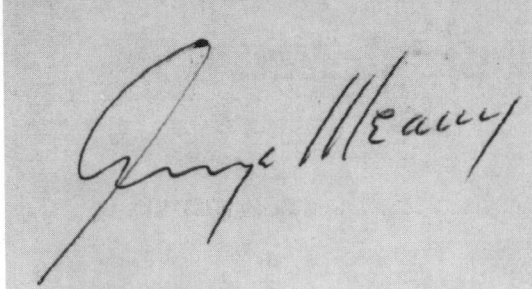
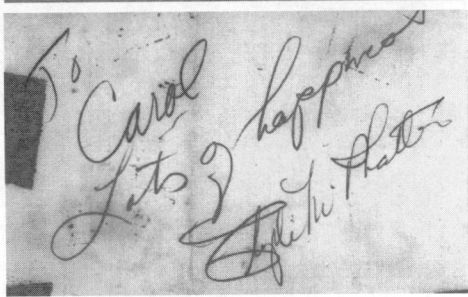

Rocker Clyde McPhatter—stamp and sig.

Labor leader George Meany. Top, photo of Meany, far left, with George Sanders, far right (and we refuse to touch *that* one!). Also shown are Meany sig, FDC, and stamp.

Singer Ethel Merman—stamp and sig.

Big band leader Glenn Miller with George. Also shown are sig and stamp.

Cartoonist Dale Messick—stamp and signed drawing of Brenda Starr.

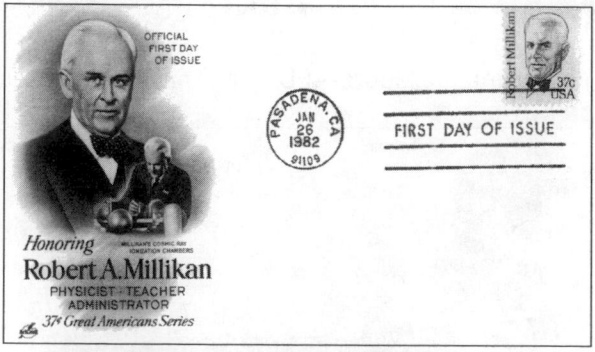

Physicist Robert A. Millikan—FDC and sig.

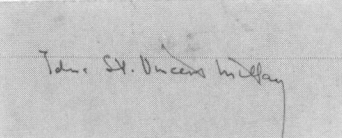

Poet Edna St. Vincent Millay—FDC and sig.

Poet Marianne Moore—FDC and sig superimposed on FDC.

Painter Grandma Moses—FDC and sig.

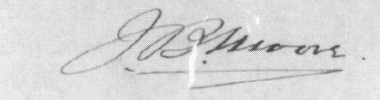

John Bassett Moore, expert in international law—stamp and sig.

Newsman Edward R. Murrow—stamp and sig.

Marilyn Monroe's last autograph was on this check. It was written on August 4th, 1962. A few hours later, she was dead (just after midnight on August 5th). Above is a sheet and detail of the U.S. stamp honoring her. Upper right (since George has so many photos with beautiful actresses) is coauthor Ralph Roberts with Marilyn in Hollywood. Okay! So it's really just a Marilyn look alike, but it was the best he could do. Below that is a photo of George and Ralph with some of the Marilyn items in George's collection.

President Nasser of Egypt—stamp and sig.

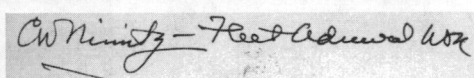

Admiral Chester W. Nimitz—stamp and sig.

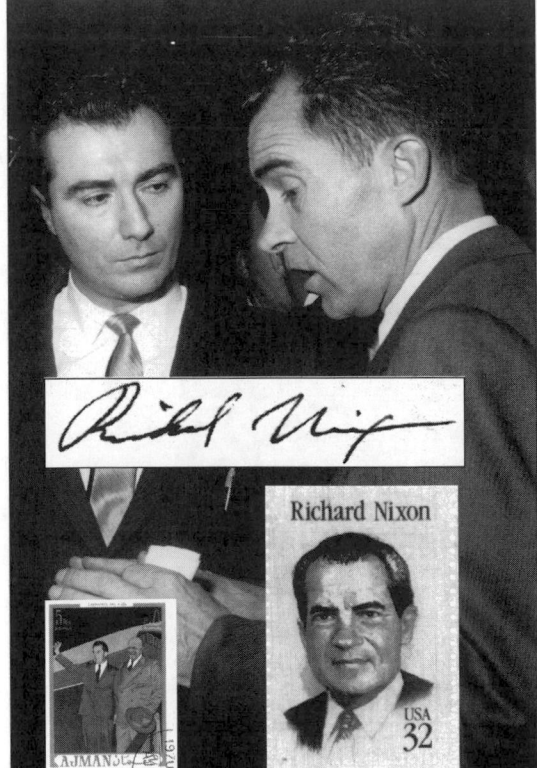

President Richard M. Nixon was the subject of stamps both as president and vice-president. Shown to the left is photo of George and Nixon, sig, and various stamps of the many that Nixon appears on.

citations of those who have "survived" with
me, and I deeply appreciate your good wishes
for my continued survival. The same to you,
and many thanks!

Yours faithfully,

Adolph S. Ochs, publisher of the N.Y. *Times*—
FDC and sig.

Francis Ouimet, French
golfing great—stamp
and sig.

Senator George W. Norris—FDC and signed
silhouette.

Olympic champ Jesse Owens with George—sig and stamp.

PHILOGRAPHY JOINS PHILATELY   131

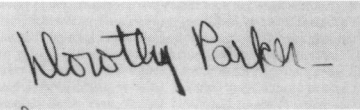

Dorothy Parker, author and well-known wit—stamp and sig.

General George S. Patton, Jr.—stamps and sig.

General John J. Pershing of World War I and chasing Pancho Villa fame—stamp and sig.

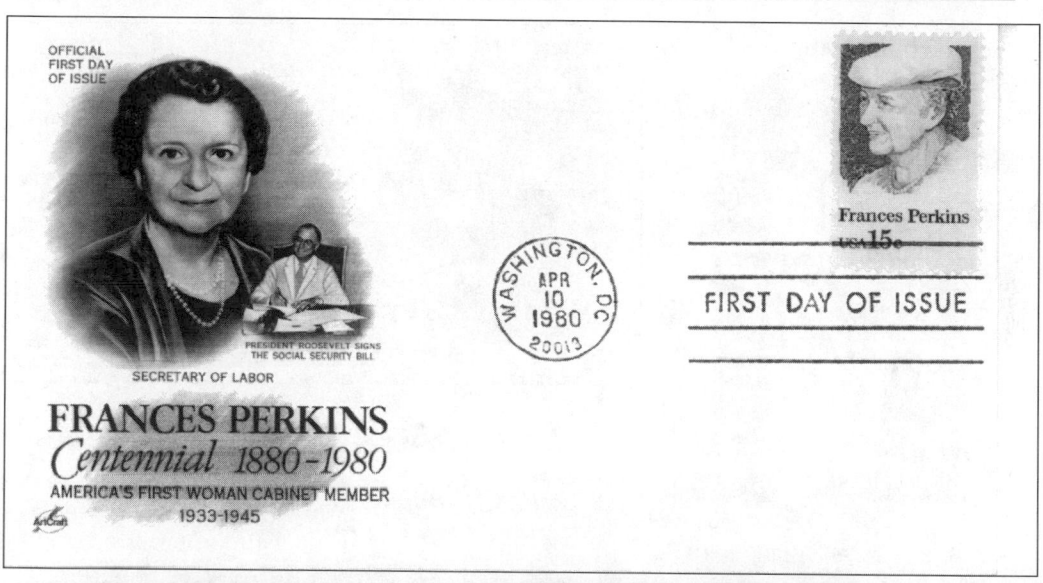

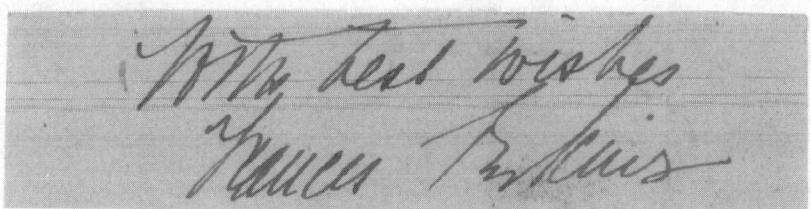

Frances Perkins, first woman member of the U.S. Cabinet—FDC and sig.

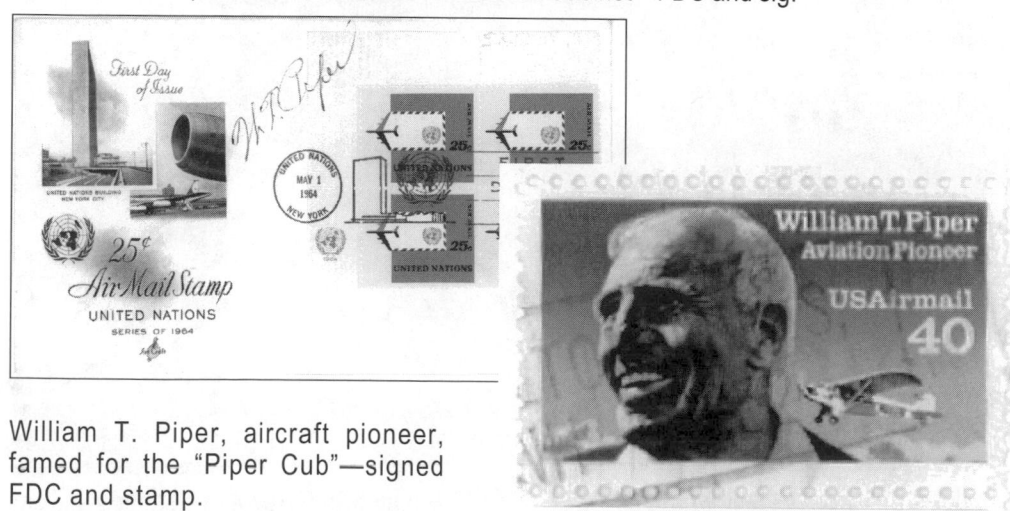

William T. Piper, aircraft pioneer, famed for the "Piper Cub"—signed FDC and stamp.

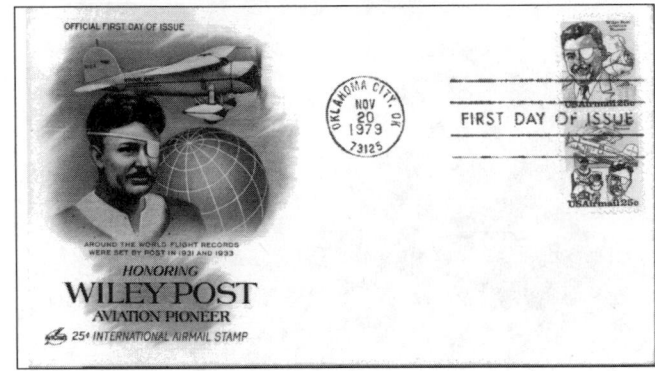

Aviator Wiley Post (died in crash with Will Rogers)—stamp and sigs of Post and his wife.

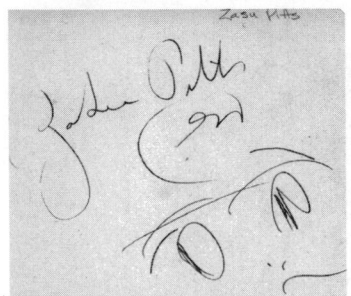

Actress Zasu Pitts—stamp and sig.

Composer Cole Porter—stamp and sig.

Senator Sam Rayburn—stamps and sig.

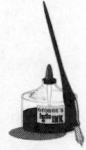

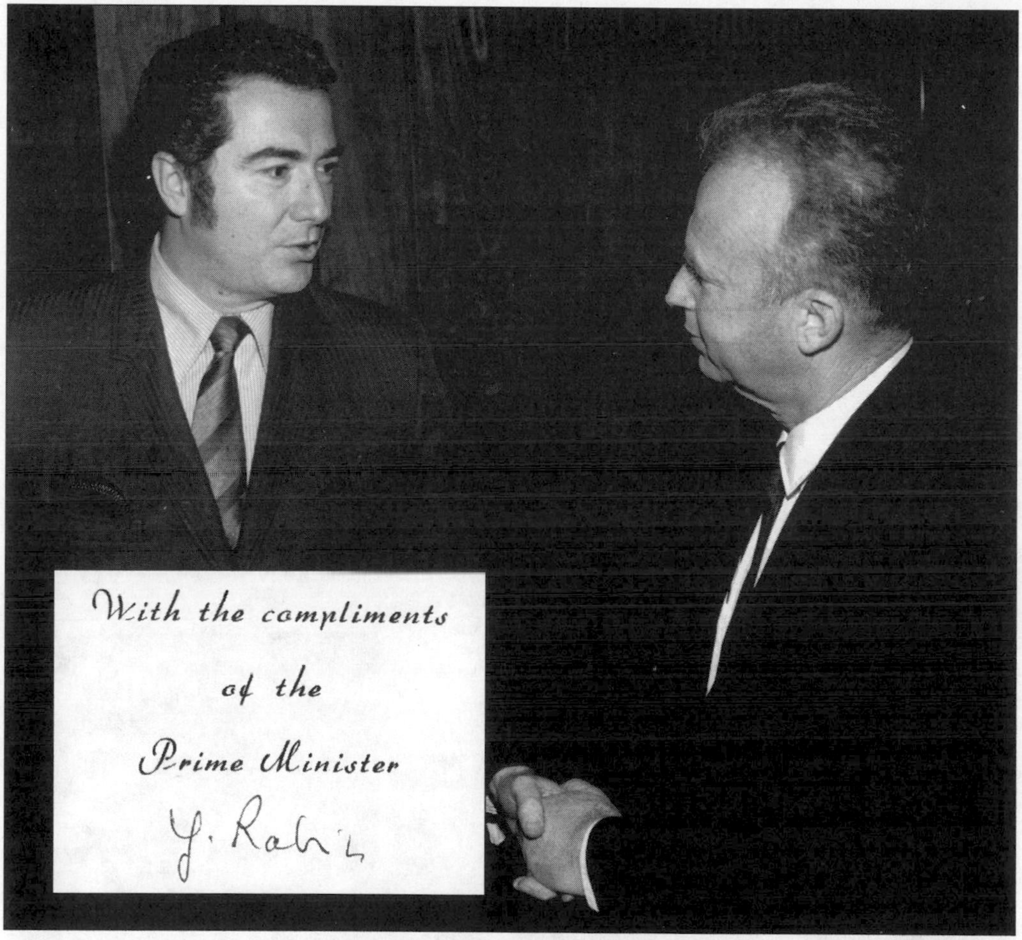
With the compliments
of the
Prime Minister
Y. Rabin

WASHINGTON, D.C.
SEP 10 1974
SMITHSONIAN STA.
THE NATIONAL MUSEUM OF HISTORY AND TECHNOLOGY
UNITED STATES 10
President Ford Confers with Prime Minister Rabin
Yitzhak Rabin, Israel's prime minister and for almost five years its ambassador to the United States, returned to Washington, D.C. to a 19-gun salute and a pledge from President Ford that America stands "committed to Israel's suvival and security".

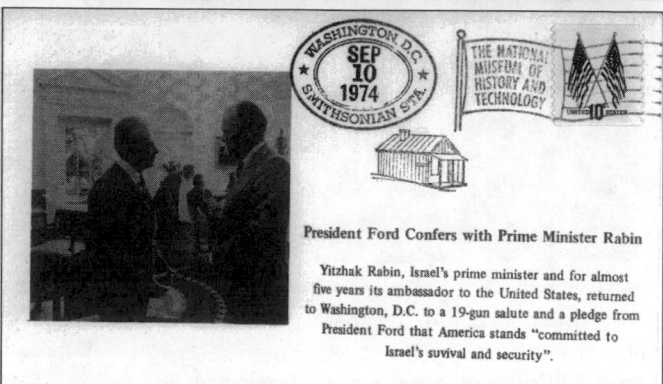

Recently assassinated Israeli Prime Minister Rabin with George Sanders. Also shown (inset in photo) Rabin's sig and (right) a First Day Cover honoring Rabin and President Gerald Ford.

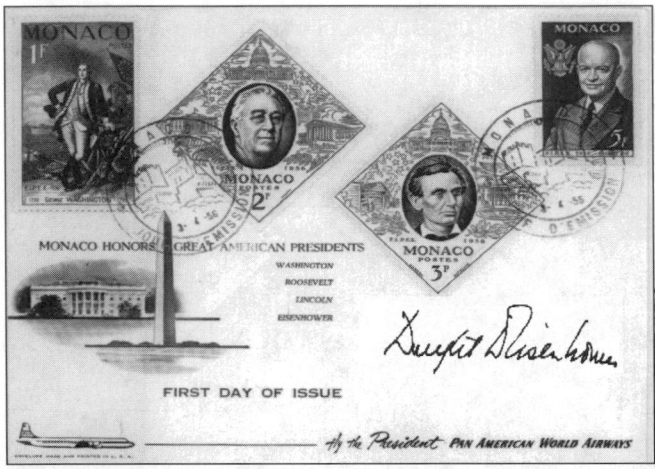

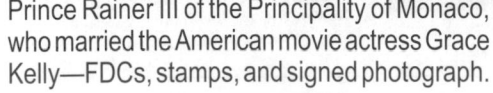

Prince Rainer III of the Principality of Monaco, who married the American movie actress Grace Kelly—FDCs, stamps, and signed photograph.

Above signed photo by President Ronald Reagan showing himself with Nancy Reagan and George Sanders. Also a photo of Reagan and George, plus a stamp and sig.

World War I ace and airline executive Eddie Rickenbacker— signed check and photo with George (stamp not depicted).

Jackie Robinson, first African-American player in major league baseball in modern times. Now enshrined in the Baseball Hall of Fame. Top left, photo with George, top right HoF postcard, left stamp, above sig.

Artist Norman Rockwell—stamp and signed card.

Astronaut Stuart Roosa with George, stamps, FDC, and sig.

FDR's First Lady, Eleanor Roosevelt—stamp and signed photograph.

President Franklin D. Roosevelt—two FDCs honoring FDR, a FDR sig, and a rare FDC signed by FDR's son, John.

Carl Sandburg—stamp and sig.

Senator Richard Russell—FDC and sig.

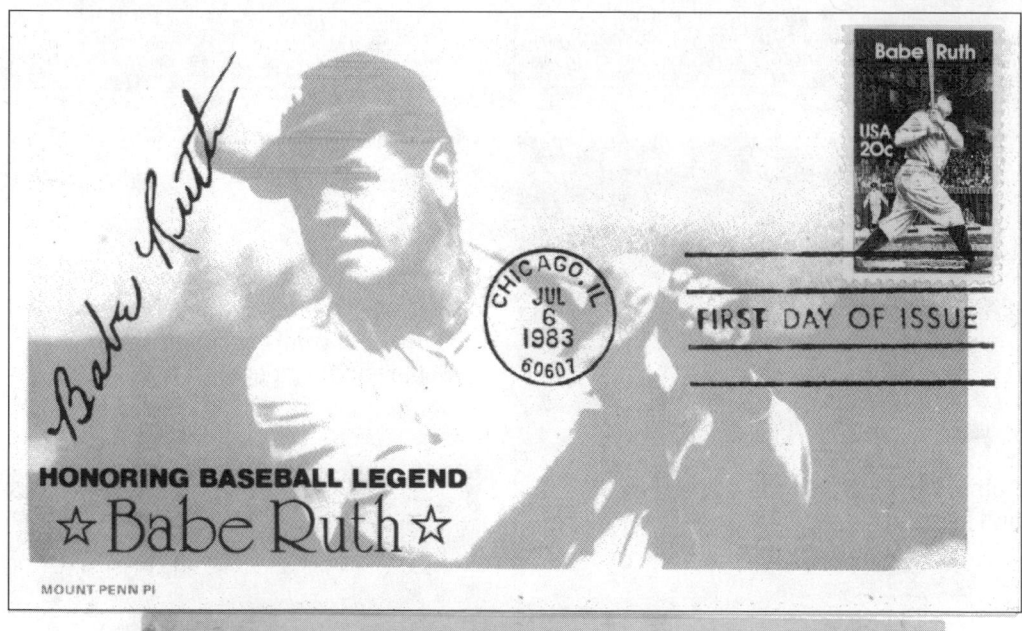

Baseball immortal Babe Ruth—FDC and sig.

The Sanders Price Guide to Autographs

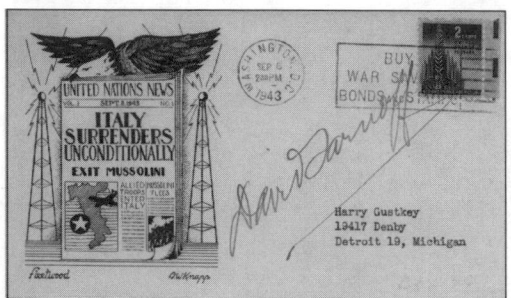

David Sarnoff of RCA—signed FDC.

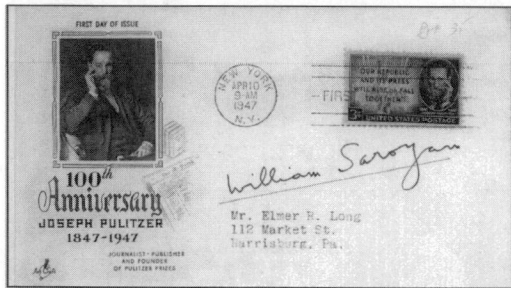

Naval heroes of the Spanish-American War era, Admirals Schley, Simpson, and Dewey. Shown are stamp and sigs of Schley and Simpson.

Author William Saroyan—signed FDC and stamp.

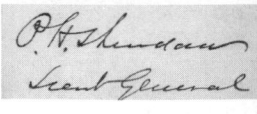

Civil war generals William "Burn, Atlanta, Burn" Sherman, U.S. Grant, and Phil Sheridan on stamp with sigs above of Sheridan and Sherman.

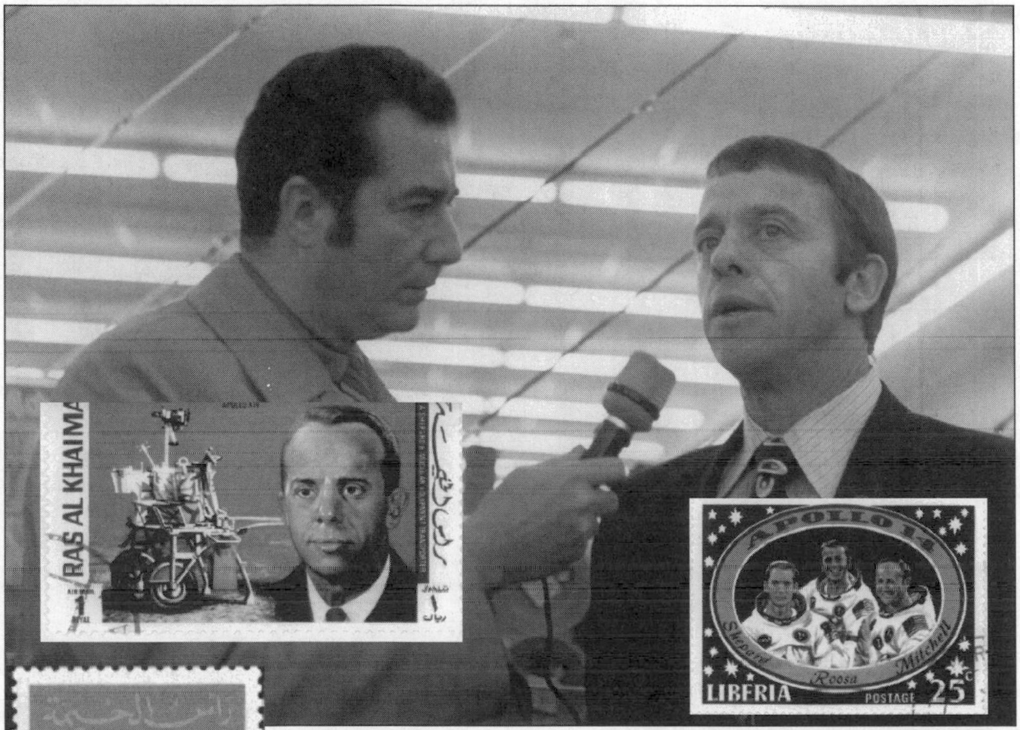

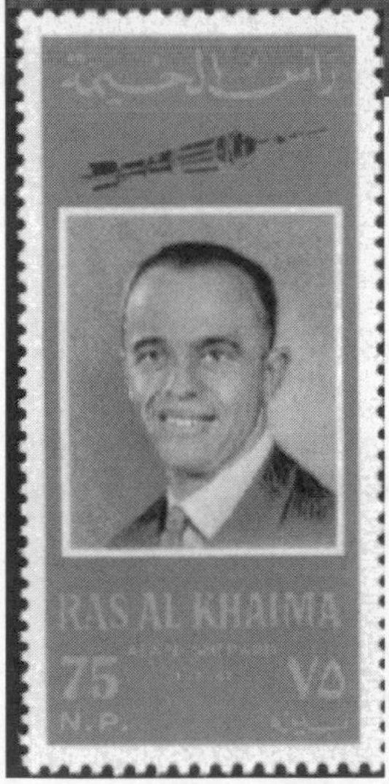

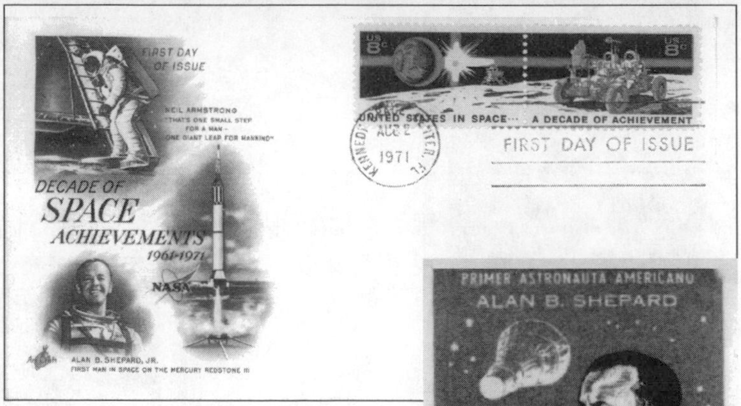

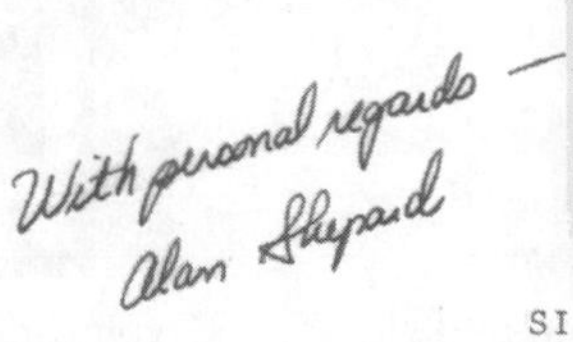

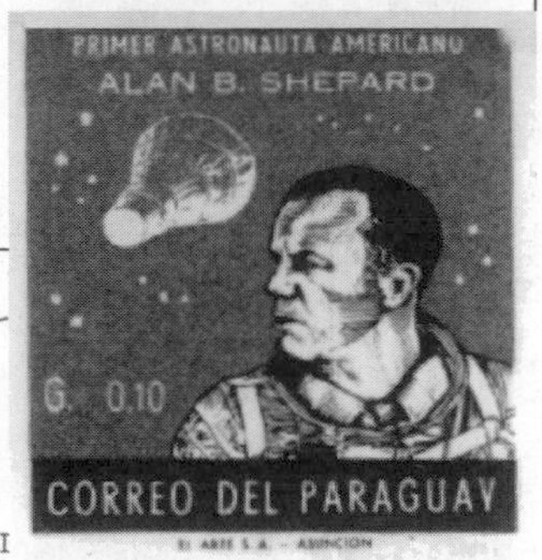

Astronaut Alan Shepard with
George (top), stamps, FDC,
and sig.

The Sanders Price Guide to Autographs

Baseball Hall of Famer George Sisler—stamp and sig.

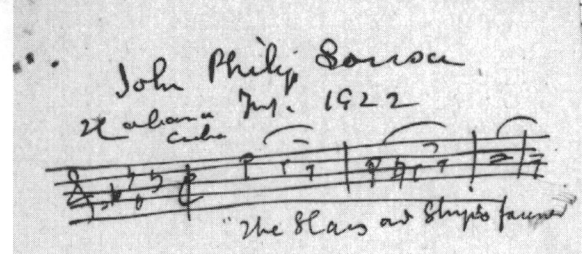

John Philip Sousa, the March King—stamp and sig.

Author John Steinbeck—stamp and sig.

Explorer Vilhjalmur Stefansson—stamp and sig.

Above, George with two-time presidential candidate and U.N. ambassador Adlai S. Stevenson. Also shown are sig and stamps.

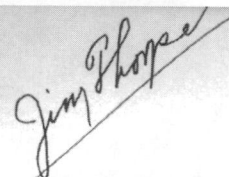

Women's rights advocate Lucy Stone—stamp and sig.

Jim Thorpe, ledgendary Native American athelete—sig and stamp.

"Mr. Republican" Senator Robert A. Taft—signed FDC and stamp.

The Sanders Price Guide to Autographs

A 1 111

Great conductor Arturo Toscanini—signed FDC and block of stamps.

Harold von Schmidt, stamp designer—stamp and sig.

Singer Ethel Waters— stamp and sig.

George Sanders in the White House with Navy Sec. Dan Kimball and President Harry S. Truman. Also shown, Truman stamps and sig.

Jazz great Muddy Waters—SP and stamp.

American statesman Daniel Webster—stamp and sig.

Actor John Wayne with George—sig and stamp.

Definer of the modern dictionary Noah Webster—FDC and sig.

Author Edith Wharton—stamp and sig.

Eisenhower's doctor, Dr. Paul Dudley White—sig and stamp.

Tennis great, Hazel Hotchkiss Wightman—stamp and sig.

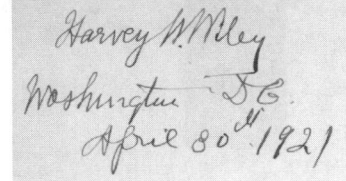

First Federal Food and Drug Administrator, Dr. Harvey W. Wiley—stamp and sig.

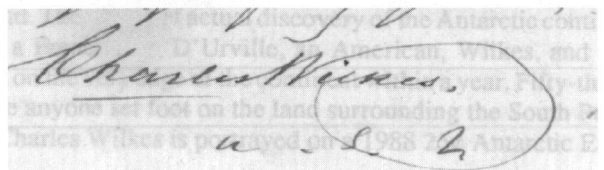

Explorer Charles Wilkes—stamp and sig.

Temperance crusader Frances Willard—stamp and sig.

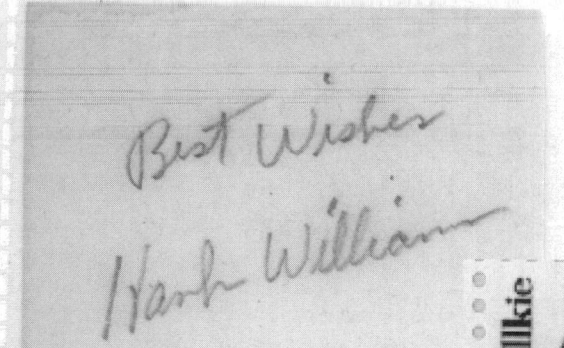

Country music legend Hank Williams, Sr.—FDC and sig.

Playwright Tennesse Williams—stamp and sig.

Presidential candidate Wendell Willkie—stamp and sig.

Aviation pioneer Orville Wright—
signed FDC and stamp.

Top, photo of George with
architect Frank Lloyd Wright
and Wright's granddaughter,
Oscar-winning actress Anne
Baxter. Also shown, Wright
stamp and (left) sig.

Civil rights leader Whitney Young—FDC and signed photograph.

And for a glimpse into the future—

As announced in the October 7, 1996 issue of *USA Today*, the U.S. Postal Service plans to honor the late Chicago Bears coach and owner George Halas. The stamp—whose design was revealed appropriately at a Chicago Bears football game—is to be issued in 1997 as part of the "Legendary Football Coaches" set. Shown here is the forthcoming stamp and a sig of George Halas.

Philography and Philately—A Stamp of Approval

As this 85-page chapter so vividly and interestingly shows, the combination of autograph and stamp collecting adds wonderful dimension to both hobbies. Go forth and enjoy!

Helen and George Sanders give back to their beautiful North Carolina mountain community of Enka by helping to keep the roads clean, and have won several well-deserved awards for doing so.

THE TOP 100!

Featuring the 100 Most Valuable Signatures

by George and Helen Sanders

Ever since the publication of our first edition of **The Price Guide to Autographs** in 1988, we have been asked to list the top signature values. Fellow collectors and dealers seem to enjoy reading about the BIG SIGS just for the fun of learning whose signature is earning the highest price on the current market.

In our previous edition, we only listed the top 60 values. This time, we do you even better. Hot from our million-plus pieces of information autograph data warehouse come the top 100 most valuable autographs in all of our pricing computers.

Most of us will probably never own all of the top 100 heavy hitters but we all dream of owning at least a couple of them. After all, aren't the catalogs of dealers and auction houses our ultimate "wish books?"

The autograph market has expanded to approximately six million collectors competing, in one fashion or another, for the handwritten treasures of U.S. Presidents, vice presidents, movie and television stars, composers, artists, scientists, astronauts, sports stars, military leaders, clergy, world leaders and other categories too numerous to mention. Our hobby has become one of the most frequently mentioned col-

lectibles throughout the world. Hence, the intense interest in what items cost and what actual value they might sustain in the 21st Century .

In the past decade, all of us have become acutely aware that the once "lowly" signature that had heretofore played second fiddle to the obviously more important ALS, document, quotation or precious manuscript was fast becoming a valuable adjunct to our respective collections. In the good, old days, most dealers seldom listed such scrawls in the front of their catalogs but did offer, at very reasonable prices, signatures for the fledgling collector in the back of their respective price lists. Many still do but not with the former casual nonchalance they had mustered when there was so much good material readily available.

Good Items Are Disappearing From the Market

In today's frenetic marketplace, we are more likely to acquire a signature of Greta Garbo than one of her childlike handwritten or hand-printed letters. It's easier to purchase an Abraham Lincoln autograph than to locate one of his letters that hasn't been priced beyond the means of Mr. or Ms. Average Collector. Rare and outstanding signatures are now listed in the front of most top dealers' fine catalogs and are no longer considered a cheap or relatively unappealing item.

As we've warned so many times in our various books or articles, as this exciting hobby grows, good items are fast disappearing from the market. The modern collector has to be quick, educated, sure-footed and carry a respectable wallet. Yes, there are still wondrous "bargains" to be found but today we face much stiffer competition for those low-cost items than ever before.

In short, the SIG is in! When all else becomes too pricey or totally unavailable to average folk, the signature of your

most favorite celebrity continues to be accessible for a valued spot in your binders or carefully framed with an attractive photo or engraving. Collectors and/or dealers no longer turn up their respective noses to a good signature when that SIG might be the only available piece awaiting your attention and your investment. By comparison, most signatures are relatively reasonable in cost. However, we are about to list for your edification the Top Signature Values selected by our computers from from over 60,000 prices in this book. Hardly a list of something for everyone but surely a clear indication that the rarest of SIGS demand the highest prices.

All of these signatures, by the way, are ones that are available to collectors. Other much more valuable autographs exist, but only in museums.

The Top 100

#	Name	Category	Value
1.	Gwinnett, Button	Revolutionary War	115000
2.	Charlemagne	Royalty	75000
3.	Ivan IV, The Terrible	Royalty	35000
4.	Edward IV (England)1442-83	Royalty	25000
5.	More, Thomas, Sir	Author	19750
6.	Toledo, Francisco, Cardinal	Clergy	15000
7.	Rain-in-the-Face	Indian Chief	13000
8.	Stuart, J.E.B. (War Date)	Civil War	12500
9.	Fritchie, Barbara (Frietschie)	Civil War	12500
10.	Luther, Martin	Clergy	10000
11.	Cervantes, Miguel de	Author	10000
12.	Sitting Bull (T. Iyotake)	Indian Leader	7175
13.	Warren, Joseph 1741-1775	Revolutionary War	6875
14.	Crockett, David 1786-1836	Military	6000
15.	Lynch, Thomas Jr.	Revolutionary War	5565
16.	Calvin, John	Clergy	5500
17.	Geronimo	Apache Chieftain	5332
18.	Poe, Edgar Allan 1809-1849	Author	5200
19.	Ferdinand I, III, IV, 1751-1825	Royalty	5200
20.	Vinci, Leonardo da	Artist	5100
21.	Jones, John Paul	Military-Rev. War	5000
22.	Galileo 1564-1642	Science	5000
23.	Beiderbecke, Bix	Entertainment	5000
24.	Beethoven, Ludwig van	Composer	4900
25.	Masterson, Wm. B. "Bat" 1853-1921	Lawman	4800

26.	Washington, George 1732-99	President	4750
27.	John II, (King of Castile) 1406-1454	Royalty	4700
28.	Lewis, Meriwether 1774-1809	Explorer	4500
29.	Racine, Jean 1639-99	Author	4500
30.	Franklin, Benjamin 1706-90	Revolutionary War	4300
31.	Ni'matullah, Hajji	Author	4200
32.	Jefferson, Thomas (As President)	President	4000
33.	Jackson, T.J. "Stonewall"(War Date)	Civil War	3975
34.	Bean, Judge Roy	Frontier Judge	3950
35.	Stuart, J.E.B. 1833-64	Civil War	3897
36.	Earp, Wyatt B.S.	Lawman	3875
37.	Lee, Robert E. (War Date)	Civil War	3822
38.	Cook, James, Capt.	Br.Naval Explorer	3800
39.	Carson, Christopher "Kit"1809-68	Frontiersman	3680
40.	Elahi, Ostad	Philosopher	3660
41.	Lincoln, Abraham (As President)	President	3583
42.	Laennec, René T.H. 1781-1826	Science	3500
43.	Dawes, William 1745-99	Revolutionary War	3500
44.	Raphael	Artist	3500
45.	Lee, Robert E. 1807-70	Military	3440
46.	Elizabeth I 1533-1603	Royalty	3400
47.	Custer, George A. (War Date)	Civil War	3380
48.	Jefferson, Thomas 1743-1826	President	3260
49.	Paine, Thomas	Revolutionary War	3200
50.	Lincoln, Abraham 1809-1865	President	3200
51.	Borgia, Francesco Card'l	Clergy	3200
52.	Beatles (all four) on one piece	Entertainment	3025
53.	Jackson, T.J. "Stonewall" 1824-63	Civil War	3012
54.	Smith, Adam 1723-1790	Economist	3000
55.	Swedenborg, Emanuel 1688-1772	Science	3000
56.	Mao Tse Tung	Head of State	3000
57.	Middleton, Henry 1717-84	Revolutionary War	3000
58.	Moore, Alfred	Supreme Court	3000
59.	Durer, Albrecht	Artist	3000
60.	Hill, Ambrose P. (War Date)	Civil War	2950
61.	Hardin, John Wesley	Outlaw	2900
62.	Custer, George A. 1839-76	Civil War	2850
63.	Jonson, Ben 1572-1637	Author	2850
64.	Capone, Al	Criminal	2850
65.	Jefferson, Thomas & Madison,James	President	2825
66.	Rembrandt van Rijn	Artist	2800
67.	Garrett, Patrick R. (Pat)	Western Lawman	2700
68.	Swift, Jonathan 1667-1745	Author	2500
69.	Younger, Bob	Outlaw	2500
70.	Oersted, Hans Christian 1777-1851	Science	2500
71.	Mozart, Wolfgang A.	Composer	2500
72.	Doors & Jim Morrison (4)	Entertainment	2500
73.	Hewes, Joseph 1730-1780	Revolutionary War	2500
74.	Bach, Johann Sebastian	Composer	2500
75.	Oakley, Annie 1860-1926	Markswoman	2283

76.	Michelangelo (Buonarroti)	Artist	2250
77.	Dean, James 1931-55	Entertainment	2250
78.	Hanson, John	Revolutionary War	2250
79.	Smith, John	Colonial Am.	2200
80.	Schubert, Franz	Composer	2200
81.	Hall, Lyman 1724-90	Revolutionary War	2200
82.	Goya, Francisco	Artist	2200
83.	Hancock, John 1737-93	Revolutionary War	2200
84.	Haydn, Joseph	Composer	2200
85.	Otto I (The Great) 912-973	Royalty	2150
86.	Garbo, Greta 1905-91	Entertainment	2150
87.	Henry VIII 1491-1547	Royalty	2150
88.	Starr, Belle	Outlaw	2000
89.	Tchaikovsky, Piotr I. 1840-93	Composer	2000
90.	Younger, Cole (Thomas Coleman)	Civil War	2000
91.	Rubens, Peter Paul	Artist	2000
92.	Ringo, John	Outlaw	2000
93.	Rasputin, Gregori E.	Clergy	2000
94.	Gogh, Vincent van	Artist	2000
95.	Hill, Ambrose Powell 1825-65	Civil War	2000
96.	Hirohito	Head of State	2000
97.	Augustus I, Duke of Saxony	Royalty	2000
98.	Boone, Daniel 1734-1820	Revolutionary War	2000
99.	Oswald, Lee Harvey 1939-63	Assassin	1950
100.	Standish, Myles	Colonial America	1885

Two men who "did it their way," George Sanders with Frank Sinatra.

General Robert E. Lee.

AUTOGRAPHS OF THE WAR BETWEEN THE STATES

by Michael J. Masters, M.D.

As they were marching through the Pennsylvania countryside on the invasion that would culminate in the battle of Gettysburg, General Robert E. Lee's Army of Northern Virginia passed the front terrace of an elegant mansion where a group of well-dressed Northern women had gathered to watch the passing Confederate army. One of the group, an attractive young woman, defiantly waved a small United States flag at the dust-covered gray and brown columns as they marched by the estate. The soldiers passed silently, offering no rebuke, and the young lady flourished the flag even more impudently.

In a short time General Robert E. Lee appeared, moving slowly on horseback beside his troops. When he was in front of the young woman, Lee paused momentarily and looked calmly into her face, saying nothing. She slowly dropped the flag to her side. Lee rode on and the young woman turned back to her friends, exclaiming, "Oh! I wish he were ours!"

If you are trying to collect autographs from the War Between the States (also known in some quarters as the Civil War), you might find yourself in deep-felt agreement with the young woman's comments from long ago.

The Civil War area of autographs continues to be "hot,"

and because it is still extremely popular, it is fortunate that a great deal of signed paper was generated by both armies.

"Wardate" Documents

Documents signed as part of the fabric of the war are considered "wardate" and usually are priced at much higher values than non-wardate items signed by the same people. These commonplace requests for leave, reports on foraging, or letters by ordinary soldiers asking for permission to do some mundane action had to go up and down the military chain of command so the documents were often endorsed on the verso by a dazzling array of generals and near-generals. Such documents are less available than in the recent past, but you have to grin when you hold a document that has been signed by several generals and by officers who before the end of the war attained the rank of general. These documents really are fun. You might also find wardate ALSs and signatures clipped from wardate documents.

Checks and Other Financial Instruments

Another source of Civil War autographs that has become very popular over the past two years is financial instruments--mainly checks but also other documents such as signed stocks/bonds or promissory notes. Checks are especially desirable because they are a convenient size for storage and framing and they are often self-validating. (Secretarial signed checks are not prevalent in Civil War material.)

Checks that are signed on the front are much more desirable and expensive than checks endorsed on the back only. Stocks signed by Civil War notables are rarer but are often colorful and offer interesting insights into the non-war pursuits of war participants. Promissory notes are often mistaken for checks. They are check-sized drafts that are essentially IOUs ("90 days after the above date, I promise to

pay....") signed by the person making the promise, hence the term promissory notes. A reference list of currently known checks and bonds signed by Civil War generals is included at the end of this chapter.

Autograph Notebooks

It was fashionable to pass autograph books through prisons and prison camps, and these may be a source of wardate documents. Another source of non-wardate autographs is from generals who served in the U. S. Congress before or after the war. Especially after the war autograph notebooks were circulated through the Congress, and attempts were made to get as many representatives or senators to sign as possible. Dealers often take out the signatures of generals or future presidents to sell separately, but over the past two years a number of intact Congressional autograph books have surfaced. In other "piles" of Congressional documents you might find generals' autographs if you are aware of the Congressional service of the various generals. A reference list of the generals who served in the U. S. Congress is also included at the end of this chapter.

Carte de Viste

Additionally, because the War Between the States was the first war to be photographed, signed photographs called CDVs (short for "carte de visite" or "visiting card") are sometimes still obtainable. CDVs were paper prints made from glass negatives and mounted to cardboard cut to the size of the French calling cards, usually about 2-1/2 inches by 4 inches. They were most popular during the Civil War years, although they were made until the early 1880s. Because the cards were easy to write on, soldiers often signed their names and many times their rank and military unit as well. They signed on the front either on the picture or

below on the card as well as on the back.

CDVs became a sort of forerunner of baseball cards in that they were collected and traded, especially those featuring notables of the war. Many times collectors identified their CDVs by writing the name of the person depicted beneath the picture in the same area that somebody might autograph a CDV, so not all signatures on CDVs are authentic.

True autographed CDVs were usually signed with name then rank as on military documents. Identifications by collectors tend to begin with rank such as "General Sterling Price." Price actually signed his CDVs as "Sterling Price, Maj Genl," sometimes adding "Comdg" for Commanding after "Genl." Unidentified wartime soldiers' CDVs are collectible, but identified CDVs command a premium, especially if they are signed by the soldier himself. As with most of Civil War collecting, items involving generals are most sought after. Unsigned CDVs of generals, especially prominent or rare Confederate generals, have become pricey.

Signed CDVs of generals (signatures on the front are more desirable and sell at a higher price than the same item signed on the back) are understandably even more desirable and costly. The term "from life" refers to a CDV contact print from the original plate for which the subject posed. CDVs that are reproductions of paintings or engravings are less desirable. Signed, from-life CDVs are what most collectors seek.

Confederate Autographs and Dead Union Generals

Confederate autograph material continues to command higher prices than similar Union material. Generals killed in action (KIAs) are eagerly sought after. My impression is that obscure Confederate KIA generals are more avidly sought after than obscure Union KIA generals; however, Union KIA

generals have become "hotter" over the last two years. Price guides in this area are limited in their ability to accurately reflect true market value because there are so many private sales with undisclosed terms.

Many transactions in the Civil War subculture involve trades as well as cash, and with premium items involving rare generals or uncommon content, very high prices may skew price "averages." It is not uncommon for there to be only one sale over several years of a particular general's autograph, and if a collector is eager to "fill a missing slot," he may pay an otherwise exorbitant price, which is then "the value" for that general. Fresh material not previously seen in the marketplace is always highly desirable. For that reason "shopping" of items to many different dealers or collectors may actually work against obtaining a higher price. Likewise, material that has been on a dealer's list for a long time because of overvalued pricing ultimately may be sold at a much lower price to enable the dealer to "get his money" out of it.

Civil War Collecting Since the Last Edition

Sometimes a Civil War notable wrote so much postwar material that even wardate material by that person never realizes as high a price as others who wrote less extensively after the war (unless, of course, the general is extremely desirable). For example, generals such as John T. Morgan or Francis Marion Cockrell, who served many postwar years in Congress, do not produce much excitement even in wardate. On the other hand, John S. Mosby wrote a great deal of postwar material, but because of the nature of his guerrilla command, his wardate material is virtually nonexistent.

So what's been happening in the Civil War arena since the last edition?

As a young teenager, General T.J. "Stonewall" Jackson,

who did most of his studying before the fireplace at night (his West Point colleagues used to say he "burned" the material into his brain) made an agreement with his uncle's young slave. Jackson would teach the slave to read if he would keep Jackson supplied in pine boughs and other materials to keep his evening fires going. Jackson kept his bargain and taught the young man to read and write. The first thing he did when he learned to write was to forge a pass and escape!

Forgeries and Other Bad Material

Unfortunately, the most disheartening aspect of War Between the States collecting in the last few years has been the influx of forgeries and bad material. A collector has to face the fact that authentic Civil War material is definitely diminishing in supply but the demand continues to be strong. A collector cannot hope to enter the field of Civil War collecting and quickly amass a large collection. Patience in obtaining material is warranted, and because of the great increase in forgeries, it is helpful to know some of the forgery trends that are operative in the current market.

Very popular and highly sought after Civil War participants with short names, such as R.E. Lee, are natural targets for forgers. While clipped signatures have been very popular because of their attractiveness when framed with a photo or drawing and lower cost, they are also much more easily forged. Forgers often obtain the proper paper from extra pages at the ends of period books or from integral sheets from routine documents or letters of the period. This authentic old paper is then cut into appropriate "clipped" sizes and forged signatures are applied. The signatures may not be of just the superstars, as I have seen more common generals on these little pieces of paper. You might feel better about a clipped endorsement if there is other writing on it, especially

wardate writing, but unfortunately I have seen the "other writing" forged as well. You must certainly buy from a very trusted Civil War document dealer or be very secure in your own knowledge. Otherwise in today's market you might very quickly become the proud owner of a fake.

Unfortunately, other items are being forged as well. Routine wardate documents may have the signatures of desirable generals forged at the bottom or as an endorsement on the back. Some of these forged documents, as well as a good number of the fake clips, have a magenta hue to the ink, which is often a giveaway of a forgery. Also there is a tendency for the signature to be "squeezed" into a small space at the bottom of the document, which gives a plausible explanation for a signature variation. I used to see forgeries that were fairly crude, with obvious feathering of ink or incongruous content, such as a general's signature on an item that was usually handled only by subordinates, but forgers are getting more clever and deceptive. Their counterfeit inks are also improving.

Joshua Chamberlain's signature has enjoyed a meteoric rise in price since the movie "Gettysburg." (His signature has finally cooled somewhat recently.) Forgeries of Chamberlain's, Mosby's, Lee's, and, to a lesser extent, Jackson's signatures are being seen in books that are advertised to have been part of their libraries. These forgeries are put in genuine period books, especially volumes of classic literature or military texts. Some of these forged inscribed books may enter the market from rare book dealers who may be less knowledgeable about certain autographs but who acquire such items in "collections."

CDVs are another area involving forgeries. Even without signatures these increasingly collectible items are being forged. One of the new wrinkles involves using a laser

copying machine to photocopy the image of a genuine CDV that is then attached to either period card stock or even preprinted modern card stock. These often have an orange cast, but since the laser copying machines have multiple color adjustment mechanisms, more experienced forgers can with practice get the correct sepia hue.

Authentic CDVs of generals such as Lee are also being fraudulently signed (which shows a certain chutzpah since genuine Lee CDVs may cost $600-$900 even without a signature). Backmarks from lesser or unimportant genuine CDVs are being transferred to CDVs with no backmarks to enhance their value. A Brady backmark on a general's CDV would increase its value. For these reasons, unless you know and are very confident of a dealer's integrity and expertise, I would be very careful buying old framed items. Take a laser photocopy with a forged signature, frame it, use old dirty glass, and let it be exposed to "age" it and you have a piece that could fool most people unless you examine the item unframed.

There are several ways that fraudulent material enters the Civil War market: gun shows, short lists, and "backwoods" auctions. Gun shows are a common denominator for Civil War enthusiasts and gun dealers. Many times a gun dealer may have obtained manuscript material in trade or in "collections." He may claim that he "got it from an old Civil War collector" and he just wants "to get his money out of it" since guns are his main area of expertise. He can then disclaim any responsibility since that is not his area of expertise.

Short lists involve small catalogs of what sounds like very good material often from a "dealer" that you have never dealt with or heard of before. The catalog just suddenly shows up in your mailbox one day. I have had similar

offerings with a story about someone dying and the heirs wanting to get cash for the deceased's collection because of financial problems. (Actually this is often a way genuine material is obtained, but caution is in order.)

A more disturbing trend involves the offering of bad material in small, local (sometimes called "farm" or "backwoods") auctions that are unknown outside that region. Auctions of this type that may be known regionally for having quality pieces at good prices in the past are being "seeded" with bad material hoping that the good material or reputation of good material will sell the fake material. I have to think in some of these circumstances that avarice is operative. Uninitiated collectors may think it is possible to get a Robert E. Lee for $500 or a T. J. Jackson for $800, but many people buying these items at these prices are very much aware of more representative values and are buying them to resell even though they might suspect the items are not "right."

Civil War Material Prices

A captured Union soldier was found taking hairs from Little Sorrell, Stonewall Jackson's horse. When questioned about this seemingly odd behavior he said, "I can get $1.00 on the streets of New York for anything associated with Stonewall Jackson." (There were War Between the States memorabilia entrepreneurs even then.) This sentiment basically expresses the national mania for Civil War material. So apart from the influx of counterfeit autograph material, what's new?

Just when I have convinced myself that Civil War material is not appreciating as fast as it had been, an auction with significant Civil War material realizes very high prices. If there has been any slowing, it has generally

been the result of high prices for Confederate material which may have priced itself out of the reach of many collectors. Prime material continues to be snapped up, however, in spite of high prices.

The gold standard of Civil War collecting is still the wardate document, especially letters from notables or documents with multiple endorsements of generals. The current thinking is that these documents will always hold their value (at least from the point of view of "collectors' prices" as distinguished from extraordinarily high prices that were paid by certain individuals at auctions in the recent past). They are still the most voraciously sought after items, and their supply, which was not very great two years ago, is even smaller now.

Price guides are usually not helpful in determining the value of multiple endorsed wardate documents because each is decidedly unique. Prices of these items will reflect unusual generals, unusual in wardate generals, or unusual combinations of generals. I have heard a variety of guidelines for calculating the price of a document with multiple generals' wardate signatures.

Personally I do not think these historically unique treasures lend themselves to any kind of pricing formula. To be honest, most of the time you ask what the price is and if you think it's too much, you don't buy it, and if you think the price is in the ballpark, you do. Constant dealing in the marketplace can give you a good feel for correct pricing. In rare material, however, there is a great deal of subjectivity. I certainly think it is possible to have price guidelines for signatures and signatures with rank. Also, a sort of bottom line guide for non-wardate and wardate ALSs is possible, but these documents are extremely content-driven and pricing is thus very subjective.

In all cases, however, if an item surfaces containing a general's signature that has not been seen for a long time, price cannot be "averaged" because there are no other sales to average. Price again becomes what the market will pay. As with most "subcultures" of autograph collecting, having a feel for current values involves constant study of recent sales and offerings. Sometimes this can only be accomplished by talking with Civil War dealers, who may be the only ones aware of many transactions.

Soldiers' letters have increased in popularity. This is partially due to the shortage of other autograph material and the increasing realization that these eyewitness accounts of the war are historical treasures even if not written by someone "famous." They can be more cost-effective. Over the past two years, I have seen an increasing number of catalogs, auctions, and dealers' lists offering soldiers' letters (with long descriptions previously reserved for autograph material) at fairly high prices especially if there is any battle content. Letters about Gettysburg especially fetch a premium, with Sharpsburg a close second. Prices in this area are also very subjective, with Confederate material realizing higher prices than Union material. Sadly, there have also been forged soldiers' letters in the marketplace.

How to Proceed

So how should you proceed in this exciting but tumultuous area? More than ever, experience is vitally necessary. If you do not have the experience, I would advise dealing with someone reputable who does.

A dealer's reputation is very important, and a tradition of selling genuine material at fair prices is worth its weight in gold. Try asking several dealers for the names of

dealers from whom they would buy manuscript material. If you end up with a name or several names on most of their lists, I would certainly start with those dealers. They in turn can recommend other reputable dealers. Cultivate a relationship with these blue chip vendors.

Personal study and knowledge of history are important, but gleaning pearls of wisdom from people who have been in this area for years is one of your best hedges against being duped. Study dealers' offerings by looking through all their autograph material. You can learn a great deal by viewing material you already have or are not even seeking because you can gain more familiarity with period inks, papers, military forms, and who (rank-wise) tended to sign them. Also the more genuine material you see, the better prepared you are to spot non-genuine material.

If you want to add a particular individual to your collection, get his signature in any form when the opportunity presents itself (prewar, postwar, or whatever) and then upgrade. Trading is alive and well and very popular for upgrading. You may never see that general again or if you do, it may be at a considerably higher price. If you have any doubts about an item, walk away. Try not to let your great desire for an item blind you to inconsistencies or other clues that it might not be "right."

Try to enjoy the War Between the States for the subject area itself even if there are items that you will not be able to obtain because of price or scarcity. Sometimes just having the information a document contains is very exciting even if you cannot own the document. Enjoy, in a social sense, the unique camaraderie of other collectors or dealers who find the War Between the States stimulating.

There are very few bargains in this area (and I would be somewhat suspicious of too good a bargain) . If you want a bargain, go to Wal Mart. If you want genuine material, you often have to pay the price.

On August 25, 1862, at Bristoe Station, before the Battle of Second Manassas, Stonewall Jackson's army had captured several Union trains and several prisoners, one of whom proved to be a civilian who had been on a visit to the army. His leg was broken as a result of a train crash.

While he was lying on the ground near a fire, he inquired whose forces had captured him. When he was informed that it was Stonewall Jackson's army, he expressed a great desire to see Jackson. At this point in the war shortly following his dazzling Valley Campaign, Jackson was arguably the most famous military person in the world, a subject of discussion in the parlors of Europe and the North as much as in the South. However, very few images of him existed.

The captured civilian learned that Jackson was a short distance away on the other side of the fire interrogating one of the train engineers. He asked to be lifted up to view the famous general. When he was lifted up, he observed the great Confederate general for half a minute, noting his rumpled appearance in his dingy gray uniform with his cap pulled down on his nose. In a tone of disappointment and disgust he exclaimed, "O my God! Lay me down! Lay me down!"

I hope you will not feel the same way about Civil War autograph collecting after this brief snapshot of the current marketplace but that you will to continue to delight in the subject matter while heeding appropriate caution.

Confederate Generals Who Served in Congress Before the War

Anderson, James Patton .... House 1855-1857
Barksdale, William .... House 1853-1861
Beale, Richard Lee Turberville .... House 1847-1849
Bonham, Milledge Luke .... House 1857-1860
Branch, Lawrence O'Bryan .... House 1855-1861
Breckinridge, John Cabell .... House 1851-1855
Breckinridge, John Cabell President of .... Senate 1856-1860 (as VP)
Breckinridge, John Cabell .... Senate 1861
Chesnut, James, Jr. .... Senate 1858-1860
Clingman, Thomas Lanier .... House 1843-1845, 1847-1858
Clingman, Thomas Lanier .... Senate 1858-1861
Cobb, Howell .... House 1843-1851, 1855-1857
Colquitt, Alfred Holt .... House 1853-1855
Featherstone, Winfield Scott .... House 1847-1851
Gartrell, Lucius Jeremiah .... House 1857-1861
Gholson, Samuel Jameson .... House 1836-1838
Hatton, Robert Hopkins .... House 1859-1861
Hindman, Thomas Carmichael .... House 1859-1861
Jenkins, Albert Gallatin .... House 1857-1861
Marshall, Humphrey .... House 1849-1852, 1855-1859
Preston, William .... House 1852-1855
Price, Sterling .... House 1845-1846
Pryor, Roger Atkinson .... House 1859-1861
Rust, Albert .... House 1855-1857, 1859-1861
Scales, Alfred Moore .... House 1857-1859
Smith, William .... House 1841-1843, 1853-1861
Toombs, Robert .... House 1845-1853
Toombs, Robert .... Senate 1853-1861
Whiffield, John Wilkins .... House 1854-1857
Wigfall, Louis Tresvant .... Senate 1859-1861
Wise, Henry Alexander .... House 1833-1844
Zollicoffer, Felix Kirk .... House 1853-1859

Confederate Generals Serving in Congress After the War

Bate, William Brimage .... Senate 1887-1905
Beale, Richard Lee Turberville .... House 1879-1881
Bratton, John .... House 1884-1885
Bullock, Robert .... House 1889-1893
Butler, Matthew Calbraith .... Senate 1877-1895
Chalmers, James Ronald .... House 1877-1882, 1884-1885
Clark, John Bullock, Jr. .... House 1873-1883
Clark, John Bullock, Jr. Clerk of .... House 1883-1889
Cockrell, Francis Marion .... Senate 1875-1905
Colquitt, Alfred Holt .... Senate 1883-1894
Cook, Philip .... House 1873-1883
Cox, William Ruffin .... House 1881-1887
Dibrell, George Gibbs .... House 1875-1885

DuBose, Dudley McIver .... House 1871-1873
Finley, Jesse Johnson .... House 1876-1877, 1879, 1881-1882
Forney, William Henry .... House 1875-1893
Gibson, Randall Lee .... House 1875-1883
Gibson, Randall Lee .... Senate 1883-1892
Gordon, George Washington House 1907-1911
Gordon, John Brown .... Senate 1873-1880, 1891-1897
Hampton, Wade .... Senate 1879-1891
Hunton, Eppa .... House 1873-1881
Hunton, Eppa .... Senate 1892-1895
Johnston, Joseph Eggleston .... House 1879-1881
Lee, William Henry Fitzhugh .... House 1887-1891
Mahone, William .... Senate 1881-1887
Maxey, Samuel Bell .... Senate 1875-1887
Morgan, John Tyler .... Senate 1877-1907
Pettus, Edmund Winston .... Senate 1897-1907
Ransom, Matt Whitaker .... Senate 1872-1895
Scales, Alfred Moore .... House 1875-1884
Shelley, Charles Miller .... House 1877-1881, 1882-1885
Terry, William .... House 1871-1873, 1875-1877
Vance, Robert Brank .... House 1873-1885
Walker, James Alexander .... House 1895-1899
Walthall, Edward Cary .... Senate 1885-1894, 1895-1898
Wheeler, Joseph .... House 1881-1882, 1883, 1885-1900
Williams, John Stuart .... Senate 1879-1885
Young, Pierce Manning Butler .... House 1868-1869, 1870-1875

Confederate Cabinet Members Who Served in Congress

Benjamin, Judah Philip .... Senate 1853-1861
Bragg, Thomas .... Senate 1859-1861
Davis, Jefferson Finis .... House 1845-1846
Davis, Jefferson Finis .... Senate 1847-1851, 1857-1861
Mallory, Stephen Russell .... Senate 1851-1861
Seddon, James Alexander .... House 1845-1847, 1849-1851
Stephenson, Alexander Hamilton .... House 1843-1859, 1873-1882

Union Generals Who Served in Congress Before the War

Baker, Edward Dickinson .... House 1845-1847, 1849-1851
Baker, Edward Dickinson .... Senate 1859-1861
Banks, Nathaniel Prentice .... House 1853-1857
Blair, Francis Preston, Jr. .... House 1857-1864
Campbell, William Bowen .... House 1837-1843
Cooper, James .... House 1839-1843
Cooper, James .... Senate 1849-1855
Craig, James .... House 1857-1861
Curtis, Samuel Ryan .... House 1857-1861
Denver, James William .... House 1855-1857
Dix, John Adams .... Senate 1845-1849

Dumont, Ebenezer .... House 1863-1867
Famsworth, John Franklin .... House 1857-1861, 1863-1873
Ferry, Orris Sanford .... House 1859-1861
Fremont, John Charles .... Senate 1850-1851
Garfield, James Abram .... House 1863-1880
Gorman, Willis Arnold .... House 1849-1853
Hamilton, Andrew Jackson .... House 1859-1861
Keim, William High .... House 1858-1859
Logan, John Alexander .... House 1859-1862
Marston, Gilman .... House 1859-1863
McClernand, John Alexander .... House 1843-1851, 1859-1861
Morgan, Edward Denison .... Senate 1863-1869
Phelps, John Smith .... House 1845-1863
Schenck, Robert Cumming .... House 1843-1851, 1863-1871
Shields, James .... Senate 1849-1855, 1858-1859
Sibley, Henry Hastings .... House 1848-1849, 1849-1853
Sickles, Daniel Edgar .... House 1857-1861
Smith, Green Clay .... House 1863-1866
Stevens, Isaac Ingalls .... House 1857-1861
Stuart, David .... House 1853-1855
Todd, John Blair Smith .... House 1861-1863, 1864-1865
Vandever, William .... House 1859-1861
Van Wyck, Charles Henry .... House 1859-1863
Ward, William Thomas .... House 1851-1853
Washburn, Cadwallader Coiden .... House 1855-1861

Union Generals Who Served in Congress After the War

Ames, Adelbert .... Senate 1870-1874
Arthur, Chester AlanPresident of .... Senate 1881 (as VP)
Banks, Nathaniel Prentice .... House 1865-1873, 1875-1879, 1889-1891
Beatty, John .... House 1868-1873
Blair, Francis Preston, Jr. .... Senate 1871-1873
Bragg, Edward Stuyvesant .... House 1877-1883, 1885-1887
Buckland, Ralph Pomeroy .... House 1865-1869
Burnside, Ambrose Everett .... Senate 1875-1881
Butler, Benjamin Franklin .... House 1867-1875, 1877-1879
Campbell, William Bowen .... House 1866-1867
Clark, William Thomas .... House 1870-1872
Clayton, Powell .... Senate 1871-1877
Cox, Jacob Dolson .... House 1877-1879
Curtis, Newton Martin .... House 1891-1897
Dodge, Grenville Mellen .... House 1867-1869
Dumont, Ebenezer .... House 1863-1867
Duval, Isaac Harding .... House 1869-1871
Edwards, John .... House 1871-1872
Ewing, Thomas .... House 1877-1881
Famsworth, John Franklin .... House 1863-1873
Ferry, Orris Sanford .... Senate 1867-1875

Garfield, James Abram .... House 1863-1880
Harding, Abner Clark .... House 1865-1869
Hawley, Joseph Roswell .... House 1872-1875, 1879-1881
Hawley, Joseph Roswell .... Senate 1881-1905
Hayes, Rutherford Birchard .... House 1865-1867
Hovey, Alvin Peterson .... House 1887-1889
Hurlbut, Stephen Augustus .... House 1873-1877
Ketcham, John Henry .... House 1865-1873, 1877-1893, 1897-1906
Logan, John Alexander .... House 1867-1871
Logan, John Alexander .... Senate 1871-1877, 1879-1886
Manson, Mahlon Dickerson .... House 1871-1873
Marston, Gilman .... House 1865-1867
Marston, Gilman .... Senate 1889
Miller, John Franklin .... Senate 1881-1886
Morgan, Edward Denison .... Senate 1863-1869
Morgan, George Washington .... House 1867-1868, 1869-1873
Negley, James Scott .... House 1869-1875, 1885-1887
Oglesby, Richard James .... Senate 1873-1879
Paine, Halbert Eleazer .... House 1865-1871
Palmer, John McAuley .... Senate 1891-1897
Pile, William Anderson .... House 1867-1869
Raum, Green Berry .... House 1867-1869
Rice, Americus Vespucius .... House 1875-1879
Robinson, James Sidney .... House 1881-1885
Rousseau, Lovell Harrison .... House 1865-1866, 1866-1867
Schenck, Robert Cumming .... House 1863-1871
Schurz, Carl .... Senate 1869-1875
Shields, James .... Senate 1879
Sickles, Daniel Edgar .... House 1893-1895
Slocum, Henry Warner .... House 1869-1873, 1883-1885
Smith, Green Clay .... House 1863-1866
Spinola, Francis Barretto .... House 1887-1891
Taylor, Nelson .... House 1865-1867
Thayer, John Milton .... Senate 1867-1871
Vandever, William .... House 1887-1891
Van Wyck, Charles Henry .... House 1867-1869, 1870~1871
Van Wyck, Charles Henry .... Senate 1881-1887
Viele, Egbert Ludoricus .... House 1885-1887
Washburn, Cadwallader Colden .... House 1867-1871
West, Joseph Rodman .... Senate 1871-1877
Williams, Alpheus Starkey .... House 1875-1878

Union Cabinet Members Who Served in Congress

Bates, Edward .... House 1827-1829
Cameron, Simon .... Senate 1845-1849, 1857-1861, 1867-1877
Chase, Salmon Portland .... Senate 1849-1855
Fessenden, William Pitt .... House 1841-1843
Fessenden, William Pitt .... Senate 1854-1864, 1865-1869
Hamlin, Hannibal .... House 1843-1847

The Sanders Price Guide to Autographs

Hamlin, Hannibal .... Senate 1848-1857, 1857-1861, 1869-1881
Johnson, Andrew .... House 1843-1853
Johnson, Andrew .... Senate 1857-1862, 1875
Johnson, AndrewPresident of .... Senate 1864-1865 (as VP)
Seward, William Henry .... Senate 1849-1861
Smith, Caleb Blood .... House 1843-1849

Known Stock/Bonds Signed by Civil War Generals

G. T. Beauregard (Confed.) .... State of Louisiana Bond
.... New Orleans, Jackson & Great Northern Railroad
A. E. Bumside (Union) .... Indianapolis & Vincennes Railroad Company
.... Narragansett Steamship Co.
.... U.S. Freehold Land & Emigration Co.
Lawrence O'B. Branch (Confed.) .... Raleigh and Gaston Railroad
Benjamin F. Butler (Union) .... Meigs Elevated Railway Construction Co.
.... Georgia & Alabama Land Co.
Daniel Butterfield (Union ....)Utica, Clington & Binghamton Railroad Co.
Joshua L. Chamberlain (Union) .... Ocala and Silver Springs Company
Charles Cruft (Union) .... Terre Haute, Alton & St. Louis Railroad Company
R. E. Colston (Confed. ....)N.C. Military and Polytechnic Academy
John A. Dix (Union ....)Mississippi & Missouri Railroad Company
Grenville Dodge (Union) .... Fort Worth and Denver City Railway
.... Missouri, Kansas & Texas Railway
.... International & Great Northern Railroad
.... Oregon & Transcontinental Co.
Thomas Drayton (Confed.) .... Charleston & Savannah Railroad
John Echols (Confed. ....)Short Route Railway Transfer Company
.... Paducah Union Depot Company
.... Troy and Tiptonville Rail Road Company
.... Owensboro, Falls of Rough & Green River Railroad Co.
.... Vulcan Contract and Improvement Co.
.... Chesapeake & Ohio Railroad Co.
Thomas Ewing (Union) .... Florida Land & Improvement Co.
Nathan Bedford Forrest (Confed.) .... Selma & Marion Railroad
J. C. Fremont (Union) .... Southwest Pacific Railroad
.... Cincinnati Railway Tunnel Co.
.... Southern Trans-Continental Railroad
Joseph Johnston (Confed.) .... National Express & Transportation Co.
William Mahone (Confed.) .... Atlantic, Mississippi & Ohio Railroad Company
George McClellan (Union) .... Grand Belt Copper Co.
James S. Negley (Union) .... New York, Pittsburgh & Chicago Railway
H. E. Paine (Union) .... Ivanhoe Mining Company
Horace Porter (Union) .... Pullmans Palace Car Co.
.... Chicago, Rock Island & Pacific Railroad Co.
Sterling Price (Confed.) .... Sate of Missouri Bond
W. E. Quarles (Confed.) .... Memphis, Clarksville & Louisiana Railroad
Thomas E. Rosser (Confed.) .... West Waynesboro Land Company
Jones Withers (Confed.) .... State of Alabama Bond

Known Checks Signed by Civil War Generals

Confederate
J. R. Anderson
Tumer Ashby

Union
Adelbert Ames
Chester A. Arthur

Rufus Barringer
William B. Bate
G. T. Beauregard
S. B. Buckner
Charles Clark
John R. Cooke
G. G. Dibrell
R. S. Ewell
Randall L. Gibson
Henry Heth
A. P. Hill
A. S. Johnston
William E. Jones
R. E. Lee
L.. L.. Lornax
James Longstreet
William Mahone
George Maney
J. H. Morgan
Albert Pike
E. Klrby Smith
David A. Weisinger
Joseph Wheeler

Mason Braymon
E. A. Carr
Joshua L. Chamberlain
John A. Dix
James A. Garfield
George W. Getty
Ulysses S. Grant
Henry W. Halleck
Schuyler Hamilton
Rutherford B. Hayes
John P. Hawkins
Joseph R. Hawley
William B. Hazen
E. D. Morgan
H. E. Paine
Thomas G. Pitcher
Winfield Scott
Phillip H. Sheridan
William T. Sherman
Lorenzo Thomas
Henry G. Thomas
C. C. Washburn
John G. Wool

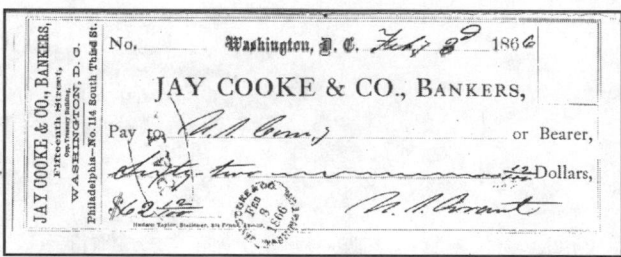

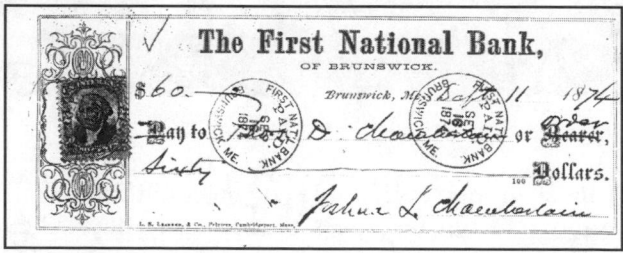

Some examples: above left, sig of General A.P. Hill, immediate left, CDV of General George Thomas, above Grant and Chamberlain checks signed on the front.

A most unique collectible (if you could fine it and get him to sign it) would be this billboard from George's broadcasting days. Actually, there is at least a signed photograph of this board in the offices of Alexander Books.

THE U.A.C.C.

(UNIVERSAL AUTOGRAPH COLLECTORS CLUB)

by Bob Erickson, UACC President

The Universal Autograph Collectors Club (UACC) is the world's largest organization for autograph collectors with over 2,000 members in the United States, Canada, and more than 25 other countries. Founded in New York in 1965, the UACC is a Federally recognized nonprofit educational organization whose purpose is to inform UACC members and the public at large about all aspects of autograph collecting through its publications, shows, and seminars.

By joining the UACC, you will receive our renowned 64-page bimonthly journal *The Pen and Quill* which features articles and news on autographs in all areas, including U.S. Presidents, authors, scientists, aviators, astronauts, royalty, entertainers, athletes, military leaders, Nobel Prize winners, and explorers, to name a few. Studies of authentic, secretarial, Autopen, rubber-stamped, facsimile, and forged signatures help collectors to make informed decisions when purchasing autographic material. Celebrity addresses are published in each issue to assist collectors who enjoy writing for autographs. The UACC also sponsors annual literary awards in addition to paying for articles published in *The Pen and Quill*

You may also have your name and address published as a new member in *The Pen and Quill* By so doing, you will

receive free autograph catalogues from our dealer members and auction houses. Or you can place a free classified ad in *The Pen and Quill* to list your wants, sell your extra material, or just communicate with other members about your common interests.

All members are required to abide by a strict Code of Ethics and violations of that Code are enforced by the UACC Ethics Board. By dealing with other UACC members, you can be assured that the Ethics Board will assist you in any dispute involving another member who has violated the Code of Ethics. Members who refuse to abide by an Ethics Board decision are subject to sanctions, including expulsion, with notice to members published in *The Pen and Quill.*

The UACC also offers its members the opportunity to purchase uncommon autographic material and reference works at affordable prices through the " UACC Warehouse" page in *The Pen and Quill.* The UACC sponsors autograph shows in major U.S. cities and London, England featuring educational displays, autograph dealers who abide by the UACC Code of Ethics, and celebrity guests. Seminars are occasionally held in conjunction with the shows to educate our members and the public on all aspects of collecting, preservation, and identification of non-authentic material.

Finally, the UACC sponsors mail auctions through *The Pen and Quill as* well as an annual live floor auction near Washington, DC. These auctions are another avenue to assist our members who buy and sell autographs.

To learn more about the UACC, send your request for a brochure and membership application to UACC, Dept. PG, PO Box 6181, Washington, DC 20044-6181. You can also get membership information and an application by visiting our Internet web site at http://www.uacc.org. We hope you will join our universe of fellow collectors soon.

Chapter 9

OLD VERSUS HISTORIC

by Stuart Lutz and John Reznikoff

There is an old cliche that "A little knowledge is a dangerous thing" and this is very true in the autograph and document field.

We get dozens of calls from people who know nothing about autographs but find them while reviewing their grandfather's papers or cleaning the attic. For example, a person finds their great-grandfather's military commission signed by Lincoln. They tell their friends about it and one of them inevitably mentions that a few Lincoln pieces have fetched nearly one million dollars at auction. Well, needless to say, there is a great difference between one of the thousands of common Lincoln signed commissions and a unique Lincoln autograph letter signed discussing the Emancipation Proclamation. So this starry-eyed person calls me to describe the Lincoln commission and I tell them that we purchase them for four or five thousand dollars. Almost on cue, the caller will say "No, it has to be worth much more! There was a Lincoln piece that sold at auction for nearly one million dollars!" A little knowledge is a dangerous thing indeed!

This is an example of people who can't differentiate between old material and historic material. A Lincoln com-

mission is a commodity; people buy, sell and trade them. A unique Lincoln letter about the historic Emancipation Proclamation is far more valuable. It is a true historic item whereas a routine commission is merely old [yet it still has value]. Lincoln's commission of Grant, however, is historic since it changed history.

This differentiation is true throughout the field Compare a Benedict Arnold signed receipt to his signed pledge to the United States of America. It is obvious which is routine and which is truly historic.

Also, people fail to understand that there must be a collector for something to have value beyond sentimentality. You can own a unique item, but if there is no collector of that item, it is monetarily worth very little. Think about your first grade report card. It is a unique item, but who would pay money for it? To you, it has great sentimental value but to everyone else, it is just a piece of paper. Now, imagine John Kennedy's first grade report card. It is very valuable since there are many Kennedy and Presidential collectors who would pay money for it. The ultimate determination of a collectible's value is what a collector will pay for it.

What exactly qualifies as historic? Well, it generally has to be rare, if not unique. Washington's handwritten acceptance of the Presidency is remarkable and historic. There are several souvenir copies of the Emancipation Proclamation signed by Lincoln, so they are not unique. But they are historic and very valuable since they commemorate one of his greatest achievements. There is only one signed Declaration of Independence which is priceless. There are about twenty-four Dunlap Declarations of Independence that were printed on the night of July 4, 1776 and are the first issue of the Declaration. While not unique, they are extremely historic and worth over a million dollars each. A facsimile copy

of the Declaration bought at the National Archives for a few dollars is worth only a few dollars, even if the facsimile itself is one hundred years old.

Of course, historic material does not have to be old. The National Archives has the original Nixon resignation [see illustration]. It is less than twenty-five years old, but no one would argue that it is not historic. The same is true with Gerald Ford's pardon of Nixon; it is relatively 'new' yet very historic. There are many souvenir copies of this on the market and they are very much in demand.

Hopefully, after reading this chapter, you will have a better understanding of the difference between historic and old material. And the old cliche about "a little knowledge" will no longer apply to the autograph and document field.

THE WHITE HOUSE
WASHINGTON

August 9, 1974

Dear Mr. Secretary:

I hereby resign the Office of President of the United States.

Sincerely,

Richard Nixon

11.35 AM

The Honorable Henry A. Kissinger
The Secretary of State
Washington, D.C. 20520

HK

John Reznikoff (right) with his father, Dr. Marvin Reznikoff.

George with author Jacqueline Susann.

Chapter 10

P.A.D.A

The Professional Autograph Dealers Association

The Professional Autograph Dealers Association, Inc. ("Pada") was organized in 1995 by many of the nation's leading dealers in historic autograph material. Concerned by the proliferation of new "dealers" lacking expertise, experience, integrity, and fiscal responsibility, PADA's purpose is to raise the standards of the autograph profession by requiring members to adhere to a strict code of ethics when conducting business with collectors, institutions, the general public, and other colleagues.

In addition to a track record of integrity, all members must provide a life-time guarantee of authenticity on the material they sell. Prospective members

undergo a rigorus screening process, during which their business history is carefully reviewed and comments by current PADA members are solicited.

PADA members are in all parts of the United States. It is

anticipated that as the organization grows, foreign dealers will also join. The present membership includes many of the leading dealers whose specialties include American and world history, science, literature, music, art, and the performing arts. Dealers who handle primarily contemporary sports and entertainment personalities are ineligible for membership in PADA.

Believing that PADA fills a strong need in the autograph community, the organization anticipated rapid growth, both in membership and stature. Current plans include a trade show, an internet WEB site, and publications designed to increase collector's and dealers' knowledge of autographs.

Please see the P.A.D.A. ad on page 604 of this book for additional information.

Russian Autographs

(a bonus mini-chapter)

The breakup of the former Soviet Union has created economic havoc in Russia and the other parts of the former "evil empire." Lots of items are coming onto the open market—MiG jets, nuclear weapons, and whatever else someone somewhere can sell to survive the cold Russian winters.

Antiquities and collectibles are not the least of these items suddenly available in the West. This signed document of Czar Nicholas II (right) is just one example. We at the **Sanders Price Guide to Autographs** are keeping an eye on this expanding part of the autograph market and those prices will be included in our next edition.

The SANDERS 4

4th Edition

PRICE GUIDE TO AUTOGRAPHS

THE WORLD'S LEADING AUTOGRAPH PRICING AUTHORITY

Section II:
PRICES

Republican U.S. Congressman Charles Taylor of North Carolina received his copy of the Sanders Price Guide to Autographs in 1990 twice, once from Helen (top) and once from George (bottom).

HOW TO USE THIS PRICE GUIDE

by Helen Sanders

With *some* changes, this chapter (of necessity) will be as in the past, somewhat of a reprise of a similar chapter printed in the previous editions of our Price Guide. As before, uncountable hours have gone into the preparation of this book and we have made every effort to be as accurate as possible so that we can bring to you figures that realistically reflect market changes, if any.

Again, we remind you, however, that *price guide* means exactly that. The prices indicated in this book are not set in cement. They are very flexible in all directions, both up and down. Two Autograph Letters Signed (ALS) by the same person, in the same year, in the same condition, even the same length are not necessarily going to be worth the same amount of money because the variables that affect their value are so diverse.

The averages used in this book are for similar types of pieces, in similar condition, signed in ink with a full signature of at least the last name and one initial. They are gathered from all geographical areas of this country and overseas as well.

This is not an exact science, as we have said in previous editions, and there are 264 shades of gray. You must be

prepared to use them. Just as condition and content guide you as to the buying price and/or selling price of a particular piece, I repeat, the figures contained herein represent an average and are there to *guide* your decisions.

We have found that some dealers have opposed a single price given for an item within a category. Some do not realize, however, what great latitude there is depending, of course, on a dealer's particular offering. The clientele to which the material is offered, as well as the guarantee included, makes a difference in this latitude.

In the last year you have no doubt seen much duplication of material offered in auction catalogues; dozens of George Washingtons, Edisons, Einsteins, etc. So the collector says to himself that there is no rarity here, maybe I'll wait. I can pick one up any old time. In fact, you have seen so many things on the market this past year that are in such quantity you feel these offerings to be superfluous and certainly redundant.

What you must also consider is the fact that the autograph market is growing so fast that these pieces are quickly absorbed into the marketplace and perhaps will not to be seen again for another generation or two or even three.

CONDITION

Just as it is in the collecting of coins, stamps, antiques, vintage cars and any collectible, condition is only one of the important considerations in autograph collecting. The prices quoted in this guide are for autographs in fine condition. Extra-fine letters, documents, cut signatures and so forth demand a higher price. Tattered, foxed, stained paper, wrinkled signed photographs and the like, decrease the value.

PRICING

Because this is not a manufactured item, there is no

Manufacturers List Price or Fair Traded Price or a discount off of either one. Also, this is not a commodities product or a stock listed on an open exchange. It is also not an object quoted at so much an ounce that can be purchased at an internationally quoted price. Therefore, we have to carefully study available retail, wholesale, auction, and private offering prices and confer with many dealers and collectors in the field. We weigh these and other factors before determining the price for each piece within its category. The prices in this guide represent the figures that we have calculated to be the **average** price for a fine item offered by an informed dealer to an informed buyer.

The sale of a particular Item can be higher if the celebrity whose signature is being offered has a local or personal interest, if the item has exceptional content or if the item is in short supply due to a sudden surge of interest. A collector might also be in need of something specific to complete a topical collection or a set and, of course, rarity, most assuredly, will send a piece well over book value.

Conversely, sales are often made *under* book value due to overstocking, a change in popularity, lack of current interest and shrewd bargaining. This edition still reflects average prices and we continue to present them rounded off. In the Entertainment category the more common lower priced material is frequently basically unchanged and is found within $1.00-$5.00 or $5.00-$10-00 range.

It is important to stress that because the prices for all categories are averages, you must take into consideration a **trading range**. What I have discovered in this current edition (as in the previous edition) is that even though the basic printed average of a group of pieces may not have changed more than a few dollars, the **range** in which these pieces are traded is, again, considerably wider. The better quality

material is higher due to more knowledgeable and affluent collectors searching the market for a smaller pool of that kind of material. At the lower end of the range the prices reflect the entrance of newer, sometimes younger, collectors who are looking for and are willing to accept a little less quality until they are better informed, at which time they begin to upgrade.

Although the singular pieces averaged together are similar, the prices for them can be very dissimilar because of the personal assessments and appraisals given by the individual sellers. Even the locale of the various dealers and their financial condition at the time of their offering can make considerable difference in a price. So, again I stress, the important thing to remember is that these averages in this fourth edition are going to give you a wider price range in which you may work than ever before, even though the quoted price may have remained *unchanged*. I even see that in many cases the price quoted is slightly lower but the prices from which that value is derived has come from higher highs and lower lows. Use this type of information to your own advantage.

There is, as there always is, an exception to the averaging rule. If, after going through all the pricing material that is available to us, we have found only *one* price to report, then that is the price you will see. Such is often the case when there is a new listing or when there is great rarity. There are also price changes on a private sale or trade basis of which we have no knowledge.

There is no common denominator! To bring it down to its simple terms, let us assume that a single ALS is listed in its category for $1,000. That ALS might just as easily sell for $1,500 or as low as $750, but it could be a tremendous bargain at any of the three prices. Yes, it certainly could. We just want you all to know that each of you is the final judge (both as buyer

or seller) as to the value of any piece.

Because this hobby is growing so fast it is difficult to document all that is happening. We hope that this book keeps you abreast of the market. Like purchasing any other collectible, use care in choosing your dealer. There are so many good, honest, knowledgeable ones, please use your common sense when making a choice.

The prices given in this book are retail prices—that is, the price you would *pay* for a given item. If you are going to *sell* to a dealer, a legitimate offer to you would be about half of the retail price taking into consideration the price range that we have already discussed. This is not much different than selling any collectible to a dealer, be it a work of art, jewelry, or an oriental rug. Since the dealer may have to hold the piece for an indeterminable number of months or years before selling it plus whatever his costs may be in its sale, this is a fair markup. You may, of course, always bargain and haggle.

While every effort has been made to ensure the accuracy of the information in this book, the authors and publisher will in no event be liable for any loss of profit or any other damage, including but not limited to special, incidental, consequential, or any other damages.

PRICING CATEGORIES

Although there are more than four pricing categories in autographs, we have chosen the four most important ones for this guide. They will cover the vast majority of autograph items, and exceptions may be interpolated from these prices. Following are the definitions we shall use:

Signature (**SIG**). This is the price that a signature is worth— that is, just the actual signature itself on a card, cut out of a letter, a page from an autograph album; may or may not be accompanied by date and/or place, etc.

Letter Signed or Document Signed (**LS/DS**). An example of more recent pieces might be a typed letter or document signed by a celebrity. During the nineteenth century, before the invention of the typewriter, it was common for secretaries or clerks to prepare handwritten letters or documents for signatures. These also fall within the LS/DS category.

Autograph Letter Signed (**ALS**). Generally the most important category except in the entertainment field where a signed photograph seems to take priority. This is a letter (or document) completely written in the hand of and signed by the important personage.

Signed Photograph (**SP**). This Category can also include signed portrait engravings, woodcuts, photo reproductions. Signed original cartoon drawings are designated with an asterisk (*) after the cartoonist's name and are found in the SP column. Reproductions of works of art and signed by the artist are shown in the Comment column.

MAJOR AUTOGRAPH CATEGORIES

The current format for autograph categories will please many and upset some. We have maintained a column to identify the category of each entry. In many cases the person is notable in more than one classification. We have identified him, her or them with the category in which the person(s) is most commonly known or collected. In addition, we have given you a "Comment" column to further enhance the information.

In some cases we have included *prices* in that "Comment" column for special material that could not be included in the averages because they were outside the normal trading range or for material that is not listed as a Category. Unfortunately, because of its size and the amount of information we would like to use, we have had to abbreviate much of what it contains.

It has become increasingly more and more difficult to manage the LS/DS column due to its inclusion of two different categories. We hope to divide it in the future so that we can more clearly delineate the prices.

A FINAL WORD ON PRICING

Every effort has been made to provide as accurate an accounting of prices as is humanly and electronically possible. We have retrieved thousands and thousands of figures, tabulated them, averaged them, and entered them into what has become our permanent database.

These raw numbers have come from every corner of our country as well as from Great Britain, France, Germany, Switzerland and Scandinavia. We have selectively incorporated the prices of non-specialized material. That is, signed original autograph manuscripts and signed books with values over and above the signature are not included. The comment column contains (whenever applicable) prices for items over and above those carried in the averages as well as musical quotations signed. These all reflect a special added value.

Please note that *some* presidential entries have both presidential and non-presidential records. We have, however, found that in many cases the values do not fluctuate greatly between the two.

Some Civil War letters and documents etc., have both war and non-war prices. If it works for the Civil War collectors we shall continue to add more in our next edition. As before, in the case of extreme rarity in any category we have reported the price(s) available to us.

We have presented to you "The Market". We have not created this market: therefore you may find incongruities, whereby an Autograph Letter Signed is priced lower than a Letter/Document Signed and sometimes Signed Photographs are signifi-

cantly more valuable in a specific category because of a particular group interest. We have not created this market but we have given you an unbiased list of collectible autographs.

Because the number of collectors and dealers in this field has grown so tremendously, much more material has come into the marketplace; therefore, please keep in mind that when you see a price that has been either raised or lowered it has been done within a much wider base than in our previous books. As a result, a price of $500 could well have been averaged at prices ranging from $300 to $600 or even $700 giving both the buyer and the seller far greater latitude in establishing a fair price for their individual piece.

Usually, the higher the price, the wider the fluctuation (both up and down) of prices within the average. Not to be ignored is the **relative** value among autographs. It should be of interest and help in your judgments.

If a price was not changed, it indicates there has been no current sale or the change (either up or down) was too minor to record so it was left unaltered. As regards new entries: Frequently only one price was available which, of course, was recorded in its proper column.

These figures are not reflections of a particular autograph personality's ability, talent, intelligence, greatness or beauty. They represent an unbiased presentation to the public of material from all over the world and are given to you so that you can make knowledgeable judgments regarding purchases and sales.

Bargains are available when certain autographs in a category are priced far below others of equal importance, rarity and collectibility, i.e., when a new category is suddenly discovered and becomes very popular. Certainly Civil War comes to mind; when you consider the prices of Confederate Generals of a few years ago compared to their current value.

Perhaps we have opened your eyes to Autographs on Stamps which we have tried to call your attention to in this edition's current chapter. In any case, there is always a burgeoning subject which you can look for.

Because of the vastness and ad infinitum concept of this publication and the electronic contribution that is made, there may be errors. For these we apologize! Further, we take no responsibility for quoting others' published prices in the compilation of our data.

Thank You!

We hope you will find this book helpful to you. Thanks, and we hope you find our price guide an enjoyable tool to use and one that is of great benefit to you. As always, we welcome your suggestions on improving our autograph price guides. Please send your comments to us at :

Autograph House
George Sanders - Helen Sanders
P.O. Box 658
Enka, NC 28728
704-667-9835

KEY

NAME	Name of a person or group
CATEGORY	Artist, entertainer, writer, etc.
SIG	Signature
LS/DS	A signed letter (either written by someone else or typed) or a signed document.
ALS	Autograph Letter Signed, i.e. written entirely in the hand of the celebrity
SP	Signed photograph
*	Signed art instead of photograph

PRICES

NAME	CATEGORY	SIG	LS/DS	ALS	SP	Comment
Aadland, Beverly	Entertainment	3	6		8	Errol Flynn's paramour
AAlton, Alvar	Architect	110	250		125	Finnish Architect-Designer
Aames, Willie	Entertainment	5	7		12	
Abba	Entertainment	20			35	
Abba, Marta	Entertainment	15		40	82	It. Actress
Abbado, Claudio	Entertainment	10			50	Symph. & Opera Conductor
Abbe, Cleveland 1838-1916	Science	15		50		Co-Founder US Weather Service 1869
Abbey, Edwin Austin	Artist	15	30	50		Am.Portraitist, Illustrator
Abbot, Charles Greeley	Science	15	50		25	Am. Astrophysicist
Abbott & Costello	Entertainment	475			917	Radio, Film, TV Comedy Team
Abbott, Bessie	Entertainment	25			40	Opera
Abbott, Bud 1895-1974	Entertainment	198	245	295	450	Radio, Film, TV Comedian
Abbott, George 1887-1995	Entertainment	15	20	45	122	Producer/Director/Playwright
Abbott, Henry Larcom	Civil War	25	45	70		Union Gen.
Abbott, Henry Livermore	Civil War	90	205			Union Gen.
Abbott, John S.C.	Author, Clergyman	12		40		
Abbott, Lyman 1835-1922	Clergy	25	45	75	45	Congregational Minister-Author
Abbott. John	Entertainment	8			20	
Abdnor, James	Congress	5	15		10	Senator SD
Abdul, Paula	Entertainment	25		55	75	
Abel, I.W.	Labor	10	25	40	10	Pres. United Steel Workers
Abel, Walter	Entertainment	10	20	25	25	
Abercrombie, John J (War Date)	Civil War	55	90	135		Union Gen. ALS '64 $525
Abercrombie, John J. 1798-1877	Civil War	45	75	105		Union Gen. ALS '64 $525
Aberdeen, Lord, 4th Earl	Head of State	35	40	85		Br. Prime Minister
Abernathy, Ralph D.	Clergy	30	75	120	60	Civil Rights Leader
Abernathy, Thomas Gerstle	Congress	5	10		10	Congressman MS
Abernethy, John 1764-1831	Science	45		185		Br. Surgeon
Abraham, F. Murray	Entertainment	10	15	35	30	
Abrahamson, James	Military-Astro.	10			30	
Abrams, Creighton W. 1912-74	Military	15	30	45	70	Gen. WW II Tank Commander
Abrams, Elliott	Diplomat	10	20		25	State Dept.
Abruzzo, Ben A.	Aviation	32			80	
Abt, Franz	Composer	70		200		
Abzug, Bella	Politician	10	15	60	15	Lawyer, Congresswoman NY
AC/DC	Entertainment	35			105	Rock
Acheson, Dean	Cabinet	25	65		40	Sec'y State
Acheson, George R.	Military	5		20	15	

The Sanders Price Guide to Autographs

NAME	CATEGORY	SIG	LS/DS	ALS	SP	Comment
Acland, Arthur Wm. 1805-77	SEE Hood, Arth.W.					
Acosta, Bert	Aviation	35	60	135	90	
Acquanetta, Burna	Entertainment	10			35	Pin-up $45
Acton, Loren	Astronaut	5		35	25	
Acuff, Roy	Country Music	10			40	
Adair, Allen	Military	20		55	65	Br. Gen.Operation Mkt. Garden
Adair, John	Governor	40	125	185		Early Gov. KY
Adair, Red	Celebrity	15	35	55	28	Oil Well Fires
Adam 12 (Cast Of)	Entertainment				50	Kent McCord, Martin Milner
Adam, Adolphe-Charles	Composer	40	120	337	90	Opera & Ballet (Giselle)
Adamic, Louis	Author	15	58	107	37	Am. Novelist. Born Yugoslavia
Adamowski, Timothee	Composer	10			20	AMusQS $45
Adams, Abigail	First Lady	505	1820	6875		
Adams, Alva	Governor	5		15	10	Gov. CO
Adams, Andrew	Revolutionary War	105	388	440		Continental Congress
Adams, Ansel 1902-84	Artist	100	345	600	375	Photographer, TLS/Content $450
Adams, Brooke	Entertainment	5	10	20	12	
Adams, Bryan	Entertainment	20			50	Rock
Adams, Charles Francis	Author-Diplomat	35	152	190		Civil War Ambassador to G.B.
Adams, Clara	Aviation	20	35		50	
Adams, Daniel W. 1821-72	Civil War	150	270	825		CSA Gen.
Adams, Dawnn	Entertainment	4			15	Actress
Adams, Don	Entertainment	2	8	20	15	Get Smart
Adams, Edie	Entertainment	5	5	8	10	
Adams, Edwin 1834-77	Actor	12			45	
Adams, Gerry	Head of State	60	75			Leader Sinn Fein, IRA
Adams, Harriet	Author	35	45	55		
Adams, Henry Brooks 1838-1918	Author	110	385	367		Am. Historian, Philosopher, Critic
Adams, J. Q. and J. Monroe	Presidents		2283			Signed by Both
Adams, James S.	Business	10	35	45	25	
Adams, Joe E.	Entertainment	10			25	Comedian
Adams, Joey	Entertainment	4	5	9	10	
Adams, John 1735-1826	President	1775	5494	16700		AMsS $33,350, FF as Pres. $3200
Adams, John 1778-1854	Congress	25		40		Repr. NY
Adams, John 1825-64	Civil War	235	488			CSA Gen. KIA (War Date) DS $2350
Adams, John Couch	Astronomer	20	45	125		Discoverer of Neptune
Adams, John Q. & Monroe, James	Presidents		2500			Signed By Both Presidents
Adams, John Quincy 1767-1848	President	350	1242	2450		Engr.S $2990-12,500.ALS/Cont.$25,000
Adams, Julie	Entertainment	4	5	9	25	
Adams, Louisa Catherine	First Lady	200	450	1115		Wife of John Q. Adams
Adams, Mason	Entertainment	3			8	
Adams, Maud (current)	Entertainment	8	9	20	25	
Adams, Maude 1872-1953	Entertainment	35	50	82	125	Am. Stage Actress. Peter Pan
Adams, Nick	Entertainment	125			350	
Adams, Samuel 1722-1803	Revolutionary War	605	1566	3750		Signer Decl. of Indepen.AMsS $9500
Adams, Sherman	Governor	25	75	110	45	Eisenhower Asst., Gov. NH
Adams, Stanley	Composer	15	25	40	25	Lyricist
Adams, William T. (Oliver Optic)	Author	20	25	55	58	Various Series Books For Boys
Adams, William Wirt (War Date)	Civil War	375		1325		CSA General
Adams, William Wirt 1819-88	Civil War	275	525	538		CSA Gen.
Adamson, James C.	Astronaut	5	15		15	
Adamson, William C.	Congress	5	15		30	19th Cent. Congressman GA
Addams, Charles*	Cartoonist	50			650	Addams Family
Addams, Dawn	Entertainment	5			15	Actress
Addams, Jane 1860-1935	Am. Social Worker	67	300	310	300	Social Reformer, Nobel Peace
Addinsell, Richard 1940-77	Composer	10	30	150	30	Br. Warsaw Concerto

NAME	CATEGORY	SIG	LS/DS	ALS	SP	Comment
Addis, Don*	Cartoonist	10			35	
Addison, Joseph 1672-1719	Author	80	205	360		Br. Poet, Essayist, Playwright
Ade, George 1866-1944	Author	25	70	155	65	Am. Humorist, Dramatist.AQS $50
Adelaide, HRH Queen England	Royalty	40		112		Queen of William IV
Adenauer, Konrad (der Alte)	Head of State	25	205	225	140	1st Chan. Fed. Rep. of Germany
Ader, Rose	Entertainment	20			95	Opera
Adjani, Isabelle	Entertainment	20			75	Opera
Adler, Alfred 18870-1937	Science	110	560	1117	192	Psychiatrist. ALS/Content $2,000
Adler, Buddy	Entertainment	10			25	Film Producer
Adler, Felix B.	Entertainment	20			45	Professional Clown
Adler, Larry	Entertainment	20			35	Harmonica Virtuoso
Adler, Luther	Entertainment	10	15	25	25	Vintage Actor-Stage & Film
Adler, Max	Business	9	26	40	30	Pres.Sears, Roebuck. Philanthropy
Adler, Richard	Composer	15	35	65	30	AMusQS $35-$135
Adler, Stella	Entertainment	15	15	25	35	Drama Teacher & Coach
Adoree, Renee	Entertainment	30	40		70	
Adrian, Edgar Lord 1889-1977	Science	25	45	130	65	Nobel Physiology
Adrian, Iris	Entertainment	8	10		20	
Aerosmith (All)	Entertainment	45			93	Rock
Aga Khan III	Royalty	95	300			
Aga Khan IV	Royalty	15	40	110	35	
Agar, John	Entertainment	4	4	9	12	
Agassiz, Alexander 1835-1910	Science	20		40		Son of Louis. Naturalist
Agassiz, Jean Louis 1807-73	Science	85	145	275	625	Swiss-Am. Zoologist, Biologist
Agnew, Spiro (V)	Vice President	35	173	170	80	
Agnus, Felix 1839-1925	Civil War	20	45			165th NY. Union Gen'l. War Date ALS $250
Aguinaldo, Emilio	Head of State	100	140	165	140	Filipino Leader Againt Spain
Agutter, Jenny	Entertainment	5	6	15	15	
Aherne, Brian	Entertainment	15	20	30	55	
Ahidjo, Ahmadou	Head of State	15		120	40	(Cameroon)
Ahlfors, Lars V., Dr.	Science	10	25		25	
Aiello, Danny	Entertainment	10	25	30	30	
Aiken, Conrad 1889-1973	Author	30	72	155	40	Am.Novelist, Poet. Pulitzer
Aiken, George D.	Senate	20	25		30	Senator & Gov. VT
Aiken, John W.	Political	20			30	Social'st Pres. Cand.1936
Aiken, William	Governor	10	15	30	20	Gov. & Congressman SC
Ainger, Alfred	Clergy	10	15	30	25	
Airy, George B. 1801-92	Science	35	130	330		Br. Royal Astronomer
Aitken, Robert 1734-1802	Printer	75	180	360		!st English Bible Printed in Am
Aitken, Robert Grant	Science	10	20	45		Astronomer
Aitken, Robert Ingersoll	Artist	25	75	190		Am. Sculptor Military Statues
Akbar, Taufik	Astronaut	5			20	Indonesia
Akers Peter	Clergy	35	45	60		
Akers, Elizabeth	Author	5		20	10	
Akihito & Machiko (Both)	Royalty	410				Emperor & Empress of Japan
Akihito, Emperor of Japan	Royalty	475	540	675	350	
Akin, Susan	Celebrity	4	7	12	10	
Akin, Warren	Civil War	40	55	90		CSA Congress
Akins, Claude	Entertainment	9	10	14	35	
Akins, Zoe	Author	10	25	50		Poet, Playwright. Pulitzer
Akroyd, Dan	Entertainment	10	15	20	35	Comedian-Actor
Al-Said, Sultan	Astronaut	10			35	Saudi Arabia
Alabama (signed by all 4)	Country Music	35			80	
Alard, Nelly	Entertainment	4			10	
Albanese, Licia	Entertainment	35	40	55	65	It. Soprano. Opera, Concert
Albani, Emma, Dame	Entertainment	50	60	100	200	Canadian Soprano. Opera

NAME	CATEGORY	SIG	LS/DS	ALS	SP	Comment
Albee, Edward	Author	20	65	118	90	Am. Dramatist. Pulitzer
Alberghetti, Anna M.	Entertainment	15			30	
Albert I (Belgium)	Royalty	25	115	195	50	
Albert III (Rainier-Monaco)	Royalty	90	200	445	120	
Albert Victor, Duke of Athlone	Royalty	150		1250	550	Eldest Son Edward VII
Albert, Carl	Congress	15		40	25	Speaker of the House. OK
Albert, Don	Entertainment	25			50	Trumpet & Bandleader
Albert, Eddie	Entertainment	10	15	20	20	Actor. Green Acres. 100's Versatile Roles
Albert, Marv	Entertainment	5	7		10	TV Host
Albert, Prince (Monaco)	Royalty	25			40	
Albert, Prince (Victoria)	Royalty	125	292	442		Consort of Queen Victoria
Albert, Stephen	Entertainment	20			30	Pulitzer, AMusQS $75
Albertson, Frank	Entertainment	15	20		30	
Albertson, Jack 1910-81	Entertainment	20	40		55	
Albertson, Joseph A.	Business	8	10	20	20	
Albright, Charles (C.W.)	Congress	15	20	30		Union Col. CW, Congressman PA
Albright, Lola	Entertainment	9	10	20	20	Early TV Series Star
Albright, Madeleine	Statesman	15			35	1st woman Secretary of State
Albritton, Louise	Entertainment	15	15	25	30	Promising Actress. Early Death
Albury, Charles Donald, Capt.	Aviation	20	45	60	55	
Alcock, J. & Brown A..W.	Aviation				923	Signed by Both
Alcock, John William 1892-1919	Aviation	235	495	685	600	Pioneer Aviator/A.W. Brown
Alcorn, James Lusk 1816-94	Civil War	55	145	250		CSA Gen.
Alcott, Amos Bronson	Author	40	85	135		Social, Civil, Education Reform
Alcott, Louisa May 1832-88	Author	202	290	435		1 pg AMsS $3500
Alda, Alan	Entertainment	15	15	30	20	Mash TV Star
Alda, Frances 1883-1952	Entertainment	20			80	Opera. New Zealand Born Soprano
Alda, Robert	Entertainment	10	10	15	25	
Aldasoro, Eduardo	Aviation	15		55	35	
Aldasoro, J. Pablo	Aviation	15		55	35	
Aldington, Richard 1892-1962	Author	25	110	176		Br. Poet, Novelist,Biographer
Aldred, Joel	Aviation-WWII	18	38	55	45	Canadian ACE
Aldrich, Bess Streeter 1881-1954	Author	5	15	35	40	Am. Novelist,Short Story Writer
Aldrich, Louis 1843-1901	Entertainment	10			40	Vintage Actor
Aldrich, Nelson W.	Senate	10	15		15	Senator NY
Aldrich, Thomas Bailey 1836-1907	Author	20	30	70	225	Novels, Poetry, Editor
Aldridge, Kay	Entertainment	4			10	
Aldrin, Edwin 'Buzz'	Astronaut	79	238	300	270	2nd Moonwalker
Aleichem, Shalom 1859-1916	Author			3750		Rus.Born Jewish Writer-Humorist
Aler, John	Entertainment	10			40	
Alexander I (Rus) 1777-1825	Royalty	265	1228	895		
Alexander II (Rus)	Royalty	225	775	1760		Assassinated
Alexander III (Pope)	Clergy		45000			
Alexander III (Rus)	Royalty		375	600		
Alexander, Albert, Sir	Statesman	20				Br.M.P
Alexander, Barton S. 1819-78	Civil War	45	65	95		Union Gen.
Alexander, Ben	Entertainment	40	50		125	Jack Webb Sidekick Dragnet
Alexander, Cecil Frances	Clergy	10	20	25	35	
Alexander, Clifford	Activist	10		25	15	Afro-Am Activist
Alexander, Edward 1835-1910	Civil War	242	712	1242		CSA General
Alexander, Edward Porter (War Date)	Civil War	535	920	3075		CSA General
Alexander, George	Entertainment	6	8	15	15	
Alexander, Harold R.L., Sir 1891-1969	Military	65	90	162	95	Alexander of Tunis, WW II
Alexander, Henry	Business	3	7	15	10	
Alexander, J. B.	Governor	20	25		25	Guam
Alexander, Jane	Entertainment	10	10	15	25	

NAME	CATEGORY	SIG	LS/DS	ALS	SP	Comment
Alexander, Jason	Entertainment	10			50	Seinfeld. Emmy
Alexander, John	Entertainment	20			40	Played T.Roosevelt Arsenic & Old Lace
Alexander, Joshua Wallis	Cabinet	15	40		25	Sec'y Commerce, Congress MO
Alexander, Lamar	Governor	9			15	Gov. TN. Pres. Candidate
Alexander, Robert	Revolutionary War	30	65			
Alexander, William (Lord Stirling)	Military-Rev. War	200	725	1575		Gen. in Continental Army
Alexander, William, Archbishop	Clergy	20	30	40	35	
Alexanderson, Ernst F. W.	Science	45	115	195		Father of Television
Alexandra (Edw VII) 1844-1925	Royalty	95		330	432	Queen of Edw.VII (Eng.)Coronation SP $1500
Alexandra (Nich. II Rus.)	Royalty	110	235	675	175	ALS/Content $5,000
Alexis, Kim	Entertainment	10			20	
Alfano, Franco	Composer					AMusQS $285
Alfieri, Carlo	Entertainment	10		35	35	Opera
Alfono, Heradio	Aviation	15			35	
Alfonso V 1396-1458	Royalty		2500			Naples & Sicily. Magnanimo
Alfonso XIII (Sp)1886-1941	Royalty	140	500	625	500	
Alfonso, Kristian	Entertainment	5			18	Pin-up $25
Alford, Henry	Clergy	10	20	30	25	
Alfred, Prince	Royalty	20	35	78		2nd Son of Queen Victoria
Alfven, Hannes	Science	20	30	45	30	Nobel Physics
Alger, Horatio 1832-99	Author	138	215	340	240	Popular Books For Boys
Alger, Russell Alexander 1836-1907	Civil War,Cabinet	50	55	85	90	Union Gen., Gov. MI, Sec'y War
Algren, Nelson	Author	25	60	185	50	Am.Novelist.Naturalistic Novels
Ali Khan, R. (Prince)	Royalty	15		90		
Alice, Princess	Royalty	15		65		2nd Daughter of Queen Victoria
Alicia, Ana	Entertainment	5	6	15	15	
All in the Family (Cast)	Entertainment	45			110	4 Leading Characters
Allan, Buddy	Country Music	5	10		12	Buck Owens' son
Allen, Adrienne	Entertainment	5	10	20	15	
Allen, Amos L. 1837-1911	Congress	10			40	Repr. ME
Allen, Andrew	Astronaut	7	10		15	
Allen, Barbara Jo(Vera Vague)	Entertainment	25			50	Comedienne AKA Vera Vague
Allen, Charles L.	Clergy	20	35	50	35	
Allen, Debbie	Entertainment	6	8	15	20	
Allen, Elizabeth	Entertainment	8	9	15	15	
Allen, Ethan 1738-89	Military-Rev. War	650	1835	3200		Col. Green Mounain Boys
Allen, Frank A., Jr.	Military	10	20	45		
Allen, Fred	Entertainment	50	65	110	100	Popular Radio Comedian/Portland Hoffa
Allen, Ginger Lynn	Model	5			30	Pin-up $35
Allen, Gracie	Entertainment	50	60	75	150	
Allen, Grant	Author	5	15	30	10	
Allen, Henry J.	Congress	5	20			Senator, Kansas
Allen, Henry T.	Military	25	70	125	50	General WW I
Allen, Henry Watkins(War Date)	Civil War	235	395	912		CSA Gen. 1820-66
Allen, Horatio	Business	65		115		
Allen, Ira (Brother of Ethan)	Military-Rev. War					Rev. War Date LS $15,000
Allen, Irwin	Entertainment	5			12	Director
Allen, Joseph P.	Astronaut	10			25	
Allen, Karen	Entertainment	15	10	20	25	
Allen, Marty	Entertainment	3	3	6	10	Bushy Haired Comedian
Allen, Peter	Composer	35			125	
Allen, Rex	Entertainment	10	10	15	25	Cowboy Singer-Actor
Allen, Robert (War Date)	Civil War	38	60	90		Union Gen. (1811-86)
Allen, Robert F.	Business	5			10	Pres., CEO Carrier Corp.
Allen, Roderick R.	Military	10	20	35		
Allen, Steve	Entertainment	10	15	15	20	Composer, Pianist,TV-Radio Host

NAME	CATEGORY	SIG	LS/DS	ALS	SP	Comment
Allen, Tim	Entertainment	15			62	Home Improvement
Allen, Valerie	Entertainment	4	4	9	10	
Allen, Viola	Entertainment	15	20	25	25	Vintage Stage Star 1898
Allen, William M.	Business	20	40	55	30	
Allen, William Wirt 1835-94	Civil War	190	375			CSA Gen., War Dte DS $510, ALS $1,275
Allen, Woody	Entertainment	20	30	45	44	Actor, Comedian, Playwright, AA Director
Allenby, Edmund 1861-1936	Military	30	95	150	220	Br.Fld Marshal, ALS/Cont.$750
Allende Gossens, Salvador	Head of State	35	120	285	60	1st Marxist Pres. Chile
Alley, Kirstie	Entertainment	10	15	25	40	
Allgood, Sara	Entertainment	10		35	50	Vintage Screen Character Actress
Allingham, Margery	Author	30	65	150		Br. Mystery Writer
Allison, Fran	Entertainment	10	12	15	25	Early TV Children's Show.Kukla,Fran & Ollie
Allison, May	Entertainment	15			40	
Allison, Mose	Composer	15			30	Jazz Pianist-Vocalist
Allison, W.B.	Senate	10	15	20	15	Senator IA
Allizard, Adolphe	Entertainment	12		35		Opera. Bass
Allman, Greg	Entertainment	20			50	Rock
Allred, Gloria	Entertainment	20			30	Feminist Att'y. Brown vs O.J. Simpson
Allston, Washington 1779-1843	Artist	275	400	825		Pioneered Romantic Landscapes. Author
Allyson, June	Entertainment	5	10	15	20	MGM Star. 2nd Career in TV Commercials
Alma-Tadema, Lawrence	Artist	20	62	132		Br. Painter of Roman Scenes
Almond, Edw. M.	Military	12	35	50		
Almonte, Juan Nepomuceno 1804-69	Military	50	200	305		Mex. General, Politician
Almy, John J.	Civil War					Union Adm. Cont. ALS $1900
Alonso, Maria Conchita	Entertainment	10	15	25	22	
Alpert, Herb	Entertainment	8	10	12	25	Big Band Leader-Trumpet
Alphand, Nicole H.	Celebrity	8			15	
Alsop, Joseph	Author	5	13	30	10	Journalist, Synd. Columnist
Alsop, Stewart	Author	10	26	35	15	Journalist, Synd. Columnist
Alt, Carol	Entertainment	10	15	25	27	Pin-up $40
Altchewsky, Ivan	Entertainment				250	Opera (Rare)
Altgeld, John P.	Governor	15	45			Gov. IL
Altieri, Albert (Johnny)	Celebrity	4			10	Philip Morris Trademark
Altman, Robert	Entertainment	5	6	15	20	
Alvarez, Luis W., Dr.	Science	15	35	85	30	Nobel Physics
Alvarez, Roma	Entertainment	3	3	6	10	
Alvary, Lorenzo	Entertainment	10	12	25	25	
Alvord, Benjamin 1813-84	Civil War	25	45	65		Union General
Aly Khan, Prince	Royalty	75				
Alyn, Kirk	Entertainment	10			25	Original Superman in movies.
Amani, Giorgio	Designer	10		35	25	Fashion
Amara, Lucine	Entertainment	15		55	45	Opera
Amato, Pasquale	Entertainment	25			125	It. Baritone. Opera
Ambler, Eric Clifford	Author	50	160			Br.Novelist
Ambrose, Bert 1896-1971	Entertainment	15			45	Notable Br. Bandleader
Ameche, Don	Entertainment	20	35	45	55	
American President, The (Cast Of)					135	Bening, Douglas
Ames, Adelbert 1835-1933	Civil War	60	65	210		Union Gen., CMH Bull Run
Ames, Ed	Entertainment	10	15		20	
Ames, Fisher 1758-1808	Statesman	110		500		Organized Federalist Party
Ames, Leon	Entertainment	15	15	20	30	Life With Father Star. TV
Ames, Nancy	Entertainment	5	6	15	10	
Ames, Oakes	Financier			1500		Founder Union Pac. RR
Ames, Oliver	Business.	30	173	190		Union Pacific RR. Rare DS $575
Amherst, Jeffrey, Lord 1717-97	Revolutionary War	455	850	1100		Gov. Gen. Br. No. Amer. Br.Gen.
Amin Dada, Idi	Heads of State	50	275		75	

NAME	CATEGORY	SIG	LS/DS	ALS	SP	Comment
Amis, Kingsley	Author	15	30	65	25	
Ammen, Daniel 1820-	Civil War	36	60	95	175	Union General
Ammen, Jacob 1806-94	Civil War	20	35	75		Union Gen.
Amos & Andy (Corell & Gosden)	Entertainment	100	150		250	Signed by Both
Amos, Wally 'Famous'	Business	4	10	20	10	Afro-Am. Cookie King
Amparan, Belen	Entertainment	10			35	Opera
Ampere, Andre Marie	Science	170	420	1400		Fr. Physicist, Mathematician
Amsden, Ben	Aviation	10	22	38	28	Navy ACE WW II
Amsterdam, Morey	Entertainment	5			15	
Amundsen, Roald	Explorer	95	195	450	395	Nor. Polar Explorer
Ancerl, Karel	Entertainment	3	4	8	5	
Ancona, Mario	Entertainment			65		
Ancona, Sydenham E.	Senate/ Congress	15		45		Civil War Congressman PA
Anders, Luana	Entertainment	10	15		20	
Anders, Merry	Entertainment	5			15	
Anders, Pamela	Entertainment	20			35	
Anders, William A.	Astronaut	40			95	
Andersen, Hans Christian	Authors	350	650	1662	1685	AQS on CDV $1450
Anderson, 'Bronco Billy'	Entertainment	105	175	200	375	
Anderson, Bill	Country Music	4			12	
Anderson, Brad*	Cartoonist	15		35	25	Marmaduke
Anderson, C.E. Bud	Aviation	12	28	45	35	WW II ACE
Anderson, Carl David	Science	20	35		70	Nobel Physics 1936
Anderson, Carl T.*	Cartoonist	15	45		60	Henry
Anderson, Clifford	Civil War	70	130	95		CSA Congress
Anderson, Clinton	Cabinet	15	20		25	Sec'y Agriculture. Senator NM
Anderson, Eddie Rochester	Entertainment	40		210	150	
Anderson, Elizabeth G.,Dr. 1836-1917	Science	55	175	175		1st Eng. Hospital for Women
Anderson, George Burgwyn	Civil War	235	425			CSA Gen., War Dte DS $525
Anderson, George T. Tige 1824-1901	Civil War	130	130	470	250	CSA Gen.
Anderson, George W.	Military	10	30	40	25	
Anderson, Gillian	Entertainment				87	X Files. With Duchevny
Anderson, Harry	Entertainment	5	8	20	35	
Anderson, Henry James	Educator	12				
Anderson, Jack	Author	3	5	15	15	Syndicated Newspaper Columnist
Anderson, James Patton (War Date)	Civil War	400		3080		CSA General
Anderson, James Patton 1822-72	Civil War	80	285	375		CSA Gen.,ALS/Content $475
Anderson, John B.	Military	5	10	20		
Anderson, John Jr.	Governor	12	15		15	Governor KS
Anderson, Joseph 1757-1837	Revolutionary War	60	235	390		Early Senator TN
Anderson, Joseph R.(War Date)	Civil War	380	702	880		CSA General
Anderson, Joseph Reid 1813-92	Civil War	85	225	385		CSA Gen.
Anderson, Judith	Entertainment	25	35	45	55	
Anderson, June	Entertainment	5			25	Opera
Anderson, Laurie	Entertainment	10	15		25	
Anderson, Leroy	Composer	25	75	195	45	AMusMsS $325
Anderson, Les 'Carrot-top'	Country Music	10	12		20	
Anderson, Loni	Entertainment	9	10	25	23	
Anderson, Louie	Entertainment	5			20	Stand-up & TV Comic
Anderson, Lynn	Country Music	4			12	
Anderson, Marian 1902-93	Entertainment	150	200	250	342	1st Afro-Am Singer Perform at Met. '58
Anderson, Martin B.	Clergy	10	15	25		
Anderson, Mary (American)	Entertainment	30	45	50	100	
Anderson, Mary (English)	Entertainment	10	20	30	30	
Anderson, Maxwell	Author	30	70	140	50	Am. Dramatist. Pulitzer
Anderson, Melissa Sue	Entertainment	10	35		35	

NAME	CATEGORY	SIG	LS/DS	ALS	SP	Comment
Anderson, Michael, Jr.	Entertainment	7			20	Producer
Anderson, O.A.	Aviation	10	25	40	30	General
Anderson, Pamela Lee	Entertainment	20			60	SP Nude $75
Anderson, Philip W.	Science	45		95	50	Nobel Physics
Anderson, Poul	Author	10	35	45		Sci-Fi. Award Winner
Anderson, Richard	Entertainment	4	5	10	12	
Anderson, Richard Dean	Entertainment	5	10	25	40	
Anderson, Richard Heron	Civil War	55	120	245		CSA Gen.,War Dte DS $375
Anderson, Robert	Author	10	20	45	15	
Anderson, Robert 1805-71	Civil War	115	325	520	1950	Cmdr.Ft. Sumter,Wardte ALS$3500
Anderson, Robert B.	Cabinet	10	17	35	20	Sec'y Treasury
Anderson, Robert H. (War Date	Civil War	205	391			CSA General
Anderson, Robert H.1835-88	Civil War	110	345	348		CSA Gen.
Anderson, Roy A.	Business	5	15	20	10	
Anderson, Samuel	Military	40	130	220		Early Congressman PA 1827
Anderson, Samuel E.	Military	5	10	20		
Anderson, Samuel R.	Civil War	125	300	350		CSA Gen.
Anderson, Sherwood	Author	35	95	150	40	Novelist, Journalist, Poet
Anderson, Tim	Entrtainment	4			20	
Anderson, W.R.	Military	15	35		50	Cmdr. N/S Nautilus
Anderson, Willie Y.	Aviation	10	22	35	30	WW II ACE
Andes, Keith	Entertainment	5	6		10	
Andre, John	Revolutionary War	1200	3500	7875		Br. Officer. Hanged as Spy
Andreotti, Guilio	Head of State	10	20	35	20	It. Journalist, Prime Minister
Andress, Ursula	Entertainment	15	20	30	35	
Andrew, A. Piatt	Senate/Congress	5	10		10	Congressman MA
Andrew, John A.	Governor	45	65	120		Civil War Gov. MA
Andrews Sisters (All Three)	Entertainment	85			170	
Andrews, Arkansas Slim	Entertainment	3	5	9	10	
Andrews, Chris. C. 1829-1922	Civil War	35	70	195		Union Gen. ALS '64 $265
Andrews, Dana	Entertainment	12	35		45	
Andrews, George Leonard	Civil War	35	55	90		Union Gen.
Andrews, Harry	Entertainment	7			25	
Andrews, Julie	Entertainment	12	12	20	40	SP Sound of Music $125
Andrews, Landaff W. 1803-87	Congress	10				Repr. KY
Andrews, Maxine 1918-95	Entertainment	12	17	19	25	
Andrews, Patti	Entertainment	10			25	
Andrews, Roy Chapman 1884-1960	Science	75		135	125	Naturalist, Explorer, Author
Andrews, V.C.	Author	4			10	Novelist
Andrews, William Frederick	Business	4	10		10	CEO Scoville, Inc.
Andriola, Alfred*	Cartoonist	5			30	Kerry Drake
Andros, Edmund, Sir	Revolutionary War			7500		Only Reported Amount Shown
Andrus, Cecil D.	Cabinet	5	10	35	15	Sec'y Interior
Anduran, Lucienne	Entertainment	10			35	Fr. Operatic Mezzo-Sopr.
Anfinsen, Christian	Science	15	25	45	20	Nobel Chemistry
Angel, Heather	Entertainment	10	12	15	30	Br. Leading Lady of 30's-40's
Angel, Vanessa	Entertainment	5			15	Actress TV's Wierd Science
Angeli, Pier	Entertainment	40	55	195	100	
Angelici, Marthe	Entertainment	20			75	Corsican Lyric Sopr.
Angell, Norman, Sir	Author	25	60	95	65	Nobel Peace Prize
Angelou, Maya	Author	25	40	35	35	Black Am. Poet
Angelyne	Celebrity	10			20	
Anglesea, Marquis of	Military	15	35	60		
Angus, Joseph	Clergy	10	20	25		
Animals, The	Entertainment	50			150	Rock HOF
Aniston, Jennifer	Entertainment	15			54	Friends

NAME	CATEGORY	SIG	LS/DS	ALS	SP	Comment
Anka, Paul	Composer	3	5	12	15	
Ankers, Evelyn	Entertainment	15	30	60	40	
Ann-Margret	Entertainment	6	8	15	32	
Anna Ivanovna (Rus)	Royalty	265	900	2250		Empress of Russia
Annabella	Entertainment	10	15	25	40	
Annaloro, Antonio	Entertainment	10		35	40	It. Tenor, Opera
Anne, Princess	Royalty	95	250		140	Daughter of Elizabeth II
Anne, Queen (Eng) 1665-1714	Royalty	365	1500	2150		
Annenberg, Walter H.	Business	10	25	40	35	Publisher
Annesley, H.N.	Law Enforcement	5	10		15	Northern Ireland
Annseau, Fernand	Entertainment	20			75	Opera
Anouilh, Jean	Author	30	95	220	40	Fr. Dramatist, Screenwriter
Ansara, Michael	Entertainment	6	8	15	25	
Anselmi, Giuseppe	Entertainment	40			125	Idolized Tenor Star
Ansermet, Ernest	Entertainment				200	
Ant, Adam	Entertainment	30			75	Punk Rock
Anthonly, Robert N.	Nobel	15	25		25	Nobel
Anthony, Henry B.	Congress	10	15	35		Editor, Gov., Senator RI
Anthony, HRH	Royalty	30	100			King of Saxony
Anthony, Ray	Entertainment	6	10	13	12	Big Band Leader
Anthony, Robert N.	Science	10			20	Nobel
Anthony, Susan B. 1820-1906	Woman Suffrage	230	1200	1638	1302	Reformer, Women's Rights
Antokolski, Mark Matveyevich	Artist	30	65	155		Russ. Sculp. 1843-1902
Anton, Susan	Entertainment	7	8	10	20	
Antonelli, Laura	Entertainment	18	20	45	50	
Antonioni, Michelangelo	Entertainment	15			150	Film Director
Anwar, Gabrielle	Entertainment	20			45	
Aoti, Rocky	Business	6	15	30	15	Benihana Japanese Resaurants
Apollinaire, Guillaume 1880-1918	Author	125	400	1200		Avant Garde Poet, Critic
Apollo 11 (Crew)	Astronaut				1264	Entire Crew (3) $900
Apollo 13 (Cast Of Movie)	Entertainment				250	Bacon, Hanks, Paxton
Apollo 15	Astronaut		175			Entire Crew FDC S $250
Apollo 9	Asttronaut					Entire Crew (3) $225
Apollo I	Astronauts				3000	Signed by All Three
Apollo II	Astronauts	280			575	Signed by All Three
Apollo XIII (Crew Of)	Astronauts				1400	FDC Signed All 3 $395
Apollo/Soyuz Mission	Astronaut	175			400	All 5
Apollonia	Entertainment				28	Purple Rain
Appleby, Ray	Entertainment	3	3	5	5	
Applegate, Christina	Entertainment	10	15		40	Actress-Model
Appleton, Daniel 1785-1849	Publisher	12				Appleton's Cyclopaedia
Appleton, Edward, Sir	Science	25	35		55	Nobel Physics
Apt, Jay	Astronaut	5	10		15	
Aquino, Corazon	Head of State	20			45	Pres. Philippines
Arafat, Yassir	Head of State	95	195		150	PLO Leader
Araisa, Francisco	Entertainment	5			35	Opera, Concert, Mexican Tenor
Arambula, Roman*	Cartoonist	40			200	Mickey Mouse
Araujo, Arturo	Head of State	15	40		30	Salvador
Arber, Werner	Science	20	35		30	Nobel Medicine
Arbos, E. Fernandez	Composer	20				AmusQS $350
Arbuckle, Maclyn	Entertainment	15	15	30	25	
Arbuckle, Roscoe 'Fatty'	Entertainment	335	400	750	775	
Archbold, John	Financier		1850			A Founder Standard Oil
Archer, Anne	Entertainment	12	15	15	30	
Archer, James J.	Civil War	200	375	825		CSA Gen.
Archer, Jeffrey	Author	5	15		15	Novelist

NAME	CATEGORY	SIG	LS/DS	ALS	SP	Comment
Archer, Jules	Author	7			10	
Archer, William S. 1789-1855	Congress	12				Sen. & Repr. VA
Archi, Attila	Entertainment	10	15	40	45	Opera
Arden, Elizabeth	Business	30	65	145	40	Founder & Owner Eliz. Arden Co.
Arden, Eve	Entertainment	20	25	50	45	
Arden, Nicke	Entertainment	3	3	5	5	
Arena, Angelina	Entertainment	5		30	25	Australian Soprano
Arens, Moshe	Diplomat-Author		80		20	Israeli
Argento, Dominick	Composer	10	30	65	20	Pulitzer, AMusQS $175
Argyll, 9th Duke, John D. Campbell	Head of State	30	45	60		Governor-General Canada
Arias Sanchez, Oscar	Head of State	35		65	50	Nobel Peace, Pres.Costa Rica
Arias, Harmodio	Head of State	25	50		30	
Arie, Raffaele	Entertainment	5			25	Bulgarian Basso
Ariyoshi, George R.	Governor	15			25	Governor Hawaii
Arkell, Bartlett	Business	5	27	45	15	
Arkell, W.J. (Judge Publ)	Business	5	15	30	10	
Arkin, Adam	Entertainment	5	7		10	
Arkin, Alan	Entertainment	5	8	15	25	
Arledge. John	Entertainment	5			20	2nd Leads 40's
Arlen, Harold	Composer	50	175	95	55	AMusQS $1,600
Arlen, Richard	Entertainment	27	30	70	65	
Arletty	Entertainment	25			75	Fr. Actress
Arliss, Florence	Entertainment	15	30	40	35	
Arliss, George	Entertainment	45	45	70	100	
Armani, Giorgio	Designer	5			30	
Armendariz, Pedro	Entertainment	30	35	45	65	
Armetta, Henry	Entertainment	25	30	50	65	
Armey, Dick	Congress	5	70		45	Majority Leader
Armistead, Lewis Addison	Civil War	600				CSA Gen., Last recorded sale_
Armour, Philip D.	Business	50	975		75	Meat Packing. Armour & Co.
Arms, Russ	Entertainment	3	3	6	10	
Armstead, Henry Hugh	Artist	10	20	35		Br. Sculptor.Albert Memorial
Armstrong, Bess	Entertainment	5			30	actress
Armstrong, Edw. R., Dr.	Science	30	75	150		Inventor Seadrome
Armstrong, Edwin H.	Science	75	250			Invented FM Broadcasting System
Armstrong, Frank Crawford	Civil War	290	365			CSA Gen.
Armstrong, Harry	Composer	80		195		Sweet AdelineAMusQS $365
Armstrong, John 1758-1843	Cabinet	45	125	872		Sec'y War.Cont. Congr.,War of 1812
Armstrong, Louis 1900-71	Entertainment	250	444	695	466	Satchmo.Jazz Trumpet
Armstrong, Martin	Author	5	10	15	10	
Armstrong, Neil A.	Astronaut	175	607	700	449	1st Moonwalker.Special SP $995
Armstrong, Robert	Entertainment	55	60	75	350	Actor King Kong
Armstrong, Robert	Military	175	450			Gen. TN Vols, Indian Fighter
Armstrong, Samuel Chapman	Civil War	55	120	350		Union Off. Cmdr. Black Regiment
Armstrong, William, Dr.	Science	20	50	110	35	
Arnaz, Desi 1915-86	Entertainment	35	45	50	200	
Arnaz, Lucie	Entertainment	5	10	15	20	
Arness, James	Entertainment	25			88	
Arnett, Peter	TV News	5			10	CNN News
Arngrim, Alison	Entertainment	6	8	15	10	
Arnheim, Gus	Bandleader				45	
Arno, Peter	Cartoonist	15	30	75	25	Drew for The New Yorker
Arno, Sig	Entertainment	10			25	
Arnold, Archibald	Military	20	62	102		
Arnold, Benedict 1741-1801	Revolutionary War	1300	1975	5875		Am. Army Officer. Traitor
Arnold, Eddy	Country Music	10	48		30	

NAME	CATEGORY	SIG	LS/DS	ALS	SP	Comment
Arnold, Edward	Entertainment	30	40		65	
Arnold, Edwin, Sir 1832-1904	Author	50	90	150	80	Br. Poet, Journalist
Arnold, Fredric	Aviation	20	35		50	ACE, WWII P-38
Arnold, Henry 'Hap' 1886-1950	Military	45	318	450	200	Air Force Gen. WW II
Arnold, Leslie P.	Aviation	10	295		30	Pioneer Pilot. '24 Round the World Flight
Arnold, Lewis Golding	Civil War	55	90	205		Union Gen.
Arnold, Matthew	Author	40	65	125		Br. Poet, Critic
Arnold, Richard	Civil War	40	95			Union Gen.
Arnold, Tom	Entertainment	20			42	
Arnot, William	Clergy	10	20	25		
Arnt, Charles	Entertainment	10			25	
Arntzen, Heinrich	Aviation		60			Br.. Ace WW I
Arp, Jean	Artist	75		275		Fr. DaDa Artist, Sculptor
Arquette, Cliff	Entertainment	20	25		40	
Arquette, Patricia	Entertainment	4			25	Actress.Color Pin-up $75
Arquette, Rosanna	Entertainment	15	15		35	
Arrau, Claudio	Entertainment		45		135	Chilean Pianist
Arrhenuis, Svante A. 1859-1927	Science	95	295	725		Nobel Chemistry 1903
Arrington, A. H.	Civil War	75	130			CSA Congress
Arriola, Gus*	Cartoonist	5			25	Gordo
Arrow, Kenneth J.	Economist	35	55			Nobel Economics
Arthur, Beatrice	Entertainment	5	10	20	20	
Arthur, Chester A. (As President)	President	375	725	2765		WH Card S $500
Arthur, Chester A. 1829-86	President	262	1167	1292	625	ALS as Actg Pres $2,500
Arthur, Chester A.& Ellen Arthur	Pres. & 1st Lady		2500			Rare as Palr
Arthur, Duke of Connought	Head of State	10	18	25		Prime Minister
Arthur, Ellen Lewis	First Lady	600	1000	1200		
Arthur, George K.	Entertainer	6		15	10	Comedian, Producer
Arthur, Jean	Entertainment	125	150	325	285	
Arthur, Julia	Entertainment	15			25	Pioneer Film Star
Arthur, Timothy Shay	Temperance Author	20	45			Am. 10 Nights In A Barroom
Artot, Desiree	Entertainment	35		150	70	Opera, Concert
Arvin, Newton	Author	18	40	85		
Asboth, Alexander S. 1811-68	Civil War	60	190	178		Union Gen. ALS '64 $330
Asbury, Francis, Bishop	Clergy	175	290	625		
Asgeirsson, Asgeir	Head of State	25				4x Premier of Iceland
Ash, Mary Kay						SEE Kay, Mary
Ash, Roy L.	Business	10	20	50	35	
Ashby, Hal	Entertainment	8	8	15	15	
Ashby, Turner (War Date)	Civil War	440	785	2792		CSA General
Ashby, Turner 1828-62	Civil War	358	625	1250	750	CSA Gen.
Ashcroft, Dame Peggy	Entertainment	20	25	35	65	
Ashe, John	Revolutionary War	75	225	450		NC General
Ashe, William Shepperd	Senate/Congress	35	90			CW Blockade Runner
Ashford and Simpson	Entertainment	15			40	
Ashley, Alfred 1835-1913	Author	15			50	Br. Poet Laureate after Tennyson
Ashley, Edward	Entertainment	3			15	
Ashley, Elizabeth	Entertainment	6	8	15	15	
Ashley, John	Entertainment	5			15	
Ashley, William	Celebrity	200	750			Pioneer. Route for Oregon Trail
Ashurst, Henry 1874-1962	Congress	25			75	First Arizona senator
Ashworth, Ernie	Country Music	10			20	
Asimov, Isaac 1920-92	Author	45	168		98	Rus-Am Biochemist.Sci-Fi Writer
Askew, Reubin	Governor	12			15	Governor FL
Asner, Ed	Entertainment	4	4	10	15	
Aspin, Les	Cabinet	5			20	Clinton Sec'y Defense

NAME	CATEGORY	SIG	LS/DS	ALS	SP	Comment
Asquith, Herbert H.	Head of State	35	70	125	150	Prime Minister
Assad, Hafez	Head of State	15	40	105	65	
Assante, Armand	Entertainment	6	8	15	32	
Astaire, Adele	Entertainment	30			75	Dancer Sister of Fred Astaire
Astaire, Fred 1899-1987	Entertainment	87	200	135	261	
Asther, Nils 1897-19??	Entertainment	25	35	65	160	
Astin, John	Entertainment	7	10	15	25	
Astley, Rick	Entertainment	4			10	Singer
Aston, Francis W.	Science	35	80	155		Nobel Chemistry 1922
Astor, Brooke	Author	5	15		10	
Astor, John J. Lord of Hever	Publisher	15	40	60	35	1st Baron of Hever 1886-1971
Astor, John Jacob 1763-1848	Business	405	1908	4850		Fur Trader-Capitalist, Financier
Astor, John Jacob Jr.	Business	40	135	360	125	Union Gen., Financier
Astor, John Jacob Mrs.	Business	35	100	195		
Astor, Mary	Entertainment	35	75		135	AA
Astor, Nancy (Viscountess) 1879-1964	Celebrity	30	55	95	35	1st Woman To Sit As Br. M.P.
Astor, Vincent	Business	8	20	45	20	
Astor, Waldorf 1879-1952	Politics	15	35	80	55	Br. M.P., Publisher Observer
Astor, William Backhouse 1792-1875	Business	138	682	400		Administered Astor Estate
Astor, William Waldorf	Business	65	200	350		Journalist-Capitalist-Financier
Astronauts (Deceased)	Astronaut				1500	Chaffee, White, Grissom (All)
Asturias, Miquel Angel	Author	50	135	285		Guatamala. Nobel Literature
Atchison, David Rice 1807-66	President for 1 Day	350	800	975		Pres.for a day.ALS/Cont $4500
Ates, Roscoe	Entertainment	25	30	60	65	
Athenagoras, Archbishop	Clergy	25	40	55	50	
Atherton, Chas. G.1804-53	Congress	20	30			Senator NH
Atherton, Gertrude	Author	30	55	150	75	Am. Novelist
Athlone, Earl, Prince Alex.of Teck	Head of State	15	25	40		Governor-General of Canada
Atholl, Katharine, Duch. of 1874-1960	Political	65				Br. Anti-Nazi.1st Woman Cabinet Member
Atkins, Chet	Country Music	5	15		20	Guitarist
Atkins, Christopher	Entertainment	6	8	15	22	
Atkins, Gaius Glenn	Clergy	15	30	45		
Atkinson, Brooks	Author	15	45		30	Theater Critic, Columnist
Atkinson, Joseph H.	Military	10	25	30		
Atlantov, Vladimir	Entertainment	20		75	55	Opera. Rus. Tenor
Atlas, Charles	Business	15	30	35	35	Mail Order Phys. Culture
Atlee, Clement 1883-1967	Head of State		150			Br. Prime Minister
Attenborough, Richard	Entertainment	25	30	35	50	AA Br. Actor-Director
Attenborough, Sir David	Science		70			
Atterbury, William W. 1866-1935	Military	15	50			Gen. WW I, Pres. Penn. RR
Attlee, Clement	Head of State	40	180	250	75	Prime Minister
Atwill, Lionel	Entertainment	100			250	
Auber, Daniel François	Composer	110		130		Father of Fr.Opera, AMusQS $350
Auberjonois, René	Entertainment	5	5	10	22	
Aubert, Lenore	Entertainment	5	8	15	20	
Aubrey, M. E.	Clergy	10	15	20		
Aubry, Cecile	Entertainment	15			20	Fr. Actress
Auchincloss, Janet L.	Business	3	5	10	5	
Auchincloss, Louis	Author	15	35	75	30	U.S. Novelist, Short Story
Auchinleck, Claude J.E., Sir	Military	45	75		95	Br. Fld. Marshal WW II
Auckland, Baron (Geo.Eden)	Head of State	40	50	100		Gov-Gen India
Audemars, Edmund	Aviation	27			48	
Auden, W(ystan) H(ugh) 1907-93	Author	75	325	517	700	Br.-Am. Poet, Pulitzer
Audran, Edmond	Composer	45	85	175		Fr. Operettas
Audran, Marius	Entertainment	12		75		Opera. Tenor
Audubon, John J. 1785-1851	Artist	785	2200	3350		Ornithologist

The Sanders Price Guide to Autographs

NAME	CATEGORY	SIG	LS/DS	ALS	SP	Comment
Auel, Jean M.	Author	6	10	25	25	Novelist
Auer, Leopold	Entertainment	25	200		40	Hungarian Violinist
Auer, Mischa	Entertainment	30	30	45	60	
Auger, Arleen	Entertainment	25			55	Opera. Am Soprano
Auger, Christopher C.	Civil War	50	125	170		Union General
Augereau, P.F.C. de Castiglione	Military	100	350	525		Marshal of Napoleon
Augsburg, Alex. S.,Prince 1663-1737	Royalty		323			Prince Bishop of Augsburg
Augusta, Queen of Prussia	Royalty		135			Consort William I. Empress of Ger.
Augustus I, Duke of Saxony	Royalty	2000				1526-1586
Augustus III	Royalty	145	425	345		King Poland
Auld, Georgie	Entertainment	5	6	15	10	
Aumont, Jean Pierre	Entertainment	45	12	20	95	
Aurand, Henry S.	Military	5	10	20	15	
Auric, Georges	Composer					Fr. Member The Six. AMusQS $395
Auriol, Jacqueline	Aviation	15	35	70	45	
Auriol, Vincent 1884-1966	Head of State	50	60	85		1st Pres. 4th Republ. France
Ausensi, Maurel	Entertainment	15			50	Opera, Sp. Baritone
Auslander, Joseph	Author	25	125		50	Poet. Harvard Lecturer Poetry
Aust, Abner	Aviation	10			20	US Ace
Austen, Jane	Author	625	2250	7500		Br.Novelist.Pride & Prejudice
Austin, Bobby	Country Music	10			20	
Austin, Charlotte	Entertainment	4			15	
Austin, Horace	Governor	10			15	Governor MN
Austin, Karen	Entertainment	5	6	10	10	
Austin, Moses 1761-1821	Merchant	425	1600	2995		Orig. Founder of TX. Mine Owner
Austin, Stephen F. 1793-1836	Texas Colonizer	800	1925	6500		Historical DS $6500,$7500
Austin, Teri	Entertainment	5	8	10	10	
Austin, Warren R.	Senate	5	10		20	Senator VT
Autry, Gene	Entertainment	25	55		87	Singing Cowboy, Businessman
Avallone, Michael	Author	5	15		10	
Avalon, Al	Entertainment	5			20	TV and film
Avalon, Frankie	Entertainment	6	8	15	25	
Avebury, John Lubbock	Science	20		150		1834-1913. Naturalist.Paleolithic
Avedon, Richard	Artist	40	175	90	167	Photographer
Average White Band	Entertainment	15			25	Rock
Averell, William W. 1832-1900	Civil War	65	160	195		Union Gen. ALS '62 $360
Avery, John, Jr.	Revolutionary War	40	77			
Avery, Margaret	Entertainment	3	3	6	10	
Avery, Sewell L.	Business	35	55	105	40	CEO Montgomery Ward
Avery, Tex*	Cartoonist	25			400	Animator. (*Original Cell)
Avery, William W.	Civil War	75	140			CSA Congress
Avildsen, John G.	Entertainment	5			20	Film Director
Axelrod, Julius	Science	35	60	95	35	Nobel Medicine
Axtell, George	Aviation	12	25	45	35	Marine ACE
Axton, Hoyt	Country Music	4	25		15	
Ayckbourn, Alan	Author	10	15	30	25	Br. Prolific Playwright
Aykroyd, Dan	Entertainment	10	12	15	25	
Ayres, Agnes	Entertainment	60	75	150	125	Silent Film Star
Ayres, Lew	Entertainment	10	15	25	25	
Ayres, Romeyn B. (War Date)	Civil War	70	135	440		Union Gen.
Ayres, Romeyn Beck 1825-88	Civil War	45	75	110		Union Gen.
Ayub Khan, General	Head of State	20	35	75	100	Afghan Prince. General
Aznavour, Charles	Entertainment	10			35	

NAME	CATEGORY	SIG	LS/DS	ALS	SP	Comment

NAME	CATEGORY	SIG	LS/DS	ALS	SP	Comment
B 52's	Entertainment	30			75	Rock
Babbage, Charles 1792-1871	Science-Math.	80	245	735		Br. Pioneer of Modern Computers
Babbitt, Bruce	Cabinet	10	20		15	Gov. AZ
Babbitt, Harry	Entertainment	10			20	Band Vocalist, Radio
Babbitt, Milton	Composer	25		70	30	AMusQS $150
Babcock, Alfred, Dr. 1805-71	Congress					Repr. NY
Babcock, Barbara	Entertainment	4	4	9	10	
Babcock, Joseph W.	Senate/Congress	5		30		Congressman WI
Babcock, Orville E. (War Date)	Civil War	40	160	255		Union Gen.LS as Grant ADC $385
Babcock, Orville E. 1845-84	Civil War	30	75	168		Union Gen.
Babcock, Tim	Governor	12	20	25	15	Governor MT
Babcock, Verne C.	Aviation	16			40	
Babilee', Jean	Entertainment	30	45		70	Ballet
Baby Peggy	Entertainment	5	6	15	15	
Bacall, Lauren	Entertainment	10	10	20	30	
Baccaloni, Salvatore	Entertainment	20	25	40	45	Opera, Concert, Films
Bach, Barbara	Entertainment	10	12	15	25	
Bach, Catherine	Entertainment	6	8	15	20	
Bach, Johann Sebastian	Composer	2500	22670	35000		Conservative Estimates
Bach, Richard	Author	25	100	175		
Bach, Sebastian	Entertainment	20			50	Rock
Bacharach, Burt	Composer	13	25	40	25	
Bacharach, Fabian	Artist	50	100	150	75	
Bache, Alexander D.	Science	25	50	110	40	1st Pres. Nat'l Acad. Science
Bache, Harold L.	Business	15	45	110	65	US Stockbroker. J.S.Bache & Co.
Bacheller, Irving	Author	25	60	65	75	Am. Novelist, Editor
Bachman, Nathan L.	Congress	10				Senator, TN
Back, George, Sir	Explorer	20	105	140		Arctic Navigator
Backhaus, Wilhelm	Entertainment	36			100	Ger. Concert Pianist
Backhouse, James	Clergy	20	35	50		
Backus, Jim	Entertainment	20	35	25	40	Mr. McGoo & Many Others
Baclanova, Olga	Entertainment	10			25	
Bacon, Edmund	Celebrity	10			15	
Bacon, Francis, Sir	Author	1500	3650	10500		Br. Philosopher, Statesman
Bacon, Frank	Entertainment	10	12	20	15	
Bacon, Kevin	Entertainment	9	10	20	40	
Bacon, Leonard	Clergy	10	15	20	25	
Bacon, Lloyd	Entertainment	12			20	Film Director
Bacon, Peggy	Artist	35	65	150		
Bacon, Robert	Senate/Congress	15	25		30	Congressman NY. Military
Bacon, Walter W.	Governor	10		25	15	Governor DE
Baddeley, Hermione	Entertainment	12	15	22	30	
Badeau, Adam (War Date)	Civil War	50		275		Union Gen.

NAME	CATEGORY	SIG	LS/DS	ALS	SP	Comment
Badeau, Adam 1831-95	Civil War	35	88	195		Union General
Baden-Powell, Robert, Sir, 1857-1941	Military	125	408	367	662	Br. Gen., Founder of Boy Scouts
Bader, Douglas, Sir	Aviation	45	130	205	70	Br. Ace
Badger, Charles J. 1853-	Military	20	45	70	30	U.S. Navy Adm.
Badger, George E. 1795-1866	Cabinet	10	62	40		Sec'y Navy, Sen. NC. Jurist
Badger, Oscar C. 1890-1958	Military		45		50	Adm. USN WW II
Badham, John	Entertainment	10			20	Film Director
Badham, W.L.	Aviation	25	50	75	55	Bi-plane , WW I
Badler, Jane	Entertainment	5	8	20	25	
Badoglio, Pietro	Head of State	30		135	55	It. Gen.,succeeded Mussolini
Baekeland, L. H. Dr.	Science-Inventor	30	50	125		Invented Bakelite. 1st Plastic
Baer, Arthur Bugs * 1886-1959	Journalist	10			40	Syndicated Columnist, Cartoonist
Baer, George F.	Business	10	25	45	30	Pres. Reading Railroad
Baer, John	Entertainment	5	6	15	15	
Baer, Max, Jr.	Entertainment	15		85	35	
Baez, Joan	Entertainment	10	12	20	28	
Bagian, James P.	Astronaut	5	10		120	
Baglioni, Bruna	Entertainment	10		45	35	Opera
Bagnold, Enid	Author		75		70	National Velvet, Chalk Garden
Bagot, Charles, Sir 1781-1843	Statesman		45	125		Br. Diplomat.. Gov.-Gen. Canada
Bailey, Buster	Entertainment	30			75	Jazz Clarinet, Sax
Bailey, Carl E.	Governor	10	15			Governor AR
Bailey, F. Lee	Legal	12	25	45	15	Noted Trial Attorney
Bailey, Jack	Entertainment	5	5	6	10	Early Radio-TV M.C.
Bailey, James Anthony	Circus	250	950	1100		Barnum & Bailey Circus
Bailey, Joseph 1825-67	Civil War	95	195			Unlon Gen. ALS '64 $1265
Bailey, Mildred C.	Military	6			70	Brigadier General
Bailey, Pearl	Entertainment	15	15	20	48	
Bailey, Razzle	Country Music	5			20	
Bailey, Temple	Author	30	45	110		
Bailey, Theodorus	Civil War	35	70	145		Union Naval Officer
Bailey, Walter R.	Business	10	35	45	20	
Baillie, Joanna 1762-1851	Author	15	50	95		Scottish Dramatist, Poet
Baillie, John	Clergy	35	75	110	50	
Bailly, Jean-Sylvain 1736-93	Astronomer	40	90	160		& Fr. Politician. Guillotined
Bain, Barbara	Entertainment	5	6	15	15	
Bain, Conrad	Entertainment	5			10	
Bainbridge, William 1774-1833	Military	150	325	650		US Naval Officer War 1812
Bainter, Fay	Entertainment	70	85	135	125	
Baio, Scott	Entertainment	5	6	15	15	
Bair, Hilbert L.	Aviation	10				US Ace. WW I
Baird, Absalom 1824-1905	Civil War	32	45	70		Union Gen. ALS '64 $200
Baird, John Logie	Science	150	295	150	600	1st TV Picture of Moving Object
Bairnsfather, Bruce 1888-1959	Cartoonist	15	30	110	25	Br. WW I Old Bill Cartoons
Bakaleinikoff, Constantin	Composer	200				
Baker, Alpheus	Civil War	135	275	475		CSA Gen.
Baker, Anita	Entertainment	4			25	Singer
Baker, Art	Entertainment	5	10		20	Early Radio-TV M.C.
Baker, Benny 1907-94	Entertainment	5		15	22	Comic Actor
Baker, Blanche	Entertainment	5	8	15	20	
Baker, Bob	Entertainment	50	70		100	Singing Cowboy 1930's
Baker, Bonnie Wee	Entertainment	6	8	15	15	Big Band Vocalist
Baker, Carroll	Entertainment	15	20	40	25	
Baker, Charles S.	Senate/Congress	5	10		5	Congressman NY.
Baker, Chauncey	Military	10		25	15	General WW I
Baker, Diane	Entertainment	5			18	

NAME	CATEGORY	SIG	LS/DS	ALS	SP	Comment
Baker, Edward D.	Civil War	85	160	200		Union Gen.
Baker, Ellen	Astronaut	5			25	
Baker, George* 1915-75	Cartoonist	30			295	Sad Sack
Baker, Howard Henry, Jr.	Senate	5		25	15	Senator TN. WH Chief of Staff
Baker, James A., III	Cabinet	10	25		50	Bush Sec'y State
Baker, Janet, Dame	Entertainment	10	15		35	Opera. Br. Mezzo Soprano
Baker, Jehu 1822-1903	Congress	7		25		Repr. IL
Baker, Josephine 1906-75	Entertainment	188	378	388	762	Highest Paid Entertainer in Eur. '20's
Baker, Kenny	Entertainment	12	15	25	50	Jack Benny Show Vocalist
Baker, La Fayette Curry	Civil War	115	165	235		Union Gen.
Baker, Laurence S. 1830-1907	Civil War	130	135	415		CSA Gen.
Baker, LaVerne	Entertainment	10			25	Jazz Vocalist
Baker, Lucien	Senate	10		30		Senator KS
Baker, Mark	Entertainment	5	10		25	Opera
Baker, Michael	Astronaut	4	10		12	
Baker, Newton D. 1837-1937	Cabinet	15	135	100	55	Wilson Sec'y War
Baker, Phil	Entertainment	7			25	Early radio comic
Baker, Royal N.	Aviation	25		95	50	Air Ace Korea, WW II
Baker, Samuel, Sir	Explorer	30	65	150		Br. Located Sources of Nile
Bakewell, William	Entertainment	15			40	Gone With The Wind (Cast)
Bakker, Jim	Clergy	20	25	35	40	
Bakst, Leon 1868-1924	Artist	95		822		Rus. Painter, Scenic Designer
Bakula, Scott	Entertainment	20			42	Quantum Leap
Balakirev, Mily 1837-1910	Composer			865		Russian
Balanchine, George 1904-83	Entertainment	170		250	312	Ballet-Choreographer
Balbo, Italo	Aviation	125	160	200	195	It. Air Marshal & Pioneer
Balch, Emily Greene 1867-1961	Sociologist	35	30	60		Nobel Economist, Reformer, Pacifist
Balchen, Bernt	Aviation	30	40	75	45	
Balck, Hermann	Military	20			75	Ger. Panzer General
Baldridge, Howard Malcolm	Congress	10	15		20	Repr. NE
Baldridge, Malcolm 1922-887	Cabinet		145			Sec'y Comm. Reagan.
Baldwin, Abraham 1754-1807	Statesman		3375			Signer Constitution, Rare
Baldwin, Alec	Entertainment	12			40	
Baldwin, Faith	Author	35	25	60	20	Novelist
Baldwin, Henry (SC)	Supreme Court	25	40	110		
Baldwin, James	Author	50	417	500	230	ALS/Content $975
Baldwin, Judy	Entertainment	3	3	6	8	
Baldwin, Raymond E.	Governor	10	20		20	Governor, Senator CT
Baldwin, Roger Sherman	Senate	35		50		Early Gov.1844, Senator CT 1847
Baldwin, Stanley 1867-1947	Head of State	50	90	125	125	3 Term Br. Prime Minister
Baldwin, Stephen	Entertainment				38	
Baldwin, William	Entertainment				38	
Baldwin, William E. 1827-64(War Date)	Civil War	395	685	2975		CSA General
Balewa, A. T., Sir	Head of State	10	35	80	25	Nigeria
Balfe, Michael William	Composer	18	55	125		
Balfour, Arthur J. 1848-1930	Head of State	50	117	120	90	Br. Prime Minister
Balfour, Howard, Lord	Aviation			75		Br. Ace WW I
Balistier, Elliot	Editor	4	15			Liberty Magazine
Ball, Albert	Aviation	125	225	330	275	Brit. RAF ACE WW I
Ball, Joseph H.	Congress	12			75	Senator
Ball, Lucille (Lucy)	Entertainment		150			
Ball, Lucille 1910-89	Entertainment	155	410		505	Full Signature
Ballard, Kaye	Entertainment	15	20	20	25	Comedienne
Ballard, Robert, Dr.	Science	17	40	85	25	Oceanographer. Found Titanic
Ballentine, John J.	Military	15	35	60		
Ballew, Smith	Entertainment	15	20		40	

NAME	CATEGORY	SIG	LS/DS	ALS	SP	Comment
Ballinger, Richard A.	Cabinet	10	25	50	25	Sec'y Interior 1909
Ballou, Charles	Military	30	110			General WW I
Balsam, Martin	Entertainment	12	15	20	50	
Baltimore, David, Dr.	Science	15	25	40	15	Nobel Medicine
Balzac, Honore de 1799-1850	Author	600	1250	1500		Fr. Novelist
Bampton, Rose	Entertainment	20	35	45	50	Opera, Concert
Bananarama	Entertainment	20			50	
Bancroft, Anne	Entertainment	6	8	15	30	
Bancroft, George	Cabinet-Author	30	85	140		Polk Sec'y Navy, Historian
Bancroft, George 1882-1956	Entertainment	19	25	45	95	
Band, The	Entertainment					Rock HOF. No Price Available
Bandaranike, S.W.R.D	Head of State	10	25	45	30	Prime Minister Sri Lanka
Banderas, Antonio	Entertainment	15			70	Latin Actor
Bangles, The (All)	Entertainment	40			85	Rock
Bangs, John Kedrick	Author	5	45		20	Humor EditorHarper's Magazine
Banisadr, A.	Head of State	10	30	80	40	Iran
Bank, C. D.	Cabinet	10	25			
Bankhead, Tallulah	Entertainment	85	140	220	265	Orig. Wilding Ph. SP $600
Bankhead, Wm. B. 1874-1940	Congress	10	40			Speaker of the House
Banks, Billy	Entertainment	80			250	Jazz
Banks, Joseph, Sir	Science-Explorer	30	110	560		Br. Naturalist.Sailed/Capt.Cook
Banks, Leslie	Entertainment	20			35	
Banks, Michael A.	Author	4	10	25	10	
Banks, Nathaniel P. (War Date)	Civil War	150	546	485		Union Gen.
Banks, Nathaniel P. 1816-1894	Civil War	75	160	125		Gov. MA, MOC, Union Gen.
Banks, Tyra	Entertainment	10			40	Model/actress
Banky, Vilma	Entertainment	45	75	190	160	
Banner, John	Entertainment	70			150	
Banning, Henry Blackstone	Civil War	30	65			Union Gen., Congressman OH
Banning, Margaret C.	Author	5	12	25	10	
Banting, Frederick G. 1891-1941	Science	600	762	1650	980	Discoverd Insulin with Best
Bantock, Granville	Composer				125	Br. Composer
Bar-Lev, Chaim	Military	20	60		52	Israeli Military Leader
Bara, Theda	Entertainment	145		300	275	
Baraka, I.A.(LeRoi Jones)	Author	35	50	75	40	
Barbara, Agatha	Head of State	10			20	Pres. of Malta
Barbarigo, St. Gregorio L. 1625-97	Clergy		3500			Saint. Canonized 1960
Barbarin, Paul	Entertainment	25		65		Bandleader, Drummer
Barbarolli, John, Sir	Entertainment	30	35	55	150	Br. Conductor
Barbe-Marbois, Francois de	Napoleon Cabinet	30	75	250		Louisiana Purchase
Barbeau, Adrienne	Entertainment	6	8	15	15	
Barbee, John Henry	Entertainment	35				Blues Vocalist
Barbejacque, Prince	Entertainment	3	3	6	10	
Barber, Rex T.	Aviation	12	35	75	35	Am. ACE, Downed Yamamoto
Barber, Samuel 1910-81	Composer	60	260	300	70	Opera, Songs, String Music
Barber, William	Military	25			70	Marine CMH Korea
Barbera, Joe	Cartoonist				140	Flintstones, Yogi Bear
Barbera, Joe	Entertainment	10	12	15	20	
Barbier, George	Entertainment	10	15	25	25	
Barbieri, Fedora	Entertainment	25			75	Opera, Concert
Barbour, Dave	Composer	15			40	Jazz Guitar
Barbour, James 1775-1842	Cabinet, Congress	50		155		Sec'y War, Senator, VA
Barbour, Philip (SC)	Supreme Court					NRPA
Barbour, William Warren	Senate	10	35		15	Senator NJ
Barclay, Thomas	Revolutionary War	25	55			Adj.-Gen'l Nova Scotia
Barclay, William	Clergy	40	75	95	75	

 # The Sanders Price Guide to Autographs

NAME	CATEGORY	SIG	LS/DS	ALS	SP	Comment
Barcroft, Roy	Entertainment	50			150	
Bard, Ralph A.	Cabinet		25		20	FDR. Navy
Bardeen, John	Science	25	50	95	35	Nobel. Signed Bio Card $55
Bardot, Brigitte	Entertainment	25	25	45	55	
Bardshar, F.A.		10	25	40	35	Navy ACE, WW II
Barere de Vieuzac, B.	Fr. Revolution	30	120	150		Anacreon of Guillotine.Exiled
Baretti, Giuseppe	Author	25	80	155		Friend of Burke, Johnson
Bari, Lynn	Entertainment	5	8	15	20	
Baring, Alexander 1774-1848	Banking	130		750		Formalized Webster-Ashburton Treaty
Baring, Francis, Sir	Business	25	35	95		Dir. East India Co.ALS/Cont.$1975
Baring-Gould, Sabine 1834-1929	Author	20	120	245	60	Onward Christian Soldiers AMS $2400
Barker, Bob	Entertainment	3	3	6	10	The Price is Right
Barker, Clive	Author	15	25		25	Br. Horror Novelist
Barker, Lex	Entertainment	65	75	130	200	
Barker, William George	Aviation	125	225	350	295	Canadian ACE, WW I
Barkhorn, Gerhard	Aviation	50	185		125	Ger. ACE, #2 Worldwide
Barkin, Ellen	Entertainment	15			48	
Barkley, Alben W. (V)1877-1956	Vice President	30	82	175	65	Truman VP
Barks, Carl*	Cartoonist	20			300	Donald Duck, Scrooge
Barksdale, Ethelbert	Civil War	30	50	65		CSA Congress
Barksdale, William (War Date)	Civil War	850				CSA General
Barksdale, William 1821-63	Civil War	412		1565		CSA General. KIA Gettysburg '63
Barlow, Francis C. 1834-96	Civil War	55	85	235		Union Gen.
Barlow, Howard	Conductor	40			45	Popular Radio/TV Conductor
Barlow, Jane	Author	5	10	25		
Barlow, Joel	Diplomat	40	120	245		Author, Chaplain Rev. War
Barnabee, Henry Clay	Entertainment	6	15	25	15	Operatic Comedian
Barnaby, Ralph S.	Aviation	27			35	
Barnard, Christian, Dr.	Science	20	35	85	55	Heart Specialist
Barnard, Daniel D. 1797-1861	Congress	12				Repr. NY, Minister Prussia
Barnard, Frederick A.P.	Educator	75	165	275		Barnard College.For Women's Ed.
Barnard, John Gross 1815-82	Civil War	25	60	235		Union Gen.
Barne, Michael	Celebrity	12	35	90	40	
Barnes, Binnie	Entertainment	6	8	15	15	
Barnes, Demus	Senate/Congress	5	15	25		Congressman NY. Writer
Barnes, Djuna	Author	45	110	260	85	Am. Novelist-Short Story Writer
Barnes, James	Civil War	50	115	170		Union Gen.
Barnes, Joanna	Entertainment	5	6	15	15	
Barnes, Joseph K. 1817-83	Civil War	150	448	550		Union Surgeon Gen.
Barnes, Julius H. 1873-1939	Business		20			Corporation Off'l. Pres. US C of C
Barnes, Priscilla	Entertainment	8	10	20	15	Pin-up $25
Barnet, Charlie	Entertainment	15			30	Big Band Leader-Tenor Sax
Barnet, Isaac	Political		25			Mayor Cincinnati
Barnett, Ross R.	Governor	10		25	15	Governor MS
Barnette, Vince	Entertainment	15	20	35	45	
Barneveld, Jan Van Olden	Dutch Statesman		2000			Father of Dutch Independence
Barney, Natalie 1876-1972	Author	110	315	412		Am. Poet, Translator, Parisian Hostess
Barnhart, George 'Eddie'	Aviation	16	35		50	
Barnum, Henry A. 1833-92	Civil War	45	90	145		Union Gen. ALS '64 $190
Barnum, Malvern H.	Military	10		35	25	General WW I
Barnum, Phineas T. 1810-1891	Business-Circus	184	470	668	1042	ALS/Content $1,100-1,500-$2,000
Baronova, Irina	Entertainment	20			70	Rus.-Br. Ballerina
Barr, Candy	Stripper	10			55	Prison for Shooting Husband
Barr, Doug	Entertainment	3	3	6	8	
Barr, Joseph Walker	Cabinet	5	15	30	15	Sec'y Treasury, Congressman IN
Barr, Roseanne	Entertainment	20	25	50	60	

NAME	CATEGORY	SIG	LS/DS	ALS	SP	Comment
Barras, Paul-Francois-Jean	Fr. Revolution	85	250			Jacobin Club.Exiled From Paris
Barrault, Jean-Louis	Entertainment	40			125	
Barrett, John	Military	20		50		WW I Victoria Cross
Barrett, Lawrence 1838-91	Civil War	20			45	Union Officer, Actor
Barrett, Majel	Entertainment	10			30	Star Trek
Barrett, Rona	Entertainment	6	8	15	15	
Barrett, Wilson 1846-1904	Entertainment	15		95	65	Br. Playwright, Actor, Manager
Barrie, Barbara	Entertainment	4	6	10	10	
Barrie, James M., Sir 1860-1937	Author	75	265	304	280	Peter Pan etc.
Barrie, Mona	Entertainment	15	15	35	30	
Barrie, Wendy	Entertainment	20	25	30	45	
Barrier, Edgar	Entertainment	4	7	10	15	
Barringer, Daniel M. 1806-73	Congress	12				Repr. NC, Minister Spain
Barringer, Rufus 1821-95	Civil War	105	305	470		CSA Gen.
Barrington, Shute	Clergy	10	15	25	20	
Barrios, Justo R. 1835-1885	Head of State	40	125			Pres. Guatemala
Barron, Blue	Bandleader	25			10	
Barron, Clarence	Business	25			40	Editor, Publisher Barron's
Barrow, Clyde 1909-34	Criminal			3325	21850	Bonnie & Clyde
Barrow, Edward G.	Business	100	300		150	Gen'l Mgr. NY Yankees
Barrow, John, Sir 1764-1848	Statesman	60	170	325		Explorer, Traveller, Author
Barrow, Robert H.	Military	10	30	50	20	
Barrows, Lewis O.	Governor	12		25	15	Governor ME
Barrows, Sydney Biddle	Celebrity	10			30	Mayflower Madame
Barry, Charles, Sir 1795-1860	Architect	20	45	135		Br. Houses of Parliament
Barry, Dan*	Cartoonist	10			100	Flash Gordon
Barry, Dave	Author	10			20	Creator Dave's World
Barry, Don 'Red'	Entertainment	22	45	35	58	
Barry, Gene	Entertainment	8	10	15	15	
Barry, John	Revolutionary War	1150	2000			Ir. Born US Naval Officer
Barry, John Decatur	Civil War	145		475		CSA Gen.
Barry, John Wolfe, Sir	Celebrity	6	12	35	20	
Barry, Marion	Politician	5	8	15	15	Mayor Washington, D.C.
Barry, Sy*	Cartoonist	10			50	Phantom
Barry, Thomas	Military	35		150		General WW I
Barry, Wesley	Entertainment	6	12	25	20	
Barry, Wm. Farquhar	Civil War	60	145	190		Union Gen.
Barrymore, Diana	Entertainment	30	35	45	30	
Barrymore, Drew	Entertainment	20			50	Nude Pin-up $135
Barrymore, Ethel	Entertainment	110	150		200	
Barrymore, John 1882-1942	Entertainment	212	287	300	550	The Great Profile.
Barrymore, Lionel 1878-1954	Entertainment	80	308		175	Member 1st Family of Am. Theatre
Barrymore, Maurice	Entertainment	15			50	
Bartato, Elisabeth	Entertainment	15			40	Opera
Bartel, Jean	Entertaiment	3			12	Miss America '43, Actress
Bartel, Jean	Entertainment					Miss American '43, Actress
Barth, John	Author	35	40	85	30	Am. Novelist
Barth, Karl	Clergy	40	95	125	75	
Barthelmess, Richard	Entertainment	20	30	80	80	
Bartholdi, Fred. Auguste, 1834-1904	Artist	450	725	575	973	Statue of Liberty Print S $700- $1395
Bartholomew, Freddie	Entertainment	30	35	40	75	
Bartle, Joyce	Entertainment	5	6	10	10	
Bartlett, Bonnie	Entertainment	5	6	10	10	
Bartlett, Joseph Jackson	Civil War	45	110			Union Gen.
Bartlett, Josiah 1729-95	Revolutionary War	215	555	908		Signer.ALS/Cont. $7200
Bartlett, Paul Wayland	Artist	10	15	30		US Sculptor

NAME	CATEGORY	SIG	LS/DS	ALS	SP	Comment
Bartlett, Robert Abram	Explorer	50	175	125		Cmdr. Ship on Peary Arctic Exp.
Bartlett, Thomas	Clergy	15	20	35		
Bartlett, William F.	Civil War	45	80	170		Union Gen.
Bartoe, John David	Astronaut	7	20		30	
Bartok, Bela 1881-1945	Composer	375	590	1950	1570	Hung.Pianist-Comp.AmusQS $1800
Bartok, Eva	Entertainment	5			15	Actress
Barton, Bruce	Business	10	30	40	20	Advertising Exec.. BBD&O
Barton, Clara 1821-1912	Humanitarian	155	775	781	800	Founder Am. Red Cross
Barton, Derek H. R., Sir	Science	20	30	40	25	Nobel Chemistry
Barton, James	Entertainment	40			125	
Barton, Seth M. (War Date)	Civil War	205		935		CSA General
Barton, Seth Maxwell 1829-1900	Civil War	95	248	308		CSA Gen.
Bartow, Francis Stebbins 1816-61	Civil War	70		360		CSA Congress
Barty, Billy	Entertainment	6	10	20	20	
Baruch, Bernard M. 1870-1965	Statesman	25	150	225	135	Financier, Pres. Advisor
Baryshnikov, Mikail	Entertainment	70	85	130	202	Ballet
Barzun, Jacques	Author	7	12	25	15	
Basehart, Richard	Entertainment	6	10	20	15	
Basie, Wm. 'Count' 1904-84	Composer	72	200		238	Big Band Leader-Pianist
Basinger, Kim	Entertainment	20	25	40	41	Actress
Baskett, James	Entertainment	200			600	
Basov, Nickolay	Science	20	45		30	Rus. Nobel Physicist
Basquette, Lina	Entertainment	15			25	1920's Star
Bassett, Angela	Entertainment	10			32	Singer
Bassett, Charles A.	Astronaut	40			65	
Bassett, Leslie	Composer	15	30	65		Pulitzer,AMusQS $100
Bassett, Richard	Revolutionary War	375	800			Signer Constitution
Bassi, Amedeo	Entertainment	35			150	Favorite Tenor of Toscanini
Bate, William B. War Date)	Civil War	130		1045		CSA Gen.,Senator, Gov. TN
Bate, William Brimage 1826-1905	Civil War-Senate	65	135	175		CSA General-Also Gov. Tenn.
Bateman, Jason	Entertainment	15			25	
Bateman, Justine	Entertainment	15	15	25	30	
Bates, Alan	Entertainment	5			20	Br. Actor
Bates, Arthur Laban	Senate/Congress	5	10		20	Congressman PA
Bates, Blanche	Entertainment	15	25	40	45	
Bates, Edward	Cabinet	35	125	250	450	Lincoln Att'y Gen.
Bates, John C.	Civil War	25		110		Union General
Bates, Katharine Lee 1859-1929	Author	80		300	125	AMsSAm.The Beautiful $6,500
Bates, Kathy	Entertainment	15			41	
Bates, Peg-Leg	Entertainment	10			20	Dancer
Bates, Sanford	Law Enforcement	10	35			Commissioner of Prisons
Bates. Florence	Entertainment	10			25	
Bathori, Jane 1876-1970	Entertainment			75	125	Opera. Legendary Fr. Soprano
Bathurst, Henry	Clergy	15	25	40	30	
Batista, Fulgencio 1901-73	Head of State	165	350	475	175	Cuban Dictator-Pre Castro
Batiuk, Tom*	Cartoonist	5			25	Funky Winkerbean
Battaglia, Franco	Entertainment	15			50	Opera, Concert
Battaille, Charles 1822-72	Entertainmment	10		50		Opera
Batten, Hugh	Aviation	10	25	40	30	Navy ACE, WW II
Batten, Jean	Aviation	40	75			Pioneer NZ Aviatrix
Battle, Cullen Andrews	Civil War	200	405			CSA Gen.
Battle, Kathleen	Entertainment	20	40		52	Opera, Concert
Battu, Marie 1838-88	Entertainment	15		75		Opera. Sang in World Premiere of L'Africaine
Batz, Willhelm	Aviation	35			95	Ger. ACE, #7 Worldwide
Baucus, Bob	Aviation	10	20	35	25	
Baudelaire, Charles-Pierre 1821-67	Author	300	1000	2367		Fr. Modernist Poet, Critic

NAME	CATEGORY	SIG	LS/DS	ALS	SP	Comment
Baudouin, King (Belg)	Royalty	35	100	250	125	King of Belgium
Baudry, Patrick	Astronaut	12	25		25	
Bauduc, Ray	Entertainment	10			25	Big Band Bassist
Bauer, Harold	Entertainment	45	80			Pianist
Bauer, Jaime Lyn	Entertainment	6	8	10	15	
Bauer, Steven	Entertainment	6	8	15	20	
Baulieu, Etienne	Science	20		45	40	Inventor RU486 Abortion Pill
Baum, Kurt	Entertainment				40	Operatic Tenor
Baum, L. Frank	Author	500	925	1175		The Wizard of Oz books
Baum, Vicki	Author	20				Novelist. Grand Hotel
Baum, William W., Cardinal	Clergy	35	55	70	50	
Baumer, Steven	Entertainment	10	15	20	25	
Baur, Hans	Aviation	20	45	90	125	Hitler's Pilot
Baur, Harry	Entertainment	30			150	Fr. Star Executed by Nazis
Bauvais, Garcelle	Entertainment				40	Models, Inc.
Bavier, Frances	Entertainment	55	60	95	150	
Baxley, Barbara	Entertainment	4	4	10	10	
Baxter, Anne	Entertainment	20	20	40	45	AA
Baxter, Henry	Civil War	35	95	160		Union Gen.
Baxter, James P. III	Author	5	15	30	10	
Baxter, Keith	Entertainment	3	3	6	10	
Baxter, Les	Bandleader	26		40		Arranger, Composer
Baxter, Percival P.	Governor	12		25		Governor ME
Baxter, Warner	Entertainment	45	50		85	
Baxter-Birney, Meredith	Entertainment	8	8	15	15	
Bayard, George D. (War Date)	Civil War	295		1222		Union Gen.
Bayard, George Dashiell	Civil War	135	170	558		Union Gen.,
Bayard, John	Revolutionary War	40	160	185		Continental Congress
Bayard, Richard Henry	Senate	20	40	85		Senator DE
Bayard, Thomas F., Sr.	Cabinet	25	35	80		Sec'y State, Senator DE
Bayard, William	Revolutionary War	85	220	450		
Bayh, Birch	Senate	10	25		20	Senator IN
Bayne, Barbara	Entertainment	20			55	
Bayne, Beverly	Entertainment	9	10	20	20	
Beach Boys (4)	Entertainment	120			450	Alb. Cover. S by 5 Living Members $395
Beach, Amy M.	Composer	45		500	225	Pianist-Composer AMQS $175
Beach, Rex 1877-	Author	20	35	95	35	Am. Novelist
Beacham, Stephanie	Entertainment	5	6	10	10	
Beadle, George Wells, Dr.	Science	20	30	45	40	Nobel Medicine
Beakley, Wallace M.	Military	5	15	25		
Beal, George Lafayette 1825-96	Civil War	42	112	135	270	Union Gen. ALS '64 $440
Beal, John	Entertainment	15	15	25	25	
Beale, Rich'd Lee T. (War Date)	Civil War	150		550		CSA General
Beale, Richard Lee Turberville	Civil War	85	105	225		1819-93. CSA General
Beall, William N.R.(War Date)	Civil War	175	325	850	700	CSA General
Beals, Jennifer	Entertainment	20	20	40	45	
Bean, Alan L.	Astronaut	15	145		95	Moonwalker Astro.
Bean, L.L. 1872-1967	Inventor-Business				300	Unique Business Empire
Bean, Roy, Judge	Frontier Judge	3950	4500			The Law West of the Pecos
Beane, Hilary	Entertainment	5	10	15	10	
Beard, Charles A. 1874-1948	Author	5	30	65		Am. Historian
Beard, Daniel C. 1850-1941	Author	100	300	105	130	Founder Boy Scouts of America
Beard. Stymie	Entertainment	75			175	
Bearden, Romare*	Artist	20	225		200	Am. Artist
Beardslee, Lester Anthony	Military	20		100		Admiral Spanish American War
Beardsley, Aubrey 1872-98	Artist	175	375	675	2300	Br. Illustrator. Art Nouveau

The Sanders Price Guide to Autographs

NAME	CATEGORY	SIG	LS/DS	ALS	SP	Comment
Beardsley, Samuel 1790-1860	Congress	10				Repr. NY, Assoc. Judge NY Supr. Ct.
Beatles (all four) on one piece	Entertainment	3025				Set of 4 Separate Sigs. $2,650
Beaton, Cecil 1904-80	Photographer	35	150	168	372	Br.Portrait,Theatrical Designer
Beatrice, Princess	Royalty	20	125	115	120	Youngest Daughter Q. Victoria
Beatrix, Queen	Royalty	100		450		Netherlands
Beatty, Clyde 1903-1965	Business-Circus	50	95	175	150	Animal Trainer. Circus Performer
Beatty, David, Adm.	Military	30	78	115	100	
Beatty, Ned	Entertainment	7	10	15	12	
Beatty, Samuel	Civil War	25	45	70		Union Gen.
Beatty, Warren	Entertainment	30	80		85	SP as Dick Tracy $45
Beatty. John	Civil War	27	55	80		Union General
Beauharnais, Eugene de 1781-1824	Royalty	45	350	430		Son of Josephine, Adopted by Napoleon
Beauharnais, Hortense de 1783-1837	Royalty	50		435		Wife of Louis Bonaparte
Beaumont, Hugh	Entertainment	75			150	
Beauregard, Pierre G.T.(War Date)	Civil War	390	2258	2125	3500	CSA Gen.
Beauregard, Pierre G.T.1818-93	Civil War	330	940	1244	850	CSA Gen.Stock Cert. S $3950
Beauvais, Garcelle	Entertainment	5			40	Actress, Models, Inc.
Beauvoir, Simone de	Author	25	60	125		Fr. Novelist. Existentialist
Beaux, Cecilia 1855-1942	Artist	75	60	60		Am. Portrait Painter
Beaver, James A.	Civil War-Gov.	30	55	110		Union Gen., Gov. PA
Beaverbrook, Max, Lord						SEE MAXWELL. WM.
Beavers, Louise	Entertainment	60			150	Popular Afr.-Am. Film Actress
Bechet, Sidney 1897-1959	Entertainment	125	575		175	Jazz Clarinetist-Saxaphonist
Bechi, Gino	Entertainment	25			55	Opera
Beck, C.C*	Cartoonist	10			100	Captain Marvel
Beck, Dave 1894-1993	Labor Leader	20	50	50	48	Sent to Prison for Union Fraud
Beck, James M. 1861-1936	Congress		25			Repr. PA
Beck, Jeff	Entertainment	20			45	Rock Guitarist
Beck, John	Entertainment	3	3	6	8	
Becker, Barbara	Entertainment	3	3	6	8	
Beckett, Samuel 1906-89	Author	155	548	385	345	Nobel Lit.Waiting for Godot
Beckett, Scotty	Entertainment	15			92	Child Actor
Beckwith, Edward G.	Civil War	45				Union General
Beckwith, Geo. Sir 1753-1823	Revolutionary War		390			Br. Gen. in the American War
Beckwith, J. Carroll	Artist	35	80	145		
Becquerel, Edmond 1820-91	Science			2750		Fr. Physicist
Becquerel, Henri 1852-1908	Science	175	450	520		Nobel Curies' Radioactivity
Beddoe, Don	Entertainment	8			20	
Bedelia, Bonnie	Entertainment	3	4	10	10	
Bedford, Brian	Entertainment	5	12		20	Actor
Bedford, Gunning, Jr.	Revolutionary War	285	700			Signer of Constitution. Scarce
Bedford, Gunning, Sr.	Revolutionary War	175	325			Cousin of above, Scarce
Bee Gees (3)	Entertainment	35			85	
Bee, Barnard E.	Civil War	275	725	2075		CSA Gen., Sec'y War Rep. Texas
Bee, Carlos	Senate/Congress	10	20		20	Congressman TX
Bee, Hamilton Prioleau (War Date)	Civil War	265				CSA General
Bee, Hamilton Prioleau 1822-97	Civil War	80	110	317		CSA Gen.
Bee, Molly	Country Music	6			20	
Beebe, Charles William 1877-1962	Explorer	25	60	135	75	Bathysphere.Naturalist.Author
Beebe, Marshall	Aviation	18	35	55	42	ACE, WW II
Beech, Olive Ann	Aviation	20	45		50	Beechcraft Airplane Mfg.
Beecham, Thomas, Sir	Conductor	35	195			Flamboyant Br. Conductor
Beecher, Henry Ward 1813-87	Clergy	55	120	185	633	Abolition, Temperance Activist
Beecher, Lyman	Clergy	40	55	65	45	Early Anti Slavery
Beems, Patricia	Entertainment	3	3	6	8	
Beene, Geoffrey	Business	10	25		25	Fashion Designer

NAME	CATEGORY	SIG	LS/DS	ALS	SP	Comment
Beerbohm, Max	Author	55	135	220	65	Humorist, Caricaturist
Beery, Noah 1884-1946	Entertainment	78		250	175	
Beery, Noah Jr.	Entertainment	15	20	25	35	
Beery, Wallace 1885-1949	Entertainment	115	130	350	300	
Beeson, Jack	Composer	15	35	95	20	
Beethoven, Ludwig van	Composer	4900	19250	25000		ALS/Content $35,000
Begin, Menachem 1914-92	Head of State	108	210	245	148	Prime Minister Israel
Begley, Ed, Jr.	Entertainment	4	7	9	15	
Begley, Ed, Sr.	Entertainment	25	45	70	75	
Behan, Brendan F.	Author	160	400	645		Ir. Author-Playwright
Behrman, S. N.	Author	15	25	60	25	Am. Playwright, Screenplays
Beichel, Rudolph	Science	20			55	Rocket Pioneer/von Braun
Beiderbecke, Bix	Entertainment	5000				Jazz Musician
Beinhorn, Elly	Aviation	10	22	40	30	Ger. Aviation Pioneer
Belth, Ian Hay (John)	Author	10	30	60	20	Br. Novelist, Playwright
Beke, Charles Tilstone	Explorer	20	50	125		Br. Geographer. Nile Source
Bekhterev, Vladimir 1857-1927	Science			2000		Russ. Neuropathologist/Pavlov
Bekhterev, Vladimir 1857-1927	Science		1750	2500		Russ. Neuropathologist/Pavlov
Bekins, Milo	Business	35	45	160	125	Bekins Van & Storage Co.
Bel Geddes, Barbara	Entertainment	10			25	Dallas. NY Drama Critic Award
Bel Geddes, Norman	Artist	20	50	155	35	Scenic Designer Theater
Bela, Magyar	Astronaut	10			25	Hungary
Belafonte, Harry	Entertainment	10	15		30	
Belafonte, Shari	Entertainment	5	6	15	20	
Belasco, David	Entertainment	35	30	70	95	Theatrical Producer
Belaunde, Fernando T.	Head of State	10	20	50	25	
Belcher, Edward, Sir	Military-Navy	15	35	60		Arctic Exped.for J. Franklin
Belcher, Jonathan 1681-1757	Colonial America	225	325	650		Colonial Gov. MA, NH, NJ
Belita	Entertainment	15	25	45	45	
Belknap, George	Civil War	15		50		Union Naval Officer
Belknap, William W.	Civil War,Cabinet	65	160	175		Union General, Sec'y War
Bell, Alexander Graham 1847-1922	Science	350	1198	2550	3040	Inventor of Telephone
Bell, Charles H.	Civil War	50	95	140		Union Naval Captain
Bell, Digby	Entertainment	12			20	Vintage Actor
Bell, Eric Temple (John Taine)	Author	30		130	55	Scot., Math Books, Sci-Fi
Bell, Griffin	Cabinet	10			25	Att'y General
Bell, Henry H. 1808-1868	Civil War	60	150			Rear Adm under Farragut
Bell, Herbert A.	Business	15	20	75	50	
Bell, John	Cabinet	95	145			W.H. Harrison, Tyler Sec'y War
Bell, Lauralee	Entertainment	4	7		15	Soaps
Bell, Peter Hansborough	Governor		195			Gov. TX 1849-53
Bell, Rex	Entertainment	50			125	
Bell, Terrel H.	Cabinet	5	15	26	15	Sec'y Education
Bell, Tyree Harris	Civil War	55	130	215		CSA Gen.
Bellamy, Edward 1850-1898	Author	25	75	150		Novelist
Bellamy, Elizabeth W.	Author	3	9	18		
Bellamy, Madge	Entertainment	10	15	40	35	
Bellamy, Ralph 1904-91	Entertainment	15	15	25	40	
Bellanca, Giuseppe M.	Aviation	40	85	160	125	Bellanca Aircraft Designer-Mfg.
Belle, Lulu	Entertainment	10			20	C & W
Beller, Kathleen	Entertainment	6	8	15	15	
Belleri, Marguerite	Entertainment	5		30	25	Metropolitan Opera 1917-20
Bellew, John Chippendall	Clergy	10	20	25	20	
Belli, Melvin	Law	10	15	35	20	Trial Attorney
Belliard, A.D. (Count)1769-1832	Military	25	55	175		Fr. Gen. under Napoleon
Bellincioni, Gemma	Entertainment	35		150	100	It. Soprano

NAME	CATEGORY	SIG	LS/DS	ALS	SP	Comment
Bellini, Vincenzo 1801-35	Composer	575		4050		It. Opera
Bellmer, Hans 1902-75	Artist	55	160	500		Ger. Surrealist
Bellmon, Henry Louis	Senate	15	20		20	Senator OK, Gov. OK
Belloc, Hilaire 1870-1953	Author	25	55	150	50	Versatile Novelist, Poet,Critic
Belloc-Lowndes, Marie	Author	15	40	110	30	Br.Author of Historical Works
Bellon, Leoncadia	Entertainment	16			45	Opera, Film
Bellonte, Maurice	Aviation	75	145	270	345	
Bellow, Saul	Author	20	145	85	35	Nobel Literature. Novelist
Bellows, George 1882-1925	Artist	95	225	375		Urban Scenes, Sports, Landscape
Bellows, Henry W. 1814-82	Clergy	20		45		Founder Antioch College
Bellson, Louis	Entertainment	25		55	70	Jazz Drummer
Bellwood, Pamela	Entertainment	6	8	15	15	
Belmont, August	Business	55	75	210	185	Banker, Diplomat, Sportsman
Belmont, August, Jr.	Business	45	120			
Belmont, August, Mrs.	Socialite	15	25	40		
Belsham, Thomas	Clergy	15	20	35	30	
Belushi, James	Entertainment	10	15	20	35	
Belushi, John	Entertainment	250			750	
Bemelmans, Ludwig	Author	45	105	255	50	Wrlter-Illustrator. Novelist
Ben-Gurion, David 1886-1973	Head of State	175	1050	1892	462	1st Prime Minister of Israel
Ben-Yehuda, Eliezer	Author	35	175	425		Jewish Scholar
Ben-Zvi, Itzhak 1884-1963	Head of State	75	185	225	95	2nd President Israel
Benacerraf, Baruj	Science	27	55		40	Nobel Medicine-Physiology
Benatar, Pat	Entertainment	20			70	
Benavidez, Roy	Military	10	25	40	20	
Benchley, Peter	Author	15	25	50	20	Sketch of Jaws S $15-$35
Benchley, Robert	Author	40	80	195	75	Am. Drama Critic, Humorist
Bendix, William 1906-64	Entertainment	35	30	60	142	
Benederet, Bea	Entertainment	40			100	
Benedict XV. Pope	Head of State	125		450	550	
Benedict, Dick	Entertainment	9	10	20	30	
Benedict, Julius, Sir	Composer	15			25	Br. Pianist
Benedict, William	Entertainment	25			60	
Beneke, Tex	Entertainment	30			65	Sax for Glenn Miller. Big Band
Benes, Eduard 1884-1948	Head of State	85	90	145	200	P.M. & President Czech.
Benet, Stephen Vincent 1898-1943	Author	80	140	175	150	Poet, Novelist. Pulitzer (2)
Benham, George W. (War Date)	Civil War	120	225	389		Union Gen.
Benham, Henry W. 1813-84	Civil War	55	125	150		Union Gen.
Bening, Annette	Entertainment	10	25	50	50	Actress, Pin-up 65
Benjamin, Judah P. 1811-84	Civil War	290	885	1200		CSA Gen. & Sec'y of State
Benjamin, Judah P.(War Date)	Civil War	395	3500	1750		CSA Sec'y of State
Benjamin, William, Jr.	Supreme Court	40	1925		60	
Bennett, Arnold	Author	40	175			Br. Novelist
Bennett, Bruce (Herman Brix)	Entertainment	15	12	20	35	Early Tarzan
Bennett, Constance	Entertainment	30	60	120	65	
Bennett, Floyd	Aviation	300	370	750	500	Pilot with Byrd over North Pole
Bennett, James Gordon	Publisher	45	195			Financed Stanley-Livingstone
Bennett, Joan	Entertainment	18	20	25	75	
Bennett, Johnstone	Entertainment	15			35	Actress with Mansfield
Bennett, Julie	Entertainment	3	3	6	10	
Bennett, Richard	Entertainment	15			35	Stage & Silent Films
Bennett, Robert Russell	Composer	40			95	Great Broadway Composer
Bennett, Samuel F.	Composer	30	75	150		In the Sweet Bye & Bye
Bennett, Spencer Gordon	Entertainment	10			25	
Bennett, Tony	Entertainment	5	10	20	30	
Bennett, Wallace F.	Senate	5	10	20	15	Senator UT

NAME	CATEGORY	SIG	LS/DS	ALS	SP	Comment
Bennett, William J.	Author-Cabinet	20	60	75	55	Book of Virtues.Sec'y Ed.
Bennett, Wm. Andrew	Head of State	4	10	15	10	
Benning, Henry Lewis	Civil War	145	275	350		CSA Gen.
Benny Show, The Jack	Entertainment	120				6 Principals
Benny, Jack 1894-1974	Entertainment	65	288		158	Great Radio-TV Comedian
Benois, Alexander	Artist	45	195	425		Rus. Designed Sets, Costumes
Benson, Edward Frederic	Author	15	35	75		Satirical, Macabre Novels
Benson, Edward W., Archbishop	Clergy	20	35	55	35	
Benson, Egbert	Revolutionary War	35	75	160		Continental Congress
Benson, Elmer A.	Governor	5	12	20	15	Governor & Senator MN
Benson, Ezra Taft 1899-1994	Cabinet	15	25	55	40	Sec'y Agriculture, Pres. Mormon Church
Benson, Frank Robert, Sir	Entertainment	15	20	35	20	Vintage Br. Actor
Benson, George	Entertainment	15			25	
Benson, Jodi	Entertainment	10			35	
Benson, Richard Meux	Clergy	35	55	65	75	
Benson, Robbie	Entertainment	5	6	15	15	
Benson, William S.	Military	10	20	35	25	Adm. USN WW I
Bent, James Theodore	Explorer	5	10	25	10	Archaeologist
Benteen, Frederick W.	Civil War		3500		2500	
Bentham, Jeremy 1748-1832	Jurist-Philosopher	85				English
Benton, Barbi	Entertainment	5	6	15	15	
Benton, Robert	Entertainment	6			20	AA Film Director
Benton, Samuel	Civil War	345	540			CSA Gen.
Benton, Thomas Hart 1782-1858	Senate/Congress	90	95	205		30-Year Senator From Missouri
Benton, Thomas Hart 1889-1975	Artist	100	250	875		ALS/Content $1,350
Benton, William	Senate	10	30	65	20	Publisher, Statesman, Sen. CT
Benton, William Plummer	Civil War	95	130			Union Gen.
Bentsen, Lloyd	Senate-Cabinet	10	30		25	Senator TX, Sec'y Treas.
Benzell, Mimi	Entertainment	15			35	Opera
Benét, William Rose 1886-1956	Author	15	35	65	40	Poet, Editor. Pulitzer
Berdyaev, Nikolai	Clergy	75	100	130	175	
Berenger, Tom	Entertainment	10			45	Actor
Berenson, Marisa	Entertainment	9	10	15	25	
Berenstain, Stan*	Cartoonist	20			75	Berenstain Bear
Beresford, Charles, Lord 1846-1919	Military	15	35	125	80	Br. Admiral
Berfson, Henri-Louis	Author	30	80	155		
Berg, Alban	Composer	135	485	1425		Atonal Music. Orchestral, Songs
Berg, Gertrude	Entertainment	18	15	20	35	
Berg, Moe 1902-72	Celebrity	225				Lawyer, Mathematician,Spy, Noted Jewish
Berg, Paul	Science	27	35	65	30	Nobel Chemistry
Berganza, Teresa	Entertainment	6			35	Opera
Bergdorf, Gary	Entertainment	10			35	'Radar'. Mash
Bergen, Candice	Entertainment	10	15	25	35	
Bergen, Edgar 1903-78	Entertainment	55	80	125	122	Am. Ventriloquist-Comedian-Actor
Bergen, Frances	Entertainment	5	6	10	10	
Bergen, Polly	Entertainment	6	8	15	15	And Cosmetics Mfg.
Berger, Erna	Entertainment	10			30	Opera
Berger, Gottlob	Military	40	120	200	75	
Berger, Senta	Entertainment	10	15	35	30	
Bergere, Lee	Entertainment	4	4	9	10	
Bergeron, Marion	Beauty Queen	15			75	Miss America 1934
Berggrav, Eivind Josef	Clergy		50			Bishop of Norway. World Council of Churches
Bergh, Henry	Reformer	70		400		Founder ASPCA
Bergland, Bob	Cabinet	4	10	20	15	Sec'y Agriculture, Congress MN
Bergman, Ingmar	Entertainment	35	40	50	125	
Bergman, Ingrid 1913-82	Entertainment	100	178	260	354	3x Academy Award Winner

NAME	CATEGORY	SIG	LS/DS	ALS	SP	Comment
Bergman, Sandahl	Entertainment	6	8	15	20	
Bergner, Elizabeth	Entertainment	20	35	60	30	
Bergonzi, Carlo	Entertainment	30			65	Opera
Bergson, Henri 1859-1941	Author	40	125			Nobel for Lit.. 1927
Berio, Luciano	Composer	20	30	75		
Berjerac, Jacques	Entertainment	15			30	Fr. Actor of Am. Films.40's-50'2
Berkeley, Busby	Entertainment	100	155	300	295	Dance Choreographer-Director
Berkley, Elizabeth	Entertainment	10			33	Showgirls Pin-up $100
Berkowitz, David	Criminal	95	90	250		Son of Sam, Serial Murderer
Berle, Milton	Entertainment	15	15	25	35	
Berlier, Jean Baptiste	Science	15	27	45		Fr.Engineer. Undergr. RR System
Berlier, Theophile, Count	Fr. Revolution	50	150	295		
Berlik, Jan	Entertainment	25			50	Czech. Operatic Tenor
Berlin, Irving 1888-1990	Composer	201	1112	1473	1642	AMusQS $2,300
Berlioz, Hector 1803-69	Composer	245	1248	1622		AMusQS $3,900
Berlitz, Charles	Business	16	20		35	Language Educator
Berman, Eugene 1899-1972	Artist	40	105	195		Rus.-Born Painter-Designer
Berman, Pandro S.	Entertainment	5	10		15	Film Producer
Berman, Shelley	Entertainment	3	3	6	8	
Bernadotte, Jean-Baptiste	Royalty	120	575	650		Charles XIV John. Marshal of Nap.
Bernard, Claude 1813-78	Science	145		800		Fr. Fndr. Experimental Medicine
Bernard, Crystal	Entertainment	10			40	Wings
Bernard, Francis, Sir 1712-79	Colonial Governor	175	522	750		Col.Gov. Mass. Bay Colony
Bernard, John Henry, Archbishop	Clergy	30	45	50	40	
Bernard, Simon	Civil War	45	115			Fr. Engineer, Nap.& US Gen.
Berndt, Walter*	Cartoonist	10			50	Smitty
Bernhard, Sandra	Entertainment	4	6		10	Comedienne
Bernhardt, Sarah 1844-1923	Entertainment	137	275	562	1045	The Divine Sarah
Bernie, Ben	Entertainment	20		25	25	Big Band Leader
Bernsen, Corbin	Entertainment	18	20	45	40	
Bernstein, Elmer	Composer	15	25	45	20	
Bernstein, Leonard 1918-90	Composer	128	462	672	245	AMusMsS $1,600, $4,500
Berosini, Josephine	Entertainment	5	10	20	30	
Berrien, J. Macpherson 1781-1856	Cabinet	20	55	105		Jackson Att'y General
Berrigan, Daniel, Fr.	Clergy	15	30	65	25	
Berringer, Tom	Entertainment	12			50	
Berry, Chuck	Entertainment	50			140	Rock. Alb. S $115
Berry, Halle	Entertainment	15			50	
Berry, Hiram G. (War Date)	Civil War	445	595			Killed in Action
Berry, Hiram G. 1824-63	Civil War	325	680			Union Gen.
Berry, Ken	Entertainment	5	6	15	15	
Berry, Lucien	Military	15	50			General WW I
Berry, Richard 1936-1997	Entertainment	30			60	Composer "Louie, Louie"
Berry, Sidney M.	Clergy	10	15	25		
Berry, Tom	Governor	5			25	Gov. SD
Berry, William H.	Civil War	15				6th Missouri Survivor
Berryman, Clifford	Artist	55	75	95		The Teddy Bear
Berryman, Clifton K.Jr.	Cartoonist		45			Pulitzer.Political Cartoonist
Bertelson, Richard L.	Aviation	10	22	38	28	Navy ACE, WW II
Berthier, L. Alexandre 1753-1815	Napoleonic Wars	75	225	425		Marshal of Napoleon
Berthold, Rudolf	Aviation	200	350	650	450	ACE, WW I, The Iron Knight
Berthollet, Claude-Louis, Count	Science	60	150	330		Fr. Chemist.Senator of Napoleon
Bertinelli, Valerie	Entertainment	6	8	15	26	
Bertolucci, Bernardo	Entertainment	15			35	Film Director
Berwick, Duke (J.Fitzjames)	Fr. Military	150	400			Gen. of Louis XIV, Marshal Fr.
Berzelius, Jons Jacob	Science	70	165	475		Swe. Chemist. Chemical Symbols

NAME	CATEGORY	SIG	LS/DS	ALS	SP	Comment
Besant, Annie Wood 1847-1933	Clergy	50	115	195		Radical Free-Thinker
Besant, Walter 1836-1901	Author	35	125	190		Br. Novelist Ams $9000
Besch, Bibi	Entertainment	3	4	8	8	
Beser, Jacob	Aviation	50	100		100	Both Atomic Missions
Bess, Gordon	Cartoonist	5			25	Redeye
Bessell, Ted	Entertainment	10	20		25	Boyfriend in "That Girl"
Bessemer, Henry, Sir 1813-98	Metallurgist-Inventor	35	60	200	90	Inventor Blast Furnace.Steel
Besser, Joe	Entertainment	10	10	20	40	
Bessieres, Bertrand	Fr. Revolution	55	100			
Bessieres, Jean-Baptiste 1766-1813	Fr. Military	175	375			Marshal of Napoleon
Best, Charles H.	Science	125	225	310	75	Discovered Insulin/Banting
Best, Edna	Entertainment	15	15	30	45	
Best, James	Entertainment	5	6	15	15	
Best, Pete	Entertainment	40			150	Pre Ringo. Beatles Drummer
Best, Willie	Entertainment	50			150	Vintage Afro-Am. Film Actor
Bestor, Don	Bandleader	15				Jack Benny's 1st Bandleader
Beswick, Martine	Entertainment	5	6	15	10	
Betham-Edwards, Matilda	Author	5	10	22		
Bethe, Hans, Dr.	Science	35	55		45	Nobel Physics
Bethune, Mary McLeod 1875-1955	Educator	125	325	500	175	Black Teacher, Activist. Cont. TLS $895
Betjeman, John, Sir 1906-82	Author	40	85	132	50	Br. Poet Laureate
Bettelheim, Bruno	Science	35	65		150	Psychiatrist researched Autism
Bettger, Lyle	Entertainment	7			20	
Betz, Carl	Entertainment	40			75	
Beugnot, J.C., Count	Fr. Military	85	160			
Beverage, John	Civil War	30	85			Union Gen., Gov. IL
Beveridge, Albert J. 1862-1927	Congress	5	20	35		US Sen., Historian
Bevin, Ernest	Statesman	25	55	125	45	Br. Powerful Union Leader
Bewick, Thomas 1753-1828	Artist	105	275	625		Br. Illustrator, Wood Engraver
Bey, Turhan	Entertainment	20	19	35	35	
Bhutto, Benazir	Head of State	35	120	175	200	Pakistan, Prime Minister
Bhutto, Zullikar Ali	Head of State	20			90	Pakistan, Prime Minister
Biaggi, Mario	Senate/Congress	5	15		10	Congressman NY. NY Police MOH
Bialik, Chaim	Author	65	225	425	80	Jewish Poet
Biasini, Piero	Entertainment	10			35	Opera
Bibb, George M. 1776-1859	Cabinet	25	45	80		Early Sec'y Treas.,Senator KY
Bibb, Wm. Wyatt 1781-1820	Governor	20	45			Gov. GA
Bickel, Theodore	Entertainment	5			35	
Bickersteth, Edward H., Bishop	Clergy	15	25	35	35	
Bickford, Charles	Entertainment	30	45	65	100	
Biddle, Clement 1740-1814	Revolutionary War	220	895	1150		Revolutionary Officer, Merchant
Biddle, Clement Carroll 1784-1855	Military	20	30	70		Col. of 1st Inf. PA. 1812. Political Science
Biddle, Francis	Cabinet	20	35	75		Att'y General
Biddle, George	Artist	26	85	210		
Biddle, Nicholas 1786-1844	Business	125	431	712		Pres. U.S. Bank, Financier
Biden, Joe	Senate/Congress	5	15		20	Senator DE
Bidwell, Daniel D. 1819-64	Civil War	225		825		Union Gen. ALS '63 $1595
Bidwell, John	Western Pioneer	20	100			Calif. Pioneer, Pres. Candidate
Biehn, Michael	Entertainment	9	10	20	40	
Bierce, Ambrose 1842-1914	Author	275	670	588		Journalist, Short Stories
Bieri, Ramon	Entertainment	10			35	
Bierstadt, Albert	Artist	125	220	540		Of the Hudson River School
Biery, James S.	Senate/Congress	10	15		25	Congressman PA
Big Man, Chief Max	Native American	30			60	Chief
Bigard, Barney	Entertainment	70			150	Jazz Clarinet, Ten. Sax
Bigelow, Erastus B.	Business-Inventor	100	290	595		Power Looms for Carpet Weaving

The Sanders Price Guide to Autographs

NAME	CATEGORY	SIG	LS/DS	ALS	SP	Comment
Bigelow, John 1817-1911	Publisher	5	10	52	15	Editor NY Evening Post. Diplomat
Bigelow, Poultney 1855-1954	Journalist	5		22		Traveller, Author. Son of John
Bigge, Arthur, Sir	Military	10	30	65		
Biggers, Earl Derr	Author	150	210	365	350	Am. Novelist, Mystery Writer
Biggs, Asa	Civil War	25	60			CSA Judge, US Senator NC
Biggs, Ronnie	Criminal	25			95	Train Robber
Bikel, Theodore	Entertainment	5			15	Actor-Singer
Bilbo, Theodore G.	Senate	20	30		25	Senator MS, Gov. MS
Bill, Max	Celebrity	8	20	40	15	
Bill, Tony	Entertainment	5			20	Actor, Film Director
Billings, Josh 1818-85	Author	25	80	165	40	American Humorist. (H.W.Shaw)
Billingsley, Barbara	Entertainment	3	3	6	10	
Billo, James D.	Aviation	10	22	38	28	Navy ACE, WW II
Billroth, Theodor 1829-94	Science	45	225	295		Ger. Surgeon. Use of Antisepsis
Binci, Mario	Entertainment	15			45	Opera
Bing, Herman	Entertainment	20			40	
Bing, Rudolph	Entertainment	15	20	35	35	Metropolitan Opera Leader
Bingham, Amelia	Entertainment	6	8	15	25	
Bingham, Henry	Civil War	85		160		Union Gen., CMH Wilderness
Bingham, John A.	Congress	25	35	90		Repr. OH, Lincoln Judge Adv.
Bingham, Judson David	Civil War	45	140	185		Union General
Bingham, William	Revolutionary War	120	315	340		Continental Congr. Senator PA
Binney, Thomas	Clergy	20	30	45	35	
Binnig, Gerd, Dr.	Science	20	60		45	Nobel Physics
Binns, Edward	Entertainment	4	4	9	9	
Binoche, Juliette	Entertainment	12			68	Actress
Bird, Billie	Entertainment	7			15	Character actress
Birdseye, Clarence	Business	100	340	550	150	Birdseye Frozen Foods
Birdwood, William, Sir	Military	45	145			Br. Fld. Marshal, WW I
Birendra, Bir B.	Head of State	10	15		20	Prime Minister Nepal
Birney, David	Entertainment	5	6	15	10	
Birney, David Bell 1825-64	Civil War	225	295	775		Union Gen. ANS '63 $990
Birney, William	Civil War	35	70	90		Union General
Bisbee, Horatio, Jr.	Civil War	25	45	105		Union Officer & MOC
Bishop, Barry	Celebrity	7	14			
Bishop, Elizabeth 1911-79	Author	35	125			Am. Poet. Pulitzer Prize '55
Bishop, J. Michael, Dr.	Science	25	40		35	Nobel Medicine
Bishop, Jim	Author	15	35	45	20	Journalist. Best Selling Novels
Bishop, Joey	Entertainment	3	3	6	10	
Bishop, Julie	Entertainment	6	8	15	15	
Bishop, Stephen	Entertainment	4			10	Rock Star
Bishop, Wm. 'Billy'	Aviation	150	225	300	220	ACE, WW I, 72 Kills
Bismark, Prince Otto von	Royalty	250	600	745	920	The Iron Chancellor
Bispham, David	Entertainment	60	80	110	120	Opera
Bissell, Clayton L.	Aviation	25	40	100		
Bissell, Emily P. 1861-1948	Humanitarian	125				Introduced U.S Xmas Seals
Bissell, Whit	Entertainment	7		15	20	
Bissell, William H.	Governor	10	28	60		Governor IL, MOC
Bisset, Jacqueline	Entertainment	15	20	30	35	
Bissett, Josie	Entertainment	10			45	Actress, Melrose Place
Bissit, J.E.	Br. Navy	10	25		15	Commander HMS Queen Eliz.
Bitter, Karl Theodore	Artist	25	75	155	100	Am. Sculptor
Bittrich, Wilhelm	Military	27	70	135	60	
Bixby, Bill	Entertainment	5	10	25	30	
Bizet, Georges 1838-75	Composer	350	890	1650		Carmen, L'Arlesienne Suite
Bjerknes, Jacob A.B. 1887-1975	Science	35				Discovered Origin of Cyclones

NAME	CATEGORY	SIG	LS/DS	ALS	SP	Comment
Bjoerling, Jussi 1911-69	Entertainment	500	650	1000	900	
Bjornson, Bjornstjerne 1832-1910	Author	50	55	140		3rd Nobel for Literature
Bjornstad, Alfred	Military	10	20	35		General WW I
Blacher, Boris	Composer	40				Rus-Ger. Classical & Experimental Music
Black, Alexander	Author	5	10	20	5	
Black, Clint	Entertainment	20			50	Country-Western
Black, Eugene R.	Business	5	20	30	15	
Black, Frank, Dr.	Conductor	5			30	NBC Dir. of Music in '40's
Black, Hugo (SC) 1886-1966	Supreme Court	40	120	285	95	
Black, Jeremiah	Cabinet	25	60	115		Att'y General (Buchanan)
Black, John Charles	Civil War	50	126	155		Union General, MOH
Black, Karen	Entertainment	6	8	15	18	
Black, Richard B.	Military	10	25	45		
Black, William	Military	20			45	General WW I
Blackburn, John T.	Aviation	12	24	38	30	ACE, WW II
Blackburn, Luke P.	Governor	15	35			Governor KY
Blackett, Patrick M.	Science	20	35	50	30	Nobel Physics. Cosmic Rays
Blackman, Honor	Entertainment	10	15	25	25	
Blackmer, Sidney	Entertainment	10	15	20	35	
Blackmon, Fred L.	Senate/Congress	10	20		15	MOC AL
Blackmore, Richard D.	Author	15	40	95		Br. Novelist. Lorna Doone
Blackmun, Harry A. (SC)	Supreme Court	40	225	270	75	
Blackstone, Harry	Entertainment	150	375	475	175	Self Sketch Signed $375
Blackstone, Harry, Jr	Entertainment	5	5	10	15	Magician
Blackton, J.Stuart & Smith, Albert E.	Entertainment		20			Co-Fndrs Vitagraph Films. Inventor
Blackwell, Alice Stone	Reformer	200		95		Woman's Suffrage
Blackwell, Mr.	Business	8	10		15	Fashion Critic
Blackwell, Otis	Composer	25	85	175		
Blaha, John E.	Astronaut	5	10		15	
Blaine, James G. 1830-93	Cabinet	57	65	140	45	U.S.Sen. ME,Garfield Sec'y St.
Blaine, Vivian	Entertainment	5	6	15	25	
Blair, Charles	Aviation	45			60	
Blair, Francis P., Jr.	Civil War	45	80	145		Union General, U.S.Sen. MO
Blair, Frank	Entertainment	3	3	6	6	Radio-TV News
Blair, Janet	Entertainment	9	10	20	20	
Blair, John (SC)	Supreme Court	150	775	1200	48	Signer of Constitution
Blair, Linda	Entertainment	9	10	20	20	
Blair, Montgomery	Legal	75	205	545		Counsel to Dred Scott
Blake, Amanda	Entertainment	60	85	115	175	Veteran Gunsmoke Actress
Blake, Bud*	Cartoonist	4			50	Tiger
Blake, Eubie 1883-1983	Composer	75	175	175	117	AMusQS $385-$650
Blake, Eugene Carson	Clergy	50	95	150	70	
Blake, Madge	Entertainment	100			250	
Blake, Robert	Entertainment	6	10	10	15	
Blake, William	Artist					Content ALS $30,000
Blakely, Susan	Entertainment	6	8	15	20	
Blakeslee, Don	Aviation	10	25	38	30	ACE, WW II
Blanc, Louis	Author	12	25	45		Fr. Socialist, Journalist
Blanc, Mel 1908-89	Entertainment	60	85	145	160	Voice of Bugs Bunny etc.
Blanchard, Albert G.(War Date)	Civil War	195	1595			CSA General
Blanchard, Albert G.1810-91	Civil War	120	205			CSA Gen.
Blanchard, Nina	Entertainment	4			8	
Bland, Richard P. 1835-99	Congress	15				Repr. MO, Defeated by W.J.. Bryan for Pres.
Bland, Schuyler Otis	Senate/Congress	5	15	25		MOC VA
Bland, William T.	Senate/Congress	5	15	20		MOC MO
Blandick, Clara	Entertainment	200			650	

NAME	CATEGORY	SIG	LS/DS	ALS	SP	Comment
Blane, Ralph	Composer	5			40	AMusMsS 36
Blane, Sally	Entertainment	6	8	15	15	
Blanks, Mary Lynn	Entertainment	3	3	6	6	
Blanton, Leonard Ray	Governor	10			15	Governor TN, MOC TN
Blanton, Thomas L.	Senate/Congress	10	20		20	Senator TX, MOC TX
Blaschka, Rudolph	Artist	10	35	75		Bohemian Artist in Glass
Blasco-Ibanez, Vicente	Author	100			450	Sp. Novelist. Self Exiled
Blaslev, Lisabeth	Entertainment	10			25	Opera
Blass, Bill	Business	10	15		25	Fashion Designer
Blatchford, Samuel (SC)	Supreme Court	45	135	190		
Blatty, William Peter	Author	15	30	45	20	The Exorcist, AA . TsS $150
Bledsoe, Tempest	Entertainment	15	35		35	
Bleeth, Yasmine	Entertainment	10			40	Baywatch, Pin-up $60
Blenker, Louis (Ludwig)1812-63	Civil War	100	210			Union Gen LS '61 $800
Blennerhassett, Harman	Revolutionary War	115	330	575		Funds, Refuge-Burr Conspiracy
Bleriot, Louis 1872-1936	Aviation	250	500	595	538	1st To Fly Englist Channel
Bless, Frederick	Aviation	10	22	38	32	ACE, Korea
Bletcher, Billy	Entertainment	50			200	
Bligh, William, Capt.	Military	770	5900	2500		Br. Adm. Capt. HMS Bounty
Bliss, Arthur, Sir	Composer	25		175		Brit. Opera, Orch. works
Bliss, Cornelius	Cabinet	10	25	55	40	Sec'y Interior
Bliss, George Jr.	Civil War	8	15	25		MOC OH
Bliss, J. S.	Civil War	5	10	20		
Bliss, Tasker H.	Military	15	25	50	25	US Gen.1st Cmdr. War College
Bliss, William Wallace S.	Military	130	435	500		Pvt. Sec'y Zachary Taylor
Bliss, Zenas R.	Civil War	35	110	160		Union Officer
Blitzstein, Marc	Composer	80	100	250		Opera. Brilliant US Composer
Blixen, Karen (Isak Dinesen)	Author	110	500		200	Danish Novelist Out of Africa
Bloch, Ernest 1880-1959	Composer	80		300	250	Swiss-Am. Composer, Teacher
Bloch, Ernst	Author	55	140	425	90	Ger. Philosopher.
Bloch, Felix	Science	25	40	100	30	Nobel Physics
Bloch, Konrad, Dr.	Science	20	30	45	30	Nobel Medicine
Bloch, Raymond	Composer	10	20	35	10	
Bloch, Robert	Author	20	50	60	20	Novelist. TMsS $450
Block, Henry W.	Business	20	45		30	H & R Block
Block, Herb*	Cartoonist	15			100	Herblock-political
Block, John R.	Cabinet	5	10	15	10	
Block, Joseph L.	Business	4	6	9	6	
Block, Martin	Entertainment	5			15	Early radio deejay
Block, Richard	Business	20	35	90	25	H & R Block
Blocker, Dan	Entertainment	200			550	
Blodget, Samuel Jr.	Revolutionary War	285	750	1540		Inventor, Soldier, Judge
Bloembergen, Nicolaas Dr.	Science	20	35	40	30	Nobel Physics
Blomberg, Werner Von	Military	30	75	165	125	Ger. Fld. Marshal WW II
Blomfield, Ezekial	Clergy	35	45	60		
Blondell, Joan	Entertainment	35	40	65	55	
Blondin, Charles 1824-97	Entertainment	30	450	175	60	Tightrope walker Niagara Falls
Blood, Robert O.	Governor	5		25		Governor NH
Blood, Sweat and Tears	Entertainment	35			80	
Bloom, Claire	Entertainment	6	8	15	20	
Bloom, Lindsay	Entertainment	8	9	12	15	
Bloomer, Amelia	Reformer	275	350			Pioneer Dress & Social Reformer
Bloomfield, Joseph	Revolutionary War	30	95	157		Officer, Attorney, Gov. NJ
Bloomfield-Zeisler, Fannie	Entertainment	25			75	Concert Pianist
Blore, Eric	Entertainment	20	25	65	60	
Blossom Rock	Entertainment	40			75	

NAME	CATEGORY	SIG	LS/DS	ALS	SP	Comment
Blough, Roger	Business	5	15	25	15	
Blount, James H.	Civil War	25	40			CSA Officer, MOC GA
Blount, William	Senate	320	900			Continental Congr. Senator TN
Blount, Winton M.	Cabinet	5	15	25	10	P.M. General
Bloustein, Edward J.	Celebrity	5	12	20	10	
Blucher, Gebhard L. von	Military	200	550	2200		Pruss. Fld. Marshal vs Napoleon
Blue, Ben 1901-75	Entertainment	26	30	60	55	
Blue, Monte 1880-1963	Entertainment	19	25	45	75	Griffith Great Silent Star
Bluford, Guion S. Jr.	Astronaut	10			30	
Blum, Leon (Fr)	Head of State	25	40	110	35	Pres. France WW II
Blum, Norbert	Statesman	5			10	German Minister & Statesman
Blumberg, Baruch S.	Science	20	30	55	25	Nobel Medicine
Blumenfeld, Felix	Composer		150		300	Russ. Conductor, Teacher
Blumenthal, Jacques	Composer	40		350		And Pianist
Blumenthal, W. Michael	Cabinet	5	10	15	10	
Blunt, Asa P.	Military	25		200		General
Blunt, James G., Dr.	Civil War	46	75			Union General
Blunt, John Henry	Clergy	15	25	35	25	
Blyden, Larry	Entertainment	3	3	6	6	
Blyth, Ann	Entertainment	11		15	20	
Blythe, Betty	Entertainment	35		50	175	Silent Star
Boardman, Eleanor	Entertainment	10	15	25	25	Vintage Actress
Boardman, Russell	Aviation	25	55	95	80	
Bob & Ray	Entertainment	25			50	
Bobbitt, John Wayne	Media Celebrity	25			50	Viotim of Angry Wife
Bobbltt, Lorena	Media Celebrity					Penis Slasher. NRPA
Bobkins, Addie	Entertainment	5	6	9	8	
Bobko, Karol J.	Astronaut	7			15	
Bochco, Steven	Entertainment	10	15		20	TV Emmy Award Producer
Bochner, Lloyd	Entertainment	4	4	9	15	
Bock, Feodor von	Military	100	295		150	Ger.Gen. WW II. Failed
Bock, Jerry	Composer	40	16	35	80	Fiddler.... AMusQS $250
Bocock, Thomas S.	Civil War	20				CSA Speaker of the House
Bodenschatz, Karl	Aviation	30	75	150	95	
Bodwell, Joseph R.	Governor	8	12		10	Gov. ME
Boe, Nils A.	Governor	10	15			Governor SD
Boerhaave, Herman 1668-1738	Science		2188			Dutch Physician, Medical Educator
Boesch, Ruthilde	Entertainment	5	10		20	Opera
Bogard, Dirk	Entertainment	10		30	25	
Bogart, Humphrey 1899-1957	Entertainment	981	1350	1750	2750	
Bogdanovich, Peter	Entertainment	10	30		20	Controversial Film Director
Boggs, Charles	Civil War	45	90	115		Union Adm.
Boggs, Hale	Senate/Congress	10	25			MOC LA
Boggs, Lindy (Mrs. H.Boggs)	Congress	10	15		15	MOC LA
Boggs, William R. (War Date)	Civil War	170		495		CSA General
Boggs, William R. 1829-1911	Civil War	85	195	315		CSA General
Bohay, Heidi	Entertainment	5	6	15	10	
Bohm, Karl	Entertainment	15		75	85	Conductor. Dir. Vienna State Opera
Bohnen, Carl	Artist	20	35			
Bohr, Aage Niels 1922-	Science	25			55	Nobel Physics 1975
Bohr, Niels H.D. 1885-1962	Science	500	1175		2238	Danish Physicist. Nobel 1922
Boisrond-Canal	Haitian Statesman	30	95			
Boito, Arrigo	Composer	45	110	325		& Verdi Librettist. AMusQS $750
Bok, Edward W.	Author-Business	30	55	140	40	Editor, Curtis Publishing, Pulitzer
Bokor, Margit	Entertainment	10			30	Hung. Soprano
Boland, Frederick	Celebrity	5	15	40	10	

The Sanders Price Guide to Autographs

NAME	CATEGORY	SIG	LS/DS	ALS	SP	Comment
Boland, Mary	Entertainment	15	75		70	
Bolcom, William	Composer	15	25	65		Pulitzer, AMusQS $75
Bolden, Charles F. Jr.	Astronaut	5			18	
Boles, John	Entertainment	20	30	45	40	
Bolet, Jorge	Entertainment	20			120	Pianist
Bolger, James	Head of State	10			20	P.M. New Zealand
Bolger, Ray 1904-87	Entertainment	63	60	327	172	Wizard of OZ. SP as Scarecrow $250-500
Bolger, Ray and Haley, Jack	Entertainment		1500			SP (OZ) $595
Bolingbroke, Henry (St.John)	Author	30	150	250		1st Viscount, Politician,Writer
Bolivar, Simon	Head of State	385	3075	4975		Statesman, Revolutionary Leader
Boll, Heinrich	Author	35	30	95	25	Nobel Lit., Novelist, Poet
Bolling, Tiffany	Entertainment	3	3	6	15	
Bolt, John	Aviation	12	30	50	35	ACE, WW II & Korea
Bolton, Frances Payne	Senate/Congress	10	25			MOC OH
Bolton, Guy	Author	15	100			Playwright
Bolton, James	Inventor	20	70		20	Sewing Machine
Bolton, Michael	Entertainment	125			150	Singer, Composer
Bolton-Jones, Hugh	Artist	10	25	45		Am. Landscape Painter
Bombeck, Erma	Author	5	20	50	10	Humorous Columnist
Bomford, George	Military Engineer	65	200			Invented Howitzer Bomb Cannon
Bomford, James Voty	Civil War	37	80	116		
Bon Jovi, Jon	Entertainment	10			40	Rock
Bonaduce, Danny	Entertainment	10			25	
Bonaparte, Caroline	Royalty	35	95	275		Marie-Annonciade
Bonaparte, Charles 1851-1921	Cabinet	30	70			Sec'y Navy, Att'y Gen. Gr.Nephew Napol.
Bonaparte, Elisa (Maria Ana)	Royalty	400		500		Oldest Sister of Napoeon
Bonaparte, Eugene Napoleon	Royalty	75	200	435		Adopted by Napoleon
Bonaparte, Jerome	Royalty	60	135	240		Brother of Napoleon
Bonaparte, Joseph 1768-1844	Royalty	120	262	350		Elder Brother of Napoleon
Bonaparte, Letizia	Royalty		1500	2700		Mother of Napoleon
Bonaparte, Louis Napoleon	Royalty					SEE Napoleon III
Bonaparte, Lucien	Royalty	50	105	165		Brother. Opposed Nap., Exiled
Bonaparte, Marie Louise	Royalty	195	815	2795		Wife of Napoleon
Bonaparte, Napoleon	Royalty					SEE Napoleon I
Bonar, Horatius	Clergy	15	20	25		
Bonci, Alessandro	Entertainment	35			115	Opera
Bond, Carrie Jacobs	Composer	35	110	170	45	Am. Composer Art Songs
Bond, Charles	Aviation	10	28	40	30	ACE, WW II, Flying Tigers
Bond, Christopher Kit	Senate	5	10		10	Senator MO
Bond, Ford	Entertainment	10			15	Early Network Radio Ann'cer
Bond, Johnny	Country Music	10			20	
Bond, Julian	Politician	10	20	50	15	Afro-Am. Activist. Poet
Bond, Tommy Butch	Entertainment	10			25	
Bond, Ward 1903-60	Entertainment	95	80	95	225	GWTW, Wagon Train
Bond, William C.	Science	45	190	350		Am. Astronomer. Harvard Observ.
Bondi, Beulah	Entertainment	15	15	30	38	
Bondur, Roberta	Astronaut	10			20	Canadian Astro
Boner, Edmond 1500-69	Clergy	650				Appealed to Pope for Henry VIII
Bonerz, Peter	Entertainment	3	3	6	6	
Bonesteel, Charles H.	Military	11	35	58		
Bong, Richard	Aviation	500	1200	2000	1800	ACE, WW II, Top U.S. Ace
Bonham, Joe 'Bonzo'	Entertainment	75			125	
Bonham, Milledge L.(War Date)	Civil War	185	255	455		CSA General
Bonham, Milledge L.1813-90	Civil War	100	205			CSA General
Bonheur, Rosa 1822-1899	Artist	110	155	325		Fr. Horse Fair & Rural Scenes
Bonjovi, John	Entertainment				40	Rock

NAME	CATEGORY	SIG	LS/DS	ALS	SP	Comment
Bonnard, Pierre 1867-1947	Artist	105	280	887		Fr. Post-impressionist,Illustrator
Bonneville, Benj. L. E. de 1795-1878	Military	225	600	897		Pioneer Explorer NW Territory
Bonney, Barbara	Entertainment	15			30	Opera
Bono, Sonny	Entertainment	10			20	Mayor Palm Springs, Congressman
Bonstelle, Jessie	Entertainment	25		40		Stage Actress, Producer
Bontemps, Arna	Author	20	175			Am. Novels, Non-Fiction, Poetry
Bonvalot, Gabriel	Celebrity				155	
Bonynge, Richard	Conductor	15			50	Dame Sutherland's Conductor Husband
Book of Love (4)	Entertainment	15			30	Rock Group
Book, Sorrell	Entertainment	3	3	6	6	
Boone, Daniel 1734-1820	Revolutionary War	2000	9333	21500		Am. Pioneer Cumberland Gap
Boone, Debbie	Entertainment	5	20		20	
Boone, Pat	Entertainment	3	3	6	8	
Boone, Richard	Entertainment	85	80	95	150	Actor. Palladin
Boone, Squire	Revolutionary War			1150		NC Farmer. Father of Daniel
Boorda, Jeremy M. 19xx-96	Military	30				Adm. US Navy. Suicide 1996
Boorstin, Daniel J.	Author	25				The Creators
Boosler, Elayne	Entertainment	15		35	35	Comedienne
Booth, Adrian	Entertainment	5			20	
Booth, Ballington	Clergy	24	75	150		Co-Cmdr. Salvation Army
Booth, Bromwell	Clergy	25	50	75		
Booth, Edwin 1833-93	Entertainment	115		300	250	Great 19th Century Actor
Booth, Evangeline	Reformer	35	115	360	90	Salvation Army
Booth, John Wilkes	Civil War	1550	3050	4000	4500	Assassin of Lincoln
Booth, Junius Brutus, Jr. 1821-83	Entertainment	35	85			Actor Brother of John Wilkes
Booth, Maude 1865-1948	Reformer	45	80	225		Fndr. Vols. of Am. & PTA
Booth, Newell S., Bishop	Clergy	20	35	50	50	
Booth, Newton	Senator	15	25	60		Governor CA, Senator CA
Booth, Shirley	Entertainment	25	40		45	
Booth, William 1829-1912	Clergy	125	160	350	175	Founder & Gen'l Salvation Army
Booth, William Bramwell	Clergy	40	75	100	65	Eldest Son & Organizer
Boothe, Powers	Entertainment	5	6	15	15	
Boozer, Brenda	Entertainment	4	5	10	10	
Bor, Tadeusz	Military	15	45	75		
Borah, William E.	Senate	20	30		45	Senator ID
Borch, F.J.	Business	4	10		10	Pres. General Electric
Borchers, Adolf	Aviation	10	15	30	25	
Bordaberry, Juan M	Head of State	7	15	25	10	Uraguay
Bordelon, Guy	Aviation	8	20	35	25	ACE, Korea
Borden, Lizzy	Celebrity			15000		Alleged Ax Murderess
Borden, Olive	Entertainment	30	35	45	150	
Borden, Robert L. 1854-1937	Head of State	35				P.M. Canada 1911-20
Bordogni, Giulio-Marco	Entertainment			40		Opera. Tenor. Teacher
Bordoni, Irene	Entertainment	15	15	35	30	
Borge, Victor	Entertainment	5	7	15	10	
Borges, Jorge Luis 1899-1986	Author	75	350			Argentinian.Fiction, Poetry
Borghese, Camillo	Head of State					SEE Paul V, Pope
Borghese, Pauline Bonaparte	Royalty			575		Sister of Napoleon
Borgia, Francesco Card'l	Clergy	3200	2200			
Borglum, Gutzon 1867-1941	Artist	225	375	535	814	Creator Mt. Rushmore Sculptures
Borglum, Lincoln	Artist	25	60	85		Son of Gutzon. Sculptor
Borglum, Solon	Artist	15		45		
Borgnine, Ernest	Entertainment	5	10	12	25	
Bori, Lucrezia 1887-1960	Entertainment	35	95		88	Opera. Sp. Lyric Soprano
Boring, Wayne*	Cartoonist	30			400	Superman
Boris III	Royalty	120			185	King & Dictator Bulgaria

NAME	CATEGORY	SIG	LS/DS	ALS	SP	Comment
Bork, Robert A.	Jurist	5	20		30	
Borkh, Inge	Entertainment	10			25	Opera. Salome
Borlaug, Norman, Dr.	Science	20	35	80	30	Nobel Peace Prize
Borman, F. & Lovell, J.	Astronaut	35			75	Signed by Both
Borman, Frank	Astronaut	30			115	
Bormann, Martin 1900-45	Military	350	971	1500	850	Nazi Private Sec'y to Hitler
Born, Max 1882-70	Science	175	350	575		Nobel, Ger.-Br. Physicist
Borne, Hermann von Dem.	Military	20	45	90		
Borno, Louis	Head of State	15	75			Pres. Haiti
Borodin, Alexander	Composer	250	450	1100		Rus. Composer & Prof. Chemistry
Borowski, Felix	Composer	15	40	100	50	
Borso, Umberto	Entertainment	15			45	It. Tenor
Borzage, Frank	Entertainment	40			150	Film Director-Producer
Bosanquet, Helen D.	Author	8	15	22		
Bose, Jagadis, Sir	Science	27	40	150		Indian Physicist
Boshell, Louise	Entertainment	6	8	15	15	
Bosley, Tom	Entertainment	5	13	20	12	
Bosson, Barbara	Entertainment	5	5	10	20	
Bostic, Earl	Bandleader	15				Jazz Saxaphonist
Bostwick, Barry	Entertainment	6	8	15	20	
Bostwick, George	Aviation	10	25	40	30	ACE, WW II
Boswell, Connie	Entertainment	10	10	25	10	
Boswell, James	Author	750		4545		Biographer of Sam'l Johnson
Bosworth, Hobart 1867—1970	Entertainment	25	30	40	65	Films Actor from 1909-43
Botha, Louis	Head of State	60	110	95		S. Afr. Soldier, Statesman
Bottolfsen, C.A.	Governor	12		25	15	Governor ID
Bottome, Margaret	Author	15	45	100	25	Lecturer
Bottoms, Joseph	Entertainment	4	4	9	12	
Bottoms, Sam	Entertainment	6	8	15	12	
Bottoms, Timothy	Entertainment	7			15	
Boucher, Voucher	Military	5	25			
Boucicault, Dion	Entertainment	20	35	50	40	19th Cent. Am. Actor-Playwright
Bouck, William C.	Governor	15	25			Governor NY
Boudin, Eugene-Louis	Artist	105	280	575		Fr. Sea & Beach Scenes
Boudinot, Elias 1740-1821	Revolutionary War	240	1980	785		Washington's Att'y Gen.
Boudinot, Elias C. 1835-90	Civil War	95	250	1210		Cherokee Leader. Murdered
Boughton, Rutland 1876-19??	Composer					Opera, Etc. AMusQS $125
Boulanger, Nadia	Composer			115	375	Fr. Conductor, Teacher
Boulard, Georges	Aviation	15		60	35	
Boulez, Pierre	Composer	40	45	75	25	Fr. Composer-Conductor
Boulle, Pierre	Author	10	15	30	15	
Boult, Adrian, Sir	Conductor		45	100	75	Esteemed Br. Conductor
Boult, Sir Adrian	Composer	20		75	30	Noted Brit. Conductor
Bourbon-Parma, Zita 1892-1989	Royalty				450	Last Austrian Empress
Bourguiba, Habib	Head of State	15	40	100	25	Pres. Tunisia
Bourke-White, Margaret 1904-71	Artist	100		192		Special SP $770.Photo Essays Life Mag.
Bourmont, Louis A.V. 1773-1846	Fr. Military		80	160		General under Napoleon
Bourne, Francis, Cardinal	Clergy	35	45	60	40	
Bourrienne, L.A.F. de	Fr. Revolution	45	60	120		Pvt. Sec'y to Napoleon
Bouton, Chas. Marie	Artist	110	165	400		
Boutwell, George S.	Cabinet	15	45	150	40	Grant Sec'y Treasury
Bow, Clara 1905-1965	Entertainment	165	175	330	492	It Girl
Bowden, Doris	Entertainment	3	3	6	6	
Bowditch, Nathaniel 1773-1838	Science	100	310	610		Astronomer, Mathematician
Bowe, Rosemarie	Entertainment	4	4	9	10	
Bowen, Elizabeth	Author	25	75	170	30	Ir.-Br. Psychological Novelist

NAME	CATEGORY	SIG	LS/DS	ALS	SP	Comment
Bowen, George F., Sir	Head of State	10	25	35		Governor Australia, New Zealand
Bowen, Ira Sprague	Science	10	25	35	15	Dir. Mt.Wilson-Palomar Obs.
Bowen, John S. 1830-63	Civil War	110	245	450		CSA General.
Bowen, John Stevens (War Date)	Civil War	175	260	1265		CSA Gen.Early Prisoner
Bowen, Louise de Koven	Social Reformer	12	20			Pres. Hull House
Bowen, Otis	Cabinet	5	10			Sec'y Health & Human Services
Bowen, Thomas Meed	Civil War	45				Union General, Senator CO
Bower, Antoinette	Entertainment	3	3	6	8	
Bowers, George M.	Senate/Congress	10	20		10	MOC WV
Bowes, Major Edward	Entertainment	12	15	19	25	
Bowie, David	Entertainment	35			115	Rock
Bowie, James (Jim)	Military		15000			Co-Cmdr. Alamo. Bowie Knife
Bowie, Sydney J.	Senate/Congress	10	20	35		MOC AL
Bowker, Judi	Entertainment	10	8	16	22	
Bowler, Metcalf	Jurist	50	135	250		Opponent of The Stamp Act 1765
Bowles, Chester	Governor	10	25	85	40	Diplomat, Advertising Exec.
Bowlin, James B.	Senate/Congress	15	30	45		MOC MO
Bowman, Lee	Entertainment	10	20	25	25	
Boxcar Willie	Country Western	6	12		15	Singer
Boxer, Barbara	Congress	5			20	Sen. CA
Boxleitner, Bruce	Entertainment	8	9	19	35	
Boy George	Entertainment	15	30	45	50	
Boyd, Alan S.	Cabinet	4			10	Sec'y Trans., CEO Amtrak
Boyd, Belle	Western Outlaw	1025			9650	Confederate Spy
Boyd, Linn 1800-59	Congress	20	30	55		Repr. KY, Speaker of House
Boyd, Steven	Entertainment	25	29	70	70	
Boyd, William Hopalong Cassidy	Entertainment	150			315	
Boyer, Charles	Entertainment	30	40	75	95	Fr. Actor.Hollywood Screen Lover
Boyer, Jean-Pierre	Head of State	35	125			Pres. Haiti
Boyesen, Hjalmar H.	Author	15	35	70	20	
Boyington, Gregory 'Pappy 1912-88	Aviation	78	155	215	162	ACE WW II Marine, #4 US, CMH
Boyle, John J.	Artist	5	10	20		
Boyle, Kay	Author	20	75	150	30	Am. Short Story Writer, Novels
Boyle, Lara Flynn	Entertainment	20			50	
Boyle, Peter	Entertainment	6	8	15	15	
Boynton, Henry Van Ness	Civil War	45	80	165		Union Officer & MOH winner
Boze, Marie	Entertainment	15			50	Vintage Actress 1879
Brabazon-Moore, John T.	Aviation	25	60	85	50	1st Licensed. WW I Pilot
Bracken, Eddie	Entertainment	5	6	9	10	
Brackett, Charles	Entertainment	20			70	Producer. 2 Oscars as Screenwriter
Bradbury, James W. 1802-1901	Congress	12				Sen. ME
Bradbury, James Ware	Senate/Congress	20	25	40		Senator ME 1847
Bradbury, Norris E.	Science	15		25		
Bradbury, Ray	Author	30	155	275	45	Am. Sci-Fi Writer
Bradford, Augustus W. 1805-81	Civil War		85			Unionist Gov. MD
Bradford, Barbara P.	Author	5			10	
Bradford, William 1729-1808	Senate	125	350	590		Sen. RI 1793
Bradford, William 1755-1856	Cabinet		250			G. Washington Att'y Gen'l
Bradlee, Ben	Editor	18	30		45	Ed. Washington Post
Bradley, Bill	Senate/Congress	5	10		20	Sen. NJ., Pro. Basketball
Bradley, Ed	Entertainment	3	7	20	10	TV News
Bradley, James	Military	11	35	58		
Bradley, John H.	Military	35	95		50	Iwo Jima Flag Raiser FDC $200 S
Bradley, Joseph P. (SC)	Supreme Court	55	100	200		
Bradley, Kathleen	Entertainment	4			10	Price is Right Model
Bradley, Omar N. 1893-1981	Military	95	229	325	185	5 Star General WW II

NAME	CATEGORY	SIG	LS/DS	ALS	SP	Comment
Bradley, Tom	Political	6	15	30	15	Mayor Los Angeles
Bradna, Olympe	Entertainment	10	75		25	
Bradshaw, Tiny	Bandleader	10				
Bradstreet, John	Colonial	60	140	295		Br. Soldier. Ticonderoga
Brady, Alice	Entertainment	90		95	175	
Brady, Charles	Astronaut	5			10	
Brady, James B. 'Diamond Jim'	Business	185	340	715	385	Financier. TLS $3800
Brady, James S.	Celebrity	20	65		30	
Brady, Mathew B.	Photographer	275	1050	2300		Presidential & Civil War Photos
Brady, Pat	Entertainment	100			250	
Brady, Scott	Entertainment	12	15	25	35	
Brady, William A.	Entertainment	25			65	
Braga, Gaetano	Composer				312	Cello Music. 8 Operas
Braga, Sonia	Entertainment	10	15	30	30	
Bragg, Braxton (War Date)	Civil War	450		1363		CSA General
Bragg, Braxton 1817-76	Civil War	365	695	912	900	CSA General
Bragg, Edward Stuyvesant	Civil War	45	85	135		Union Gen., Statesman, MOC
Bragg, Thomas	Civil War	135	225			CSA Att'y General
Bragg, Wm. Henry, Sir	Science	45	95			Nobel Physics with son Wm. L.
Bragg, Wm. Lawrence, Sir	Science	48	85			Nobel Physics with father W.H.
Braham, John (Abraham) 1774-1856	Entertainment	15		100		Supreme Br. Opera, Concert Performer
Brahms, Johannes 1833-97	Composer	1000	1350	2919	4350	AMusQS $2,750-$12,500
Brailowsky, Alexander	Entertainment	53			85	Concert Pianist.. Chopin Specialist
Brainard, David	Explorer			125		Arctic Explorer/G.B.Grinnell
Braithwaite, Wm. Stanley	Author	35	120	235	45	
Bramesfeld, Heinrich	Military	10		25		Ger. Capt. of See. RK Winner
Branagh, Kenneth	Entertainment	20			50	Br. Actor
Branch, John 1782-1863	Cabinet	25	75	165		Sec'y Navy, Gov. NC, Gov. FL
Branch, Lawrence O. 1820-62	Civil War	180	405			CSA General
Branch, Lawrence O.(War Date)	Civil War	470		1060		CSA Gen. KIA 1862
Brand, Christopher Q., Sir	Aviation	75	150	300	200	ACE, WW I, Only night Ace
Brand, Harry	Entertainment	5			20	Motion Picture Producer
Brand, Max 1892-1944	Author	50				Destry..., Dr. Kildare
Brand, Neville	Entertainment	75			150	
Brand, Vance D.	Astronaut	10	40		195	Apollo Soyuz
Brandauer, Klaus Maria	Entertainment	15	15	30	40	
Brandegee, Augustus	Senate/Congress	15	35	200		Repr. CT. Civil War Member
Brandeis, Louis D. (SC)1856-1941	Supreme Court	150	615	777	1272	1st Jewish Supr. Ct. Judge
Brandenstein, Daniel	Astronaut	5			15	
Brando, Marlon	Entertainment	200	525	365	673	
Brandon, Henry	Entertainment	5			10	
Brandon, Michael	Entertainment	8				Actor
Brandt, Marianne	Entertainment	25		80	75	Opera
Brandt, Willy 1913-92	Head of State	25	175	210	85	Ger.Chanc. Nobel Peace Prize
Brangwyn, Frank 1867-1956	Artist			125		Br. Painter-Decorator
Branigan, Laura	Entertainment	10			30	
Branly, Edouard 1844-1940	Science		625	635	475	Fr. Physicist, Inventor
Brann, Louis J.	Governor	5	15		10	Gov. ME
Brannan, Charles F.	Cabinet	10	15		15	Sec'y Agriculture
Branzell, Karin	Entertainment	40			145	Opera
Braque, Georges	Artist	420	675	1225		Developed Cubism with Picasso
Brattain, Walter	Science	25	50	90	45	Nobel Physics. Transistor
Bratton, John, Dr. 1831-98	Civil War	95	317	390		CSA Gen.
Brauchitsch, Walter von	Military	75	155	210	125	Hitler Fld.Marshall
Braun, Eva	WWII Nazi	1000		2750		Hitler's Mistress-Wife
Braun, Wernher von	Science					see Von Braun

NAME	CATEGORY	SIG	LS/DS	ALS	SP	Comment
Brautigan, Richard	Author	45	150			Counter-Culture Classic
Braxton, Carter 1736-97	Revolutionary War	275	550	2167		Signer Decl. of Indepen.
Braxton, Toni	Entertainment	5			15	Pinup SP $60
Brayman, Mason	Civil War	30	78			Union General, Gov. Idaho
Brayton, Charles Ray	Civil War	40	65	100		Union General
Brazzi, Rossano 1916-95	Entertainment	8	9	19	75	Romantic Italian Actor
Brearley, David	Revolutionary War	375	800			Continental Congress
Breathed, Berke*	Cartoonist	20			175	Bloom County
Brecht, Bertolt	Author	400	1750	3100		Ger.-Jewish Playwright, Poet
Breckinridge, John Cabell 1821-75	Civil War & VP US	360	400	990		CSA Gen., Sec'y War, US Congr.
Breckinridge, Joseph Cabell	Military	25	40			1842-1920
Breckinridge, Wm. C.	Civil War	110	250	275		CSA Officer
Breeding, J. Floyd	Senate/Congress	5	15		10	MOC KS
Breen, Bobby	Entertainment	8	15	35	25	Child Singer.
Breese, Lou	Entertainment	15	40	45	70	Big band leader
Breese, Vance	Aviation	30	115		40	Aviator & Aircraft Designer
Brefoort, H. B.	Military	15	30			
Bremer, Lucille	Entertainment				25	Astaire Dancing Partner
Brendel, El 1890-1964	Entertainment	15	35		60	Stage & Film Comedy Roles
Breneman, Tom	Entertainment	15	15	30	25	
Brennan, Eileen	Entertainment	4	4	9	15	
Brennan, Francis J., Cardinal	Clergy	30	45	55	50	
Brennan, Walter 1894-1974	Entertainment	100	150	300	225	AA x 3
Brennan, William J., Jr. (SC)	Supreme Court	75	105	155	85	
Brennecke, Kurt	Military	15	35	60	35	
Brenner, Victor D. 1871-1924	Artist	295	240	675		Designer Lincoln Penny -V.D.B.
Brent, Charles H., Bishop	Clergy	25	40	55	40	
Brent, Evelyn	Entertainment	15	20	25	35	
Brent, George	Entertainment	25	30	35	60	
Brent, George Wm.	Civil War	100	210	300		
Brent, Joseph Lancaster	Civil War	90	145	345		CSA Colonel
Brent, Robert	Military	35	100	165		
Brereton, Lewis Hyde	Aviation	45	140		55	Cmdr. 1st Allied Airborne WW II
Bres, Edward S.	Military	10	30	50		
Breslau, Sophie	Entertainment	35			90	Opera
Breslin, Jimmy	Celebrities	5	15	40	10	Journalist, Novelist
Bresser-Gianoli, Clotilde	Entertainment	20			55	Opera
Breton, Andre	Author	60	175	325		Fr. Poet, Essayist, Critic
Brett, George H. 1886-	Military		125			Air Corps Gen. WW II
Brett, Jeremy 1935-95	Entertainment	20			195	Portrayed Sherlock Holmes
Breu, Paul	Aviation				25	Ger. Bomber Pilot. RK
Breuer, Marcel	Architect	20	60	125	150	Bauhaus School/Gropius
Brewer, David J. (SC)	Supreme Court	75	95	160		
Brewer, Teresa	Entertainment	3	3	10	15	Big Band Singer
Brewerton, Henry (d. 1879)	Civil War			125		Union Gen. Corps of Engineers
Brewster, Benjamin	Cabinet	10	35			Arthur Att'y General
Brewster, David, Sir 1781-1868	Science	30	55	180		Physicist. Invented Kaleidoscope
Brewster, Kingman Jr	Educator	5	15	25	15	Diplomat
Brewster, Ralph Owen	Senate	10	25	40	30	Senator, MOC ME
Breyer, Stephen	Supreme Court	20			40	
Brezhnev, Leonid I.	Head of State	375	975		400	Soviet Communist Party Leader
Brian, Mary	Entertainment	5	7	15	25	
Brice, Benjamin W.	Civil War	15	45			Union Paymaster General
Brice, Fanny 1891-1951	Entertainment	131	185	375	375	Stage, Radio, Film Top Comedienne
Brickell, Edie	Entertainment	7			30	
Bricker, John W.	Senate	15	30		20	Gov. Ohio

The Sanders Price Guide to Autographs

NAME	CATEGORY	SIG	LS/DS	ALS	SP	Comment
Brico, Antonia, Dr.	Conductor	15			75	Eccentric Female Conductor
Bridges, Beau	Entertainment	5	6	15	20	
Bridges, H. Styles	Senate	7	15		10	Senator NH
Bridges, Harry	Labor Leader	70	180		140	Pres. Longshoreman Union
Bridges, Jeff	Entertainment	5	6	15	25	
Bridges, Lloyd	Entertainment	5	6	15	15	
Bridges, Robert 1844-1930	Author	15				Poet Laureate England
Bridges, Roy D. Jr.	Astronaut	7			25	
Bridges, Todd	Entertainment	15			40	Troubled child actor
Bridgman, Laura D.	Celebrity	110		235		Blind, Deaf, Mute
Bridy, Pat	Cartoonist			25		Rose is Rose
Briggs, Austin*	Cartoonist	25			200	Flash Gordon
Briggs, Charles F.	Author	15	40	125		Editor NY Times
Briggs, Claire	Cartoonist	15			50	Mr. & Mrs.
Briggs, James E.	Military	10	25	50	20	
Briggs, Le Baron Russell 1855-1934	Educator	4		18		Legendary Harvard Professor
Briggs, Roxanne Dawson	Entertainment	10			20	Actress, Star Trek
Brigham, Louis S.	Business	10	35	45	20	
Bright, John	Statesman	35	50	155		Radical Br. Orator.(Corn Laws)
Brightman, Sarah	Entertainment	15			50	Star Andrew Lloyd Weber's Musicals
Brigitte, Simone	Entertainment				20	Model-Actress
Brimmer, Andrew F.	Government	10	15		12	Afro-Am. Gov. Fed. Res. Board
Brinegar, Paul	Entertainment	10	15	20	25	
Brinkley, Christie	Entertainment	10	15	25	45	
Brinkley, David	Entertainment	5			15	News Anchor-Commentator
Brinley, Wilford	Entertainment	5			20	
Brinson, Samuel Mitchell	Senate/Congress	10	20	45		MOC NC
Brisbane, Arthur	Author	15	35	100	30	Influential Editorial Writer
Brisebois, Danielle	Entertainment	3	3	6	6	
Brissette, Tiffany	Entertainment				10	Child Actress
Brisson, Carl	Entertainment	15	15	25	15	Danish Actor
Bristol, Mark	Military	20	25			Admiral WW I
Bristow, Benjamin Helm 1832-96	Cabinet	20	65	110		Civil War Commanded 25th KY
Britt, Mai	Entertainment	10			25	
Britt, Maurice L., Capt.1912-84	Military	22	35			WW II Hero CMH & Football Star
Brittany, Morgan	Entertainment	10	15	25	30	
Britten, Benjamin 1913-76	Composer	115	390	512	195	Br. Conductor
Britton, Pamela	Entertainment	12			15	Actress
Britton, Barbara	Entertainment	6	8	15	25	
Britton, Sherry	Entertainment	5	6	15	15	
Brix, Herman	Entertainment	10	12	15	20	SEE Bruce Bennett
Broadhead, James Overton	Law	25		65		Att'y Friend of Lincoln
Broca, Paul 1824-1880	Science	110		917		Fr. Pathologist, Surgeon, Anthropologist
Broccoli, Cubby	Entertainment	10	15	20	25	Film director
Brochler, Jan	Entertainment	10			35	Opera, Dutch Baritone
Brock, William	Clergy	15	25	40	25	
Brock, William G. Sen.	Business	20	70	125	40	
Broderick, Helen	Entertainment	25			70	
Broderick, Matthew	Entertainment	9	10	20	35	
Brodhead, James E.	Entertainment	5	6	15	15	
Brodhead, Richard	Senator	15	35	75		Senator from PA
Brodie, Benjamin C.	Science		60	90		Br. Orthopedic Surgeon
Brodie, Steve 1856-1901	Entertainment	100				World Champion. Jumped off Brooklyn Bridge
Brody, Lane	Entertainment	4			10	
Broglie, Duke A-C-L-V	Statesman	135	270	540		Fr. Politician. Author
Broglie, Louis Victor de 1892-1987	Science	20	55	105	345	Nobel Physics

NAME	CATEGORY	SIG	LS/DS	ALS	SP	Comment
Brokow, Tom	Entertainment	5	12	25	15	TV News Anchor-Commentator
Brolin, James	Entertainment	15	15	30	25	
Bromberg, J. Edward	Entertainment	30			65	
Bromfield, John	Entertainment	8			15	
Bromfield, Louis	Author	35	75	170	65	Am. Novelist. Pulitzer
Bronk, Detlev W.	Science	10	22	40	20	Pres. Nat'l Adademy of Sci.
Bronson, Betty	Entertainment	35			75	
Bronson, Charles	Entertainment	10	15	25	37	
Bronson, David 1800-63	Congress	10				Repr. ME, Collector Customs
Bronte, Charlotte	Author			8250		Br. Novelist. Jane Eyre
Brook, Alexander	Artist	25	40	75		
Brook, Clive 1887-1974	Entertainment	40	55	75	92	Br.Actor. 1st Talky Sherlock Holmes
Brooke, Alan, Fld Marshal, Sir	Military	40	110	205	75	Cmdr. Br.II Corps WW II,Dunkirk
Brooke, Edward W.	Senate	10	15		25	Senator MA
Brooke, Hilary	Entertainment	10	15	25	25	
Brooke, John Rutter 1838-1926	Civil War	45	65	193		Union Gen.
Brooke, Rupert	Author	450	550	1045		Br. Poet
Brooke-Popham, Robert	Military	30	65	95	50	Br. Air Chief Marshal WW II
Brookhart, Smith W.	Senate	10	15		15	Senator IA
Brooks, A. Raymond	Aviation	35	60	90	75	Bi-Plane ACE, WW I
Brooks, Albert	Entertainment	5			10	
Brooks, Angie	Stateswoman	12				Pres. U.N. Assembly
Brooks, Arthur	Aviation	15		30	35	
Brooks, Avery	Entertainment	30			100	Star Trek
Brooks, Diok*	Cartoonist	5			35	Jackson Twins
Brooks, Foster	Entertainment	5	6	15	10	
Brooks, Fred Emerson	Author	10	15	35		Poet
Brooks, Garth	Country Western	15			55	
Brooks, Gwendolyn	Author	20	40		25	Afro-Am. Poet
Brooks, James L.	Entertainment	10			20	
Brooks, John	Military	55	125	275		Am. Revolution Gen., Gov. MA
Brooks, Leslie	Entertainment	10	12	15	15	
Brooks, Louise 1906-1985	Entertainment	150	612	425	595	One of the Screen's Great Beauties
Brooks, Mel	Entertainment	10	30	25	22	Actor-Comedian. Director AA
Brooks, Peter H.	Clergy	15	25	35		
Brooks, Phillips 1835-93	Clergy-Author	58	120	130	75	O Little Town of Bethlehem
Brooks, Rand	Entertainment	10	15	30	35	GWTW
Brooks, Randi	Entertainment	6	8	15	15	
Brooks, Richard	Entertainment	20	30		60	AA Film Director
Brooks, Wm. Thos. H.	Civil War	42	65	105		Union Gen. ALS '64 $245
Broom, Jacob	Revolutionary War	350	900	2000		Continental Congress
Broomall, John M.	Senate/Congress	10	15	40		MOC DE 1863. CW Officer
Brophy, Ed	Entertainment	25				Character Actor
Brophy, Kevin	Entertainment	3	3	6	9	
Brophy, Theodore F.	Business	4	5		10	CEO GTE
Brosnan, Pierce	Entertainment	25	40	50	72	Newest James Bond
Brothers, Joyce	Science	4	10	25	10	Early TV Psychiatrist
Brough, Candi & Randi	Entertainment	10			25	
Brough, Fanny	Entertainment	4	4	9	10	
Brough, Lionel	Entertainment	4	4	9	10	
Brougham, Henry, Lord 1778-1868	Statesman	95	115	271		Attr. One Horse Brougham. Author
Brougham, John	Entertainment	12			30	Am. Actor-Playwright
Broughton, Joseph M.	Senate/Congress	5	12		10	Senator/MOC NC
Broun, Heywood 1888-1939	Author	10	35	70	15	Journalist, Novelist, Columnist
Browder, Earl	Political	15	35	65	20	US Communist Party Leader
Brown, A. Roy	Aviation WWI	250				Can. Ace. Downed Richtofen

The Sanders Price Guide to Autographs

NAME	CATEGORY	SIG	LS/DS	ALS	SP	Comment
Brown, Aaron V. 1795-1859	Cabinet	45	125			PMG, Repr.& Sen. TN
Brown, Albert Gallatin	Governor	45	60	90		CSA Senator, Gov. Miss.
Brown, Alice	Author	15	35	100		Prolific Novelist, Poet
Brown, Arthur Whitten	Aviation	300	395	575	575	Alcock & Brown
Brown, Benjamin Gratz 1826-85	Congress	15				Sen. MO
Brown, Blair	Entertainment	6	8	15	15	
Brown, Bo	Cartoonist	5			20	Magazine Cartoonist
Brown, Bothwell	Entertainment	10	15	25	25	
Brown, Charles Brockden 1771-1810	Author	975		6500		Father of the American Novel
Brown, Clarence	Entertainment	10			25	
Brown, Curt	Astronaut	7			15	
Brown, David	Entertainment	10			20	Producer. Oscar Winner
Brown, Down Town Julie	Entertainment	5			15	TV Host
Brown, Edmund G. 'Jerry'	Governor	10	25		20	Governor CA, Pres. Candidate
Brown, Edmund G. 'Pat'	Governor	10	25		20	Governor CA
Brown, Edward N.	Business	15				RR Exec.
Brown, George	Military	25				
Brown, George Stan	Entertainment	6			15	Afr.-Am Actor
Brown, Harold, Dr.	Science-Cabinet	10	20		15	Sec'y Defense
Brown, Harry Joe	Entertainment	25	40	65		Film Producer, Director
Brown, Helen Gurley	Author	5	10	20	10	Editor, Publisher
Brown, Henry B. (SC)	Supreme Court	50	175	250		
Brown, Henry W.	Aviation	12	25	42	32	ACE, WW II
Brown, Herbert C., Dr.	Science	25	30	45	35	Nobel Chemistry
Brown, Jacob	Military	50	135			Gen. War 1812
Brown, James	Entertainment	40			75	Rock. Alb. S $70
Brown, James	Entertainment	5			15	Actor
Brown, Jim Ed	Country Music	5			15	
Brown, Joe E. 1892-1973	Entertainment	35	50	40	75	Vintage Film Comedian
Brown, John 1800-1859	Civil War	775	2225	8500	2530	Abolitionist-Hung for treason
Brown, John Calvin 1827-89	Civil War	110	165	350		CSA Gen. Sig/Rank $200
Brown, John George	Artist	10	30	45		
Brown, John Y.	Business	10	25	51	19	
Brown, Johnny Mack	Entertainment	50	75		125	Cowboy Actor
Brown, Joseph Emerson	Civil War	45	60	85		Civil War Gov. Georgia
Brown, Julie	Entertainment	4			10	Singer
Brown, Les	Entertainment	15			35	Big Band Leader
Brown, Lt. John	Revolutionary War	72	175	400		
Brown, Mark N.	Astronaut	5			15	
Brown, Moses	Revolutionary War	45		265		Naval Commander
Brown, Nicholas 1729-91	Revolutionary War	35	80	195		Supplied Army. Brown University
Brown, Norma	Military	10	20	30	15	
Brown, Norman	Entertainment	4			10	
Brown, Phyllis George	Entertainment	5	8	20	15	
Brown, Prentiss M.	Senate	10	25		15	Senator MI
Brown, Preston	Military	22	35		45	General WW I. Chief of Staff
Brown, Robert	Military	20		75	125	General WW I
Brown, Robert	Science	135		775		Scot. Living Cells Nucleus
Brown, Ron 19xx-96	Cabinet	15	40		60	Clinton Cabinet.Tragic Plane Crash
Brown, Ruth	Entertainment	20			45	Rock & Roll HOF
Brown, Sam J.	Aviation	18	40	55	45	ACE, WW II
Brown, Tom	Entertainment	10	15	25	25	
Brown, William Wallace	Congress	10	15	30		Repr. PA. CW Officer
Brown-Sequard, Chas. E. 1817-94	Science			488		Fr. Physician.Father of Endocrinology
Browne, Charles Farrar						SEE Ward, Artemus
Browne, Chris*	Cartoonist	20			75	Hagar

The Sanders Price Guide to Autographs

NAME	CATEGORY	SIG	LS/DS	ALS	SP	Comment
Browne, Coral	Entertainment	10	15	18	25	
Browne, Dik*	Cartoonist	20			60	Hi & Lois, Hagar
Browne, Hablot Knight	Artist	25	90	150		Watercolor. Illustrator Dickens
Browne, Jackson	Entertainment	20			55	Rock
Browne, Leslie	Entertainment	5	7	12	10	
Brown, Reno	Entertainment	15			50	Early westerns actress
Brownell, Herbert Jr.	Cabinet	10	18	40	125	Att'y Gen., Eisenhower
Browning, Eliz. Barrett	Author	400	1085	2750	2500	
Browning, George	Business	195	580			Browning Arms Mfg.
Browning, John B.	Business	50	160		75	Pres. Browning Arms Co.
Browning, John Moses	Inventor-Business	195	1200	575		Inventor, Designer of Fire Arms
Browning, Orville H. 1806-81	Cabinet	25	125			Sec'y of Interior, Sen.IL
Browning, Ricou	Entertainment	15			40	Creature, Olympic Swimmer
Browning, Robert 1812-89	Author	240	470	1025	1150	Br. Poet. AMsS $3250
Browning, Tod	Entertainment	75			250	
Brownlee, John	Entertainment	10		45	30	Opera, Australian/Am. Baritone
Brubeck, Dave	Entertainment	10	15	25	25	Jazz
Bruce, Andrew D. 1894-	Military	35	200			Gen. 77th Infantry Div. So. Pacific
Bruce, Blanche K.	Senator	350	600			1st Afro-Am.Full Term Senator
Bruce, Carol	Entertainment	5	5	10	30	Vocalist. Content ALS $95
Bruce, David	Entertainment	10			20	
Bruce, Lenny 1926-66	Entertainment	450	675		1200	ALS/Typescript Archive $5750
Bruce, Nigel 1895-1953	Entertainment	150	175	300	310	Noted for Dr. Watson. Caricature S $250
Bruce, Thos.(7th Earl Elgin)	Diplomat	50	190	340		Conveyed Elgin Marbles
Bruce, Virginia	Entertainment	15			25	
Bruce, Wallace	Author	35		120		
Bruce, Wm. Cabell 1860-1946	Congress	7	15	30	15	Sen. MD, Aut;hor
Bruch, Max 1838-1920	Composer	90	200	475	95	Ger. Opera,AMusQS $1,100-2,500
Bruckner, Josef Anton	Composer	1200	2750	5500	2500	Aus. 10 Symphonies.
Brummel, Geo. B. 'Beau'1778-1840	Dandy	90	220	750		Br. Man of Fashion
Brummer, Renate	Astronaut	5			20	Germany
Bruna Rasa, Lina	Entertainment	65			350	Opera
Brune, G.M.A. 1763-1815	Napoleonic Wars	85	350	450		Marshal of Nap. Assassinated
Brunel, Marc Isambard, Sir	Science	70	145	315		Fr.-Br.Inventor, Engineer
Brunet, Isambard Kingdom	Science	40	145	325		Br. Engineer, Broad Gauge RR
Bruning, Heinrich 1885-1971	Head of State			100	425	Ger. Chancellor. Fled to U.S. '34
Brunner, Emil	Clergy	45	75	110	50	
Bruscantini, Sesto	Entertainment	10			25	Opera
Bruson, Renato	Entertainment	10			30	Opera
Bry, Ellen	Entertainment	3	3	6	6	
Bryan, Charles W.	Governor	12	27			Governor NE
Bryan, George	Revolutionary War	120	350	750		Jurist. Proposed Abolition 1777
Bryan, Goode	Civil War	140		440		CSA Gen.
Bryan, Jane	Entertainment	5	10	20	15	
Bryan, William E.	Aviation	10	22	38	28	ACE, WW II
Bryan, William Jennings 1860-1925	Cabinet	125	372	375	575	Nominated 3 Times for Presidency
Bryant, Alys McKey	Aviation	35	60	140	75	
Bryant, Anita	Entertainment	5	50	10	10	Controversial Singer
Bryant, William Cullen 1794-1878	Author	67	325	461	750	Am. Poet, ALS/Content $1,750
Brynner, Yul 1915-85	Entertainment	50	50	70	142	AA
Buber, Martin	Clergy	75	175	250	90	
Buchan, John, Lord	Author	20	185			Gov. Gen. Canada, Novelist
Buchanan, Edgar	Entertainment	30	40	55	75	
Buchanan, Franklin 1800-74	Civil War	160	495	388		CSA Admiral
Buchanan, James 1791-1868	President	356	858	1632	750	Special SP $12,500
Buchanan, James M.	Economics	35	45	85	40	Nobel Economics

The Sanders Price Guide to Autographs

NAME	CATEGORY	SIG	LS/DS	ALS	SP	Comment
Buchanan, Patrick	Political	12	15		125	Political Commentator
Bucher, Lloyd M.	Military	35	90	150	90	Captured Capt. of USS Pueblo
Buchli, James F.	Astronaut	5	15		25	
Buchman, Franklin	Clergy	20	35	65		
Buchwald, Art	Author	10	15	25	15	Syndicated Humor Column
Buck, Clayton Douglass	Senate	11	15	25	20	Senator-Governor DE
Buck, Dudley 1839-1909	Composer	10				Organist
Buck, Frank	Big Game Hunter	50	80	145	85	Bring 'Em Back Alive
Buck, Paul H.	Author	4	10	15	5	
Buck, Pearl S. 1892-1973	Author	40	145	198	50	Am. Novelist. Nobel, Pulitzer
Buckingham, Catharinus P. 1808-88	Civil War	30		95		Union Gen. LS '62 $745
Buckingham, William A.	Governor	40	65	140		Civil War Gov. CT.
Buckland, Ralph P. (War Date)	Civil War	130		250		Union Gen.
Buckle, Henry Thomas	Author	5	10	25		
Buckley, James	Senate/Congress	6	15		10	
Buckley, William F., Jr.	Author	7	15	45	20	National Revue, Conservative Journalist
Buckner, Simon Bolivar (War Date)	Civil War	450	2500	4608		CSA General
Buckner, Simon Bolivar 1823-1914	Civil War	225	275	375	295	CSA Gen.
Buckstone, John B. 1802-79	Entertainment	5		25		Br. Actor, Comedian, Playwright
Budd, Julie	Entertainment	3	3	6	6	
Buell, Don Carlos 1818-98	Civil War	88	155	251	150	Union Gen. ADS '62 $400
Buffalo Bill Jr.	Entertainment	25			50	
Buffett, Jimmy	Entertainment	10			35	Rock
Buffington, Thomas Mitchell	Old West	350	550			Chief of Cherokee Nations
Buford, Abraham	Civil War	125	234	789		CSA Gen. 1990 Price Averages
Buford, John 1826-63	Civil War	300	2090			Union Gen.Sig/Rank $400 (1993)
Buford, Napoleon Bonaparte	Civil War	65	145	375		Union Gen. ALS '62 $320
Bugliosi, Vince	Legal	16				Manson Trial Att'y
Buhari, Mohammed	Head of State	15	50	130	25	
Buick, David D.	Business	170	675	885	275	Buick Motor Co.
Bujold, Genevieve	Entertainment	6	8	15	20	
Bulfinch, Charles	Architect	130	375			Fanueil Hall, Completed WH
Bulfinch, Thomas	Author	20	45	100		Bulfinch's Mythology
Bulkley, John D.	Military	20	65		35	Adm. USN WW II
Bull II, William	Governor	55	80			Governor SC
Bull, John S.	Astronaut	15			25	
Bull, Ole B.	Composer	15		125	125	Nor. Violin Virtuoso
Bull, William, II	Governor	60		240		Governor SC 1760
Bullard, Robert Lee	Military	20	75	130	100	General WW I
Bullard, William	Military	15	35			Admiral WW I
Buller, Redvers, Sir	Military	40	110	250	45	Cmdr-in-Chief South Africa
Bullet Boys (4)	Entertainment	10			40	
Bullitt, William P.	Diplomat	10	20		25	Ambassador To USSR
Bulloch, Terrence	Aviation	20			35	Br. Aviator WWII
Bullock, Sandra	Entertainment	15			60	Actress
Bullock, Walter	Author	3	4	7	5	
Bulow, Bernhard H.M.K. von	Head of State	15	35	90	40	Prussian Imperial Chancellor
Bultmann, Rudolph	Clergy	70	90	165	80	
Bulwer, Elizabeth	Author			25		
Bulwer, Wm. Henry Lytton 1801-72	Diplomat	15	40	75		Clayton-Bulwer Treaty. US & Eng
Bulwer-Lytton, Edward	Author	60	220	460		
Bumbry, Grace	Entertainment	10	15		55	Opera
Bumpers, Dale	Governor	12	15		20	Senator AR
Bunce, Francis M.	Military	25	55	125	65	Admiral Spanish-American War
Bunche, Ralph J. 1904-71	Diplomat	50	130	225	125	Nobel Peace Prize
Bundy, McGeorge	Law	20	35	45	25	Director FBI

NAME	CATEGORY	SIG	LS/DS	ALS	SP	Comment
Bundy, Omar	Military	35	90		55	General WW I
Bunner, Henry C. 1855-96	Journalist	65	70	135		Editor Puck Magazine
Bunny, John	Entertainment	100	130	160	200	
Bunsen, Christian K.J., Baron	Diplomat	15	45	110		Prussian Theologian, Scholar
Bunsen, Robert W. 1811-99	Science	175	480	1019	1380	Ger. Chemist, Bunsen Burner
Bunting, Mary	Celebrity	10	28		15	
Bunting, William M.	Clergy	49	100	150		
Buntline, Ned 1823-86	Author	140	185	250	912	Novelist,Adventurer,Dime Novel
Buono, Sonny	Entertainment	5	10		20	
Buono, Victor	Entertainment	30			100	
Burbank, Luther 1849-1926	Science	115	275	298	165	Pioneer, Experimental Botanist
Burder, George	Clergy	10	15	20	15	
Burdette, Robert J.	Author	20	55	135	40	
Burge, V.L.	Aviation	18			35	
Burger, Warren E. (SC)	Supreme Court	50	175	195	75	Chief Justice
Burgess, Anthony b.1917	Author	40	55		150	Br. Novelist.Clockwork Orange
Burgess, Thomas, Bishop	Clergy	15	25	35		
Burgess, Thornton W.	Author	30	100	225		Peter Rabbit
Burghley, Wm. Cecil, Lord	Head of State	1725				Elizabeth I, Tudor Statesman
Burghoff, Gary	Entertainment	10			40	
Burgoyne, John 1722-92	Revolutionary War	1100	2850	4050		Br. Gen. vs Am. Colonies
Burke, Arleigh 1901-1996	Military	35	60	110	100	Adm. USN WW II
Burke, Billie (Ziegfield)1885-1970	Entertainment	150	203	187	270	Wizard of Oz
Burke, Delta	Entertainment	10	15	25	30	
Burke, Edmund	Senate/Congress	5	12	20		MOC NH
Burke, Edward A.	Celebrity	45			150	
Burke, Paul	Entertainment	5	6	15	15	
Burke, Selma	Artist	10	20	75	15	
Burke, Yvonne B.	Congress	10			20	Afro-Am 3 Term Repr CA
Burleigh, Harry Thacker	Composer	25		150		AMusQS $200, Spirituals
Burleigh, Walter A. 1820-96	Congress	10				Delegate from Dakota Terr.
Burleson, Albert S.	Cabinet	10	25	35		P.M. General, MOC TX
Burleson, OmarTruman	Senate/Congress	5	15		10	MOC TX
Burmester, Willy	Entertainment	90		275		Ger. Violinist. AMusQS $350
Burne-Jones, Edward 1833-98	Artist	125	235	455		Pre-Raphaelite Painter,Designer
Burnet, David G. 1788-1870	Head of State	275	635	1200		1st Pres. Republic TX
Burnet, William 1688-1728	Colonial	145	465			Br. Gov. NY & NJ
Burnett, Carol	Entertainment	5	6	15	20	
Burnett, Frances Hodgson 1849-1924	Author	50	145	285		Little Lord Fauntleroy
Burnett, Leo	Business	5	10	25	10	Advertising
Burnett, Peter H.	Governor	200		550		California Pioneer & 1st Gov.
Burnette, Smiley	Entertainment	40	50		75	
Burney, Cecil, Sir	Military	15	35			Br. Adm. WW I
Burnham, Hiram	Civil War	60	195			Union Gen.
Burns & Allen	Entertainment	160			200	
Burns, Bob	Entertainment	25	25	45	45	Bazooka
Burns, Edmund	Entertainment	30			75	Silent Screen Star
Burns, Geo. & Gracie Allen		272			372	
Burns, George 1896-1996	Entertainment	20		50	57	
Burns, James MacGregor	Author	20	30			Educator, Political Science
Burns, John 1791-1872	Civil War	350			1250	Vet. War 1812. Vol. Gettysburg
Burns, John A.	Governor	12	15		15	Hawaii
Burns, Ken	Entertainment	5			15	Documentary Film Maker
Burns, Robert 1759-96	Author	500	1450	3650		Scottish Poet
Burns, William Chalmers	Clergy	25	40	50	35	
Burns, William J.	Business	35	10	175		Chief FBI 1921-24, Det. Agency

NAME	CATEGORY	SIG	LS/DS	ALS	SP	Comment
Burns, William Wallace	Civil War	35	75	95	150	Union General
Burnside, Ambrose E. (War Date)	Civil War	145	389	569	725	Union Gen. ALS $2,500
Burnside, Ambrose E.1824-81	Civil War	115	275	324	650	ALS war date $2,500
Burpee, David	Business	25	35	70	35	Burpee Seed Co.
Burpee, Jonathan	Business	10	25	50	20	Burpee Seed Co.
Burr, Aaron (V) 1756-1836	Vice President	330	856	1495		ALS's/Content $7,000-12,000+
Burr, Raymond 1917-93	Entertainment	20	38	30	65	
Burritt, Elihu 1810-79	Am. Linguist	20		125		Peace Advocate. AQS $150
Burroughs, Edgar Rice 1875-1950	Author	250	448	675	625	Tarzan. TLS/Cont. $1900
Burroughs, John	Governor	10		25	15	Governor NM
Burroughs, John 1837-1921	Author	50	100	200	525	Am. Naturalist, Philosopher
Burroughs, Sherman Everett	Senate/Congress	5	15	30	10	MOC NH
Burrows, Abe	Author	10	15	25	20	Playwright, Pulitzer
Burrows, J. C.	Senate	10		25		Senator MI
Bursch, Daniel	Astronaut	7			15	
Burstyn, Ellen	Entertainment	10	8	15	25	
Bursum, Holm Olaf	Senate	5	15	25		Senator NM
Burton, Charlotte	Entertainment	8	9	12	15	
Burton, Harold H. (SC) 1888-1964	Supreme Court	40	170	325	85	
Burton, Isabel, Lady	Author	25	85	180		
Burton, LeVar	Entertainment	6	8	10	15	
Burton, Richard	Entertainment	100	300		231	
Burton, Richard F., Sir 1821-90	Explorer	150	275	1350		Orientalist, Linguist, Author
Burton, Theodore E.	Senate/Congress	7	10	35		Senator, MOC OH
Burton, Tim	Entertainment	15			50	Film Director
Busby, George Henry	Governor	11	15			Governor GA
Buscalia, Leo	Author	16	25	40	20	Educator, Author, Lecturer
Busch, Adolphus	Business	55		225		Anheuser-Busch.TLS $5800
Busch, August A.	Business	25	90	175	50	Anheuser-Busch Brewery
Busch, Fritz	Entertainment	45		135	250	Ger. Conductor
Busch, Niven	Author	12		25		Dramatist, Screenwriter
Busch, Wilhelm 1832-1908	Artist			1400		Painter & Poet.
Busell, Darcey	Entertainment	15			40	Ballet
Busey, Gary	Entertainment	6	8	15	20	
Bush, Barbara	First Lady	58	145		100	
Bush, George (As President)	President	160	613	1230	400	W. H. Cd. S $500,President'l Cd. $950
Bush, George 1924-	President		335	828		
Bush, George W.	Business	4			10	Baseball Exec.
Bush, Irving T.	Business		35			Owned Largest Shipping Terminal
Bush, Owen	Entertainment	4			8	Character Actor
Bush, Prescott	Senate	25	75		90	Senator CT
Bush, Vannevar 1890-1974	Science	58	180	255	125	Pioneer In Analog Computers.Atom Bomb
Bushkin, Joe	Entertainment	6	8	10	12	
Bushman, Francis X.	Entertainment	42	75	110	100	Silent Star of Ben Hur
Bushmiller, Ernie*	Cartoonist	20			125	Nancy
Bushnell, David 1742?	Science	250	750	1250		Invented 1st Submarine
Bushnell, Horace 1802-76	Clergy	25	35	45		New Engl.Congregational Minister
Bushyhead, D.W.	Celebrity	200		1500		
Busoni, Ferruccio 1899-1924	Composer	120		340	425	Pianist, AMusQS $175-$650
Busse, Henry	Entertainment	20			50	Big Band Leader
Bustamante, Jose Luis	Celebrity	9	35	60		
Butcher, Susan	Ididorod	5	10		15	Dog Breeder
Bute, John Stuart	Royalty	85	130			Earl of Bute
Butenandt, Adolf F.J.	Science	20	30	45	25	Nobel Chemistry
Buthelezi, Gatsha Mangosuthu	Head of State	20			35	Chief of Zulu Nation
Butler, B.F. 1795-1858	Cabinet			150		PMG for Jackson

NAME	CATEGORY	SIG	LS/DS	ALS	SP	Comment
Butler, Benjamin F. 1818-93	Civil War	185	355	229		Union Gen., LS '62 $2750
Butler, Carl & Pearl	Country Music	15			30	
Butler, Daws	Entertainment	15	15	20	40	
Butler, Dean	Entertainment	5	8	12	15	
Butler, Ellis Parker 1869-1937	Author	10	60	92	40	Pigs is Pigs
Butler, John	Clergy	10	15	20	20	
Butler, John	Revolutionary War	75	185	375		Am. Loyalist.Butler's Rangers
Butler, Matthew C. (War Date)	Civil War	155	345	670		CSA General
Butler, Matthew C. 1836-1909	Civil War	90	170	285		CSA General, US Sen. SC
Butler, Nicholas Murray	Educator	12	35	90	30	Nobel Peace Prize
Butler, Pierce (SC)	Supreme Court	35	90	275	45	
Butler, Pierce 1744-1822	Revolutionary War	60	180	385		Signer of Constitution
Butler, Samuel 1835-1902	Author	20	60	125		Br. Author, Artist, Musician
Butler, Smedley D.	Military	15	35	75	35	Marine Corps Gen/2 CMH
Butler, Thomas S.	Senate/Congress	5	15			MOC PA
Butler, Walter 1752-81	Revolutionary War		550	675		Captured,escaped. Butler's Rangers
Butler, William Orlando	Military	45	210			Hero Battle of New Orleans
Butler, Zebulon	Military	70	200			Col. Revolutionary War
Butt Rumford, Clara	Entertainment	35			150	Opera
Buttafuco, Joey	Celebrity	12				
Butterfield, Billy	Entertainment	25			45	Jazz Trumpet, Bandleader
Butterfield, Daniel (War Date)	Civil War	150	260	315	450	Union General .Composed TAPS
Butterfield, Daniel 1831-1901	Civil War	70	675	240		Union Gen. Composed Taps
Butterworth, Charles	Entertainment					
Buttlar-Brandenfels, F.H.	Military	5	15	25	15	
Buttons, Red	Entertainment	5	7	15	40	
Buttram, Pat	Entertainment	20	95		45	Gene Autry Movie Sidekick
Buttrick, George A.	Clergy	25	45	75	45	
Butts, Alfred M.	Inventor	35	50			Scrabble
Butz, Earl L.	Cabinet	6	18	30	15	Sec'y Agriculture
Buzzi, Ruth	Entertainment	3	6	10	15	
Byers, Samuel Hawkins	Author	25	40	60		Union Soldier-Author
Byington, Spring	Entertainment	20			55	
Byner, John	Entertainment	3	3	6	8	
Byng, Geo. Viscount Torrington	Military	25	75			Br. Adm.Destroyed Sp.Fleet 1719
Byrd, Charlie	Entertainment	15			25	Jazz Guitar
Byrd, Harry F. Byrd, Sr.	Governor	25				Gov. VA
Byrd, Harry F., Jr.	Senate	10	25		25	Senator VA
Byrd, Jerry	Country Music	10			20	
Byrd, Ralph	Entertainment	100	150		350	
Byrd, Richard E. 1888-1957	Aviation-Explorer	70	335	560	375	Adm. USN, Polar Expl.
Byrd, Robert C.	Senate	15	30	100	25	Senator WV
Byrds, The (Entire Group)	Entertainment					Rock. Alb S $120
Byrne, Bobby	Entertainment	20			70	Big band leader
Byrne, Jane	Politician	5	10	28	10	Mayor
Byrnes, Edd	Entertainment	5			15	
Byrnes, James F. (SC)	Supreme Court	30	125	235	55	
Byrns, Joseph Wellington	Senate/Congress	15	25		20	MOC TN
Byron, Arthur	Entertainment	15	15	20	35	
Byron, Geo. Gordon, Lord 1788-1824	Author	1638	2750	8950		Influential, Romantic Br. Poet
Byron, Jean	Entertainment	5			15	

NAME	CATEGORY	SIG	LS/DS	ALS	SP	Comment

NAME	CATEGORY	SIG	LS/DS	ALS	SP	Comment
Caan, James	Entertainment	11	8	15	35	
Cabana, Robert D.	Astronaut	6			20	
Cabell, Earle	Mayor	10				Dallas JFK Assassination TLS $475
Cabell, James Branch 1879-1958	Author	30	120	165		Novels Attacked for Immorality
Cabell, William L.	Civil War	175	405			CSA General
Cable, George Washington 1844-1925	Author	35	50	75	45	CSA Soldier, Short Story Writer
Cabot, Bruce 1904-72	Entertainment	50	55	90	150	John Wayne Sidekick
Cabot, George 1751-1823	Congress		45	100		Sen. MA.Ratified US Constitution
Cabot, Sebastian	Entertainment	25	30	90	75	
Caceres, Andreas A.	Head of State	10	25	65	20	Peru
Cadbury, George	Business	35		170	50	Cadbury Chocolate Mfg.
Cadbury, Richard	Business	30	45	160	50	Cadbury Chocolate Mfg.
Cade, Robert, Dr.	Business	10	15		10	Inventor of Gatorade
Cadman, Chas. Wakefield	Composer	60	215	360	100	AMusQS $195
Cadman, S. Parkes	Clergy	20	35	50	35	
Cadmus, Paul	Artist	36	85	120		
Cadwalader, George	Civil War	50	110	160		Union Gen. LS '63 385
Cadwalader, Lambert	Revolutionary War	55	140	335		Continental Congress
Cady, Daniel	Congress	20	35	50		MOC NY 1815
Caesar, Irving	Composer	26	55	125	45	Lyricist (Tea for Two)
Caesar, Sid	Entertainment	5	6	15	20	
Cage, John M. 1912-92	Composer	95	95	200	55	AMusQS $125-$250. AMsS $3750
Cage, Nicholas	Entertainment	15			48	AA
Cagney, James 1899-1987	Entertainment	40	60	100	223	AA Actor
Cagney; Jeanne	Entertainment				20	Jimmy Cagney's Actress Sister
Cahier, Madame Charles	Entertainment	25			90	Early Opera
Cahn, Sammy	Composer	15	80	125	50	AMusQS $250
Cain, Dean	Entertainment				42	Superman
Cain, James	Author	40	55	90		Novelist. Hard Boiled Fiction
Caine, Michael	Entertainment	10	15	25	38	
Caine, Thos. Hall, Sir 1853-1931	Author	15	45	92	25	Br. Novelist, Dramatist
Calder, A. Stirling 1870-1945	Artist			65		Sculptor. Father of Alexander Calder
Calder, Alexander (Sandy)1898-1976	Artist	125	225	850	150	Sculptor, ALS/Cont. $1000
Calder, William M.1869-1945	Congress		20			Sen..NY
Calderon, A. W. Gen.	Head of State	5	15	35	10	
Caldwell, Erskine 1903-	Author	35	150	210	75	Tobacco Road
Caldwell, George A. 1814-66	Congress	10				Repr. KY, Officer Mexican War
Caldwell, John Curtis	Civil War	35	75		95	Union Gen.
Caldwell, Sarah	Conductor	15			20	1st Woman Conductor NY Met.
Caldwell, Taylor	Author	35	150	225	50	Novelist
Caldwell, Zoe	Entertainment	5	25	15	15	
Calhern, Louis	Entertainment	30	25	45	45	Eminent Stage-Film Actor

NAME	CATEGORY	SIG	LS/DS	ALS	SP	Comment
Calhoun, Alice	Entertainment	15	15	35	30	
Calhoun, Eleanor	Entertainment	3	3	6	8	
Calhoun, John C. (V) 1782-1850	Vice President	145	350	475	375	Andrew Jackson VP
Calhoun, Rory	Entertainment	7	40	12	15	
Calhoun, William Barron	Congress	10	15	35		Repr. MA 1835
Calhoun, William M.	Senate/Congress	5	10			
Calkin, Dick*	Cartoonist	75			500	Buck Rogers
Callaghan, James	Head of State	40	75	140	45	Br. Prime Minister
Callahan, Laurence K.	Aviation	10	20	45	30	
Callas, Charlie	Entertainment	3	5	8	12	
Callas, Maria 1923-77	Entertainment	300	850	875	1188	Opera, Concert. Small format SP $525
Calleia, Frank	Entertainment	19	25	45	45	
Calleia, Joseph	Entertainment	25			55	
Calley, William	Military	20	35	45	40	My Lai, Viet Nam
Calloway, Cab 1907-95	Entertainment	30	45	50	198	Afro-Am. Big Band Leader
Calvert, Louis	Entertainment	5	6	15	15	
Calvert, Phyllis	Entertainment	5	15		15	
Calvet, Corinne	Entertainment	9	10	15	15	
Calvin, John	Clergy	5500	7500	10000		
Calvin, Melvin, Dr.	Science	25	35	55	20	Nobel Chemistry
Calvé, Emma	Entertainment	55	90	120	450	Opera
Camacho, Manuel Avila	Head of State	35		80	20	Pres. Mexico
Camargo, Alberto	Head of State	10	18	35	20	Columbia
Cambaceres, J.J.R.(Parma)	Napoleonic Wars	115	200			Prince & Duke
Cambell, James	Cabinet	35	80	120		Pierce P.M. General
Cambern, Donn	Entertainment	10			20	Actor Mayberry
Cambon, Jules	Diplomat	20	25	35		Fr. Ambassador to US
Cambridge, G.O.	Clergy	10	20	25		
Cambridge, Godfrey	Entertainment	35			80	
Cameron, Betsy	Author	5	10	20	10	
Cameron, George 1861-1944	Military	20		45		General WW I
Cameron, James D.1833-1918	Cabinet	30	35	45		Senator PA. Sec'y War
Cameron, Kenneth	Astronaut	5			15	
Cameron, Kirk	Entertainment	15			20	
Cameron, Robert A. 1828-94	Civil War	35	75			Union Gen. ALS '62 $175
Cameron, Rod	Entertainment	5			25	Actor
Cameron, Simon (War Date)	Cabinet	110	180	265	300	
Cameron, Simon 1800-89	Cabinet	102	135	170	295	Lincoln Sec'y War, Financier
Cammaerts, Emile	Author	10	20	40	15	Belgian Poet-Writer
Camp, Colleen	Entertainment	9	10	20	25	
Campanella, Joseph	Entertainment	3	3	6	6	
Campanini, Italo	Entertainment	65	80	175		
Campbell, Archibald	Revolutionary War	95	275			Br. General.
Campbell, Archie	Country Music	8			25	
Campbell, Beatrice	Entertainment	19	25	45	45	
Campbell, Charles Thomas	Civil War	35	80	110		Union General
Campbell, Colin, Sir 1792-1863	Military	16	45	75		Br. Gen. Vs U.S., War 1812
Campbell, Douglas	Aviation	45	65	80	95	ACE, WW I, Bi-plane Ace
Campbell, E. Simms*	Cartoonist	20			150	1st Black Mag. Cartoonist
Campbell, Ernest T.	Clergy	20	30	40	30	
Campbell, Geo.J.(8th Duke Argyll)	Statesman	25	60	130		Author. Br. Cabinet
Campbell, George W.1769-1848	Cabinet	55	160	310		Sec'y Treas. Senator TN 1803
Campbell, Glen	Entertainment	5	6	15	20	
Campbell, Jack M.	Governor	10	20			Governor NM
Campbell, James E.	Governor	15	25	30		Governor OH, MOC
Campbell, John	Revolutionary War	62	175	290		Br. General

The Sanders Price Guide to Autographs

NAME	CATEGORY	SIG	LS/DS	ALS	SP	Comment
Campbell, John A. (SC)	Supreme Court	100	200	300		
Campbell, John Hull 1800-68	Congress	6				Repr. PA
Campbell, Malcolm 1885-1948	Sportsman	50	225			Br Auto. & Hydroplane racer-designer
Campbell, Mary	Entertainment			50		Miss America 1922-23
Campbell, Naomi	Model	20			60	Semi-Nude Col. SP 80
Campbell, Patrick, Mrs.	Entertainment	35	60		80	Vintage Stage Actress
Campbell, Philip P.1862-1944	Congress	12				Kansas
Campbell, R. L.	Military	5	15	20	10	
Campbell, William (Bill)	Entertainment	5	5	10	12	SP As Rocketeer $35
Campbell, William B.	Civil War	40	55	95		Union Gen., Congress TN
Campbell-Bannerman, Henry, Sir	Head of State	18	45	110		Prime Minister
Campora, Giuseppe	Entertainment	10			40	It. Tenor, Opera
Camus, Albert 1913-1960	Author	75	290	794		Nobel. AMsS (Poem) $595
Canary, David	Entertainment	8			15	Actor
Canby, Edward R.1817-73	Civil War	65	292	370		Union Gen. ALS '64 $330
Cander, John	Composer		40			Pop Music
Candler, Asa Griggs	Business	475	1275		595	Founder of Coca Cola
Candler, Warren Akin	Clergy	25	35	50		
Candlish, Robert Smith	Clergy	10	15	25	35	
Candy, John	Entertainment	55			100	Died Prematurely
Canetti, Elia	Author	65	225	350		Bulg.-Br.Nobel Literature
Canfield, Dorothy (Fisher)1879-1958	Author	50	65	300		Am. Novelist, Essayist.
Canham, Erwin	Journalist	10	20			Christian Science Monitor
Caniff, Milton* 1907-88	Cartoonists	25	82	100	150	Terry & Steve Canyon
Caniglia, Maria	Entertainment	15			88	Opera. Dramatic Sopr.
Cannell, Stephen J.	Entertainment	6	10		10	TV Producer
Canning, Charles John	Head of State	15		65	45	1st Viceroy of India
Canning, Effie I.	Author	45		300		
Canning, George 1770-1827	Head of State	55	130	142		Prime Minister
Cannon, Annie Jump 1863-1941	Science			100		Great Woman Astronomer
Cannon, Dyan	Entertainment	6	8	15	20	
Cannon, Frank J.	Senate	5			10	Senator UT
Cannon, George Q.	Senate/Congress	50	140	200		Utah's 1st Congressman
Cannon, Howard W.	Senator	5	10	25	15	Senator NV
Cannon, John K.	Military	10	30	50		
Cannon, Jos. G.'Uncle Joe'	Congress	20	40	95	40	Speaker of the House
Cannon, Martha H., Dr.	Science	25	30	60	30	
Canova, Antonio 1757-1822	Artist	85	250	612		It. Sculptor. Classical Revival
Canova, Diana	Entertainment	3	3	6	10	
Canova, Judy	Entertainment	12	15	20	25	
Cantinflas 1911-95	Entertainment	33			87	
Cantor, Eddie 1892-1964	Entertainment	81	155		90	
Cantrell, Lana	Entertainment	3	3	6	10	
Canutt, Yakima	Entertainment	15	15	25	50	AA
Canyon, Christy	Entertainment				35	Porn Queen
Capers, Ellison (War Date)	Civil War	130		630		CSA General
Capers, Ellison 1837-1903	Civil War	75				CSA General
Capers, Virginia	Entertainment	3	3	6	6	
Caperton, William	Military	20			50	Adm. WW I
Capka, Carol	Entertainment	3	3	6	6	
Caplin, Mortimer	Celebrity	5	5	10	10	
Capon, Robert F.	Clergy	10	15	20	15	
Capone, Al	Criminal	2850	10750		3800	Gangster. Special DS $15,000
Capote, Truman 1924-84	Author	125	340	1088	242	Novelist, Short Story Writer
Capp, Al*	Cartoonist	85			245	Li'l Abner
Capper, Arthur	Senate	12	25		30	Senator KS

NAME	CATEGORY	SIG	LS/DS	ALS	SP	Comment
Capra, Frank 1897-1991	Entertainment	25	155		80	AA Film Director.TLS Ltr/Poem $450
Capshaw, Kate	Entertainment	6	8	15	35	
Captain & Tennile	Entertainment	5	6	15	15	
Capucine	Entertainment	25	30	70	65	
Caraway, Hattie 1878-1950	Congress	25	55	35	40	1st Woman US Senator, AR
Carberry, John J., Cardinal	Clergy	50	65	80	50	
Cardigan, 7th Earl Brudenell	Military	75	175	250	130	Br.Gen. Charge of Light Brigade
Cardinale, Claudia	Entertainment	10			35	
Cardozo, Benjamin N. (SC)	Supreme Court	150	350	875	840	
Carere, Christine	Entertainment	5			20	Actress
Carey, Harry Jr.	Entertainment	6	8	15	20	
Carey, Harry Sr.	Entertainment	100	110	175	250	
Carey, Hugh L.	Governor	10	15		15	Governor NY
Carey, Macdonald	Entertainment	10			30	
Carey, Mariah	Entertainment	30			65	Singer
Carey, Michele	Entertainment	5	6	15	25	
Carey, Ron	Entertainment	5	6	10	10	
Carias Andino, Tiburcio	Head of State	40	125		45	Pres. Honduras
Carl XIV Johan 1763-1844	Royalty	150	580			King Sweden
Carl XV 1826-72	Royalty	125	425			King of Sweden & Nor. from 1859
Carl XVI Gustaf 1946-	Royalty	55	150			King Sweden
Carl, Marion	Aviation	12	32	55	38	ACE, WW II, 1st Marine Ace
Carle, Frankie	Entertainment	15			35	Big Band Leader
Carleton, Guy, Sir (Baron)1724-1808	Military-Rev. War	250	645	800		Br. Commander-in-Chief
Carleton, James H. 1814-73	Civil War	30		110		Union Gen. LS '63 $825
Carleton, Will 1845-1912	Author	15	50	150	25	Ir. Novelist
Carlin, George	Entertainment	7	10	12	15	
Carlin, Lynn	Entertainment	3	3	6	6	
Carlisle, 7th Earl Geo.W.F. Howard	Author-Politician	20	45	115		Poet,Orator,Viceroy of Ireland
Carlisle, Belinda	Entertainment	20			50	
Carlisle, John Griffin	Senate-Cabinet	15	25	35	30	Speaker. Sen. KY,Sec'y Treas.
Carlisle, Kitty	Entertainment	8	9	12	15	
Carlisle, Mary	Entertainment	10	12	25	20	
Carlo Alberto 1798-1849	Royalty	45	150	375		King of Sardinia
Carlotta (Marie-Charlotte-Amalie)	Royalty	340	770	1700		Empress of Mex. Became Insane
Carlsen, Capt. Kurt	Celebrity	20	55	125	45	
Carlson, Frank	Governor-Senate	10	18	25	20	Governor, Senator KS
Carlson, Richard	Entertainment	20			40	
Carlton, Guy 1724-1808	Revolutionary War		1500			Br. Gen.
Carlyle, Russ	Entertainment	5			15	Bandleader
Carlyle, Thomas	Author	90	225	450	85	Br. Philosopher, Social Critic
Carman, Tex J.	Country Music	10			20	
Carmen, Jean	Entertainment	4	4	9	10	
Carmer, Carl	Author	20	45	175		
Carmichael, Hoagy 1899-1981	Composer	45	200		200	AMusQS $250, $320, $375
Carmichael, Oliver C.	Educator	20	35		25	Pres. Univ. Alabama
Carnarvon, Henry 4th Earl	Statesman	15	35	80		Created Fed. Dominion Canada
Carne, Judy	Entertainment	6	8	15	10	
Carnegie, Andrew 1835-1919	Industrialist	222	747	1106	933	Philanthropist.TLS/Cont.$4850
Carnegie, Dale 1888-1955	Author	50	35		45	Teacher.How To Win Friends...
Carnes, Kim	Entertainment	4			20	Singer
Carney, Art	Entertainment	15	45		32	'Norton' on The Honeymooners
Carney, Robert B.	Military	8	20	25		
Carnot, Lazare N.M.	Fr. Revolution	85	235	350		Min. of War. Exiled
Carnot, Marie François Sadi 1837-94	Head of State			165		Pres. France 1887-1894. Assassinated
Carnovsky, Morris	Entertainment	15		40	45	

The Sanders Price Guide to Autographs

NAME	CATEGORY	SIG	LS/DS	ALS	SP	Comment
Carol, Sue (Ladd)	Entertainment	5	6	15	15	
Caroline (Geo. IV-Eng)	Royalty	95	150	210		Estranged Queen
Caroline (Monaco)	Royalty	25			80	Princess. Daughter of Grace
Caroline 1768-1821	Royalty			459		Estranged Queen George IV
Caroline 1776-1841	Royalty		90	170		2nd Queen of Maximilian I (Bavaria)
Caroline of Anspach	Royalty	335	450	1000		Queen of George II (Eng.)
Caron, George R.	Aviation	35		100	90	Enola Gay Tail gunner
Caron, Leslie	Entertainment	15	30		40	Dancer-Actress
Carpenter, Carleton	Entertainment	5	6	10	10	
Carpenter, John	Entertainment	10			25	Film Director-Writer
Carpenter, Joseph Estlin	Clergy	40	50	60	75	
Carpenter, Karen	Entertainment	250	250		125	
Carpenter, Karen & Richard	Entertainment		485			Early Death for Karen
Carpenter, Mary-Chapin	Entertainment	5			35	Singer-Composer
Carpenter, Matthew H.	Senate/Congress	10	15	30	35	Senator WI
Carpenter, Richard	Entertainment	4	4	9	15	
Carpenter, Scott	Astronaut	25	75	125	118	Mercury 7 Astro
Carpenter, W. Boyd, Bishop	Clergy	10	20	30		
Carpenter, William B.	Explorer	10	35	60		Br. Physiologist
Carpenter, William S.	Military	10	15	45	20	
Carr, Darleen	Entertainment	3	3	6	6	
Carr, Eugene Asa 1830-1910	Civil War	35	80		220	Union Gen. CMH, ALS '63 $2200
Carr, Gerald P.	Astronaut	5			15	
Carr, Jane	Entertainment	5			15	Actress
Carr, Jerry	Astronaut	5			10	
Carr, Tommy	Entertainment	20			35	
Carr, Vicki	Entertainment	3	3	6	10	
Carradine, David	Entertainment	7			20	
Carradine, John	Entertainment	65	70	150	150	
Carradine, Keith	Entertainment	7			20	
Carradine, Robert	Entertainment	7			25	
Carranza, Venustiano	Head of State	52	205	400		Revolutionary Pres.Mex.Murdered
Carrel, Dr. Alexis	Science	75	220	300	85	Nobel Medicine
Carreno, Terresa	Composer	20		135	90	Pianist. Pupil of Gottschalk
Carrera, Barbara	Entertainment	6	8	15	19	Pin-Up SP $25
Carreras, Jose	Entertainment	25	40		65	Operatic Tenor
Carrere, Christine	Entertainment				15	Fr. Actress
Carrey, Jim	Entertainment	15			70	Comedian-Actor
Carrigain, Philip	Law	20	50			Surveyed NH, Named Granite St.
Carrillo, Leo 1880-1961	Entertainment	45	50	60	155	TLS/Content $150
Carroll, Charles 1737-1832	Revolutionary War	275	679	765		Signer Decl. of Indepen.
Carroll, Daniel	Revolutionary War	175	685	710		Continental Congress
Carroll, Diahann	Entertainment	6	8	15	20	
Carroll, Earl	Entertainment	85	105	210	190	
Carroll, Georgia	Entertainment	5			15	Pin-Up SP $20
Carroll, Gladys Hasty 1904-	Author	15				US Novelist
Carroll, John	Entertainment	10	15	20	20	
Carroll, John Lee	Governor	10		30		Governor MD
Carroll, Julian M.	Governor	10		35		Governor KY
Carroll, Leo G.	Entertainment	25			45	
Carroll, Lewis (SEE DODGSON,C)						
Carroll, Lisa Hart	Entertainment	6	8	15	19	
Carroll, Madeleine	Entertainment	35	150		83	
Carroll, Mickey	Entertainment	10			30	Wizard of Oz Munchkin
Carroll, Nancy	Entertainment	10	15	20	35	
Carroll, William	Military	25		90		Gen. TN Militia, Gov. TN 1821

NAME	CATEGORY	SIG	LS/DS	ALS	SP	Comment
Carroll, William H.	Civil War	60	145			CSA Gen.
Carryl, Guy Wetmore	Author	4	15	25		
Cars, The	Entertainment	50			85	
Carson, Christopher Kit1809-68	Frontiersman	3680			3000	Scout, Indian Agt.,Trapper etc.
Carson, Jack	Entertainment	15			50	
Carson, John	Military	10			35	General WW I
Carson, Johnny	Entertainment	15	20	30	50	Comedian. Tonight Show Host
Carson, Leonard Kit	Aviation	12	25	42	32	ACE, WW II
Carson, Rachel 1907-1964	Author-Science	70	205	285	275	ALS/Content $1,650
Carson, Sunset	Entertainment	20	25		45	
Carter, Ann S.	Aviation	25	40		45	1st Woman Helicopter Pilot
Carter, Ben	Entertainment	100			250	
Carter, Benny	Entertainment	40	60	100	90	Jazz. Sax, Trumpet
Carter, Betty	Entertainment	15			35	Lionel Hampton Vocalist
Carter, Billy	Celebrity	4	10	15	10	Pres. Carter's Brother
Carter, Boake	Radio	5	20	35	15	Radio Commentator-Vintage
Carter, Dixie	Entertainment	5		20	20	
Carter, Elliot	Composer	20		125		Pulitzer
Carter, Helen	Country Music	10			20	
Carter, Helena Bonham	Entertainment	20	30		40	
Carter, Hodding	Consultant	4	8	12	10	White House Aide
Carter, Howard	Science	125		425		Egyptologist, King Tut's Tomb
Carter, Janis	Entertainment	4	4	9	9	
Carter, Jimmy	President	125	482	1483	250	Pres. TLS/Content $3,000
Carter, Jimmy & Rosalyn	Pres. & 1st Lady	100			295	
Carter, Leslie, Mrs.	Entertainment	20	75	90	70	Vintage Stage & Early Films
Carter, Lillian	Celebrity	12	25		15	Pres. Carter's Mother
Carter, Lynda	Entertainment	6	8	15	20	Pin-Up SP $25
Carter, Mother Maybelle	Country Music	40			80	
Carter, Nell	Entertainment	5			15	
Carter, Robert	American Colonial		1400			
Carter, Rosalynn	First Lady	20	85	130	40	
Carter, Sonny	Astronaut	6			25	
Carter, Thomas H.	Senate	10		35	25	Senator MT. 1st Repr.from State
Carter, Tony	Entertainment	4	4	9	10	
Carter, Wilf	Country Music	10			20	
Carteret, George 1610-1680	Military		1600			Br. Naval Officer. Named New Jersey
Carteret, George 1610-80	Military		1600			Br. Naval Off'r. Founded State of New Jersey
Carteri, Rosanna	Entertainment	10			30	
Cartland, Barbara	Author	10	35	70	75	Br. Novelist. Romantic Novels
Cartright, Joy	Entertainment	3			15	
Cartwright, Angela	Entertainment	5	6	15	15	
Cartwright, Nancy	Entertainment	4			10	Voice of Bart Simpson
Carty, John J.	Science-Business	60	150	275	150	Telephone Pioneer. AT&T
Caruso, Anthony	Entertainment	25	29	70	52	
Caruso, David	Entertainment	10			30	NYPD Blues
Caruso, Enrico 1873-1921	Entertainment	262	550	675	961	Caricature Self-Portr.$625-1450-2250
Caruso, Enrico, Jr.	Entertainment				25	Actor Son Of Caruso Sr.
Caruthers, Robert L. 1800-82	Congress	12				Repr. TN, CW Gov. TN
Carvel, Elbert M.	Governor	10	15			Governor DE
Carver, Geo. Washington 1864-1943	Science	200	1092	757	3495	Hall of Fame, Botanist,Educator
Carvey, Dana	Entertainment	10			40	
Carville, Edward P.	Gov-Senate	12	15	40	20	Senator, Governor NV
Cary, Jeremiah E. 1803-88	Congress	10				Repr. NY
Cary, Phoebe	Author	10	15			Am. Poet/Sister Alice
Cary, Samuel Fenton	Senate/Congress	10		30	25	MOC OH

NAME	CATEGORY	SIG	LS/DS	ALS	SP	Comment
Casadesus, Robert, Dr.	Composer	45		100	100	Fr. Concert Pianist-Composer
Casals, Pablo 1876-1973	Entertainment	100	150	383	427	Spanish Cellist, AMusQS $350
Casanovo, Giacomo	Author	150	580	915		Adventurer, Gambler, Spy
Case, Clifford P.	Senate/Congress	5			10	Senator, MOC NJ
Case, Francis H.	Senate/Congress	10	25		15	Senator, MOC IA
Case, Jerome I.	Business	30	60	155		Case Tractors & Farm Implements
Case, Kenny	Entertainment			35		Tenor of 4 Ink Spots
Case, Norman S.	Governor	10	25			Governor RI
Casella, Alfredo	Composer	35	130	250		Pianist, Conductor
Casellato, Renzo	Entertainment	5			20	Opera
Caselotti, Adriana	Entertainment	4	15	35	60	Voice of Snow White
Casement, Jack	Civil War	45	170			Union Gen.
Casey, Silas 1807-82	Civil War	50	105	165		Union Gen.ALS '63 $550
Cash, Johnny	Country Music	5			10	
Cash, June Carter	Country Music	6			18	
Cash, Kellye	Celebrity	8		12	12	
Cash, Rosanne	Entertainment	5	6	15	20	Pin-Up SP $25
Cash, Tommy	Country Music 5			10		
Casimir-Perier, Jean Paul P. 1847-1907	Head of State			150		Pres. France 1894-95
Casper (Cast of)	Entertainment				100	Four Cast Members
Casper, John H.	Astronaut	8		95	20	
Cass, Lewis 1782-1866	Cabinet	50	110	152		Jackson Sec'y War, Senator MI
Cass, Peggy	Entertainment	5			10	
Cassatt, Mary	Artist	225	475	975		ALS/Content $4,500, $5,000
Cassavetes, John	Entertainment	20	15	20	45	Actor, Film Director
Cassidy, David	Entertainment	5			15	
Cassidy, Jack	Entertainment	25			55	
Cassidy, Joanna	Entertainment	5	6	15	15	
Cassidy, Shaun	Entertainment	10			35	
Cassidy, Ted	Entertainment	175	220	300	425	
Cassin, Jimmy	Composer	10	40			Songwriter
Cassin, Rene	Statesman	30	75	175	45	Founder UNESCO, Nobel Peace
Cassini, Oleg	Business	11	25	40	15	Fashion Designer
Casson, Mel*	Cartoonist	10			20	Redeye
Castagna, Bruna	Entertainment	20			100	Opera
Castanzo, Jack	Entertainment	10			30	Jazz Musician
Castelnuovo-Tedesco, M.	Composer	65		300	125	Versatile Comp.All Fields.AMuQs $325
Castle, Irene	Entertainment	50		75	75	
Castle, Irene & Castle, Vernon	Entertainment	100			425	Dance Couple
Castle, Lee	Entertainment	5	6	15	15	
Castle, Peggy	Entertainment	10			25	
Castle, Vernon	Entertainment	50			150	
Castle, William	Entertainment	40			100	
Castlereagh, R. Stewart, Visct.1769-1822	Statesman		20	83	237	Minister War vs Napol. Suicide
Castro, Emilio	Clergy	25	30	35	35	
Castro, Fidel	Head of State	850	925	1350	1135	Communist Premier of Cuba
Castro, Raul	Military				125	Younger Brother of Fidel
Castro, Raul H.	Governor	5			12	Governor AZ
Cates, Clifton B.	Military	10	25	50	18	
Cates, Phoebe	Entertainment	7	8	15	30	Pin-Up SP $35-45
Cathcart, Wm. Schaw Sir	Revolutionary War	65	125			Cmdr.British Legionin America
Cather, Willa 1873-1947	Author	400	360	600	150	Novelist.ALS/Cont $2,250
Catherine I (Rus)	Royalty	520	2000	4500		
Catherine II (The Great)1729-1796	Royalty	612	1889	2400		Empress Russia. The Great
Catherwood, Mary	Author	10	15	20		
Catlett, Walter	Entertainment	10	15	25	25	

The Sanders Price Guide to Autographs

NAME	CATEGORY	SIG	LS/DS	ALS	SP	Comment
Catlin, George 1796-1872	Artist-Author	100	310	1000		Travel Books.Indian Scenes
Catlin, Isaac	Civil War	50	95	330		Union Gen., CMH
Catt, Carrie Chapman 1859-1947	Women's Rights	60	120	250		Suffragette Leader
Catton, Bruce	Author	30	150	125	30	Historian, Editor. Pulitzer
Caulfield, Joan	Entertainment	8			25	Pin-Up SP $35
Cavalieri Muratore, Lina	Entertainment	50			220	Opera
Cavallaro, Carmen	Entertainment	15			35	Big Band Leader-Pianist
Cavanagh, Paul	Entertainment	7			20	
Cavanaugh, Hobart	Entertainment	15	18	20	35	
Cavell, Edith 1865-1915	Science	225	375	1200		Br. Nurse.Court Martial.Shot
Cavett, Dick	Entertainment	3	6	10	15	
Cavour, Camillo, Count 1810-61	Head of State		425			Architect of Italy's Unification. P.M.
Cayce, Edgar	Author	70	225			Am. Rural Healer, Seer
Cayvan, Georgia	Entertainment	6	8	15	15	
Ceausecu, Nicolae	Head of State	40	335		120	Pres. Romania. Assassinated
Cech, Thomas R., Dr.	Science	20	35		25	Nobel Chemistry
Cecil, Edg. Algernon, Lord	Diplomat	20	30			Statesman. Nobel Peace Prize
Celeste	Entertainment				34	Porn Queen
C,line, Louis Ferd. (Destouches)	Author	175		1275		Fr. Physician, Novelist
Celler, Emanuel	Senate/Congress	5	20		10	MOC NY
Cellini, Benvenuto	Artist	1000	4800	13500		Florentine Goldsmith, Sculptor
Cello, Aldo	Business	3	9	10	10	TV Ad vertising
Cenker, Robert	Astronaut	5			15	
Cerf, Bennett	Author	15	20	30	10	Random House Editor
Cermak, Anton J.	Politician	15	40	95	125	Assassinated Mayor of Chicago
Cernan, Eugene A.	Astronaut	20			102	Moonwalker Astro.
Cervantes, Miguel de	Author	10000	15000			Sp.Novelist,Poet.Don Quixote
Cesky, Charles J.	Aviation	10	22	38	28	ACE, WW II
Cetywago, King of Zulu	Afr. Leader	375				
Cezanne, Paul	Artist	1100	2300	8000		Fr. Impressionist to Cubism
Chabas, Paul Emlle	Artist	35	60	135		
Chabert, Lacey	Entertainment	5			48	Child Actress
Chabot, Phillipe de Brion, Comte	Military	1750				1480-1543. Fr.Cmdr.In Chief
Chabrier, Alexis Emmanuel	Composer	70	255	408		Fr. Opera, Orchestral, Piano
Chadwick, James, Sir	Science	80	215	450		Nobel Phys. Discovered Neutron
Chaffee, Adna R.	Civil War	35	80	115		Union General
Chaffee, Roger	Astronaut	200			400	Died Aboard Apollol I, 1-27-67
Chagall, Marc 1887-1985	Artist	280	400	1232	462	Color Repro S $125-295-395-650
Chaka Kahn	Entertainment	10			30	
Chakiris, George	Entertainment	10	15	25	25	
Chalia, Rosalia	Entertainment	25	40	65		
Chaliapin, Feodor 1873-1938	Entertainment	200	260	500	549	Opera. Rus. Basso. SPc $450
Chalker, Jack	Author	10	20	40	10	
Chalmers, James R. (War Date)	Civil War	250				CSA General
Chalmers, James R. 1831-98	Civil War	130	377			CSA General
Chalmers, Thomas	Clergy	55	60	80	75	
Chamberlain, Austen, Sir	Statesman	20	85	100	100	Nobel Peace Prize
Chamberlain, Daniel	Governor	50	125			Carpetbag Gov. SC
Chamberlain, Joseph A. 1836-1914	Br. Politician	58	85	85	90	Statesman, Nobel Peace Prize
Chamberlain, Joshua L.1828-1914	Civil War	625	1255	1862		ALS Re Gettysburg $3500
Chamberlain, Neville	Head of State	75	400	400	165	Prime Minister
Chamberlain, Owen, Dr	Science	25	35	75	30	Nobel Physics
Chamberlain, Richard	Entertainment	15	15	30	35	
Chamberlain, S.J.	Military	10	30	50		
Chamberlaine, William	Military	10		35	20	General WW I
Chamberlin, Clarence	Aviation	50	250	375	250	Record Non-Stop Flight NY-Ger.

NAME	CATEGORY	SIG	LS/DS	ALS	SP	Comment
Chambers Brothers (All)	Entertainment	50			200	Rock Group
Chambers, Marilyn	Entertainment	10	15	25	30	Pin-Up SP $50
Chambers, Robert Wm.	Author-Artist	10	15	20		Novelist.Life Mag Illustrator
Chambers, Whittaker	Journalist	15	50	150	25	Charged Alger Hiss as Communist
Chaminade, Cecile 1857-1944	Composer	85	195	300	232	AMusQS $125
Champion, Gower	Entertainment	25	30	60	75	
Champion, Gower & Marge	Entertainment	50			75	Both Dancers
Champion, Marge	Entertainment	10	12	15	20	Dancer
Chan, Genie*	Cartoonist	10			35	Conan
Chan, Jackie	Entertainment				75	Karate-Judo Films
Chancellor, John	News	15			30	Radio-TV News Commentator
Chandler, A.B. 'Happy'	Senate-Gov.	15	35		50	Sen., Gov. KY.Baseball Comm.
Chandler, Christopher	Celebrity	6		40		
Chandler, Dorothy 'Buff'	Business	8	20	45	25	Buffums Dept. Stores
Chandler, George	Entertainment					
Chandler, Helen	Entertainment	30			75	
Chandler, Jeff	Entertainment	40	75	150	120	
Chandler, Joseph Ripley	Congress	15		35		Repr. PA 1843. Editor US Gazette
Chandler, Lane	Entertainment	20			40	
Chandler, Norman	Business	15	35	75	30	L.A. Times
Chandler, Otis	Business	20	45	95	40	Founder L.A. Times
Chandler, Raymond	Author	190	540	975		Novelist. Detective Fiction
Chandler, William E.	Cabinet-Senate	20	38	65		Senator NH, Sec'y Navy
Chandler, Zachariah	Cabinet-Senate	25	35	50		Senator NH, Sec'y Int.,Att'y Gen'l
Chandrasekhar, Subrahmanyan	Science	30	110	225		Nobel, Astrophysicist
Chandu the Magician	Entertainment	5	7	25	20	
Chanel, Coco	Business	50	110	235	85	Fashion Designer, Perfumer
Chaney, Lon, Jr. 1906-73	Entertainment	338	642	500	675	
Chaney, Lon, Sr. 1883-1930	Entertainment	1050			1950	Man of a 1000 Faces
Chang	Entertainment	15			45	Chinese Giant
Chang, Franklin R.	Astronaut	5			15	
Channing, Carol	Entertainment	4	24		10	
Channing, Stockard	Entertainment	4	4	9	10	
Channing, William Ellery	Clergy-Author	40	70	120		
Channing, William Henry	Clergy	35	45	65	50	
Chaparral, John and Paul	Country Music	20			40	
Chapin, Harry	Composer	100			295	Singer-Songwriter
Chaplin, Charles, Sir 1889-19xx	Entertainment	310	538	450	1083	Legendary Film Comedian
Chaplin, Geraldine	Entertainment	10	15	28	30	
Chaplin, Lita Grey 1908-95	Entertainment	20	25	45	25	
Chaplin, Sydney	Entertainment	15	15	35	30	
Chapman, Graham	Entertainment	15	20	25	30	
Chapman, Leonard, Jr.	Military	15	30		55	USMC General, WW II
Chapman, Marguerite	Entertainment	10			20	Pin-Up SP $25
Chapman, Mark David	Criminal	75	155			Murdered John Lennon
Chapman, Oscar L.	Cabinet	15	20	30	35	Sec'y Interior 1849
Chapman, Philip K.	Astronaut	6			20	
Chappell, Clovis G.	Clergy	20	25	30	30	
Chappell, William 1809-1888	Business	20	45	110	35	Music Publisher
Chaptal, Jean Antoine, Count	Napoleonic	135	200			Chemist.Min.Agri., Interior
Charcot, Jean Martin 1825-93	Science	90	225	575		Fr. Neurologist and Teacher
Charisse, Cyd	Entertainment	5	6	15	20	Pin-Up SP $30
Charlemagne	Royalty	75000				Price Estimate Only
Charles & Diana	Royalty		1700		1430	Prince & Princess of Windsor
Charles Albert (Sardinia)	Royalty			225		Count of Savoy
Charles Edw. Stuart	Royalty	110	350	815		Bonnie Prince Charlie

NAME	CATEGORY	SIG	LS/DS	ALS	SP	Comment
Charles Emmanuel I	Royalty		400			King Sardinia
Charles Emmanuel I 1562-1630	Royalty	595	900			The Great
Charles I (Eng) 1600-49	Royalty	625	1750	4000		Important DS (1642) $4500
Charles II (Eng) 1630-85	Royalty	875	1854	2825		
Charles II (Sp)	Royalty	275	395			
Charles IV (Eng)	Royalty	245	1100			
Charles IV (Sp)	Royalty	185		600		
Charles IX (Fr) 1560-74	Royalty	292	1283	1700		
Charles V (Charles I {Sp})	Royalty	580	2100	5000		
Charles VI (Charles III {Sp})	Royalty	375	1200			Holy Roman Emperor 1711-1740
Charles X (Fr)	Royalty	150	450	725		
Charles XIV John (Swe)	Royalty	145	675	880		See also Bernadotte
Charles XV (Swe-Nor)	Royalty	45	140	320		
Charles, Ernest	Composer	20	80		45	
Charles, Prince of Wales 1948-	Royalty	775		1500	756	Philip Arthur George
Charles, Ray	Entertainment		200			Blind Afro-Am. Singer-Musician
Charles, Suzette	Entertainment	5	6	15	20	Miss American 1984
Charlotte Sophia 1741-1818	Royalty	145	275	452		Queen of George III (Eng)
Charlotte, Grand Duchess	Royalty	20	75	180	50	Luxembourg
Charo	Entertainment	3	3	6	10	
Charpentier, Gustave 1860-1956	Composer	100	250	297	300	AMusQS $450-$625
Charteris, Leslie	Author	20	55	135	85	The Saint. FDC S $75
Charvet, David	Entertainment				40	Baywatch
Chase, Charley	Entertainment	20			150	Vintage Film Comedian
Chase, Chevy	Entertainment	5	6	15	35	
Chase, Ilka	Entertainment	12	15	20	25	Author
Chase, Mary Ellen	Author	25	70	150	35	Educator, Essayist,Novelist
Chase, Salmon P. (SC)	Supreme Court	90	150	352	300	Chief Justice Supr. Ct.,Cabinet
Chase, Samuel	Revolutionary War	275	775	1550		Signer Decl. of Indepen.
Chase, William C.	Military	6	20	35		
Chase, William Merritt 1849-1916	Artist	95				US Painter of Western Scenes
Chateaubriand, Francois Rene de	Author	120	305	650		Fr. Novelist, Diplomat
Chatterton, Ruth	Entertainment	12			55	
Chauncey, Isaac 1772-1840	Military	20	95	90		Am. Naval Off. Tripoli, War1812
Chausson, Ernest	Composer	50	145	345		Fr. Opera, Symphonies
Chauvel, Henry, Sir	Military	25	75			Aussie General WW I
Chavez, Carlos	Composer	15	35	70	40	Mexican Conductor-Composer
Chavez, Cesar E. 1927-93	Labor	40			110	Migrant Labor Organizer
Chavez, Dennis	Senate	10	25		30	NM. 1st Hispanic Rep & Senator
Chavez, George A.	Aviation	45	58	175	65	
Chayefsky, Paddy (Sidney)	Author	75	150	250	125	Plays, TV Dramas, Screenplays
Cheap Trick	Entertainment	35			40	
Cheatham, Benj. Franklin 1820-86	Civil War	225	400			CSA General
Cheatham, Benjamin F.(War Date)	Civil War	390		652		CSA General
Checker, Chubby	Entertainment	10	20	25	32	Rock
Cheek, John	Entertainment	10			25	Opera
Cheers (Cast) (6)	Entertainment				335	
Cheever, Charles A., Dr.	Science	40	100		75	
Cheever, George B. 1814-90	Clergy	10		30		Author
Cheever, John	Author	45	125	250	100	Subtle, Ironic Novels. Pulitzer
Chekhov, Anton 1860-1904	Author	560	1815	5800		Rus.Dramatist. Novelist, Physician
Chen, Joan	Entertainment	15			60	Model-Actress
Chen, Tina	Composer	10	10		15	
Cheney, Dick	Cabinet	10			25	Sec'y Defense
Cheney, Sherwood	Military	5		25		General WW I
Chennault, Anna	Celebrity	20	25	50	25	Wife of Claire Chennault

NAME	CATEGORY	SIG	LS/DS	ALS	SP	Comment
Chennault, Claire L. 1890-1958	Aviation	500	362	660	525	Flying Tigers. USAAF Gen.
Cher	Entertainment	10	15	28	55	Pin-Up SP $80
Cherkassky, Shura	Entertainment	20			60	Opera
Chernov, Vladimir	Entertainment	10			30	Opera, Rus. Baritone
Cherry, R. Gregg	Governor	5	15		10	Governor NC
Cherubini, Luigi	Composer	175	250	595		It. 29 Operas, 15 Masses
Chesebrough, George M.	Science		750			
Chesebrough, Robert	Business	15	30	50		Vaseline Products
Cheshire, Leonard	Military	15	50	65	40	Br. RAF
Chester, Bob	Entertainment	20			40	Big Band Leader
Chester, Colby M.	Business	10			55	CEO General Foods
Chester, John	Revolutionary War	35	80			Continental Army. Judge
Chesterfield, Fourth Earl of						SEE STANHOPE, P.D.
Chesterton, Gilbert Keith	Author	52	390	325	190	Father Brown, Detective
Chestnut, James	Civil War	250				CSA Gen.
Chevalier, Albert 1861-1923	Composer	6	25	40	25	Br. Actor,Singer,Humorist
Chevalier, Maurice 1888-1972	Entertainment	35		151	122	Fr. Film & Vaudeville Actor
Chevrolet, Louis	Business	750	4875			Chevrolet Auto Mfg.
Chiao, Leroy	Astronaut	7			15	
Chicago	Entertainment	35			85	
Chichester, Francis, Sir	Celebrity	35	100	165	75	Aviator, Sailed Gypsy Moth IV
Chickering, Thos.E. 1824-71	Civil War-Business	70	90	175		Union Gen. Chickering Piano
Chierel, Micheline	Entertainment	10				Actress
Child, Julia	Celebrity Chef	5	12	15	15	TV Chef. Cookbook Author
Child, Lydia Maria	Author	30	90	155		Abolitionist, Reformer, Editor
Childress, Alvin	Entertainment	50			125	
Childs, George Wm.	Publisher	10	15	25		
Chiles, Lawton Mainor, Jr.	Senate	10	15	20	15	Senator FL
Chiles, Lois	Entertainment	5	6	15	15	
Chilton, Kevin P.	Astronaut	4			12	
Chilton, Robert Hall (War Date)	Civil War	390	3125			CSA General
Chilton, Robert Hall 1815-79	Civil War	185				CSA General
Chilton, Samuel 1804-67	Congress	50				Repr. VA. John Brown's Att'y
Chirac, Jacques	Head of State	25	75	185	35	Fr. Prime MInister, Mayor Paris
Chirico, Giorgio de 1888-1978]	Artist			780		Major Italian Surrealist
Chisholm, Shirley A.	Senate/Congress	5			12	Afro-Am. Congresswoman NY
Chittenden, Thos. C. 1788-1866	Congress	10				Repr. NY
Choate, Joseph H. 1832-1917	Diplomat	15	60	95	25	Prosecuted Tweed Ring
Choate, Rufus 1799-1859	Senate	20	35	55		Boston Statesman,Orator, NY Sen
Choiseul, Leopold C. de, Cardinal	Clergy	100	165			
Chong, Rae Dawn	Entertainment	6	8	15	20	
Chong, Tommy	Entertainment	8			15	Cheech & Chong
Chopin, Frederic	Composer	1200	3500	8000		ALS/Cont. $16,500
Chou En-Lai	Headsof State	1155	4000	10000	2500	Chinese Communist Premier
Chouteau, Rene Auguste	Revolutionary War	350	800	1515		American Pioneer. Fur Trader
Chretien, Jean-Loup	Astronaut	10			20	France
Christian IX (Den) 1818-1906	Royalty	90	250			
Christian VII (Den & Nor) 1749-1808	Royalty	125	325	625		King of Denmark
Christian, George B.	Senate	5	20		10	Senator OH
Christians, Mady	Entertainment	25	30	65	60	
Christie, Agatha 1891-1976	Author	242	775	588	920	Classic Detective Novels
Christie, Julie	Entertainment	10	15	28	55	Pin-Up SP $60
Christina, Queen (Swe)	Royalty	250	1675	2300		
Christine, Virginia	Entertainment	4	4	9	15	
Christo	Artist	5	12	20	85	
Christophe, Henry 1767-1820	Head of State	1375	1500			Haitian Revolutionary, Sovereign.

NAME	CATEGORY	SIG	LS/DS	ALS	SP	Comment
Christopher, Dennis	Entertainment	3	3	6	6	
Christopher, Warren	Cabinet	15	35		25	Sec'y State
Christopher, William	Entertainment	5	6	15	15	
Christy, Eileen	Entertainment	5			25	Vintage Actress
Christy, Howard Chandler 1873-1952	Artist	55	125	220	488	Illustrator, Portraitist. Books
Christy, June	Entertainment	10			20	Stan Kenton Vocalist
Chrysler, Walter P. 1879-1940	Business	317	925	850	732	Chrysler Motors.TLS $3500
Chun Doo-Hwan	Head of State	25		50		
Chung, Connie	TV News	5	10	20	12	TV News Anchor
Chung, Kyung-Wha	Entertainment	10			60	Contemporary Violin Sensation
Chung, Myung Whun	Conductor				75	Controversial Korean Maestro
Church, Benjamin 1734-38	Revolutionary War	195	530	1010		Am. Physician & Spy
Church, Frank	Congress	5	15		25	Senator ID
Church, Frederick E. 1826-1900	Artist	150	425	1188		Am.Dramatic Landscapes
Church, Frederick S.	Artist	40	65	120		ALS/Sketch $500
Church, R.W.	Clergy	20	35	50		
Churchill, Clementine S.	First Lady, Br.	85	200	235	160	Wife of Winston S.
Churchill, Jennie(Jerome)	Celebrity	15	75	235	95	W.S. Churchill's Mother
Churchill, John 1650-1722	Military	1100				1st Duke of Marlborough
Churchill, Mary	Celebrity	5		25		
Churchill, Randolph, Lord	Br. Statesman	45	95	285		Father of Winston S.
Churchill, Sarah	Entertainment	20	35	30	35	Actress-Daughter of Winston S.
Churchill, Thomas J.1824-1905	Civil War	75	80	200		CSA Gen., Gov. AR
Churchill, Thomas James (War Date)	Civil War	192				CSA General
Churohill, Winston	Author	15	35	60	35	
Churchill, Winston S.1874-1865	Head of State	800	2504	4750	3350	WW II P.M. 3x5 SP $1500
Ciannelli, Eduardo	Entertainment	20			45	
Ciano, Galeazzo, Conte	Royalty	65	295			Son-in-Law of Mussolini
Clcognani, A.G., Cardinal	Clergy	35	50	75	60	
Cigna, Gina	Entertainment	55	70		25	Opera
Cimaro, Pietro	Entertainment	10	25	50		It. Conductor
Cimino, Michael	Entertainment	6	8	15	20	Film Director
Citroen, André 1878-1935	Business	75	350		744	Citroen Auto Mfg.
Civiletti, Benjamin	Cabinet	5	10	20	10	
Clair, René 1898-1981	Entertainment			362		Fr. Film Maker
Clairborne, Liz	Business	10			20	Clothing Designer
Claire, Ina	Entertainment	15	15	35	25	
Claire, Marion	Entertainment	10			25	Am. Soprano
Clamorgan, Jacques	Explorer-Trader		750			Missouri Co. 1795
Clancey, Tom	Author	10	15		10	Am. Novelist
Clanton, Jimmy	Entertainment	20			25	Rock
Clanton, N.H.	Celebrity	1100				
Clapton, Eric	Entertainment	30			82	Rock
Clark, Abraham 1726-94	Revolutionary War	320	800	4500		Signer Decl. of Indepen.
Clark, Barzilla W.	Governor	5	12	20		Governor ID
Clark, Bruce C.	Military	6	20	35	15	
Clark, Buddy	Entertainment	10			25	40's Singer
Clark, Candy	Entertainment	3	3	6	15	
Clark, Carol Higgins	Author	5	15		20	All Around the Town
Clark, Charles	Civil War	110	275	350		CSA General, CW Gov. of Miss.
Clark, Clarence D.	Senate	10		35	15	Senator WY
Clark, Cottonseed	Country Music	15			30	
Clark, Dane	Entertainment	7	7	10	13	
Clark, Dick	Entertainment	6	8	15	19	
Clark, Edward 1815-80	Civil War		195			CSA Gen. 8th Gov. TX
Clark, Francis E.	Clergy	10	15	25	20	

The Sanders Price Guide to Autographs

NAME	CATEGORY	SIG	LS/DS	ALS	SP	Comment
Clark, Frank	Senate/Congress	5	15		10	Congressman FL
Clark, Fred	Entertainment	25			50	
Clark, George Rogers 1752-1818	Revolutionary War	675	2900	3750		General, Frontier Leader
Clark, James B. Champ 1850-1921	Congress	60	40	145	95	Speaker of the House. MO
Clark, James, Sir	Medical	15	35	85		Phys.to Queen Victoria & Albert
Clark, John Bullock,Sr.(War Date)	Civil War					CSA Gen. ALS/Content $8250
Clark, Kenneth B.	Activist	20				Brown vs Board of Education
Clark, L. Gaylord	Author	20	35	95		Editor Knickerbocker Magazine
Clark, Marguerite	Entertainment	20			50	Stage.Film Rival Mary Pickford
Clark, Mark W. 1896-1984	Military	35	190	275	103	Gen. WW II 5th Army.
Clark, Mary	Military	5	8	15	15	
Clark, Mary Higgens	Author		25		20	Suspense Novels
Clark, Myron H.	Governor	10	20	35	15	Governor NY
Clark, Petula	Entertainment	10			25	Br. Singer
Clark, Ramsay	Cabinet	15	35	60	20	Att'y Gen.
Clark, Roy	Country Music	6			20	
Clark, Susan	Entertainment	5	10	12	15	Pin-Up SP $25
Clark, Tom C. (SC)	Supreme Court	40	108	125	125	
Clark, Walter J.	Aviation	10	22	38	28	ACE, WW II
Clark, William 1770-1838	Explorer	375	1900	2500		Lewis & Clark Expedition
Clark, William A.	Senate	35	135	195		Railroad & Mining Magnate
Clarke, Adam	Clergy	75	145	350		
Clarke, Annie	Entertainment	15	15	25	25	
Clarke, Arthur C.	Author	15	35	75	40	2001
Clarke, Charles G.	Entertainment	6			10	Director
Clarke, Charles G.	Entertainment	6			15	Film Director
Clarke, Charles Mansfield	Medical	20	65	140		Br. Obstetrician
Clarke, George	Colonial Gov. N.Y	85	350			
Clarke, Henri J.G. Duc de	Napoleonic Wars	50	275	345		Marshal of Napoleon
Clarke, James Freeman	Clergy	30	50	75	60	
Clarke, James McClure	Senate/Congress	5			10	MOC NC
Clarke, Mae	Entertainment	40			60	
Clarke, Robert	Entertainment	20			50	
Clarke, Thomas	Revolutionary War	165	550			
Clarkson, Mathew 1758-1825	Military-Rev. War	45	95	175		Rev. Soldier, Philanthropist
Clarkson, Thomas 1760-1846	Reformer			100		Br. Devoted Entire Life to Abolition of Slavery
Clary, Alice	Author	15	25		15	
Clary, B. A.	Military	5	15	20	10	
Clary, Robert	Entertainment	4	4	9	12	
Clavell, James	Author	10	25	55	15	Novelist
Clay, Cassius Marcellus	Civil War	80	220	450		Union Gen., Senate, Abolition.
Clay, Henry 1777-1852	Cabinet	138	431	1275	350	Sec'y State, ALS Auct. $9,300
Clay, Lucius D. 1897-1978	Military	30	125	145	105	Gen. WW II
Clay, William L., Sr.	Senate/Congress	10			40	Afro-Am. Congressman MO
Clayburgh, Jill	Entertainment	5	6	15	20	
Clayton, Henry D.	Senate/Congress	5	10			MOC AL
Clayton, Jan	Entertainment	5	6	15	15	
Clayton, John M.	Cabinet	30	65	140		Taylor Sec'y State
Clayton, Joshua 1744-1798	Revolutionary War	220	425			1st Gov. DE. Senator DE
Clayton, Powell	Senate/Congress	10	25			Senator AR
Clayton, S. J.	Senate/Congress	5	10			
Clear Sky, Chief	Native American	20			50	Iroquois Chief
Cleave, Mary	Astronaut	12			25	
Cleaveland, Moses	Revolutionary War	170	850			Cleveland, Ohio Namesake
Cleburne, Patrick R.	Civil War	1050	1650			CSA General
Cleese, John	Entertainment	9	20		32	

NAME	CATEGORY	SIG	LS/DS	ALS	SP	Comment
Clem, John L. Johnny 1851-1937	Civil War	150	185	220	2760	Union Drummer Boy, Chicamauga
Clemenceau, Georges	Head of State	110	140	175		Prime Minister France
Clemens, Orion (Brother of Samuel)	West	125		160		Sec'y of Nevada Territory 1861
Clemens, S. as Mark Twain	Author	699			4250	ALS/Content $19,500
Clemens, S.L. and Twain, Mark	Author	1025		4500		Both Signatures
Clemens, Samuel L.1835-1910	Author	750	1724	3292	4465	ALS Content $19,000
Clement IX, Pope 1600-69	Clergy		1367			Guilio Rospigliosi
Clement VIII, Pope	Head of State	550	1300			
Clement, Martin Withington	Business	3	8	16	6	Pres. CEO Pennsylvania RR
Clements, Stanley Stash	Entertainment	10			20	
Clervoy, Jean-François	Astronaut	5			15	France
Cleveland, Carleton A.	Business	10	35	45	20	
Cleveland, Charles	Clergy	20	25	45		
Cleveland, Frances F.1864-1947	First Lady	52	80	216	225	ALS As 1st Lady $300
Cleveland, Grover & Francis F. Cleveland		President	418			
Cleveland, Grover (As Pres.)	President	245	562	750		WH Card S $325
Cleveland, Grover 1837-1905	President	250	614	1088	795	ALS/Content $1,250-$3,500
Clewes, Henry	Business	25	45			Banker
Cliburn, Van	Entertainment	25	28	55	95	Am. Pianist
Clifford, Clark M.	Cabinet	10	15	25	15	Sec'y Defense
Clifford, John Henry	Governor	10	55	95		
Clifford, Nathan (SC)1803-81	Supreme Court	75	175	240	150	Att'y Gen., Ambassador
Clifford, Rich	Astronaut	7			15	
Clift, Montgomery	Entertainment	250	355	600	760	
Clifton, Joseph C.	Aviation	15	35	60	40	
Cline, Patsy	Country Music	475			1450	Early Death
Clinger, Debora	Entertainment	3	5	7	8	
Clingman, Thomas Lanier 1812-97	Civil War	95	295	440		CSA General
Clinton, De Witt 1769-1828	Statesman	65	230	225		Promoted Erie Canal. Mayor NYC
Clinton, George (V) 1739-1812	V.P.-Military	135	500	385		Historical ALS $7,000
Clinton, Henry, Sir	Military-Rev. War	425	925	2200		Br. Soldier
Clinton, James	Military-Rev. War	200	490			General Revolutionary War
Clinton, James G. 1804-49	Congress	15		35		Repr. NY
Clinton, William Bill	President		295		315	42nd President. TLS/AN $1500
Clinton, William J. (Bill) (As Pres.)	President	150	275		455	42nd U.S. President
Clive, Colin	Entertainment	250			438	
Clive, E.E.	Entertainment	20			50	
Clive, Robert	Military	250	600	1200		Baron Clive of Plassey
Cloggers, Stoney Mtn.	Country Music	30			60	
Clokey, Art*	Cartoonist	20			150	Gumby. SP $35-45
Clooney, Geo./A. Edwards	Entertainment				80	Scene E.R. SP
Clooney, Rosemary	Entertainment	5	6	15	15	
Close, Glenn	Entertainment	10	15	20	37	
Clostermann, Pierre	Military	55	85	125	75	
Clover, Richardson	Military	35	125			USN Admiral
Clovio, Giorgio Guilio 1498-1578	Artist	650	1400	2000		It. Miniaturist
Clyde, Andy	Entertainment	50			150	Vintage Comedian
Clyde, June	Entertainment	8	9	15	20	
Clymer, George 1739-1813	Revolutionary War	125	505	900		Signer Decl. of Indepen. FF $900
Coase, Ronald	Economist	20	35		25	Nobel Economics
Coates, Eric	Composer	25	55	85	130	
Coates, Phyllis	Entertainment	10			20	
Coats, Bob	Aviation	10	22	38	30	ACE, WW II
Coats, Michael L.	Astronaut	5			15	
Cobain, Kurt	Entertainment				185	Rock
Cobb, Calvin H.	Military	15	40	75		

NAME	CATEGORY	SIG	LS/DS	ALS	SP	Comment
Cobb, Howell (War Date)	Civil War	225			950	CSA General
Cobb, Howell 1815-68	Civil War	112	192	490		Speaker, Sec'y Tres.,CSA Gen.Gov. GA
Cobb, Irvin S. 1876-1944	Author	25	45	150	95	Journalist-Humorist-Playwright
Cobb, Jerrie	Aviation	5	10	19	21	
Cobb, Lee J.	Entertainment	35	50	75	85	
Cobb, Sylvanus 1823-87	Author	12			40	
Cobb, Thos. Reade R. (War Date)	Civil War	1200		2000		CSA Gen. KIA '62
Cobb, Thos. Reade R. 1823-62	Civil War	500	1950	1910		CSA Gen. KIA '62
Cobham, Alan J., Sir	Aviation	25	65	85	45	Br. Aviation Pioneer
Cobham, Gov. Gen. NZ	Head of State	5	8	15	10	New Zealand
Cobo, Albert E.	Celebrity	10	15	45	15	Detroit's Cobo Hall
Coburn, Charles 1877-1961	Entertainment	45	90	155	125	AA
Coburn, James	Entertainment	10	15	25	25	
Coca, Imogene	Entertainment	15			25	Comedienne
Cochran, Eddie 1938-60	Entertainment	220			595	Star of Early Rock. Died at 22
Cochran, Jacqueline	Aviation	45	175		150	Speed record holder
Cochran, John L. Johnny	Legal	10			20	O.J. Simpson Trial Lawyer
Cochran, Robert L.	Governor	12	20	30	15	Governor NE
Cochran, Steve	Entertainment	15	15	30	28	
Cochrane, Basil, Sir	Military	15	25	30		
Cochrane, John 1813-98	Civil War	30	45	100		Union Gen. ALS '62 $345
Cochrane, Ralph	Military	5	15	25	20	NRPA
Cockburn, George, Sir	Military	40	100	140		Br. Admiral War 1812
Cockcroft, John Douglas, Sir	Science	60	110	245	75	Nobel Physics
Cocke, Philip St. George (War Date)	Civil War			5500		CSA Gen. Suicide '61
Cocke, Philip St. George 1809-61	Civil War	410				CSA Gen.
Cocker, Joe	Entertainment	20	40		35	Rock
Cockrell, Francis Marion 1834-1915	Civil War	70	110	200		CSA General, US Sen. MO
Cockrell, Ken	Astronaut	5			10	
Coco, James	Entertainment	15	20	25	35	
Cocteau, Jean	Author-Artist	75	175	800	640	Orig. Sketch S $795, 900
Coda, Eraldo	Entertainment	5			25	Opera
Cody, Buck	Entertainment	3	3	6	6	
Cody, Iron Eyes	Entertainment	15	40	25	65	
Cody, John P., Cardinal	Clergy	25	35	50	45	
Cody, Lew	Entertainment	15	20	25	35	
Cody, William F. & Buffalo Bill	Celebrity	732		1950	4175	Signed both Ways. AQS $1550
Cody, William F. 1846-1917	Celebrity	750	1375	1800	1550	CW Scout, Pony Expr.,Showman
Coffin, Charles Carleton 1823-1896	Civil War-Author	92				Only Journalist to Cover Entire War
Coffin, Henry Sloane	Clergy	25	35	40	50	
Coffin, Howard C.	Manufacturer	30				Pioneer Auto Manufacturer
Coffin, Isaac, Sir 1759-1839	Military	20		75		Boston Born Br. Naval Officer
Coffin, John 1756-1838	Revolutionary War	175	500			Loyalist General
Coffin, Tris	Entertainment	20			35	
Coffin, William Sloane	Clergy	18	30	35	50	
Coffyn, Frank	Aviation	40	65		95	
Coggan, Donald, Archbishop	Clergy	35	45	50	50	
Coghlan, Frank, Jr.	Entertainment	5			20	GWTW
Coghlan, Joseph B.	Military	25			60	Adm USN-Spanish American War
Cogswell, William 1838-1895	Civil War	15	35	75		Repr. MA
Cohan, Alexander	Entertainment					
Cohan, George M. 1878-1942	Composer	110	155	275	280	Actor, Composer, Playwright, Director
Cohen, Octavus Roy	Author	15	30	45	25	Novels, Screenplays, Radio
Cohen, Stanley, Dr.	Science	20	35		25	Nobel Medicine
Cohen, Wilbur J.	Cabinet	5	14	22	10	Sec'y HEW
Cohen, William S.	Cabinet	10		25	40	Senator ME, MOC ME, Sec. Defense

NAME	CATEGORY	SIG	LS/DS	ALS	SP	Comment
Cohn, Harry	Business	35	85	165	65	Co-Founder Columbia Pictures
Cohn, Jack	Business	25	70	140	55	Co-Founder Columbia Pictures
Cohn, Roy	Lawyer	15	25	40	20	Legal Aide Sen. McCarthy
Coit, James Brolles	Civil War	25		125		Union General
Coke, Edward, Sir 1552-1634	Law		2162	3500		Eminent Eng. Jurist. Lord Chief Justice
Coke, Thomas, Bishop	Clergy	250	350	750		
Coker, Jack	Entertainment	6	8	15	20	
Colbert, Claudette	Entertainment	40	110		75	
Colby, Bainbridge	Cabinet	10	30	55		Sec'y State
Colby, Leonard	Military	40	90			General. Indian Fighter
Colden, Cadwallader	Revolutionary War	100	240			Am. Colonialist
Cole, Cornelius	Senate/Congress	15	25	40		MOC CA 1863, Senator CA
Cole, Edward N.	Business	5	12	30	10	Pres. General Motors
Cole, Michael	Entertainment	3	3	6	8	
Cole, Nat King 1919-65	Entertainment	160	275		316	Am. Jazz Pianist, Singer
Cole, Natalie	Entertainment	15			40	Singer
Cole, Sterling	Congress/Senate	5	10			Congressman NY
Coleman, Booth	Entertainment	10			40	Planet of the Apes
Coleman, Cy	Composer	25			30	Arranger
Coleman, Dabney	Entertainment	5	6	15	15	
Coleman, Gary	Entertainment	5	7	12	15	
Coleman, George	Entertainment	7			40	Jazz Sax
Coleman, Nancy	Entertainment	6	8	15	10	
Colenso, John W., Bishop	Clergy	20	25	35		
Coleridge, John Duke	Celebrity	8	12	25		
Coleridge, Samuel Taylor 1772-1834	Author	325	575	1250		Br. Poet, Critic. AMsS $7,500
Coleridge-Taylor, Samuel 1875-1912	Composer	30	70	162	40	Choral, Musical Theatre, Songs
Colette, Sidonie-Gabrielle 1873-1954	Author	65	315	375	805	1873-1954. Fr. Novelist , Journalist, Critic
Colfax, Schuyler (V) 1823-85	Vice President	95	125	631	250	Speaker of House, Grant VP
Colgate. James C.	Business	10	25	50	40	Colgate University. Donor
Colgrass, Michael	Composer	20	35	85		Pulitzer, AMusQS $100
Collamer, Jacob	Cabinet	20	55	80		Taylor P.M. General
Collier, Constance	Entertainment	25			75	Vintage Br. Actress
Collier, James W.	Senate/Congress	5	15		10	MOC MS
Collier, Peter F.	Business	14	35	70		
Collinge, Patricia	Entertainment	6	8	15	19	
Collingwood, Charles	Journalist	5	35	60	15	News Analyst, War Correspondent
Collins, Cardiss	Senate/Congress	5	15		10	MOC MO
Collins, Eileen	Astronaut	5			10	
Collins, J. Lawton	Military	15	50	80	35	General WW II
Collins, Jackie	Author	10	15	20	15	Novelist
Collins, Joan	Entertainment	15	15	30	25	Pin-Up SP $30
Collins, Judy	Entertainment	5	6	15	20	Singer
Collins, LeRoy	Governor	5	10		14	Governor FL
Collins, Lottie	Entertainment	15	15	25	25	
Collins, Michael	Astronaut	90	160	250	135	Apollo XI
Collins, Phil	Entertainment	30			55	Singer
Collins, Ray	Entertainment	50	60	150	175	
Collins, Wilkie	Author	100	309	530	1380	Br. Novelist,Biography,Mystery
Collis, Charles	Civil War	25		60		Union Gen., CMH
Collishaw, Raymond	Aviation	75	175	375	225	Brit. ACE, WW I
Collyer, Robert, Dr. 1823-1912	Clergy	35	55	73		Unitarian. Lecturer. Author
Colman, Ronald	Entertainment	50	65	130	150	
Colman, Samuel 1832-1920	Artist	20		95		Landscapes. Fdr, 1st Pres. AM. Watercolor
Colombo, Scipio	Entertainment	10			30	Opera
Colonna, Jerry	Entertainment	20	9	19	35	Buggy-Eyed Comedian

NAME	CATEGORY	SIG	LS/DS	ALS	SP	Comment
Color Me Badd	Entertainment	10			25	Rock
Colquitt, Alfred H.	Civil War	85	165	275	250	CSA Gen., US Sen. GA
Colson, Charles W. 'Chuck'	Clergy	35	50	75	30	Convicted Watergate Figure
Colston, Raleigh E.	Civil War	70	425			CSA Gen.
Colt, Samuel 1814-1862	Business-Inventor	450	2188	3975		Founder Colt Firearms
Coltrane, John	Entertainment					Great Jazz Saxophonist. NRPA
Colum, Padraic	Author	30	150		40	Irish Poet & Playwright
Columbo, Russ	Entertainment	50	90	200	165	
Comden, Betty & Green, A.	Composers	10	45		30	Collaberators Broadway Musicals
Comiskey, Charles	Business	400				Owner Chicago White Sox
Commager, Henry Steele	Civil War	25	60	105		Union General
Command Performance (5)	Entertainment	20			50	
Commodores	Entertainment	25			60	
Como, Perry	Entertainment	12			60	
Compson, Betty	Entertainment	15	30	60	70	
Compton, Arthur H. 1892-1962	Science	90	205	275	100	Nobel Physics. Atomic Bomb
Compton, Fay	Entertainment	5			15	Br. Actress
Compton, Joyce	Entertainment	8	9	19	15	
Compton, Karl T. 1887-1954	Science	90	200		110	Physicist, Pres. M.I.T.
Conant, A. Roger	Aviation	10	22	38	28	ACE, WW II, Marine Ace
Conant, James Bryant	Diplomat	10	15	30	20	Educator, US Ambassador
Conati, Lorenzo	Entertainment	20			65	Opera
Conchita, Maria	Entertainment	4			10	
Conde', Louis II 1621-1686	Military		750			One of France's Most Celebrated Generals
Condon, Eddie	Composer	40			60	Guitarist
Condon, Richard	Author	5	15	35	10	
Cone, Fairfax M.	Business	10	35	45	20	Foote,Cone & Belding, Adv.
Cone, Hutchinson	Military	25	35			Admiral WW I
Confalonieri, Carlo, Cardinal	Clergy	50	75	90	65	
Conforti, Gino	Entertainment	3	3	6	6	
Congreve, William 1670-1729	Author	190	575	1050		Br. Drama. Restoration Comedy
Congreve, William, Sir.2nd Baronet	Science	45	125	235		Artillerist, Invented Rocket
Coningham, Sir Arthur	Aviation	35	60			Cmdr. RAF 1st Tactical
Conklin, Chester	Entertainment	100	115	220		
Conkling, Roscoe	Senate	15	25		20	MOC, Senate NY Political Boss
Conlee, John	Entertainment	4			10	
Conley, Eugene	Entertainment	20	30		50	Opera
Conley, Joe	Entertainment	3	3	6	8	
Connally, John B.	Cabinet	25	60	95	45	Gov. TX, Sec'y Treasury
Connally, Tom 1877-1963	Senate	20	25		70	Senator TX. Gov. TX
Connelly, Jennifer	Entertainment	15			35	
Connelly, Marc 1890-1980	Author	20	75	75	35	Am. Dramatist. Pulitzer
Connelly, Matthew J.	White House Staff	10	25	35	15	Pres. Truman Aide
Conner, James 1829-1883	Civil War	90	210	270		CSA General. 1st Bull Run, Seven Pines
Conner, Nadine	Entertainment	10			33	Am. Opera, Radio, Records
Connery, Sean	Entertainment	45	50	65	131	Best Known for James Bond Films
Conness, John	Senate	45	85			Civil War Senator CA
Connick, Harry, Jr.	Entertainment	25	45		45	Big Band Leader-Singer-Pianist
Conniff, Ray	Entertainment	25	35	65	45	
Connolly, Walter	Entertainment	70		90	85	
Connor, Harry P.	Aviation	15	30	45	50	
Connor, James	Civil War	95	205	260		CSA General
Connor, John T.	Cabinet	7	20	35	20	Sec'y Commerce
Connor, Patrick Edward	Civil War	35	58			Union General
Connors, Chuck	Entertainment	20	25	30	35	
Connors, Mike	Entertainment	7			15	

NAME	CATEGORY	SIG	LS/DS	ALS	SP	Comment
Connors, Norman	Entertainment	4			10	
Connors, Patti	Entertainment	3	3	6	6	
Conover, Harry	Business	10	17	25	15	Top Modeling Agency
Conquest, Ida	Entertainment	15	15	25	30	
Conrad, Charles Magill 1804-78	Cabinet	45	55	190		Sec'y War
Conrad, Charles, Jr.	Astronaut	10	285		70	3rd Moonwalker.
Conrad, Gerhard	Aviation	10	25	45	25	
Conrad, Joseph 1857-1924	Author	230	1125	1450	1250	Br. Novelist. Lord Jim etc.
Conrad, Michael	Entertainment	15	20	40	35	
Conrad, Robert	Entertainment	7	10		20	
Conrad, William	Entertainment	8			25	
Conried, Hans	Entertainment	15	20	40	40	
Conroy, Kevin	Entertainment	3	3	6	6	
Conroy, Pat	Author					Signed 1st Ed. $125-$200
Consigny, Eugene F.	Banker		20			
Constable, Archibald 1774-1827	Publisher	30				Encyclopaedia Britannica
Constable, John 1776-1837	Artist	258	610	2400		Br. Landscapes, Rural Life
Constantine I, 1868-1923	Royalty	90				King of Greece. Resigned-Recalled
Constantino, Florencio	Entertainment	75			365	Opera
Conte, John	Entertainment	4	5	9	12	
Conte, Richard	Entertainment	7	10	15	15	
Conti, Bill	Composer	60	85	100	40	
Conti, Joseph	Entertainment	4			10	
Contino, Dick	Entertainment	3			8	Accordianist
Convy, Bert	Entertainment	10			20	Broadway, TV Star
Conway, Henry Seymour 1721-95	Military	25	60	135		Br. Fld. Marshal. MsDs $250
Conway, Martin F. 1827-82	Congress	10				Repr. KS, U.S. Consul France
Conway, Rose A.	Cabinet	3	5	10	5	
Conway, Thomas	Revolutionary War	65	105	250		Maj. Gen. Rev. War
Conway, Tim	Entertainment	5	6	15	20	
Conway, Tom	Entertainment	50			128	The Saint
Conwell, Russell H. 1843-1925	Clergy	35	45	40		Baptist Fndr. & 1st Pres. Temple Univ.
Cony, Samuel	Governor	30	45	60		Civil War Gov. ME
Conyers, John	Senate/Congress	3	12		5	Afro-Am. Congressman MI
Coogan, Jackie	Entertainment	20	25	30	50	
Coogan, Richard	Entertainment	5	6	15	15	
Cook, Ann T.	Model	10			25	Model For Gerber Baby Products
Cook, Elisha Jr. 1902-95	Entertainment	15	25	35	82	
Cook, Eliza	Author				75	Poet
Cook, Everett R.	Aviation	10	30		50	ACE WW I
Cook, Francis Augustus	Military	75		55	30	Spanish American War
Cook, Frederick Albert, Dr.	Explorer	75	145	175	150	Claimed 1st at North Pole
Cook, James, Capt.	Br.Naval Explorer	3800	8850	27000		Captain Cook
Cook, Joseph, Sir	Politician	10	20	40		Australian Statesman
Cook, Philip 1817-94	Civil War	150	318	395		CSA Gen.
Cook, Robin	Author	5			10	Novelist
Cook, Thomas	Business	35	110	545		Founder British Tourist Company
Cook, Tommy	Entertainment	15			30	Child Actor
Cook, Walter V.	Aviation	8	20	38	28	ACE, WW II
Cooke, Alistair, Sir	Author	20	95	140	75	TV Host. Masterpiece Theatre
Cooke, Jack Kent	Business	10	22		15	
Cooke, Jay 1821-1905	Business	100	1112	2450	175	Banker, Financier
Cooke, Nicholas	Revolutionary War		1100			Rev. War Gov. Rhode Island
Cooke, Philip St. George	Civil War	50				Union Gen. ALS/Cont.$935
Cooke, Sam	Entertainment	267	688		512	Rock
Cooke, Terence J., Cardinal	Clergy	60	75	100	95	

NAME	CATEGORY	SIG	LS/DS	ALS	SP	Comment
Cool, Harry	Entertainment	4	4		6	
Cooley, Denton A., Dr.	Science	20	40	90	40	Heart Transplant Surgeon
Cooley, Lyman E.	Science	10		35		Civil Engineer
Cooley, Spade	Country Music	15			35	King of Western Swing
Coolidge, Calvin & Entire Cabinet	President	295				
Coolidge, Calvin (As President)	President	210	874	2633	568	WH Card S $200-325.ALS $6450
Coolidge, Calvin 1872-1933	President	177	634	1075	655	Autogr. Speech Signed $6000
Coolidge, Grace 1879-1957	First Lady	80	240	150	165	
Coolidge, John	Celebrity	40	65			Father Of Pres. Coolidge
Coolidge, Rita	Entertainment	15			25	
Coolidge, T. Jefferson	Statesman	4	10	20		
Coolidge, William David, Dr.	Science	45	85	165	125	Dir. Research G.E., Inventor
Coombs, Patricia	Artist	10	20	35	15	
Cooper, Alfred Duff	Statesman	10	25	60	15	1st Viscount Norwich. Author
Cooper, Alice	Entertainment	25		35	90	Rock
Cooper, Emil	Composer	30	180	80	72	Rus.Internat'l Cond.-Violinist
Cooper, Gary 1901-61	Entertainment	220	415	375	498	3x5 SP $325. Orig.Spurr PH SPI $600
Cooper, Gladys, Dame	Entertainment	30	35	65	55	
Cooper, Gordon	Astronaut	25	75		85	Mercury 7 Astro.
Cooper, Jackie	Entertainment	20	25	35	55	Child to Mature Actor. Director
Cooper, James Fennimore 1789-1851	Author	90	180	1125		Am. Novelist.ALS/Cont.$1,750
Cooper, Jeanne	Entertainment	8			18	Actress. Soap Star
Cooper, John Sherman	Senate/Congress	10	25			Senator KY, Statesman, Diplomat
Cooper, Leon N., Dr.	Science	20	35	60	30	Nobel Physics
Cooper, Leroy, Jr.	Astronaut	40				Apollo VII (Early Sig.)
Cooper, Merian C.	Entertainment	100			250	King Kong, Four Feathers
Cooper, Miriam	Entertainment	35			75	
Cooper, Peter 1791-1883	Industrialist	75	200	310	175	Am. Inventor, Philanthropist
Cooper, Prentice	Governor	10	16			Governor TN
Cooper, Rick	Entertainment	5			10	Actor
Cooper, Samuel (War Date)	Civil War	158		818		CSA Gen.Special Content ALS $6325
Cooper, Samuel 1798-1876	Civil War	120	230	445		CSA Ranking Gen.
Cooper, Thos. Sidney	Artist	10	20	35		
Coors, W. K.	Business	20	60	95	50	Coors Brewery
Coots, J. Fred	Composer	35	45	100	40	AMusQS $150-$195
Copas, Cowboy	Country Music	100			225	
Copeland, C.C.	Clergy	30	80	225		
Copeland, L. du Pont	Business	20		50		
Copeland, Royal S., Dr.	Senate	15	70			Senator NY. Author
Copeland, William John	Clergy	20	25	35		
Copland, Aaron 1900-90	Composer	65	165	300	150	AMusQS $300-$800
Copley, John Singleton 1738-1815	Artist	350	710	4875		Outstanding Am. Portraitist
Copley, Teri	Entertainment	5			15	Pin-Up SP $20
Copmpanari, Giuseppe	Entertainment	35			125	Opera
Coppens, Willy (Baron de H)	Aviation	20	40	125	50	
Copperfield, David	Entertainment	10	15		25	Illusionist
Coppola, Francis Ford	Entertainment	25	40		50	AA Film Director
Coppée, François E. 1842-1908	Author	15	45	45		Fr. Poet, Novelist, Dramatist
Coquelin, Benoit-Constant(Aine')	Entertainment	25	60	55		Fr. Actor-Manager, Cyrano
Coquelin, Ernest-Alex.-H.(Cadet)	Entertainment	15	30	50		Comedie-Francaise. Author
Corbett, Boston	Civil War	965		1800		Shot John Wilkes Booth
Corbett, Henry Winslow	Senate/Congress	10	15	25	20	Senator OR
Corbett, Michael	Entertainment	4			10	Actor Young and the Restless
Corbin, Henry Clarke	Civil War	50		115		Union General
Corbusier, Le 1887-1965	Architect	85	575		575	Jeanneret, Charles Edouard
Corby, Ellen	Entertainment	10			20	

NAME	CATEGORY	SIG	LS/DS	ALS	SP	Comment
Corcoran, Michael (War Date)	Civil War			1723		Union Gen. RARE
Corcoran, William W.	Business	20	50			Banker, Philanthropist
Cord, Alex	Enteretainment	8			12	
Corden, Henry	Entertainment	25	55		40	Fred Flintstone (Voice)
Corea, Chick	Entertainment	15			35	
Corelli, Franco	Entertainment	25	35	100	110	Opera
Corelli, Marie 1855-1924	Author	45	55	65	70	Eng. Romantic Novelist
Corena, Fernando	Entertainment	20			45	Opera
Corey, Elias	Science	20	35		30	Nobel Chemistry
Corey, Jeff	Entertainment	5			15	
Corey, Wendell	Entertainment	35	45	80	75	
Cori, Carl F.	Science	15	25	47	20	Nobel Medicine
Corio, Ann	Entertainment	12	15	20	30	
Corlett, Irene	Entertainment	3	3	6	6	
Cormack, Allan M.	Science	20	35	50	25	Nobel Medicine
Corman, Roger	Entertainment	5			20	
Cornbury, Edward Hyde, Lord	Colonial Gov.	200	450			1st Colonial Gov. NJ, Gov. NY
Corneliano, Mario N. di	Clergy	35	45	60	50	
Cornelius, Peter (Carl August)	Composer	55		325		Opera, Choral Works, Song Cycle
Cornell, Ezekiel	Military	60	200			Brig. Gen. American Rev.
Cornell, Ezra	Business	30	80	165	75	Financed Western Union Telegr.
Cornell, Joseph 1903-1972	Artist	135	1200	700		Am. Surrealist Sculptor
Cornell, Katharine 1898-1974	Entertainment	20	35	75	75	Superb Am. Leading Actress
Cornell, Lydia	Entertainment	3	3	10	10	Pin-Up SP $30
Corner, George W.	Science	75	150		100	
Cornfeld, Bernard	Business	10	20	55	35	
Cornforth, John W., Sir	Science	15	35	45	20	Br. Nobel Laureate in Chemistry
Corning, Erastus 1794-1872	Business	70	175	295		1st Pres. NY Central Railroad
Cornwallls, Charles E.1738-1805	Revolutionary War	175	400	1238		Br. General Am. Revolution
Corot, J.B. Camille	Artist	212	490	1120	3000	Barbizon School. Impressionist
Corrigan, Douglas 1907-95	Aviation	65	80	187	100	Wrong Way
Corrigan, Mairead/B. William	Irish Activists	35	40	100	50	Nobel Peace Prize 1976
Corrigan, Michael A.	Clergy	10		30	20	Bishop
Corrigan, Ray Crash	Entertainment	40			150	
Corsaut, Aneta	Entertainment	25			90	Actress Andy Griffith
Corse, John Murray	Civil War	35	245	80		Union General
Corse, Montgomery D. 1816-95	Civil War	120		325		CSA General
Corson, Fred P., Bishop	Clergy	20	30	50	45	
Cortelyou, George B.1862-1940	Cabinet	50	150	220		Served two Presidents.
Cortes, Hernando (Cortez)1485-1574	Explorer		44300			Sp. Conqueror of Mex.
Cortez, Ricardo	Entertainment	25			40	
Cortina, Juan	Military		1500			Mexican General
Corwin, Thomas	Cabinet	30	55	125		Fillmore Sec'y Treasury
Cosby, Bill	Entertainment	9	10	20	30	
Cosby, George B.	Civil War	60	130	200		CSA General
Cosby, N. Gordon	Clergy	20	30	45		
Cosell, Howard	Entertainment	15			65	Radio-TV Sports News
Cosgrave, William T. 1880-1965	Head of State	70	150	275		Sinn Fe'in Easter Uprising.
Coslow, Sam	Composer-Author	50	200	300	350	Academy Award 1943
Cosmovici, C. B.	Astronaut	12			25	
Cossotto, Fioranza	Entertainment	10			30	Opera
Cossutta, Carlos	Entertainment	5			25	Opera
Costa Lo Giudice, Silvio	Entertainment	40			100	Opera
Costa, Michael, Sir	Composer	15	40	95	25	Br. Conductor.Opera, Ballet
Costa-Gavras, Constantin	Entertainment	15			35	AA
Costa-Gavras, Constantin	Entertainment	20			40	Film Director

The Sanders Price Guide to Autographs

NAME	CATEGORY	SIG	LS/DS	ALS	SP	Comment
Costas, Bob	TV Host	5			10	TV Host & Sports Commentator
Coste, Dieudonne	Aviation	125	235	385	275	
Coste, Dieudonne & Bellonte, M.	Aviation	210			365	
Costello, Delores (Barrymore)	Entertainment	28	35	65	60	
Costello, Elvis	Entertainment	10			30	
Costello, Lou 1906-59	Entertainment	200	375		400	Radio, Film, TV Comedian
Costner, Kevin	Entertainment	25			50	AA Actor-Director-Producer
Coswell, Henry T.	Aviation	55	105	150		1st Balloon ascent 1844
Cotsworth, Staats	Entertainment	8			15	
Cotten, Joseph 1905-94	Entertainment	20	25		35	
Cotton, Carolina	Country Music	15			30	
Coty, François	Business	100	400	475		Coty Perfume & Cosmetics
Couch, Darius Nash	Civil War	65	80	145		Union General
Couch, Virgil	Urban Designer	10	20	15		Dir. National Civil Defense
Cougar, John	Entertainment	10			35	
Coughlin, Charles E.	Clergy	25	50	60		Activist Catholic Priest
Coulouris, George	Entertainment	10			25	Character Actor
Coulter, Jessie	Country Music	6			15	
Coulter, Richard	Civil War	42	75	95		Union Bvt. General
Courbet, Jean D. Gustave	Artist	225	600	1090		Leader of Realist School
Couric, Katie	TV Host	5			16	Host Today
Court, Hazel	Entertainment	10			35	
Courtney, Inez	Entertainment	15			35	
Cousins, Norman	Author	10	25	40	15	Saturday Review Editor, Author
Cousins, William E., Archbishop	Clergy	20	35	45	35	
Cousteau, Jacques	Science-Author	50		175	125	Underwater Explorer, Films
Cousteau, Jim (Son of Jacques)	Science	25			150	Underwater Explorer (Deceased)
Couter, John B.	Military	15	47			
Couve de Murville, M.	Celebrity	5	12	20	15	
Couzens, James	Senate/Congress	10	30		15	Senator MI
Coué, Emile 1857-1926	Science	175		500		Fr. Psychotherapist, Hypnotism
Covarrubias, Miguel	Artist	150	325			Mex. Book & Magazine Illustr.
Covey, Richard O.	Astronaut	5			15	
Cowan, Edgar	Senate	15	25	35		Civil War Senator PA
Cowan, Jerome	Entertainment	10			35	
Coward, Noel, Sir 1899-1973	Author-Composer	155	203	340	306	AMusQS $275,Playwright,Actor
Cowl, Jane	Entertainment	22		35	45	
Cowles, Gardner	Business	12		25	15	Publisher Des Moines Register
Cox Family, The	Entertainment	25			45	Bluegrass
Cox, Archibald	Cabinet	15	185	55	20	Att'y Gen., Watergate Prosecutor
Cox, Courtney	Entertainment	15			50	Actress Friends
Cox, George H.	Author	5	15	30		Br. Historical Writer
Cox, Jacob D. 1828-1900	Civil War	25		95		Union Gen., Sec'y Interior, Gov. OH
Cox, James M.	Governor	15	60	75	25	Pres. Candidate,MOC,Gov. OH
Cox, Palmer*	Cartoonist	50	140	275	225	Author, Illustrator Brownies
Cox, Samuel S. 1824-89	Congress	25		125		Civil War Repr. OH
Cox, Wally	Entertainment	25		78	40	
Cox, William R.	Civil War	60	85	105		CSA Gen.
Coxe, Tenche	Revolutionary War	40	100	170		Continental Congress
Coxey, Jacob S.	Reformer	20	55	140	30	Led Coxey's Army to Wash. D.C
Coyote, Peter	Entertainment	10			35	
Crabbe, Buster 1909-83	Entertainment	30	15	40	68	Actor. Flash Gordon,Tarzan
Crabtree, Lotta (Charlotte)	Entertainment	25	70	125	130	Am. Musical Comedy Actress
Craddock, Crash	Country Music	5	8	20	18	
Craig, Edward Gordon 1872-1966	Entertainment	15	40	155	190	Br. Stage Designer, Actor
Craig, James	Civil War	45	75	95		Union General

NAME	CATEGORY	SIG	LS/DS	ALS	SP	Comment
Craig, James	Entertainment	15			35	
Craig, James, Sir	Head of State	60	185			1st Prime Minister No. Ireland
Craig, Jenny	TV Personality	4			10	Talk Show Host
Craig, Malin	Military	6	15	30		
Craig, Yvonne	Entertainment	7			15	Pin-Up SP $30
Craigavon, James C. 1871-1940	Head of State	20		35		1st P.M. Northern Ireland
Crain, Jeanne	Entertainment	15	20	40	45	Pin-Up SP $50
Cram, Donald J., Dr.	Science	20	35		30	Nobel Chemistry
Cramer, Floyd	Country Music	5			12	Pianist
Cramer, Grant	Entertainment	6	8	15	15	
Cranch, Christopher P.1813-92	Artist	5		25	35	
Crane Frank	Clergy	15	20	35		
Crane, Bob	Entertainment	150			200	Murdered TV Star Hogans Heroes
Crane, Charles Henry	Civil War	25	175	210		Union General.Surgeon
Crane, Cheryl	Celebrity	30			40	Killed Mother's Friend
Crane, Daniel (Scandal)	Congress	5		25	20	MOC IL
Crane, Frank	Clergy	15	25	45		
Crane, Fred	Entertainment	15			35	
Crane, Hart	Author	130	600	1500	350	Am. Poet, The Bridge
Crane, Henry Hitt	Clergy	25	30	50	35	
Crane, John	Military	100	250			Gen. Revolutionary War
Crane, Richard	Entertainment	20			45	
Crane, Roy*	Cartoonists	30			200	Wash Tubbs, B. Sawyer
Crane, Stephen	Author	370	1100	4350		Died at 28.Red Badge of......
Crane, Walter 1845-1915	Artist - Poet	45	140	300		Br. Painter-Illustrator. Cont. ALS $600
Crane, William H. 1845-1928	Entertainment	30	45	90	55	Vintage Actor
Crane, William M.1784-1846	Military	15				War 1812 Navy
Crane, Winthrop M.	Senate-Business	10	25		35	Crane Stationery, Gov., Sen. MA
Cranston, Alan	Senate	15	20		22	Senator CA
Cranston, Henry Young 1789-1864	Congress	10				Repr. RI
Crass, Franz	Entertainment	5			25	Opera
Craven, Frank	Entertainment	20			55	Vintage Film & Stage Actor
Craven, Wes	Entertainment	10			25	Director
Cravens, Jordan E.	Civil War	25		80		CSA Officer, MOC AR
Crawford, Broderick 1911-86	Entertainment	35	50	40	85	
Crawford, Christina	Author	6	10	20	15	Daughter of Joan Crawford
Crawford, Cindy	Model	10			55	Pin-Up SP $50
Crawford, Francis M. 1854-1909	Author	12	15	25		Am. Novelist
Crawford, Geo. W. 1798-1872	Cabinet		40	95		Sec'y War.Gov. GA Secessionist
Crawford, J. W. Capt. Jack	Military-Author	35		250		Indian Wars Scout.The Poet Scout
Crawford, Joan 1908-77	Entertainment	45	181	170	177	Pin-Up SP $200
Crawford, Johnny	Entertainment	15			30	
Crawford, Michael	Entertainment	20		35	70	
Crawford, Robert	Composer	25				Air Force Song AMusQS $275
Crawford, Samuel W.	Civil War	48	85	210		Union Gen.
Crawford, William H. 1772-1834	Cabinet	40	155	150		Madison Sec'y War. ALS/Cont. $1500
Crawford-Frost, Wm. A.	Business	15	25	70	20	
Cream	Entertainment	35			75	
Creedence Clearwater Revival	Entertainment	40			90	
Creeley, Robert 1926-	Contemp. Poet	5	12		10	Am. Poet. The Charm—1st Ed. S $150
Cregar, Laird 1916-44	Entertainment	115	120	250	318	300 lb. Character Actor. Died at 28
Creighton, John O.	Astronaut	5			15	
Creighton, Johnston B.(War Date)	Civil War	65	350			Union Adm.
Creighton, Mandell	Clergy	10	15	20		
Cremer, Peter Erich	Military	75		120		
Crenna, Richard	Entertainment	5	6	15	15	Versatile Film-TV Actor

The Sanders Price Guide to Autographs

NAME	CATEGORY	SIG	LS/DS	ALS	SP	Comment
Cresap, Mark	Business	4	6	15	7	
Crespin, Régine	Entertainment	10			60	Opera
Creston, Paul	Composer	10			125	
Creswell, John A. J.	Cabinet	20	25	40		Senator MD,CW MOC. P.M. Gen.
Crews, John R.	Military	10			20	Award CMH, WWII
Crews, Laura Hope 1880-1942	Entertainment	165			350	Aunt Pittypat-Gone With the..
Crichton, Michael	Author	15	150		95	Jurassic Park, etc.
Crick, Francis, Dr.	Science	50	75			Nobel in Medicine, DNA
Crier, Katherine	TV News	5			10	TV Commentary, Special Analysis
Crimson Tide (Cast Of)	Entertainment				130	Gene Hackman
Crippen, Hawley Harvey	Criminal		415	500		Murdered Wife.Executed in Eng.
Crippen, Robert L.	Astronaut	7			115	Shuttle Orbiter 102 Crew
Cripps, Richard Stafford, Sir	Statesman	30	90	210		Br.Economist, King's Counsel
Crisp, Charles Frederick	Senate/Congress	20		35		CSA Officer,' Speaker of House
Crisp, Charles Robert	Senate/Congress	12	20		15	MOC GA
Crisp, Donald	Entertainment	50	60	90	150	
Cristal, Linda	Entertainment	10	15	30	22	Pin-Up SP $25
Crittenden, John J. 1787-1863	Cabinet	25	60	125		Sen.,MOC KY, Att'y General
Crittenden, Thomas L. (War Date)	Civil War	85			2500	Union Gen.
Crittenden, Thomas L. 1819-93	Civil War	50	135	285	250	Union Gen.
Croce, Benedetto	Author-Philos.	25	35	80		It.Statesman, Critic, Historian
Crocker, Charles	Business	20	55	100		Am.Financier. Pres. S.P. RR
Crockett, David 1786-1836	Military	6000	9250	29500		Am. Frontiersman.Died at Alamo
Crockett, Samuel R.	Author	7	15	35		Scot.Abandoned Ministry
Croft, Dwayne	Entertainment	5			25	Opera
Croghan, George	Colonial America	195	420	850		Trader,Indian Agt,Treaty Maker
Croker, Richard Boss	Politician	20	45	80		Tammany Hall Leader
Croly, George	Clergy	15	25	40		
Crompton, Richmal	Author	15	40	80	30	
Cromwell, James	Entertainment	10			40	SP Col./Babe $70
Cromwell, Oliver 1599-1658	Head of State	1200	7000	10225		Named Lord Protector Eng.
Cromwell, Richard	Entertainment	7	9	20	15	
Cronenberg, David	Entertainment	10			25	Film Director
Cronin, A. J.	Author	25	85	170	30	Br. Physician-Novelist.
Cronin, James W.	Science	15	25	35	20	Nobel Physics
Cronkite, Walter	TV News	10	20	35	20	TV News Anchor, Commentator
Cronyn, Hume	Entertainment	10	15	25	35	Cronyn & Jessica Tandy SP $100
Crook and Chase	Entertainment	5			10	Lorianne & Charlie
Crook, George 1818-90	Civil War	112	438	375	400	Union Gen. Sig/Rank $385
Crookes, William, Sir 1832-1919	Science	132	125	180		Br.Phys., Chem., Nobel. Thallium
Crooks, Richard	Entertainment	19	38	45	50	Opera
Crosby, Bing 1901-77	Entertainment	75	360	395	194	AMusQS $75
Crosby, Bob	Entertainment	15			25	Big Band Leader
Crosby, Cathy Lee	Entertainment	9	10	20	25	Pin-Up SP $30
Crosby, Gary	Entertainment	3	3	6	6	
Crosby, Howard	Clergy	15	20	25		
Crosby, J.T.	Aviation	10	22	38	28	ACE, WW II, Navy Ace
Crosby, Kathryn	Entertainment	10	15	25	25	
Crosby, Mary	Entertainment	3	5	10	15	
Crosby, Norm	Entertainment	5	6	15	10	
Crosby, Percy*	Cartoonist	40	90		200	Skippy
Crosby, Stills & Nash	Entertainment					Alb. S $125
Crosley, Powel Jr.	Business	20	75	95	35	Crosley Radio Corp.
Crosman, Henrietta	Entertainment	10			25	40 Years on Stage. Silent Films
Cross, Christopher	Entertainment	5			10	Composer, Singer
Cross, Marcia	Entertainment	15			50	Actress, Melrose Place

NAME	CATEGORY	SIG	LS/DS	ALS	SP	Comment
Cross, Wilbur L.	Governor	4	10			Gov. CT
Crosse, Andrew 1784-1855	Science			165		Br. Electrical Pioneer/Copper-Zinc Battery
Crossfield, A. Scott	Aviation	15	30	45	55	1st U.S. Test Pilot of X-15
Crossman, George H.	Civil War	20		80	48	General
Crothers, Rachel	Author	7	30	45	15	Am. Playwright. Susan & God
Crothers, Scatman 1910-86	Entertainment	25	30	45	65	Black Character Actor
Crouse, Lindsay	Entertainment	15	15	30	30	
Crouse, Russell	Author	10	15	45	60	Playwright. Life With Father
Croves, H. (B.Traven)(Torsvan)	Author	250	800			Ger. Novelist, Actor, Pacifist
Crow, Sheryl	Entertainment	20			90	Rocker, Grammy winner
Crowe, Eyre	Statesman			20		British Circa 1923
Crowe, William	Military	15	45		25	Admiral U.S. Navy
Crowley, Leo	Cabinet	3	5	10	5	Chm. FDIC. 9 Gov't Posts
Crowley, Pat	Entertainment	5	6	15	15	
Crowninshield, Benj. W.	CabinetP	30	85	185		Sec'y Navy 1814
Crozier, William	Military	35			60	General WW I, Inventor
Cruikshank, Eliza	Celebrity			60		Mrs. George Cruicshank
Cruikshank, George*	Artist	160	115	345	375	Illustrator,Caricaturist,Etcher
Cruise, Tom	Entertainment	20	25	60	85	
Crumb, George	Composer	25		375		Pulitzer, AMusQS $200, $320
Crumb, Robert*	Cartoonist	25			260	Underground Cartoons
Crume, Dillard	Entertainment	5			20	Blues Bassist/Koko Taylor
Crummit, Frank	Entertainment	5			15	Vintage Radio/Julia Sanderson
Cruz-Romo, Gilda	Entertainment	5			30	Opera
Cruzen, Richard H.	Explorer	20		50	75	Adm. Arctic-Antarctic/Byrd
Crystal, Billy	Entertainment	20			45	Stand-up Comedian-Actor
Cuberli, Lella	Entertainment	10			35	
Cudahy, Michael F.	Business	25	65	135	50	Meat Packer. Refrigeration
Cuellar, Javier P.	Diplomat	5			15	Sec'y Gen. UN
Cugat, Xavier	Entertainment	20	30	35	100	Big Band Rhumba King
Cui, Cesar 1835-1918	Composer	95	200	450		And Russian Military Engineer
Cukor, George	Entertainment	25	95		95	Stage and Screen Director
Culbertson, Ely 1891-1955	Author	25	80		150	Invented Culbertson Contract Bridge
Culbertson, Frank L. Jr.	Astronaut	6			20	
Culkin, Macaulay	Entertainment	20			42	Child Actor
Cullen, Countee 103-46	Author	200	410	400		Am. Black Poet
Cullom, Shelby M. 1829-1914	Congress	35	60			MOC 1865, Senator, Gov. IL
Cullum, George W. 1809-92	Civil War	25		70		Union Gen.
Culp, Julia	Entertainment	35			150	Opera
Culp, Robert	Entertainment	9	10	25	25	
Culver, Roland	Entertainment	10	15	25	25	
Culverhouse, Hugh	Business	10		15		
Cumming, Alfred 1829-1910	Civil War	100	295	330		CSA General
Cummings, e.e.(Edw. Estlin)	Author	200	350	500	690	Am. Poet, Painter
Cummings, Homer 1870-1956	Cabinet	25	40	75	125	FDR Att'y Gen.
Cummings, Robert	Entertainment	15			38	
Cunard, Samuel, Sir	Business	90	130	210		Br. Shipowner.Cunard Line
Cunningham, Andrew B. 1883-1963	Military		100	200		Br. Adm. S. Afr. & WW I
Cunningham, E.V. (Howard Fast)	Author	20			35	Suspense Novels & Sci-Fi
Cunningham, John W.	Clergy	10	15	20	35	
Cunningham, Merce 1922-	Entertainment	40		200	60	Dancer/Choreogr. Kennedy Award
Cunningham, R. Walter	Astronaut	10	20	30	25	
Cunningham, Randy Duke	Aviation	12	25	45	38	ACE, Nam, Only Navy Ace
Cuomo, Mario	Governor	15	35		65	Governor NY
Curie, Marie 1867-1934	Science	1050	2753	3400	3315	Curie Laboratory DS $9,500
Curie, Pierre 1859-1906	Science	440	895	3750		Content ALS $9,000

The Sanders Price Guide to Autographs

NAME	CATEGORY	SIG	LS/DS	ALS	SP	Comment
Curless, Dick	Country Music	10			20	
Curley, Michael J., Archbishop	Clergy	45	55	65		
Curley, Pauline	Entertainment	4			20	Vintage Actress
Currie, Donald, Sir	Business	10	20	40		Scot. Shipowner. Castle Line
Currier, Moody	Governor	4			10	Gov. NY
Currier, Nathaniel	Artist	225	800			Currier & Ives, Lithographers
Curry, B.	Civil War	30	70			CSA Officer
Curry, Charles Forrest	Senate/Congress	10	15	35		MOC CA
Curry, George	Military	30	105			1st Territorial Gov. NM
Curry, Jabez L.M. 1825-1903	Civil War			40		CSA Congr. Lt. Col. Cavalry
Curry, John Steuart	Artist	65		370		Orig. Ink Sketch S $750,Murals
Curry, Tim	Entertainment	15			45	Rocky Horror Show
Curtin, Andrew G.	Governor	30	45			Civil War Gov. PA.
Curtin, Jane	Entertainment	10	15	20	25	
Curtis, Alan	Entertainment	12	15	35	25	
Curtis, Benjamin R. (SC)	Supreme Court	35	150	250		Resigned. Protest of Dred Scott
Curtis, Charles (V) 1860-1936	Vice President	55	125	175	90	Native Am. Descent
Curtis, Cyrus H. K.	Business	35	55	140	95	Curtis Publishing Co.
Curtis, Edward Sheriff 1868-1952	Artist		500		1300	Photographer, Native Americans
Curtis, George Wm. 1824-92	Author	60	130	55		Editor Harper's Weekly.Civil War
Curtis, Jamie Lee	Entertainment	9	10	20	35	Pin-Up SP $40
Curtis, Ken 1916-91	Entertainment	25			70	Festus. Country Music
Curtis, Newton M.1835-1910	Civil War	30	85			Union Gen. ALS '62 $155
Curtis, Robin	Entertainment	6	8	15	15	
Curtis, Samuel Ryan 1817-66	Civil War	50	60	235		Union Gen'l. Hero of Pea Ridge
Curtis, Tony	Entertainment	10	10	20	28	
Curtis, Verna Maria	Entertainment	10			30	Am. Soprano
Curtis, Wilfred A.	Aviation	10	25	40	25	
Curtiss, Glenn	Aviation	285	400	650	850	Am. Inventor. Pioneer Aircraft
Curtiz, Michael	Entertainment	30	75		100	Film Director
Curzon, Robert (Zouche)	Br. Explorer	10		25		
Cusack, John	Entertainment	15			35	
Cushing, Caleb 1800-79	Cabinet	25	55	100		Pierce Att'y Gen., Diplomat
Cushing, Harvey, Dr.	Science	165	475	675		Specialist in Neurosurgery
Cushing, Peter	Entertainment	15	19	38	40	
Cushing, Richard 1895-1970	Clergy	35	98	80	55	Rom. Cath. Cardinal
Cushing, Thomas 1725-1788	Colonial Am.	565	1100			Patriot.Prominent in Col.Congr.
Cushman, Charlotte S.	Entertainment	15	20	35	75	19th Century Stage Actress
Cushman, Robert E.,Jr. 1914-	Military				40	Gen. U.S. Marines. Vietnam War
Cushman, Samuel	Senate/Congress	10	20	35		MOC NH 1835
Custer, Elizabeth	Author-Civil War	80	200	775	360	Wife of George A. Custer
Custer, George A. (War Date)	Civil War	3380	3630	13000	8625	Union Gen., Indian Fighter
Custer, George A. 1839-76	Civil War	2850	8250	8500		Union Gen.
Custine, Adam Philippe, Count de	Revolutionary War	100	350			Fr.Gen.Fought in Am. Revolution
Cutler, Lysander	Civil War	90	185	260		Union General
Cutler, Manasseh 1742-1823	Revolutionary War	425	550			Am.Clergyman, Botanist, Pioneer
Cuvier, Georges, Baron 1769-1832	Science	70	350	365		Fr. Comparative Anatomy
Cuyler, Theodore L.	Author	10	15	35		
Cyrus, Billy Ray	Country Music	25	70		55	
Czerny, Carl	Composer	75	255	460		Master of Liszt. Etudes

NAME	CATEGORY	SIG	LS/DS	ALS	SP	Comment
Czerny, Vincenz	Science	110		900		Ger. Leader Abdominal Surgery
Czerwenka, Oskar	Entertainment	5			25	Opera

D

D'Abo, Maryan	Entertainment	10			20	Pin-Up SP $25
D'Abo, Olivia	Entertainment	20			40	
d'Albert, Eugen	Composer	130	190		150	Ger. Pianist.Opera. AMusQS $150
D'Albert, Eugene F.C.	Composer	55	75	130		Ger. Opera, Piano Concertos
D'Amato, Alfonse	Senate/Congress	4			10	Senator NY
D'Amato, Alfred	Congress	12			75	NY
D'Angelo, Beverly	Entertainment	10			30	
D'Annunzio, Gabriele 1863-1938	Author	75	175	150	467	It. Writer, Pro-Fascist Soldier
D'Arclee', Hariclee'	Entertainment	100				Fr. Soprano
D'Artagnan, Comte de	Military			6500		Capt.Louis XIV Musketeers
D'Arville, Camille	Entertainment	15			45	Actress-Vintage
D'Eon, Charles de Beaumont	Adventurer	100		400		Louis XV's secret agent to Russ
D'Estaing,V. Gistard	Head of State	15	40	100	60	Pres. France
D'Indy, Vincent 1851-1931	Composer	40	125	358	400	Fr.Opera,Orchestral,Vocal Music
D'Orsay, Alfred, Count	Society Leader	25	65	175		Fr.Wit, Fashion Arbiter, Artist
D'Orsay, Fifi	Entertainment	15	20	25	35	
D'Oyly Carte, Rupert	Entertainment	20	70	125	135	Producer of Gilbert & Sullivan
D'Oyly, George	Clergy	15	20	35		
Da Ponte, Lorenzo	Librettist		1500			Don Geiovanne, Cosi fan tutte, Marriage of
Dache, Lilly	Business-Designer	55	70	130	150	Coutourier.Specialty-Hats
Daddi, Francesco	Entertainment	5	8	15		
Dafoe, Allan Roy, Dr.1883-1943	Science	75	60	135	225	Delivered Dionne Quintuplets
Dafoe, Willem	Entertainment	8	11	40	35	
Dagmar	Entertainment	20			35	
Dagover, Lil 1897-19??	Entertainment				195	Ger. Actress
Daguerre, Louis	Science	150	490	1250		Fr. Inventor Daguerreotype
Dahl, Arlene	Entertainment	10		15	20	Pin-Up SP $25
Dahl, Perry	Aviation	10	22	38	28	ACE, WW II
Dahl, Roald	Author	12	20	35	15	Br. Short Stories, Children's
Dahlberg, Edward	Author	15	25	35	20	Am. Writer & Critic
Dahlberg, Ken	Aviation	15	30	50	40	ACE, WW II
Dahlgren, John A.1809-70	Civil War	85	350	415		Adm. Union Navy. Dahlgren Gun
Dahlgren, Ulric	Civil War	270		1375		Union Col.Planned Capture Jeff. Davis
Dailey, Dan	Entertainment	20	25	45	40	
Dailey, Janet	Author	5	10		10	
Dailey, Peter F.	Entertainment	6	8	15	15	
Dal Monte, Toti	Entertainment	25			95	Opera
Daladier, Edouard	Head of State	30	85	150	50	Premier Fr.Arrested-Liberated
Dalai Lama XIV	Head of State	75	160	200	100	Tibetan Religious Leader
Daley, Cass	Entertainment	7	9	20	15	

NAME	CATEGORY	SIG	LS/DS	ALS	SP	Comment
Daley, Richard J.	Political	20	40	85	40	Mayor Chicago.Last Big City Bos
Daley, Richard M.	Political	5			10	Mayor Chicago
Dali, Salvador 1904-89	Artist	200	680	650	982	Sp. Surrealist Painter
Dali, Tracey	Entertainment	10			45	Model/actress
Dallapozza, Adolf	Entertainment	5			25	Vienna Operettas
Dallas, Alexander J. 1759-1817	Cabinet	42	150	190		Madison Sec'y Treasury
Dallas, George M. (V)	Vice President	50	200	300		Dallas, Texas Named for Him
Dalmores, Charles	Entertainment	25			85	Opera
Dalton, Abby	Entertainment	5	6	15	15	
Dalton, Charles	Entertainment	5	6	10	10	
Dalton, Dorothy	Entertainment	20	25	65	60	
Dalton, Emmett 1871-1937	Outlaw	600	1700	4050	2500	Western Train Robber
Dalton, Frank	Lawman	850	2500			U.S.Marshal-Old West
Dalton, John	Science	135	400	750		Br. Chemist & Philosopher
Dalton, Lacy J.	Entertainment	5			18	
Dalton, Timothy	Entertainment	20			48	
Daltry, Roger	Entertainment	15			45	Rock
Daly, James	Entertainment	5	6	15	15	
Daly, John Charles	Entertainment	5			10	Broadcaster, News Commentator
Daly, Tyne	Entertainment	9	10	20	25	
Damita, Lili	Entertainment	40	80	95	85	Fr. Film Star. Mrs. Errol Flynn
Damon, Cathryn	Entertainment	5	6	15	15	
Damon, Les	Entertainment	5			25	Radio Actor. Nick Charles Thin Man
Damone, Vic	Entertainment	5			10	Singer
Damrosch, Walter 1862-1950	Composer-Cond.	50	195	115	200	Pioneer of Symphonic Broadcasts
Dana, Charles A. 1819-97	Publisher-Editor	20	35	70	35	Owner & Editor NY Sun
Dana, James D.	Science	15		45		Scientific Observer Antarctic
Dana, James Jackson	Civil War	40	140			Union General
Dana, Napoleon J.T. 1822-1905	Civil War	30	55			Union Gen. ADS '64 $300
Dana, Richard Henry, Jr.1815-82	Author	50	200	215		Sailor,Law. Prosecutor J.Davis
Danaher, John A.	Senate/Congress	5	15		10	Senator CT
Dandridge, Dorothy 1923-65	Entertainment	45	50	75	375	
Dandridge, Ruby	Entertainment	35			90	
Dandy, George B. 1830-1911	Civil War	40	95			Twice Brevetted Union Gen.Georgian
Dane, Karl	Entertainment	10			15	Actor
Dane, Nathan	Revolutionary War	25	65	130		Continental Congress
Danei, Paul Francis 1694-1775	Clergy		7500			Saint Paul of the Cross 1867
Danenhower, John Wilson	Explorer	15	45	115		De Long Arctic Expedition 1879
Danes, Claire	Entertainment				48	Actress
Danforth, John C.	Senate	5			10	Senator MO
Danforth, Thomas 1622-1699	Colonial America	390	470			Deputy Governor MA
Dangerfield, George	Author	5	10	25		
Dangerfield, Rodney	Entertainment	10	15	25	20	
Danges, Henry 1870-1948	Entertainment	35				Opera. Baritone. Sang in World Prem. Louise
Daniel, John W.	Senate	10	25			Senator VA, Disabled in CW
Daniel, Peter Vivian (SC)	Supreme Court	40	125	230		
Daniel, Price	Senate/Congress	15	40		20	Senator, Gov. TX
Daniell, Henry	Entertainment	50			150	
Daniels, Bebe	Entertainment	20	25	65	75	
Daniels, Billy	Entertainment	10			20	Vocalist
Daniels, Charlie	Country Music	6			12	
Daniels, Jeff	Entertainment	5			30	Actor.
Daniels, Josephus	Cabinet	25	48	160	125	Sec'y Navy WW I. Diplomat
Daniels, William	Entertainment	5			20	
Daniloff, Nick	Celebrity	20		25		
Danilova, Alexandra	Entertainment	20	35	60	75	Rus-Am Ballerina, Teacher

NAME	CATEGORY	SIG	LS/DS	ALS	SP	Comment
Dankworth, Johnny	Bandleader				20	
Dannay, Frederick 1905-19F2	Author	50	160	300		ELLERY QUEEN
Dannenberg, Konrad	Science	20			55	Rocket Pioneer/von Braun
Danner, Blythe	Entertainment	5	6	15	15	
Dannihill, Albert	Entertainment	3	3	6	8	
Danning, Sybil	Entertainment	9	10	20	25	
Dano, Royal	Entertainment	8	10	20	25	
Danova, Cesare	Entertainment	6	8	15	25	
Danson, Ted	Entertainment	15			35	
Dantine, Helmut	Entertainment	12	15		40	Autrian Actor of 40's-50's
Danton, Georges-Jacques	Fr. Revolution	1080	2800			Guillotined Leader of Revolution
Danton, Ray	Entertainment	7			15	
Danza, Tony	Entertainment	10	15	28	30	
Darby, Kim	Entertainment	15			35	
Darcy, Emery	Entertainment	15			45	Met Tenor
Darden, Christopher	Law	20	125			O.J.Simpson Prosecuting Att'y
Darin, Bobby	Entertainment	50			150	
Darion, Joe	Composer	10			30	AMusQS $50
Darlan, Francois 1881-1942	Military			448		Fr. Adm. Vichy. Assassinated
Darling, J.N. 'ding'*	Cartoonist	25			150	Political Cartoonist
Darlington, William 1782-1863	Naturalist-Author	25		155		Many Swiss & US plants named for him
Darnell, Linda 1923-65	Entertainment	45	145		180	Died Tragically in Fire
Darrah, Thomas	Military	35	50			General WW I
Darrall, Chester B.	Senate/Congress	10	30	55		MOC LA. Union Surgeon CW
Darrell, Johnny	Country Music	10			20	
Darren, James	CelebrityEntertainment	10			20	
Darrieux, Danielle	Entertainment	5			25	Fr. Actress. Film & Stage
Darro, Frankie	Entertainment	50			150	
Darrow, Charles B. 1889-1967	Designer		995			Developed Best Seller Monopoly
Darrow, Clarence 1857-1938	Celebrity	472	1733	2338	1327	Scopes Trial, Loeb & Leopold
Daschle, Thomas	Congress	10			20	Senator, SD
Dart, Justin	Business	50	100	250	75	
Darville, Camille	Entertainment	10			20	Actress
Darwell, Jane 1880-1967	Entertainment	65	100	195	200	GWTW, Grapes of Wrath
Darwin, Charles 1809-92	Science	640	2250	2586	9775	Br. Naturalist.Theory of Evolution
Dassin, Jules	Entertainment	20			45	Film Director
Daubigny, Charles Francois	Artist	95	280	410		Fr. Landscape Painter
Daudet, Alphonse	Author	35	80	175		Fr. Stories, Novels, Plays
Daugherty, Harry M.	Cabinet	25	55	125	50	Att'y Gen.Tried-Acquitted Fraud
Daumier, Honore	Artist	240	630	1470		Fr. Caricaturist & Serious Art
Dauphin, Claude	Entertainment	35			75	
Dausset, Jean, Prof.	Science	20	45		30	Nobel Medicine
Dauvray, Helen	Entertainment	3	3	6	6	
Daval, Danny	Entertainment	5	6	15	15	
Dave, Red River	Country Music	10			20	
Davenport, Addington 1670-1736	Revolutionary War	140	257	500		Am. Colonial Jurist
Davenport, Fanny	Entertainment	20			50	Vintage, 1889
Davenport, Harry	Entertainment	100			250	
Davenport, Homer C.	Cartoonist	30	60	135		Political Cartoons, Uncle Sam
David, Felicien-Cesar 1810-76	Composer	100	500			AMusMsS $650-750
David, Ferdinand	Composer	45		225		Ger. Violinist
David, Hal	Composer	20	30	65	35	
David, Jacques Louis	Artist	175	440	610		Fr. Classical Painter
David, Mack	Author	20			40	Lyricist
Davidson, Allen Turner	Civil War	25	80	125		CSA Congress. Lawyer, Banker
Davidson, Jo	Artist	35	75	135		Am. Sculptor

The Sanders Price Guide to Autographs

NAME	CATEGORY	SIG	LS/DS	ALS	SP	Comment
Davidson, John	Entertainment	3	6	6	10	
Davidson, John W. 1824-81	Civil War					Union Gen. ALS '62 $630
Davidson, Loyal	Military	35	60			
Davidson, Randall T., Archbishop	Clergy	25	35	45		
Davidson, William B.	Entertainment	10				Character Actor
Davidson, William H.	Business		2565			Son of Wm. A.& Pres.Harley-Davidson
Davies, Gail	Entertainment	4			10	Singer
Davies, Marion	Entertainment	28	50	150	112	C. Bull Original SP $275
Davies, Peter Maxwell	Composer				110	Songs of a Mad King. Opera
Davies, Rhys	Author	5	20	35	10	Welch. Novels, Stories
Davies, Ronald N.	Law	25		60	30	Nazi War Trials Jurist
Davies, Thomas F., Bishop	Clergy	30	35	45		
Davies, William	Revolutionary War	35	648	170		VA Sec'y War
Davis, Angela	Activist	10	15	25	22	Afro-Am. Activist
Davis, Ann B.	Entertainment	10			25	
Davis, Benjamin O. Jr.	Aviation	20	35	75	40	ACE, WW II, Afro-Am. Pioneer
Davis, Bette 1908-89	Entertainment	95	190	350	174	
Davis, Brad	Entertainment	20			35	
Davis, Charles Henry 1807-77	Civil War	30	65	105		Union Adm. ALS '63 $275
Davis, Clifton	Entertainment	5			15	
Davis, Cushman K.	Senate	12	25		30	Senator MN
Davis, David (SC)	Supreme Court	75	295	315		Sen. IL. Pres Pro Tem
Davis, Dwight F.	Cabinet	25	80	170	65	Sec'y War
Davis, Ellabelle	Entertainment	10			40	Great Afro-Am Singer
Davis, Ewin L.	Senate/Congress	4	10			MOC TN
Davis, Fay	Entertainment	4	4	9	9	
Davis, Gail	Entertainment	15	20	25	35	
Davis, Geena	Entertainment	10	15	35	40	Semi-Nude Pin-up Col. 85
Davis, Henry Greene	Civil War	55	130			Union General
Davis, Henry Minton 1817-65	Congress	15		50		Prevented MD from Joining CSA
Davis, James J.	Cabinet	20	50	95	75	Sec'y Labor, Founder Moose
Davis, Jefferson (War Date)	Civil War		2650	7500	5500	President CSA
Davis, Jefferson 1808-89	Civil War	764	1630	2253	3500	CSA Pres. ALS/Content $15,000,LS $55000
Davis, Jefferson C. 1828-79	Civil War	50	80	110		Union Gen. ANS '62 $330
Davis, Jim	Entertainment	45	50	70	85	
Davis, Jim*	Cartoonist	35	75	225	175	Garfield
Davis, Jimmie	Governor	30	45		60	Gov. LA, You Are My Sunshine
Davis, Jo	Entertainment	3	3	6	8	
Davis, Joan	Entertainment	25			55	
Davis, John 1761-1847	Author	30	175	290		Historian, Comptroller US Treas
Davis, John 1787-1854	Governor	25	50	70		Gov. MA
Davis, John William	Congr.-Diplomat	20	35	70	40	Dem. Presidential Candidate
Davis, Johnny 'Scat'	Entertainment	10	10	12	15	
Davis, Mack	Country Music	10			20	
Davis, Meyer	Entertainment	15			35	Big Society Band
Davis, Miles	Entertainment	165			450	Jazz Trumpet
Davis, Nancy	Entertainment	50			150	
Davis, Nancy (Reagan)	First Lady	80			170	
Davis, Nelson H. 1821-90	Civil War	25	60	78		Union Gen. Chancellorsville
Davis, Noah	Senate/Congress	10	25	60		MOC NY 1869, Jurist
Davis, Ossie	Entertainment	10			25	
Davis, Patti (Reagan)	Entertainment	5	6	15	25	
Davis, Phil*	Cartoonist	30			250	Mandrake the Magician
Davis, Phyllis	Entertainment	10	15	20	25	
Davis, Reuben 1813-90	Civil War	50		270		CSA General
Davis, Rich'd Harding	Author	10	25	40	20	Correspondent 6 Wars, Novelist

The Sanders Price Guide to Autographs

NAME	CATEGORY	SIG	LS/DS	ALS	SP	Comment
Davis, Robert	Military	5		25		General WW I
Davis, Rufe	Entertainment	25			55	
Davis, Sammy, Jr.	Entertainment	40	50	80	200	
Davis, Varina	CSA First Lady	150	290	600	750	Mrs. Jeff. Davis.ALS/Cont $6000
Davis, William W.H. 1820-1910	Civil War		55			Led 104th PA
Davison, Bruce	Entertainment	5			10	
Davison, Wild Bill	Entertainment	30			75	Jazz Cornet-Bandleader
Davisson, Clinton Joseph	Science	25	75			Nobel Physics.Bell Laboratories
Davout, Louis Nicolas, Duke	Fr. Revolution	45	210	248		Marshal of Napoleon
Davy, Humphry, Sir	Science	90	270	585		ALS Content $8,500,AMsS $2500
Dawber, Pam	Entertainment	9	10	20	25	
Dawes, Charles G. (V)	Vice President	30	150	295	275	Nobel Peace Prize
Dawes, William 1745-99	Revolutionary War	3500				Patriot. Rode with Paul Revere
Dawson, George	Clergy	20	35	60		
Dawson, John B. 1798-1845	Congress	10				Repr. LA, Maj. General of Militia
Dawson, John L.	Congress	20		70		Governor Kansas Terr. ,MOC PA
Dawson-Briggs, Roxanne	Entertainment				40	Actress. Star Trek
Day, Chon*	Cartoonist	10	35		50	Brother Sebastian
Day, Dennis	Entertainment	10	15	25	30	Vocalist-Comedian. Jack Benny
Day, Doris	Entertainment	10			40	Pin-Up SP $30
Day, Frank	Celebrity	10		25		
Day, J. Edward	Cabinet	4	5	15	10	P.M. General
Day, Jeremiah	Clergy	15	20	35		
Day, Laraine	Entertainment	10			40	
Day, Linda (George)	Entertainment	6	8	15	19	
Day, William R. (SC)1849-1923	Supreme Court	40	90	135	65	Sec'y State
Day-Lewis, Daniel	Entertainment	25			85	
Dayan, Moshe 1915-1981	Military	100	235	220	195	Israeli Soldier, Politician
Dayan, Yael	Author	5			25	And Daughter of Moshe
Daymond, Gus	Aviation	12	25	55	40	ACE, WW II, Eagle Squadron
Dayne, Taylor	Entertainment	5			35	Rock
Dayton, Elias	Revolutionary War	90	210	395		General. Continental Congress
Dayton, Jonathan	Revolutionary War	175	450	657		Continental Congress
Dayton, William L.1807-67	Senator NJ	25	40	110		John C. Fremont Running Mate
De Acosta, Mercedes	Author	10	25	45		Intimate of Greta Garbo
de Almeida, Antonio	Conductor	10			45	Specialist in Fr. Music
De Beauvoir, Simone	Author	35	95	200		Fr. Writer,Philosopher,Feminist
De Bono, Emilio	Military	75	225		375	It. Fascist Politician & Gen.
De Bray, Xavier B. 1818-95	Civil War	125				CSA Gen. ALS/Cont.$2500
De Corsia, Ted	Entertainment	20	25		40	
de Duve, Christian R.	Science	10			40	Nobel
De Falla, Manuel 1876-1946	Composer	425	1200			Sp. AMusQS $2000
De Forest, Lee, Dr. 1873-1961	Science	350	1405	1412	1200	ALS Scientific Content $12,500
De Gaulle, Charles 1890-1969	Head of State	375	1088	1650	2530	Gen., Pres. Fr.Karsh SP $1395
De Havilland, Geoffrey	Aviation	70	140	205	125	De Havilland Aircraft Co.
De Kooning, Elaine*	Artist	50			275	Willem's Wife.Artist on her own
De Kooning, Willem	Artist	140	200	450	125	Repro Two Women S $285
De La Beckwith, Byron	Activist	12		35	28	White Supremicist
De La Cierva, Juan	Aviation	90		295	350	Inventor Autogyro
De La Grange, Anna	Entertainment			80		Opera
De La Mare, Walter	Author	20	65	90	30	Br. Poet.Songs of Childhood
De La Pena, George	Entertainment	3	3	6	6	
De La Renta, Oscar	Business	10	15	35	20	Fashion Designer.Elegant Gowns
De La Rue, Warren 1815-89	Science			200		Br. Astron., Inventor Silver-Chlor. Battery
De Lancey, Stephen	Revolutionary War	75	180	225		Loyalist. Lawyer. Imprisoned
De Leo, Sarafina	Entertainment				40	Opera

PRICES   275

NAME	CATEGORY	SIG	LS/DS	ALS	SP	Comment
De Luca, Giuseppe	Entertainment	25	35	95	175	Opera
De Mornay, Rebecca	Entertainment	7	25		35	Pin-up Color $60
De Palma, Brian	Entertainment	15		30	30	Film Director
De Paul, Saint Vincent	Clergy	1100	1600	4500		
De Peyster, John W. Jr.	Civil War	10	20	55		Aide to Gen.Kearny
De Quincey, Thomas	Author	145	310	650		AMs $650-$2,250
De Quincy, Thomas 1785-1859	Author	45				AMs $650
De Reszke, Edouard 1853-1917	Entertainment	68			150	Opera-Vintage. AMusQS $75
De Reszke, Jean 1850-1925	Entertainment	100	120	75	345	Opera-Vintage
De Reszke, Marie	Entertainment			125		Opera
De Ridder. Anton	Entertainment	10		45	35	Opera
De Rita, Joe	Entertainment	15			35	
De Russy, Gustavus A.(War Date)	Civil War	50	250	233		Union Gen.
De Seversky, Alex. 1894-1973	Aviation	90	250	205	238	TLS/Historical Cont. $1,200
De Smet, Pierre 1801-73	Jesuit Missionary	225		800		Missionary to Western Indians
De Toth, Andre'	Entertainment	10			20	Film Director
De Trobriand, Philippe R.(War Date)	Civil War	50	325	395		Union Gen.
De Valera, Eamon (Ire)1882-1975	Head of State	45	125	325	110	Pres. P.M. Cont.TLS $550
De Vere, Aubrey T.	Author	20	60	140		Ir. Poet,Critic,Hymns
De Wilde, Brandon	Entertainment	100			300	
De Windt, Harry 1856-1933	Explorer	30	15	75	50	Br. Explorer
De Witt, Alexander	Senate/Congress	5		20		MOC MA
Deacon, Richard	Entertainment	25			50	
Dean, Billy	Country Music	5			20	
Dean, Donald J.	Military	15	45			WW I Victoria Cross
Dean, Eddie	Country Music	10	10	20	25	
Dean, Gilbert 1819-70	Congress	9				Repr. NY
Dean, James 1931-55	Entertainment	2250	6875	3250	7500	
Dean, Jimmy	Country Music	5			12	Sausages & CW Singer
Dean, John W.	Law	5	15	25	95	Special Counsel to Nixon. Watergate
Dean, Julia	Entertainment	6	8	15	15	
Dean, Maureen	Author	10	35			(Mrs. John Dean)
Dean, William F.	Military	15	35	45	35	Gen. WW II
Deane, Silas	Revolutionary War	230	550	1050		Diplomat. Negotiated Treaties
DeAngelis, Jefferson	Entertainment	10				Actor
Dearborn, Henry (1751-1829)	Cabinet	110	402	580		Rev. War. Jefferson's Sec'y War.
Dearborn, Henry A.S.1783-1851	Senate/Congress	55	175	250		Collector Port Boston 1812-29
Dearden, John, Cardinal	Clergy	30	35	45	40	
Death on the Nile (Cast)	Entertainment				75	Signed by 6
Debakey, Michael, Dr.	Science	20	35		35	1st Coronary Artery Bypass Op.
Debar, William J.	Senate	10	15			Senator KY
DeBeaune, Charlotte	Celebrity		525			Mistress of Henry IV
DeBeck, Billy*	Cartoonist	30			260	Barney Google, Snuffy Smith
DeBlanc, Jeff	Aviation	12	28	52	38	ACE, WW II, CMH
DeBray, Xavier B. 1818-95	Civil War	95		248		CSA General
Debre, Michael	Head of State	5	20	50		
DeBroglie, Louis-C-V- Maurice	Science	35	90			Physicist. Pioneer in X-Rays
Debs, Eugene	Labor	70	225	255	135	U.S. Socialist Leader.Organizer
Debussy, Claude 1862-1918	Composer	388	1625	1188		AMusQS $7,500
DeButts, John D.	Business	10	35	45	20	
Debye, Peter J.W.	Science	55	110	175		NobelChemistry-Discovered Rayon
Decamp, Rosemary	Entertainment	5			40	Am.Radio & Film Star
DeCarlo, Yvonne	Entertainment	10	9	20	40	
DeCasseres. Benjamin	Author	5	15	25		Columnist, Editorials NY Mirror
Decatur, Stephen	Military	1100	3100	5710		American Naval Hero, War 1812
DeCisneros, Eleanora	Entertainment	40			185	Opera

NAME	CATEGORY	SIG	LS/DS	ALS	SP	Comment
DeCordova, Fred	Entertainment	5	8	15	15	
Dee, Francis	Entertainment	5	6	15	25	
Dee, Ruby	Entertainment	5	6	15	20	
Dee, Sandra	Entertainment	6	8	15	20	Pin-Up SP $25
Deems, 'Cousin'	Country Music	4			15	And His Goat Herders
Deems, Charles Force	Celebrity	5	10	20		
Deere, Allan Christopher	Aviation-Ace	15	40	50		N.Z. Ace WWII, 22 confirmed
Deere, John 1804-86	Business	300		1422		Steel Plow.Deere Check $4750
Deering, James	Business	10	25	45	25	
Deering, Olive	Entertainment	15			35	
Dees, Rick	Country Western	3	5	15	10	Singer
Defoe, Daniel 1660-1731	Author	1500	7500			Br. Journalist, Novelist
DeFore, Don	Entertainment	10			15	
Defore, Don	Entertainment	5			15	
DeFranco, Buddy	Entertainment	12			25	Bandleader, Clarinetist
Degas, Edgar (Hilaire Germain)	Artist	250	760	2042		Fr.Impressionist. Ballet Scenes
DeGeneres, Ellen	Entertainment	10			40	Comedienne
DeHart, John	Revolutionary War	30	65	140		
DeHaven, Gloria	Entertainment	6	8	15	20	
DeHaven, Robert	Aviation	10	20	40	30	ACE, WW II
DeHavilland, Olivia	Entertainment	30	60	30	55	As Melanie, SP $150 in GWTW
Dehmelt, Hans G., Dr.	Science	20	35		30	Nobel Physics
Dehner, John	Entertainment	10		10	15	
Deisenhofer, Johann	Science	27	36		35	Nobel
Dekker, Albert	Entertainment	6			10	
DeKlerk, F.W.	Head of State	75	150		90	Nobel Peace, Pr.Minister S.A.
DeKoven, Reginald 1859-1920	Composer	25	45	150	100	Versatile American Composer
Del Fuegos, The	Entertainment	20			50	
Del Monaco, Marlo	Entertainment	45	65	125	175	Opera
Del Rio, Delores	Entertainment	30	35	55	65	
Del Tredici, David	Composer	15	35	80		Pulitzer, AMusQS $100
Delacroix, F.V. Eugene 1798-18863	Artist	175	385	717		Brilliant Colorist.Great Murals
DeLaCroix, Raven	Entertainment	3	3	6	8	
Delafield, John R.	Military	8				General
Delafield, Richard	Civil War	38	65	95		Union General. Engineer
DeLagnel, Juius A. 1827-1912	Civil War	85		200		CSA General
DeLancie, John	Entertainment				45	Actor. Star Trek
DeLand, Margaret	Author	12	25	75	25	Am. Novelist.Old ChesterTales
Delaney, Kim	Entertainment	10	35	70	50	Actress "NYPD Blue"
Delano, Columbus	Cabinet	20				Sec'y Interior, Grant
Delany, Dana	Entertainment	10		25	40	Actress
Delbridge, Del	Entertainment	10			15	Radio Announcer
Deledda, Grazia	Author	45	105	320		Nobel Literature 1926
DeLiagre, Alfred	Entertainment	5	7	12	10	
Delibes, Leo	Composer	85	220	340		Light Opera, Ballet
Delius, Frederick 1862-1934	Composer	300	395	770		Br.Orchestral, Concerti, Songs
Dell, Gabriel	Entertainment	15	20	25	35	
Dell, Myrna	Entertainment	5	6	10	10	Pin-Up SP $15
Della Casa, Lisa	Entertainment	10			25	Swiss Soprano. Opera
Della Chiesa, Vivian	Entertainment	5	6	15	15	Soprano
Della Joio, Norman	Composer	35	115	240	55	Pulitzer, AMusQS $50-$175
Dellums, Ronald B.	Senate/Congress	10	15		15	Afro-Am. Congressman CA
Delna, Marie	Entertainment	25			90	Fr. Contralto. Opera
DeLong, Phillip C.	Aviation	12	25	40	30	ACE, WW II
Deluise, Dom	Entertainment	10			30	
DeLuise, Dom	Entertainment	5	6	15	15	

NAME	CATEGORY	SIG	LS/DS	ALS	SP	Comment
DeMarco, Antonio	Entertainment	10	25			Producer
DeMarco, Tony	Entertainment		25			Dancer
Demarest, William	Entertainment	15		25	35	
DeMille, Agnes	Entertainment	50	200		150	Dancer,Innovative Choreographer
DeMille, Cecil B. 1881-1959	Entertainment	55	233	395	275	Director, Producer, Film Giant
DeMille, Katherine	Entertainment	10	12	15	25	
DeMille, William C.	Entertaiment	15	45		50	Early Dir.,Playwright,Producer
DeMonvel, Boutes	Artist	25	70	125		
Dempsey, John	Governor	12				Gov. CT
Dempsey, Patrick	Entertainment	10			15	
Dempsey, Stephen W.	Congress	4	25			Repr. NY
Demslow, W.W.*	Cartoonist	50			175	Illustrator Of Wizard Of Oz
Demzn, Lev	Cosmonaut	20	30			
Denby, Edwin	Cabinet	20	50	75	45	Sec'y Navy
Deneuve, Catherine	Entertainment	10	15	25	35	Pin-Up SP $40
Denfeld, Louis E.	Military	10	25	40	25	Adm.Chief Naval Operations WWII
DeNiro, Robert	Entertainment	15	25	40	85	
Denison, Charles S.	Senate	5	10	15		Senator IL
Denison, John H.	Clergy	10	15	25		
Denman, G. Tony	Aviation	10	20	35	25	ACE, WW II, Navy Ace
Denman, Thomas, 3rd Baron	Head of State	7	15	35		Gov. General Australia
Dennehy, Brian	Entertainment	15	35		25	
Denning, Richard	Entertainment	6	8	15	15	
Dennis, Sandy	Entertainment	38	45		85	
Dennison, Jo Carroll	Entertainment	5	6	10	10	
Dennison, William	Cabinet	145		600		Lincoln P.M. Gen. CW Gov. OH
Dent, Elliott	Aviation	10	22	38	30	ACE, WW II
Dent, Frederick T.	Civil War	35	90	225		Union Gen.
Dent, S. Hubert	Senate/Congress	5	15		15	MOC AL
Denton, Jeremiah A., Jr.	Military-Congress	10	20	30	20	Admiral WW II, MOC AL
Denver, Bob	Entertainment	7	7	10	20	
Denver, James W.	Civil War	100	210	450		Denver, CO. Union Gen.
Denver, John	Country Music	5	6	15	25	
Denza, Luigi 1846-1922	Composer					AMusQS $50-$110
Depardieu, Gerard	Entertainment	10			35	
Depew, Chauncey M.	Financier	30	158		70	Orator,NY Central RR, U.S. Sen.NY
Depp, Johnny	Entertainment	20		40	75	
Derain, Andre'	Artist	125	210	425		Repro Femme Nu Assise $285
Derby,14thEarl (Edward Stanley)	Head of State	50	35	95		Br. Prime Minister
Derby,16th Earl(Fred Stanley)	Head of State					
Derek & Dominoes (all)	Entertainment	50			150	
Derek, Bo	Entertainment	10	15	25	20	Pin-Up SP $50
Derek, John	Entertainment	15	28	35	25	
Deringer, Henry 1786-1868	Arms Mfg.	450		6500		Invented Derringer Pistol
Derleth, August	Author	20	75			
Dern, Bruce	Entertainment	6	8	15	15	
Dern, George H.	Cabinet	10	20	35		Sec'y War, Mining Exec.,Gov. UT
Dern, Laura	Entertainment	5	8	25	25	
Dershowitz, Alan M.	Law	16	20		30	Trial Attorney
Desai, M.R.	Head of State	5	15	25		Prime Minister India
Desanto, Sugar Pie	Entertainment	15			35	James Brown Vocalist
Descartes, Rene	Philosopher	950	4035	10000		Mathematician.Analytic Geometry
Deschanel, Paul Eugène L. 1856-1922	Head of State			100		Pres. France 1920. Resigned
Descher, Sandy	Entertainment				30	Child Actress
DeSilva, Howard	Entertainment	10	12	20	25	
Desmond, Johnny	Entertainment	3	5		8	Singer

NAME	CATEGORY	SIG	LS/DS	ALS	SP	Comment
Desmond, Shaw 1877-1960	Author	25	75			Irish Playwright. Pioneered Paranormal
Desmond, William	Entertainment	40				Vintage Film Actor
Despretz, César	Science	5		30		Fr. Physician. Inventor Electric Arc Furnace
Dessalines, Jean-Jacques 1750-1806	Revolutionary		2500			Haitian Ruler
Destinn, Emmy 1878-1930	Entertainment	100		225	190	Czech Soprano
Detaille, Edwouard 1848-1912	Artist	110		325		Fr. Military & Portr. Painter
DeTreville, Yvonne	Entertainment	20			85	Opera, Light Opera
Deutekom, Cristina	Entertainment	10			35	Dutch Coloratura Soprano. Opera
Deutsch, Emery	Bandleader	5				
Deutsch, Patti	Entertainment	3	3	6	8	
DeVane, William	Entertainment	10	5	10	30	
Devens, Charles, Jr.1820-91	Military -Cabinet	32	50	150	150	Union Gen.-Att'y Gen.
Devereux, James P.S.	Military	35	70	90	150	Gen. WW II, Congress MD
Devers, Jacob L.	Military	10	20	35	35	General WW II
Devine, Andy 1905-77	Entertainment	30	35	50	162	Comic Sidekick of Roy Rogers etc.
DeVito, Danny	Entertainment	8	10	20	25	As The Penguin $75
Devo	Entertainment	30			60	
DeVos, Rich	Business	18			25	Founder Amway
DeVries, William, Dr.	Science	15	25	40	20	
Dew, William, Bishop	Clergy	20	30	45		
Dewey, George	Military-Civil War	80	160	200	300	Span. American War. Admiral
Dewey, John	Author	60	155	250	75	Philosopher, Educator, Psychol.
Dewey, Orville	Clergy	15	20	25		
Dewey, Thomas E. 1902-1971	Governor	40	65	165	90	Presidential Candidate,Gov.NY
Dewhurst, Colleen	Entertainment	10		35	40	
DeWitt, Joyce	Entertainment	5	8	15	25	
DeWolf, H.G.	Military	5	15		20	Canadian Adm. WW II
DeWolfe, Billy 1907-74	Entertainment	25	40	50	45	
Dexter, J.M.	Clergy	10	15	20		
Dey, Susan	Entertainment	9	10	20	25	
DeYoung, Russell	Business	5			10	CEO Goodyear Tire & Rubber Co.
Di Stefano, Giuseppe	Entertainment	25		65	75	It. TenorOpera
Diaghilev, Sergei 1872-1929	Entertainment			2250		Ballet Impresario
Diamond, David	Composer	25		35		AMusQS $200
Diamond, Neil	Entertainment	5	6	15	15	Composer-Singer
Diamond, Selma	Entertainment	30	40	55	75	
Diana, Princess (Eng)	Royalty	548				Princess Di
Diaz, Armando Vittorio	Military	35	100	175	120	It. General WW I
Diaz, Cameron	Entertainment				38	Actor
Diaz, Porfirio	Head of State	100	196	250	225	Dictatorial Pres. of Mexico
Dibrell, George Gibbs (War Date)	Civil War	290				CSA General
Dibrell, George Gibbs 1822-88	Civil War	155	365	317		CSA General, MOC TN
Dick, Fred	Aviation	10	22	40	30	ACE, WW II
Dick, Samuel	Revolutionary War	50	170	225		Continental Congress NJ
Dickens, Charles 1812-70	Author	612	1038	2038	3342	Br. Novelist.Christmas Carol,Oliver Twist
Dickens, Jimmy	Country Music	5			10	
Dickenson, Don M.	Cabinet	15	20	45	20	P.M. General 1888
Dickerson, Mahlon 1770-1853	Cabinet-U.S. Sen.	25	85	150		Jackson Sec'y Navy. Gov. NJ
Dickey, James	Author	12	30	65	50	Am. Poet, Novelist *Deliverance*
Dickinson, Angie	Entertainment	6	14	15	25	Pin-Up SP $30
Dickinson, Anna Eliz.1842-1932	Author	25	70	142		Abolitionist-Lecturer
Dickinson, Clement C.	Senate/Congress	5			15	MOC MO
Dickinson, Daniel S.	Senate/Congress	15	25			Senator from NY
Dickinson, Don M.	Cabinet	10	20			P.M. Gen. 1888
Dickinson, Emily	Author	615	2560	6275		
Dickinson, Jacob M. 1851-1928	Cabinet	25	45	125		Taft Sec'y of War

 # The Sanders Price Guide to Autographs

NAME	CATEGORY	SIG	LS/DS	ALS	SP	Comment
Dickinson, James S.	Civil War	25	40	75		CSA Congressman
Dickinson, John P.	Revolutionary War	200	575			Continental Congress
Dickison, J. J.	Civil War	75	155	195		CSA Cav'ry Off.,Florida's Mosby
Dickman, Joseph	Military	50				General WW I
Dicks, Jacob	Governor	15	25	40		Governor NY
Diddley, Bo	Entertainment	20			52	Rock
Didier-Pouget, W.	Artist	30	65	95		
Diefenbaker, John	Head of State	15	35	110	20	Prime Minister Canada
Diem, Ngo Dinh	Head of State	50				Pres. So. Viet Nam
Diemer, Louis	Composer	25			45	Fr. Pianist. AMusQS $100
Diemer, Walter E.	Business	20		75	90	Inventor Dubble Bubble Gum
Dies, Martin	Senate/Congress	15	50		25	MOC TX. Un-American Activities
Diesel, Rudolf	Science	900		3250		Ger. Mech. Engineer. Diesel Eng
Diesenhofer, Johann, Dr.	Science	20	25		40	Nobel Chemistry
Dieterle, William	Entertainment	30			75	Film Dirctor
Dietrich, Dena	Entertainment	5			10	Mother Nature (Commercial)
Dietrich, Marlene 1901-92	Entertainment	40	40	288	139	Bull Vint. Portrait $595
Dilke, Charles W. 2d Baronet	Author	10	25	45		Br. Travel Books, Politician
Dillards	Entertainment	25			60	Herb, Dean, Rodney, Merle
Diller, Phyllis	Entertainment	6	9	19	15	
Dillman, Bradford	Entertainment	8	9	15	15	
Dillon, C. Douglas	Cabinet	10	20	30	20	Ambassador, Diplomat
Dillon, Matt	Entertainment	10	15	20	35	
Dillon, R. Crawford	Clergy	15	45	60		
Dimitrova, Ghena	Entertainment	10			35	Opera
Dinesen, Isak (Karen Blixen)1885-1962	Author	100	500		500	Danish. Out of Africa
Dingley, Nelson, Jr.	Congress	10	20	35		Governor, Repr. ME
Dinkins, David	Political	10	35		15	Mayor NYC
Dinning Sisters (3)	Entertainment	10			15	Jean, Jayne, Ginger
Dior, Christian	Fashion	110	400		225	Fashion Designer
Dippel, Andreas	Entertainment	35			125	Ger. Tenor. Impresario. Opera
Dire Straits	Entertainment	30			75	
Dirks, Rudolph* 1877-1968	Cartoonist	70		175	400	Katzenjammer Kids
Dirksen, Everett M.	Senate	20	80		50	Senator, MOC IL
Disney, Roy E.	Business	20	55		30	Brother of Walt. Disney Exec.
Disney, Walt* 1901-1966	Cartoonist		2975		12500	M.Mouse, D.Duck, etc.
Disney, Walter Walt Elias	Business	1135	2767	3650	3718	Animated Film Producer
Disraeli, Benjamin, (Beaconsfield)	Head of State	175	350	1012		Prime Minister, Novelist
Disraeli, Isaac	Author	25	80	160		Br. Man of Letters. Novels
Ditmars, Raymond L. 1876-1942	Science	85				Herpetologist, Zoo Curator, Author
Divine	Entertainment	35			75	Rock
Divine, M.J., 'Father'(Geo. Baker)	Clergy	150	525	700	200	Founded Communal Religious Soc.
Dix, Dorothea L. 18802-87	Civil War	105	250	490		Union Superintendent of Nurses
Dix, Dorothy (Eliz. Gilmer)	Author	15	30	45	25	Am. Journalist, Editor, Advice
Dix, John Adams (War Date)	Civil War	115		370		Union Gen.
Dix, John Adams 1798-1879	Civil War-Cabinet	65	295	158	500	Union Gen., Sec'y Treasury
Dix, Morgan	Clergy	25	35	50		Abolitionist
Dix, Richard	Entertainment	25	40	65	75	
Dix, Robert	Entertainment				25	
Dixey, Henry E. 1859-1943	Entertainment	10	20	30	25	1st Success as Adonis
Dixon, Donna	Entertainment	9	10	20	25	
Dixon, Jeane	Celebrity	10			15	Forecasts the Future
Dixon, Julian C.	Senate/Congress	10	15		12	Afro-Am MOC CA
Dixon, Thomas 1864-1946	Author-Clergy	15	30	75		The Clansman.Social Critic
Dixon, Willie	Entertainment	50			100	Rock HOF. Late Blues Man
Dizengoff, Meir	Celebrity	48	150			

NAME	CATEGORY	SIG	LS/DS	ALS	SP	Comment
Dmytryk, Edward	Entertainment	20			40	Film Director
Doane, G.W.	Clergy		20	25	35	
Dobbin, James C.1814-57	Cabinet	30	75	150		Pierce Sec'y Navy
Dobbin, John F.	Aviation	20	40	65	45	ACE, WW II, Marine Ace
Dobehoff, F.L.	Aviation	15	150		75	
Dobie, Charles Cald.	Author	5	10	15	5	
Dobie, J. Frank	Author	20	50	130	75	Folklorist & Western Author
Dobrinyin, Anatole	Head of State	40	130	375	75	U.S.S.R. Political Power
Dobson, Kevin	Entertainment	5	6	15	15	
Dockery, Thomas P. 1833-98	Civil War	95		300		CSA General
Dockery, Thomas P.(War Date)	Civil War	275	350			CSA Gen.
Docking, Robert	Governor	5	12	20		Governor KS
Dockstader, Lew	Entertainment	75				
Doctorow, E. L.	Author	15	35	90	30	Am. Novelist. Ragtime
Dodd, Christopher J.	Senate/Congress	5	15		10	Senator, MOC CT
Dodd, Thomas J.	Senate & Congress	20	40	65	30	Chief of Counsel at Nuremberg
Dodd, William E.	Historian	15	60	75	25	Ambassador to Nazi Germany
Dodderidge, Philip	Clergy	25	35	45		
Dodge, Charles C. 1841-1910	Civil War	40				Union Gen.
Dodge, Grenville M.(War Date)	Civil War	75	160	235		Union Gen.,Repr. IA.LS/Cont. $1950
Dodge, Grenville M.1831-1916	Civil War	50	65	135		Union Gen.
Dodge, Henry 1782-1867	Congress			45		Gov. Wisc.Terr.,1st Sen.,Indian Fighter
Dodge, Jerry	Entertainment	3	3	6	6	
Dodge, Joseph M.	Business	10	25	50		Banker, Built Jap. Economy
Dodge, Mary Abigail	Author	12	20			
Dodge, Mary Mapes	Author	15	40	75	30	Children's Books.
Dodge, William Earl 1805-83	Business	10	25	340		Phelps, Dodge & Co. YMCA Fndr.
Dodge, William G.	Civil War	25	55	85		
Dodgson, Charles L.(Lewis Carroll)	Author	210	715	1500		Alice in Wonderland
Dods, Marcus	Clergy	40	45	60		
Dodson, Jack	Entertainment	6	8	15	15	
Doenitz, Karl 1891-1980	Military	85	300	350	172	Ger. Adm., WW II.TLS/Cont. $7500
Doerflinger, Joseph	Aviation	10		75	45	
Doering, Arnold	Aviation	10	20	35	25	
Dohanos, Stevan	Illustrator	5	15			
Doherty, Shannen	Entertainment	25			50	Pinup, SP $95
Dohnanyi, Erno von	Composer	50	135	225		Hung. Conductor. AMQS $350
Doi, Takao	Astronaut	15	25		25	
Doig, Andrew Wheeler	Senate/Congress	10	20			MOC NY 1839, Banker, Mining
Doisy, Edward A.	Science	20	45	165	30	Nobel Medicine. Vitamin K
Dolby, Ray	Science	20	35			Inventor Dolby Sound
Dolby, Thomas	Entertainment	20			40	
Dole, Charles F	Clergy	10	15	20		
Dole, Elizabeth	Cabinet	6	15	30	20	Sec'y Labor. Head Red Cross
Dole, James D.	Business	55	145	235	75	Fdr.Hawaiian Pineapple Industry
Dole, Robert	Senate	10	20		85	Senator KS
Dole, Sanford B. 1844-1926	Business	45	358	390	100	Financier, Pres. Repub. HI. Dole Pineapple
Dolenz, Mickey	Entertainment	10		25	35	Monkees
Dolin, Anton	Entertainment	25	40	95	75	Ballet
Dollar, Robert	Business	20	55	130	50	Dollar Steamship Line.
Dolliver, Jonathan P.	Senate & Congress	20	35		25	Senator, MOC IA 1889
Domenici, Pete	Senate	5			15	Senator NM
Domerque, Faith	Entertainment	10			35	
Domingo, Placido	Entertainment	20		40	50	Opera, Concert
Dominguez, Oscar 1906-57	Artist			250		Sp. Surrealist Artist
Dominick, Fred H.	Senate & Congress	5	15		10	MOC SC 1917-33

NAME	CATEGORY	SIG	LS/DS	ALS	SP	Comment
Domino, Fats	Entertainment	25	25	35	55	Rock. AMusQS $125
Donahue, Al	Entertainment	15			75	Big Band Leader
Donahue, Archie	Aviation	12	25	50	35	ACE, WW II, Ace in one day
Donahue, Elinor	Entertainment	5	6	15	15	Pin-Up SP $20
Donahue, Phil	Entertainment	5			30	TV Talk Show Host
Donahue, Troy	Entertainment	5	6	15	25	
Donaldson, Jesse M.	Cabinet	10	15	35	15	1st Postman Becomes P.M. Gen.
Donaldson, Sam	TV News	7			16	TV News Anchor, Commentator
Donat, Peter	Entertainment	5	6	15	15	
Donat, Robert 1905-1958	Entertainment	65	75	100	235	
Donat, Zdislawa	Entertainment	5			25	Opera
Donath, Ludwig	Entertainment				25	Played Father of Al Jolson
Doniphan, Alexander William	Military	120	250	475		Fought Mex.,Indians,Mormans
Donizetti, Gaetano 1797-1848	Composer	500	800	1858		AMusQS $2,750,AMusMs $3,000
Donlan, Roger	Military	10	25	40	15	
Donlevy, Brian	Entertainment	20			100	
Donnell, Jeff	Entertainment	5	6	10	10	
Donnelly, Ruth	Entertainment	10	15	25	25	
Donner, Clive	Entertainment	5			25	Film Director
Donner, Richard	Entertainment	10			20	
Donner, Vyvyan	Editor	5				Fashion
Donovan, Hedley	Editor	5	6	15	10	Time-Life Editor
Donovan, King	Entertainment	15			35	
Donovan, Raymond J.	Cabinet	8	15	35	16	Sec'y Labor
Donovan, Wm. J.Wild Bill	Military	80	225	325	95	Fighting 69th,OSS-CIA
Doobie Brothers	Entertainment	40			80	
Doohan, James 'Scotty'	Entertainment	10	12	20	25	Star Trek
Dooley, Paul	Entertainment	5	6	15	15	
Dooley, Thomas A., Dr.1927-61	Science	125	185	400	125	Jungle Physician, SE Asia
Doolittle, Hilda 1886-1961	Author	75	205	475		Imagist Poet. Ed.The Egoist
Doolittle, James H. 1896-1993	Aviation	85	204	275	75	Gen. WW II, Test Pilot. Bombed Tokyo
Doolittle, James Rood	Senate	15	25	40		Civil War Senator WI
Doors & Jim Morrison (4)	Entertainment	2500				Rock
Doors, The (3)	Entertainment	100				Rock
Doran, Ann	Entertainment	15	15	25	20	
Dorati, Antal	Conductor	15	25		85	Hung.-born
Dornan, Robert K.	Congress	4			24	Rep. CA
Dornberger, Walter R.	Military	40	100	120	75	Rocket Engineer. Bell Aircraft
Dorr, Julia C. R.	Author	3	5	15		
Dors, Diana	Entertainment	20			150	
Dorsey, Jimmie	Entertainment	30	150		250	Big Band Leader-Saxophone
Dorsey, Tommy 1905-56	Entertainment	55	140		125	Big Band Leader-Trombone
Dortch, William T.	Civil War	25	40	75		CSA Senator NC
Doré, Paul Gustave 1833-83	Artist	55	170	675		Fr. Book Illustrator
Dos Passos, John	Author	20	50	90	30	Am. Novelist
Dostoevsky, Fyodor	Author	1500	5700	13800		Rus.Novelist.Crime & Punishmen
Doubleday, Abner 1819-93	Civil War	375	2200	1450		Union Gen.-Credit for baseball
Doubleday, Frank Nelson	Business	65	185	375		Book Publisher
Doucette, John	Entertainment	6	8	15	15	
Dougherty, Dennis, Cardinal	Clergy	35	40	50	40	
Douglas, Beverly B.	Civil War	30	40	55		CSA Officer, MOC VA
Douglas, Chas. W.H. 1850-1914	Military	25	70	195		Br. Gen.
Douglas, Donald W. Jr.	Business	25	60		45	Douglas Aircraft
Douglas, Donald W. Sr.	Aviation	150	295	450	360	Pioneer Aircraft Mfg.
Douglas, Donna	Entertainment	6	8	10	15	Pin-Up SP $20
Douglas, Eric	Entertainment	9			18	Son of Kirk Douglas

NAME	CATEGORY	SIG	LS/DS	ALS	SP	Comment
Douglas, Helen Gahagan	Congress-Entertainment	30	60	120	55	Repr. CA, Opera, Actress
Douglas, Kirk	Entertainment	10		15	25	
Douglas, Leon	Country Music	10			20	
Douglas, Lloyd C.	Author	25	45	65	30	Retired Minister. "The Robe", etc
Douglas, Melvyn	Entertainment	14	20	25	40	
Douglas, Michael	Entertainment	15		25	40	
Douglas, Mike	Entertainment	4	5	9	20	Singer. Early TV Host
Douglas, Paul	Entertainment	10	12		35	
Douglas, Paul H.	Senate	10	20		15	Senator IL
Douglas, Paul P.	Aviation	10	22	42	32	ACE, WW II
Douglas, Robert	Entertainment	10			25	
Douglas, Stephen A. 1813-61	Senate	198	290	762	270	Statesman, Pres. Candidate
Douglas, William O. (SC)	Supreme Court	75	175		200	
Douglas, William Taylor	Clergy	15	20	25		
Douglass, Frederick 1817-95	Abolitionist	275	1348	5825	6325	Afro-Am. Author, Lecturer, Editor
Douglass, Robyn	Entertainment	4	4	9	10	
Doulton, Henry, Sir	Potter-Inventor	20	35	70		Royal Doulton China
Doumer, Paul 1857-1932	Head of State	60		100		Pres. France 1931-32. Assassinated
Doumergue, Gaston 1863-1937	Head of State			195		Pres. France. P.M. France
Dove, Billie	Entertainment	15	15	35	75	
Dow, Neal 1804-97	Civil War	45	75	400		Union Gen., Temperance Reformer
Dow, Tony	Entertainment	4	6	10	20	
Dowden, Edward	Author	10	15	25		Ir. Critic, Editor, Professor
Dowling, Eddie 1895-1975	Entertainment	20	25	53	45	Major Broadway Star
Down, Lesley-Anne	Entertainment	5	6	15	15	
Downey, Morton	Entertainment	10	15	20	25	
Downey, Robert, Jr.	Entertainment	20			70	Actor
Downey, Sheridan	Senate	10	25		20	Senator CA 1938-50
Downing, Big Al	Entertainment	3	3	6	6	
Downing, George, Sir 1623-84	Statesman-Diplomat	850	475			2nd Graduate Harvard College
Downliners Sect	Entertainment				72	Br. Rock Group (All 5)
Downs, Hugh	Entertainment	10		25	22	TV Co-Host 20/20
Downs, Johnny	Entertainment	10			35	
Doyle, Arthur Conan, Sir 1859-1930	Author-Physician	450	775	1689	1763	Br. Novelist. Sherlock Holmes
Doyle, Dinty	Journalist		20			Columnist
Dozier, James	Military	12	30	45	15	
Dr. Seuss*	Cartoonists	25			450	Cat In The Hat-early
Drabble, Margaret	Author		20	50		Br. Novelist, Editor
Dragonette, Jessica	Entertainment	18	20		45	Soprano. Radio, Stage Star
Dragoni, Maria	Entertainment	10			30	Opera
Drake, Alfred	Entertainment	7			10	Musical Theatre
Drake, Betsy	Entertainment	5			15	Mrs. Cary Grant (Once upon a Time)
Drake, Frances	Entertainment	8	9	15	25	
Drake, Francis M.	Governor	5	250			Gov. IA. RR Builder. Fndr. Drake Univ.
Drake, Michele	Entertainment	4			15	Pin-Up SP $20
Drake, Samuel Adams	Civil War	45		75		Union General, Author
Drake, Stan*	Cartoonist	20			100	Blondie
Drake, Tom	Entertainment	3	3	6	10	
Draper, Eben S.	Governor	5	12			Governor MA
Draper, Rusty	Country Music	5			12	
Draper, Ruth	Entertainment	10	45	70	50	Am. Monologuist
Draper, William F.	Civil War		50			General
Draper, William H.	Clergy	20	35	40		
Drayton, Thomas F. 1808-91	Civil War			230		CSA Gen..Sig./Rank $175
Drayton, Gracie*	Cartoonist	20			250	Created Campbell Soup Kids
Drees, Willem	Head of State	20	35	100		Survivor Buchenwald

NAME	CATEGORY	SIG	LS/DS	ALS	SP	Comment
Dreiser, Theodore 1871-1945	Author	70	200	300	300	American Tragedy
Drescher, Fran	Entertainment	10			58	Actress. The Nanny
Dresser, Louise	Entertainment	30			55	Stage. Major Silent Film Star
Dressler, Marie	Entertainment	130			250	
Drew, Ellen	Entertainment	4	6	9	10	
Drew, John 1853-1927	Entertainment	60	75	185	100	
Drexel, Anthony	Banker	45	65	145		Philanthropist
Drexel, J. A.	Aviation	43	60	100	65	
Dreyfus, Alfred 1859-1935	Military	140	310	800	1955	Framed for Treason, Devil's Isl
Dreyfus, Julia Louis	Entertainment	10			45	Actress, Seinfeld
Dreyfuss, Henry	Business		12	20		Self Sketch Henry $25
Dreyfuss, Richard	Entertainment	8	15	25	40	
Dribrell, George G.	Civil War	95	250	300		
Drinan, Robert, Father	Senate/Congress	4			15	Catholic Activist Priest
Drinkwater, John 1882-1937	Author	20	50	125	25	Poet
Driscoll, Bobby	Entertainment	125	155	190	250	
Driver, Samuel Rolles	Clergy	85	100	125		
Drouet, Robert	Entertainment	25	30	60	68	
Dru, Joanne	Entertainment	10			25	
Druckman, Jacob	Composer	20	50	95		Pulitzer, AMusQS $250
Drum, Hugh A. Lt.Gen	Military	25	55	120	50	General WW I, WW II
Drum, Richard C.	Civil War	27	50	80		
Drummond, Henry	Clergy	50	60	80		
Drummond, James	Clergy	25	35	50		
Drury, Allen	Author	10	30	65	35	
Drury, Frank	Aviation	10	25	40	30	ACE, WW II, Marine Ace
Drury, James	Entertainment	15			35	The Virginian
Dryer, Fred	Entertainment	10		25	25	
Du Barry, Jeanne, Comtesse	Royal Mistress	285	960	1200		Banished, Arrested, Guillotined
Du Chaillu, Paul B. 1831-1903	Explorer	35	80	65	75	Brought 1st Gorillas out of Afr
Du Maurier, Daphne, Dame	Author	45	140	150	50	Br. Novelist. Rebecca
Du Maurier, George	Author	15	45	125		And Illustrator of Punch
Du Pont, Alfred I.	Business	10				Banking
Du Pont, Elizabeth H	Business	20	75	110	30	
Du Pont, Henry A. 1838-1926	Business	55	345			CW,MOH. RR Pres.
Du Pont, Lammot	Business	20			50	CEO Du Pont Chemical
Du Pont, Pierre S.	Governor	15	35		50	Governor DE, Du Pont Chemical
Du Pont, Pierre-Samuel 1739-1817I	Economist	45	110	240		Progenitor of Du Pont Lineage
Du Pont, R.	Aviation	40	110			Am Aviation Exec.
Du Pont, Samuel Francis(War Date)	Civil War	150	215	556		1803-1865, Union Adm.
Du Vigneaud, Vincent	Science	25	55	145	45	Nobel, Synthesized Penicillin
Duane, James 1733-1797	Revolutionary War	110	325	750		1st Continental Congress
Dubcek, Alexander	Head of State	80	130			Czech. Reformer
DuBois, W. E. B.	Author	300	750		425	Black Rights, Educator-Writer
Dubose, Dudley	Civil War	95	275			CSA Gen., MOC GA
DuBridge, Lee, Dr.	Science	30	100	145	50	Pres. Cal-Tech
Dubuffet, Jean 1931-85	Artist	150	400	950		Swiss proponent of raw art
Dubuque, Julien	Am. Pioneer	600	2500			1st White Settler Near Dubuque
Duchamp, Marcel 1887-1968	Artist	125	350	575	1368	Fr. Avante Garde Artist
Duchin, Eddie	Entertainment	25	40		120	Big Band Leader, Pianist
Duchin, Peter	Entertainment	5	6	15	15	Pianist, Band Leader
Duchovny, David	Entertainment				675	X Files With G. Anderson
Duckworth, John T., Sir 1748-1817	Military	55	180			Br. Admiral, Gov. Newfoundland
Ducos, Jean Francois	Fr. Revolution	36	100	205		
Dudayev, Dzhokhar	Head of State	15			45	Pres.. Chechen Republic
Dudicoff, Michael	Entertainment	10	12		25	

NAME	CATEGORY	SIG	LS/DS	ALS	SP	Comment
Dudley, Dave	Country Music	6			15	
Dudley, Joseph 1647-1720	Colonial America	450	895	1500		Col.Gov.MA.Philos.Scholar,Divin
Dudley, Paul 1675-1751	Colonial America	115	310			Jurist. Religious Activist
Dudley, Thomas V., Bishop	Clergy	35	50	45	50	
Duer, William 1747-99	Revolutionary War					War Dte/Cont. $1500
Duesenberg, Frederick S.	Business	550	1350			
Duff, Arthur, Sir	Military	15	45	70		Br. Admiral
Duff, Howard	Entertainment	15		25	35	Actor. Film & Radio
Duff, James H.	Senate	5	15		10	Governor, Senator PA
Duffer, Candy	Entertainment	20			45	Rock
Duffie, Alfred Napoleon A.(War Date)	Civil War		207			Union Gen.
Duffie, Alfred Napoleon A.1835-80	Civil War	35	72	85		Union Gen. Cavalry
Duffy, Brian	Astronaut	5			15	
Duffy, Francis P.	Clergy	15	20	25		
Duffy, Julia	Entertainment	9	10	20	20	
Duffy, Patrick	Entertainment	7			20	
Dufranne, Hector	Entertainment	18				Opera. Fr. Baritone
Dufy, Raoul 1877-1953	Artist	300	450	873	500	Fr. Impressionist, Fauvism
Duggan, Andrew	Entertainment	15			25	
Dukakis, Michael S.	Governor	10			20	Governor MA. Presidential Cand.
Dukakis, Olympia	Entertainment	15	25	35	30	
Dukas, Paul 1865-1935	Composer	55	160	355		Fr. Sorcerer's Apprentice
Duke, Basil Wilson (War Date)	Civil War			3917		CSA General
Duke, Basil Wilson 1838-1916	Civil War	78	170	500		CSA Gen.
Duke, Charles M., Jr.	Astronaut	20	115	125	76	Moonwalker
Duke, Clarence	Celebrity	4	10	25	5	Sports Announcer
Duke, David	Activist	40			95	Ex KKK Grand Wizard
Duke, Patty	Entertainment	8	9	15	20	
Duke, Vernon 1903-69	Composer	20	50	145		AMusQS $175-$400
Dulbecco, Renato	Science	20	35	60		Nobel Physiology-Medicine
Dullea, Keir	Entertainment	8	12	15	20	
Dulles, Allen W.	Diplomat	30	165	225	75	State Dept., OSS, CIA
Dulles, John Foster 1888-1959	Cabinet	30	120	150	75	Sec'y State, Diplomat, UN
Dumas, Alexandre (Fils)	Author	55	105	175	425	Fr. Dramatist, Novelist
Dumas, Alexandre (Pere)	Author	110	225	550	750	Fr. Novelist.Three Musketeers
Dumbrille, Douglass	Entertainment	40			75	
Dummar, Melvin E.	Celebrity	20	30	45		Fraudulent H. Hughes Heir
Duna, Steffi	Entertainment	10		15	25	
Dunagin, Ralph	Cartoonist	5			20	The Middletons
Dunaway, Faye	Entertainment	10	15	25	30	
Dunbar, Charles E. 1888-1959	Law		20			Chairman WW I War Trade Board
Dunbar, Bonnie J.	Astronaut	5			15	
Dunbar, Charles E., Sr.	Bureaucrat	10	25			Chm. US War Trade Board 1914-18
Dunbar, Dixie	Entertainment	6	8	15	15	
Dunbar, Paul Lawrence 1872-1906	Author	750				Afro-Am. Poet, Novelist etc.
Duncan, Charles T.	Celebrity	4	10	25	10	
Duncan, Isadora 1878-1927	Entertainment	400		1150	1035	Am. Interpretive Dancer
Duncan, James 1811-49	Military	75				Mexican War Hero
Duncan, Johnny	Country Music	10			20	
Duncan, Lee (Rin Tin Tin)	Entertainment	100				Dog Trainer & Actor
Duncan, Sandy	Entertainment	5			20	
Duncan, Thomas	Civil War	20	50	80		Union General
Duncan, Todd	Entertainment	25			100	First Porgy
Dundas, Henry 1742-1811	Statesman	25	40	85		Br. Sec'y War.Pro War with Am.
Dunham, Sonny	Entertainment	15				Bandleader, Trumpet
Dunlap, John	Am. Printer	150	575			1st To Print Decl. of Ind. etc.

NAME	CATEGORY	SIG	LS/DS	ALS	SP	Comment
Dunlap, Robert P. 1794-1859	Congress	12				Repr. ME, Gov. ME
Dunlop, John T.	Cabinet	5	10	15	15	Sec'y Labor
Dunn, Artie	Entertainment	10			36	Music. The Three Sons
Dunn, Emma	Entertainment	20			35	
Dunn, Holly	Country Music	10			25	
Dunn, James	Entertainment	60		120	125	
Dunn, William McKee	Civil War	25	40	70		Union Gen.(Judge, Adv. Gen.'75)
Dunne, Dominick	Author		30		35	Columnist
Dunne, Irene	Entertainment	20	15	30	52	
Dunne, Phillip	Author	5	20	35	15	Novelist
Dunne, Stephen	Entertainment				25	
Dunning, Debbie	Entertainment	5				Actress. Pin-up 67
Dunnock, Mildred	Entertainment	7			20	
Dunsany, Edw.J.Plunkett, Lord	Author	50		225	120	Traveller, Hunter, Playwright
Dunst, Kirsten	Entertainment	10			75	Actress
DuPonceau, Pierre	Military	25	60	140		
Duportail, Louis le Begue	Revolutonary War		750			Fr. Gen. in Continental Army
Dupre, Marel	Composer	45			125	Celebrated Organist
Durais, C.	Artist	10	20	50		
Duran Duran	Entertainment	60			100	
Durand, Asher Brown	Artist	85	175	200		Hudson River School. Engraver
Durant, Ariel (Ida)	Author	25	50	115	35	Historian with Husband Will
Durant, Thomas C. 1820-85	Business	35	262			Pioneer Builder & Financer of Railroads
Durant, Will	Author	30	30	135	45	Historian with Wife Aerial
Durant, William Crapo	Business	250	850	1075		Durant Motor Car. GM, Chevrolet
Durante, Jimmy 1893-1980	Entertainment	25	85		60	
Durbin, Deanna	Entertainment	22			42	Child Singing Star. Retired Early
Durenberger, David	Senate	5			15	Senator MN
Durer, Albrecht	Artist	3000	8200	21000		Foremost Ger.Renaissance Artist
Durham, Bobby	Country Music	10			20	
Durkin, Martin P.	Cabinet	10	25			Sec'y Labor, Eisenhower
Durning, Charles	Entertainment	5	6	15	25	
Duroc, Geraud C.M.	Military	25	65	185		Napol. Grand Marshal-Diplomat
Durrell, Lawrence	Author	25	70	190	40	Br-Ir Poet,Playwright,Travel
Duryea, Charles E. 1861-1938	Science-Business	290	625		2300	Built 1st Am.Gasoline Motor Car
Duryea, Dan	Entertainment	15	15	30	35	
Duryea, Hiram	Civil War					Union Gen. ANS '61 $310
Duse, Eleanora 1859-1924	Entertainment	200	400	795	575	Great Italian Stage Actress
Dussault, Nancy	Entertainment	3	3	6	10	
Dussek, Jan L 1760-1812	Composer	30	90	145		Marie Antoinette was Patron
Dustinn, Emmy	Entertainment	30			170	Opera
Dutra, Enrico Gaspar	Head of State	10	20	50	35	Pres. Brazil.Outlawed Communist
Duval, Gabriel (SC)	Supreme Court	45	115	245		
Duvalier, Francois	Head of State	75	650		150	Papa Doc. Haitian President
Duvall, Robert	Entertainment	10	15	25	35	
Duvall, Shelley	Entertainment	6	8	15	18	
Duv,, Christian de, Dr.	Science	20	35		30	Nobel Medicine
Duyckinck, Evart A.	Editor	40		150		Literary World
Dvorak, Ann	Entertainment	10		30	35	Actress. Vintage
Dvorak, Antonin	Composer	475	895	2500		Czech.Slavonic Dances,Symphonie
Dwan, Allan	Entertainment	15			35	
Dwight, Theodore 1764-1846	Journalist	35	50	150		Harvard Wits, Hartford Convention
Dwight, Timothy 1752-1817	Author-Clergy	20	55			President Yale. Equal Education of Women
Dyer, Edward 1543-1607	Author		1000			Br. Poet and Courtier
Dyer, Eliphlet	Revolutionary War	50	155			Continental Congress
Dyer, George C.	Military	15	40	60		Admiral USN

NAME	CATEGORY	SIG	LS/DS	ALS	SP	Comment
Dyer, Leonidas Carstarphen	Senate/Congress	5			10	MOC MO 1915-1933
Dyer, Nehemiah 1839-1910	Military	25				Admiral
Dyke, Leroy Van	Country Music	5			15	
Dylan, Bob	Entertainment	175	225	400	638	Songwriter, Poet, Folksinger
Dymally, Mervyn M.	Congress	5			15	Afr-Am. Congressman CA
Dysart, Richard	Entertainment	10	15	25	18	

NAME	CATEGORY	SIG	LS/DS	ALS	SP	Comment
Eadie, Betty J.	Author	5			10	Non-Fiction
Eadie, John	Clergy	10	15	25		Scot. Theologian & Scholar
Eads, James Buchanan	Civil War	105	330	500		Engineer, Shipbuilder for Union
Eagleburger, Lawrence	Diplomat	4			10	State Dept., Ambassador
Eagles	Entertainment	40			80	Alb. S/Frey,Henley,Walsh $185
Eagleston, Glenn	Aviation	20	42	70	45	ACE, WW II
Eagleton, Thomas F.	Senate	20	50		10	Senator MO
Eaker, Ira 1896-	Aviation	20	80	95	145	WW II Air Force Cmdr
Eakins, Thomas	Artist	375		3250		Am. Painter-Sculptor
Eames-Story, Emma, Mme.	Entertainment	35				Opera
Earhart, Amelia 1898-1937	Aviation	540	1432		1562	TLS/Content $2,495
Earle, George H.	Governor	10	15			Governor PA
Earle, Virginia	Entertainment	6	8	15	15	
Early, Jubal 1816-94	Civil War	485	662	988		CSA General
Early, Jubal A. (War Date)	Civil War	780		2500		CSA General
Earp, Virgil	Lawman	500	4500	6800		US Marshal. S Auction $8,250
Earp, Wyatt B.S.	Lawman	3875		27500		Legendary Gambler, Gunfighter
East, James	Lawman	250	750			Western Cowboy
East, John	Senate	10	20	40	35	Senator NC, Suicide
Eastlake, Charles L., Sir	Artist	50	150	850		Pres. of Royal Academy, Critic
Eastland, James	Congress	10			15	Senator MS 1943-78
Eastman, George 1854-1932	Business	190	1892	825	1380	Fndr Eastman Kodak.Rare DS $4900
Eastman, John	Artist	40		185		Am. Artist. Portraits & Genre
Eastman, Max 1883-169	Author	35	95	115		Editor-Fdr. The Masses
Easton, Florence	Entertainment	45			175	Opera
Easton, Sheena	Entertainment	12	15	25	45	
Eastwood, Clint	Entertainment	20			61	Actor-Producer-Dir. AA
Eaton, Amos Beebe	Civil War	25	50	90		Union General
Eaton, Dorman 1823-99	Reformer	10	25	55		Jurist, Nat'l Civil Service Act
Eaton, John Henry	Cabinet	20	55	100		Senator TN 1818, Sec'y War
Eaton, Joseph H.	Civil War					Union Gen. ALS '65 $605
Eaton, William 1764-1811	Military-Diplomat	30		75		U.S.Consul Tunis,Tripoli Action
Eban, Abba	Diplomat	15	75	75	65	Israeli Diplomat, Ambass. UN
Ebb, Fred	Composer	10		35	20	AMusQS $50 New York, NY..
Ebbets, Charles H.	Business	150			175	Orig. Brooklyn Dodgers Field
Eben Emael	Military	30	85	140	60	

NAME	CATEGORY	SIG	LS/DS	ALS	SP	Comment
Eberhart, Adolph O.	Governor	5	22			Governor MN
Eberhart, Richard	Author	10	20	45	15	Major Poet 20th Cent.,Pulitzer
Eberlein, Gustav 1847-1926	Artist				80	Ger. Sculptor
Eberly, Bob	Entertainment	3	3	10	40	Band Singer, Records
Eberly, Ray	Entertainment				60	Singer. Band, Records
Ebert, Roger	Entertainment	16				TV Critic
Ebsen, Buddy	Entertainment	5	6	15	29	
Eccles, John C.	Science	20	30	40	30	Nobel Medicine
Echols, John (War Date)	Civil War	190	695			CSA General
Echols, John 1823-96	Civil War	95	195	372		CSA General
Echols, Leonard Sidney	Senate/Congress	5	15			MOC WV 1919
Eckels, James H. 1858-1907	Statesman	15	50	100		U.S. Comptroller of Currency
Eckener, Hugo von 1868-1954	Aviation	215	525	650	450	Ger. Aeronaut, Built G.Zeppelin
Eckert, Thomas T. (War Date)	Civil War	475				Union Gen.Telegraph Giant.
Eckstine, Billy	Entertainment	20			50	Vocalist-Trumpet-Bandleader
Ed, Carl	Cartoonist	10			30	Harold Teen
Eddington, Arthur Stanley, Sir	Science	25	140	185		Mathematician, Astrophysicist
Eddy, Duane	Entertainment	30			45	Rock Guitarist. HOF
Eddy, Mary Baker	Clergy	1275	2125	3890		
Eddy, Nelson	Entertainment	50	175		120	
Eden, Anthony, Sir	Head of State	48	140	190	75	Prime Minister
Eden, Barbara	Entertainment	10	15	25	40	Pin-Up SP $45
Ederle, Gertrude Trudy	Entertainment	25			60	And Showgirl
Edeson, Robert	Entertainment	20			45	Silent Star. Ten Commandments
Edge, Walter E.	Senate/Congress	15	25		20	Gov.NJ 1917, Senator PA, Ambass
Edison, Charles 1890-1969	Cabinet	55	95	110	60	Sec'y Navy. Son of Thos. A.
Edison, Thomas Alva 1847-1931	Science	467	1224	3312	2166	Prolific Am. Inventor
Edmonds, Walter Dumanx	Author	5	25	40	20	
Edmunds, Geo.Franklin 1828-1919	Congress	10	15	30		Senator VT 1866-91
Edmundson, Henry A.	Civil War	40	55	80		CSA Officer, MOC VA
Edward & Wallis (See Windsor)	Royalty					Duke and Duchess of Windsor
Edward III (Reign of...)	Royalty					Doc. Written 1340 $450
Edward IV (England)1442-83	Royalty	25000				
Edward VI (Reign of...)	Royalty					Land Grant 1551. $1750
Edward VII (Eng) (As King)	Royalty					King From 1901-10
Edward VII (England) 1841-1910	Royalty	110	475	289	625	As Albert Edw., Q.Vict. Eldest Son
Edward VIII 1894-1972 (As King)	Royalty	300	1875	1750	750	
Edward VIII, as Prince of Wales	Royalty	150	475	660	675	Content TLS $1250
Edward, Duke of Kent	Royalty	50	135	350		Father of Queen Victoria
Edward, Duke Windsor 1894-1972	Royalty	200	642	1950	655	FDC 12/7/64 $300
Edwards, Anthony	Entertainment	20	50	70	50	Actor. See Clooney, G
Edwards, Arthur (See Clooney, Geo.)						
Edwards, Blake	Entertainment	10			25	Film Producer-Director
Edwards, Clarence	Military	35				General WW I
Edwards, Cliff (Ukele Ike)	Entertainment	50	70	100	125	
Edwards, Douglas	News	3	3	6	15	Radio-TV News
Edwards, Edward Irving	Senate	10	15			Senator, Governor NJ
Edwards, Elaine S.	Senate	7	20		10	Senator LA, 8/1/72-11/13/72
Edwards, Gail J.	Entertainment	5	6	15	15	
Edwards, George	Congress	10				
Edwards, Gordon	Business	4			10	Business Exec., U.S. Steel
Edwards, James B.	Cabinet	10	15	35	10	Governor SC, Sec'y Energy
Edwards, Joan	Entertainment	5			10	
Edwards, Jonathan	Clergy-Author	110	350	380		Great Theologian Am.Puritanism
Edwards, Oliver	Civil War	25	60	100		Union General
Edwards, Penny	Entertainment	10			20	Westerns Leading Lady

NAME	CATEGORY	SIG	LS/DS	ALS	SP	Comment
Edwards, Ralph	Entertainment	4	4	9	10	This Is Your Life
Edwards, Vince	Entertainment	10			25	Dr. Ben Casey
Egan, Richard	Entertainment	5	6	15	15	
Egan, William A.	Governor	5	12		10	Governor AK
Egbert, H.C.	Military	45				Gen. Spanish-Am. War
Egbert, Sherwood	Business	3	14	35	15	
Eggar, Samantha	Entertainment	6	8	15	19	
Eggert, Nicole	Entertainment				40	Actress. Baywatch
Eggerth, Marta	Entertainment	10			45	Opera, Operetta
Eggleston, Benjamin 1816-88	Congress	12	20	25		Repr. OH
Eggleston, Edward 1837-1902	Author	5		30		Am. Regional Classic Novels
Eggleston, Geo. C. 1839-1911	Author	10	25			Editor. Civil War & Boy's Books
Eglevsky, André	Entertainment	40	55	110	75	Rus-Am Ballet Teacher-Dancer
Ehrlich, Paul, Dr. 1854-1915	Science	150	1250	1850	1380	Nobel. Diphtheria, Syphillis
Eichelberger. Robert L.	Military	20	45	70	40	Gen. WW II. Cmdr I Corps
Eichelbrenner, E. A.	Science	45	95	225		
Eichmann, Adolf	Military	275	500	1250	750	ALS/Cont.Offered $50,000-60,000
Eick, Alfred	Military	26		50		
Eiffel, Alexandre-Gustave 1832-1923	Arch.-Engineer	275	525	1450	1430	ALS/Content $1,750
Eigen, Manfred	Science	20	35	80	40	Nobel Chemistry
Eilers, Sally	Entertainment	15	15	30	38	
Eilshemius, Louis Michel 1864-1941	Artist	35	60	525		Am. Landscape Expressionist
Einstein, Albert 1879-1955	Science	1105	2552	3375	3735	ALS/Sci. Content $25,000
Eisele, Donn F.	Astronaut	50			85	
Eisenberg, Maurice	Entertainment	10	15		20	Cellist
Eisenhower, Arthur B.	Business	5	15		10	Brother to Ike. Banker
Eisenhower, Barbara	Celebrity	5	15		10	Daughter-in Law to Ike
Eisenhower, Dwight D.(As President)	President	445	990		392	
Eisenhower, Dwight D.1890-1969	President	257	766	3220	739	ALS/Content $3.750-$17,500
Eisenhower, Edgar N.	Law	5	20		15	Brother & Lawyer to Ike
Eisenhower, John S. D.	Military	10	20	35	15	General & Only Son of Ike
Eisenhower, Julie Nixon	Celebrity	5	10	25	25	Daughter & Inlaw Two Presidents
Eisenhower, Mamie Doud	First Lady	58	122	165	50	White House Card S $65
Eisenhower, Milton	Educator	10	30		20	Brother. Pres. Penn. State U.
Eisenman, Robin G.	Entertainment	4	4	9	10	
Eisenstaedt, Alfred	Photographer	15	40		125	Celebrity Photographer
Eisley, Anthony	Entertainment	7			12	
Eisner, Michael O.	Business	30			45	CEO Walt Disney Co.
Eisner, William J.	Business	10	35	45	20	
Eizenstat, Stuart E.	Government	4	10	15	12	White House Staff
Ekberg, Anita	Entertainment	10			20	
Ekland, Britt	Entertainment	10	12	25	30	Pin-Up SP $35
Ekwall, William A.	Senate/Congress	5	10		10	MOC OR
El Fadil, Siddig	Entertainment				50	Actor. Star Trek
Elahi, Ostad	Philosopher	3660		15150		Musician, Judge
Elam, Jack	Entertainment	5	6	15	15	
Elbert, Samuel 1743-1788	Revolutionary War		110	170		Distinguished Officer. Gov. GA
Elder, Ruth (Camp)	Aviation	100	190	310	350	Pioneer Aviatrix
Elder, Will*	Cartoonist	30			400	Annie Fanny
Elders, Joycelyn	Cabinet	15	30		20	Clinton Surgeon General
Eldridge, Florence	Entertainment	10			35	Vintage Stage & Film
Eldridge, Louise	Reformer	10	15	30		Aunt Louisa AQS $25
Eldridge, Roy	Entertainment				65	Jazz Trumpet
Electric Light Orchestra	Entertainment	35			75	
Eleniak, Erika	Entertainment	10			35	Actress-Model. Nude SP 100
Elg, Taina	Entertainment	10			30	Ballet-Actress/Gene Kelly

The Sanders Price Guide to Autographs

NAME	CATEGORY	SIG	LS/DS	ALS	SP	Comment
Elgar, Edward, Sir 1857-1934	Composer	100	350	767	525	AMusQS $1,500
Elgart, Les	Bandleader	32				
Elgin,7th Earl (T.Bruce)	Diplomat					SEE Bruce, Thomas
Elijah, Muhammad	Celebrity	385			425	Religious Activist
Elion, Gertrude, Dr.	Science	20	65		35	Nobel Medicine
Eliot, Charles W. 1834-1926	Educator	15	50	65		Pres. Harvard
Eliot, George (Pseud.)1819-80	Author	160	595	1250		Br. Novelist. (Mary Ann Evans)
Eliot, T(homas) S(tearns) 1888-1965	Author	165	446	2362	768	Br. Poet, Critic, Editor, Nobel
Eliot, Thos. Dawes 1808-770	Congress	5		15		CW Repr. MA
Elizabeth I 1533-1603	Royalty	3400	29000			
Elizabeth II & Philip	Royalty		1340		1025	
Elizabeth, II	Royalty	350	775	800	775	
Elizabeth, Queen Mother	Royalty	80	390	425	500	Queen of George VI
Elkins, Stephen B.	Cabinet	15	25	60	25	Sec'y War, Senator WV
Ellender, Allen J.	Senate	4	5		10	Senator LA
Ellerbee, Linda	TV News	10	35		15	TV News, Commentator
Ellery, William 1727-1820	Revolutionary War	175	360	785		Signer Decl. of Indepen.
Ellicott, Andrew	Revolutionary War	60	185	320		Surveyor, Mathematician
Ellington, Buford	Governor	10	12	20		Governor TN
Ellington, Duke 1899-1974	Composer	200	538		467	AMusQS $300-$1,200
Elliott, Bob	Entertainment	3	3	6	10	
Elliott, Carter	Composer	40	125	280		
Elliott, Cass (Mama)	Entertainment	300	375			Rotund, Sweet-Voiced Singer
Elliott, Maxine	Entertainment	30	40	75	70	
Elliott, R.W.B., Bishop	Clergy	25	35	40	40	
Elliott, Robert B.	Senate/Congress	10	15		15	MOC SC
Elliott, Sam	Entertainment	9	10	20	35	
Elliott, Washington L. 1825-88	Civil War	30				Union Gen. ALS '63 $200
Elliott, Wild Bill	Entertainment	50			150	Vintage Cowboy
Ellis, F. H.	Aviation	15	35		30	
Ellis, Havelock 1859-1939	Science	35	380	155	275	Br. Pioneer Advocate Sex Ed.
Ellis, Robert H.	Military	10	25	45		
Ellison, James	Entertainment	10		15	30	Vintage Cowboy
Ellison, Ralph W. 1914-94	Author	45	285			Afr.-Am. Author of The Invisible Man
Ellsberg, Daniel	Activist	20	35	50	25	Leaked Pentagon Papers
Ellsworth, Ephraim E.(War Date)	Civil War			3750		Union Zouave Col. 1st CW Martyr
Ellsworth, Ephriam E.1837-61	Civil War	595	1550	2500		Union Zouave Col.
Ellsworth, Oliver (SC)1745-1807	Supreme Court	100	268	575		Chief Justice. Constitutional Conv.
Ellul, Jacques	Clergy	25	30	45		
Elman, Mischa 1891-1967	Entertainment	28	225		80	Rus.-Am. Violinist
Elman, Ziggy	Entertainment	25			75	Trumpet
Elmore, E.C.	Civil War	55	105			Treas. CSA. ALS $3,500
Elrod, Jack*	Cartoonist	10			35	Mark Trail
Elson, Edward L.R.	Clergy	15	20	25		
Elssler, Fanny 1810-84	Entertainment	250				Austrian Ballerina
Elston, John A.	Congress	5	15			Congressman CA
Eltinge, Julian	Entertainment	25	20	35	40	Female Impersonator,Silent Film
Eluard, Paul	Author	110	225	375		Fr. Poet. Exponent Surrealism
Elvira	Entertainment	8	9	19	25	Pin-Up SP $35
Ely, Joseph Buell	Governor	15	35	70		Gov. MA, Anti New Dealer
Ely, Paul, General	Military	65		140	90	Fr. Cmdr. Indochina.Dienbienphu
Ely, Ron	Entertainment	10	12	15	25	
Ely, Smith	Congress	15				Mayor NYC, Repr. NY
Elzey, Arnold (Jones)(War Date)	Civil War	350		1700		CSA General
Emberg, Kelly	Model	10			25	Pin-Up SP $40
Embry, Joan	Zoologist	5			24	

NAME	CATEGORY	SIG	LS/DS	ALS	SP	Comment
Emerson, Faye	Entertainment	5			30	Film Actress-TV Panel Show Member
Emerson, George	Entertainment	6			30	
Emerson, Hope	Entertainment	15			35	
Emerson, Lake and Palmer	Entertainment	35			122	Rock
Emerson, Ralph Waldo 1803-82	Author-Clergy	267	300	850	2530	ALS/Content $3,500
Emery, Ralph	Entertainment	1			6	TV Host
Emma, Queen (Ne, Rooker)	Royalty	100				Wife of King Kamehameha IV
Emmett, Daniel D.	Composer	300	425	600		1st Minstral Show. Dixie
Emmons, Ebenezer 1799-1863	Science	25	40	70		Early Prof. of Natural History
Emory, William H.(War Date)	Civil War	65	170	330		Union General
Empey, James W.,Lt.Col.	Aviation		25			Ace WW II
Enders, John Franklin, Dr.	Science	25	60	110	45	Nobel Medicine.
Endicott, William C. 1826-1900	Cabinet	25	30	55	40	Sec'y War
Enesco, Georges	Composer	125	275	550	550	AMusQS $850
Enevoldson, Einer	Astronaut	10			20	
Engel, Georgia	Entertainment	5	6	15	15	
Engel, Samuel G.	Entertainment	10			15	Producer
England, Anthony W.	Astronaut	5			15	
England, Sue	Entertainment	5			20	1940's Moppet
Engle, Frederick	Civil War	45				Union Commodore
Engle, Joe Henry	Astronaut	5			45	Engle & Truly SP $195
Engler, Irvin	Author		25	30		Poet
English, Thos. Dunn 1819-1902	Author-Congress	25	30	45		Ben Bolt.Dr.,Lawyer, Poet
Englund, Robert	Entertainment	10			35	Horror Movies
Ennis, Skinnay	Bandleader				65	Singer, Musician
Enos, Roger 1729-1808	Military	55	175	295		General, Honored VT Citizen
Enright, Richard E.	Law	12	24			Police Commissioner
Enriques, René	Entertainment	10			35	Hill Street Blues
Enriquez, Rene	Entertainment	12	15	30	35	
Ensley, F. Gerald, Bishop	Clergy	20	35	50	25	
Ensor, James Sydney, Baron	Artist	50	160	390		Belg. Painter, Etcher. Bizarre
Ephron, Henry	Entertainment	15			25	Playwright
Ephron, Nora	Author	16				
Ephron, Phoebe	Author	10		20		Playwright
Ephron, Phoebe	Entertainment	15			25	Playwright Mother of Nora
Epp, Franz Xaver von	Military	15	40		75	Gen. WW I. Sturmabteilung Army
Epstein, Brian	Entertainment	350	1500			Beatles Manager & Promoter
Epstein, Jacob, Sir 1880-1959	Artist	150	210	392		Controversial Br.-Am. Sculptor
ER (Cast)	Entertainment					All 6 $295
Erdrich, Louise	Author	5			10	Novelist. The Bingo Palace
Erhard, Ludwig	Head of State	20	70	170	50	Chancellor W. Germany
Erickson, Leif 1911-86	Entertainment	20			50	
Ericsdotter, Siw	Entertainment	25			60	Opera
Ericson, B.A.	Aviation	10	25			Piloted XC-99
Ericsson, John 1803-89	Civil War	75	195	468		Designed & Built Monitor
Ernest Augustus II 1771-1851	Royalty			285		1st Hanover King
Erni, Hans	Artist	65		225		ALS=FDC/sig'd art
Ernouf, Manuel L.J(Baron)	Fr. Revolution	35	85	160		
Ernst, Max 1891-1976	Artist	235	355	775		Surrealist-Dada Movement
Errol, Leon	Entertainment	35			65	
Erskine, Graves B.	Military	15	35	65	40	Led US Marines at Iwo Jima
Erskine, John 1879-1951	Author	35	125	175		Novelist, Pres. Juilliard, Musician
Erté	Artist	80	210	350	90	
Ervin, Sam J.	Senate/Congress	10	20		15	MOC, Senator NC
Ervine, St. John	Author	15	50			Br. Controversial Drama Critic
Erwin, Durward	Country Music	10			20	

NAME	CATEGORY	SIG	LS/DS	ALS	SP	Comment
Erwin, James	Military	45				General WW I
Erwin, Sam J.	Congress	20	80			Sen. Watergate Investigator
Erwin, Stuart	Entertainment	20			45	
Esaki, Leo	Science	20	35	50	45	Nobel Physics
Escobedo, Mariano	Military	50	225			Captured Maximillian
Eshkol, Levi 1895-1969	Head of State	295	250	560	120	Israeli P.M., Fndr. Histadrut
Esnault-Pelterie, Robert 1881-1957	Aviation	75	250			Pioneer Aviator. Invented Aileron
Esperian, Kalen	Entertainment	10			30	Opera
Essame, Hubert	Military	25	41			
Estaing, Charles Hector T. de	Revolutionary War	175	500	750		Fr.Gen-Adm. Pro American Hero
Estavez, Emelio	Entertainment	5			35	Actor
Este, Isabella d' 1474-1539	Royalty			10000		(Mantua) Art Patron, Diplomat
Estefan, Gloria	Entertainment	10			45	
Esterhasy, Gunt A.	Head of State	20	70			Austria
Esterhazy, Prince Pal A. 1786-1866	Statesman	25		70		Austro-Hung. Diplomat
Estes, Billy Sol	Celebrity	5	20	45	15	Grain Storage Scandal
Estevez, Emilio	Entertainment	10	15	25	30	
Estil, Benjamin	Congress	15	25			Congressman VA 1825
Estrada, Erik	Entertainment	4	4	9	15	
Etter, Philippe	Head of State	15	50			Switzerland
Etting, Ruth	Entertainment				60	Major Vint. Singing Star
Eubanks, Bob	Entertainment	4	4	9	10	
Eugenie, Empress(Nap.III)	Royalty	195	305	375		Influenced Nap. Fashion Leader
Euler (-Chelpin), Ulf Svante von	Science	20	35	60	40	Nobel Medicine
Eurythmics	Entertainment	40			90	
Eustis, Abraham	Military	40		350		War 1812. Promoted to Br. Gen.
Eustis, William 1753-1825	Cabinet	35	142	185		Sec'y War, MOC MA 1801
Evans, Clement A. (War Date)	Civil War	175	850	925		CSA General
Evans, Clement A. 1833-1911	Civil War	90		363		CSA General
Evans, Dale	Entertainment	10	12		25	
Evans, Daniel J.	Senate-Gov.	15	18		20	Gov., Senato Washington
Evans, De Lacy	Military	150	220			Br. Col. Who Burned White House
Evans, Edith, Dame 1888-1976	Entertainment	15	30		35	
Evans, Edw. R.G.,Lord Mountevans	Explorer	35			75	Admiral, Arctic Explorer
Evans, Gene	Entertainment	5	6	15	30	
Evans, Geraint, Sir	Entertainment	10			35	Opera
Evans, Joan	Entertainment	7	10	15	10	
Evans, John V.	Governor	10	15			Governor ID
Evans, Linda	Entertainment	9	10	20	35	Actress
Evans, Lt. Col. D. M	Civil War	15	25	40		
Evans, Madge	Entertainment	15	15	35	30	
Evans, Maurice	Entertainment	20	25	35	55	
Evans, Nathan G. Shanks	Civil War	175		575		CSA Gen.
Evans, Nicholas	Author		40			The Horse Whisperer
Evans, Ray	Composer	15	35	45	40	
Evans, Robley D.	Civil War	30	65	110	150	Capt. USN, Fight'n Bob
Evans, Ronald E.	Astronaut	40			100	
Evarts, William M. 1818-1901	Cabinet	75	82	167	45	Att'y Gen., Sec'y State, Sen NY
Everest. F.K. 'Pete'	Aviation	15	30	45	35	
Everett, Chad	Entertainment	5	6	15	18	
Everett, Edward 1794-1865	Sen.-Cab.-Clergy	75	165	187	95	Fillmore Sec'y State, Sen. MA
Everly Brothers	Entertainment	30			75	
Evers, Charles	Celebrity	5	20	40	10	
Evers, Medgar 1925-63	Activist		2800			AM. Civil Rights Leader
Evigan, Greg	Entertainment	3	3	6	10	
Ewell, I.R.L.	Civil War	190	395			

NAME	CATEGORY	SIG	LS/DS	ALS	SP	Comment
Ewell, Rich'd Stoddert (War Date)	Civil War	686		1850		CSA General
Ewell, Rich'd Stoddert 1817-72	Civil War	375	550	1275		CSA General
Ewell, Tom	Entertainment	6	8	15	25	
Ewing, James	Military	45	142			Officer Am. Revolution
Ewing, Thomas 1789-1871	Cabinet	40	110	245		Sen. OH,Sec'y Treas. & Interior
Exelmans, Rene' J.I., 1775-1852	Fr. Revolution	20	35	135		Marshal of France
Exile (4)	Entertainment	20			50	Rock
Exon, J. James	Senator-Gov.	5	10		10	Senator, Governor NE
Eyre, Edward John 1815-1901	Explorer	55		150		Gov. Australia. Eyre Rock
Eythe, William	Entertainment	10	15	20	20	
Eytinge, Rose 1838-1911	Entertainment	25		50	45	19th Cent./Laura Keene, Booth

NAME	CATEGORY	SIG	LS/DS	ALS	SP	Comment
Fabares, Shelley	Entertainment	7	10	15	21	Actress. Coach
Faber, John Eberhard	Business	134	500	725		Eberhard Faber Pencil Co.
Fabian	Entertainment	5			20	
Fabian, John M.	Astronaut	10			15	
Fabio	Model	16			40	Fashion Model
Fabray, Nanette	Entertainment	5	6	15	30	
Factor, Max	Business	25	125	175	60	Cosmetic Mfg.
Factor, Max Jr.	Business	10	30	55	45	Cosmetic Mfg.
Fagan, James F.	Civil War		1625			CSA Gen.& U.S.Marshal
Fagerbakke, Bill	Entertainment	8			35	Actor Coach
Fagoaga, Isidodo	Entertainment	15			50	Opera
Fahey, Jeff	Entertainment	5			36	Actor. The Marshal
Fair, James G.	Senate	30	145	110		Mining, Financier, CA Developer
Fairbank, Calvin	Abolitionist	40	85	150		Freed Fugitive Slaves
Fairbanks, Charles W. (V)	Vice President	50	100	275	150	T. Roosevelt VP
Fairbanks, Douglas, Jr.	Entertainment	20	85		45	
Fairbanks, Douglas, Sr. 1883-1939	Entertainment	122	50		299	Swashbuckling Silent Film Mega Star
Fairbanks, Erastus 1792-1864	Governor	35		80		CW Gov. VT. Mfg.Platform Scales
Fairchild, Charles S.	Cabinet	20	35	55	40	Sec'y Treasury 1887
Fairchild, David G.	Science	5	10	20	10	Am. Botanist. Books on Plants
Fairchild, Lucius	Civil War	20	45	65		Union Gen., Gov. WI, Statesman
Fairchild, Morgan	Entertainment	10	15	20	25	Pin-Up SP $30
Fairchild, Sherman	Business	25	60	115	40	Fairchild Camera & Equipment Co
Fairfax, George Wm. 1787	Post Rev. War	75	210	395		Companion of Geo. Washington
Fairfax, Thomas Lord 1691-1782	Colonial America	220	550			Historically Important Family
Fairfield, Charles 1842-1924	Cabinet	25		40		Sec'y Treas. under Cleveland
Fairfield, John 1797-1847	Gov.-Senate	15	20	30		Senator, Gov. ME
Fairless, Benjamin F.	Business	35	95	190	70	CEO US Steel
Faisal, King	Royalty	25	50	95	125	King Saudi Arabia
Faith, Percy	Composer	15			150	Conductor-Arranger
Faithfull, Emily	Reformer	25	45	55		Br.Printer-Publisher Q.Victoria

NAME	CATEGORY	SIG	LS/DS	ALS	SP	Comment
Falck, Wolfgang	Aviation	20	45	60	40	
Falconer, William 1732-1769	Author	45	350			Brit. Poet. Shipwrecked,Univer.Marine Dict'y
Falk, Peter	Entertainment	5	6	15	25	
Falkenburg, Jinx	Entertainment	5	6	10	25	
Fall, Albert B.	Cabinet	40	85	150	60	Sec'y Interior.Teapot Dome
Fall, Leo 1873-1925	Composer				105	Austrian Operetta Composer
Falla, Manuel de 1876-1946	Composer	175	510		900	AMusQS $1,000-1200
Fallon, Walter A.	Business	4			10	CEO Eastman Kodak Co.
Falstaff, John, Sir	Military		8000			Model for Shakespeare's Play
Falwell, Jerry	Clergy	15	20	25	35	Far Right—Politically-Theologically
Fancourt, Darell	Entertainment	15				D'Oyly Carte Gilbert & Sullivan Baritone Star
Faneuil, Peter	Revolutionary War	125	225	555		Faneuil Hall, Boston
Fang, Wu Ting, Dr.	Statesman	10			20	Chinese Statesman
Fantin-Latour, Henri	Artist	35	90	175		Fr. Illustrator, Lithographer
Far, Frances	Composer	4	13	30	10	
Faraday, Michael 1791-1867	Science	160	400	712	650	Br. Physicist, Chemist.ALS/Cont.$1800
Farentino, James	Entertainment	16			25	Actor
Fargo, Donna	Country Music	6	10		20	Singer
Fargo, James C.	Business	150	685			Pres.-Fndr. Wells, Fargo & Co.
Fargo, William G. 1818-81	Business	285	613	1250		Wells-Fargo, Am. Expr. LS $2950
Farina, Dennis	Entertainment	15	35		25	
Farinelli, Patricia	Model	4			15	Pin-Up SP $20
Farley, James A.	Cabinet	15	40	70	25	FDR P.M. General
Farman, Henri	Aviation	60	110	175	165	Pioneer Aviator. Airplane Mfg.
Farman, Maurice	Aviation	75		190		Pioneer Aviator. License #6
Farmer, Art	Entertainment	10			25	Jazz Fluegelhorn-Trumpet
Farmer, Fannie Merritt	Author	190			250	Cookery Expert
Farmer, Frances	Entertainment	165	190	250	618	
Farnol, J. Jeffrey	Author	4	25			British
Farnsworth, Charles	Military	25			65	General WW I
Farnsworth, Daniel W.	Business		15	30		Founder Woolen Mills
Farnsworth, John F.	Civil War	45	110			Union Gen.
Farnsworth, Philo T.	Inv.1st TV Camera					Rare NRPA
Farnsworth, Richard	Entertainment	8	9	15	20	
Farnum, Dustin	Entertainment	50	45	90	130	Silent Star. The Virginian
Farnum, William	Entertainment	40			195	Vintage Leading Man. Silent Films
Farquhar, John Hanson	Senate/Congress	10	20	30		MOC IN, Capt. Union Army
Farr, Jamie	Entertainment	6	8	15	20	MASH cast
Farragut, David G. 1801-70	Civil War	162	453	875	1182	Union Adm. LS/Cont. $1,300
Farrakhan, Louis	Activist	70			150	Leads Nation of Islam
Farrar, Frederick W.	Clergy	25	35	50	50	
Farrar, Geraldine 1882-1967	Entertainment	65		120	110	Opera, Concert
Farrell, Charles	Entertainment	15	20	30	42	Leading Man 30's-40's
Farrell, Eileen	Entertainment	10			95	Opera, Concert
Farrell, Glenda	Entertainment	25	30		75	
Farrell, Mike	Entertainment	5	6	15	15	
Farrimond, Richard	Astronaut	10			25	
Farrow, Mia	Entertainment	10	30		28	
Farwell, Chas. B. 1823-1903	Congress	15				Senator
Fassbaender, Brigitte	Entertainment	10			25	Ger. Mezzo Soprano,Opera
Fast, Howard (E.V.Cunningham)	Author	15	125		20	Historical Novelist, Screenplays
Faster Pussy Cat	Entertainment	25			50	Rock
Fauber, Bernard M.	Business	5	10		10	Pres. K Mart
Faubus, Orval E.	Governor	35		70	50	Gov. AR, Blocked Integration
Faulkner, Charles J., Jr.	Senate	15	25			Sen. WV. Battle of New Market
Faulkner, Chas. J. 1806-84	Congress		40	150		Repr. WV. Authored Fugitive Slave Act

The Sanders Price Guide to Autographs

NAME	CATEGORY	SIG	LS/DS	ALS	SP	Comment
Faulkner, William 1897-1962	Author	350	1500	2500	3680	Nobel Lit., Pulitzer Fiction
Fauquier, Francis	Colonial Gov. VA	200	575			Colonial Administrator
Fauré, Felix 1841-99	Head of State	30		125		Pres. France 1895-99
Fauré, Gabriel 1845-1924	Composer	100	220	192	550	Fr. 100's Songs,Chamber Music
Fausto, Cleva	Entertainment	30			65	Opera
Faversham, William 1868-1940	Entertainment	25			40	Created Role 'Jim Carson' in Squaw Man
Fawcett, Edgar	Author	45	105	225		
Fawcett, Farrah	Entertainment	9	10	20	25	Pin-Up SP $35
Fawcett, Millicent, Dame 1847-1929	Reformer	35	35	100		Br. Women's Suffrage Leader
Fay, Frank	Entertainment	15	25	45	45	
Faye, Alice	Entertainment	10	15	25	25	
Faye, Julia	Entertainment	4	6	10	12	
Faylen, Frank	Entertainment	45			75	
Fazenda, Louise	Entertainment	25			75	
Featherston, Winfield Scott	Civil War	85	225	215		1920-91.CSA Gen.
Fegelein, Hermann Otto	Military	500				Ger. SS Gen. WWII
Feiffer, Jules	Cartoonist	10			50	Mag. Cartoonist
Feinhals, Fritz	Entertainment	30			50	Ger. Baritone, Opera
Feinstein, Diane	Senate	5	12	25	20	Senator CA
Feld, Fritz	Entertainment	8	9		20	
Feldany, Eric	Entertainment	3	3	6	10	
Felder, Rodney Dr.	Celebrity	5	8	17	5	
Feldman, Charles K.	Business	10	20	40	15	Fndr. Famous Artists Corp.
Feldman, Marty	Entertainment	35			85	
Feldon, Barbara	Entertainment	5	6	15	35	
Feldshuh, Tovah	Entertainment	5	6	10	12	
Feliciano, Jose	Entertainment	5	6		20	Guitar-Vocalist
Felix, Maria	Entertainment	10			30	
Fellini, Frederico 1920-93	Entertainment	50	295		188	AA Film Director-Producer
Fellows, Edith	Entertainment	10			20	Teen Singer-Actress of 30's
Fels, Joseph	Business	95	210	490		Fels Naptha Soap
Felt, Harry, Adm.	Military	10	30	50	25	
Felton, Cornelius C. 1807-82	Educator	10	25	70		President Harvard 1860-62
Felton, Happy	Bandleader	15				
Felton, Rebecca L.	Senate	25	45	150		Sen. GA For 1 Day 11/21-11/22
Fenn, Sherilyn	Entertainment	10			38	Pin-Up SP $45
Fenneman, George	Entertainment	10			20	
Fenton, Ruben E.	Governor	30	50	80		Civil War Gov. NY
Fenwick, B.J., Bishop	Clergy	20	25	30		
Fenwick, Millicent 1910-1992	Senate/Congress	20	30		50	MOC NJ. Lampooned in Doonsbury
Feoktistov, Konstantin	Cosmonaut	20			75	Pioneer Russian Cosmonaut
Ferber, Edna 1887-1968	Author	110	458	425		Novelist, Screenplays,Pulitzer
Ferdinand I 1503-1564	Royalty	400	1235			Holy Roman Emperor
Ferdinand I 1793-1875	Royalty	70	245			Emperor of Austria
Ferdinand I 1865-1927	Royalty				580	King of Roumania, Prince of Hohenzollern
Ferdinand I, III, IV, 1751-1825	Royalty	5200				King of Naples, Two Sicilies
Ferdinand II 1578-1637	Royalty	100	460			Holy Roman Emperor from 1619
Ferdinand II, The Catholic	Royalty	450	1700	4385		Spain
Ferdinand V 1452-1516	Royalty		3700			King of Spain
Ferdinand VII (Sp)	Royalty	125	475			
Ferebee, Thomas	Aviation	50	125	250	100	Major. Bombadier of Enola Gay
Ferenczi, Sandor	Science	70	180	350		Hung.Psychoanalyst.Freud Friend
Ferguson, Homer	Congress	5	15		10	Senator MI. Ambass. Philippines
Ferguson, Maynard	Entertainment	10			30	Trumpet Player
Ferguson, Miriam A. 'Ma'	Governor	60	150			Governor TX
Ferguson, Samuel W. (War Date)	Civil War	270		700		CSA General

NAME	CATEGORY	SIG	LS/DS	ALS	SP	Comment
Ferguson, Samuel W. 1834-1917	Civil War	180	350	775		CSA Gen.
Ferguson, William J.	Entertainment	175	225	425		Actor Our American Cousin
Ferkauf, Eugene	Business	7	10	14	10	
Ferlinghetti, Lawrence	Author	20	75	90	25	Am.Poet,Publisher.Beat Movement
Fermi, Enrico 1901-1954	Science	475	1950			Nobel Phys.Nuke Chain Reaction
Ferrar, Geraldine	Entertainment	35			130	Opera. Famous for Puccini Roles
Ferrara, Franco	Entertainment	45			250	Conductor
Ferrare, Cristina	Entertainment	6	8	15	15	Model. TV Host
Ferrari, Enzo 1898-1988	Business	300	662		528	Auto Mfg. Race Car Driver
Ferraro, Geraldine	Congress	20	45	55	25	Congresswoman NY
Ferrer, Jose	Entertainment	20	25	40	58	AA Actor
Ferrer, Mel	Entertainment	5			20	
Ferrer, Miguel	Entertainment	4			15	Actor son of Jose
Ferrero, Edward (War Date)	Civil War	75	245			Union General
Ferrero, Edward 1831-99	Civil War	45	145	235		Union General
Ferrigno, Lou	Entertainment	5		10	12	
Ferris, Scott	Senate/Congress	12	15		15	MOC OK
Ferry, Orris S.(War Date)	Civil War	50	80	140	300	Union Gen., U.S. Sen. NY
Ferry, Thomas White 1827-96	Senate	70	95			Sen. MI,Pres. Pro Tem Senate
Fersen, Hans-Axel, Count de	Revolutionary War		1250			With Rochambeau at Yorktown
Fesch, Cardinal	Clergy		220	450		Married Napoleon & Josephine
Fess, Simeon Davison	Senate/Congress	10	15	25		MOC, Senator MI
Fessenden, Francis (War Date)	Civil War	75	172			Union Gen.
Fessenden, Francis 1839-1906	Civil War	48	90	212		Union Gen.
Fessenden, James	Civil War	20	52	70		Union Gen.
Fessenden, William P.1806-69	Cabinet	40	65	175		Lincoln Sec'y Treasury
Fetchit, Stepin	Entertainment	30			150	Early Afro-Am. Actor
Few, William	Revolutionary War	200	450	750		Continental Congress.1st GA Sen
Feynman, Richard P.	Science	25	40	85	30	Nobel Physics.
Fibich-Hanusova, Betty	Entertainment			250		Opera. Great Czech Alto
Fiderkiewicz, Alfred J., Dr.	Statesman	25	50			Polish Statesman
Fidler, Jimmy	Entertainment	5	6	15	15	Hollywood Gossip Columnist
Fiedler, Arthur	Entertainment	32			50	Conductor Boston Pops
Fiedler, John	Entertainment	3	3	6	10	
Field, Charles E	Clergy	20	35	45	25	
Field, Cyrus W. 1819-92	Business	50	306	275		Atlantic Cable, Financier
Field, Eugene 1850-95	Author	110	230	525	200	Children's Poet, Journalist
Field, Henry Martyn 1822-1907	Clergy	10		35		Presb. Younger Brother Cyrus Field
Field, Kate	Author	10	15			
Field, Marshall, III 1893-1956	Business	95	160	350		Communications Empire
Field, Marshall, Jr.1916-1965	Business	30	110	170	75	Pres.,CEO Field Entertprises
Field, Marshall, Sr.1834-1906	Business	300	245	550		Marshall Field & Co.
Field, Mary French	Author	5	15	20	15	
Field, Rachel	Author	20	100			Am. Novelist, Children's Books
Field, Sally	Entertainment	7	15	28	25	Pin-Up SP $30
Field, Stephen J. (SC)1816-99	Supreme Court	75	150	300	225	
Field, Virginia	Entertainment	5	6	15	15	
Fielder, James F.	Governor	10	15	25	15	Governor NJ
Fielding, Copley	Artist			12		Brit. Watercolorist
Fields, Debbi	Entertainment	2			8	
Fields, Gracie	Entertainment	15	35	55	80	Br. Singer & Comedienne
Fields, James T. 1817-81	Author		20	35		Publisher
Fields, Lew M. 1879-1946	Entertainment	50				SEE Weber & Fields
Fields, Shep	Entertainment	15			40	Big Band Leader
Fields, Stanley	Entertainment	15	15	35	40	Vintage Character Actor
Fields, W. C. 1879-1946	Entertainment	400		925	1775	Comedian-Actor Stage & Screen

	CATEGORY	SIG	LS/DS	ALS	SP	Comment
	Business	90	150	410		Co-Founder Fisher Body (GM)
	Astronaut	5			20	
	Civil War	55	70	95		Union Gen. Founded Fisk Univ.
1872	Business	50	115	190	95	Robber Baron.Stock Cert. S $19500
·rn	Entertainment	15			35	Stage. Silent Films
	Military	15		35		Admiral WW I
	Science	20	35		30	Nobel Physics
343-1913	Science			331		Physician. Identified Cause of Appendicitis
	Entertainment	125	135	195	250	
·d	Author	90	250	760		Poet.Translator Rubaiyat....
	Entertainment	30	35	80	85	
· 1896-1940	Author	375	1635	2944	2250	ALS/Content $5,500
	Statesman	10	30			Irish Statesman
·ne	Entertainment	6	8	15	15	
	Revolutionary War	35	90	190		
·.(Honey Fitz)	Political	20	55	95		Mayor Boston. JFK Grandfather
	Business	2	5	12	5	
·k E.	Celebrity	3	8	25	10	
·mas 1741-1811	Revolutionary War	200	315	400		Continental Congress
	Entertainment	25			80	
	Author-Runner	15	35			
	Entertainament	15			35	Rock
	Entertainment	5	10	20	15	Also Author, Playwright
·ntgomery	Artist	60	190	265	422	Self Caricature S. $950
	Military	15	20	25	20	
· 1830-1913	Business		2925			Stand. Oil Pioneer. Fndr. So. FL
	Entertainment	100			263	Nor. Soprano
·Count	Fr. Revolution	15		25		Gen. Exploits in Gallantry
·, Cardinal	Clergy	35	40	60	40	
·945-	Congress	4	10			Congressman NY
·olas-Camille	Science	40	65	165		Fr. Astronomer
· 1646-1719	Clergy-Science	800	975			Br. 1st Astronomer Royal
·d, Fr. 1886-1948	Clergy	45	125		250	Boy's Town Founder
·Patrick	Entertainment				38	Actor
·s & Lester	Country Music	50			125	
·e	Author	175	635	1500		Fr. Novelist. Realist School
	Entertainment	4	4	9	10	
	Entertainment	102			217	Signed by All 6
	Entertainment	30				Member Fleetwood Mad
·es	Entertainment	10			15	Voice of Roger Rabbitt
·re	Author	15		40	30	Shadowlands
1883-1972	Cartoonist	50	295		375	Animator. Creator of Betty Boop
·rd	Entertainment	5			20	Film Director
·harles L.	Business	95	450			Fleischmann's Yeast
	Business	10			50	Oldest Biz, Hollywood Madame
·der, Sir 1881-1955	Science	200	300	2000	800	Nobel for Penicillin
	Entertainment	225	250		350	Original Rawhide
·s	Aviation	10	22	38	28	ACE, WW II
	Author	300	895	1100	1400	1st Ed. Signed $5,000
·Ambrose, Sir	Science	25	65	145		Br. Electrical Engineer
·la	Entertainment	10	25	25	42	Pin-Up SP $55
	Entertainment	150			450	Veteran Film Director
·s, Alfred	Military	10	50			WW I Victoria Cross
	Entertainment	45			250	Opera
·well	Entertainment	30			75	
· Jack	Military	25	60	120	60	

NAME	CATEGORY	SIG	LS/DS	ALS	SP
Fiennes, Ralph	Entertainment	15			40
Fiennes, Ranulph	Explorer	10			30
Fieseler, Gerhard	Aviation	25	55	85	85
Fifteen (15)	Entertainment	35	15	30	55
Figner, Medea (See Mei-Figner)					
Figueres, Jose	Head of State	15	45	110	20
Filacuridi, Nicola	Entertainment	15			45
Filippeschi, Mario	Entertainment	25			85
Fillmore, Caroline	First Lady	600	950	800	
Fillmore, Millard (As Pres.)	President	450	1462	2975	
Fillmore, Millard 1800-74	President	243	1348	1283	10000
Finch, Peter	Entertainment	75		110	165
Findlay, William 1768-1846	Governor	45	60	115	
Fine, Janine	Entertainment				40
Fine, Jeanna	Entertainment				40
Fine, Larry	Entertainment	108			350
Finegan, Bill (William J.)	Entertainment	20			40
Finkel, Fyvush	Entertainment	3			20
Finlay, Frank	Entertainment	5	6	15	15
Finletter, Thomas A.	Cabinet	5	12	30	15
Finley, Jesse J. (War Date)	Civil War				
Finley, Jesse J.1812-1904	Civil War	85	115	220	
Finley, John	Astronaut	5			15
Finney, Albert	Entertainment	9	10	20	25
Finney, Charles G.	Clergy	50	75	110	
Finnie, Linda	Entertainment	10			30
Finston, Nat W.	Composer-Author	10			20
Fio-Rito, Ted	Entertainment	15			35
Fiorella, Pascal A.	Rev.War Era	20	55	125	
Fiorentino, Linda	Entertainment				40
Firestone, Harvey S. 1868-1938	Business	135	1725	1550	619
Firestone, Jr., Harvey S.	Business	25	50	85	35
Firestone, Leonard K.	Business	15	40	70	25
First Ladies (Four Repub.)	First Ladies	250			900
First Ladies (Kennedy thru Bush)	First Ladies	750			
Fischer, Annie	Entertainment				250
Fischer, Bobby	Celebrities	40	85	200	75
Fischer, Edmond H., Dr.	Science	20	45		30
Fischer, Harold E.	Aviation	10	25	45	35
Fischer, Siegfried	Aviation	10	15	25	15
Fish, Hamilton 1808-1893	Cabinet	20	95	100	
Fish, Nicholas	Revolutionary War	40	120	245	
Fish, Preserved	Colonial	45	165		
Fisher, Amy	Criminal	20		155	
Fisher, Anna L.	Astronaut	10			25
Fisher, Bud* (Harry C.)	Cartoonist	75	95		425
Fisher, Carrie	Entertainment	5	10	20	20
Fisher, Cindy	Entertainment	4			10
Fisher, Eddie	Entertainment	5	10	20	25
Fisher, Fred J.	Business	90			
Fisher, Freddie	Entertainment	5			
Fisher, Geoffrey F. 1887-1972	Clergy	35			
Fisher, Ham*	Cartoonist	100		225	250
Fisher, Harrison	Artist	40			
Fisher, John S.	Governor	10	15	35	
Fisher, John, Lord	Military	15	25		

NAME	CATEGORY	SIG	LS/DS	ALS	SP	Comment
Fletcher, Harvey 1884-1981	Science	225				Stereo Sound 1934
Fletcher, James	NASA	10	20	35		Whistle Blower
Fletcher, James Cooley	Clergy	5		25		Missionary
Fletcher, John Gould	Author	15	30	100		Pulitzer Poet
Fletcher, Louise	Entertainment	6	8	15	25	
Flindt, Flemming	Ballet					Royal Danish Ballet Star
Flint, Austin 1812-86	Physician	70	215	400		Eminent Physician-Teacher
Flint, Lawrence	Aviation	10	16	35	25	
Flippen, Jay C.	Entertainment	25			60	
Floege, Ernest	Military		45		70	Commandant Paul.Fr.Resistance
Floren, Myron	Entertainment	2			8	Accordian. Lawrence Welk
Florence, William J., Mrs.	Entertainment	10		25	15	Appeared With Husband
Florence, William Jermyn 1831-91	Entertainment	15	25	40	75	Actor, Songwriter, Playwright
Flores, Juan Jose	Head of State		775			1st President of Equador
Florey, Howard Walter	Science	25	40	75	35	Nobel Medicine, Penicillin
Florey, Robert	Entertainment	15			35	
Flory, Paul J., Dr.	Science	20	35	70	30	Nobel Chemistry
Flotow, Frederich von	Composer	75	220	450		Ger. Opera, Ballet, Concertos
Flourens, Marle-Jean P.1794-1867	Science		50			Fr. Physiologist
Flower, R.P	Governor	10	15			Governor NY
Flower, Wm.Henry, Sir	Science	10	25	50		Br.Zoologist
Flowers, Bess	Entertainment	6	8	15	20	Extra in over 1,000 films
Flowers, Wayland	Entertainment	12	15		23	
Floyd, John Buchanan (War Date)	Civil War			1850		CSA Gen.
Floyd, John Buchanan 1806-63	Civil War	182	320	409		Gov. VA. Sec'y War, CSA General
Floyd, William	Revolutionary War	400	1295	1500		Signer Decl. of Indepen.
Fluckey, Gene	Military	45		110	90	Top US Submarine Cmdr.
Flunger, Anna	Entertainment	6	8	15	15	
Fluster, Lafayette	Senate	40				Pres. Pro Tem of Senate
Flynn, Edward J.	Political	5	10	25	10	Democratic Boss NY
Flynn, Errol 1909-59	Entertainment	307	600	510	650	Warner Bros. DS $1,500
Flynn, James	Entertainment	4	5	9	9	
Flynn, Joe	Entertainment	50	60	110	125	
Flynt, Larry	Publisher	15	75	100	65	Hustler Magazine
Foale, Mike	Astronaut	4			12	
Foch, Ferdinand	Military	50	125	280	235	Fr. General WWI, Marshal
Foch, Nina	Entertainment	8	5	10	15	
Fogelberg, Dan	Entertainment	6			20	
Fogerty, John	Entertainment	15			40	Rock
Fokker, Anthony	Aviation	200	295	530	500	Am. Aircraft Designer-Builder
Foley, Red	Country Music	30			85	
Folger, Charles J.	Cabinet	7	15	30		Sec'y Treasury
Follett, Ken	Author	4	10		15	Br. Mystery Novelist
Folsom, Marion B.	Cabinet	15	25		20	Sec'y HEW. Drafter Soc.Sec.Adm.
Folsom, Nathaniel	Revolutionary War	125		450		Am. Gen., Continental Congress
Foltz, Frederick	Military			45	100	General WW I
Fonck, Paul-Rene'	Aviation	1000	1900			ACE, Fr. WW I. Top Allied Ace
Fonda, Bridget	Entertainment	25			47	Col. Pin-up 70, Art Print S 100
Fonda, Henry 1905-1982	Entertainment	30	100		120	AA
Fonda, Jane	Entertainment	6	195	30	23	Pin-Up SP $35
Fonda, Jelles	Revolutionary War	50	155	225		Colonial Leader,Rev.War Officer
Fonda, Peter	Entertainment	6	8	15	25	
Fonda, Ten Eyck H.	Civil War	50		95		Military Telegrapher Hero
Fong, Benson	Entertainment	25			40	
Fong, Hiram L.	Senate	5	10		10	Senator HI
Fonseca, Roberto A.	Head of State	5	16	40	20	

NAME	CATEGORY	SIG	LS/DS	ALS	SP	Comment
Fontaine, Joan	Entertainment	12	15	40	35	Pin-Up SP $45
Fontanne, Lynn	Entertainment	15			40	
Fonteyn, Margot 1919-91	Entertainment	40	55	135	194	Premier Ballerina
Foot, Solomon	Congress	15	30	45		Repr. VT 1843, CSA Congress
Foote, Andrew Hull 1806-1863	Civil War	45	110	300		Union Adm '63 $3,500
Foote, Arthur	Composer	30	85	195		Organist. Church Music, Songs
Foote, H.R.B.	Military	8	20			Br. Maj. Gen. Victoria Cross WW II
Foote, Henry S.	Civil War	25	40	70		US Senator, CSA Congress
Foote, Horton	Author	5		20	15	Playwright, Scriptwriter
Foote, Shelby	Author	15	35			
Foraker, Joseph B.1846-1917	Senator-Gov.	10	35			Governor, Senator OH
Foran, Dick	Entertainment	15	20	35	45	
Foray, June	Entertainment	5			10	Voice of Rocky & Bullwinkle
Forbes, Bertie Chas.1880-1954	Business	35	225	175	65	Founder Forbes Magazine
Forbes, M. Steve	Publisher	5			15	Presidential Candidate
Forbes, Malcolm S.	Business	30	70	175	75	Publ., Motorcyclist,Balloonist
Forbes, Ralph	Entertainment	15	15	30	25	
Forbes-Robertson, John 1853-1937	Entertainment	22		150	50	Leading Br. Actor Shakespeare, Films
Force, Manning F. 1824-99	Civil War			100		Union Gen. Shiloh, Vicksburg, Atlanta
Ford, Benson	Business	5	15	30	15	Ford Motor Car
Ford, Betty	First Lady	35	117		50	
Ford, Edsel 1893-1943	Business	250	600		500	Ford Motor Co.
Ford, Edsel B. II	Business	5	10	20	10	Ford Motor Co.
Ford, Eileen	Business	5	30		10	Ford Modelling Agency
Ford, Elaine	Business	24			30	
Ford, Gerald & Ford, Betty	Pres.-1st Lady				100	FDC S. $250
Ford, Gerald R.	President	88	262	433	60	Content: ALS $5,500,TLS $1,500
Ford, Gerald R. (As President)	President	228	660	1442	273	Served Only 2½ Years
Ford, Glenn	Entertainment	30			52	
Ford, Harrison	Entertainment	50			133	
Ford, Henry 1863-1947	Business	1098	4200	4500	2500	Pioneer Auto Mfg.Important DS $28500
Ford, Henry II	Business	10	15	30	55	Ford Motor Co.
Ford, John	Entertainment	150			300	Classic Western Film Director
Ford, John Anson	Business	5	10	20	10	
Ford, John Thompson	Theatre Owner	475	600	750		Ford's Theater, Wash. D.C.
Ford, Lita	Entertainment	15			45	Singer
Ford, Michael	Entertaiment				15	Br. Actor
Ford, Paul	Entertainment	15			35	
Ford, Sewell 1868-1946	Author		15	35		Short Story Writer
Ford, Tennessee Ernie	Country Music	12			38	
Ford, Wallace	Entertainment	20			50	
Fordney, Joseph W.	Senate/Congress	15		30		MOC MI. Lumber, Banking
Forepaugh, Adam 1831-90	Business-Circus	50				Early Circus Owner
Forester. C[ecil] S[cott]	Author	75	260	90	95	Br.Novelist.Horatio Hornblower
Forgy, Howell M. !908-83	Military Chaplain					And Pass the Ammunition S Book $395
Forman, Milos	Entertainment	20			75	A A Director
Forman, Thomas M.	Revolutionary War	45	100			
Formes, Karl	Entertainment	5	6	15	15	
Formica, Fern	Entertainment	15	25		30	Munchkin, Wizard of Oz
Forney, John H. 1829-1902	Civil War					CSA Gen. ALS '62 $975
Forney, William H. 1823-94	Civil War	90	135	297		CSA Gen., Repr. AL
Forrest, Edwin 1806-1972	Entertainment	30	80	125	150	Early Great Am. Actor
Forrest, Frederick	Entertainment	4			15	Actor
Forrest, French (War Date)	Civil War	165	658			CSA Naval Commander
Forrest, French 1796-1866	Civil War	95	140	187		CSA Naval Commander
Forrest, Hal*	Cartoonist	25			125	Tailspin Tommy

NAME	CATEGORY	SIG	LS/DS	ALS	SP	Comment
Forrest, Nathan B. (War Date)	Civil War	805		14800		CSA Gen.
Forrest, Nathan B. 1821-77	Civil War	650	2048	4700		CSA General
Forrest, Sally	Entertainment	5			12	
Forrest, Steve	Entertainment	7			15	Actor
Forrestal, James 1892-1949	Cabinet	45	115		25	Sec'y Navy. 1st Sec'y Defense. Suicide
Forslund, Constance	Entertainment	5	6	15	15	
Forster, Edw. Morgan 1879-1970	Author	65	240	338		Br. Novelist. Howard's End
Forster, John 1812-76	Author	20	25	50		Br. Historian, Biographer
Forster, Robert	Entertainment	6			12	Actor
Forsyth, Frederick	Author	10	40	80	20	Br., Master of Spy Novels
Forsyth, James William	Civil War	35	105	175		Union Gen., Wounded Knee
Forsyth, John 1780-1841	Cabinet	25	55	150		Sec'y of State (Jackson)
Forsythe, James W.	Civil War	40	120	185		Un. Gen. TLS/Cont. $250
Forsythe, John	Entertainment	9	10	20	25	
Fort, George F.	Governor	15	35	50		Governor NJ 1850
Fort, John Franklin	Governor	5	15			New Jersey
Fort, Luigi	Entertainment	20			45	Opera
Fortas, Abe (SC)	Supreme Court	25	150	200		Resigned from Court
Forte, Fabian (Fabian)	Entertainment	5	8	25	20	
Forti, Carmen Fiorella	Entertainment	25			60	Opera
Forward, Walter 1786-1852	Cabinet	15	50	80		Sec'y Treasury 1841
Fosbury, Dick	Sportsman	20			40	Eponym for Fosbury Flop
Fosdick, Harry Emerson 1878-1969	Clergy	35	62	90	50	Baptist Minister, Author
Foss, Joe	Aviation	30	75	85	55	ACE, WW II, Medal of Honor
Foss, Sam Walter	Author	5	10	20	10	
Fosse, Bob 1927-1987	Entertainment	35	120	90	60	AA. Choreographer-Film Director
Foster, Abiel 1735-1806	Clergy-Political	120	345			Cont. Congress. 1st MOC NH '89
Foster, Charles 1828-1904	Cabinet	35	55	100		Gov. OH, Sec'y Treas.
Foster, Dianne	Entertainment	4			20	Actress
Foster, Hal*	Cartoonist	100			500	Tarzan
Foster, Hal*	Cartoonist	100			600	Prince Valiant
Foster, Jodie	Entertainment	40			90	Actress, Dir., AA. Pin-up $135
Foster, John Gray (War Date)	Civil War	45	90	273		Union General
Foster, John Gray 1823-74	Civil War	35	42	65		Union Gen.
Foster, John W. 1836-1917	Cabinet	25		65	140	Sec'y State 1892, Diplomat
Foster, Lafayette S. 1806-80	Senate	25	60	95		Civil War Senator CT
Foster, Lawrence	Entertainment	3	5	8	10	
Foster, Myles B.	Artist	17	40	70		
Foster, Norman	Entertainment	15	15	35	45	Directer
Foster, Preston	Entertainment	20	85		65	
Foster, Stephen	Composers	1000	3500	10000		
Foster, Susanna	Entertainment	12	30		25	
Foucauld, Charles E. 1858-1916	Explorer-Clergy	300		875		Fr. Priest & Explorer
Fouche', Jos. Duc d'Otrante	Fr. Revolution	125	400	680		Politician, Advisor Nap.
Foulois, Benj. D. 1880-1967	Aviation	50				General. Pioneer Aviator
Fountain, Pete	Entertainment	6	10	20	25	Jazz-Dixieland Clarinetist
Four Seasons, The (4)	Rock Group				125	60's Rock Group. Sherry
Four Tops	Entertainment	40			95	Rock Singing Group
Fournier, G.	Military	55	85			
Fowler, Gene	Author	20	90		30	Journalist, Biographer,Novelist
Fowler, Henry H.	Cabinet	5	20	35	15	Sec'y Treas.
Fowler, William, Dr.	Science	20	30	45	30	Nobel Physics
Fowles, John	Author	30	70	150	35	Br.Novelist.Fr. Lieut's Woman
Fowley, Douglas	Entertainment	10			30	
Fox, Charles 1749-1806	Statesman	30	65	175		Br.Reformer, Orator, Libel Bill
Fox, Edward	Entertainment	6			15	Br. Actor

NAME	CATEGORY	SIG	LS/DS	ALS	SP	Comment
Fox, Fontaine T.	Cartoonist	35	50		200	Toonerville Trolley
Fox, Fred S.	Entertainment	10		45		Actor Mayberry
Fox, Michael J.	Entertainment	20	25	40	35	
Fox, Samantha	Entertainment	10			45	
Fox, Samuel	Clergy	15	20	25	35	
Fox, William	Business	185	550		375	Founder Fox Film Corp.
Foxworth, P. E.	Celebrity	5	15	35		
Foxworth, Robert	Entertainment	4	4	9	10	
Foxworthy, Jeff	Entertainment	7			35	Comedian-Red Neck
Foxx, Redd	Entertainment	20	30		35	
Foy, Eddie, Jr.	Entertainment	20	25	40	45	
Foy, Eddie, Sr.	Entertainment	25			60	
Foy, Maximilian S., Count	Fr. Revolution	15	35	80		Statesman, General. Waterloo
Fradona, Ramon*	Cartoonist	15			50	Brenda Starr
Frakes, Jonathan	Entertainment	8	9	19	20	Star Trek
Frampton, George, Sir 1860-1928	Artist	15		35		Brit. Sculp. Edith Cavell Mem.
France, Anatole	Author	50	130	235	300	Fr.Novels, Poetry,Critic. Nobel
Franchetti, Alberto	Composer	35		130	90	Wrote 9 Operas
Franchi, Sergio	Entertainment	10			32	
Franciosa, Anthony	Entertainment	4	4	9	15	
Francis I (1494-1547) Fr.	Royalty	500	750			France. Special DS $2,750
Francis I (1777-1830)	Royalty		185			King Two Sicilies
Francis II (1768-1835)	Royalty	95	300	425		Last Holy Roman Emperor(Aus)
Francis V (1819-75)	Royalty	40	100			Duke of Modena
Francis, Anne	Entertainment	4	6	15	16	
Francis, Arlene	Entertainment	5	6	15	10	
Francis, Connie	Entertainment	3	5	12	15	Singer
Francis, David R.	Cabinet	15	30	50	25	Sec'y Interior 1896
Francis, Dick	Author	25	72	80	40	Jockey Turned Mystery Writer
Francis, Genie	Entertainment	5	6	15	15	
Francis, Kay	Entertainment	25	30	70	95	
Franciscus, James	Entertainment	10	12	15	20	
Franck, César 1822-1920	Composer	340	1100	700		AMusMsS $5,000
Franco, Francisco	Head of State	175	750	1300	275	Sp. Soldier & Dictator
Frank, August	Military	10	30	45		
Frank, Hans	Nazi Lawyer	275	500			Nazi Administrator of Poland
Frank, Otto	Celebrity WWII		1500			Ann Frank
Franken, Rose	Author	10	25	40		Playwright
Frankenheimer, John	Entertainment	10		30	25	Film Director
Frankfurter, Felix (SC) 1882-1965	Supreme Court	145	1250	1195	750	Founder Am. Civil Liberties Un.
Franklin, Benjamin 1706-90	Revolutionary War	4300	11404	21450		Rev. War Dte. DS $25,000
Franklin, Bonnie	Entertainment	4	5	12	20	
Franklin, Herbert H. 1867-1956	Business	35	125			Pioneer Auto Manufacturer
Franklin, Jane 1792-1875	Author	65		395		Wife of John Franklin,Traveller
Franklin, John, Sir 1786-1847	Explorer	125	320	610		Proved NW Passage
Franklin, William	Colonial & Revol.	145	475	865		Brit. Gov. NJ, Son of Benj.
Franklin, Wm. Buell (War Date)	Civil War	120		220		Union Gen. AES/3 Gen'ls $825
Franklin, Wm. Buell 1823-1903	Civil War	75	155	178	195	Union Gen.
Frann, Mary	Entertainment	5	6	15	15	
Frantz, Charton C.	Business	10	35	45	20	
Franz Ferdinand 1863-1914	Royalty				1380	Archduke Austria.Assassinated
Franz Josef II, Crown Prince	Royalty	40	75	140	45	Liechtenstein
Franz Joseph I, 1830-1916	Royalty	155	540	875		Emperor of Austria
Franz, Arthur	Entertainment	10			20	
Franz, Dennis	Entertainment	5			35	NYPD Blue
Fraser, Douglas A.	Labor	10	15		15	Union President

NAME	CATEGORY	SIG	LS/DS	ALS	SP	Comment
Fraser, James Earle	Artist	540	662			Am. Sculptor of Buffalo Nickel
Fraser, Malcolm	Head of State	10			30	P.M. Australia
Fraser, Peter	Head of State	10	25		20	Prime Minister New Zealand
Frasier (Cast of)	Entertainment				250	All Five
Frawley, William	Entertainment	225	250		450	
Frazer, John Wesley	Civil War	165	255			CSA General
Frazer, Joseph W.	Business	275	600			Kaiser-Frazer Auto Mfg.
Frazetta, Frank*	Cartoonist	50			450	Johnny Comet
Frazier, Brendon	Entertainment	5			30	Actor
Freddy & The Dreamers (All)	Entertainment	95				
Frederic, Harold	Author	10	35	70		Am. Novelist, Correspondent
Frederic, Prince (Hohenz.)	Royalty	10	25			
Frederick Augustus I, 1750-1827	Royalty		275			The Just Saxony
Frederick Augustus II (1797-1854_	Royalty		175			King Saxony
Frederick I (Wurttemburg)	Royalty	25	95			
Frederick II, The Great (Prussia)	Royalty	400	1362	2185		1712-86
Frederick III 1831-1888	Royalty	65	260	550	500	Prussia
Frederick IV 1671-1730	Royalty		320	805		Denmark
Frederick IX 1899-1972	Royalty	50	175	350		Denmark
Frederick V 1723-66	Royalty	90	270	500		Denmark
Frederick VI 1768-1839	Royalty	80	238			Denmark
Frederick VII 1808-63	Royalty	45	150			Denmark
Frederick Wm. I 1688-1740	Royalty	145	420			Prussia
Frederick Wm. III 1770-1840	Royalty	65	450	475		Prussia
Frederick Wm. IV 1795-1861	Royalty	100	425	750		Prussia. Insane
Frederick, Pauline	Entertainment	15	30		80	Silent Cinema Star
Frederick, Prince of Wales 1707-51	Royalty		110			Son of Geo.II. Father of Geo. III
Fredericks, Fred*	Cartoonist	10		85	50	Mandrake The Magician
Fredericks, R.N.	Banker	12				
Freed, Bert	Entertainment	5	6	15	15	
Freeland, Paul van	Head of State	5	16	40	20	Prime Minister
Freeman, Kathleen	Entertainment	7	10		15	
Freeman, Mona	Entertainment	6	8	15	18	
Freeman, Morgan	Entertainment	15		50	40	
Freeman, Orville	Cabinet	7	15	25	10	Sec'y Agriculture
Freeman, Samuel	Revolutionary War	15	45	100		Rev. War Patriot
Freeman, Ted	Astronaut	10			48	
Fregeville, C.L.J.Marquis	Fr. Rev. War	15	35	75		
Freleng, Frizz*	Cartoonist	30			168	Animator, Crazy Cat
Frelinghuysen, Frederick T.	Cabinet	20	59	105	40	Sec'y State, Senator NJ
Frelinghuysen, Joseph S	Senate/Congress	5	15			Senator NJ
Fremont, Jessie Benton	Author	35	80	270		Wife of John C.
Fremont, John C. (War Date)	Civil War	265	875	1595		Union Gen.
Fremont, John C. 1813-90	Civil War	225	644	1108		Union Gen.-Content ALS $6,500
Fremstad, Olive	Entertainment	95			375	Opera. Europe & Met 1903-1917
French, Daniel Chester 1850-1931	Artist	95	200	225	125	Sculptor, Lincoln Memorial
French, Samuel Gibbs 1818-1910	Civil War	155	285	309		CSA General
French, Victor	Entertainment	15			40	
French, William H.	Civil War	40	125	250		Union General
Freni, Mirella	Entertainment	10			40	Opera
Freron, Louis M.S.	Fr. Revolution	20	45	90		Revolutionary
Fresnay, Pierre	Entertainment	10			45	Fr. Actor/Director
Freud, Anna 1895-1982	Science		570	350		Daughter of Sigmund Freud
Freud, Sigmund 1856-1939	Science	1650	5000	5070	9475	ALS/Content $7,500-$22,500
Frey, Richard	Aviation	25	50	100	65	
Friant, Louis, Count	Fr. Revolution	30	75	150		

NAME	CATEGORY	SIG	LS/DS	ALS	SP	Comment
Frick, Henry Clay	Business	95	1125	320		Carnegie Steel.Frick Art Museum
Fricke, Janie	Entertainment	5			10	Singer
Fricke, Richard I.	Business	10	35	45	20	
Fricker, Brenda	Entertainment	20	35	65	100	
Friedan, Bette	Feminist	15		25	20	
Friedgen, A.E.	Business	10	35	45	20	
Friedkin, William	Entertainment	7	10		20	
Friedman, Herbert	Science	15	35	55	20	
Friedman, Jerome I.	Science	20	35		30	Nobel Physics
Friedman, Milton	Economist-Author	20	35		25	Nobel Economics
Friends (Cast Of)	Entertainment				240	Cast of 6
Friganza, Trixie	Entertainment	4	4	9	10	
Friml, Rudolf 1879-1972	Composer	100	275	325	242	AMusS $750
Frisch, Karl von	Science	15	30	40	25	Nobel Medicine
Fritchie, Barbara (Frietschie)	Civil War	12500				Patriotic Heroine
Frith, William P.1819-1909	Artist	25	45	110		Crowded Scenes Contemporay Life
Fritsch, Werner von	Military	55	150	210	175	
Frizzell, Lefty	Country Music	25			65	
Frobe, Gert	Entertainment	30			80	
Frohman, Daniel	Entertainment	15		40	35	Dean of Am.Theatrical Producers
Froman, Jane 1907-80	Entertainment	15	15	20	45	Major Singing Star. Suffered Air Crash
Fromm, Erich	Science	45	150		75	Psychoanalist-Social Philosophe
Fromme, Lynette 'Squeaky'	Assassin	50	120	210	60	Charles Manson Follower
Frondizi, Arturo	Head of State	15	35	75	55	President Argentina
Frontenac, Louis, Comte 1620-1698	Statesman			5400		Gov. La Nouvelle France(Canada)
Frontiersmen, The	Country Music	25			50	
Frost, A.B.*	Cartoonist	40			250	Illustrator
Frost, Daniel Marsh	Civil War	170	245	450		CSA General
Frost, David	Entertainment	5			15	
Frost, Edwin B.	Science	10	25	45		Am. Astronomer
Frost, Robert 1874-1963	Author	150	683	2500	735	Poet. Pulitzer 1924,'31,'37,'43
Frost, Terry	Entertainment	10			40	Vintage cowboy actor
Frothingham, Octavius B.1822-95	Clergy	25	35	50		Am. Unitarian. Desciple of Theodore Parker
Fry, Christopher	Author	20	95	150		
Fry, Elizabeth	Clergy-Philanthro	40	125	185		Br. Quaker Philanthropist
Fry, Franklin C.	Clergy	20	25	35		
Fry, James Barnet 1827-94	Civil War	30	50	100		Union Gen. Shiloh, 1st Bull Run....
Frye, Dwight	Entertainment	650			1750	
Frye, Wm. P. (Actg V.P.)	Acting V.P.	15				
Fuchida, Mitsuo	Military-Aviation	300	350	500		Led Attack on Pearl Harbor 1941
Fuchs, Rutger	Military	40	125	195	95	
Fuchs, Vivian E. Sir	Explorer	25	75	150		Br. Antarctic Expl.
Fukuda, Takeo	Head of State	15		50	30	Prime Minister Japan
Fukui, Kenichi	Science	20	30	45	25	Nobel Chemistry
Fulbright, James W.	Congress	20	45	100	55	Senator AR, Fulbright Scholarship
Fulford, Millie Hughes	Astronaut	10			15	
Fulgham, Robert	Author	5			15	
Fulkerson, Abraham 1834-1902	Congress	20	35			CSA Col. Repr. TN
Fuller, Alfred C.	Business	125		195	150	Founder Fuller Brush Co.
Fuller, Alvan T.	Governor	15	25		20	Governor, MOC MA
Fuller, Buckminster R. 1895-1933	Science	25			102	Architectural Engin'r, Geodetic Dome
Fuller, Delores	Entertainment	20			50	Actress/Ed Wood
Fuller, Eduard	Author	6	20	40		
Fuller, John G.	Celebrity	10	16			
Fuller, Loie 1862-1928	Entertainment	50	124	200	350	Am. Dancer
Fuller, Margaret 1810-1850	Reformer-Author	140	250	450		Feminist, ALS/Content $2,500

NAME	CATEGORY	SIG	LS/DS	ALS	SP	Comment
Fuller, Melville W. (SC)	Supreme Court	50	150	275	175	
Fuller, R. Buckminster 1895-1983	Architect	30	85	140	245	Engineer, Geodesic Dome
Fuller, Robert	Entertainment	4	4	9	9	
Fuller, Sam	Entertainment	35			80	Film Director
Fullerton, Chas. Gordon	Astronaut	10	30	35		
Fullerton, Gordon	Astronaut	5			10	
Fulton, Fitz	Astronaut	10		15	25	
Fulton, Robert 1765-1815	Inventor	325	1062	3481		Submarine, Steamboat
Fulton, William S. 1795-1844	Congress	12				Sen. AR, Gov. AR
Funicello, Annette	Entertainment	10	15	20	25	Pin-Up SP $30
Funk, Casimer	Science	25	65		30	Biochemist Discovered Thiamin
Funk, Isaac K.	Publisher	25	80	135		Funk & Wagnalls Dictionary
Funk, Larry	Bandleader	10			30	
Funston, Frederick	Military	75	195	300		Cuba, Span.-American War. CMH
Furcolo, Foster	Governor	10	25			Governor MA
Furnas, Robert W.	Governor	5	10			Governor NE
Furness, Betty	Entertainment	15	15	25	25	
Furness, William H.	Clergy	10	15	20		
Furrer, Reinhard	Astronaut	15			95	Germany
Furstenberg, Betsy von	Entertainment	5	10		10	Fashion Designer
Furtwangler, Wilhelm 1886-1954	Entertainment	400	505	800	775	Controversial Ger. Conductor WW II
Fuseli, Henry 1741-1825	Artist	200	525			Br.-Swiss Romantic Painter
Futrell, J.M.	Governor	5	12		10	Governor AR

Gabet, Sharon	Entertainment	5	6	15	15	
Gable, Clark 1901-60	Entertainment	375	462	850	1209	
Gable, Kay	Entertainment	8	9	25	25	
Gabor, Eva	Entertainment	25	12	25	20	
Gabor, Zsa Zsa	Entertainment	5	6	15	15	Pin-Up SP $20
Gabreski, Frances	Aviation	35	95	125	72	ACE, WW II, #3 US
Gabriel, Peter	Entertainment	15			50	Rock
Gabrielle, Monique	Entertainment	15			25	Pin-Up SP $35
Gabrilowitsch, Ossip 1878-1936	Entertainment	110	135	240	110	Rus.-Am. Pianist, Conductor
Gacy, John Wayne	Celebrity	50	100	150	175	serial killer_paintings $1,000
Gadsden, James	Diplomat-Business	110	350	625		Gadsden Purchase
Gadski-Tauscher, Johanna	Entertainment	50		50	112	Ger.-Born Wagnerian Soprano
Gaffney, Drew	Astronaut	4			12	
Gagarin, Yuri & Gherman, Titov	Cosmonauts					SP's (2) $1,725
Gagarin, Yuri & Leonov, Alleksei	Cosmonauts				2995	SP/Both Cosmonauts
Gagarin, Yuri 1934-68	Astronaut	150	350		1500	First Man To Travel In Space
Gage, Lyman J.	Cabinet	12	25	50	30	Sec'y Treasury 1897
Gage, Nicholas	Author	10	25		15	
Gage, Thomas	Revolutionary War	225	885	950		Br. General. Commander-in-Chief

NAME	CATEGORY	SIG	LS/DS	ALS	SP	Comment
Gagnon, Ren, A.	Military	25	30		40	Iwo Jima Flag Raising FDC $225
Gail, Max	Entertainment	3	5	10	15	
Gaines, John P. 1795-1857	Congress	20				Rep. OR, Soldier, Gov. OR
Gainsborough, Thomas	Artist	270	760	1850		Br. Portraitist. Landscapes
Gajdusek, D. Carleton, Dr.	Science	20	35		30	Nobel Medicine
Galanos, James	Business	12	30	50	25	
Galard, Genevieve de	Celebrity	40			50	
Galbraith, John Ken.	Economist	15	35		20	Author Books Economics
Gale, Zona 1874-1938	Author	10	55	75	15	American Novelist Short Story Writer
Galella, Ron	Photographer	5	10		10	Celebrity Photographer
Galer, Robert E., Jr.	Aviation				50	Gen'l WW II. MOH. Air Ace
Galileo 1564-1642	Science	5000		25000		It. Astronomer
Gall, Bob	Business	4			10	Business Exec.
Gallagher, Megan	Entertainment	5			35	Actress
Galland, Adolf	Aviation	40	75	150	135	ACE, Ger. WW II, Luftwaffe Head
Gallatin, Albert 1761-1849	Cabinet	75	338	390		Served both Jefferson & Madison
Gallatin, Albert E. 1881-1952	Artist					Pencil Sketch $250
Galle, Emile 1846-1904	Artist	100	325	645		Fr. Artist in Glass & Furniture Mfg.
Galli-Curci, Amelita 1889-1963	Entertainment	62	190	385	200	Opera
Gallian, Ketti	Entertainment	8	9	19	19	
Gallico, Paul W.	Author	15	110		35	Am.Novelist. Poseidon Adventure
Galligan, Zach	Entertainment	4			10	
Gallinger, Jacob Harold 1837-1918	Congress	10	20	35	15	Repr.,Senator NH 1891-1919
Gallo, Ernest & Julio	Business	40			65	Gallo Winery, Sonoma, CA
Gallo, Gustavo	Entertainment	20			50	Opera
Gallo, Robert, Dr.	Science	20	35		45	Research. Co-Discoverer HIV Virus
Galloway, Joseph 1731-1803	Revolutionary War		3500			Continental Congr.& Army. Tory Loyalist
Gallup, Benadam	Military	25	75			Colonel French-Indian War
Gallup, George, Jr.	Pollster	10	20		25	Gallup Poll
Galsworthy, John 1867-1933	Author	30	85	175	240	Br. Novelist, Playwright
Galvan, Elias G., Bishop	Clergy	20	25	35	35	
Galvin, Robert	Business	12	17	25	15	
Galway, James	Entertainment				40	Irish Flutist. AMusQS $50
Gam, Rita	Entertainment	5	6	15	18	
Gambee, Charles R.	Civil War	15	55			Col. 53rd Ohio Vol. KIA Reseca
Gamble, Hamilton R. 1798-1864	Civil War	25		190		CW Gov. MO. Cmmdr.-in-Chief MO Militia
Gance, Abel 1889-1981	Entertainment		190	500		Fr.Historically, One of Greatest Directors.
Gandhi, Indira 1917-84	Head of State	150	350	350	1950	Assassinated P.M. India. TLS/Cont.$600
Gandhi, Mohandas K. 1869-1948	Political Leader	550	1375	2150	2810	Spiritual Leader India
Gandhi, Rajiv	Head of State	40		85	150	P.M. of India, Assassinated
Gandier, D.M., Rev.	Clergy	10	20	35		Temperance Advocate
Gann, Ernest K.	Author	10	20	35		
Gannett, Frank E.	Business	20	55	140	35	Newspaper, TV, Radio Empire
Ganz, Rudolph	Conductor	15			45	Swiss/Am. Pianist/Conductor
Garat, Pierre (Fils)	Entertainment	45		120		Tenor Son
Garat, Pierre (Pere)1762-1823	Entertainment	125		300		1st Great French Tenor
Garber, Jan	Entertainment	15			35	Big Band Leader
Garbo, Greta 1905-91	Entertainment	2150	3500	7225	10000	Internat'l Film Star. Cont. ALS$16,500
Garcelon, Alonzo	Governor	5	12			Governor ME
Garcia, Andy	Entertainment		10		40	
Garcia, Jerry	Entertainment	60	75	150	172	Rock
Garcia-Robles, Alfonso, Dr.	Diplomat	35		130	60	Nobel Peace Prize, Disarmament
Gardanne, Gaspard A.	Fr. Revolution	40	115	250		
Garden, Mary 1874-1967	Entertainment	25	35	60	142	Opera. Scottish Born Soprano
Gardiner, Reginald	Entertainment	10			35	
Gardner, Ava 1922-90	Entertainment	45	60	110	110	Pin-Up SP $150

NAME	CATEGORY	SIG	LS/DS	ALS	SP	Comment
Gardner, Dale A.	Astronaut	10			25	
Gardner, Erle Stanley 1889-1970	Author	85	225	275	175	Lawyer & Detective Novelist
Gardner, Franklin (War Date)	Civil War	375	500	1510		CSA Gen.
Gardner, Franklin 1823-73	Civil War	225	215	850		CSA General
Gardner, Guy S.	Astronaut	6			10	
Gardner, John L.	Civil War	25		155		Union Gen.
Gardner, John W.	Cabinet	5	35	30	10	Sec'y HEW. Fndr. Common Cause
Gardner, O. Max	Governor	15	20	35	20	Gov. NC. Lawyer, Industrialist
Garfield, James A. (As President)	President	330	2475			Assassinated July 1881
Garfield, James A. 1831-81	President	250	1166	1400	1900	Union Gen.,DS/War Dte $2,500
Garfield, James R. 1865-1950	Cabinet	20	35	70	35	Sec'y Interior 1907
Garfield, John 1913-1952	Entertainment	75	90		395	Warner Bros. Star. Died at 39
Garfield, Lucretia R. 1832-1918	First Lady	95	180	135		
Garfunkel, Art	Entertainment	5			10	
Gargan, William	Entertainment	15	15	35	50	
Garibaldi, Giuseppe 1807-82	Head of State	155	370		705	It. Nationalist Leader, Soldier
Garland, Augustus H. 1832-99	Cabinet & CW	70	145	215		Att'y Gen. & CSA Congress,Gov.
Garland, Beverly	Entertainment	5	10		20	Actress
Garland, Hamlin	Author	20	35	50	85	Pulitzer. Novelist, Essayist
Garland, Judy 1922-69	Entertainment	460	657		925	Special DS $950
Garn, Jake	Senate-Astronaut	15	40		15	Senator UT
Garneau, Marc	Astronaut	15			35	
Garner, Erroll	Entertainment	75			150	Jazz Pianist
Garner, Francoise	Entetainment	10			35	Opera
Garner, James	Entertainment	10	10	20	30	
Garner, John Nance (V)	Vice President	55	195	225	175	VP & Speaker.FDR VP
Garner, Peggy Ann	Entertainment	30			75	
Garnett, Francis H.	Author	20	60	125		
Garnett, Richard Brooke 1817-63	Civil War	650	535	615		CSA Gen. RARE. ALS 1861 $6600
Garnett, Tay	Entertainment	10	26		30	Director-Producer
Garr, Terri	Entertainment	10	15	25	25	
Garrard, Kenner	Civil War	45	75	160		Union Gen. War Date ALS $575
Garrett, Betty	Entertainment	7			18	Film & Stage Comedienne
Garrett, Finis J.	Senate/Congress	10	15	25	20	MOC TN 1905
Garrett, Patrick R. (Pat)	Western Lawman	2700	3350	4000		Killed Billy the Kid
Garrett, Thomas	Emancipation	100	250	395		Chief Engineer Underground RR
Garriott, Owen I.	Astronaut	5			20	
Garrison, Lindley M. 1864-1932	Cabinet	35	85	140	50	Sec'y War 1913
Garrison, Vermont	Aviation	12	25	45	35	ACE, WW II & Korea
Garrison, Wm. Lloyd 1805-79	Abolitionist	80	120	250	200	Reformer.ALS/Cont. $1200
Garros, Roland	Aviation	125			425	Fr.ACE.1st To Fly Mediterranean
Garroway, Dave	Entertainment	10			25	
Garson, Greer 19xx-1996	Entertainment	20	35	45	58	Pin-Up SP $95
Garth, Jennie	Entertainment	15			50	Actress. Beverly Hills 90210
Gartrell, Lucius J. 1821-91	Civil War	95	285	317		CSA Gen.
Garvey, Marcus 1887-1940	Black Nationalist		1512			Back to Africa Movement
Gary, Elbert Henry	Business	25	90	175	35	U.S.Steel, Gary, Ind., TLS on Ltrhd.$985
Gary, James Albert	Cabinet	15	25	40		P.M.Gen.Owned Cotton Mills 1897
Gasdia, Cecilie	Entertainment	10	15		35	
Gasser, Heber S.	Science	20	35	60	50	Nobel Medicine
Gassman, Vittorio	Entertainment	25			85	
Gately, George	Cartoonist	5			20	Heathcliff
Gates, Bill	Business	20	75		35	Microsoft Genius.
Gates, Daryl	Law Enforcement	15			30	Chief Police of L.A.
Gates, Horatio	Revolutionary War	250	475	1050		General, Continental Army
Gates, Seth 1800-77	Congress	25	40	80		Anti-Slavery Repr. from NY

NAME	CATEGORY	SIG	LS/DS	ALS	SP	Comment
Gatlin, Larry & Brothers	Entertainment	10			20	C & W
Gatlin, Richard C. 1809-96	Civil War	90	248			CSA Gen.
Gatling, Richard J.1818-1903	Inventor	285	565	1908		Gatling Gun.Gat Slang for Gun
Gatti-Casazza, Giulio	Entertainment	50	150	250		It. Impresario. Opera Director
Gatty, Harold	Aviation	75	275	462	175	Australian. Wiley Post Navigator
Gaugin, Paul	Artist	585	1235	3450		Fr. Post-Impressionist
Gauguin, Paul 1848-1903	Artist			12750		Fr. Post Impressionist
Gautier, Dick	Entertainment	5			12	
Gavarni, Paul	Artist	85		300		
Gavassi, Father Allesandro	Clergy	75	100	150		
Gavaudan, Pierre 1772-1840	Entertainment			135		Opera. Tenor
Gavin, James M. 1907-1993	Military	45	100	275	125	Gen. WW II, Diplomat,Ambassador
Gavin, John	Entertainment	5			20	Ambassador to Mexico
Gavin, Leon	Senate/Congress	5	10		10	MOC PA 1943
Gaxton, William	Entertainment	10	15	25	25	
Gay, Enola	Aviation	150			350	Tibbets,Van Kirk,Ferebee
Gay, George A.	Civil War	15	25	45		Nat'l Commander GAR 1934
Gay, Sydney Howard	Author	3	10	20		
Gaye, Marvin	Entertainment	75			125	
Gayle, Crystal	Country Music	5			15	
Gayle, John	Governor	10	35			Statesman, Jurist
Gaynor, Janet	Entertainment	25	35	55	85	
Gaynor, Mitzi	Entertainment	10			20	Pin-Up SP $25
Gaynor, William J.	Celebrity	20	55	115	30	
Gazzara, Ben	Entertainment	5			15	
Ge'ricault, Theodore 1791-1824	Artist			3000		Broke Classical Tradition.
Gear, John Henry 1825-1900	Congress	10	20	25		Senator IA 1887
Geary, Anthony 'Tony'	Entertainment	6	8	15	15	
Geary, John W.	Civil War	55	125	275	250	Un.Gen.,1st Mayor San Francisco
Gebel-Williams, Gunter	Entertainment	15			50	Circus animal trainer
Gedda, Nicolai	Entertainment	15		35	35	Swe. Tenor, Opera
Gee, Edwin A., Dr,	Business	5	10		10	CEO International Paper Co.
Geer, Ellen	Entertainment	4			12	Actress
Geer, Will	Entertainment	25			55	
Geezinslaw, Sam & Dewayne	Country Music	15			30	
Geffrard, Nicholas Fabre	Head of State	35	125			Pres. Haiti
Gehlen, Reinhard	Military	15	40	45		
Geiger, Johannes H.1882-1945	Science	125	350	750		Ger. Physicist. Geiger Counter
Geisel, Ernesto	Head of State	12	20	25	15	
Geisel, Ted	Author					SEE Dr. Seuss
Gell, William, Dr.	Science	25	40			Br. Archaeologist
Gelston, David	Revolutionary War	85	170			
Gemar, Charles	Astronaut	4			12	
Gemini 5 (3 Sigs)	Astronauts					US $1 Bill.Aboard Gem.5 Signed $2595
Gene't, Jean	Author	175	295	450		Fr. LS/Content $1,275
Geneen, Harold S.	Business	5	10	25	10	
Genesis	Entertainment	40			85	
Genet, Edmond Citizen1763-1834	Fr. Revolution	55	150	850		1st Fr. Minister to U.S.
Genn, Leo	Entertainment	10	15	25	25	
Gentilini, Amerigo	Entertainment	15			45	Opera
Gentry, Bobbie	Country Music	5			12	
Gentry, Jerauld R.	Astronaut	5	25		15	
George (Prince Denmark) 1653-1708	Royalty		270			Consort of Queen Anne
George I (Eng) 1660-1727	Royalty	230	1088	2700		Created Cabinet System of Gov.
George I (Gr) 1845-1913	Royalty	45	85	130		
George II (Eng) 1683-1760	Royalty	390	780	1515		

The Sanders Price Guide to Autographs

NAME	CATEGORY	SIG	LS/DS	ALS	SP	Comment
George II (Greece)	Royalty	35	80	195	400	
George III (Eng) 1738-1820	Royalty	230	825	3500		
George IV (Eng) 1762-1830	Royalty	110	446	695		13 pp. Warrant 1815 $3,500
George V (Eng) 1865-1936	Royalty	110	475	780	585	
George V And Queen Mary (Teck)	Royalty	250			800	
George VI (Eng) 1895-1952	Royalty	190	462	300	450	
George VI and Queen Elizabeth	Royalty	275	660		1370	
George, Chief Dan	Entertainment	20			45	
George, Christopher	Entertainment	20	25	65	75	
George, Duke of Cambridge 1819-1904	Military	40				Br. Cmdr. Crimean War
George, Gladys	Entertainment	20	25	40	40	
George, Grace	Entertainment	25			60	
George, Harold L.	Military	35	90	170	75	
George, Henry	Economist	30	105	200	35	Author, Reformer, Editor
George, Phyllis	Entertainment	4	4	9	10	Miss America
George, Susan	Entertainment	6	8	15	15	
George, Walter F. 1878-1957	Congress	15	35		20	Senator GA 1922-57
Gerard, James W.	Diplomat	12				Ambassador
Gerard, Francis R.	Aviation	10	22	38	28	ACE, WW II
Gerard, Gil	Entertainment	9	10	20	20	
Gerard, Richard	Composer	50	95	165		AMusQS $235
Gerardy, Jean	Entertainment	125			190	Belg. Violin-Cellist
Gere, Ashlyn	Entertainment					Actress-Model. Nude Pin-up 45
Gere, Richard	Entertainment	20	25	55	75	Uses paint pen
Gerlache de Gomery, Adrien V.J.	Explorer	85	180	300		Belg. Naval Off'r., Antarctic
Gerland, Alfred	Aviation	15	35	55	40	
German, Edward, Sir 1862-1936	Composer	35	105	175	85	Operettas. AMusQS $200
Gernreich, Rudi	Business	10	15	40	25	Fashion Designer
Geronimo	Apache Chieftain	5332			4500	
Gerri, Toni	Entertainment	4	4	9	9	
Gerry, Elbridge (VP) 1744-1814	Revolutionary War	265	675	2880		Signer Decl. of Ind.FF $750
Gerry, James 1796-1873	Congress	10				Repr. PA, Physician
Gerry, Peter G. 1879-1957	Congress	10	15		20	MOC, Senator RI 1913
Gersel Cemal	Head of State	20	65	170	35	Turkey
Gershwin, George & Gershwin, Ira	Composer		4850			
Gershwin, George1898-1937	Composer	941	2134	4650	4400	
Gershwin, Ira 1896-1983	Composer	75	162	250	180	Lyrics AQS $880
Gerson, Betty Lou	Entertainment	3			20	Major Radio Actress.Voice of Cruella de Vil
Gervais, John L. 1753-98	Revolutionary War			100		Continental Congress
Gerville-Reache, Jeanne	Entertainment				275	Opera. Tragic French Mezzo
Gessendorf, Mechthild	Entertainment	10			25	Opera
Getty, Estelle	Entertainment	5	9	20	15	
Getty, George F.	Business		50			Founder Getty Oil Company
Getty, George W. 1819-1901	Civil War	30	48			Union Gen. ALS/Cont. $740
Getty, George Washington (War Date)	Civil War	40	95			Union Gen. Div. Cmdr.
Getty, J. Paul 1892-1976	Business	185	645	1025	505	Billionaire Oil Mogul. Check S $400-$900
Getz, J. Laurence	Senate/Congress	10	200	20		MOC PA 1867. Publisher
Getz, Stan	Entertainment	85			225	Am. Jazz Saxophonist
Ghali, Boutros Boutros	Head of State	10			30	Pres. U.N.
Ghiaurov, Nicolai	Entertainment	10			25	Opera
Gholson, Samuel J. 1808-83	Civil War	95	292	575		CSA Gen.
Ghostley, Alice	Entertainment	5		15	15	Comedienne
Giancana, Antoinette	Celebrity	15			50	'Mafi Princess'
Giannini, A. P.	Business	150	290	500		Bank of America Founder
Gibb, Cynthia	Entertainment	5	6	15	35	Pin-Up SP $20
Gibbon, Edward	Author	300	885	1800		Br. Decline & Fall Roman Empire

NAME	CATEGORY	SIG	LS/DS	ALS	SP	Comment
Gibbon, John 1827-96	Civil War-Indian Fighter	50	185	330		Union Gen.ALS/Cont. $1760
Gibbon, John (War Date)	Civil War	120		870		Union Gen.
Gibbons, Barry	Business	5			20	Founder Burger King
Gibbons, Cedric	Art	95	225	450		Hollywood Art Dir. 11 Awards
Gibbons, Floyd 1887-1939	Aviation-Journalist	55	182	320	155	Pioneer Aviator. Radio News
Gibbons, Herbert Adams	Celebrity	10	20	45		
Gibbons, James, Cardinal	Clergy	45	115	125	175	Established Washington Univ.,DC
Gibbons, Leeza	Entertainment	5			12	Pin-up $20
Gibbs, Addison C.	Governor	10	40			Governor OR
Gibbs, Alfred 1823-68	Civil War	30	80	95		Union Gen. ALS '64 $655
Gibbs, Georgia	Entertainment	15			35	Big Band Vocalist
Gibbs, Marla	Entertainment	6	8	15	10	
Gibran, Kahlil	Author-Artist	125	325	750	150	Syrian Poet, Novelist, Essayist
Gibson, Charles Dana 1867-1944	Artist	45	250	275	325	Illustrator-Gibson Girl
Gibson, Charles H.	Congress	5		15		Repr., Senator MD 1885
Gibson, Debbie	Entertainment	10			30	
Gibson, Edward G.	Astronaut	10			20	
Gibson, George	Military	5	15	25		
Gibson, Henry	Entertainment	5			12	
Gibson, Hoot	Entertainment	105	145		225	Vintage Film Cowboy
Gibson, Horatio G.	Civil War	50				General
Gibson, James	Military	75	230	425		Officer War 1812. Wounded, Died
Gibson, Mel	Entertainment	30			125	With Pocahontas Cast SP 130
Gibson, Randall Lee (War Date)	Civil War	190		2688		CSA Gen.
Gibson, Randall Lee 1832-92	Civil War	90	360	675		CSA General, US Sen. LA
Gibson, Robert L.	Astronaut	5			20	
Gibson, William	Author	20		170		Playwright. The Miracle Worker
Giddings, De Witt C.	Senate/Congress	15	25	40		MOC TX. Served in CSA Army
Giddings, Joshua R. 1795-1864	Congress	12				Repr. OH
Gide, Andre	Author	175	350	590		Nobel Lit.,Moralist,Philosopher
Gielgud, John, Sir	Entertainment	25	45		78	
Gies, Miep	Celebrity	40	125	250		Befriended Anne Frank's family
Gieseking, Walter	Entertainment	22			135	Concert Pianist
Giesler, Jerry	Law	10	20	40	15	Brilliant Trial Lawyer
Gifford, Francis	Entertainment	5	7	12	10	
Gifford, Kathie Lee	Entertainment	5			20	Pin-Up SP $25
Gifford, Walter S.	Business-Diplomat	5	15	25	10	Pres. AT&T 1925-48, Chm.-'50
Gigli, Beniamino 1890-1957	Entertainment	95	190	300	345	Opera, Concert
Gil, Brendan	Author	16			20	Writer New Yorker Mag.
Gilbert, A. C.	Business	60	95	175		Inventor Erector Set.
Gilbert, Billy	Entertainment	20	25	45	45	
Gilbert, Cass	Architect	20	60		35	Woolworth Bldg., Supr. Court...
Gilbert, H. E.	Celebrity	5	11	28	8	
Gilbert, John	Entertainment	120		275	250	
Gilbert, L. Woolfe	Composer	20	50	95	25	
Gilbert, Lynn	Entertainment	3	3	6	10	
Gilbert, Melissa	Entertainment	10			35	
Gilbert, Sara	Entertainment	16			25	Actress Rosanne
Gilbert, William. S., Sir 1836-1911	Composer	165	365	742	690	Gilbert & Sullivan Operettas
Gilbreth, Lillian	Engineer	30		100		1st Woman Engineer
Gilder, Richard Watson	Civil War	125				Editor Century Magazine
Giles, Sandra	Entertainment	5			10	Pinup $30
Giles, William Branch	Senate	30	80	115		Early, influential VA Sen. 1801
Gilford, Jack	Entertainment	15			35	
Gill, Eric	Artist	20	70	150		Br. Sculptor, Engraver
Gill, Vince	Country Music	10			30	

The Sanders Price Guide to Autographs

NAME	CATEGORY	SIG	LS/DS	ALS	SP	Comment
Gillespie, Dizzy 1917-93	Entertainment	50			70	Jazz. Trumpet
Gillett, Frederick H. 1851-1935	Speaker of House	15	35	95		MOC, Senator MA
Gillette, Anita	Entertainment	3	3	6	10	
Gillette, Francis	Senate	20	60			Free-Soiler Senator CT
Gillette, King Camp	Business	40	115	250	75	Gillette Co. (Safety Razor)
Gillette, William 1855-1937	Entertainment	55	175	215	150	Portrayed Sherlock Holmes Originally
Gilley, Mickey	Entertainment	4			20	C/W Singer
Gillis, J. H.	Military	5	15	25		
Gillmore, Joseph A.	Governor	35	90			Civil War Gov. NY
Gillmore, Quincy A. (War Date)	Civil War	55	140	205		Union Gen. LS '63 $7975
Gillmore, Quincy A. 1825-88	Civil War	30	95	178		Union Gen.
Gilman, John T. 1753-1828	Revolutionary War		100	140		Cont. Congr.Gov. NH
Gilman, Nicholas	Revolutionary War	110	285	550		Continental Congress
Gilmer, Jeremy F. 1818-83	Civil War	125		412		CSA Gen.
Gilmer, John H.	Civil War	20		85		CSA Congress from NC
Gilmer, Thomas W.	Cabinet		95	145		Tyler Sec'y Navy
Gilmore, Gary	Celebrity	15	27	35		
Gilmore, James R. 1822-1903	Author	20	60	194		Merchant, Abolitionist, Novelist, Songwriter
Gilmore, Joseph A.	Civil War Gov.	35	135			Gov. NH
Gilmore, Laura E. 1832-	Celebrity			50		Wife of James R. Noted Medium
Gilmore, P.S.	Composer-CW	35	80	180		When Johnny Comes Marching...
Gilmore, Virginia	Entertainment	10	15	30	28	
Gilmour, Patrick S.1829-92	Bandleader					Bandmaster. Sig & Music 30
Gilpin, Henry D.	Cabinet	25	50	75		Van Buren Att'y Gen. 1840
Gilruth, Robert R.	Astronaut	10			20	
Gimbel Brothers (6)	Business	475				Gimbel Department Stores
Gimbel, Bernard F.	Business	60	175	375	90	Gimbel Bros. Dept. Stores
Giminez, Eduardo	Entertainment	10			30	Opera
Ginastera, Alberto	Composer		90	175		Opera, Ballet
Gingold, Hermione 1897-1987	Entertainment	10			25	Br. Comedienne
Gingrich, Newt	Senate/Congress	10	45		40	MOC GA Since 1973
Ginsberg, Allen	Author	30	200	225	75	Beat Poet TMsS $575
Ginsberg, Ruth Bader	Supreme Court	30	40		40	Clinton Appointment to S.C.
Giordano, Umberto	Composer	250	400	475	733	Opera Composer. AMusQS $450-$700
Girard, Stephen 1750-1831	Revolutionary War	125	350	325		Philanthropist, Merchant, Banker
Gisborne, Thomas	Author	30				
Gish, Dorothy	Entertainment	75			125	
Gish, Lillian 1896-1993	Entertainment	20	65	75	85	Silent Star. Birth of a Nation
Gissing, George Robert 1857-1903	Author	50	175	345		Br. Novelist.
Gist, States Rights 1831-64	Civil War	450		1450		CSA Gen. RARE. ALS '61 $2400
Given, Robin	Entertainment	10			25	
Givenchy, Hubert de	Business	35	70	95		Fashion Designer
Givens, Edward G. Jr.	Astronaut	10			25	
Givet, George	Entertainment	10				Comic. Greek Ambassador Good Will
Glad, Gladys	Entertainment	10	12		20	
Gladden, Adley H. 1810-62	Civil War	510	1133			CSA Gen. ALS '61 $6325
Gladden, Washington	Clergy	30	40	55		
Gladstone, William E.1809-98	Head of State	70	95	500	100	Prime Minister
Glaser, Donald A.	Science	20	35	70	30	Nobel Phys. Inv. Bubble Chamber
Glaser, Lillian	Entertainment	10				Mrs. DeWolf Hopper
Glaser, Lulu	Entertainment	10	12	20	20	
Glaser, Paul Michael	Entertainment	5			20	
Glasgow, Ellen	Author	40	180			Novelist. Pulitzer. VA Life
Glashow, Sheldon Lee, Dr.	Science	20	35		30	Nobel Physics
Glaspell, Susan	Author	25	65	110		Am. Playwright. Pulitzer
Glass, Carter 1858-1946	Cabinet	15	45	65	25	Sec'y Treas., Sen. VA 1902

NAME	CATEGORY	SIG	LS/DS	ALS	SP	Comment
Glass, Philip 1937-	Composer	30	50		190	Am.Orchestral, Opera, Film,Stage
Glass, Ron	Entertainment	5			15	
Glassman, Alan	Entertainment	5			25	Opera
Glazer, Tom Paul	Country Music	15			30	
Glazunov, Alexander	Composer	225	365	675	262	Rus. AMusQS $1,000-$2,750
Gleason, Jackie	Entertainment	50	65	90	125	
Gleason, James	Entertainment	40			75	
Gledhill, Arthur	Business	4			10	Stanley Works
Glenn, John (As Astronaut)	Astronaut	40	148	450	95	1st To Orbit Earth
Glenn, Scott	Entertainment	8	12	35	30	
Glennon, John, Cardinal	Clergy	40	50	65	45	
Gless, Sharon	Entertainment	8	9	19	22	Actress
Gliere, Reinhold 18875-1956	Composer			350		Rus. Symphony & Ballet
Globus, Yoram	Entertainment	5			16	Producer
Glossop, Peter	Entertainment	10			30	Opera
Gloucester, Henry Wm.Fred, Duke	Royalty	10	20	50	30	Son Geo. V., Gov-Gen. Australia
Glover, Danny	Entertainment	5	6	15	25	
Glover, John	Revolutionary War	240	610	1250		Gen. Continental Army. Active
Glubb, John, Sir Pasha	Military	20	45	55	30	Br. General
Gluck, Alma	Entertainment	20	35	45	115	Opera, Concert, Recording
Glueck, Nelson	Archaeologist	10	25	50	20	Uncovered 1500 Ancient Artifact
Glyn, Elinor	Author	20	70	165	45	Br. Novelist, Film Scenarios
Gnys, Wladek	Aviation	40			150	Shot Down 1st Plane in WW II
Goard, Nona	Aviation	10	15	25	15	
Gobbi, Tito	Entertainment	20			85	It. Baritone, Opera
Gobel, George 1918-91	Entertainment	10			25	
Godard, Benjamin	Composer	75	120	225	150	Fr. Opera Jocelyn Berceuse
Godard, Louis	Aviation-Balloon	200	575			ALS/Content $6,500
Goddard, Paulette	Entertainment	30	45	80	115	
Goddard, Robert H. 1882-1945	Science	355	1750	1425	2990	Am. Physicist. Rocket Pioneer
Godden, Rumer	Author	15		65		
Goderich, Fred. John Robinson	Head of State	15	40	95		Viscount Goderich. Br. P.M.
Godey, Louis A. 1804-78	Publisher	40	95	175		Godey's Ladies Book
Godfrey, A. Earl	Aviation	30	60	110	75	
Godfrey, Arthur	Entertainment	15	50	55	25	
Godfrey, Capt. Johnny	Aviation	50				Ace/29 Victories
Godolphin, Sidney, 1st Earl 1644-1712	Head of State	55	350			P.M. Eng.Queen Anne
Godoy, Manuel de 1767-1851	Head of State	295				Sp. Politician, Prime Minister
Godt, Eberhard	Military	15		70		
Godunov, Alexander 1949-1995	Entertainment	33			60	Ballet. Russian Star Defected
Godwin, Linda	Astronaut	5			15	
Goebbels, Joseph	Nazi Leader WWII	350	1025	1250	1250	Nazi Minister of Propaganda
Goebel, Arthur	Aviation	40			110	Pioneer Aviator
Goering, Hermann W. 1893-1946	Military	450	2044	2425	1475	Marshal of the Reich. Suicide
Goethals, George W.	Military-Science	175	585			Panama Canal.TLS/Cont. $1,750
Goethe, Johann W. von	Author	1200	2550	5670		Ger. Poet, Dramatist, Novelist
Goettheim, F.	Business	10	20	45		
Goff, Nathan Jr.	Cabinet	15	25	50		Hayes Sec. of Navy
Gogh, Vincent van	Artist	2000	4500	13000		Dutch Painter. Individual Style
Gogol, Nicholai	Author	500	3350	6500		Father of Rus. Realistic Lit.
Golan, Menahem	Entertainment	5	6	15	15	Film Producer
Gold, Missy	Entertainment	5			15	
Gold, Tracy	Entertainment	5			15	
Goldberg, Arthur J. (SC)	Supreme Court	50	145		115	Resigned. Became Ambass. UN
Goldberg, Reiner	Entertainment	10			30	Opera
Goldberg, Rube* 1883-1970	Cartoonist	50	95		150	Ike & Mike, Boob McNutt

NAME	CATEGORY	SIG	LS/DS	ALS	SP	Comment
Goldberg, Stan*	Cartoonist	10			50	Archie
Goldberg, Whoopi	Entertainment	10	15	28	32	
Goldblum, Jeff	Entertainment	6	8	15	35	
Golden Eye (Cast Of)	Entertainment				160	Brosnan,Scorupco, Janssen
Golden Girls, The (Cast Of)	Entertainment	20			90	All Four
Golden, Charles, Bishop	Clergy	15	25	30	30	
Goldenson, Leonard H.	Business	10	20	30	15	TV Broadcasting Exec.
Golding, Louis	Author	55	85	125	50	Br. Verse, Stories, Novels
Golding, William 1911-1994	Author	55	225	585	65	Nobel Lit.,Lord of the Flies
Goldman, Edwin Franco	Composer	25	50	75		Bandmaster
Goldman, Emma	Anarchist	60	240	640	75	Deported. Author-Editor
Goldman, Michael	Author	5	10	15	10	
Goldman, Nahum	Zionist	15		50		Pres. World Zionist Org.
Goldman, William	Author			125		Soldier in the Rain, Princess Bride
Goldmark, Peter C.	Science	25		40		Inventor. LP Records
Goldowsky, Boris	Conductor	5			35	Opera Coach. Dir. of own Opera Theatre
Goldsboro, Bobby	Country Western	4			10	Singer
Goldsborough, Louis M.	Civil War	65	135	200		Rear Admiral USN
Goldschmidt, Berthold 1903-	Composer				175	Ger. Works Banned by Nazis WW II
Goldschmidt, Neil E.	Cabinet	4	10	25	15	Sec'y Transportation
Goldschmidt, Richard, Dr.1890-1958	Science		20	40		World Famous Geneticist
Goldsmith, Jerry	Entertainment	4			10	
Goldwater, Barry	Congress	10			33	Sen. AZ. Presidential Candidate
Goldwyn, Sam	Business	100	124	255	195	Goldwyn Studios
Goldwyn, Sam, Jr.	Entertainment	4			12	Producer
Golino, Valerie	Entertainment	15			45	Actress
Gollob, Gordon	Aviation		165		200	WWII Ger. Air Ace. RK
Golonka, Arlene	Entertainment	4	4	9	15	
Gombell, Minna	Entertainment	25	30	55	55	
Gomes, Carlos 1836-96	Composer	25		175		Brazilian. Opera
Gomes, Francisco	Head of State	15	55	135	25	
Gomez, Aurea	Entertainment	5			20	Opera, Brazilian Soprano
Gomez, Thomas	Entertainment	20			50	
Gompers, Samuel 1850-1924	Labor Leader	150	225	450		Founder & 1st Pres. A.F.of L.
Good, James W.	Cabinet	25	50		30	Hoover Sec'y of War
Goodman, Al	Bandleader				45	
Goodman, Benny 1909-1986	Entertainment	50	188		162	Big Band Leader-Clarinetist
Goodman, Dody	Entertainment	4	4	9	10	
Goodman, John	Entertainment	15			25	
Goodpaster, Andrew	Military	15	35	50	25	Gen. WW II
Goodson, Mark	Entertainment	10			30	Producer TV
Goodwin, E. S.	Aviation	3	5	10		
Goodwin, Hugh H.	Military	25	65	126	50	
Goodwin, Nat C.	Entertainment	20			30	Vintage Actor
Goodyear, Charles 1800-60	Inventor	300	1750	4400		Developed Rubber Vulcanization
Goodyear, Charles Jr.	Business	20	60	150	30	Goodyear Tire & Rubber Co.
Gookin, Dan	Author	10		35	20	Dos For Dummiesetc.
Goosens, Eugene, Sir	Composer	15	45	90	65	Br.Conductor. Opera/Orchestral Works
Goossens, Eugene	Entertainment	15			45	
Gorbachev, Mikhail (USSR)	Head of State	500		895	1200	Instituted Perestroika,Glasnost
Gorbachev, Raisa	Rus. 1st Lady	50			125	
Gorcey, Leo	Entertainment	90	100		155	
Gordon, Alex., 4th Duke of	Revolutionary War	20		35		
Gordon, C. Henry	Entertainment	20				Actor
Gordon, Charles G. 1833-85	Military	110	350	1217	600	Chinese Gordon,Gordon Pasha
Gordon, Charles W.	Clergy	20	25	30		

NAME	CATEGORY	SIG	LS/DS	ALS	SP	Comment
Gordon, Gale	Entertainment	15			50	Versatile Radio, TV, Film Actor
Gordon, Gavin 1901-83	Entertainment	40				Vintage
Gordon, George H.	Civil War	35	65	95		Union General
Gordon, George W. 1836-1911	Civil War	225	377	472		CSA General
Gordon, Gray	Entertainment	20			50	Big band leader
Gordon, Huntley 1897-1956	Entertainment	15	22		45	Silent Film Star
Gordon, John Brown (War Date)	Civil War	185	1200	3750		CSA Gen.
Gordon, John Brown 1832-1904	Civil War	192	215	400		CSA Gen., Gov. & US Sen. GA
Gordon, John F.	Business	4	6	15	5	
Gordon, Mack	Composer	30	60	130	40	Lyricist
Gordon, Richard F. Jr.	Astronaut	20			35	
Gordon, Ruth	Entertainment	15	15	35	30	AA Rosemary's Baby
Gore, Albert A., Jr.1948-	Vice President	15	25		80	Vice President
Gore, Albert A., Sr.1907-	Congress	15	95			Repr., Senator TN 1939-44, 53-71
Gore, Christopher	Senate	85	205	350		Gov. MA, Senator MA 1813
Gore, Howard W.	Cabinet	4	30			Sec'y Agriculture
Gore, Tipper	2nd Lady	5	12		10	
Gorgas, Josiah (War Date)	Civil War		1488	725		CSA Gen.
Gorgas, Josiah 1813-83	Civil War	195	382			CSA Gen. War Dte. LS $1200
Gorgas, William C., Dr.	Science	125	225	325		Eradicated Yellow Fever
Gorham, George H.(cont)	Senate/Congress	10	20	35		
Gorham, Nathaniel 1738-96	Revolutionary War	375	425	1750		Pres. Continental Congress
Goritz, Otto 1873-1929	Entertainment	30			65	Operatic Baritone
Gorki, Maxim 1868-1936	Author		1250	1512	1265	Rus.Writer emerged from lower classes.
Gorky, Maxim 1868-1936	Author	400	1200	1750	1050	Russ.Novels, Dramas, Stories
Gorman, Arthur P. 1839-1906	Senate	10	15	25		Senator MD 1881-99
Gorman, Margaret	Entertainment	40				1st Miss America 1921
Gorney, Karen Lynn	Entertainment	3	3	6	6	
Gorshin, Frank	Entertainment	10	15	20	25	As The Riddler $45
Gosse, Aristid V.	Science	30		80		
Gosse, Edmund, Sir	Author	20	35	50	30	Br. Poet, Man of Letters
Gossett, Louis, Jr.	Entertainment	15	80		70	
Gottfrederson, Floyd*	Cartoonist	100			500	Mickey Mouse Strip Art
Gotti, John	Crime	20			75	Mafia Boss
Gottschalk, Louis Moreau 1829-69	Composer	500	1200	1875	2990	Pianist , AMusQS $4500
Goudal, Jetta	Entertainment	10	10	20	40	
Goudsmit, Samuel A.	Science	15	25	40	20	Dutch Born Atomic Physicist
Gough, John B. 1817-86	Clergy	20	45	55	25	Temperance Advocate, Reformer
Gould, Charles L.	Business	10	35	45	20	
Gould, Chester*	Cartoonist	50			508	Dick Tracy
Gould, Elliott	Entertainment	5	6	15	15	
Gould, George	Business	10	15	25	15	Son of Jay. Lost Inheritance
Gould, Glenn	Entertainment				3250	Eccentric, Legendary Pianist. RARE
Gould, Gordon	Inventor	15	40			Commercial Laser Inventor
Gould, Harold	Entertainment	5	6	15	15	
Gould, Jay 1836-92	Business	215	1512	1125		Financier, Pres. Erie RR
Gould, John 1804-81	Science	110		750		Br. Ornithologist
Gould, Morton	Composer	20	45	70	40	AMusQS $200
Gould, Robert Simonton	Civil War	25	65	90		CSA Cmdr. Gould's Battalion
Gould, Samuel B.	Celebrity	4	8	20	10	
Goulding, Ray	Entertainment	3	3	6	10	
Goulet, Robert	Entertainment	10			20	Handsome Baritone Broadway, Concert Star
Gounod, Charles 1818-93	Composer	150	365	533	560	AMusQS $650-$2,500
Gourard, Henri J.E. 1867-1946	Military				75	Fr. Gen. WW I
Gouraud, Henri-Joseph E.	Military	40	150		75	Fr. Gen. WW I
Govan, Daniel C. 1829-1911	Civil War	90		540		CSA Gen.

NAME	CATEGORY	SIG	LS/DS	ALS	SP	Comment
Gowdy, John	Clergy	15	15	25		
Goya, Francisco	Artist	2200	7900	18750		Sp.Painter,Etcher,Lithographer
Goz, Harry	Entertainment	6	8	15	18	
Grabe, Ronald J.	Astronaut	5			20	
Grable, Betty 1916-73	Entertainment	60	100	200	322	GI's WW II #1 Pin-up girl
Grace and Prince Rainier	Royalty	175	300		350	PC SP $225-350
Grace de Monaco (Grace Kelly)	Royalty	200	295	425	320	As Princess
Grace, Eugene G.	Industrialist	25	65	140	40	Pres.,Chmn. Bethlehem Steel
Grace, William R.	Business	15	30	45	30	Mayor NYC. W.R. Grace & Co.
Gracen, Elizabeth Ward	Entertainment	5			10	Miss America '82, Pin-Up SP $25
Grady, Don	Entertainment	5			12	
Graf, Herman	Aviation	35			85	Ger. ACE. #9 Worldwide
Graham, Billy	Clergy	15	95	60	45	World-Wide Evangelist. Baptist Preacher
Graham, C.J.	Entertainment	4			10	Horror
Graham, Donald	Business	10	25	40	15	
Graham, Elizabeth Candler	Author	5	7	10	15	Books about Coca-Cola
Graham, George 1772-1830	Military-Cabinet	20	50	85		Monroe Sec. War (ad int)
Graham, John 1774-1820	Diplomatist	65	215	430		Aided Jefferson, Madison,Monroe
Graham, Katherine	Publisher	15	30	60	20	Chm. CEO Washington Post
Graham, M. Gordon	Aviaton	25			50	ACE WW II
Graham, Martha 1895-1986	Entertainment	65	375	395	270	Dancer, Teacher, Choreographer
Graham, Sheila	Author	25		40	35	Journalist, Gossip Columnist
Graham, Sylvester	Inventor			100		The Graham Cracker
Graham, Virginia	Entertainment	5			10	TV Host, Commentator
Graham, William A. 1804-75	Cabinet	20	40	65		Fillmore Sec. Navy 1850
Grahame, Gloria	Entertainment	50	100		150	AA
Grahame, Kenneth	Author	75	110	195		Br.Writer Wind in the Willows
Grahame-White, Claude	Aviation	62	100	250	120	1st Br. School of Aviation
Grahm	Entertainment	5			15	
Grainger, Percy	Composer	40	110	215	125	Pianist
Gramegna, Anna	Entertainment	45			95	Opera
Gramm, Phil	Senate	7			15	Senator TX
Grammer, Kelsey	Entertainment	10			40	TV Series-Frasier
Gran, Tryggve	Celebrity	12	30			
Granados, Enrique	Composer			700		Sp. Pianist. Piano Works, Opera
Grandi, Dino, Count 1895-1988	Diplomat	25	45	90	40	Mussolini Cabinet
Grandval, Marie F.C.	Composer	10		95		Fr. Woman Composer
Grandy, Fred	Entertainment	5	10		10	Congressman IA- Love Boat
Grange, E. R.	Aviation	10	25	45	35	
Granger, Farley	Entertainment	5	7	12	20	
Granger, Francis	Cabinet	10	35	50		Wm. H. Harrison P.M. General
Granger, Gideon 1767-1822	Cabinet	65	100	325		P.M. General 1801
Granger, Gordon	Civil War	45	95	145		Union General
Granger, Robert S. 1816-94	Civil War			65		Union Gen. Captured 1861
Granger, Stewart	Entertainment	20			50	
Granit, Ragnar	Science	20	45	110	35	Nobel Medicine
Granlund, Nils T. (NTG)	Entertainment	20			40	Producer Radio,TV,Night Club
Grant, Amy	Entertainment	5	6	15	15	
Grant, Cary 1904-86	Entertainment	238	402		417	AA
Grant, Duncan 1885-1978	Artist	70		300		Scot. Impressionist.Bloomsbury Grp.
Grant, Frederick Dent	Military	20				Son Of U.S. Grant
Grant, Gogi	Entertainment	3	5	10	10	
Grant, Hugh	Entertainment	15			60	Br. Actor
Grant, Julia Dent 1826-1902	First Lady	140	375	750		
Grant, Kathryn	Entertainment	8			30	Actress-Widow of Bing Crosby
Grant, Kirby	Entertainment	15		25	35	

NAME	CATEGORY	SIG	LS/DS	ALS	SP	Comment
Grant, Lee	Entertainment	10	30		30	Oscar winner
Grant, U.S. III	Military	10	30	50		
Grant, Ulysses S. (War Date)	President	836	1000	5500	3750	ALS/Spec,Cont. $15000-16000
Grant, Ulysses S. 1822-85	President	631	1650	2708	1900	CDV In Uniform S $3000-$6000
Grant, William T.1876-1972	Business	50	138	350	275	1176 W.T. Grant Stores
Granville, Bonita	Entertainment	12	15	20	35	
Grapewin, Charles	Entertainment	150			350	
Grappelli, Staphane	Entertainment	15			80	Unique Violinist
Grass Roots, The	Rock Group				250	60's Group (5)
Grass, Gunter	Author	40	135	260	130	Ger. Novelist. Nazi Era
Grasse, Francois-Jos., Comte de	Revolutionary War					Kept Aid From Cornwallis. NRPA
Grasser, Hartmann	Aviation	14	25	50	30	
Grassi, Rinaldo	Entertainment	35	95			Opera
Grassle, Karen	Entertainment	4	4	9	10	
Grasso, Ella	Governor	10	35		20	1st Woman Governor CT
Grateful Dead (All)	Entertainment	100			250	Rock HOF
Gratiot, Charles	Military	150	205			War 1812. General 1828
Gratz, Barnard	Revolutionary War	75	212	400		
Graue, Dave*	Cartoonists	10			65	Alley Oop
Grauman, Sid	Entertainment	30	45	90	75	Owner of Opulent Theaters
Gravatte, Marianne	Entertainment	4	4	9	10	
Gravel, Maurice Mike	Senate	5			20	Senator Alaska
Graveline, Duane E.M.D.	Astronaut	5			20	
Graves, Peter	Entertainment	9	10	20	25	Mission Impossible
Graves, Robert	Author	65	175	365	110	Br. Poet, Novelist, Critic
Graves, William	Military	50				General WW I
Gray, Asa 1810-88	Science	35	60	168		Am. Botanist.Darwin Supporter
Gray, Billy	Entertainment	8			20	
Gray, Bowman	Business	7	15	35	15	
Gray, Colin	Aviation	35		90		Top New Zealand ACE
Gray, Colleen	Entertainment	15	25	45	30	
Gray, Delores	Entertainment	40			85	Am. Singer, Dancer
Gray, Elisha 1835-1901	Inventor	80		1188		Founder Western Electric Mfg.
Gray, Erin	Entertainment	9	10	20	20	
Gray, George 1840-1925	Congress	10		35	30	Senator DE. Jurist. Diplomat
Gray, Gilda 1901-59	Entertainment	40			120	Popularized the Shimmy
Gray, Glen	Entertainment	15			35	Big Band Leader
Gray, Harold*	Cartoonists	100			500	Little Orphan Annie
Gray, Harry Jack	Business	5	10	20	10	CEO United Technologies
Gray, Horace (SC)	Supreme Court	30	75	170	40	1882
Gray, Isaac P.	Governor	10	15			Governor IN
Gray, Jack Stearns	Aviation	150				TLS/Content $950. AVIATRIX
Gray, Linda	Entertainment	6	20	12	20	Dallas. Pin-Up SP $20
Gray, Oscar L.	Senate/Congress	5	15		10	MOC AL 1915
Gray, Thomas 1716-71	Author	950	2100	5100		Br. Poet
Grayco, Helen	Entertainment	3	3	6	12	Vocalist & Wife Spike Jones
Grayson, Cary T. 1878-1938	Medical	95				White House Physician to 3 Presidents
Grayson, Kathryn	Entertainment	8	10	20	30	
Greco, Jose	Entertainment	10	15		40	Dance
Greeley, Andrew, Rev.	Clergy	4	15		10	
Greeley, Horace 1811-72	Journalist	65	342	290	825	Go West, Young Man...
Greely, Adolphus W. 1844-1935	Explorer	85	200	212	150	Union Gen., Arctic Explorer
Green, Adolph	Composer	10	15		20	Collaborated/Betty Comden
Green, Al	Entertainment	10			20	
Green, Anna Katherine 1846-1935	Author	95	50	65		Pioneer Am. Detective Fiction
Green, Charles 1785-1870	Aeronaut	40	100	250		Br. Balloonist

NAME	CATEGORY	SIG	LS/DS	ALS	SP	Comment
Green, Dorothy	Entertainment	5	6	15	15	
Green, Dwight H.	Governor	10	15			Governor IL
Green, Henrietta (Hetty) H.1834-1916	Financier					Wall St. Speculator. LS $7500
Green, Herschel	Aviation	12	28	48	35	ACE, WW II, Triple Ace
Green, John(ny)	Composer	25	80	145	35	AMsS $250, $150, $350
Green, Mitzi 1920-69	Entertainment	8	15	25	20	Actress.Musicals-Stage & Film
Green, Paul	Author		45			Playwright, Lost Colony. Pulitzer
Green, Richard	Entertainment	30			75	
Green, Theodore 1867-1966	Senate	10		20	15	Gov., Senator RI
Green, Thomas (War Date)	Civil War	175	725	3250		CSA Gen. KIA
Green, Thomas 1814-64	Civil War	112	200			CSA Gen. KIA
Green, William F.	Labor Leader	40	95	195	125	Pres. A.F.of L.
Greenaway, Kate 1846-1901	Artist	1000	1500			Orig. Pencil Drawing S $1,200
Greene, Frank L.	Senate/Congress	10		20	15	MOC, Senator VT
Greene, George S.	Civil War	30	70			Union Gen.
Greene, Graham 1904-1991	Author	95	342	615	385	Br. Novelist, Dramatist, Critic
Greene, Lorne 1915-87	Entertainment	33			83	Bonanza
Greene, Michele	Entertainment	5	8	25	22	
Greene, Nathanael 1742-86	Military-Rev. War	900	2672	3065		Am.Rev. War Gen.ALS/Cont. $4800
Greene, Richard	Entertainment	10			40	Vint.Brit. Actor. Robinhood
Greene, Sarah Pratt Mc.	Author	20				1856-1935
Greene, Shecky	Entertainment	5	6	15	15	
Greenleaf, John	Clergy	30	50	85		
Greenspan, Alan	Economist	15	30		35	Chairman Fed. Reserve Bd.
Greenstreet, Sidney 1879-1954	Entertainment	180		450	635	Casablanca, Maltese Falcon
Greenwood, Charlotte 1893-1978	Entertainment	18			40	Long-legged Comedienne-Dancer
Greenwood, Edward D.	Science	10	15	35		
Greenwood, G.(Lippincott)	Author	10	30	75	15	
Greenwood, Lee	Country Music	5			10	
Greer, Dabbs (Bill)	Entertainment	10			20	
Greer, Jane	Entertainment	5	6	15	15	
Gregg, Andrew 1755-1835	Congress	40	155			Sen., MOC PA ALS/Content $475
Gregg, David M. (War Date)	Civil War	105	188	428		Union Gen.
Gregg, David M. 1833-1916	Civil War	40	73	170	125	Union Gen.
Gregg, John 1828-64	Civil War					CSA Gen. KIA. AES '63 $880
Gregg, John R.	Business	65	85	150	90	Inventor Gregg Shorthand System
Gregg, Maxcy (War Date)	Civil War	565	4000			CSA Gen. KIA
Gregg, Maxcy 1814-62	Civil War	410	600			CSA Gen. KIA
Gregg, Virginia	Entertainment	10	12	20	25	
Gregor XVI, Pope 1765-1846	Clergy		1200			Roman Catholic Pope 1831-46
Gregory, Bill	Astronaut	7			15	
Gregory, Dick	Entertainment	8	9	19	20	
Gregory, F. H. (War Date)	Civil War	60	95	115		Union Naval Captain
Gregory, F.H.	Civil War	20		72		Union Gen.
Gregory, Frederick D.	Astronaut	5	15		15	
Gregory, James	Entertainment	5	6	15	15	
Gregory, Thomas W. 1861-1933	Cabinet	20			45	US Att'y Gen. Woodrow Wilson
Greico, Richard	Entertainment	10			45	
Grell, Mike*	Cartoonist	10			75	Tarzan
Grenfell, Wilfred T.	Physician-Clergy	35	75	75	130	Medical Missionary, Author
Grenville, George	Head of State	200	750			Br. P.M., Author of Stamp Act
Grenville, Wm. W., Baron.1759-1834	Statesman	95	285	650		Br. Pro Rom.Cath. Emancipation
Gresham, Walter Q.1832-95	Cabinet-CW	45	70	100		Union Gen. ALS '62 $310
Gretchaninoff, Alexander T.	Composer	65	180	395		AMsS $350
Grew, Joseph C.	Diplomat	10	25		35	Ambassador Japan 1931-41
Grey, Chas. 2nd Earl of	Head of State	50	75	160		Prime Minister

The Sanders Price Guide to Autographs

NAME	CATEGORY	SIG	LS/DS	ALS	SP	Comment
Grey, George Sir 1799-1882	Diplomat	5	25	55		Br. Statesman
Grey, Jennifer	Entertainment	5			40	Actress
Grey, Joel	Entertainment	6	8	15	20	
Grey, Nan	Entertainment	4	8	12	15	
Grey, Virginia	Entertainment	10	15	15	20	
Grey, Zane 1875-1939	Author	79	250	600	398	Dentist Turned Western Writer
Gridley, Chas. Vernon 1844-98	Military	250	410	895		Cmdr. of Adm. Dewey Flagship
Gridley, Richard 1711-96	Revolutionary War	170	450	790		Gen.Continental Army, Artillery
Grieg, Edvard 1843-1907	Composer	350	600	1125	1095	AMusQS $1,800-$2,800-$3,250
Grier, Pam	Entertainment	5	6	15	15	Pin-Up SP $20
Grier, Robert C. (SC)1794-1870	Supreme Court	80	235	420		
Grierson, Benjamin H.(War Date)	Civil War	120	235	545		Union General
Grierson, Benjamin H.1826-1911	Civil War	45		235		Union Gen.
Griesbach, Franz	Military	20			50	Ger. Infantry General
Griffes, Charles T.	Composer	175	380			ALS/Content $3,000
Griffin, Charles 1826-67	Civil War	35	120			Union Gen., Indian Fighter
Griffin, Chris	Entertainment	10			25	Jazz Trumpet
Griffin, Cyrus	Revolutionary War	360	765			Continental Congress
Griffin, Merv	Entertainment	5			15	
Griffin, S. Marvin	Governor	10		30		Governor GA
Griffin, W.E.B.	Author	5			10	Fiction
Griffith, Andy	Entertainment	15	20	30	35	
Griffith, Corinne	Entertainment	35	45	90	100	
Griffith, D(avid) W(ark) 1874-1948	Entertainment	350	665	875	1025	Pioneer Film Producer-Dir.
Griffith, Hugh 1912-80	Entertainment	190	275		450	SP PC $200
Griffith, Melanie	Entertainment	20	30	55	70	
Griggs, John W.	Cabinet	12	45	110		Politician-Jurist, Gov. NJ
Griggs, S. David	Astronaut	60	150		140	
Grillo, Joann	Entertainment	4			10	
Grimes, Tammy	Entertainment	4	5	9	15	
Grimm, Jacob	Author	565	1840	3760		Grimm's Fairy Tales
Grimm, Wilhelm	Author	500	1425	3150		Grimm's Fairy Tales
Grinnell, Henry 1799-1874	Financier	45	160			Financed Arctic Expeditions
Grinnell, Josiah 1821-91	Congress	25				Repr. IA, Founder Grinnell, IA & University
Grinnell, Moses H.	Business	25	60	120		MOC NY. Merchant Prince NY
Gris, Juan 1887-1927	Artist	175		1500		Sp Cubist Painter
Grisham, John	Author	20	70		45	The Firm, The Pelican Brief
Grisi, Giulia	Entertainment	250		300	195	It. Ballerina
Grismer, Joseph R.1849-1922	Entertainment	4	15			Actor-Manager
Grissom, Virgil I.'Gus' 1926-67	Astronaut	275	725		1195	Merc. 7. FDC S $750 (Deceased)
Griswald, O.W.	Military	15	35			
Griswold, John A.	Senate/Congress	10		25		MOC NY 1869
Griswold, Matthew	Senate/Congress	12	20	25		MOC PA 1891
Griswold, Putnam	Entertainment	20			50	Opera
Grizzard, George	Entertainment	5	6	15	15	
Grizzard, Lewis	Author	20				Southern humorist
Grodin, Charles	Entertainment	6	8	15	15	
Groener, Harry	Entertainment	4			20	Dear John
Groening, Matt*	Cartoonist	35			140	Simpsons
Grofé, Ferde	Composer	100	200	245	125	AMusMsS $1,850, AMusQS $360
Gromyko, Andrei A.	Statesman	125	160	295	150	Rus.Diplomat. Ambass. to US
Gronau, Wolfgang von	Aviation	75	135	235	195	
Groom, Victor	Aviation	20	45	75	55	
Groom, Winston	Author	20				Forrest Gump
Gropius, Walter 1883-1969	Architect	125	150	600	408	Co-Founder of the Bauhaus
Gropper, William	Artist	30	80	200		Am. Social Protest Artist

NAME	CATEGORY	SIG	LS/DS	ALS	SP	Comment
Gross, Calvin	Celebrity	8	20		15	
Gross, Chaim	Artist	50	85	165		4x6 Repro. Peace S $75
Gross, Clayton K.	Aviation	8	16	28	22	ACE, WW II
Gross, Courtlandt	Business	5	10	15	10	
Gross, Milt*	Cartoonist	20			100	Nize Baby
Grosser, Heinz	Science	15			45	Rocket Pioneer/von Braun
Grossinger, Jennie	Business	23	60	135	35	Grossinger's Hotel,Catskill Mts
Grossmith, George 1874-1935	Entertainment	10			25	Br Musical Comedy,Films, Revues
Grosvenor, Charles H.	Civil War	25	40	55		Union Gen., MOC OH
Grosvenor, Gilbert H.1875-1966	Business	135	100	195	95	Pres.National Geographic.Editor
Grosz, George 1893-1959	Artist	55	250	250		Expressed Hatred of Bourgeoisie
Grouchy, Marquis E. de	Napoleonic Wars	100	250			Marshal of Napoleon. Exiled
Grover, Cuvier	Civil War	30	65	85		Union General
Groves, Leslie R.	Military	55	145	220	85	Gen.WW II. Manhattan Project
Grow, Galusha A. 1822-1907	Congress	10	175	145	35	Repr. PA, Speaker of the House
Gruberova, Edita	Entertainment	15			40	Opera
Gruelle, Johnny	Cartoonist	35			250	Raggedy Ann & Andy
Gruen, George John	Business	30	80	150	55	Chm. Gruen Watch Co.
Gruenther, Alfred M.	Military	15		30	25	Gen. WW II, Pres. Am. Red Cr.
Grumman, Leroy R.	Business	50	145		70	Grumman Aircraft
Grévy, Jules 1807-91	Head of State	40				Pres. France 1879-87
Guardia, R.A.C.	Head of State	15	50		25	Costa Rica
Guardino, Harry	Entertainment	6	15		20	
Guden, Hilde	Entertainment	25		75	50	Opera
Guderian, Hans	Military	30	55	100	45	
Guderian, Heinz	Military	50	175	285	500	Ger. Panzer Gen. WW II
Gudger, V. Lamar	Senate/Congress	10	30		15	MOC NC
Gudin de la Sablonniere	Fr. Revolution	120	235			
Gudunov, Alexander	Entertainment	15		40	35	Rus. Ballet
Guelfi, Piero	Entertainment	10			25	Opera
Guerin, Jules 1866-	Artist	10		35		Muralls at Lincoln Mem'l, Penn.RR Station
Guest, Edgar A.	Author	25	75	165	50	Am.Journalist-Poet of the Peopl
Guest, Lance	Entertainment	6	8	15	19	
Guest, Winston Mrs.	Business	5	10	15	10	
Guevaro, Ernesto Che	Revolutionary	340	895			Aide to Fidel Castro in Cuba
Gueymard-Lautiers, Pauline 1834-?	Entertainment	30		120		Opera, Fr. Mezzo-Soprano
Guffey, Joseph F.	Senate/Congress	5	10		10	Senator PA
Guggenheim, Daniel 1856-1930	Business	20	198	85	35	Guggenheim Foundation
Guggenheim, Harry F.	Aviation		75			Pres. Guggenheim Fund (Aeronautics)
Guggenheim, Peggy	Business	15	25	70	20	Patron of Arts. Collector
Guggenheim, William	Business	55	125		75	Industrialist, Philanthropist
Guilbert, Yvette	Entertainment	40	65	130	150	
Guild, Curtis Jr.	Governor	12	15			Governor MA
Guild, Nancy	Entertainment	6	8	15	15	
Guilfoyle, Paul	Entertainment	10	15	35	30	
Guillaume, Robert	Entertainment	5	10	18	20	
Guillemin, Roger C.L.	Science	20	55	110	35	Nobel Medicine
Guillotin, Joseph-Ignace	Science	275	1650			Fr. Doctor Supported Guillotin
Guinan, Texas (Mary Louise)	Entertainment	25	70	90	40	Actress, Hostess of Speakeasies
Guiney, Louise Imogen	Author	50		300		Poet-Essayist
Guingand, Francis	Military	15	35	50		Fr. General
Guinness, Alec, Sir	Entertainment	18	25	30	60	Br. Screen Actor. AA
Guinness, Benjamin L. 1798-1868	Business	30	50	110		Guinness Brewing Co.
Guinness, Edward C. 1847-1927	Business	15	25	45	20	Guinness Brewing Co.
Guisewite, Cathy*	Cartoonists	25			85	Cathy
Guiteau, Charles 1842-82	Assassin	460	850	6000		Shot Pres. Garfield

NAME	CATEGORY	SIG	LS/DS	ALS	SP	Comment
Gulager, Clu	Entertainment	6		15	20	
Gumbel, Bryant	Entertainment	5			10	
Guns 'N Roses (all)	Entertainment	80			135	
Gunsche, Otto	Military	50		85	55	
Gur, Mordechai	Military	20	75			Israeli Gen. 6 Day War
Gurie, Sigrid	Entertainment	20	25	60	45	
Gurrag-gchaa,Jugderdemidij	Astronaut	15	50		35	Mongolian Astro.
Gusmeroli, Giovanni	Entertainment	5			15	Opera
Gustavus II Adolphus(Swe)	Royalty-Military	350	2250	2300		Saved Protestantism in Germ.
Gustavus III (Swe)	Royalty	115	700	985		
Gustavus IV Adolphus(Swe)	Royalty	150				
Gustavus V (Swe)	Royalty				275	
Guston, Philip 1913-80	Artist			175		Canadian-born Am. Painter
Guthrie, Arlo	Country Music	5	6	15	15	
Guthrie, James 1792-1869	Cabinet-Senate	22	45	80		Pierce Sec'y Treas. Sen. KY
Guthrie, Thomas	Clergy	15	20	25		
Guthrie, Woody	Entertainer	300				Folksinger, Poet, Songwriter
Gutierrez, Sid	Astronaut	5			15	
Guttenberg, Steve	Entertainment	5		30	25	
Guy, Thomas	Celebrity	15	40	105		
Guynemer, Georges	Aviation	225	400	650	500	ACE, WW I. A French Legend
Guyot, Arnold 1807-1884	Science	25	45	195		Geographer, Mapmaker, Educator
Guyot, Pierre	Fr. Revolution	25	55	125		
Guyton-Morveau, L.B.Baron 1737-?	Science	20	50	95		Fr. Chemist
Gwenn, Edmund 1875-1959	Entertainment	75	105		175	SP Miracle 34th St. $1,650
Gwin, William M. 1805-1885	Senate/Congress	20	45	60		MOC MS, Senator CA
Gwinnett, Button	Revolutionary War	115000	165000			Rare Signer Decl. Independence
Gwynne, Anne	Entertainment	6	8	15	15	
Gwynne, Fred	Entertainment	20			45	
Gye, Albani	Entertainment	10			25	

NAME	CATEGORY	SIG	LS/DS	ALS	SP	Comment
Haab, Robert	Head of State	25	70			Switzerland
Haag, Carl 1820-1915	Artist		30	80		Ger.-Born Br. Court Painter to Victoria
Haakon VII (Nor)	Royalty	120	205			1st King Independent of Sweden
Haakon VII and Maud	Royalty	200			450	King & Queen of Norway
Habberton, John	Author	10	15	25		
Habersham, Joseph 1751-1815	Revolutionary War	95	260	540		Continental Army,Cont.Congress
Hack, Shelley	Entertainment	4	7	12	15	Pin-Up SP $20
Hackett, Bobby	Entertainment	20			45	Cornet/Benny Goodman
Hackett, Buddy	Entertainment	5	10	20	25	Comedian
Hackett, James K.	Entertainment	12	15		30	Vintage Actor
Hackett, Joan	Entertainment	10	15	25	25	
Hackman, Gene	Entertainment	20		35	52	SP/Denzel Washington 130

The Sanders Price Guide to Autographs

NAME	CATEGORY	SIG	LS/DS	ALS	SP	Comment
Hadley, Jerry	Entertainment	10			35	Concert, Opera
Hadley, Reed	Entertainment	15			30	
Haenschen, Gus	Entertainment	15		25	30	Big Band
Hagar, Sammy	Entertainment	15			50	Rock
Hagegard,Hakan	Entertainment				30	Opera
Hagen, Jean	Entertainment	5			10	
Hagen, Johannes 1847-1930	Science	15	40	100		Austr. Astron.Hagen's Clouds
Hagen, Uta	Entertainment	7	12	20	20	
Haggard, Henry Rider 1856-1925	Author	103	130	275	270	King Solomon's Mines
Haggard, Merle	Country Music	10			30	
Haggerty, Dan	Entertainment	5	6	15	15	
Haggin, James Ben Ali	Business	35	205			Am Financier, Anaconda Copper
Hagman, Larry	Entertainment	6	8	15	25	
Hagood, Johnson 1829-98	Civil War	103	295	383		CSA Gen.War Date S $200
Hague, Frank	Politician	10	25	40	15	Headed Major Dem. Machine
Hahn, Jessica	Playboy Cover	4			15	Pin-Up SP $20
Hahn, Otto 1879-1968	Science	140	345	2000	350	Ger.Nobel Chem. Nuclear Fission
Hahn, Reynaldo	Composer	70	160			Ven. Critic, Dir. Paris Opera
Haider, Michael	Business	15			40	Pres. Standard Oil NJ
Haig, Alexander M.	Military	20	45	50	45	Gen. WW II, Sec'y State
Haig, Douglas. 1st Earl 1861-1924	Military	25	75	135	60	Br.Gen., Boer War, India, WW I
Haig, Lady Dorothy	Celebrity	4		25		Wife of Sir Douglas Haig
Haight, Edward 1817-85	Congress	10				Repr. NY, Founder NY Bank
Haight, Henry H.	Governor	15				San Francisco's Haight-Asbury Distr.
Halle, William 1797-1837	Congress					Repr. MS
Halley, Arthur	Author	25	40	65	35	Am. Novelist.Hotel,Airport
Haines, Connie	Entertainment	20			50	Big Band Vocalist
Haines, Daniel 1801-1877	Governor	30	45	90		Governor NJ
Haines, William 1900-73	Entertainment	15	15	35	40	
Hairston, Jester	Entertainment	10			30	
Haise, Fred W. Jr.	Astronaut	10			95	
Halaby, Najeeb	Celebrity	10	30		15	
Halban, H.H., Dr.	Science	30	65			Fr. Pioneer Of Uranium Fission
Haldane, John B.S. 1892-1964	Science		125	195		Br. Geneticist & Author
Haldeman, George W.	Aviation	30	55	105	75	
Haldeman, H. R.	Political	10	20	45	15	Nixon-Watergate
Halder, Franz	Military	55	95	160	115	Ger.Gen.Opposed Hitler.Prison!
Hale, Alan Jr.	Entertainment	40	55	75	100	
Hale, Alan Sr.	Entertainment	50	55	95	100	
Hale, Barbara	Entertainment	10	15	25	30	Pin-Up SP $30
Hale, Edward Everett 1822-1909	Clergy	40	190	255	240	Author Man Without a Country
Hale, Eugene 1836-1918	Senate	10	15	30		MOC 1869-75, Senator ME
Hale, George E.	Science	20	100			Invented Spectroheliograph
Hale, John Parker 1806-1873	Congress	15	45	100		Abolitionist., Senator NH
Hale, Lucretia Peabody	Author					1820-1900
Hale, Monte	Entertainment	6	10	20	25	Big Time Cowboy Star
Hale, Richard	Entertainment	6	8	15	15	
Hale, Robert	Entertainment	10			30	Opera
Hale, Sarah J. B.	Author	50	155	225		Editor.Mary Had A Little Lamb
Halevy, Fromental	Composer	30		125		La Juive
Halevy, Jacques 1799-1862	Composer	45	80	135		Opera. Taught Gounod, Bizet
Halevy, Ludovic	Author	25	70	120		Novels, Libretti For Operas
Haley, Alex 1922-92	Author	48	125	150	140	Roots, Malcom X.ALS/Cont. $2900
Haley, Bill	Entertainment	175			450	
Haley, Jack 1899-1979	Entertainment	172	150		233	Tin Man in ....Oz
Halifax, Edw. Frederick L.1881-1958	Statesman	15	50			1st Earl of...Viceroy of India, U.S. Ambassa-

NAME	CATEGORY	SIG	LS/DS	ALS	SP	Comment
dor						
Hall and Oates	Entertainment	20			40	
Hall, Abraham Oakey 1826-98	Politician	4	7	100	10	NY Mayor, Tweed Ring, Tammany Hall
Hall, Alvin W.	Celebrity	5	10		35	
Hall, Arsenio	Entertainment	10			20	TV Talk Show Host
Hall, Charles M.	Clergy	10	15	20		
Hall, David	Governor	12			15	Governor OK
Hall, Deidre	Entertainment	10			35	Soaps
Hall, Fawn	Entertainment	12	15	50	25	Pin-Up SP $30
Hall, Gus	Communist	30	55	150	30	US Communist Party Leader
Hall, Harry	Entertainment	3	3	6	6	
Hall, Huntz	Entertainment	10	15	25	40	
Hall, Jerry	Entertainment	10			30	Pin-Up SP $35
Hall, Jon	Entertainment	35	45	85	50	
Hall, Josephine	Entertainment	6	8	15	15	
Hall, Joyce C.	Business	50	600		132	Hallmark Greeting Cards
Hall, Juanita	Entertainment	55			75	Bloody Mary inSouth Pacific
Hall, Lyman 1724-90	Revolutionary War	2200	2950	3500		Signer Decl. of Indepen.
Hall, Monty	Entertainment	3	3	6	15	
Hall, Nathan	Cabinet	20	35	110		Fillmore P.M. General
Hall, Pauline	Entertainment	10			30	Vintage Actress
Hall, Radclyffe	Author		45	135		Well of Loneliness
Hall, Robert, Sir 1761-1831	Clergy	25	30	35	35	Br. Baptist Minister. Great Pulpit Orator
Hall, Tom T.	Country Music	5			12	
Hall, William	Civil War	40		100		Union Gen., CW Gov. MO
Hallam, Henry 1777-1859	Author	35	115	175		Br. Historian
Halle, Wilhelmine	Entertainment	6	8	15	15	
Halleck, Fitz-Greene 1790-1867	Poet	25	80			Member of Knickerbocker Group
Halleck, Henry Wager (War Date)	Civil War	189	800	866	200	Union Gen.ALS/Cont. $4,500
Halleck, Henry Wager 1815—72	Civil War	108	250	670		Union Gen.
Hallett, Mal	Entertainment	20			35	Big Band Leader
Halliburton, Richard 1900-1939	Explorer-Author	32	200		50	World Traveller, Lecturer
Halop, Billy	Entertainment	75	75	120	150	One of Orig. Dead End Kids
Halpern, Seymour	Congress	5			15	MOC NY
Halpine, Charles G.	Author	20	35	90		
Halsey, Wm. F. 'Bull' 1882-1959	Military	75	198	210	200	Adm. WW II
Halstead, Murat	Editor	5	20	35		Journalist
Halston	Business	15	20	40	30	Designer
Halstrom, Holly	TV Model	5			10	Price is Right Model
Hamblen, Stewart	Country Music	15			30	
Hamel, Veronica	Entertainment	5	10	20	20	
Hamer, Frank	Military	110	465			
Hamer, Rusty	Entertainment	35		55	75	
Hamill, Mark	Entertainment	8	9	20	55	Actor Star Wars
Hamilton, Alex. Jr.1786-1875	Military	15	40	150		Officer War 1812
Hamilton, Alexander 1754-1804	Cabinet	1175	3065	3500		Washington Sec'y Treas. FF $1600-2000
Hamilton, Andrew J.	Civil War					Union Gen. Offic'l Report '63 $5060
Hamilton, Charles Smith	Civil War	32	65	110		Union Gen.ALS/Content $575
Hamilton, Donald	Author	7	15	30	10	
Hamilton, Emma, Lady	Celebrity	150		575		Mistress of Lord Nelson
Hamilton, Gail	Author					See Dodge, Mary A.
Hamilton, George	Entertainment	5			20	
Hamilton, George Alexander, Sir	Diplomatist	75	540			Archaeologist, Husband Emma H.
Hamilton, Ian, Sir 1853-	Military	15				Brit. General. Led Gallipoli Exp.
Hamilton, James	Colonial Am.	65	160			Colonial Gov. PA
Hamilton, James Alex. 1788-1878	Military	45	140			Officer War 1812

NAME	CATEGORY	SIG	LS/DS	ALS	SP	Comment
Hamilton, John	Entertainment	15				Character Actor
Hamilton, Lee	Congress	5	20		10	Congressman IN
Hamilton, Linda	Entertainment	20			50	Pin-Up SP $50
Hamilton, Margaret 1902-85	Entertainment	75	125		168	SP 'Wicked Witch of West' $300
Hamilton, Neil	Entertainment	25	125	65	100	'Commissioner Gordon' in Batman
Hamilton, Ian, Sir	Military	50				Br. General WW I
Hamlin, Hannibal (V)1809-91	Vice President	85	285	312		Lincoln VP, US Sen., Gov.
Hamlin, Harry	Entertainment	8	15	28	20	
Hamlin, V.T.*	Cartoonist	50			325	Alley Oop
Hamlisch, Marvin	Composer	10		65	35	AMusQS $35, $85
Hammarskjold, Dag	Head of State	95	650	725		Sec'y General United Nations
Hammer	Entertainment	25			45	Rap
Hammer, Armand	Business	50	535	275	150	Occidental Petroleum
Hammerstein, O., II & Kern, Jerome	Composer		1200			
Hammerstein, Oscar, II 1895-1960	Composer	250	515		260	Lyricist-Librettist
Hammett, Dashiell 1894-1961	Author	450	1825	2750	575	Hard-Boiled Detective Fiction
Hammond, James B.	Inventor	20	100			Typewriter
Hammond, James H. 1807-64	Congress		45	115		US Sen., Gov.SC.Cotton is King
Hammond, Jay S.	Governor	10	15			Governor AK
Hammond, L. Blaine	Astronaut	5			15	
Hammond, William A.	Civil War	50	120	400		Union Gen. /Surgeon Gen.Author
Hampden, Renn D.	Clergy	10	25	30		
Hampden, Walter	Entertainment	20		45	45	
Hampson, Thomas	Entertainment	10			40	Opera
Hampton, Hope	Entertainment	40			70	
Hampton, Lionel b.1913	Entertainment	40			65	Big Band Leader-Vibes
Hampton, Wade (War Date)	Civil War	400	1930	4633		CSA Gen.
Hampton, Wade 1818-1902	Civil War	270	575	960		CSA General, Gov., US Sen. SC
Hamsun, Knut (Pedersen)	Author	38	80	135	75	Nobel Lit. Neo-Romantic Novels
Hanami, Kohei	Military	80	250			
Hancock, Clarence E. 1885-1948	Congress	5	25			Repr. NY
Hancock, Herbie	Composer	10	15	45	20	
Hancock, John 1737-93	Revolutionary War	2200	5428	8491		First Signer.ALS/Cont. $15,000
Hancock, Winfield Scott (War Date)	Civil War	220		1375	675	Union General
Hancock, Winfield Scott 1824-86	Civil War	147	325	248	675	Union Gen.ALS/Cont. $3300
Hand, Edward	Revolutionary War	185	475	1000		Gen. Cont. Army. Repr. PA 1784
Handel, George Frederick	Composer	1000	5800	22000		
Handelman, Stanley M.	Entertainment	3	3	6	6	
Handler, Ruth	Business	40	75			Founder Mattel Toys
Handy, W. C. 1873-1958	Composer	275	475	575	700	AMusQS $2200, Sheet Music S $795
Hanks, Tom	Entertainment	20			120	Actor. Forrest Gump, Oscar winner
Hanna & Barbera	Cartoonists	30			100	Animators
Hanna, Bill	Cartoonist				85	Flintstones, Yogi Bear
Hanna, Marcus A. 1837-1904	Industrialist	25	385	225	35	Sen. OH. Political Power Broker
Hannah, Daryl	Entertainment	10	35	40	50	Pin-Up SP $60
Hannah, John A.	Educator	7			10	Pres. Michigan State Univ.
Hansbrough, Henry C.1848-1933	Congress	10	15	30		MOC, Senator ND
Hansen, William	Entertainment	6	8	15	15	
Hanson, Howard	Composer	15	35	80		Pulitzer. Dir.Eastman Sch. Musi
Hanson, John	Revolutionary War	2250				Pres. Continental Congress
Haralson, Hugh A. 1805-54	Congress	10				Repr. GA, Maj. Gen'l State Militia
Harbach, Otto 1873-1963	Entertainment	125	100		175	Playwright,Lyricist, Music Publ
Harbaugh, Gregory J.	Astronaut	5			15	
Harbison, John	Composer	20		75		Pulitzer, AMusQS $150
Harbord, James G.	Military	60	145	185	125	Chief of Staff AEF WW I, RCA
Harburg, E. Y. 'Yip'	Composer	100	175	375		Over the Rainbow

The Sanders Price Guide to Autographs

NAME	CATEGORY	SIG	LS/DS	ALS	SP	Comment
Harcourt, Edward Venables	Clergy	25	30	40		
Hardee, William J.(War Date)	Civil War	300	875	1110	950	CSA General
Hardenberg, K.A.von Furst	Statesman	15	60	125		Prussian Politician
Hardie, James Allen 1823-1876	Civil War	45	205	245		Union General
Hardie, James Allen 1823-76	Civil War	55	155			Union Gen.
Hardie, Russell	Entertainment	10	15	25	25	
Hardin, Clifford M.	Cabinet	5	10	18	15	Sec'y Agriculture
Hardin, Gus	Entertainment	4			10	Female Singer
Hardin, John Wesley	Outlaw	2900	6500			
Hardin, Ty	Entertainment	6	8	15	19	
Harding, Ann	Entertainment	15	15	35	30	
Harding, Florence Kling	First Lady	60	180		75	White House Card S $85
Harding, Tonya	Celebrity	75				Infamous Ice Skater
Harding, Warren G. (As President)	President		628	1950	948	ALS/Cont.$15000.WH Cd S $400-500
Harding, Warren G. 1865-1923	President	125	492	1450	425	
Hardinge, Chas., 1st Baron	Diplomat	10	750	35	25	Br.Viceroy India, Ambass.Russia
Hardinge, Henry, Sir 1785-1856	Military			585		Br. Field Marshal
Hardwicke, Cedric, Sir	Entertainment	35	65	90	95	
Hardy, Oliver 1892-1957	Entertainment	250	300	500	550	
Hardy, Thomas 1840-1928	Author	275	1000	1425	1400	Br. Novelist, Poet, Dramatist
Hardy, Thomas Masterman, Sir	Military	70	295			1769-1839 Br. Adm./Nelson
Hare, John, Sir	Entertainment	20	30		50	
Hare, WIlllam Hobart	Clergy	35	50	65	50	
Haring, Keith*	Artist	25	40	95	350	Pop Artist-Cartoonist
Harkins, Paul	Military	15	30	50	30	
Harkness, Georgia	Clergy	35	50	95	65	
Harlan, James A.1820-	Cabinet	20	55	98		A. Johnson Sec'y Interior 1865
Harlan, John Marshall 1833-1911	Supreme Court	55	95	175		
Harland, Marion	Author	7	15	20		
Harley, William S.	Business		2615			Co-Fndr. Harley-Davidson Motorcycles
Harlfinger II, Frederick J.	Military	10			25	
Harlow, Jean	Entertainment	925	1400	3000	2500	
Harlow, Jean (Mama)	Entertainment	25	30		45	
Harman, Fred*	Cartoonist	25			250	Red Ryder
Harmon, Judson	Cabinet	10	25	40	20	U.S. Att'y Gen., Gov. OH
Harmon, Mark	Entertainment	9	10	20	25	
Harmonica Rascals	Entertainment	10			25	Borah Minovitch and the......
Harned, Virginia	Entertainment	15			35	Vintage Actress, Mrs. Sothern
Harney, William S. (War Date)	Civil War	50		330		Union Gen.
Harper, Joseph W.	Celebrity	10	30	80		
Harper, Robert G.	Revolutionary War	65		150		Gen. Rev. War, Statesman
Harper, Tess	Entertainment	9	10	20	25	
Harper, Valerie	Entertainment	5	6	15	15	
Harrel, Scotty	Entertainment	8			15	C & W
Harrell, Costen J., Bishop	Clergy	20	25	40	35	
Harrelson, Woody	Entertainment	15			45	Cheers
Harridge, Will 1883-1971	Business		125			Pres. Org. Known as American League
Harries, George	Military	20	35	80		General WW I
Harriman, Edw. Henry 1848-1909	Business	35	55	90	45	U.S. RR Magnate. S RR Bonds $575+
Harriman, Edward Roland	Business	20	55	120	35	CEO Union Pacific RR. Banker
Harriman, W. Averell 1891-1986	Governor	25	70	100	50	Gov. NY, Statesman, Diplomat
Harrington, Pat	Entertainment	4	5	10	15	
Harris	Cartoonist	5			18	The Better Half
Harris, Arthur T., Sir Bomber...	Military	30	85	110	150	Cmdr.-in-Chief RAF WW II
Harris, Barbara	Entertainment	5			12	
Harris, Bernard A., Jr.	Astronaut	10			20	Afro-Am. Astronaut

NAME	CATEGORY	SIG	LS/DS	ALS	SP	Comment
Harris, Cecil	Aviation	14	25	50	40	ACE, WW II
Harris, Ed	Entertainment	5	6	15	15	
Harris, EmmyLou	Entertainment	10			35	
Harris, Fred R.	Senate/Congress	3	10			Senator OK
Harris, George E.	Senate/Congress	5	10			CSA Officer. MOC NC
Harris, Isham 1818-97	Civil War	45	65			Civil War Gov. TN. ALS '64 $450
Harris, Jean	Criminal	40	70	375		Murdered Dr. Herman Tarnower
Harris, Jed	Entertainment	5	20			Producer. Theatre
Harris, Joel Chandler 1848-1908	Author	175	390	700		Books on Black Folklore
Harris, John 1726-91	Frontier Leader	125	265	850		Founder Harrisburg, PA
Harris, John A.	Senate/Congress	3		15		
Harris, Jonathan	Entertainment	3			10	Actor
Harris, Julie	Entertainment	6	8	15	15	
Harris, Louis	Pollster	20	35		25	
Harris, Mel	Entertainment	5			40	Actress. 30 Something
Harris, Neil Patrick	Entertainment	10			35	
Harris, Patricia Roberts	Cabinet	5	15	25	20	Sec'y Health & Human Services
Harris, Paul Percy	Business	20	45		25	Fndr. & Pres. Emeritus Rotary
Harris, Phil	Entertainment	5			20	
Harris, Richard	Entertainment	15		35	40	
Harris, Robert	Author		50			Enigma
Harris, Robert H.	Entertainment	3	3	6	10	
Harris, Sam H.	Entertainment	4	25			Producer-Manager
Harris, Thomas	Author		55			Silence of the Lambs
Harris, Thomas S.	Aviation	15	45			ACE WW II, Test Pilot
Harris, William A. 1841-1909	Congress-Civil War	30				Repr.& Sen. KS, CW Adj. Gen'l
Harris, William L., Bishop	Clergy	15	25	35		
Harrison, Albertis S. Jr.	Governor	10	20			Governor VA
Harrison, Anna Symmes	First Lady	675	975	2500		Free Frank $975
Harrison, Benj. & Roosevelt, T.	Presidents					Civ.Serv.Commission S $2250
Harrison, Benj.& Harrison Caroline	Pres.-1st Lady	600				Together
Harrison, Benjamin (As President)	President	362	1012	1900		Exec. Mansion Card S. $450
Harrison, Benjamin 1726-91	Revolutionary War	450	674	2750		Signer Decl. of Indepen.
Harrison, Benjamin 1833-1901	President	200	581	695	2100	TLS/Cont. $1600
Harrison, Burton, Mrs.	Celebrity	10			35	1890's Socialite
Harrison, Byron Patton 'Pat'	Senate/Congress	5	15		10	MOC, Senator MS
Harrison, Caroline Scott 1832-1892	First Lady	160	250	1150	750	
Harrison, Carter H.	Mayor	15	35	45		Mayor Chicago 1897
Harrison, George	Entertainment	200	450	275	448	Beatle
Harrison, George P.,Jr. 1841-1922	Civil War	90		278		CSA Gen.
Harrison, George P.,Jr.(War Date)	Civil War		220			CSA Gen..
Harrison, Gregory	Entertainment	5	10	20	15	
Harrison, Helen	Aviation	40	125			Am Aviatrix
Harrison, Henry B.	Governor	12		20		Governor CT 1885
Harrison, Jenilee	Entertainment	4	4	9	12	Pin-Up SP $15
Harrison, Mary Lord 1858-1948	First Lady	70	130	175	120	
Harrison, Noel	Entertainment	5			15	
Harrison, Rex 1908-90	Entertainment	40	55	70	98	Br. My Fair Lady
Harrison, Richard B. 1865-1935	Entrtainment	25	85		150	Am.Black Actor. The Green Pastures
Harrison, Robert Hanson	Revolutionary War	210	400	750		Sec'y to G. Washington
Harrison, William Henry 1773-1841	President	570	1575	3236		President Only 1 Month
Harrold, Kathryn	Entertainment	8	9	19	20	Pin-Up SP $25
Harry, Debbie	Entertainment	25			75	Rock
Harry, Jackee	Entertainment	5			15	
Harryhausen, Ray	Entertainment	10			35	Film Director
Harshaw, Margaret	Entertainment	10	12	40	65	Opera. U.S. Soprano

NAME	CATEGORY	SIG	LS/DS	ALS	SP	Comment
Hart, Corey	Entertainment	6	8	15	15	
Hart, Dolores	Entertainment	4	4	15	20	
Hart, Dorothy	Entertainment	15		25	35	
Hart, Gary W.	Senate/Congress	5			15	Senator CO
Hart, John	Entertainment	10			25	SP as the Lone Ranger $50
Hart, John 1711-1879	Revolutionary War	320	644	1300		Signer Decl. of Indepen.
Hart, Johnny*	Cartoonist	20			200	B.C. & Wizard Of Id
Hart, Lorenz	Composer	500	7500			Rogers & Hart
Hart, Mary	Entertainment	5	8	15	15	Pin-Up SP $15
Hart, Moss	Authors	20	55	105	30	
Hart, Paul	Entertainment	6	8	15	15	
Hart, Roxanne	Entertainment	10			20	Pinup $30
Hart, Terry J.	Astronaut	5	15		30	
Hart, Thomas C.	Military	40			65	Adm. WW II
Hart, Veronica	Entertainment	10	15	35	35	Pin-Up SP $40
Hart, William S.1870-1946	Entertainment	145	180	235	605	1st Western Movie Star
Harte, Francis Brett 1836-1902	Author	90	185	150		Frontier Life, AMsS $25,000
Hartford, George L.	Business	40	295	280		Great Atlantic & Pacific Tea Co
Hartford, Huntington	Business	15	30	45	20	Patron of the Arts. Playboy
Hartford, John	Composer	10	45	70		AMusQS $95
Hartley, Fred A.	Congress	20		50		Congressman NJ
Hartley, Mariette	Entertainment	5	6	15	15	
Hartley, Nina	Entertainment	20			45	
Hartley, Roland H.	Governor	5	12		10	Governor WA
Hartley, Thomas 1748-1800	Revolutionary War					Lt. Col. War Content ALS $6500
Hartline, Haldan K.	Science	25	80	140	35	Nobel Medicine
Hartman, David	Entertainment	4	8	12	10	Early Host Good Morning Am.
Hartman, Don	Entertainment	10			35	Producer
Hartman, Lisa (Black)	Entertainment	10	15	25	28	Pin-Up SP $40
Hartmann, Erich	Aviation	40	105	190	345	Ger.Ace WW II. #1 Worldwide
Hartranft, John F. 1830-89	Civil War	80	122	165		Union Gen. ALS/Cont. $1045
Harts, William	Military	10		35		General WW I
Hartsfield, Henry W. Jr	Astronaut	10	40		15	
Hartsuff, George L. 1830-74	Civil War	45	75	95		Union Gen. S/Rank $75
Hartwell, Alfred S. 1836-1912	Civil War	24	80	105		Union General
Harvey, George B. M.	Journalist-Dipl.	20	70		100	Fostered W. Wilson Nomination
Harvey, Lawrence	Entertainment	90			150	
Harvey, Lilian	Entertainment	5	6	15	25	
Harvey, Marilyn	Entertainment	10			35	Star of "The Astounding She Monster"
Harvey, Paul	Journalist	10	25		15	
Harvey, William 1578-1657	Science	750	3750	11000		1st Theory Blood Circulation
Hasbrouck, Robert W.	Military	50	165		75	Am. Gen. WW II
Hasen, Irwin	Cartoonist	5			20	Dondi
Haskell, James K.	Entertainment	10	15	30	25	
Haskell, Peter	Entertainment	5			10	Actor
Haskin, Joseph Abel	Civil War	50				Union General
Hassam, Childe 1859-1935	Artist	150	350	480		Foremost in Am. Impressionism
Hassam, Crown Prince	Royalty	15	35	80	50	Morocco
Hassan, al Bakr, Ahmad	Head of State	10	35	90	18	Last Price Availble
Hassan, Crown Prince	Royalty	10	15	50	20	
Hasselhoff, David	Entertainment	15	8	15	40	
Hasso, Signe	Entertainment	5			20	
Hastings, Daniel H.	Governor	10	25			Governor PA
Hastings, Warren 1732-1818	Head of State	70	155	235		Gov. Gen. India. Colonial Adm.
Haswell, Charles H.	Civil War	25	35	55		Union Naval Architect
Hatch, John Porter 1822-1901	Civil War	30	50	80	75	Union Gen. CMH. ADS(Gen.Orders 62)$4180

The Sanders Price Guide to Autographs

NAME	CATEGORY	SIG	LS/DS	ALS	SP	Comment
Hatch, Orrin	Senate	5			10	Senator UT
Hatcher, Richard G.	Political	5	10		15	Afro-Am. Mayor, Gary IN
Hatcher, Teri	Entertainment	10			60	Actress. Lois & Clark
Hatfield, Hurd	Entertainment	15	20	30	35	
Hatfield, Lansing	Entertainment	12			95	Opera, Concert, Recital Artist
Hatfield, Mark O.	Senate	10	15		15	Senator OR, Governor Oregon
Hathaway, Henry	Entertainment	40			95	
Hatlo, Jimmy 1898-1963	Cartoonist	10	45		80	Little Iodine
Hatton, Frank	Cabinet	50				Arthur PMG
Hatton, Raymond	Entertainment	50			125	
Hatton, Robert	Civil War	125	265	365		No Current Price
Hatton, Rondo	Entertainment	450			1200	
Hauck, Frederick H.	Astronaut	10			25	
Hauer, Rutger	Entertainment	10			35	
Haught, Helmut	Aviation	10	15	30	20	
Haupt, Herman 1817-1905	Civil War	35				Union Gen. ALS '62 $440
Hauptman, Herbert A., Dr.	Science	20	35		30	Nobel Chemistry
Hauptmann, Bruno Richard	Kidnapper	425				Convicted Killer Lindbergh Baby
Hauptmann, Gerhart	Author	90	295	575	375	Nobel Prize Literature 1912
Hauser, Dr. Gayelord	Medical	20				Healthfood Advocate. Garbo Lover
Hausner, Jerry	Entertainment	4	4	9	9	
Havel, Vaclav	Head of State	20			45	Czech. Poet
Haven, Annette	Entertainment	9	10	20	25	Pin-Up SP $40
Havens, Beckwith	Aviation	18	40	55	50	
Haver, June	Entertainment	5	10	12	20	Pin-Up SP $25
Havoc, June	Entertainment	6	8	15	15	
Hawes, Elizabeth	Artist	10	20	35		
Hawke, Ethan	Entertainment	10			42	
Hawke, Robert	Head of State	15	40	130	25	Prime Minister Australia
Hawkins, Anthony Hope, Sir	Author	10	35	70	30	Br.Novelist.Prisoner of Zenda
Hawkins, Coleman	Entertainment	138			250	Jazz Tenor Sax
Hawkins, Jack	Entertainment	45			100	
Hawkins, John	Civil War	35		125		Union Gen.
Hawkins, Paula	Senate/Congress	3	10		10	Senator FL
Hawkins, Rush C.	Civil War					Union Gen. DS '61 /Union Gen. DS '61 $200
Hawkins, William 1770-1819	Governor	35	85			Governor NC. War 1812
Hawks, Frank Monroe 1897-1938	Aviation	80	135	325	248	Pioneer Aviator
Hawks, Howard	Entertainment	85			150	
Hawley, Joseph R. 1826-1905	Civil War	45	90	120		Union Gen., Gov. CT, Sen CT
Hawley, Steven A.	Astronaut	5			20	
Hawn, Goldie	Entertainment	10	15	30	40	Pin-Up SP$65
Haworth, Jill	Entertainment	4	4	9	10	
Hawthorn, Alex. Travis	Civil War	155	295	445		
Hawthorne, Julian 1846-1934	Author	30		225		Son of Nathaniel Hawthorne
Hawthorne, Nathaniel 1804-65	Author	400	1350	2080		Novelist, Short Story,US Consul
Hay, Bill (Announcer)	Entertainment	10	1625	20		
Hay, John H.	Military	5			15	
Hay, John Milton 1838-1905	Cabinet	50	150	225	135	ALS/Content $950 War Dte
Hay, William Henry	Military	5	15	30		
Hayakawa, Sessue	Entertainment	120			250	
Hayden, Carl	Senate/Congress	10	25		20	MOC, Senator AZ. 42 Years
Hayden, Charles 1870-1937	Banker	20	45			Philanthropist. Hayden Planetarium
Hayden, Mellisa	Entertainment	5	6	15	15	
Hayden, Russell	Entertainment	25			75	Cowboy
Hayden, Sterling	Entertainment	25			50	
Hayden, Tom	Congress	5	15		20	MOC CA

The Sanders Price Guide to Autographs

NAME	CATEGORY	SIG	LS/DS	ALS	SP	Comment
Haydn, Franz Jos. 1732-1809	Composer					Working Draft 4 String Quartets $1.04 Mil.I
Haydn, Joseph	Composer	2200	15500	24000		
Haydon, Benj. R. 1786-1846	Artist			212		Br. Historical Painter,Author,Teacher
Hayek, Salma	Entertainment				80	Actress-Desperado
Hayes, George 'Gabby'	Entertainment	128	165		450	
Hayes, Helen 1900-94	Entertainment	20	40	45	65	First Lady of American Theatre
Hayes, Ira H., Corporal	Military	400				Iwo Jima Flag Raising FDC $550
Hayes, Isaac	Entertainment	6	8	15	20	
Hayes, Isaac Israel 1832-81	Explorer-Civil Wa	95	190	275		ALS/Cont.$1,500.War Dte. DS $375
Hayes, Joseph	Civil War	55	95	170	150	
Hayes, Lucy Webb	First Lady	230		400	700	
Hayes, Margaret	Entertainment	9	10		15	
Hayes, Patrick, Cardinal	Clergy	35	45	75	50	
Hayes, Roland	Entertainment	80			250	Am. Tenor, Spingarn Medal '25
Hayes, Rutherford B. (As Pres.)	President	225	700	995	1375	ALS/Cont. $7,500, WH Cd. $350
Hayes, Rutherford B. 1822-93	President, CW	203	575	786	2762	Union Gen.
Hayne, Paul Hamilton	Author	65		850		ALS/Literary Content $2,500
Hayne, Robert Young 1791-1839	Congress	65				Sen. SC, Gov. SC
Haynes, Linda	Entertainment	4	4	9	9	
Hays, Frank A.	Aviation	35	55	95	65	ACE, SS II
Hays, Harry Thompson (War Date)	Civil War	302	1015			CSA Gen.
Hays, Harry Thompson 1820-76	Civil War	185	450			CSA General
Hays, Robert	Entertainment	6	8	12	12	
Hays, Wayne L.	Senate/Congress	5	20		15	MOC OH
Hays, Will H. 1879-1859	Motion Pic. Exec.	30	42		40	Film Czar. Enforced Hays Code
Hays, William 1819-75	Civil War	35	85	145		Union Gen. ALS '64 $385
Hayward, George	Science	10	20	35	15	
Hayward, Louis	Entertainment	10	15	25	50	
Hayward, Susan 1917-75	Entertainment	142	200	525	542	
Haywood, Thomas	Military	5	8	15	10	
Hayworth, Rita 1918-87	Entertainment	150		390	565	
Hazelwood, John 1726-1800	Revolutionary War	75	190	370		Commodore Continental Navy
Hazelwood, Joseph	Navy Captain	20			45	Capt. Exxon Valdez-Oil Spill
Hazen, Wm. Babcock	Civil War	25	45	95		Union Gen.
Head, Edith	Entertainment	25			125	8 Academy Awards
Headle, Marshall	Aviation	25	70		85	Lockheed Chief Test Pilot
Healey, Robert C.	Author	10	15	25		
Healy, George Peter	Artist	125	310	725		Eminent 19th Cent. Portraitist
Healy, Ted	Entertainment	25		40	45	
Hearnes, Warren E.	Governor	4	10		15	Governor MO
Hearst, George 1820-1891	Business-Senate	200		490		Fathered Newspaper Dynasty. CA
Hearst, Patricia	Celebrities	275				Kidnapped daughter
Hearst, Phoebe A.(Mrs. George..)	Business	20	40	90		Philanthropies
Hearst, Wm. Randolph 1863-1951	Business	225	545	575	695	Repr.NY.Powerful Publisher
Hearst, Wm. Randolph, Jr.	Business	10	20	45	20	
Heart	Entertainment	35			125	Rock
Heath, Edward	Head of State	40	90	115	45	Br.Prime Minister
Heath, William 1737-1814	Revolutionary War	160	742	1500		Gen.Cont'l Army.DS War Dte.$1275,$1400
Heatherton, Joey	Entertainment	9	10	20	25	
Heatherton, Ray	Entertainment	20			70	Big band leader
Heber, Reginald	Clergy	85	100	200		
Hebert, Louis (War Date)	Civil War	187	488			CSA Gen.
Hebert, Louis 1820-1901	Civil War	100	250			CSA Gen.
Hebert, Paul O.	Civil War	105	200	260		
Hecht, Ben 1894-1964	Author	15	45		45	AA.Playwright, Novelist, Newsman
Heckart, Eileen	Entertainment	5	6	15	15	

NAME	CATEGORY	SIG	LS/DS	ALS	SP	Comment
Heckerling, Amy	Entertainment	5	6	15	15	
Heckman, Charles A. 1822-96	Civil War	30	85			Union Gen. ALS (Autobiog.)$550
Hedin, Sven 1865-	Explorer	55		225	125	Swe. Asian Explorer
Hedison, David	Entertainment	4	4	9	10	
Hedl, Walter	Composer	15	55	90		AMusQS $175
Hedman, Robert Duke	Aviation	20	45	75	45	ACE, WW II, Flying Tigers
Hedouville, G.M.T.J,Count	Fr. Revolution	70	125			
Hedren, Tippi	Entertainment	5	6	15	22	
Hedrick, Roger	Aviation	12	25	40	32	ACE, WW II
Heflin, Howell	Senate	5	15	15		Senator AL
Heflin, James Thomas	Senate/Congress	10	20		15	MOC, Senator AL
Heflin, Van 1910-71	Entertainment	35	75	95	100	
Hefner, Christie	Business	5	10	30	20	Publisher Playboy Magazine
Hefner, Hugh	Business	8			10	Playboy Magazine. TLS/Cont. $500
Heft, Bob	Designer	20				Designed US 50 Star Flag
Hefti, Neal	Composer	16	35	50	40	AMusQS $195
Hegel, Geo. Wilhelm F.1770-1831	Philosopher	850	1500	2050		Ger. Idealist Philos./Kant
Heggie, O.P.	Entertainment	300			750	
Heidegger, Martin 1889-1976	Philosopher			1400		Ger. Existential Phenomonologist
Heidt, Horace	Entertainment	20			40	Big Band Leader. Sigs 12 Members $45
Heifetz, Jascha 1901-87	Entertainment	130			585	Violin Virtuoso.AMusQS $700
Helgle, Katherine	Entertainment				75	Actress
Heimlich, Henry Jay, Dr.	Science	20		45	40	Created Heimlich Maneuver
Heine, Heinrich 1797-1856	Author	570	4000	6500		Ger. Poet, Critic, Essayist
Heinlein, Robert A.	Author	50	165	350		Sci-Fi Fiction
Heinrich, Albert H.	Aviation	35		120		
Heintzelman, Samuel P.(War Date)	Civil War	45	130	195		Union Gen.
Heintzelman, Samuel P.1805-80	Civil War	35	95	153		Union General
Heinz, Henry John	Business	110		800	350	A Founder H.J. Heinz Co.
Heinz, Henry John II						
Heinz, Henry John II	Business	35				Food Manufacturer
Heinz, Henry John III 1938-92	Congress		30		25	Sen. PA. Air Crash Victim
Heinz, John	Senate	10			22	Senator PA
Heinze, Karl	Astronaut	35			75	
Heise, Karl G.	Astronaut	10			20	
Heisenberg, Werner, Dr.	Science	50	225	650		Nobel Physics,ALS/Cont. $950
Helbig, Joachim	Aviation	10	20	35	25	
Held, Anna	Entertainment	65	80	135	85	Mrs. Florenz Ziegfield
Held, John, Jr.* 1889-1958	Cartoonist	165			500	Illustrator Created The Flapper
Heldmann, Aloys	Aviation		70			Ger. WW I Ace
Heldy, Fanny	Entertainment	40			110	Opera
Helena, Princess	Royalty	10	20	50	30	Third Daughter Queen Victoria
Helgenberger, Marg	Entertainment	15			35	Pin-Up SP $50
Heller, John R., Dr.	Science	12	20		15	
Heller, Joseph	Author	15	30	45	15	Catch 22
Heller, Walter E.	Business	5	15		15	Fndr.,Chm. Walter E. Heller
Heller, Walter W.	Cabinet	5	15	30	15	
Helletsgruber, Luise	Entertainment	25			75	Opera
Hellinger, Mark	Author	35	105	225	40	Columnist, Playwright
Hellman, Lillian 1905-84	Author	40	145		100	Am. Dramatist, Little Foxes
Hellyer, Paul T.	Celebrity	15	30			
Helm, Ben Hardin	Civil War	195	250			CSA General
Helm, Fay	Entertainment	15			50	Actress
Helmholtz, Hermann L.von 1821-94	Science			600		Ger. Physicist Biologist
Helmond, Katherine	Entertainment	8	6	15	20	
Helms, Jesse	Congress	5	15		15	Senator NC

NAME	CATEGORY	SIG	LS/DS	ALS	SP	Comment
Helms, Richard	Celebrity	5	15	45	20	
Helmsley, Leona	Business	10			35	Hotel Magnate
Heloise	Author	4			10	Columnist.
Helps, Arthur, Sir 1817-75	Author	10	15	40		Historian Re America
Helton, Percy	Entertainment	20			65	
Hemingway, Ernest 1899-1961	Author	988	3661	4350	2490	Nobel Lit. Pulitzer. Rosen Caric. $2500
Hemingway, Margaux	Entertainment	40			80	Daughter E. Hemingway
Hemingway, Mariel	Entertainment	10			50	Actress-Daughter E. Hemingway
Hemingway, Mary	Author	20	45	80		Mrs. Ernest Hemingway
Hempel, Frieda	Entertainment	20			70	Ger. Soprano, Opera
Hemphill, John 1803-1862	Congress	20				Sen. TX. Chief Justice Repub. TX.
Hemsley, Sherman	Entertainment	6	8	15	20	
Hemstridge, Natasha	Entertainment	20			80	Br. Actress
Hench, Philip S.	Science	20	45	90	25	Nobel Medicine
Henderson, Archibald	Military	65	195			Marine General War 1812
Henderson, Fletcher	Entertainment	16			35	Bandleader
Henderson, Florence	Entertainment	3	3	10	10	
Henderson, J. Pinckney	Statesman	390	525			Gen. TX Army, Gov. Texas
Henderson, Marcia	Entertainment	5			20	
Henderson, Skitch	Composer	16			35	Conductor, Bandleader
Hendon, Bill	Senate/Congress	3	5		5	Congressman NC
Hendricks, Barbara	Entertainment	10			30	Opera
Hendricks, Thos.A. (V)1819-85	Vice President	50	200	200	75	Cleveland VP, U.S. Sen. IN
Hendrix, Jimi 19942-1970	Entertainment	930	2950			
Hendrix, Wanda	Entertainment	10	15		35	
Hendry, Gloria	Entertainment	5			9	Afr.-Am. Actress
Heney, Hugh	Explorer	325	750			Scout for Lewis & Clark
Henie, Sonja	Entertainment	50	60		167	Gold in Olympic Figure Skating
Henize, Charles G.	Astronaut	10	15		15	
Henley, Don	Entertainment	15			35	Composer, Singer The Eagles
Henley, Thos. Jeff. 1810-65	Congress	10				Repr. IN, San Francisco Postmaster
Henner, Marilu	Entertainment	6	8	15	25	Pin-Up SP $60
Henreid, Paul	Entertainment	20			95	Film Leading Man/Dir.
Henri, Robert	Artist	80	175	215		Portr. Painter, Ashcan School
Henricks, Terence T.	Astronaut	5			15	
Henry II	Royalty	295	1050	2460		France
Henry III	Royalty	250	675	1325		France
Henry IV (Fr) 1553-1610	Royalty	180	738	2900		And Navarre. Assassinated
Henry IV (Sp)	Royalty		1750			King of CastileThe Impotent
Henry V (Fr)	Royalty	40	65	150		Pretender to Throne
Henry VI	Royalty	195	525	1350		England
Henry VII (Eng)	Royalty	875	7200	10000		
Henry VIII 1491-1547	Royalty	2150	12000	17500		
Henry, Bill	Aviation	10	25	40	30	ACE, WW II, Navy Ace
Henry, Bill	Entertainment	15	15	35	30	
Henry, Buck	Entertainment	6	6	10	12	
Henry, Gloria	Entertainment	5	7	10	15	
Henry, John 1750-1798	Revolutionary War	35	135	220		Continental Congress. Sen. MD
Henry, Joseph 1797-1878	Science	55	205	238		1st Electric Motor. 1st Dir. Smithsonian
Henry, Mike	Entertainment	10			35	
Henry, O.	Author					SEE W.S. Porter
Henry, Patrick 1736-99	Revolutionary War	1100	2606	3400		Rev. War ALS $7,800,LS $4500
Henschel, George, Sir	Composer	70			150	Br. Conductor, Singer
Henshaw, David	Cabinet	20	60	105		Tyler Sec'y Navy
Henson, Jim 1936-90	Entertainment	75	150	175	281	Created the Muppets
Henson, Matthew A.	Explorer	130	350			Afro-Am. Arctic Explorer

NAME	CATEGORY	SIG	LS/DS	ALS	SP	Comment
Henstridge, Natasha	Entertainment	10			40	Actress Pin-Up $80
Henze, Hans Werner	Composer	45			165	Ger. Opera, Theater Works
Henze, Karl	Aviation	16	37	71	45	
Hepburn, Audrey 1929-93	Entertainment	98	325	485	389	AA Belg.Born Actress-Humanitarian
Hepburn, Katharine 1907-	Entertainment	133	246	515	775	AA. 3x5 SP $650
Hepworth, Barbara, Dame	Artist	70	190		125	Br. Sculptor.Reclining Figure
Herbeck, Ray	Entertainment	5			15	Big Band Leader-Sax
Herbert, F. Hugh	Author	12	20	30	20	Am. Playwright, Producer
Herbert, Frank	Author	15	20	35	20	Am. Sci-Fi. Dune Trilogy
Herbert, Geo.E. (Carnarvon)	Archaeology	20	45	90		With Carter, King Tut Tomb
Herbert, Hilary A.	Cabinet	10	20	35	20	Cleveland Sec'y Navy
Herbert, Hugh	Entertainment	30	45	70	75	
Herbert, P.O.	Civil War	100		375		CSA General
Herbert, Sidney	Entertainment	15	25	30	25	
Herbert, Victor 1859-1924	Composer	95	198	420	348	AMusQS $275-$475
Herford,Oliver	Cartoonist	10	25			
Hergesheimer, Joseph	Author	25	65	145	30	Am. Psychological Novels
Herget, Wilhelm	Aviation	20		50		
Hering, Constantine	Science	15	25	50		1st Homeopathic School
Herkimer, Nicholas	Revolutionary War		3700			General of Militia.
Herkomer, Hubert von, Sir	Artist	20	85	130		Br. Portrait Painter
Herman, Jerry	Composer	15	40	65	30	AMusQS $85 Hello Dolly
Herman, Pee Wee	Entertainment	12	15		30	
Herman, Woody	Entertainment	20	90		65	Big Band Leader-Clarinetist
Hermann, Bernard 1911-75	Composer		567			Music for Movies,Radio.Conductor CBS
Hermann, Hajo	Aviation	25	50		60	
Herndon, William	Legal	160	450	925		Law Partner of Abraham Lincoln
Herne, James A.	Entertainment	15	15	30	28	Actor-Manager
Herres, Bob	Astronaut	5			16	
Herrick, Myron T.	Diplomat	30	135			Ambassador, Gov. OH
Herriman, George*	Cartoonist	50			600	Krazy Kat
Herring, Clyde L. 1879-1945	Congress	7			10	Senator IA
Herring, John F. 1795-1865	Artist	60		275		Br.Race Horses & Sporting Events
Herring, Thomas 1693-1757	Clergy		25	40		Archbishop York & Canterbury
Herriot, Edouard 1872-1957	Head of State	25	80	175		Premier of Fr., Nazi Prisoner
Herriot, James (Wight)	Author-Vet.	18	40	75	25	All Creatures Great & Small
Herrmann, Adelaide & Alexander	Magic	50			75	Magicians
Herrmann, Bernard	Composer		875			Film Composer
Herron, Francis J.	Civil War	45	80	125		Union Gen.
Herschbach, Dudley, Dr.	Science	25	35		40	Nobel Chemistry
Herschel, John Fred. Wm., Sir	Science	82	170	275	1265	Br. Astronomer, Mathematician
Herschel, William, Sir	Science	150	475	675		Br.Astronomer,Discovered Uranus
Hersey, John 1914-93	Author	20	75	125	25	Bell for Adano Pulitzer
Hershey, Alfred D., Dr.	Science	20	30	45	30	Nobel Medicine
Hershey, Barbara	Entertainment	20			35	
Hershey, Lewis B.	Military	15			25	Gen., Selective Service Adm.
Hersholt, Jean 1886-1956	Entertainment	20		95	65	Major Star & Humanitarian
Herter, Christian	Cabinet	15	25		25	Sec'y State
Hertz, Alfred	Entertainment	25			120	Conductor
Hervey, Irene	Entertainment	15			35	
Herzberg, Gerhard, Dr.	Science	25	65		30	Nobel Chemistry
Herzl, Theodor 1860-1904	Zionist	150	900	4500	250	Important DS $8,000
Herzner, Hans-Albrecht 1907-42	Military	700				1st Ger. Engaged in Combat WW II
Herzog, Chaim	Head of State	30	65	175	60	Pres. Israel
Hesburgh, Theodore M., Rev.	Clergy	15	30	75	25	Longtime Pres, Notre Dame
Hess, Myra, Dame 1890-1965	Entertainment	20	40	65	35	Br. Pianist

NAME	CATEGORY	SIG	LS/DS	ALS	SP	Comment
Hess, Rudolf	Military-Politici	155	450	815	750	Nazi WW II. Second to Hitler
Hess, Victor F.	Science	20	30	55	25	Nobel Physics
Hess, Walter R.	Science	20	30	50	25	Nobel Medicine
Hesse, Hermann 1877-1962	Author	90	565	550	388	Ger. Author, Artist, Poet. Nobel
Hesseman, Howard	Entertainment	5	6	15	15	
Heston, Charlton	Entertainment	10			39	
Heth, Henry (War Date)	Civil War	300	3000	3500		CSA Gen.
Heth, Henry 1825-99	Civil War	138	466	625		CSA General
Hewes, Joseph 1730-1780	Revolutionary War	2500	7250	8500		Signer Decl. of Indepen.
Hewes,Joseph & John Penn	Revolutionary War		25000			Signers Decl. of Indepen.
Hewett, Charlston	Entertainment	4			10	
Hewish, Anthony	Science	20	40	85	30	Nobel Physics. Pulsars
Hewitt, Abram S.	Business	35	60	85		Iron Manufacturing/Peter Cooper
Hewitt, H.K.	Military	20	50	85		
Hewlett, William R.	Business	25	70	145	30	Hewlett-Packard
Hexum, Jon-Erik	Entertainment	60			125	
Heydrich, Reinhard	Military	200	2500	1350	600	Specialist in Nazi Terror
Heydt, Louis Jean	Entertainment	35			80	
Heyerdahl, Thor	Explorer	30	50	95	35	Nor. Ethnologist, Adventurer
Heyman, Edward	Entertainment	3	3	6	6	
Heyman, Edward 'Eddie'	Author	5	10	25	10	
Heyse, Paul	Author	45	135	350		Ger. Novelist, Nobel Literature
Heyward, Dorothy	Author	55	325			Co-writer of Porgy
Heyward, DuBose	Author	120	400			Porgy....LS/Cont. $2,250
Heyward, Thomas Jr.1746-1809	Revolutionary War	475	1125	1400		Signer Decl. of Indepen.
Heywood, Anne	Entertainment	10			20	Br. Actress
Heywood, Eddie	Entertainment	35			100	Big Band Leader-Piano
Hichens, Robert S.	Author	15	40	150		Br. Novelist.Garden of Allah
Hickel, Walter J.	Cabinet	10	15	30	15	Governor Alaska, Sec'y Interior
Hickenlooper, Andrew	Civil War	30	55	80		Union Gen., Military Engineer
Hickenlooper, Bourke B.1896-1971	Senate	10	15		15	Governor, Senator IA
Hickman, Darryl	Entertainment	5			15	
Hickman, Dwayne	Entertainment	5			15	
Hickman, Ron	Inventor	20	50			Black & Decker Workmate
Hicks, Catherine	Entertainment	8		25	20	
Hicks, Frederick Cocks	Senate/Congress	10	15			MOC NY
Hidalgo, Miguel y Costilla	Clergy	1525				Mexican Revolutionary & Priest
Hieb, Richard	Astronaut	4			12	
Higgins, Andrew Jackson	Business	25		50		Bldr.WW II Higgins Landing Boat
Higgins, Charles	Science	15	35			
Higginson, Henry L.	Business	10	20	35		
Higginson, Thos. W. 1823-1911	Civil War-Clergy	95	575	206		Antislavery Writer, Military CW
High Eagle	Old West				1650	Sioux Indian. Survived Battle of Little Big Horn
Hildebrand, Samuel	Civil War		1750			Quantrill Raider-Murderer
Hildegarde	Entertainment	5	6	18	10	Singer, Pianist, Entertainer
Hill, Ambrose P. (War Date)	Civil War	2950	7500	11725		CSA Gen. KIA
Hill, Ambrose Powell 1825-65	Civil War	2000	3850		1350	CSA General KIA
Hill, Annie	Entertainment	6	8	15	10	
Hill, Archibald V.	Science	25	45		35	Nobel Medicine 1922
Hill, Arthur	Entertainment	5	6	15	15	
Hill, Benjamin H. 1823-82	Civil War-Senate	62	165	230		Signed CSA Constitution & GA Secession
Hill, Benjamin J. 1825-80	Civil War	110	192	335		CSA Gen.
Hill, Benny	Entertainment	25			30	
Hill, Dana	Entertainment	6	8	15	15	
Hill, Daniel H. (War Date)	Civil War	600		1865		CSA General
Hill, Daniel Harvey 1821-89	Civil War	320	500	617		CSA General

NAME	CATEGORY	SIG	LS/DS	ALS	SP	Comment
Hill, David B.	Senate	10	15			Governor NY, Senator
Hill, David Lee Tex	Aviation	12	30	42	35	ACE, WW II, Flying Tigers
Hill, Edwin C.	Commentator	10	20		15	Radio Commentator
Hill, Faith	Entertainment	10			50	C & W Singer
Hill, Frank*	Cartoonist				50	
Hill, George Roy	Entertainment	5			25	AA
Hill, George Washington	Business	80	220			American Tobacco Co.,Pres.
Hill, Grace Livingston	Author	25	40	75		Am. Novelist
Hill, Isaac 1789-1851	Senate/Congress	20	35	60		Governor, Senator NY
Hill, James J.	Business		225		950	Raild. Exec., Financier
Hill, John F.	Governor	5	15			Governor ME
Hill, Jonathan A. 1831-1905	Civil War		30			Union Gen.
Hill, Napoleon	Author	75	300			Think & Grow Rich.How to Succeed Books
Hill, Rowland 1744-1833	Clergy	50	75	175		
Hill, Rowland, 1st Viscount	Military	35	80	170		Cmdr. in Chief. England
Hill, Rowland, Sir	Inventor	145	340	785		Originator of Penny Postage
Hill, Teresa	Entertainment	5			40	Actress. Models, Inc.
Hill, Thomas 1818-91	Clergy-Educator	15	20	50		Pres. Harvard, Antioch
Hill, Tiny	Entertainment	6	8	15	15	
Hill, Walter	Entertainment	5			20	Film Director
Hill, William	Entertainment	3	3	6	6	
Hill, Wm. J. Billy	Composer	30				Last Roundup, Wagon Wheels
Hillary, Edmund, Sir b. 1919	Mountaineer	70	150	285	133	1st To Climb Mr. Everest
Hillegas, Michael	Revolutionary War	225	645			U.S. Treasurer 1777
Hillegess, C.K. Cliff	Author	10			20	Cliff's Notes Study Helps
Hiller, Arthur	Entertainment	5			15	Film Director
Hiller, Ferdinand	Composer	40	85	125		Conductor, Pianist
Hiller, Frank, Jr.	Aviation	75	150	330	160	
Hiller, Wendy	Entertainment	15		35	25	AA
Hillerman, John	Entertainment	9	10	20	25	
Hilles, Charles D.	Political	8	25			Chairman G.O.P. 1924
Hilliard, Harriet	Entertainment	20			35	
Hilliard, Henry W.	Civil War	35	80	105		Conf. Commissioner to TN
Hilliard, Robert	Entertainment	20			40	
Hillig, Otto	Aviation	40	85	150	115	
Hillis, Marjorie	Author	5	10	15		
Hills, Carla A.	Cabinet	7	20	35	15	Sec'y HUD
Hilmers, David C.	Astronaut	5			20	
Hilton, Barron	Business	10	15	25	15	
Hilton, Conrad	Business	60	90	190	110	Fndr. Hilton Hotel Dynasty
Hilton, James, Sir	Author	35	120	205	35	Lost Horizon
Himmler, Heinrich 1900-45	Military	250	750	1500	775	Nazi Head of the Gestapo
Hinchingbrooke, Alex	Celebrity	10	20	45	15	
Hinckley, John, Jr.	Assassin	35	150	200		Attempt on Pres. Reagan
Hincks, Edward W.	Civil War	50	185			Union General
Hindemith, Paul	Composer	100	295	425		Ger. Teacher, Theorist, Critic
Hindenburg, Paul von 1847-1934	Head of State	160	380	400	575	2nd Pres. Weimar Rep. of Ger.
Hindman, Thomas C. (War Date)	Civil War	475	385	1017		CSA General
Hindman, Thomas C. 1818-68	Civil War	320				CSA Gen.
Hines, Duncan	Business	65	225		80	Duncan Hines Cake-Cookie Mix
Hines, Earl K. Fatha	Entertainment	125			250	Pianist, Composer, Bandleader
Hines, Gregory	Entertainment	9	10	25	30	
Hines, Herm	Entertainment	10			25	Jazz Sax
Hines, Jerome	Entertainment	20			40	Opera, Concert. Basso
Hines, John E.	Clergy	10	15	15		
Hines, Mimi	Entertainment	5			10	Singer, Comedienne

NAME	CATEGORY	SIG	LS/DS	ALS	SP	Comment
Hingle, Pat	Entertainment	5	6	15	15	
Hinks, Edward W. 1830-94	Civil War			75		Union Gen.
Hinshelwood, Cyril Norman, Sir	Science	20	45		35	Nobel Chemistry
Hinton, Walter	Aviation	40	85	130	90	Pilot of NC-4. MOH
Hippel, Hans Joachim von	Aviation	10			35	WW I & II Fighter Pilot. Stunt Flyer
Hirohito	Head of State	2000	8000		12000	
Hirsch, Judd	Entertainment	5	6	15	15	
Hirschfeld, Al	Caricaturist	35			250	Repro S $90-$250
Hirshfield, Harry	Cartoonist	10			125	Abie The Agent
Hirshhorn, Joseph H. 1899-1981	Financier		150	220		Art Collector. Donated 4000 works of art
Hirt, Al	Entertainment	10			25	Trumpet
Hiss, Alger 1904-	Diplomat	40	65	222		Figure in Sensational Spy Case
Hitchcock, Alfred 1899-1980	Entertainment	238	525	575	532	Self-Caricature S $450-$750
Hitchcock, Ethan Allen (War Date)	Civil War	50	150	200		Union Gen., Also Author
Hitchcock, Frank H.	Cabinet	15	30	35	30	Sec'y Interior 1898
Hitchcock, Gilbert M. 1859-1934	Congress	10	20		15	Governor NE
Hitchcock, Raymond	Entertainment	20			35	
Hitchcock, Thomas 1900-44	Aviation	120				Lafayette Escadrille.Greatest US Polo Player
Hitchings, George, Dr.	Science	20	30	70	30	Nobel Medicine
Hite, June	Research	5	15	25		Hite Research
Hite, Les	Entertainment	75			275	Saxophone. Hold Tight
Hitler, Adolf 1889-1945	Head of State	1500	2499	17000	2070	Special DS $9,500-$18,500
Hittorff, Jacques 1792-1867	Architect	5	20	30		Fr.
Hitz, John	Celebrity	10	35	90		
Hitzfeld, Otto Maximilian	Military	20			50	Ger. Infantry General
Hix, John	Cartoonist	15	50			Author Strange As It Seems
Ho Chi Minh	Head of State	600	1225	2000	2600	Vietnam
Ho, Don	Entertainment	5	6	10	12	Singer
Hoag, R. C., Major	Astronaut	5			15	
Hoagland, Everett	Entertainment	20			57	Jazz Clarinetist. Bandleaer
Hoar, Ebenezer R.	Cabinet	25		35		U.S. Att'y Gen 1869, Grant
Hoar, George F. 1826-1904	Senate	10		15		MOC, Senator MA 1877
Hoban, James 1762	Revolutionary War	255	675			Architect White House, Wash.D.C
Hobart, Garret A. (V)1844-99	Vice President	65	200	310	200	
Hobart, John Sloss 1738-1805	Senate/Congress	25	40	70		Delegate & Senator NY
Hobart, Rose	Entertainment	10			25	
Hobbes, Halliwell	Entertainment	25			45	Vint. Brit. Character Actor
Hobby, Oveta Culp	Cabinet	16	25	40	30	1st Sec'y HEW
Hobson, Richard P. 1870-1937	Military-Author	95	250			MOH Sp.-AM. War
Hobson, Richmond P.	Military	75	260	385	150	Adm.CMH. Blew up USS Merrimac
Hobson, Valerie	Entertainment	25			60	Br. Vintage Film Star
Hoche, Lazare	Fr. Revolution	205	515			General French Republic
Hock, Robt C.	Astronaut	5			15	Skylab
Hockney, David	Artist	60		75		
Hodes, Art	Entertainment	10			25	Pianist-Bandleader
Hodes, H. I.	Military	5	15	25		
Hodge, Al	Entertainment	25			200	
Hodges, Courtney 1887-	Military	15	150		25	Gen. WW II. Cmmdr. 10th, 3rd, & 1st Armies
Hodges, George H.	Governor	12				Kansas 1913-15
Hodgkin, Dorothy C.	Science	25		35		Nobel Chemistry
Hodgson, John	Clergy	20	25	35		
Hodiak, John	Entertainment	20	25	45	45	
Hoe, Richard	Business	30	55	95		Improved Hoe Rotary & Art Press
Hoe, Richard M.	Industrialist	90	310	532		Invented Rotary Press
Hoegh, Leo A.	Governor	5			12	Governor IA
Hoest, Bill	Cartoonist	10		35	40	The Lockhorns

The Sanders Price Guide to Autographs

NAME	CATEGORY	SIG	LS/DS	ALS	SP	Comment
Hoey, Clyde R.	MOC-Sen.-Gov.	10	25		15	MOC, Senator, Governor NC
Hoey, Dennis	Entertainment	75			200	
Hofer, Andreas	Military		3000			Tyrolean Patriot,executed
Hoff, Philip H.	Governor	5	15			Governor VT
Hoffa, James R.	Labor Leader	275	310		400	Teamsters Union (disappeared)
Hoffa, Portland	Entertainment	20				Comedienne, Mrs. Fred Allen
Hoffer, Eric	Celebrity	5	10	25	10	Self Made Philosopher
Hoffgen, Marga	Entertainment	10			35	
Hoffman, Dustin	Entertainment	20	25	30	35	Oscar winner
Hoffman, Harold Giles	Governor	12	30			Governor NJ
Hoffman, Jeffrey A.	Astronaut	5			15	
Hoffman, John Thompson	Governor	10	20	35		Governor NY 1868
Hoffman, Kurt-Caesar	Military	25			65	
Hoffman, Maud	Entertainment	3	5		8	
Hoffman, Paul G.	Business	10	20	35	20	Auto Mfg.-Studebaker Cars
Hoffmann, Oswald C.J.	Clergy	10	20	25		
Hoffmann, Peter	Entertainment	15			55	Opera
Hoffmann, Roald, Dr.	Science	20	30	45	25	Nobel Chemistry
Hofmann, Josef 1876-1957	Entertainment	40	100	140	168	Pianist, Composer. AmusQS $70-200
Hofstadter, Robert	Science	20	30	45	25	Nobel Physics
Hogan, Hulk	Entertainment	5			10	Wrestler
Hogan, Paul	Entertainment	10	15	20	25	Dundee
Hogarth, Burne*	Cartoonist	25			250	Tarzan-2nd Artist
Hogarth, Wm. 1697-1764	Artist	450	1665	3500		Br. Painter-Engraver.
Hogeback, Hermann	Aviation	10			40	Ger. Bomber Pilot. RK
Hoiris, Holger	Aviation	40	85	155	95	
Hoke, Robert Frederick 1837-1912	Civil War	100		368		CSA Gen. ALS '62 $625
Hokinson, Helen	Cartoonist	20			100	Mag. Cartoonist-the Ladies
Holbrook, Hal	Entertainment	6	8	15	15	
Holden, Fay	Entertainment	20			50	
Holden, Joyce	Entertainment	10			25	Singer-Dancer/Donald O'Connor
Holden, William 1918-81	Entertainment	40	90		162	
Hole, Jonathan	Entertainment	3	3	6	6	
Holiday, Billie 1915-59	Entertainment	448	925		1800	Legendary Jazz Singer
Holladay, Ben	Business	135	475	925		Indian Trade, Army Contracts
Holland, Edmund M.	Entertainment	15			45	Vintage Stage Actor
Holland, John Philip	Inventor	70	160	325		1st Sub/Internal Combustion Eng
Holland, Josiah Gilbert 1819-81	Author	15	90	75		AKA Timothy Titcomb.Co-founder Scribner's
Holland, Spessard L.1892-1971	Congress	10	20			Governor, Senator FL
Hollen, Andrea Lee	Military	10	20	35	15	
Holley, Marietta 1836-1926	Author	10	15	35		Am. Humorist
Holley, Robert, Dr.	Science	15	20	35	20	Nobel Chemistry
Holliday, Fredeerick W.M. 1828-99	Civil War			70		CSA Officer, Congress, Gov. VA
Holliday, Judy	Entertainment	125			325	
Holliday, Polly	Entertainment	5	6	15	15	
Holliman, Earl	Entertainment	5	8	10	15	
Holliman, John	TV News	5			15	TV News Commentator
Hollings, Ernest 'Fritz'	Senate	10			15	Senator SC
Hollins, Geo. Nichols 1799-1878	Civil War	275	463			Commodore CSA Navy
Holloway, Stanley	Entertainment	20			60	
Holloway, Sterling	Entertainment	25			50	
Hollowell, George	Aviation	10	22	38	30	ACE, WW II, Marine Ace
Holly, Buddy 1936-1959	Entertainment	892	912	3250	2800	Rock Singer-Songwriter
Holly, Lauren	Entertainment	11			35	Actress. Col. Pin-up 55
Hollywood Wives (Cast of)	Entertainment				65	Signed by 6
Holm, Celeste	Entertainment	5	6	15	15	

NAME	CATEGORY	SIG	LS/DS	ALS	SP	Comment
Holm, Eleanor	Entertainment	10			30	
Holman, Bill	Cartoonist		45			Smokey Stover
Holman, Libby	Entertainment	10	35		95	Vintage Torch Singer.TLS/Cont.$150
Holman, William Steele	Senate/Congress	12	20	30		MOC IN 1859
Holmes, Augusta 1847-1903	Composer	10		85		Ir./Fr. Conventional Fr. Romantic Music
Holmes, Burton 1870-1958	Author	12	20	45	25	In 1894 OriginatedTravelogues
Holmes, Christopher	Astronaut	15	25		25	
Holmes, D. Brainerd	Celebrity	10			25	
Holmes, Herbie	Bandleader	12				
Holmes, John Haynes	Clergy	15	20	30		
Holmes, Oliver W., Jr. (SC)1841-1935	Supreme Court	260	310	1592	638	
Holmes, Oliver W., Sr. 1809-94	Author-Physician	70	205	419		HOF, ALS/Content $1,800
Holmes, Robert D.	Governor	5	10		5	Governor OR
Holmes, Theophilus H.1804-80	Civil War	205	245			CSA Gen. ALS '62 $1100
Holmquest, Donald L.	Astronaut	10	15		20	
Holshouser, James E.	Governor	5		20	15	Governor NC
Holst, Gustav	Composer	35	105	300		AMusQS $275-$625
Holstrom, E.W. 'Brick'	Military	15	35	70	25	
Holt, Jack	Entertainment	40	60	100	100	
Holt, Jennifer	Entertainment	5			10	
Holt, Joseph (War Date)	Civil War	75		405		Union Gen.
Holt, Joseph 1807-94	Cabinet-Civil War	65	180	262		Lincoln Judge Adv.
Holt, Rush D.	Senate/Congress	5	10			Senator WV 1935
Holt, Tim	Entertainment	45			120	
Holt, Victoria	Author	4		15	12	
Holten, Samue 1738-1816	Revolutionary War	85	195			Patriot, Statesman, Activist. Cont'l Congr.
Holton, Linwood	Governor	7			15	Governor VA
Holyoake, Keith, Sir	Head of State	45	95	125	50	NZ Prime Minister, Gov. General
Holzer,Helmut	Science	20			40	Rocket Pioneer/von Braun
Home, A. Douglas-	Head of State	45	70	150	135	Br. Prime Minister
Homer, Louise	Entertainment	20			98	Opera. Am Mezzo
Homer, Winslow 1836-1910	Artist	362	480	1100		Remarkable Seascapes, Landscapes
Homesteaders, The	Country Music	25			50	
Homma, Masaharu	Military	75	205	340	180	Jap.Gen.Invasion of Philippines
Homolka, Oscar	Entertainment	25	30	50	55	
Honda, Soichiro 1904-94	Business					Founder Honda Motor
Honnegger,Arthur	Composer	45	130	290	50	AMusQS $575
Hood, Alexander Sir 1758-1798	Military	55	135	245		Accompanied Capt. Cook
Hood, Arthur Wm. 1805-77	Military	20				Admiral, 1st Baron
Hood, Darla	Entertainment				375	Child Actress Our Gang Series
Hood, John Bell (War Date)	Civil War	803	1870	1575	1000	CSA Gen. ALS '62 $18150
Hood, Samuel, Sir 1762-1814	Military	35	80	135		Br. Adm. with Lord Nelson
Hood, Sir Arthur W.	Military	20				1st Baron, Admiral
Hood, T. 'Tom' (Younger)	Author	15	30	70		
Hood, Thomas (Elder)1799-1845	Author	40	140	275		Br. Humorist, Poet
Hooft, W.A. Vlsser't	Clergy	15	20	25	20	
Hook, James Clarke	Artist	25		85		Brit. Royal Academy
Hooker, John Lee	Entertainment	30			88	Jazz Musician. Blues Legend
Hooker, Joseph (War Date)	Civil War	265	602	1005		Union Gen. ALS $4500
Hooker, Joseph M. 1814-79	Civil War	183	472	616		Union Gen. ALS/Content $4,500
Hooker, Richard	Author	36			60	creator of M*A*S*H
Hooks, Benjamin L.	NAACP	5	15	25	10	NAACP Exec. Director
Hooks, Kevin	Entertainment	10			20	Afr.-Am. Actor
Hooper, Dennis	Entertainment	20			50	
Hooper, William 1742-90	Revolutionary War	450	5000	6500		Signer Decl. of Indepen. ADS 3,000
Hooper, William Henry	Congress	10	15	35	30	Repr.UT 1859

NAME	CATEGORY	SIG	LS/DS	ALS	SP	Comment
Hoosier Hot Shots	Entertainment					G Ward,Hezzie,K Trietsle,F Kettering
Hoosier Hotshots	Entertainment				50	C & W Group. All 4
Hooten, Ernest A.	Science	25	65	140		Am. Anthropologist.Harvard Prof
Hoover, Herbert & Entire Cabinet	President	225				
Hoover, Herbert (As Pres)	President	331	500	3000	438	Historic TLS/Content $7,500
Hoover, Herbert 1874-1964	President	110	481	2620	325	Cont.TLS $2,500. WH Card S $450
Hoover, J. Edgar 1895-1972	Criminologist	45	208	220	172	Director of F.B.I. for 48 Years
Hoover, Lou Henry	First Lady	50	50	245	425	WH Card S $95-150
Hope, Bob	Entertainment	10		50	61	
Hopekirk, Helen	Author	15				
Hopf, Hans	Entertainment	25			65	Opera
Hopkins, Anthony	Entertainment	20		45	48	
Hopkins, Bo	Entertainment	5	6	10	10	
Hopkins, Claude	Entertainment	30			60	Pianist-Bandleader-Composer
Hopkins, Esek 1718-1802	Military	180	1200			1st Cmdr-In-Chief Continental Navy
Hopkins, Frederick G., Sir	Science	45	120	200		Nobel Medicine 1929
Hopkins, Harry L.(Harry)18900-1946	Cabinet	25	45		40	Sec'y Commerce.Important Aide to FDR
Hopkins, James H. 1832-1904	Congress	10				Repr. PA, Banker
Hopkins, Johns 1795-1873	Business	175	500	3575		Financier, Philanthropist
Hopkins, Mark 1802-87	Educator	40	105	255		Inspired Teacher, Lecturer
Hopkins, Miriam	Entertainment	35	40	75	110	
Hopkins, Samuel 1721-1803	Revolutionary War	90	280	375		Officer Cont'l Army.Theologian
Hopkins, Stephen 1707-85	Revolutionary War	250	683	1125		Signer. Important ALS $6500
Hopkinson, Francis 1737-91	Revolutionary War	250	757	1094		Signer, Author, Composer
Hopkinson, Joseph 1770-1842	Judge-Author	90	200			MOC PA. Hail Columbia
Hopper, Dennis	Entertainment	15			35	
Hopper, DeWolfe 1858-1935	Entertainment	20	40	50	85	ALS/Casey at the Bat quote $395
Hopper, Hedda	Entertainment	15		30	35	
Hordern, Michael, Sir	Entertainment	10	20	35		
Horenstein, Jascha	Entertainment	60			375	Conductor
Horina, Louise	Entertainment	15			45	Opera
Hormel, Jay C.	Business	45	95		60	Chm. George A. Hormel & Co.
Hornberger, H. Richard	Author	20	30	45	25	
Horne, L. Donald	Business	5			10	CEO Mennen Co.
Horne, Lena	Entertainment	10	25		35	Afro-Am Film & Record Vocalist
Horne, Marilyn	Entertainment	15			35	Opera, Concert
Horner, H. Mansfield	Business	5			10	Aircraft Exec.
Horner, Henry	Governor	10			20	Governor IL
Horowitz, David	Celebrity	3	7	16	5	
Horowitz, Vladimir 1903-89	Entertainment	153	150		175	Piano Virtuoso
Horrocks, Gen. Sir Brian	Military	15	25	40	25	Cmdr. XIII Corps WW II
Horsford, Eben N. 1818-74	Science	15	25	70		Am. Analytical Chemist
Horsley, John Calcott	Artist	40				Brit. Royal Academy
Horsley, Lee	Entertainment	6	8	15	19	
Horthy, Miklos, Adm.1868-1957	Head of State	55	190	485	150	Hungarian Admiral & Politician
Horton, Edw. Everett 1886-1970	Entertainment	20	25	35	85	
Horton, Edward A.	Clergy	15	20	25		
Horton, Peter	Entertainment	8	11	40	30	
Horton, Robert	Entertainment	3	3	6	15	
Hosmer, Titus 1736-80	Revolutionary War	35	95	200		Continental Congress. Judge
Hotchkiss, Benjamin J.	Inventor-CW			995		Union Arms Supplier
Hotchkiss, Charles T. 1832-1914	Civil War			85		Union Gen. Atlanta Campaign
Houdini, Harry (E.Weiss)1874-1926	Entertainment	900	1550	1785	2007	Am. Magician, Escape Artist
Hough, Lynn Harold	Clergy	15	20	35		
Houghton, Katharine	Entertainment	27			40	
Hounsfield, Godfrey	Science	20	30	40	25	Nobel Medicine

The Sanders Price Guide to Autographs

NAME	CATEGORY	SIG	LS/DS	ALS	SP	Comment
House, Edw. M.'Colonel'	Diplomat	35	100	310	45	Confidant of Pres. Wilson
Houseman, John	Entertainment	20			55	Actor/Director
Housman, Alfred Edward 1859-1936	Author	65	225	688		Br. Poet, Scholar
Houssay, Bernardo A., Dr.	Science	65	135	250	100	Nobel Medicine 1947. Activist
Houston, David	Country Music	5			10	
Houston, George	Senate	35	85			Civil War Senator AL
Houston, Sam 1793-1863	Military	600	2156	3281		Pres. Repub. TX, Soldier, Statesman
Houston, Temple	Lawyer-Outlaw	375		1667	750	Son of Sam Houston
Houston, V. S. K.	Senate/Congress	10	25	40		MOC HI 1927
Houston, Whitney	Entertainment	35			75	Singer
Houston, William C. 1746-88	Revolutionary War	30		110		Continental Congress, etc.
Hovey, Alvin	Civil War	25	55	70		Union Gen., Gov. IN
Hovhaness, Alan	Composer	70		375		Noted for Orchestral Works
Hovis, Larry	Entertainment	5			15	
How, William Walsham, Bishop	Clergy	15	20	25		
Howard, Curley	Entertainment	400	500	900	1000	
Howard, Edward, Cardinal	Clergy	35	50	75		
Howard, James H.	Aviation	15	30	55	45	ACE, WW II, CMH; Flying Tiger
Howard, John	Entertainment	10	20	40	38	
Howard, Ken	Entertainment	6	8	15	15	
Howard, Leslie 1890-1943	Entertainment	258	200		457	GWTW. WW II in Br. Secret Serv.
Howard, Milford W. 1862-1937	Congress	8				Repr. AL
Howard, Moe 1895-1975	Entertainment	200	290	650	450	Three Stooges Leader
Howard, Oliver Otis (War Date)	Civil War	142		425		Union Gen.
Howard, Oliver Otis 1830-1909	Civil War	109		178	253	300	Union Gen. MOH
Howard, Robert, Sir 1626-98	Author	95	325			Br. Restoration Dramatist/Dryde
Howard, Ron	Entertainment	10		40	35	
Howard, Shemp 1891-1955	Entertainment	595	220	400	595	Rarest of Three Stooges Autogr.
Howard, Sidney	Author	50	175	375	75	Am. Playwright. Pulitzer
Howard, Trevor	Entertainment	10			35	
Howard, Willie	Entertainment	8	9	20	18	
Howe, Albion P. (War Date)	Civil War	35	102	510		Union General
Howe, Elias 1819-67	Science	200	400	3000		Invented Sewing Machine
Howe, James Wong	Entertainment	40			65	Award Winning Cinematographer
Howe, Julia Ward 1819-1910	Author	85	150	344		Battle Hymn AQS $1,475-$3000
Howe, Louis McHenry	Political	5	20			Secretary to FDR
Howe, Richard, Earl 1726-1799	Revolutionary War	100	875	580		Br. Adm.Rev. War.LS/Cont.$1500
Howe, Samuel Gridley	Humanitarian-Mil.	10	35	80		Philanthropist, Doctor, Clergy
Howe, Timothy O. 1816-83	Cabinet	5		25		PMG(Arthur).US Sen. WI
Howe, William, Sir	Revolutionary War	200	850			Cmdr-in-Chief Br. Forces in Am.
Howell, C. Thomas	Entertainment	5		25	20	
Howells, William Dean 1837-1920	Author	30	195	575		Novelist, Critic, Editor
Howes, Barbara	Author	7	10	20	10	
Howland, Beth	Entertainment	5	6	15	15	
Howley, William 1766-1848	Clergy	25	35	40		Archbishop Canterbury
Howlin, Olin	Entertainment	20			40	
Hoxie, Al	Entertainment	35				Actor-Cowboy
Hoxie, Jack	Entertainment	150				Actor-Cowboy
Hoyle, Edmond 1671-1769	Author	130	675	820		Card Games. Established Rules
Hoyt, John W.	Governor	50	85			Gov. WY Terr.,1st Pres. U.WY
Hruska, Roman	Senate & Congress	5	15			MOC, Senator NE
Hubbard, Chester D.1814-91	Congress	10	15			MOC WV
Hubbard, Elbert	Author	50	160	275	145	Roycrofters,Message to Garcia
Hubbard, Gardiner G.	Celebrity	25	55	170		Fndr. Nat'l Geographic Society
Hubbard, L. Ron 1911-886	Author	100	1000			Religious Activist
Hubbard, Richard B.	Governor		150			Gov. TX 1876-79

NAME	CATEGORY	SIG	LS/DS	ALS	SP	Comment
Hubbard, Thomas H. 1838-1915	Civil War	15	35			Union Gen. 30th ME
Hubble, Edwin P.	Science	15	80			Am. Astronomer.
Hubel, David H., Dr.	Science	20	30	45	25	Nobel Medicine
Huber, Oscar, Fr.	Celebrity	20		30		
Hubley, Adam	Revolutionary War	75	300			Officer Cont. Army. Politician
Hubner, Herbert	Entertainment	25			75	Vintage German opera star
Huddleston, George	Senate/Congress	10	20		15	MOC AL 1915-1937
Hudson, Charles 1795-1881	Congress	10				Repr. MA, Author Religious Textbooks
Hudson, George	Financier	10	20	35		Controlled 1,000 Miles Railrd
Hudson, Rochelle	Entertainment	25	30	50	45	
Hudson, Rock 1925-85	Entertainment	25	30	80	138	
Hudson, W.H.	Naturalist-Author		135	495		Green Mansions
Huemer, Dick*	Cartoonist	15			100	Disney Artist
Huerta, Victoriano	Revolutionary	75	250	625	120	Mex. General, Politician.Exiled
Hufstedler, Shirley	Cabinet	5	10	15	10	Sec'y Education
Hug-Messner, Regula	Aviation	15	30	50	35	
Huger, Benjamin (War Date)	Civil War	175	750			CSA Gen.
Huger, Benjamin 1805-77	Civil War	90	275	308		CSA General
Huger, Isaac 1742-97	Revolutionary War	100	215	450		General Continental Army
Huggins, Charles, Dr.	Science	25			35	Nobel Medicine
Huggins, Roy	Entertainment	15			25	TV Producer Fugitive
Huggins, William, Sir	Science	35	100	210	45	Br.Astron. Stellar Spectroscope
Hughes, Carol	Entertainment	12				Actress
Hughes, Charles E. (SC)1862-1948	Supreme Court	40	210		288	Chief Justice, Sec'y of State
Hughes, Chas. E. & Court	Supreme Court				4500	
Hughes, Edwin H., Bishop	Clergy	20	25	40	35	
Hughes, Harold E.1922-	Congress	4			20	Senator IA
Hughes, Howard 1905-76	Business	1500	2500	7250	2617	Aircraft, Oil Tool. RKO. Aviator
Hughes, Hugh Price	Clergy	15	20	25	20	
Hughes, Langston 1902-67	Author	240	398	898	575	Afro-Am.Poet, Short Story Writer
Hughes, Mary Beth	Entertainment	9	10	20	15	
Hughes, Richard	Military-Rev. War	25	60			Br. Adm. during Rev. War
Hughes, Richard J.	Governor	5	15			Governor NJ
Hughes, Rupert	Author	15	50	95		Poet, Author, Historian
Hughes, Sarah T.	Law	10	95	30	15	Fed. Judge Swore In L.B. Johnson 1963
Hughes, Thomas	Author	40		115		Tom Brown's School Days
Hugo, Victor 1802-85	Author	245	375	1050	1222	Novelist-Politician-Poet
Huidekoper, Henry	Civil War	60				Union Col., Bucktails
Hull, Cordell 1871-1955	Cabinet-Statesman	47	135		125	Nobel, Father Fed.Income Tax
Hull, Henry 1890-19??	Entertainment	82	30		95	Veteran Am. Actor
Hull, Isaac 1773-1843	Military	190	570	565		Cmdr. U.S.S. Constitution1812
Hull, J.E.	Military	25				General
Hull, Josphine 1884-1957	Entertainment	150		200	275	
Hull, Warren	Entertainment	25			50	
Hull, William	Military	145	370	770		Revolutionary War Gen.
Hulse, Tom	Entertainment	9	10	20	25	
Humbard, Rex	Clergy	10	15	15	15	
Humboldt, Alexander, Baron von	Science	70	125	338		Ger. Naturalist and Traveller
Hume, Benita	Entertainment	10			25	
Hume, Joseph 1777-1855	Politician	10	30	80		Br.Physician.Radical Politician
Hume, Mary-Margaret	Entertainment	5			12	Pin-Up SP $20
Humes, William Young C.	Civil War	140	235	435		CSA General
Hummel, Johann Nepomuk	Composer	150	190	400		Child Prodigy Piano Virtuoso
Humperdinck, Engelbert	Composer	95	225	375	250	AMusQS $450-$675
Humperdinck, Engelbert	Entertainment	5	7	20	25	Contemporary Vocalist
Humphrey, George M.	Cabinet	10	20			Sec'y Treasury

NAME	CATEGORY	SIG	LS/DS	ALS	SP	Comment
Humphrey, Hubert H. (V)1911-78	Vice President	40	207		40	V.P. & Presidential Cand.
Humphrey, Muriel	Congress	10	20		15	Senator MN
Humphreys, Andrew A.1810-83	Civil War	65	180	224		
Humphreys, David	Revolutionary War	55	150	200		ADC Washington. Poet,Diplomat
Hungerford, Cy	Cartoonist				30	
Hungerford, Orville 1790-1851	Congress	10				Repr. NY, W & R Railroad Pres.
Hunnicutt, Arthur	Entertainment	15			35	
Hunt, E. Howard	Gov't Official	15	25	90	25	21 Yr. Vet./CIA. Watergate
Hunt, Earl, Bishop	Clergy	20	25	35	25	
Hunt, George W. P.	Governor					Governor AZ
Hunt, H. L.	Business	90	485	580	175	TX Oil King. Arch Conservative
Hunt, Helen	Entertainment	20			60	Twister/B.Paxton $130
Hunt, Henry J. 1819-89	Civil War	55	80	135		Union Gen. Artillery Gettysburg
Hunt, Henry Jackson (War Date)	Civil War	68	145			Union Gen. ALS/Cont. $770
Hunt, James B. Jr.	Governor	5	10			Governor NC
Hunt, James Bunker	Business	5	15	35	10	Son of Oil Magnate H.L.Hunt
Hunt, John, Sir	Celebrity	10	20	50		
Hunt, Leigh 1784-1859	Author	30				Br. Essayist, Poet
Hunt, Linda	Entertainment	15			65	AA
Hunt, Marsha	Entertainment	8	9	19	20	
Hunt, Nelson Bunker	Business	8	20	40	15	Son of Oil Magnate H.L.Hunt
Hunt, Pee Wee	Entertainment	15			45	Trombone-Vocalist
Hunt, Ward (SC)	Supreme Court	65	80	175		1872
Hunt, Washington	Governor	30		60		MOC 1842, Governor NY 1850
Hunt, William H.	Cabinet	15	30	60	25	Sec'y Navy 1881
Hunt, William Holman	Artist	55	165	330		Br. Pre-Raphaelite Painter
Hunt, WIlliam Morris	Artist	50	215	500		American Portraitist
Hunter, David 1802-86	Civil War	55	158	178	250	Union General
Hunter, David O. (War Date)	Civil War	85	220	387		Union Gen.
Hunter, Holly	Entertainment	20			55	AA
Hunter, Jeff	Entertainment	25	35	65	60	
Hunter, Kim	Entertainment	5	6	15	15	AA
Hunter, R. M. T. 1809-87	Civil War	95	170	190		CSA Sec'y State. US Sen. ALS '63 $360
Hunter, Rachel	Cover Girl	20			45	Pin-Up SP $100
Hunter, Robert	Revolutionary War	220	508	1035		Br. Gen. Colonial Gov. VA,NY
Hunter, Tab	Entertainment	8	9		35	
Hunter, William 1774-1849	Diplomat	55	80	125		Statesman, Senator RI
Huntington, Agnes	Opera	25			150	Am. & Brit. Productions
Huntington, Benjamin 1736-1800	Revolutionary War	60	175	275		Continental Congress
Huntington, Collis P.	Business	85	400			Pioneer Am. Railroad Builder
Huntington, Daniel	Artist		155	250		Portrait Painter
Huntington, Ebenezer	Revolutionary War	110	250	380		Statesman, Army General
Huntington, Henry E.	Business	65	125	200		Railroad Magnate
Huntington, Jabez W.	Senate/Congress	25	30	45		MOC 1829, Senator CT 1840
Huntington, Jedediah 1743-1818	Military	75	125	230		Gen. Revolutionary War
Huntington, Samuel 1731-96	Revolutionary War	250	869	1225		Signer Decl. of Indepen.
Hunton, Eppa	Civil War	115	285			CSA General
Huppert, Isabelle	Entertainment	15			35	
Hurd, Peter	Artist	85	225	370		
Hurlbut, Stephen A. (War Date)	Civil War	60	128	377		Union Gen., ALS/Cont.$2200
Hurley, Charles F.	Governor	12	25			Governor MA
Hurley, Patrick J. 1883-1963	Cabinet	15	45	60	25	Sec'y War Hoover
Hurrell, George	Photographer					Orig.16x20 Ltd. Ed. Dietrich $1200
Hurst, Fannie 1889-1968	Author	15	45	150	85	Popular, Sentimental Novels
Hurt, John	Entertainment	16	20	25	30	
Hurt, Mary Beth	Entertainment	6	8	15	15	

NAME	CATEGORY	SIG	LS/DS	ALS	SP	Comment
Hurt, William	Entertainment	20	25	50	60	
Hurwitz, Hank, Dr.	Science					Atomic Scientist
Husa, Karel	Composer	15	30	65		Pulitzer, AMusQS $150
Husky, Ferlin	Country Music	5			15	
Hussein, King	Royalty	75	135	385	65	King of Jordan
Hussey, Olivia	Entertainment	5	8	12	15	
Hussey, Ruth	Entertainment	4	6	12	15	
Huston, Anjelica	Entertainment	8			40	AA
Huston, John 1906-87	Entertainment	40	145	50	78	AA Film Director-Actor
Huston, Walter 1884-1950	Entertainment	100		170	200	AA
Hutchence, Michael	Entertainment	20			50	
Hutchins, Will	Entertainment	10	15		15	
Hutchinson, Frederick Sharpe	Civil War	35		130		Union General
Hutchinson, John W.	Composer	15		50		
Hutchinson, Josephine	Entertainment	10	15	25	25	
Hutchinson, Thomas	Colonial	185	450			Royal Gov. MA. Exiled
Hutchison, Pat	(see Roberts, Pat Hutchison)					
Hutton, Betty	Entertainment	8	9		30	Pin-Up SP $20
Hutton, Gunilla	Country Music	5			10	
Hutton, Ina Ray	Entertainment	20			45	All Girl Big Band
Hutton, Jim	Entertainment	40	70	110	100	
Hutton, Lauren	Entertainment	9	10	20	25	Pin-Up SP $25
Hutton, Robert	Entertainment	20	40	110	100	
Hutton, Timothy	Entertainment	12			35	AA
Huxley, Aldous 1894-1963	Author	65	400	392	350	Br. Novellst.TLS/Content $1,200
Huxley, Julian Sorell 1887-1975	Science-Author	30	148	175		Br. Biologist, Educator
Huxley, Thomas Henry 1825-95	Science	55	150	235		Br. Biologist
Hyams, Leila	Entertainment	20	25	50	40	
Hyde, Arthur W.	Cabinet	7	15	30	10	Sec'y Agriculture 1929
Hyde, Edgar R.	Clergy	10	10	15		
Hyde-White, Wilfrid	Entertainment	15	15	35	35	
Hyer, Martha	Entertainment	6	8	15	25	Actress
Hylton, Jack 1892-1965	Entertainment	15			70	Br. Bandleader
Hylton, Lord	Politician	7	15	25		Chief Whip Unionist Party
Hyman, Earle	Entertainment	5			10	Afr.-Am ctor
Hymes, Myriam	Entertainment				20	
Hynde, Chrissie	Entertainment	25			40	Rock
Hyndman, Henry Mayers	Socialist	75		350		Br. Marxist-Socialist

I Remember Mama (Cast of [5])	Entertainment	125			395	50's Popular TV Program
Iacocca, Lee A.	Business	15	50		35	CEO Chrysler Motors
Ian, Janis	Entertainment	10	40		20	
Ibert, Jacques-Francois	Composer	75		325		AMusQS $450

The Sanders Price Guide to Autographs

NAME	CATEGORY	SIG	LS/DS	ALS	SP	Comment
Ibsen, Henrik 1828-1906	Author	205	600	1500	1325	Nor. Poet & Dramatist
Icart, Louis 1888-1950	Artist	115		875		Fr. Art Deco Painter-Illusrator
Ickes, Harold L.	Cabinet	20	35	60	25	Roosevelt Sec'y Interior
Idol, Billy	Entertainment	10			25	Rock
Iglesias, Julio	Entertainment	15			50	
Ihlefedl, Herbert	Aviation	25	55		60	
Ikeda, Hayato	Head of State	15		65		Japan
Iman	Model	25			60	Model
Imboden, John Dan'l (War Date)	Civil War	500	800			CSA Gen. Spec'l ALS $4500
Imboden, John Dan'l 1823-95	Civil War	165	425	230		CSA Gen.
Immelmann, Max	Aviation	200	425	700	500	ACE, WW II, 1st German Ace
Impellitteri, Vincent	Celebrity	3	10	25	5	
Imus, Don	Entertainment	10			20	Obnoxious talk show host
Ince, John	Entertainment	40			125	
Ince, Ralph	Entertainment	40			125	
Ince, Thomas H.	Entertainment	40			125	Film Dir. Civil War Epics
Indiana, Robert	Artist	45	95	170	120	
Ingalls, John James 1833-1900	Congress	10	15			Senator KS
Ingalls, Laura	Aviation		295			Pioneer. 1st Non-Stop Transcontinental Flight
Ingalls, Rufus (War Date)	Civil War	55		526		Union Gen., Explorer
Ingalls, Rufus 1818-93	Civil War	37	75	122		Union General, Explorer
Inge, William	Author	55	120	180		Am. Playwright. Pulitzer
Inge, William R.	Clergy	50	80	150		Dean St. Paul's Cath., Writer
Ingels, Marty	Entertainment	10			35	
Ingersoll, Charles J. 1782-1862	Senate/Congress	15	25	40		MOC PA 1813
Ingersoll, Charles R.	Governor	5	15	25		Governor CT
Ingersoll, Jared 1749-1822	Revolutionary War	75	274	450		Continental Congr.,Constitution Signer
Ingersoll, Robert Green	Civil War	30	60	85	40	Agnostic Lecturer, Orator
Ingersoll, Robert H.	Business	80	175	300	225	Ingersoll $1 Watch
Ingham, Samuel D. 1779-1860	Cabinet	35	120	145		Sec'y Treasury 1829
Ingle, Red	Entertainment	25			80	
Ingle, Robert P.	Business	5	15	25	10	Ingles Grocery Chain
Inglis, James	Business	5	20			Mfg.
Ingraham, Duncan N.(War Date)	Civil War	150		1100		Capt.CSA Navy
Ingram, Rex	Entertainment	100			300	Vintage Afro-Am. Actor
Ingram, Rex	Entertainment	50			125	
Ingres, Jean-Auguste-Dominique	Artist	205		1050		Fr. Leader Among Classicists
Ingrid, Victoria (Fred. IX)	Royalty	15	40			
Ink Spots, The (4)	Entertainment	300			260	Vintage Singing Group
Inman, Henry	Artist	110	305	650		American Portraitist
Inman, Jerry	Country Music	10			20	
Innes, Roy	Activist	7	15		10	Afr.-Am. Activist
Inness, George 1824-94	Artist	75	225	425		Am. PainterCont. ALS $950
Inouye, Daniel K.	Senate	5			15	Senator HI
Inskeep, Jonathan	Revolutionary War	80	175			
Insull, Samuel 1859-1938	Financier	65	95	185		Pvt. Sec'y Edison.TLS/Cont.$685
Ionesco, Eugene	Author	35	125	195		Fr. Dramatist.Theatre of Absurd
Ireland, Jill	Entertainment	25			60	Pin-Up SP $75
Ireland, John	Entertainment	10			35	
Ireland, John M.F	Governor		150			Gov. TX 1883-87
Ireland, Kathy	Cover Girl	10			25	Pin-Up SP $50
Irish, James M.	Military	10	30	50		
Irons, Jeremy	Entertainment	10		25	35	
Irvin, James 1800-62	Congress	8				Repr. PA, Merchant, Miller, Miner
Irvin, James B. 1930—91	Astronaut	60	125	350	205	Deceased Moonwalker
Irvine, James 1735-1819	Revolutionary War	55	130	250		Gen. Militia. Cmdr. Fort Pitt

NAME	CATEGORY	SIG	LS/DS	ALS	SP	Comment
Irvine, William 1741-1804	Revolutionary War	55	570	300		Gen., Continental Congress
Irving, Amy	Entertainment	9	10	20	25	
Irving, Clifford	Author	16	60	124	25	
Irving, Henry, Sir 1838-1905	Entertainment	30	60	90	70	Vintage Actor-Manager
Irving, John	Author	5	15	29	75	Am.The World According to Garp
Irving, Washington 1783-1859	Author	150	385	1060		Rip Van Winkle
Irwin, David	Celebrity	10	20	45	15	
Irwin, James B.Jim 1930-91	Astronaut	15	222	180	130	Moonwalker
Irwin, May	Entertainment	25		35	45	Vintage Stage. 1st Film Kiss
Irwin, Will 1873-1948	Journalist			40		War Correspondent, Author
Isabella I, Of Castile 1451-1504	Royalty	850	3875	6500		Queen Spain.Columbus' Patron
Isabella II 1830-1904	Royalty	175	405	730		Spain. Strife, Intrigue. Abdicated
Isabey, Jean-Baptiste 1767-1855	Artist		115	350		Court Painter to Napoleon & Bourbons
Ish Kabibble (Merwyn Bogue)	Entertainment	15			25	Novelty Singer, Kay Kyser Band
Isherwood, Christopher 1904-86	Author	40	140	225	300	Br. Novelist, Playwright
Ishiguro, Kazuo	Author	15			35	Remains of the Day
Ismay, Hastings Lionel	Military	20	35	60		Churchill Chief-of-Staff WW II
Israels, Jozef	Artist	55	180	350		Dutch. Hague School Genre Art
Ito, Hirobumi (Prince)1841-1909	Statesman	55	140			Japan. Prime Minister 1886
Ito, Lance, Judge	Law	140				O.J. Trial Judge
Ito, Marquis	Statesman	25				Japanese Statesman
Ito, Robert	Entertainment	4			10	Actor
Iturbi, Jose	Entertainment	20			50	Classical Pianist.Jose & Amparo S $30-$95
Iturbide, Augustin de 1783-1824	Revolutionary		875			Self Proclaimed Emperor of Mex.
Ivan IV, The Terrible	Royalty	35000				No Current Price
Iverson, Alfred, Jr. 1829-1911	Civil War	130	300	500		CSA Gen. Sig/Rank $240
Ives, Burl	Entertainment	10	30		40	AA
Ives, Charles E. 1874-1954	Composer	250	1250	2000	425	Tonal Experimentation, Pulitzer
Ivey, Judith	Entertainment	10			35	
Ivins, Marsha S.	Astronaut	5			15	
Ivogun, Maria	Entertainment	45			175	Opera
Izak, Edouard	Military	20	45			WW II CMH

Jabotinsky, Vladimir	Zionist	45	120	310	60	Zionist Leader WW I
Jack, Thomas M. 1831-80	Civil War	45				CSA Col. A.D.C. to A.S. Johnston
Jacks, L.P.	Clergy	15	20	45		
Jackson, Alan	Country Music	20			60	C & W
Jackson, Alfred Eugene	Civil War			950		CSA General
Jackson, Andrew (As President)	President		2220	5300		
Jackson, Andrew & Van Buren, Martin	Presidents		3800			
Jackson, Andrew 1767-1845	President	622	2080	4000		Addr. Leaf/Free Frank $1,375
Jackson, Anne	Entertainment	6	8	15	15	
Jackson, Charles T.1805-80	Science	200				Co-Discoverer of Ether

The Sanders Price Guide to Autographs

NAME	CATEGORY	SIG	LS/DS	ALS	SP	Comment
Jackson, Clairborne F.1807-62	Civil War		175	212		CSA Gen.
Jackson, Eugene Pineapple	Entertainment				15	Our Gang
Jackson, Glenda	Entertainment	15	20	25	30	Oscar winner, Member of Parliament
Jackson, Gordon 19xx-96	Entertainment	15		50	55	Scot.'Hudson' in Upstairs, Downstairs
Jackson, Helen Hunt	Author	12	35	50	25	Am.Novelist, Poet. Ramona
Jackson, Henry M. Scoop	Senate/Congress	5	15			MOC, Senator WA
Jackson, Henry R. 1820-98	Civil War	90	195	353		CSA Gen.
Jackson, Howell E. (SC)	Supreme Court	50			110	U.S. Senator 1881, Supr.Ct.1893
Jackson, James S. (War Date)	Civil War	200				Union Gen. KIA
Jackson, James S.1823-62	Civil War	125		1320		Union Gen. KIA
Jackson, James, Dr.1777-1867	Science	7	220	500	10	1st Am. to Perform Vaccinations
Jackson, Janet	Entertainment	25			70	Rock
Jackson, Jesse	Clergy	20	65	80	35	
Jackson, Joe	Entertainment	20			35	
Jackson, John King 1828-66	Civil War					CSA Gen. AES '61 $685
Jackson, Kate	Entertainment	10	15	25	20	
Jackson, LaToya	Entertainment	20		45	60	Pin-Up SP $150
Jackson, Mahalia	Entertainment	90			175	Gospel Singer
Jackson, Maynard	Entertainment	5	10	20	15	Trumpet
Jackson, Michael	Entertainment		800		320	Legendary Pop Music Mega Star
Jackson, Rachel	First Lady	575				
Jackson, Robert H. (SC)	Supreme Court	50	295		125	Chief Prosecutor at Nuremberg
Jackson, Samuel L.	Entertainment	15			80	Afro-Am Actor
Jackson, Samuel M. 1833-1907	Civil War			600		Union Gen. Wilderness, Spotsylvania
Jackson, T.J. Stonewall 1824-63	Civil War	3012	8860	14762		CSA General
Jackson, T.J. Stonewall(War Date)	Civil War	3975	15000	28125		CSA Gen. ALS $47,375
Jackson, Thomas	Clergy	25		40		
Jackson, Victoria	Entertainment	5			10	
Jackson, Wanda	Country Music	10			20	C & W
Jackson, William 1759-1828	Revolutionary War	120	350	750		Gen. Washington Aide. Diplomat
Jackson, William Henry 1843-1942	Photographer	40	110			Indians, Union Pac. RR Route
Jackson, Wm. Hicks 'Red'	Civil War	90	185	240		CSA General
Jacob, Francois	Science	20	30	55	30	Nobel Medicine 1965
Jacob, John C.	CORE	10	15		15	Afro-Am. Leader CORE
Jacob, John J.	Governor	12	20			Governor WV
Jacobi, Derek	Entertainment	5		12	15	
Jacobi, Lou	Entertainment	5			15	
Jacobs, Andy	Congress	4	15			Indiana
Jacobs, Josef	Aviation	30	40	80	55	
Jacobs, Lou	Entertainment	50	100		100	Clown
Jacobs, William W. 1863-1943	Author	10		50		Br. Monkey's Paw
Jacobsen, Fritz	Aviation	10	20	35	40	Ace WW I
Jacquet, Illinois Jean	Entertainment	30			70	Jazz Sax, Bandleader
Jadlowker, Hermann	Entertainment	95			245	Opera
Jaeckel, Richard	Entertainment	8			20	
Jaeger, James A.	Aviation	10		30		
Jaehnert, Erhard	Aviation	5	10	20	15	
Jaffe, Sam 1893-1984	Entertainment	25			45	Gunga Din
Jagger, Bianca	Entertainment	10			25	
Jagger, Dean	Entertainment	15	25	30	35	AA
Jagger, Mick	Entertainment	50			145	
Jahn, Sigmund	Astronaut	15			35	
Jakes, John	Author	15	50	75	50	Holiday for Havoc
James I & VI (Eng)	Royalty	800	1450	4475		
James II (Eng) 1633-1701	Royalty	530	1812	1700		
James, Daniel, Jr. Chappiel	Military	20	35	85	45	AF Gen. 1st Black 4 Star Gen.

NAME	CATEGORY	SIG	LS/DS	ALS	SP	Comment
James, Etta	Entertainment	20			40	Rock
James, Frank 1844-1915	Outlaw	1038	2100	4100		
James, Harry	Entertainment	20		40	55	Big Band Leader-Trumpet
James, Henry 1811-82	Author	75		200		Theological & Social Scholar
James, Henry 1843-1916	Author	110	360	675		Novelist, ALS/Content $5,500
James, Manley	Military	10		45		WW I Victoria Cross
James, P.D.	Author	20	65			Notable Br. Mystery Writer
James, Sonny	Country Music	10			30	
James, Thomas L.	Cabinet	15	25	45		P.M. General 1881
James, Will	Author	75	250	410	750	Illustrated own Western Novels
James, William 1842-1910	Science	90	350	495	125	Psychologist, Pragmatist,Philosopher
Jan & Dean	Entertainment	20			45	Rock
Janeway, Eliot	Author-Economist	16				
Janis, Conrad	Entertainment	5			12	
Janis, Elsie	Entertainment	25		50	55	Stage, Screen Comedienne
Janney, Leon	Entertainment	35			75	Member Original Our Gang
Jannings, Emil	Entertainment	150			375	1st Academy Award Winner
Janowitz, Gundula	Entertainment	10			65	Opera
Jansen, Marie	Entertainment	15			40	Opera
Jansons, Mariss	Conductor	10			45	Newly Discovered Latvian Conductor
Janssen, David	Entertainment	70			105	
Janssen, Werner	Conductor				45	Conductor of Many US Leading Orchestras
January, Lois	Entertainment	4	5	10	15	
Jaray, Hans	Entertainment				20	Classical-Semi Classical Singer
Jardine, William	Cabinet	10	25	55	20	Sec'y Agriculture 1925
Jarman, Claude, Jr.	Entertainment	15			35	Oscar winner
Jarman, Maxie	Business	15			55	Jarman Shoes
Jaroff, Serge	Entertainment	12	6	15	35	Jaroff Ballet & Don Cossack Chorus
Jarreau, Al	Entertainment	20			40	
Jarrett, Art	Bandleader	15			30	
Jarriel, Tom	Entertainment	4	10	15	10	TV News
Jarvik, Robert, Dr.	Science	12	35	60	35	Inventor Artificial Heart
Jarvis, Anna M.	Promoter	65	175			Campaigned for Mother's Day
Jarvis, Gregory B.	Astronaut	100	600		275	
Jarvis, Howard	Reformer-Tax	5	12	30	15	Sponsor Proposition 13
Jason, Rick	Entertainment	5			15	Actor
Jason, Sybil	Entertainment	5	6	15	15	
Javits, Jacob J.	Congress	5	20		25	Repr. 1947, Senator NY 1957
Jawlensky, Aleksey von 1864-1941	Artist			600		Russ. Painter
Jaworski, Leon	Law	10	20	45	15	Dir.Watergate Prosecution Force
Jay, James, Sir 1732-1815	Science	90	275	400		Phys. to G. Washington,Inventor
Jay, John (Grandson)	Diplomat	15	25	40		Active Opposition to Slavery
Jay, John (SC) 1745-1829	Supreme Court	400	1720	2400		ALS at Auction $6,600
Jean, Gloria	Entertainment	5		20	25	Child Singer-Actress
Jean, Norma	Country Music	10			20	
Jeans, James, Sir	Science	12	30	65	20	Br. Physicist, Astron., Author
Jedlichka, Ernest	Entertainment	45			200	Rus-Pol Pianist
Jeffers, Robinson 1887-1962	Author	65	350	450	90	Prize Winning Poet, Dramatist
Jeffers, William M.	Business	25	70	135	50	Union Pacific RR
Jefferson Airplane	Entertainment	125			300	Rock-The San Francisco Sound
Jefferson, Charles E.	Clergy	20	25	40		
Jefferson, Joe 1829-1905	Entertainment	30	70	125	65	Important Am.Vintage Actor
Jefferson, Martha Wayles	First Lady					Rare. Only 2 Known
Jefferson, Thomas & Madison,James	President	2825	6865			Special Doc. S $30,000
Jefferson, Thomas (As President)	President	4000	7000	21750		Free Frank $5,000-$5950
Jefferson, Thomas 1743-1826	President	3260	7900	15875		Content ALS's $101,000-$200,00

NAME	CATEGORY	SIG	LS/DS	ALS	SP	Comment
Jefferson, Thomas 1859-1932	Entertainment				125	Stage & Silent Films/D.W. Griffith
Jeffreys, Anne	Entertainment	10	12	15	25	
Jellicoe, John R.	Military	20	65	120	50	Br.Adm.WW I,P.M. New Zealand
Jenckes, Joseph 1656-1740	Colonial Am.	90	250	520		Colonial Governor RI
Jenkins, Allen	Entertainment	25			45	
Jenkins, Butch	Entertainment	10			25	
Jenkins, Thornton Alex.	Military	10	25	35		Chief-of Staff Farragut Squad.
Jenner, Bruce	Entertainment	3	3	6	6	Olympic Decathlon Winner
Jenner, Edward, Dr.	Science	450	850	2250		Smallpox Vaccination
Jenner, William E. 1908-85	Congress	10	20			Senator IN
Jenner, William, Sir	Science	35	110	295		Phys. to Queen Victoria
Jennings, Al	Celebrity	450		850		
Jennings, Peter	Entertainment	5	15	35	15	Broadcast Journalist, Anchor
Jennings, Waylon	Country Music	10			20	
Jennison, Ralph D.	Business	10	35	45	20	
Jenrette, John W. Jr.	Congress	5	20		10	Repr. SC
Jenrette, Rita	Entertainment	4	6	15	10	Pin-Up SP $25
Jensen, Karen	Entertainment	4	4	9	10	
Jepson, Helen	Entertainment	10			40	Opera, Concert
Jergens, Adele	Entertainment	5	6	10	10	
Jeritza, Maria 1887-1984	Entertainment	30			90	Opera, Operetta, Films
Jernigan, Tamara E.	Astronaut	8			20	
Jernstedt, Ken	Aviation	10	25	40	30	ACE, WW II, Flying Tigers
Jerome III, Wm. Travers	Education	20	40		35	Pres. Bowling Green
Jerome, Jerome K.	Author	35	70	95		Humorist, Playwright
Jerusalem, Siegfried	Entertainment	15			45	Opera. Current Leading Wagnerian Tenor
Jessel, George	Entertainment	30	80		90	Noted Emcee, Comic, Toastmaster
Jesup, Thomas S.1788-1860	Military	45	125	190		Gen. LS/Content $950
Jesup, William H.	Military	5	15	25		
Jeter, Michael	Entertainment	5			20	
Jethro Tull	Entertainment	30			75	
Jethro, Homer and	Country Music	30			125	
Jett, Joan	Entertainment	20			50	Rock
Jewell, Marshall	Governor-Cabinet	40	75	195		ALS/Cont. $400
Jewett, Sarah Orne 1849-1909	Author	45	200	300		New England Life & Folklore
Jewison, Norman	Entertainment	5			20	Film Director
Jillian, Ann	Entertainment	6	8	15	20	Pin-Up SP $25
Jimenez, Enrique A.	Head of State	8	15	25	10	Panama
Jimenez, Marcos P.	Head of State	10	25	50	15	Venezuela
Joachim, Joseph 1831-1907	Composer	95	150	337	220	Hung.Violinist.AMuQS $250-$575
Jodl, Alfred	Military	150	592	550	250	Chief-of-Staff To Keitel WW II
Joel, Billy	Composer	15			70	Singer, Songwriter
Joffre, Joseph Jacques Cesaire	Military	65	155	250	225	Marshal of France WW I
Johann, Zita	Entertainment	15			35	
John II, (King Castile) 1406-1454	Royalty	4700	6000			Patron of Literature & Arts
John of Austria (Don John)	Royalty	150				1629-1679
John XXIII, Pope	Clergy	595			650	Angelo Giuseppe Roncalli
John, Augustus	Artist	50	135	330		Welch. Portraits, Landscapes
John, Elton	Entertainment	70	130	225	125	Br. Singer-Songwriter
Johns, Glynis	Entertainment	15	15	30	30	
Johns, Jasper	Artist	20	90		30	Am. Pop Artist
Johnson, Amy (Mollison)	Aviation	75	85	135	200	Br. Aviation Pioneer
Johnson, Andrew (As Pres.)	President	373	2082	7500	2750	FF $1450, 1500
Johnson, Andrew 1808-75	President	469	1218	6400	2500	ALS/Content $19,500. FF $775
Johnson, Art	Aviation	10	22	38	30	ACE, WW II, USAAF Ace
Johnson, Ben	Entertainment	15			40	Oscar winner

NAME	CATEGORY	SIG	LS/DS	ALS	SP	Comment
Johnson, Ben 1572-1637	Author	450	1500			Br. Poet, Playwright
Johnson, Betty	Entertainment	3	3	6	6	
Johnson, Bradley T.(War Date)	Civil War	200	1425	970		CSA Gen.
Johnson, Bradley T.1829-1903	Civil War	90	370	272		CSA Gen.,ALS/Content $4,500
Johnson, Bunk	Entertainment	200			550	Jazz Trumpet
Johnson, Bushrod Rust	Civil War	115	300			CSA General
Johnson, Cave 1793-1866	Cabinet	50	110	195		P.M.Gen. 1st US Postage Stamps
Johnson, Chic	Entertainment	30			55	(Olsen & Johnson)
Johnson, Crockett*	Cartoonist	50			500	Barnaby
Johnson, Don	Entertainment	15			45	
Johnson, Eastman 1824-1906	Artist	40	60	185	300	Am. Portrait & Genre Artist
Johnson, Edward	Entertainment				75	Distinguished Canadian Tenor
Johnson, Eliza M.	First Lady	750	1500			
Johnson, Frank*	Cartoonist				40	
Johnson, Fred*	Cartoonist	10			35	Moon Mullins
Johnson, Gerald	Aviation	15	30	50	40	ACE, WW II
Johnson, H. Hank	Business	4			15	Pres. Spiegel
Johnson, Harold K.	Military	12	35	50	30	WW II. Prisoner. 4 Star Gen.
Johnson, Henry A.	Business	5			15	CEO Spiegel Inc.
Johnson, Herschel	Civil War	40	110			Gov. GA, CSA Senator
Johnson, Hiram W. 1866-1945	Congress	25	60			Senator CA
Johnson, Howard B.	Business	80				Howard Johnson Inns
Johnson, Howard S.	Business	12	30		24	
Johnson, Hugh S.	Cabinet	15	90	150	25	Gen., Dir. NRA During Depression
Johnson, James Johnnie	Aviation	30	65	120	95	ACE, WW II, Br. RAF Top Ace
Johnson, James K.	Aviation	10	25	38	32	ACE, Korea, Double Ace
Johnson, James Weldon	Author	30	100	225		NAACP,1st Ed.Black Manhattan S $795
Johnson, Jesse G.	Military	35	85	170		Adm. WW II
Johnson, John H. 1918-	Publisher		50		65	1st Afro-Am Periodicals.Ebony, Jet
Johnson, Jonathan Eastman	Artist	25	150			Am. Portrait, Genre Painter
Johnson, Keen	Governor	5	15		10	Governor KY
Johnson, L.B. & Johnson, Lady Bird	Pres.-1st Lady				600	
Johnson, Lady Bird	First Lady	40	108		95	
Johnson, Leon W.	Military	10	20	35		
Johnson, LeRoy	Congress	4			10	
Johnson, Louis A.	Cabinet	10	50	55	20	Sec'y Defense 1949
Johnson, Lyndon B. 1908-73	President		532		552	
Johnson, Lyndon B.(As Pres.)	President	165	1082	3365	475	TLS as Pres. $1,250-$4,200
Johnson, Lynn	Cartoonist	7			25	For Better Or Worst
Johnson, Lynn-Holly	Entertainment	5	7	12	15	
Johnson, Martin 1884-1937	Explorer-Photogr.	15	40			With Osa, Wild Animal Films
Johnson, Nunnally 1897-1977	Author	20	68		40	Am. Playwright, Screenwriter
Johnson, Oliver	Celebrity	5	15	30		
Johnson, Osa	Explorer-Photogr.	15	15	35	30	With Martin, Wild Animal Films
Johnson, Philip	Architect	25			125	Early Skyscrapers
Johnson, Reverdy 1796-1876	Cabinet	20	95	95		Statesman, Att'y Gen.,Sen. MD
Johnson, Richard L.	Aviation	15	20	30	20	
Johnson, Richard M. (V)	Vice President	70	200	350	400	Van Buren Vice Pres.
Johnson, Robert S.	Aviation	20	25	45	80	ACE, WW II, #5 US
Johnson, Robert W..	Business					Fndr. Johnson & Johnson
Johnson, Russ	Entertainment	3	3	6	6	
Johnson, Samuel C.	Business	5			10	Pres. Johnson's Wax
Johnson, Samuel, Dr.Johnson	Author	1750	4080			Lexicographer, Critic
Johnson, Van	Entertainment	7			20	
Johnson, William B.	Business	5			10	CEO Railway Express
Johnson, William Cost	Senate/Congress	10	20	35		MOC MD 1833

The Sanders Price Guide to Autographs

NAME	CATEGORY	SIG	LS/DS	ALS	SP	Comment
Johnson, William Samuel	Revolutionary War	130	375	675		Continental Congress
Johnson, Willis, Dr. 1869-1951	Educator	10				
Johnston, Albert Sidney 1803-62	Civil War	290	1500	2179		CSA Gen.,TX Sec.War DS $9500
Johnston, Frances 1864-1952	Photographer	5	25			1st Famouse Female Photographer
Johnston, George D. 1832-1910	Civil War	95	295	312		CSA Gen.
Johnston, Harriet Lane	Acting First Lady	200		625		Buchanan's Niece
Johnston, J. Lawson	Business	15	35	60		
Johnston, Johnny	Aviation	20	45		55	
Johnston, Joseph E. (War Date)	Civil War	440	1425	1938	3500	CSA Gen.
Johnston, Joseph E. 1807-91	Civil War	290	600	706	1800	CSA ALS/Cont $3,500-12,000
Johnston, Lynn*	Cartoonist	20			75	For Better or Worse
Johnston, Mary	Astronauts	5			15	
Johnston, Olin D.	Senate/Congress	5	15			Senator SC 1945
Johnston, Richard M.	Author	5	10	20		
Joliot, Fred. & Irene Curie Joliot	Science	200				Scientific Nobel Winning Team
Joliot-Curie, Frédéric 1900-58	Science			500		Fr. Chem.Nobel '35.Son-in-law Pierre/Marie
Joliot-Curie, Irene 1897-1956	Science	40		205		
Jolley, I. Stanford	Entertainment	20			50	
Jolson, Al 1886-1950	Entertainment	173	378		430	Starred in 1st Talking Picture
Jones, Allan	Entertainment	10	15	35	30	Film & Concert Singer
Jones, Anne	Country Music	10			20	
Jones, Annisa	Entertainment	150			325	
Jones, Anson	Am. Politician	350		1200		Physician, Pres. Texas Repub.
Jones, Anthony Armstrong	Country Music	10			20	
Jones, Bob	Clergy	15	25	60	25	
Jones, Buck 1889-1942	Entertainment	157	230	300	385	Vintage Film Cowboy
Jones, Carolyn	Entertainment	100	35	65	75	
Jones, Casey	Aviation	45	90	175	150	
Jones, Chuck*	Cartoonist	25			175	Animator
Jones, Claude A.	Military	40	65			
Jones, David (Davy)	Entertainment	15			40	The Monkies
Jones, David R. (War Date)	Civil War	370	2893			CSA Gen.
Jones, David R.1825-63	Civil War	305	800			CSA Gen.
Jones, Dean	Entertainment	9	10	20	20	
Jones, Dick	Entertainment	10			35	
Jones, E. Stanley	Clergy	35	50	75	50	
Jones, Edward F.	Civil War	50	110	155	150	Union Gen.
Jones, George	Entertainment	10			25	C & W
Jones, Grace	Entertainment	18	20	30	38	Pin-Up SP $75
Jones, Grandpa	Country Music	5			12	
Jones, Gwyneth	Entertainment	15			40	Opera
Jones, Henry	Entertainment	5			15	
Jones, Howard	Entertainment	10			20	
Jones, Isham	Entertainment	15			40	Vintage Big Band
Jones, J. Carey	Military	20	45			Admiral WW II
Jones, Jack	Entertainment	5			10	
Jones, James	Author	50	240			..Here To Eternity
Jones, James Earl	Entertainment	10			30	
Jones, Janet	Entertainment	10	15	28	30	Pin-Up SP $30
Jones, Jennifer	Entertainment	142	225		275	AA
Jones, Jenny	Entertainment	10			20	TV Host
Jones, Jesse H.	Cabinet	15	10	15	10	Sec'y Commerce 1940
Jones, Jim	Clergy	250	375	650	850	
Jones, John Marshall	Civil War	225	650			CSA General
Jones, John Paul	Military-Rev. War	5000				Naval Hero
Jones, John Percival	Senate/Congress	10		25		Senator NV 1873

NAME	CATEGORY	SIG	LS/DS	ALS	SP	Comment
Jones, L.Q.	Entertainment	5			15	
Jones, Louis R.	Military	10	30			
Jones, Maj. Gen. David M.	Astronaut	10			20	
Jones, Marcia Mae	Entertainment	5	6	15	15	
Jones, Mary H. 'Mother'	Labor	60	195	430		Agitator, Speaker, Organizer
Jones, Quincy	Composer	12	20	35	30	AMusQS $50
Jones, Rickie Lee	Entertainment	20			35	
Jones, Samuel 1819-87	Civil War	95	381			CSA General
Jones, Samuel (War Date)	Civil War	180	580	765		CSA Gen.
Jones, Samuel Porter	Clergy	20	25	35		
Jones, Shirley	Entertainment	10	30		25	Pin-Up SP $30
Jones, Spike	Entertainment	25			65	Big Band Leader
Jones, Thomas	Astronaut	7			15	
Jones, Thomas V.	Business	15	30		25	
Jones, Tom	Entertainment	8	9	19	20	
Jones, Tommy Lee	Entertainment	20			35	Col. SP Batman$60
Jones, William E. (War Date)	Civil War	275		1900		CSA Gen. KIA
Jones, William E.1824-64	Civil War	140	250	600		CSA Gen.Grumble.KIA.
Jong, Erica	Author	10	12	20	15	Best Selling Bawdy Autoblograph
Jongkind, Johan 1819-1891	Artist	200	450	860		Dutch.Master of Rendering Light
Jonson, Ben 1572-1637	Author	2850				Br. Playwright, Poet
Jope, Bernhard	Aviation	10	25	40	30	
Joplin, Janis 1943-70	Entertainment	750	600	900	1000	
Joplin, Scott	Composer	650	980	2000		Rag Time Composer
Jordan, Barbara	Senate/Congress	12			30	Afr-Am.Congresswoman TX
Jordan, Dorothy	Entertainment	15	15	35	30	
Jordan, Hamilton	Gov't Official	5	15	20	15	Chief of Staff Carter Admin.
Jordan, Jim (Fibber)	Entertainment	15	20	35	25	
Jordan, Louis	Entertainment	25			65	Big Band Leader
Jordan, Thomas (War Date)	Civil War	135	380	1065		CSA Gen.
Jordan, Thomas 1819-95	Civil War	80	255	350		CSA General
Jordan, Vernon	Cabinet	5	16			
Jordanaires, The (4)	Entertainment	30				Gospel
Jordon, Richard	Entertainment	15		25	30	
Jorgensen, Christine	Celebrities	20	25	45	30	1st To Undergo Sex Change
Jorn, Carl	Entertainment	30			85	Opera
Jory, Victor 1902-82	Entertainment	35	60		102	
Jose, Richard J.	Entertainment	10			15	Singer
Joseffy, Raphael	Entertainment	25			125	Pianist, Pupil of LIszt
Joseph II 1741-1790	Royalty	125	350	875		King Ger. & Holy Roman Empire
Josephine, Empress	Royalty	1200	1510	2400		Fr. Wife of Napoleon
Joslyn, Allyn	Entertainment	25			55	
Joswig, Wilhelm	Aviation	10			30	
Jouett, James	Civil War	25	55	125		Union Naval Officer/Farragut
Jouhaux, Benjamin 1879-1954	Reformer	25	60	140	50	Nobel Peace Prize 1951
Jourdan, Jean B., Count	Napoleonic Wars	55	260	290		Marshal of Napoleon
Jourdan, Louis	Entertainment	12		20	25	
Journey	Entertainment	25			50	
Jowett, Benjamin	Scholar	10	22	35		One of Greatest Teachers
Jowett, Charles	Clergy	15	20	25		
Joy, Jimmie	Bandleader	10				
Joy, Leatrice	Entertainment	12			30	
Joyce, Alice 1890-1955	Entertainment	15	25		60	Silent Star
Joyce, Elaine	Entertainment	4	4	9	12	
Joyce, James 1882-1941	Author	400	590	3105	6325	Ir. Novelist, Poet, Playwright
Joyce, Richard	Military	40	100	175		

 **The Sanders Price Guide to Autographs**

NAME	CATEGORY	SIG	LS/DS	ALS	SP	Comment
Juan Carlos, King	Royalty	55	120	245	150	Spain
Juarez, Benito 1806-1872	Head of State	425	1325	1800	1500	Pres. Mexico. Revolutionary
Judd, Ashley	Entertainment	6			20	Actress
Judd, Naomi & Wynona	Country Music	20			40	
Judd, Norman B. 1815-78	Congress	25				Repr. IL, Nominated A. Lincoln
Judd, Walter H. 1898-	Congress	10	15			Congressman MN
Judge, Arline	Entertainment	15	15	35	30	
Julia, Raul	Entertainment	20			75	
Julian, George W. 1817-99	Congress	15	30	75		Co-Founder Free Soil Party, Repr. IN
Juliana, Queen	Royalty	100	250	710	150	Netherlands
Jumangi (Cast Of)	Entertainment				200	Williams, Hunt, Durst, Pierce
Jump, Gordon	Entertainment	5	6	15	15	
Jung, Carl Gustav 1875-1961	Science	510	1900	3850		Swiss Psychiatrist-Psychologist
Junkers, Hugo	Science	50		355		Ger. Airplane Engineer-Designer
Junot, Andache,Duc Abrantes	Military	70	235			Fr. Gen., Sec'y to Napoleon
Junot, Jean Androche	Fr. Revolution	30	90	185		
Jurgens, Curt	Entertainment	15			40	
Jurgens, Dick	Entertainment	20			45	Big Band Leader
Jusserand, Jean Jules 1855-1932	Author		20	45		Pulitzer Prize. Fr. Diplomat
Justice, Bill*	Cartoonist	25			250	The Chipmunks
Justin, A.G.	Civil War	10	25			CW Gov. PA
Juttner, Arthur	Military	10			30	Ger. RK Winner

Kabaiwanska, Raina	Entertainment	10			35	Opera
Kabalevsky, Dmitri	Composer	32	388	233		TMsS/Political Content $675
Kadar, Janos	Head of State	50	130			
Kaelin, Kato	Entertainment	35	65		80	Actor. Houseguest O.J. Simpson
Kafka, Franz	Author	850		16400		Ger. Novelist. Visionary Tales
Kahn, Julius 1861-1924	Congress	5	15			Repr. CA 1899
Kahn, Madeline	Entertainment	5	6	15	15	
Kahn, Otto H. 1867-1934	Business	95	50	135	60	Banker, Philanthropist, Arts Patron
Kahn, Yahya	Head of State	30			50	Pakistan
Kahoutek, Lubos	Science	5	15	30	15	Am. Astronomer
Kai-Shek, Chiang & Mme. Kai-Sheck	Head of State				375	
Kai-Shek, Chiang 1887-1975	Head of State	100	220	450	772	Republic of China
Kai-Shek, Mayling Soong Chiang	Author	50	120		100	Madame Chiang
Kaiser, Henry J.	Industrialist	90	150		225	S.F.Bay Bridge.Grand Coulee Dam
Kalakaua, David 1836-91	Royalty	100	425	775	1610	King Hawaii
Kallen, Kitty	Entertainment		20		25	Big Band Vocalist
Kaltenborn, H. V.	Radio	5	15	30	15	Radio Commentator
Kaltenbrunner, Ernst	Military	150	500		175	Perpetrator of Nazi Atrocities
Kamburg, Arthur, Dr	Science	10	20			Nobel
Kamehameha II, Liholiho 1797-1824	Royalty	960		3850		King Hawaii

NAME	CATEGORY	SIG	LS/DS	ALS	SP	Comment
Kamehameha III, Kauikeaouli	Royalty	750	1585			King Hawaii
Kamehameha IV 1824-63	Royalty		2500			King of Hawaii
Kaminsky, Max	Entertainment	10			30	Dixieland Jazz Bandleader
Kamio, Mitsuomi	Military	110		225		
Kamionsky, Oscar	Entertainment				350	Great Jewish Baritone
Kammhuber, Josef	Aviation	20	30	65	35	Ger. Air Defense Gen. WW II. RK
Kanaly, Steve	Entertainment	6	8	15	20	
Kander, John	Composer	5	20	35	10	
Kandinski, Vasili 1866-1944	Artist	200	795			Rus. Painter. Cont. TLS $1,500
Kane, Bob*	Cartoonist	100			485	Batman. SPI $275
Kane, Carol	Entertainment	10	12	20	25	
Kane, Elisha Kent	Explorer	95	215	450		Grinnell Arctic Expedition
Kane, Helen	Entertainment	25			60	Boop-Boop-a-Doop Girl
Kane, Richard	Military	20			90	
Kane, Thomas L. 1822-83	Civil War	48	105	160		Union Gen.ALS '63 $990
Kangaroo, Captain	Entertainment	5	6	15	25	
Kanin, Garson	Author	10	20	50	45	Playwright, Director, Screen.
Kansas	Entertainment	30			60	
Kant, Immanuel 1724-1804	Author	1005	3950	7375		Ger. Philosopher, Professor
Kantor, MacKinlay	Author	15	30	65	25	Andersonville, Pulitzer
Kantrowitz, Adrian, Dr.	Science	25	70	145	30	
Kantrowitz, Arthur, Dr.	Science	15		30		
Kaper, Bronislaw	Composer	10	30	55	15	
Kaplan, Gabe	Entertainment	5			15	
Kaplan, Gilbert	Conductor				50	Mahler Specialist
Kapliolani 1834-99	Royalty				1265	Queen Hawaii
Kappel, Frederick R.	Business	3	6	15	8	
Karajan, Herbert von	Conductor			325		Austrian Classical Conductor
Karas, Anton	Composer	25	40	85	100	Third Man Theme AMusQS $350
Karloff, Boris 1887-1969	Entertainment	262	415	500	752	Frankensteln. 3½x4½ SPI $295
Karman, Theodore von	Industrial	25	60	110	50	Designer Karman-Ghia VW
Karns, Roscoe	Entertainment	30			75	
Karpis, Alvin Creepy	Criminal	65	395	300	100	30's Public Enemy #1
Karras, Alex	Entertainment	5	6	15	15	
Karsavina, Tamara	Entertainment	50			362	Rus.-Br. Dancer
Karsh, Yousuf	Photographer	35	90	75	70	Portraits, Royalty,World Famous
Kasavubu, Joseph	Head of State	20	75	185	40	1st Pres. Dem. Repub. of Congo
Kaschmann, Giuseppe	Entertainment	60			325	Internationally Important Baritone Star
Kasem, Casey	Entertainment	5	8		12	Disc Jockey
Kasem, Jean	Entertainment	5	8		15	
Kasha, Al	Composer	15			45	
Kashfi, Anna	Entertainment	10		30	35	
Kassebaum, Nancy Landon	Senate	5	15		15	Senator KS
Kassell, Art	Bandleader	10			65	
Kastler, Alfred, Dr.	Science	15	35		40	Nobel Physics 1966
Katchinsky, Victorin	Aviation	20			45	
Katz, Bernard, Sir	Science	15	30	45	35	Nobel Medicine 1970
Katzenbach, Nicholas	Cabinet	10	20		15	Att'y General 1965
Katzenberg, Jeffrey	Business	15	20			Disney CEO
Katzir, Ephraim	Head of State	10			45	Pres. Israel '70's
Kaufman, Andy	Entertainment	150			60	Very Early Death
Kaufman, George S.	Author	30	85	175	35	Dramatist, Critic, Director
Kaunda, Kenneth	Head of State	40	150	350	70	1st Pres. Zambia
Kavelin, Al	Entertainment				20	Big Band Leader
Kawato, Masajiro Mike	Aviation	40	100		150	Ace WW II, Downed Boyington
Kay, Beatrice	Entertainment	10			25	

NAME	CATEGORY	SIG	LS/DS	ALS	SP	Comment
Kay, Dianne	Entertainment	3	3	6	6	
Kay, Herbie	Bandleader	10				
Kay, Mary (Ash)	Business	5	15	30	10	Cosmetics Empire
Kay, Mary Ellen	Entertainment				25	
Kaye, Celia	Entertainment	4	5	10	12	
Kaye, Danny	Entertainment	75			100	
Kaye, Sammy	Entertainment	15			40	Big Band Leader
Kaye, Stubby	Entertainment	10			25	
Kazan, Elia	Entertainment	10	12	20	35	Director, Producer, Author
Keach, Stacy	Entertainment	8	9		20	
Kean, Jane	Entertainment	5	6	15	12	
Keane, Bil*	Cartoonists	10			50	The Family Circus
Keane, Edward	Entertainment	10			25	
Kearny, Philip (War Date)	Civil War	360	650	850		Union General KIA
Kearny, Stephen	Military-Governor	85	195	380		War of 1812, 1st Gov. of CA
Keating, Kenneth B.	Senate/Congress	5	15		10	Gen. WW II, MOC Senator 1947-65
Keaton, Buster	Entertainment	195	225		400	Great Film Comedian
Keaton, Diane	Entertainment	15			65	
Keaton, Michael	Entertainment	10			50	As Batman SP $75
Keble, John	Clergy	75	125	350	295	Founder of Oxford Movement
Kedrova, Lila	Entertainment	10		25	40	
Keeble, John	Author	10	30	75		
Keel, Howard	Entertainment	5	6	25	20	He-Man Singer-Actor
Keeler, Ruby	Entertainment	35			55	
Keene, Carolyn	Author	5	15	30	10	Publisher Pseud.(5 Authors)
Keene, Charles S.	Entertainment	10			25	
Keene, Tom	Entertainment	25			50	Actor
Kefauver, Estes	Senate	15	40		35	Senator TN
Keifer, Joseph W.	Civil War	25	45	60		Union Gen.& Speaker
Keillor, Garrison	Author	15	25	35	20	Humorist
Keim, Betty Lou	Entertainment	5			12	Actress
Keim, George May 1805-61	Congress	10				Repr. PA, Mayor Reading, PA
Keirstead, Wilfred C.	Clergy	10	15	20	15	
Keisha	Model	5			15	Pin-Up SP $25
Keitel, Harvey	Entertainment	10			25	
Keitel, Wilhelm 1882-1946	Military	350	738	1500	650	Ger. Fld. Marshal WWII
Keith, Arthur, Sir	Author	10		35		Anthropologist, Origins of Man
Keith, Brian	Entertainment	5	8	15	20	
Keith, David	Entertainment	5	6	15	10	
Keith, George Keith E., Viscount	Military	45	135	155		Br. Admiral. 1746-1823
Keith, Ian	Entertainment	15				Vintage Actor
Keith, Rosalind	Entertainment	10			75	
Keith, William, 1680-1749	Revolutionary War	135		700		Colonial Lt. Governor PA & DE
Kekkonen, Urho	Head of State	15	45			Finland
Kelcey, Herbert	Entertainment	10			20	Vintage Stage Actor
Kelland, Clarence Buddington	Author	20	55	150	30	Am. Novelist, Short Stories
Kellar, Harry	Entertainment	15			35	Vintage Stage Actor
Kellard, Ralph	Entertainment	10			25	
Kellaway, Cecil	Entertainment	25			75	
Keller, Helen & A. Sullivan	Author-Teacher	535			2185	
Keller, Helen 1880-1968	Author	200	400	2150	875	Blind, Deaf, Mute Author
Kellerman, Annette	Entertainment	45		165	175	Aussie Dancer & Swimming Star
Kellerman, Sally	Entertainment	10			25	
Kellerman,FC,Duke Valmy	Military	75	285	405		7 Years' War. Marshal of Nap.
Kelley, Clarence M.	Celebrity	5	15	35	20	
Kelley, Deforest	Entertainment	10	15	25	35	Star Trek

The Sanders Price Guide to Autographs

NAME	CATEGORY	SIG	LS/DS	ALS	SP	Comment
Kelley, Kitty	Author	12			20	Celebrity Biography
Kelley, Patrick Henry	Senate/Congress	5	10		10	MOC MI 1913
Kellogg, Charlotte	Philanthropist	7	20			Mrs. Vernon Kellogg
Kellogg, Frank B. 1856-1937	Cabinet	32	200	95	35	Nobel Peace Prize 1929
Kellogg, John Harvey, Dr.	Food Business	15	175	75		Am. Phys.Health Reformer.Breakfast Cereal
Kellogg, Ray	Entertainment	5			9	Actor
Kellogg, W. K.	Business	110	150	325	200	Fndr. W.K. Kellogg Co.
Kellogg, William P. 1831-1918	Congress	50	100			U.S. Senator 1868, Gov. LA 1873-77
Kelly, Edward J.	Political	10			15	Mayor Chicago
Kelly, Emmett, Sr.	Entertainment	62	150		325	Circus Clown Weary Willie
Kelly, Gene 19xx-1996	Entertainment	20			52	AA
Kelly, Grace (Actress-Personal)1928-82	Entertainment	200	325	1297	438	AA, AA
Kelly, Howard A., Dr.	Science	20	35	60	40	Orig. Faculty Johns Hopkins U.
Kelly, Jack	Entertainment	15			45	
Kelly, John H.	Civil War	475	975			CSA Gen., Youngest Killed
Kelly, Moira	Entertainment	20			55	
Kelly, Nancy	Entertainment	10	20		25	
Kelly, Patsy	Entertainment	28	35	65	60	
Kelly, Paul	Entertainment	25			55	
Kelly, Paula	Entertainment	5		12	15	Pin-Up SP $18
Kelly, Thomas W.	Military	10	20		15	Gen. Desert Storm
Kelly, Walt*	Cartoonists	50			425	Pogo
Kelsey, Fred	Entertainment	25				Character Actor
Kelsey, Linda	Entertainment	5	6	15	15	
Kelton, Pert	Entertainment	15			45	
Kelvin, William T., Lord	Science	85	195	300	175	Kelvin Scale, Atlantic Cable
Kemble, Edward W.* 1861-1933	Artist-Cartoonist	25			375	Am. Illustrator Huck Finn, etc.
Kemble, Frances A.Fanny	Entertainment	20	75	90		
Kemp, Hal	Entertainment	15			40	Big Band Leader
Kemp, Jack	Cabinet	15			25	Sec'y HUD
Kempenfelt, Richard 1720-1782	Military					
Kemper, Jackson, Dr. 1789-1870	Clergy	20				Educator
Kemper, James L. (War Date)	Civil War	330				CSA Gen. AES $1150 '64
Kemper, James L. 1823-95	Civil War	125	292	420		CSA Gen.
Kemper, John M.	Celebrity	3	7	15	10	
Kendal, Madge, Dame 1848-1935	Entertainment	12			35	
Kendall, Amos	Cabinet	20	50	95		Jackson P.M. General,Journalist
Kendall, Cy	Entertainment	25			50	
Kendall, Edward C., Dr.	Science	30	55	100	35	Nobel Medicine 1950
Kendall, Henry W.	Science	20	35		30	Nobel Physics 1990
Kendall, Paul	Military	10	30			
Kendren, John C.	Science	15	20	30	20	
Keneally, Thomas	Author	10			20	Schindler's List
Kenellopoulos, Panayotis	Head of State	15	35	90		Greece
Kennan, George F.	Author	15	45			Am.Diplomat, Historian.Pulitzer
Kennedy, Anthony M.	Supreme Court	30			50	
Kennedy, Arthur	Entertainment	30	40	95	75	
Kennedy, Caroline	Celebrity-Author		25			Daughter of JFK
Kennedy, Douglas	Entertainment	4			30	AKA Keith Douglas
Kennedy, Edgar	Entertainment	125			250	
Kennedy, Edward M.Ted	Congress	15	40	75	30	Senator MA 1962
Kennedy, Ethel	Celebrity	15	50	75	35	Mrs. Robert Kennedy
Kennedy, G.A.Studdert	Clergy	20				Br. Poet, Author.Woodbine Willie
Kennedy, George	Entertainment	5			45	AA
Kennedy, George C.	Aviation	45			250	
Kennedy, Gerald, Bishop	Clergy	25	40	50	40	

NAME	CATEGORY	SIG	LS/DS	ALS	SP	Comment
Kennedy, J.& Kennedy, Jacqueline	Pres.&1st Lady		4200		2200	Engr. WH Vignette S $3500
Kennedy, Jacqueline (As 1st Lady)	First Lady	825	1250	2317	3050	
Kennedy, Jacqueline 1929-94	First Lady	300	1011	1875	1200	Auction 10/95 SP $3,300
Kennedy, Jayne	Entertainment	6	8	15	15	
Kennedy, John F. (As Pres.)	President	1650	4373		4233	TLS/Cont. As Pres. $19,500
Kennedy, John F. 1917-63	President	1250	2986	5812	3050	
Kennedy, John F., Jr.	Attorney	25			50	Magazine Publisher
Kennedy, John P.	Cabinet	35	50	95		Fillmore Sec'y Navy 1852
Kennedy, Joseph P.1888-1969	Business	75	600	300	120	Boston Financier, Father of JFK
Kennedy, Joseph Patrick II	Congress	15	800		70	Repr. MA 1987
Kennedy, Madge	Entertainment	10			30	
Kennedy, Martin John	Senate/Congress	5	15			MOC NY 1930-45
Kennedy, Robert F. 1925-68	Cabinet-Congress	200	1061		900	Att'y Gen. Brother of JFK
Kennedy, Robert F., Jr.	Author					Signed Book 112
Kennedy, Rose Fitzgerald 1890-1995	Celebrity	145	125	200	50	Kennedy Family Matriarch
Kennedy, Tom	Entertainment	50			125	
Kenney, George	Military	25	60	110	40	USAAF Gen. WW II
Kenny G.	Entertainment	20			75	Saxophonist
Kenny, Bill	Entertainment	25			75	Leader of Ink Spots
Kenny, Elizabeth, Sister	Science	175			275	Pioneer Polio Treatment
Kenny, Nick	Entertainment		20			Singer/Ink Spots
Kensit, Patsy	Entertainment	10			60	Actress
Kent, A. Atwater	Inventor	20	195	90	35	Radio Mfg., Philanthropist
Kent, Edw. Augustus, Duke 1767-1820	Royalty	45	150			Son of Geo. III. Father of Queen Victoria
Kent, J. Ford	Military	90	195			Gen., Took San Juan Hill
Kent, Jack	Cartoonist	10			35	King Aroo
Kent, James 1763-1847	Revolutionary War	80	140	250		Legal Reporting System
Kent, Rockwell 1882-1971	Artist	40	215	305	75	Am. Landscape, Figure Painting
Kent, Walter	Composer	40	105			AMusQS $200(Be Home for Xmas)
Kent, William 1864-1928	Congress	5	12		10	Repr. CA 1911
Kenton, Simon 1755-1836	Pioneer	420	1350			Hunter, Trader, Spy, General
Kenton, Stan 1912-79	Entertainment	35			110	Big Band Leader-Pianist
Kenyatta, Jomo	Head of State	125	220	525	150	Prime Min. Kenya
Kenyon, Doris	Entertainment	15	25	45	45	
Kenyon, William S.	Senate/Congress	10	15	35		MOC NY 1859
Kepford, Ira	Aviation	15	30	48	42	ACE, WW II
Kepner, Wm. E.	Military	15	35	60	25	
Keppel, Francis	Celebrity	5	15	20	15	
Keppler, Joseph 1838-1894	Publisher	15		45		Founder Puck Magazine
Kerbs, Edwin G., Dr.	Science	20	30	55	35	Nobel Medicine
Kercheval, Ken	Entertainment	5			25	
Kerensky, Alexander	Head of State	205	850	1250	475	Rus. Revolutionary Politician
Kern, Jerome 1885-1945	Composer	450	955	2100	2250	AMusQS $685-$2,500
Kern, Paul B., Bishop	Clergy	20	25	35	25	
Kernan, Francis	Senate/Congress	10		35		MOC 1863, Senator NY 1875
Kerns, Joanna	Entertainment	5		10	15	
Kerouac, Jack	Author	500	2500	4000	5500	Beat Generation Rep. Clebr. pd. 5000 for DS
Kerr, Clark	Celebrity	5	10	20	10	
Kerr, Deborah	Entertainment	15	9	20	25	Pin-Up SP $35
Kerr, John	Entertainment	8			30	Actor Tea And Sympathy
Kerr, Robert S.	Senate/Congress	5	15		10	Senator, Gov. OK
Kerr, Ruth	Business	25	35	150	100	Kerr Glass Co.
Kerrigan, J. Warren	Entertainment	25			60	
Kerry, Robert	Senate	10			20	Senator
Kershaw, Joseph B. 1822-94	Civil War	182	900	1625		CSA Gen.LS '61 $3500
Kerwin, Joseph P.	Astronaut	7			25	

NAME	CATEGORY	SIG	LS/DS	ALS	SP	Comment
Kesey, Ken	Author	30	40	55	30	One Flew Over the Cukoo's....
Kesselring, Albrecht	Military	95	525		175	Ger. Field Marshal WW II
Kestnbaum, Meyer	Business	20	30		25	Pres. Hart, Schaffner & Marx
Ketcham, Hank*	Cartoonist	20	60		90	Dennis the Menace
Ketcham, John H. (War Date)	Civil War	150		328		Union Gen.
Ketcham, John H. 1832-1906	Civil War	58				Union Gen.
Ketelby, Albert W.	Composer	15		75		In a Persian Market, ...Monastery Garden
Kettering, Charles F.	Inventor	100	160	325	125	Engineer. Sloan-Kettering Inst.
Kevorkian, Jack, Dr.	Science	25			75	Euthanasia. Dr. Death
Key, David M. 1824-1900	Cabinet	30	45	90		P.M. General. CSA Officer
Key, Francis Scott 1779-1843	Lawyer-Author	500	600	1141		Special ADS $2,500
Key, Philip Barton 1857-1815	Senate/Congress	10	30	40		MOC MD 1807
Key, Ted*	Cartoonist	10			75	Hazel
Keyes, Erasmus D. 1810-95	Civil War	50	120	307		Union General
Keyes, Erasmus, D. (War Date)	Civil War	70	250	423		Union Gen.
Keyes, Evelyn	Entertainment	15		20	82	SP in GWTW Costume $40-100
Keyes, Irwin	Entertainment	4			10	Character Actor
Keyes, Roger J.B.1st Baron	Military	15	30	55	25	Br. Adm.Fleet. Boxer Rebellion
Keynes, John Maynard 1883-1946	Economist	75	1600	585	230	Br. Economist.Content TLS $1600
Keys, Ancel	Science	5	15	30	10	
Keys, Henry W.	Governor	10	20	35		Governor NH
Keyser, Ralph S.	Military	30	55			
Keyserling, Hermann	Philosopher	15	35	60	50	Ger. Social Philosopher
Khachaturian, Aram	Composer	150		675	633	AMusQS $300, $575, $625
Khalid, King	Royalty	20	65	135	60	Saudi Arabia
Khambatta, Persis	Entertainment	10		30	25	Star Trek
Khan, Chaka	Entertainment	15			30	
Khan, Mohammad Ayub	Head of State	30	95			
Khan, Yasmin, Princess	Royalty	5			20	Daughter of Rita Hayworth
Khanh, Nguyen, Gen.	Head of State	20	60	175	35	
Khanieff, Nikhandr S. 1922-54	Entertainment				650	Leading Heroic Tenor at Bolshoi
Khomeini, Ruhollah, Ayatollah	Religious Leader	500				Iranian Moslem Leader
Khorana, Har G., Dr.	Science	15	25	45	20	Nobel Medicine 1968
Khruschchev, Nikita S.1894-1971	Head of State	300	410	550	1265	Premier Soviet Union
Kiam, Victor	Business	10	25		15	Remington Electric Razor Co.
Kibbee, Guy	Entertainment	20			40	
Kidder, Margot	Entertainment	10			30	Pin-Up SP $30
Kiddoo, Jos. Barr	Civil War	50				Union General
Kidman, Nicole	Entertainment	20			75	
Kiel, Richard	Entertainment	5			15	
Kielmansegg, Graf J.A.	Military	15			35	Gen. German Army
Kienzl, Wilhelm 1857-1941	Composer	15		50		Opera
Kiepura, Jan	Entertainment	30			125	Opera, Concert
Kilban, B.*	Cartoonist	10	25		100	Cat Cartoons, The New Yorker
Kilbride, Percy	Entertainment	100			350	
Kilby, J. S. Jack	Science	15	35	60	30	Inventor of Micro Chip
Kiley, Richard	Entertainment	6	8	15	25	
Kilgore, Harley, M.	Senate/Congress	5	15		15	Senator WV 1941
Kilgore, Merle	Country Music	10			20	
Kilham, Hannah	Clergy	50	75	100		
Kilian, Victor	Entertainment	10		20	25	
Killinger, John W.	Senate/Congress	10	15	30		MOC PA 1859
Kilmer, Joyce	Author	205	550			Poet. Trees
Kilmer, Val	Entertainment	15			45	Batman SP/Chris O'Donnell $150
Kilpatrick, Hugh J. (War Date)	Civil War	195	570	635		Union Gen.
Kilpatrick, Hugh J.1836-81	Civil War	120	228	400	415	Union Gen. Cavalry. '63 LS $1295

The Sanders Price Guide to Autographs

NAME	CATEGORY	SIG	LS/DS	ALS	SP	Comment
Kimball, Dan	Cabinet	20	30	40	25	Sec'y Navy. Aerojet General
Kimball, J. Golden	Clergy	25	150			Pioneer Mormon Leader
Kimball, John W.	Civil War	45		202		Union Gen.
Kimball, Spencer W.	Clergy	25	25	35	30	Morman Leader
Kimball, Ward	Cartoonist	25			75	Musician-Discny Cartoonist
Kimberly, John W., 1st Earl	Statesman	20	30	110		Br.Colon'l Sec'y. Kimberly S.A.
Kimberly, R. Lewis	Civil War	25	40	50		Union General
Kimbrough, Emily	Author	10	20	45	15	Our Hearts Were Young & Gay
Kimmel, Husband E.	Military	350			550	US Adm. Cmdr.At Pearl Harbor
Kindelberger, James H. Dutch	Business	45			75	Pres. No. American Aviation
Kindermann, K. B.	Aviation	5	10	15	10	
Kindler, Hans	Conductor	10			45	Conductor Wash.,DC Nat'l Symphony
King, Alan	Entertainment	5	6	15	15	
King, Andrea	Enntertainment	10			20	Actress
King, B.B.	Entertainment	20	125		90	R & B Singer, Guitarist
King, Ben E.	Composer	10			25	Stand by Me
King, Cammie	Entertainment	15		35	35	GWTW
King, Carole	Entertainment	15			25	Rock
King, Charles	Civil War	50		175		Soldler-Author
King, Charles	Entertainment	20			50	
King, Coretta Scott	Celebrity	20	40	95	20	Mrs. Martin Luther King, Jr.
King, Edward J., Bishop	Clergy	25	35	50		
King, Ernest J. 1878-1956	Military	30	117		125	Fleet Adm. Cmmdr. Chief US Fleet WW II
King, Frank*	Cartoonist	35			165	Gasoline Alley
King, Henry	Entertainment	30			75	Film Director
King, Horatio 1811-1897	Cabinet	40	175			P.M. General 1861
King, Jack 1903-43	Composer					Pop Songwriter AMusQS $35
King, John 'Dusty'	Entertainment	20	30	45	55	
King, John Alsop	Governor	10		35		Gov. NY, a Founder Repub. Party
King, Larry	Entertainment	10	20	35	15	Talk Show Host
King, MacKenzie (Wm. L.)1874-1950	Head of State	60	55	90	55	Prime Minister Canada WW II
King, Martin Luther, Jr.1929-68	Clergy	1772	4275	2600	4250	Advocate Peaceful Nonviolence
King, Martin Luther. Sr.	Clergy	35	45	60	65	
King, Pee Wee	Entertainment	5			15	C & W. Bandleader-Composer
King, Perry	Entertainment	6	8	15	18	
King, Preston 1806-65	Congress	15	45	105		Repr. 1843, Senate NY. Suicide 1865
King, Rodney	Celebrity	100				Afro-Am. L.A. Vicitim
King, Rufus (War Date)	Civil War	70				Union Gen. ALS/Cont.'62 $3200
King, Rufus 1755-1827	Revolutionary War	250	475	450		Cont'l Congr. Historical ALS $2500
King, Rufus 1814-76	Civil War	35	100			Union General
King, Stephen	Author	95	125	450	70	Master of Horror and Suspense
King, Thomas Starr	Clergy	25	35	95	40	
King, Walter Woolf	Entertainment	12		25	50	Broadway Singing Star. Villain
King, Wayne	Entertainment	15			20	Big Band Leader
King, William R. (V)	Vice President	200	340			Pierce VP. Died after 45 days
King, Wm. L. Mackenzie 1874-1950	Head of State	40	300			3 Times P.M. Canada
Kingman, Dong	Artist	25	50	100		
Kingsford-Smith, Charles	Aviation	45	250		200	FDC Trans-Tasman Fl. $175
Kingsley, Ben	Entertainment	9	10	20	35	AA
Kingsley, Charles 1819-75	Author-Clergy	45	95	160		Br. Novelist, Clergyman
Kingston, Trio	Entertainment	30				Folk Group of 59's
Kingston, William H.	Author	25		100		Br. Boy's Adventure Books
Kinks (5 Current Members)	Entertainment	40			85	Rock. LP Cover S $95
Kinsey, Alfred, Dr. 1894-1956	Science	140	230	375	240	Am. Sexologist Researcher
Kinskey, Leonid	Entertainment	7			25	
Kinski, Klaus	Entertainment	20		35	45	

NAME	CATEGORY	SIG	LS/DS	ALS	SP	Comment
Kinski, Natassia	Entertainment	15	20	90	30	Actress, Nude Pin-Up 90
Kinstler, E.R.*	Cartoonist	10			150	Illustrator
Kintner, Robert	Business	5	10	30	10	
Kip, William I., Bishop	Clergy	50	85	125		
Kipling, Rudyard 1865-1936	Author	212	885	700	1064	Nobel Lit., Novelist, Poet
Kiplinger, Austin	Business	10	20	45	15	Kiplinger Washington Newsletter
Kipnis, Alexander	Entertainment	35	75		85	Opera. Russ. Bass
Kirby, George	Entertainment	5			15	
Kirby, Jack*	Cartoonist	25			170	Captain America
Kirby, Rollin*	Cartoonist	20			90	
Kirby-Smith, Edmund	Military	65	185	295		CSA General
Kirk, Andy	Bandleader				65	
Kirk, Claude Jr.	Governor	7	15			Governor FL
Kirk, Eddie	Country Music	10			20	
Klrk, Florence	Entertainment	10			30	Opera
Kirk, George	Aviation	10	22	38	30	ACE, WW II
Kirk, Norman T.. 1888-	Military		50			U.S. Gen. WW II
Kirk, Phyllis	Entertainment	20		95	45	
Kirk, Tommy	Entertainment	10			20	
Kirkby-Lunn, Louise	Entertainment	30			95	Opera
Kirkconnell, Clare	Entertainment	4	5	9	10	
Kirkham, Ralph W.	Clvll War	27	55	75		Union General
Kirkland, Lane	Labor	8	15	30	15	Labor Leader. AFL-CIO
Kirkland, Sally	Entertainment	5			20	
Kirkpatrick, Jean J.	Cablnet	12		25	20	Ambassador U.N.
Kirkwood, Joe, Jr.	Entertainment	45	75	150	100	And Golfer
Kirkwood, Samuel J.1813-94	Cabinet	15	25	55	30	Sec'y Intertior, Gov,Senator IA
Kirman, Richard, Sr.	Governor	10		30		Governor NV
Klrschlager, Angelika	Entertainment				30	Opera. Vienna's New Rising Star
Kirsten, Dorothy	Entertainment	20			50	Am. Soprano, Opera, Concert
Kiss (Entire Group)	Entertainment	35			125	Rock. Alb. S $145
Kissinger, Henry A.	Cabinet	20	125		50	Sec'y State
Kistiakowsky, G.B., Dr.	Science	40	135			Nobel Chemistry
Kitchener, Horatio H. of Khartoum	Military	85	205	335	200	Ir.-born Br. Field Marshal
Kitt, Eartha	Entertainment	10			35	Pin-Up SP $25
Kittinger, Joe	Aviation	25	45			
Kittredge, Walter	Composer	30				Tenting Tonight...AMQS $300-$1,150
Kleber, Jean-Baptiste	Fr. Revolution	145	410	855		One of France's Greatest Gen'ls
Klee, Paul	Artist	205	615	1850		Swiss Surrealist Painter
Klein, Calvin	Business	5	15	35	25	Fashion-Accessory Designer
Klein, Robert	Entertainment	4			12	Actor, Comedian
Klemperer, Otto	Entertainment	50			170	German Conductor
Klemperer, Werner	Entertainment	15	25		25	
Kleppe, Thomas S.	Cabinet	5	15	30	10	MOC ND, Sec'y Interior
Klimt, Gustav 1862-1918	Artist	165	575	1250		Austrian. Allegorical Murals
Kline, Kevin	Entertainment	10	12	45	35	Wanda Cast $120. AA
Klose, Margarete 1902-68	Entertainment	15			65	Opera. Ger. Mezzo-Soprano
Kluge, Hans Gunther von	Military	75		250		Ger. Gen.I WW II, Suicide
Klugman, Jack	Entertainment	10			25	
Klutznick, Philip M.	Cabinet	5	12		8	Sec'y Commerce
Kmentt, Waldemar	Entertainment	10			30	Opera
Knern, H.H.*	Cartoonist	25			180	Katzenjammer Kids
Knerr, Harold H.	Cartoonist			95		Katzenjammer Kids Artist for Many Years
Knibb, William	Clergy	45	60	75		
Knievel, Evel	Celebrity	10	15	35	45	Daredevil Motorcycle Rider
Knight, Evelyn	Entertainment	10				With the Star Dusters

NAME	CATEGORY	SIG	LS/DS	ALS	SP	Comment
Knight, Fuzzy	Entertainment	50			150	
Knight, Gladys	Entertainment	15	15	35	40	Rock
Knight, Goodwin J.	Governor	10	15		15	Governor CA
Knight, John S.	Business	10	35	45	20	Publisher
Knight, Jordan	Entertainment	10			45	
Knight, June	Entertainment	8	9	20	25	
Knight, Laura, Dame 1877-1970	Artist	60	100	175		Ranked Alongside Britain's Greatest
Knight, Phil	Business	22	35	45	25	Nike Athletic Shoes Etc.
Knight, Shirley	Entertainment	9	10	20	25	
Knight, Ted	Entertainment	15		35	35	
Knopf, Alfred A.	Business	7	20	35		Knopf Publishing
Knote, Heinrich	Entertainment	20			50	Opera
Knott, Walter	Business	150			475	Founder Knott's Berry Farm
Knott, Walter And Cordelia Knott	Business	25	70		75	Co-Founders Knott's Berry Farm
Knotts, Don	Entertainment	10			20	Self Sketch S $35
Knowland, William F.	Senate	10	20		25	Senator CA, Publisher
Knowles, James S.	Author	10	25	50		
Knowles, Patrick	Entertainment	10			25	
Knox, Alexander	Entertainment	10	15	30	30	
Knox, Elyse	Entertainment	10	20	35	25	Actress-Wife Tom Harmon
Knox, Frank 1874-1944	Cabinet	50	115	95	100	Sec'y Navy. TLS/Cont $275
Knox, Henry 1750-1806	Cabinet-Military	150	724	700		Rev. War Dte. ALS $4,500
Knox, James, Cardinal	Clergy	30	30	35	35	
Knox, Philander C.1853-1921	Cabinet	12	25	70	30	Att'y Gen., Senator PA
Knudsen, William S.	Business	20	35	85	45	Pres. GM. WW II War Prod. Dir.
Knutson, Harold	Senate/Congress	5	10		10	MOC MN
Kobayashi, Takeji	Author	20		60	45	Proletarian Literary Movement
Koch, Edward I.	Political	10	20	35	15	Mayor NYC
Koch, Heinrich H. Robert	Science		1500	2259	1500	Nobel Bacteriology-Medicine'05
Koch, Howard W.	Entertainment	10			25	
Koch, Robert, Dr. 1843-1910	Science			1367	2300	Founder Modern Bacteriology
Kodaly, Zoltan 1882-1967	Composer	125	290	685	448	Content ALS $1750
Koehl, Herman	Aviation	75			250	1st East-West Crossing Atlantic
Koehler, Armin	Aviation	10	20	35	25	
Koening, Walter	Entertainment	20			45	
Kohl, Hannelove	Celebrity	5			10	Mrs. Helmut Kohl
Kohl, Helmut	Heads of State	15	30	65	25	Chancellor Germany
Kohler, Walter J.	Business	10	30			Founder Kohler Corp. Plumbing
Kohlsaat, Herman H.	Editor	3		15		
Kohner, Susan	Entertainment	5			20	
Kokoschka, Oskar 1886-1980	Artist	100		450	275	PC Repro Painting S $180
Kolff, Willem J., Dr.	Science	15	55		40	Created Artificial Kidney
Kolker, Henry	Entertainment	10			20	
Kolleck, Teddy	Political	15	25		35	Mayor of Jerusalem
Kollo, Rene	Entertainment	10		35	25	Opera
Kollwitz, Kathe 1867-1945	Artist			362		Ger. Sculptor, Graphic Artist
Komarov, Vladimir	Astronaut	125			190	
Konetzni, Anny	Entertainment	25			65	Opera
Konya, Sandor	Entertainment				40	Opera. Hung. Tenor
Kook, Abraham Isaac	Clergy	45	145			Palestinian Rabbi
Koontz, Dean	Author	25	65		70	Horror
Koop, C.Everett, Dr.	Military	7	20	50	30	Adm., US Surgeon General
Kopell, Bernie	Entertainment	5			15	
Koppel, Ted	TV News	10	15	30	20	
Korda, Alexander	Entertainment	40	45	90	85	
Koren, Edward*	Cartoonist	10			75	New Yorker Cartoonist

NAME	CATEGORY	SIG	LS/DS	ALS	SP	Comment
Korman, Harvey	Entertainment	5	6	15	15	
Kornberg, Arthur	Science	20	30	45	25	Nobel Medicine
Kornby, Arthur	Science	15		20		
Korngold, Erich W.	Composer	75	200	350	90	Opera, Orchestral, Film Scores
Korolyov, Sergei 1906-66	Science		1718	2300		Russ. Aeronautical Engineer
Korvin, Charles	Entertainment	4	4	9	10	
Kosciusko, Thaddeus	Revolutionary War	300	750	2500		Polish Patriot.
Kosleck, Martin	Entertainment	15			35	
Kossa, Frank R.	Military	7	9	12	10	
Kossuth, Lajos 1802-94	Head of State	120	825	475	90	Hungarian Patriot, Journalist
Kostal, Irwin	Composer	3	10	20	10	
Kostelanetz, Andre 1901-80	Entertainment	15	25	45	25	Conductor
Koster, Henry	Entertainment	15	35		40	Film Director
Kosygin, Aleksei	Head of State	275	1295	875	480	Premier of Soviet Union
Kovack, Nancy (Mehta)	Entertainment	4	4	9	10	
Kovacs, Ernie	Entertainment	200			400	
Kovalevskaya, Sophia 1850-91	Science			850		Rus. Mathematician, Novelist
Kovansky, Anatol	Artist	15		40	25	
Kove, Martin	Entertainment	6	8	15	15	
Kowarski, L.	Science	10	25	60		
Kozky, Alex*	Cartoonist	10			20	Apt. 3-G
Kozlovsky, Ivan 1900-	Entertainment				1500	Ukrainian Tenor. RARE
Kraft, Chris	Astronaut	15			25	
Kraft, James L.	Business	30	95	175	50	Founder Kraft Foods Co.
Kragen, Ken	Business	5	10	20	20	Entertainment Business Mgr.
Kral, Roy	Celebrity	10	25		15	
Kramer, Stanley	Entertainment	15	35		35	Film Producer, Director
Kramer, Stephanie	Entertainment	5			20	
Krantz, Judith	Author	25		40	35	Novelist
Krasner, Milton	Entertainment	20			45	Film Director. AA
Kraus, Alfredo	Entertainment	15			35	Opera
Kraus, Clemens	Entertainment	65			220	Austrian Conductor
Kraus, Robert	Artist	10	25	50	25	
Krauss, Werner	Entertainment	250				
Krebs, Hans Adolf, Sir	Science	15	26	40	20	Nobel Medicine
Kreisler, Fritz 1875-1962	Composer	103	170	300	232	Violinist, AMQS $275
Kremer, Andrea	TV News	5			12	ESPN News
Krenek, Ernst	Composer	15	35	90	55	AMusQS $95-$225
Krenn, Fritz	Entertainment	15			35	Opera
Kreps, Juanita M.	Cabinet	4	10	15	12	Sec'y Commerce
Kresge, S. S.	Business	150	250	305	100	Kresge Stores
Kretschmer, Otto	Military	45	140		185	Highest Scoring U Boat Cmdr.
Kreutzer, Conradin	Composer	125	300	650		Ger. Composer/Conductor
Krige, Alice	Entertainment	4	4	9	10	
Kristel, Sylvia	Entertainment	20			45	
Kristofferson, Kris	Entertainment	10		35	30	
Kroc, Mrs. Ray (Joan)	Business	5	15	35	15	McDonalds
Kroc, Ray A.	Business	30	90	150	100	McDonalds
Krock, Arthur	Author	7	20	40	15	Bureau Chief,Columnist NY Times
Kroesen, Fred J.	Military	4	15	20	10	
Krofft, Marty	Entertainment	40	125		50	Puppeteer
Kroft, Steve	TV Journalist	5			24	60 Minutes
Krol, John, Cardinal	Clergy	35	40	75	50	
Kroll, Gustov	Science	10			30	Rocket Pioneer/von Braun
Kropotkin, Peter A. 1842-1921	Anarchist	30	75	502		Rus. Prince Gave Up Title for Working Class
Krueger, Walter 1881-	Military		100			Sp.-Am.,WW I & Full Gen. WW II

NAME	CATEGORY	SIG	LS/DS	ALS	SP	Comment
Krug, J. A.	Cabinet	10	20	30	15	Sec'y Interior
Kruger, Kurt	Entertainment	8	9	15	35	
Kruger, Otto 1885-1974	Entertainment	30			75	Distinguished Leading & Character Actor
Kruger, Paul	Head of State	75	350		175	Pres. So. Afr., Kruger Nat'l Pk
Kruger, Stephanus J.P.1825-1904	Head of State	125	450		660	Krugerrand Named For Him
Krupa, Gene 1909-73	Entertainment	40	195		95	Big Band Leader-Drums
Krupinski, Walter	Aviation	15	30	55	60	Ger. Ace. WW II . RK
Krupp, Alfred	Business	180	450	500		Founder Krupp Works
Krupp, Friedrich Alfred	Business	125	350			Arms Manufacturer
Krylov, Ivan A.	Author	15	40	75	20	Russion Fabulist. Fables
Kschessinska, Matilda M.1872-1971	Ballet	110		580		Prima Ballerina Assoluta Imperial Theatre
Kubelik, Jan	Composer	40	115	240	225	Violinist, AMQS $200-575
Kubelik, Rafael	Conductor	15	50		50	
Kubitschek,Juscelino	Head of State	10	35	90	25	Brazil
Kubrick, Sidney	Entertainment	5	5	10	15	
Kubrick, Stanley	Entertainment	10			60	Film Director
Kuchel, Thomas 1910-	Congress	5	25			Sen. CA
Kuchta, Gladys	Entertainment	10			30	Opera
Kudrow, Lisa	Entertainment	20			60	Actress Friends
Kuhlman, Katherine	Clergy	35		50		Radio Evengelist
Kulp, Nancy	Entertainment	10			25	Comedienne-Actress
Kuncewiczowa,, Maria	Author	145		345		Escaped Nazi Ger.
Kung, Hans	Clergy	35	50	75	60	
Kunstler, William	Law	20	35	75	25	Noted For Defense of Radicals
Kupka, Frantisek 1871-1957	Artist	110	225	387		Czech.Abstract Art, Illustrator
Kuralt, Charles	TV News	8	20	35	15	Commentator
Kurtz, Swoosie	Entertainment	5			26	Actress. Sisters
Kusch, Polykarp, Dr.	Science	20	50		25	Nobel Physics
Kuykendall, Andrew J. 1815-91	Congress	10				Repr. IL, Union Officer
Kwan, Nancy	Entertainment	9	16		45	
Ky, Nguyen Cao	Head of State	30	100	250	75	
Kyne, Peter B.	Author	5	15	30	10	Homsey Family Novels
Kyser, Kay	Entertainment	15			30	Big Band Leader

NAME	CATEGORY	SIG	LS/DS	ALS	SP	Comment
L A Guns	Entertainment	15			40	Rock
L A Law (Cast of)	Entertainment				275	10 Sigs.
L'Amour, Louis 1908-88	Author	75	220	490	125	Novels Re The Old West
L'Enfant, Pierre Charles	Aviation	400	850	1500		
L'Ouverture, Toussaint 1743-1803	Statesman		2300			Led Haitian Slave Revolt 1791
La Belle, Patti	Entertainment	15			35	Singer
La Cava, Gregory	Entertainment	20			45	Film Director
La Forge, Frank	Composer	15			45	
La Marr, Barbara	Entertainment	300			800	

NAME	CATEGORY	SIG	LS/DS	ALS	SP	Comment
La Revelliere-Lepaux,L.	Fr. Revolution	25	70	145		Politician
La Rocque, Rod	Entertainment	20		45	55	
La Rue, Jack	Entertainment	10			25	
La Verne. Lucille	Entertainment	75			150	
LaBeauf, Sabrina	Entertainment				15	Actress. Bill Cosby Show
Labouisse, Eve Curie	Science	15	60	90	35	Daughter of Marie & Pierre Curie
Lacepede, Bernhard de	Science	30	75	145		Fr. Naturalist & Politician
Lachaise, Gaston 1882-1935	Artist		125	325		Fr.-Am. Sculptor
Laciura, Anthony	Entertainment	5			25	Opera
Ladd, Alan 1913-64	Entertainment	65	75		188	
Ladd, Cheryl	Entertainment	8	9	20	20	Pin-Up SP $30
Ladd, David	Entertaiinment	10			25	Producer
Ladd, Diane	Entertainment	5	6	15	15	
Ladd, Sue Carol	Entertainment	5	6	15	15	
LaDelle, Jack	Entertainment	3	3	6	6	
Laemmle, Carl	Business	95	268	825	750	Film Pioneer, Founder Universal
Laennec, René T.H. 1781-1826	Science	3500	3500	6500		Fr. Phys., Invented Stethoscope
LaFarge, John 1835-1910	Artist	40	95	175		Am. Landscape & Figure Painter
Lafayette, Marquis de 1757-1834	Revolutionary War	400	1250	2178		Gilbert Motier. Cont. ALS $4,900-9600
LaFollette, Philip	Governor	15	35		20	Governor WI
LaFollette, Robert Jr.	Senate/Congress	10	25		20	Senator WI
LaFollette, Robert M.	Senate/Congress	35	95		40	Senator WI
LaFontaine, Henri Marie	International Law	10	20	30		Nobel Peace Prize
Lagerkvist, P„r F.	Author	30	70	175	100	Nobel Literature 1951
Lagerlof, Selma 1858-1940	Author	95	305		125	Nobel Literature 1909
Lagge, James	Clergy	20	25	35		
LaGuardia, Fiorello 1882-1947	Congress	20	131	145	175	Great Reform Mayor NYC.Repr. NY
Lahm, Frank	Aviation	35	75	140	90	
Lahr, Bert 1895-1967	Entertainment	283	340		572	Comedian, Cowardly Lion of OZ
Lahti, Christine	Entertainment	6	8	15	15	
Laidlie, D. A.	Clergy	15	20	25		
Laine, Frankie	Entertainment	7			15	
Laine, J.L.J.,Viscount	Fr. Revolution	30	85	175		
Laingen, Bruce	State Dept.	5			15	Iran Hostage
Laird, Melvin	Cabinet	7		25	15	Sec'y Defense
Lake, Arthur	Entertainment	55	25	50	35	Dagwood of Blondie)
Lake, Ricki	Entertainment	30			60	TV Hostess
Lake, Simon 1866-1945	Science-Engineer	58	163	600		Inv. Even-Keel Type Submarine
Lake, Veronica 1919-73	Entertainment	175	495		255	
Laker, Freddie, Sir	Business	5			20	Airline President
Lakes, Gary	Entertainment	10			30	Opera
LaLanne, Jack	Entertainment	10	15	30	25	TV Body Builder
Lalique, Rene 1860-1929	Artist	150		600		Fr. Jeweler & Decorative Glass Artisan
Lamar, Joseph R. (SC)	Supreme Court	35	95	225		
Lamar, Lucius Q.C. (SC) 1825-93	Supreme Court	75		235		CSA Officer, US Sen.
Lamar, Mirabeau B.1789-1859	Head of State	95	395			Pres., V.P. & Sec'y State Repub. of TX
LaMarck, Jean Baptiste de	Science	400	950	1000		Forerunner of Darwin
LaMarr, Hedy	Entertainment	35	75	100	108	40's Beautiful Glamour Girl
LaMartine, Alphonse de 1790-1869	Author	90	205	225		Fr. Romantic Poet-Statesman
Lamas, Fernando	Entertainment	20	25	45	45	
Lamas, Lorenzo	Entertainment	9	10	20	25	
Lamb, Caroline, Lady 1785-1828	Celebrity			1395		
Lamb, Charles	Author	115	• 350	750		Br. Essayist, Critic
Lamb, Gil	Entertainment	8			20	Stage-Film Dancer, Comic
Lambert, Ray	Celebrity	5	14		10	
Lambert, William C.	Aviation	75	135	175	150	ACE, WW I, 2nd Leading Ace

NAME	CATEGORY	SIG	LS/DS	ALS	SP	Comment
Lamm, Richard D.	Governor	5	26			CO Gov.
Lammers, Hans	Military	95	650			Nazi Official. Hitler Legal Advisor
Lamond, Frederic	Composer	20		78	100	Scot. Pianist & Composer
Lamont, Corliss	Activist	10		25		Author.Indicted for Contempt of Congress
Lamont, Daniel S.	Cabinet	15	25	40		Sec'y War, Journalist, Politici
Lamont, Forrest	Entertainment	25			65	Opera
Lamont, Robert P.	Cabinet	25	60	95		Sec'y Commerce
Lamont, Thomas	White House	15	30	45		Lincoln Pvt. Sec'y
Lamont, Thomas S.	Business	8	25	40	10	Banker. Morgan Guaranty
LaMotta, Vikki	Entertainment	3		10	5	Model-Actress. SP Nude 45
Lamour, Dorothy	Entertainment	9	25	20	35	Pin-Up SP $35, $55
Lamphier, Tom	Aviation				125	US Ace. Shot Down Yamamoto
Lampton, Mike	Astronaut	7			15	
Lamson, C.M.	Clergy	10	10	20		
Lana,Cosmo Gordon	Clergy	10	15	25		
Lancaster, Burt	Entertainment	25	150		65	
Lance, Bert	Business	3	5	15	10	Banker
Lanchester, Elsa	Entertainment	15	20	40	45	
Land, E. S.	Military	25	65		35	Adm. Maritime Comm. WW II
Land, Edwin H.1909-1992	Science-Business	80	225		175	Polaroid Camera Inventor
Landau, Martin	Entertainment	10			45	AA. As Dracula $75
Lander, Frederick West	Civil War	180	225	475		Union Gen.ALS/Cont.'61 $1375
Landers, Ann	Columnist	8	20	30	10	Advice Column
Landers, Audrey	Entertainment	6	8	15	15	
Landers, Judy	Entertainment	5	6	15	15	Pin-Up SP $25
Landesberg, Steve	Entertainment	5			20	
Landi, Bruno	Entertainment	15			60	Opera
Landi, Elissa	Entertainment	45	30	60	70	Vintage
Landis, Carole 1919-48	Entertainment	100			198	Suicide at 29
Landis, Jessie Royce	Entertainment	25			75	
Landis, John	Entertainment	15			25	Film Director
Landis, Kenesaw Mountain	Jurist	200			525	Baseball Commissioner
Landon, Alfred M. 1887-1987	Governor	25	95	110	50	Rep. Pres. Candidate vs FDR
Landon, Melville D.	Journalist	20				(aka Eli Perkins) Columnist
Landon, Michael	Entertainment	100	125		205	
Landowska, Wanda	Entertainment	110			295	Pol-Fr Harpsichordist
Landrieu, Moon	Cabinet	6		15	10	Sec'y HUD
Landseer, Charles	Artist	30		75		R.A. & Keeper of Royal Academy
Landseer, Edwin H., Sir 1802-1873	Artist	30	65	262		Extraordinary Landscape Painter
Landseer, John	Artist	25		125		Father of Edwin H.
Landseer, Thomas	Artist-Engraver	25	40	75		Brother of E.H.
Landsteiner, Karl, Dr	Science	50	90	210		Nobel Medicine
Lane, Abbe	Entertainment	15			20	Vocalist. Mrs.Xavier Cugat. Pin-Up SP $15
Lane, Allan Rocky	Entertainment	65			250	Cowboy-Actor
Lane, Christy	Entertainment	5	6	15	15	Gospel Singer
Lane, Diane	Entertainment	10	20		15	
Lane, Evelyn	Entertainment	10			25	Brit. Actress. Vintage
Lane, Franklin K.	Cabinet	25	40		25	Sec'y Interior
Lane, Harriet	First Lady, Actg.	100	250	375		Actg. 1st Lady, Buchanan
Lane, James H. (War Date)	Civil War-Congress	172	450	540		Special DS $7,500
Lane, James H. 1814-1866	Civil War-Congress	85	135	302		Sen. KS, Union Gen.,Suicide
Lane, James Henry 1833-1907	Civil War	65	200	335	950	CSA General
Lane, Joseph	Governor	40	75	130		Gov. OR Terr.& 1st US Sen.
Lane, Lola	Entertainment	15	15	30	25	
Lane, Nathan	Entertainment	15			66	Stage, Screen Actor-Comedian
Lane, Priscilla	Entertainment	12	15	25	25	

The Sanders Price Guide to Autographs

NAME	CATEGORY	SIG	LS/DS	ALS	SP	Comment
Lane, Rosemary	Entertainment	15	15	35	35	
Lang, Anton	Entertainment	25	25	45	40	
Lang, Cosmo Gordon	Clergy	25	35	45	35	
Lang, Fritz	Entertainment	50	375		150	Ger. Innovative Film Director
Lang, June	Entertainment	10				Actress
Lang, K D	Country Music	20	20		75	
Lang, Rosa	Entertainment	4	4	9	10	
Lang, Sebastian	Entertainment	19	25	45	45	
Lang, Walter	Entertainment	20			45	Film Director. 40 Year Vet.
Langan, Glenn	Entertainment	8	15	35	25	
Langdon, Harry	Entertainment	100			225	
Langdon, John	Revolutionary War	210	400	1575		Continental Congr.,Gov. NH, Signer Const'n
Lange, David	Head of State	5	15	30	15	New Zealand
Lange, Hope	Entertainment	10			30	Pin-Up SP $30
Lange, Jessica	Entertainment	8			35	AA
Lange, Ted	Entertainment	5			15	
Langella, Frank	Entertainment	15	20		45	
Langer, Will	Senate	10	35			Senator ND
Langford, Frances	Entertainment	8			20	Big Band Vocalist-Films
Langley, Samuel P.	Aviation	205	260	500	350	1890's Aeronautical Pioneer
Langlie, Arthur	Governor	12	20		15	Governor Washington
Langmuir, Irving	Science	30	75	145		Nobel Chemistry 1932
Langtry, Lillie 1852-1929	Entertainment	350		568		Actress & Mistress of Edw. VII
Langtry, Lily	Entertainment	175	450			
Lanier, Sidney	Author	300	590	1165		Most Important So. Poet of Time
Lannes, Jean	Fr. Revolution	675				Marshal of France
Lanphier, Thomas G., Jr.	Aviation	40	70	120	85	ACE, WW II, Yamamoto Mission
Lansbury, Angela	Entertainment	5	6	15	25	
Lansing, Robert	Cabinet	40	125			Sec'y State
Lansky, Meyer 1902-83	Gangster	200	1500			Jewish Mob Boss
Lantieri, Rita	Entertainment 5	5			20	Opera
Lantz, Walter* 1900-94	Cartoonist	60	85	95	122	Woody Woodpecker
Lanza, Mario 1921-1959	Entertainment	175			798	Tragic Tenor/Cinema Star. Early Death
LaPlace, P.M.,Marquis de	Science	535				Fr. Astronomer, Mathematician
Lapoype, J.F.C., Baron	Fr. Revolution	20		125		
Larch, John	Entertainment	6	8	15	10	
Larcom, Lucy	Author	15	25	45		
Lardner, Dionysius	Author	45	175			Irish writer on Sci. & Math.
Lardner, James L.	Civil War	35	85	125		Union Naval Commodore
Lardner, Ring 1885-1933	Author	65	195	310	75	Am. Humorist, Social Satirist
Lardner, Ring Jr.	Author	10	20	35	15	
Laredo, Ruth	Entertainment	15	15	30	35	
Larmouth, Kathy	Entertainment	4	4	9	9	
LaRocca, D.J. Nick	Musician-Composer	50			225	AMusQS $250
LaRosa, Julius	Entertainment	5			10	Singer Arthur Godfey Show
LaRoushe, Lyndon, Jr.	Pres. Candidate	20		35	25	Tax Evader
Larrey, Dominick Baron	Fr. Revolution	45	155	310		
Larroquette, John	Entertainment	10			30	
Larsen-Todsen, Nanny	Entertainmnt	20			50	Opera
Larson, Gary*	Cartoonist	20			100	Far Side
Larson, Leonard, Dr.	Science	5	15	30	10	
LaRue, Lash	Entertainment	5	6	15	25	
Lasker, Mary	Business	5	10	15	10	
Lasky, Jesse L.	Business	40	75	150	75	Pioneer Film Producer
Lasser, Louise	Entertainment	6			25	
Laswell, Fred*	Cartoonist	25			150	B.Google & Snuffy Smith

NAME	CATEGORY	SIG	LS/DS	ALS	SP	Comment
Latham, Hubert	Aviation	25	35	90	75	
Latham, Louise	Entertainment	4			20	Current Character Actress
Lathrop, George P.	Author	20	50	150		Am. Journalist, Writer
Latour-Maubourg,M.V.N.F.	Napoeonic Wars	20		75		Cavalry Gen.
Latourette, Kenneth Scott	Clergy	20	30	45	30	
Latrobe, Benjamin H. 1764-1820	Artist		462	1400		Am. Arch. of the White House
Lattimore, Richard	Author	10	15	25	15	
Laubach, Frank C.	Clergy	35	50	90	60	
Lauck, Chet	Entertainment	10				Radio. Lum & Abner
Lauder, Estee	Business	10			30	Cosmetics
Lauder, Harry, Sir	Entertainment	55	90	145	70	Vintage Scottish Comedian
Laughton, Charles 1899-1962	Entertainment	85	125		275	
Lauper, Cyndi	Entertainment	25	35	85	60	Rock
Laurance, John	Revolutionary War	15		90		
Laurants, Arthur	Author	5			20	Playwright
Laurel, Stan & Hardy, Oliver	Entertainment	650			1058	SPI 3x5 $895, SP (PC) $650
Laurel, Stan 1890-1965	Entertainment	130	425	525	375	
Lauren, Dyanna	Entertainment				36	Porn Queen
Lauren, Ralph	Business	10	15	40	25	Fashion Designer.
Laurencin, Marie	Artist	125		590		Fr. Painter & Printmaker
Laurens, Henry 1724-92	Revolutionary War	1250	2310	1975		Pres. Continental Congress
Laurie, Piper	Entertainment	6	8	15	20	Pin-Up SP $30
Lausche, Frank J.	Governor	12	20		15	Governor OH
Lauter, Harry	Entertainment	5			15	
Lauterbach, Johann Christoph	Entertainment		95	195		Ger. Violinist
Lavi, Daliah	Entertainment	4			10	Pin-Up SP $10
Lavin, Linda	Entertainment	5	6	15	15	
Lavoisier, Antoine L. de 1743-94	Science	400	3625			Fr. Founder Modern Chemistry
Law, Andrew Bonar	Head of State	30	80	135		Br. Prime Minister
Law, Evander McIvor 1836-1920	Civil War	100	250	568		CSA Gen.
Law, George H.	Clergy	10		15	20	
Law, John 1671-1729	Reformer	150				Scot. Economist. LS/Cont.$5000
Law, John Phillip	Entertainment	5			15	
Law, Ruth	Aviation	30			100	
Lawden, Frank O.	Celebrity	4	12	30		
Lawes, Lewis E.	Law Enforcement	20	40	120	25	Prison Warden. Sing Sing
Lawford, Peter	Entertainment	20			55	
Lawler, Michael K. 1814-82	Civil War	30	95			Union Gen. ALS '61 $360
Lawrence, 1st Baron	Head of State	10	30	75		India
Lawrence, Abbott 1792-1855	Congress	25				MA. Financier. Lawrence MA
Lawrence, Barbara	Entertainment	5			20	
Lawrence, Carol	Entertainment	5	6	15	15	
Lawrence, D(avid) H(erbert) 1885-1930	Author	225	590	3515		Br. Novelist.Lady Chatterley's Lover
Lawrence, David L.	Governor	17	20			Governor PA
Lawrence, Elliot	Entertainment	20			40	Big Band Leader. Multiple Emmys
Lawrence, Ernest O.	Science	95	275	400	200	Nobel Physics
Lawrence, Gertrude 1902-52	Entertainment	20	50		45	1st Star of King and I
Lawrence, Herbert A., Sir	Military	10	30	50	25	
Lawrence, Jacob	Artist	15	25			Afro-Am. Painter
Lawrence, John	Colonial	35	95	175		CT Statesman, Rev. War Leader
Lawrence, Marc	Entertainment	10	15	25	25	
Lawrence, Marjorie	Entertainment	10			125	Australian Opera, Concert Soprano
Lawrence, Sharon	Entertainment	10			25	NYPD Blue
Lawrence, Steve	Entertainment	6	8	10	15	
Lawrence, Thomas, Sir 1769-1830	Artist	150	225	200		Br. Portr. Painter. Pres. Royal Academy
Lawrence, Thos.E. 1888-1935.	Author-Soldier	650	1250	4000	2917	Lawrence of Arabia

NAME	CATEGORY	SIG	LS/DS	ALS	SP	Comment
Lawrence, Vicki	Entertainment	5	6	15	15	
Lawrence, William 1819-99	Congress	8				Repr. OH, Union Colonel
Lawson, James M.	Clergy	20	25	35	25	
Lawson, Ted	Aviation	15	30		40	
Lawton, Alexander R. (War Date)	Civil War		650	897		CSA Gen.
Lawton, Alexander R.1818-96	Civil War	110	350	311		CSA Gen.
Laxalt, Paul	Senate/Congress	4	10		15	Governor, Senator NV
Lay, Herman W.	Business	10	25	50	30	Lay's Potato Chips
Layard, Austin Henry, Sir	Archaeologist	10	25	50		Br. Diplomat
Lazarev, Alexander	Conductor				65	Former Bolshoi Maestro
Lazaro, Hippolito	Entertainment					Opera. Tenor
Lazarus, Emma 1849-87	Author		2300			The New Colossus
Lazarus, Mel*	Cartoonist	5			20	Miss Peach, Momma
Lazarus, S. Ralph	Business	4	7	10	5	Pres.Benrus Watch.Philanthropis
Lazenby, George	Entertainment	10	15	28	25	
Lazzari, Virgillo	Entertainment	15			45	
Lea, Homer	Military	55	175			Predicted US-Jap. War/HI as Key
Leachman, Cloris	Entertainment	9	25	15	20	AA
Leadbetter, Danville	Civil War	150	475			CSA General
Leahy, Patrick	Senate/Congress	5	15		10	Senator VT
Leahy, William Daniel	Military	35	145	105	195	Chief of Staff-FDR & Truman
Leake, J. B.	Civil War	20	55	75		
Leakey, Louis B.	Science	45	125	225	65	Anthropologist, Archaeologist
Leakey, Mary D.	Science	15	25	70	30	Anthropologist, Archaeologist
Leakey, Meave, Dr.	Science	20	60			
Leakey, Richard, Dr.	Science	125				Br. Anthropologist
Lean, David, Sir	Entertainment	45			70	Film Director
Lear, Edward	Artist	130		550		Br. Painter & Nonsense Poet
Lear, Norman	Business	10	15	45	20	TV FIlm Producer
Lear, Tobias	Revolutionary War	75	240	325		Pvt. Secretary to G. Washington
Lear, William P. Sr.	Business	30	115	175	100	Lear Jet Aircraft
Learned, Michael	Entertainment	9	10	20	25	
Leary, Timothy, Dr.	Activist-Educator	15	35		20	Drug Cult Leader Psychologist
Lease, Mary Elizabth	Reformer	15	20	40		Orator, Writer Woman Suffrage
Leavenworth, Henry	Military	250		750		Frontier Soldier, General
LeBlanc, Matt	Entertainment	20			70	Actor.. Friends
LeBrock, Kelly	Entertainment	10	15		35	Pin-Up SP $40
Lebrun, Albert 1871-1950	Head of State	30	50	125	35	Last Pres. 3rd French Repub.
Lebrun, Chas. F. Duc de 1739-1824	Napoleonic Wars	35	100	150		3rd Consul/Bonaparte
LeCarre, John (David Cornwell)	Author	20	45	75	30	Br. Realistic Spy Novels
Lecuona, Ernesto	Composer	150			375	AMusQS $400-$600
Led Zeppelin (all-org.)	Entertainment	250			700	Alb.Cover Signed $850
Lederer, Francis	Entertainment	10			25	
Lederman, Leon M., Dr.	Science	15	25	50		Nobel Phyics
Ledoux, Harold*	Cartoonist	5			25	Judge Parker
Ledyard, John 1751-89	Explorer		475			Accompanied Capt. Cook. Wrote Adventures.
Lee, Alfred	Clergy	10	15	35		
Lee, Anna	Entertainment	5			15	
Lee, Bernard	Entertainment	15			25	
Lee, Brandon 1964-93	Entertainment		525		900	Son of Bruce Lee. Tragic Death
Lee, Brenda	Country Music	5			15	
Lee, Bruce	Entertainment	650	812		1050	Legendary Cult Celeb
Lee, Canada	Entertainment	55			125	
Lee, Charles (1731-82)	Military			2035		Turncoat Gen. Rev. War
Lee, Charles (1758-1815)	Cabinet	110	250	550		Washington's Att'y Gen.
Lee, Christopher	Entertainment	15			50	Best Known for Role in Dracula

The Sanders Price Guide to Autographs

NAME	CATEGORY	SIG	LS/DS	ALS	SP	Comment
Lee, Dixie (Mrs Bing Crosby)	Entertainment	10	15	25	25	
Lee, Dr. Tsung-Dao	Science	20	30	45	25	Nobel Physics
Lee, E. Hamilton	Aviation	10	25	50	35	
Lee, Edwin G.	Civil War	165	290	410		CSA Gen.
Lee, Fitzhugh (War Date)	Civil War	238		605		CSA Gen.
Lee, Fitzhugh 1835-1905	Civil War	157	190	311	480	CSA General. AQS $595
Lee, Francis Lightfoot	Revolutionary War	660	1050	4250		Signer Decl. of Indepen.
Lee, Geo. Wash. Custis 1832-1913	Civil War	155	590	410		CSA General
Lee, Geo. Wash.,Custis (War Date)	Civil War	270		2500		CSA Gen.
Lee, Gypsy Rose 1913-1970	Entertainment	105			565	Burlesque Queen & Sometimes Movie Star
Lee, Harper	Author	110	350			To Kill a Mocking Bird
Lee, Heather	Entertainment				35	Porn Queen
Lee, Henry 1756-1818	Revolutionary War	200	600	625		Light-Horse Harry
Lee, Lila	Entertainment	5	6	15	15	
Lee, Mark C.	Astronaut	5			20	
Lee, Mary Custis	Civil War	150		690	475	Mrs. Robert E. Lee
Lee, Michele	Entertainment	5	6	15	15	
Lee, Peggy	Entertainment	10			30	Singer-Composer
Lee, Pinkie	Entertainment	15			35	
Lee, Richard Henry 1732-94	Revolutionary War	275	2333	3350		Signer Decl. of Indepen.
Lee, Robert E. (War Date)	Civil War	3822	12012	18740	8138	As CSA Gen. Auction $23K-$36,000
Lee, Robert E. 1807-70	Military	3440	5700	10700	7250	CSA Cmmdg. Gen.
Lee, Ruta	Entertainment	4			10	Pin-Up SP $10
Lee, Samuel P.	Civil War	60	210	275		Union Adm.
Lee, Spike	Entertainment	10	25		25	Afro-Am Film Director
Lee, Stephen Dill (War Date)	Civil War	250	1800			CSA Gen.
Lee, Stephen Dill 1833-1908	Civil War	120	345	384		CSA Gen.
Lee, Tommy	Entertainment	20			50	Rock
Lee, William H. 1837-91	Civil War	183		660		CSA Gen.,ALS War Date/Cont.. $6050
Lee, William Raymond	Civil War	15	45	70		Union General
Lee, Yuan T., Dr.	Science	20	35	45	30	Nobel Chemistry
Leeb, Wilhelm R. von	Military	20		135		
Leech, John	Artist	70	125	165		Br. Caricaturist $875
Leech, Richard	Entertainment	15			35	Opera
Leeds, Andrea	Entertainment	10			25	
Leese, Oliver, Sir	Military	20	50		35	Br. Gen. WW II/Montgomery. 8th Army
Leestma, David C.	Astronaut	5			15	
Lefebvre, F.J., Duke	Fr. Revolution	160	300			Marshal of Napoleon
Lefevre, Edwin	Financial Writer	4	8	15		Panamanian Ambass. to Spain
Leftwich, John W.	Senate/Congress	10	15	30		MOC TN 1866
LeGallienne, Eva	Entertainment	5	25	50	35	
LeGallienne, Richard	Author	25	50	65		Brit. Man of Letters
LeGarde, Tom and Ted	Country Music	10			20	
Leger, Fernand	Artist	80	240	575		Fr. Abstract Painter.AMsS $2750
Leggett, Mortimer Dormer	Civil War	20	40	65		Union General
Legrand, Michel	Composer	5	45	25	20	
LeHand, M. A. (Missy)1898-1944	Gov't Exec. Aide	20	80	130	40	FDR Personal Sec'y 20 Years
Lehar, Franz 1870-1948	Composer	85	222	618	342	The Merry Widow. AMusQS $225
Lehman, Herbert H. 1882-1963	Governor	15	75			Gov. NY, Senator NY
Lehmann, Ernst August	Aviation	85		365		Ger. Aeronautical Engineer
Lehmann, Lilli 1848-1929	Entertainment	175		100		Ger. Soprano. 170 Operatic Roles
Lehmann, Lotte	Entertainment	45	75	175	120	Opera
Lehmann, Marie	Entertainment	50			175	Ger. Prima Donna. Mother Lilli
Lehr, Lew	Entertainment	15	15	35	30	
Leibman, Ron	Entertainment	5	6	15	15	
Leider, Frida	Entertainment	35			150	Opera. Great Brunhilde

NAME	CATEGORY	SIG	LS/DS	ALS	SP	Comment
Leiferkus, Sergei	Entertainment	10			25	Opera
Leigh, Janet	Entertainment	5	9	15	20	Pin-Up SP $25
Leigh, Jennifer Jason	Entertainment	10			75	
Leigh, Richard	Composer	5	18			
Leigh, Vivien (As Scarlett O'Hara)	Entertainment				1450	SP $1750 (PC)-7750
Leigh, Vivien 1913-67	Entertainment	507	600	740	874	
Leigh, Vivien and Laurence Olivier	Entertainment		475		1200	
Leighton, Frederic 1830-1896	Artist	25		200		Pres. Br.Royal Academy
Leighton, Laura	Entertainment	10			55	Actress. Melrose Place
Leighton, Margaret	Entertainment	15			40	
Leinsdorf, Erich	Conductor	15			75	Austro-Amer Conductor
Leisure, David	Entertainment	5			10	
Lejeune, John Archer	Military	35	75	150	75	Commandant US Marine Corps
Leland, Henry M. 1843-1932	Business		1580			Contract Creating Lincoln Motor Co. S $9500
Leland, W. C.	Business	20	55	140	40	
Leloir, Luis Frederico	Science	20	40	45	25	Nobel Chemistry
Lelong, Lucien	Designer	25				Fashion, Cosmetics
Lelouch, Claude	Entertainment	9	10	20	25	
LeMaire, Charles	Entertainment	15			25	Director
Lemass, Sean	Head of State	10	25	60	30	Prime Minister Ireland
LeMay, Curtis E. 1906-1990	Military	25	112		75	AF Gen. WW II. 200th Air Force, SAC
Lembeck, Harvey	Entertainment	30			75	
Lembeck, Michael	Entertainment	3	3	6	10	
Lemeshev, Sergei	Entertainment				500	Opera. Russ. Tenor of Soviet Era. RARE
Lemmon, Jack	Entertainment	6	8	15	25	AA
Lemnltz, Tiana	Entertainment	40			125	Opera
Lemnitzer, Lyman L.	Military	30	40	90	35	Supreme Allied Commd'r WW II
Lemon, Mark 1809-70	Author	15		35		Br. Playwright, Humorist, Co-Founder Punch
Lenin, Vladimir Ilyich (N.Lenin)	Head of State					ALS/Content $29,000
Lennon Sisters, The (4)	Entertainment	20			45	
Lennon, John 1940-1980	Entertainment	600	2238		1025	Assassinated Beatle
Lennon, Julian	Entertainment	20			40	
Lennox, Vera	Entertainment	12			20	Br. Actress
Leno, Jay	Entertainment	10			35	Self Caricature S $75
Lenoir, William B.	Astronaut	7			20	
Lenormand, René 1846-1932	Composer	30			175	Songs, String & Piano Music
Lenox, Lucie	Entertainment	15			40	
Lenske, Rula	Entertainment	4	4	9	15	
Lenya, Lotte	Entertainment	20	60		150	Cabaret Singer, Character Actr.
Leonard, Ada	Entertainment	20			70	Big band leader
Leonard, Elmore	Author	10			20	Author of "Get Shorty," many other novels
Leonard, George	Jurist	40	100			Colonial Am. Jurist
Leonard, Gloria	Entertainment	5	6	15	15	
Leonard, Jack	Entertainment				25	Singer/Tommy Dorsey Orch.
Leonard, Jack E.	Entertainment	5			10	Comedian
Leonard, Sheldon	Entertainment	5	6	15	15	
Leoncavallo, Ruggiero 1857-1919	Composer	175	500	512	675	AMusQS $850, $925
Leone, Sergio	Director-Movies	55			400	Master of Spaghetti Western
Leone, Tia	Entertainment					Actress. Pin-Up 45
Leonov & Gagarin (SEE GAGARIN)						
Leonov, Aleksei 1934-	Cosmonaut	130	155		275	Rus. Cosmonaut, 1st Space Walker
Leontif, Wassily, Dr.	Economist	20	35		40	Nobel Economics
Leontovich, Eugenie	Entertainment	15		30	45	
Leopardi, Giacomo	Author	80	350	475		Physically Deformed Italian Poe
Leopold I	Royalty	105	475			Belgium
Leopold I	Royalty	75	375	625		Hungary

NAME	CATEGORY	SIG	LS/DS	ALS	SP	Comment
Leopold II	Royalty	65	325	540		Belgium
Leopold, Nathan F. 1905-71	Criminal	125	385	575	150	Loeb & Leopold Case
Lermontov, Mikhail 1814-1841	Author	540	2300	4625		Novelist, Poet. Killed in Duel
Lerner, Alan Jay 1918-96	Composer	45	95	175	175	Am. Lyricist, Librettist/Loewe
Lerner, Max	Author	5	30	40	10	
LeRoy, Hal	Entertainment	7			15	Film Director
LeRoy, Mervyn	Entertainment	25	50		75	Film Director
Leslie, Frank 1821-80	Publisher	95				Founder Illustrated Newspaper
Leslie, Frank, Mrs.	Publisher	20		75	75	Leslie's Magazine
Leslie, Joan	Entertainment	6	8	15	19	
Leslie, Preston H.	Governor	10	15			Governor KY
Leslie, Thomas J. 1796-1874	Civil War	10		35		Union Gen. Paymaster's Dept. 50 Years
Lesseps, Ferdinand, de 18y05-94	Diplomat	145	225	475	700	Engineer. Promoted Suez Canal
Lester, Buddy	Entertainment	3	4	10	15	
Lesters, The (5)	Entertainment	10			25	Gospel Singers
Leszczynski, Stanislaus	Royalty	575				Stanislaw I, King of Poland
Letcher, John 1813-84	Civil War	80	265	212		CW Gov. VA, ALS/Cont. $2,500
Letterman, David	Entertainment	20			40	
Letterman, Jonathan	Civil War	95	175			Med. Services for CW Union Army
Leutze, Emanuel	Artist	75		320		Washington Crossing Delaware
Levant, Oscar	Entertainment	20			45	Pianist, Humorist, Actor
Levene, Sam	Entertainment	10			20	
Levenson, Sam	Entertainment	10	35		15	Radio, TV Comic
Leventhrope, Collett 1815-89	Civil War	90	165	1150		CSA Gen.
Lever, Asbury	Senate/Congress	5	10		5	MOC SC
Lever, Lord (Wm. Hesketh)	Business	30	100	190	60	Br. Soap Mfg. Lever Brothers
Leverett, John 1662-1724	Colonial	50	130	275		President of Harvard, Judge
Levi, Edward H.	Cabinet	7	25	45	10	Att'y General
Levi-Montalcini, Rita, Dr.	Science	20	65			Nobel Medicine
Levin, Ira	Author	25	35		30	Rosemary's Baby
Levine, David	Cartoonist	15			100	Caricaturist
Levine, Irving R.	TV News	4	10		5	Commentator
Levine, Jack	Artist	10	15	30		
Levine, James	Entertainment	7	10	35	25	Conductor
Levinson, Barry	Entertainment	5			20	
Levy, David H.	Science	15			20	Discovered Metor Crater
Lewellyn, Anthony	Astronaut	5	16		15	
Lewis, (Percy) Wyndham	Artist-Writer			400		Br. Painter & Writer
Lewis, Al	Entertainment	10			30	
Lewis, C(live) S(taples)	Author	270	575	1555		Br. Medievalist, Philosopher
Lewis, David 'Duffy'	Aviation	15	30	55	40	
Lewis, Drew	Cabinet	10		20	15	Sec'y of Transportation
Lewis, Edwin	Clergy	15	20	30		
Lewis, Emmanuele	Entertainment	6	8	15	15	
Lewis, Francis	Revolutionary War	375	1250	2500		Signer Decl. of Indepen.
Lewis, Geoffrey	Entertainment	4			10	Actor
Lewis, Gwilym H.	Aviation	20	45	80	55	
Lewis, Huey (And the News)	Entertainment	12			30	Rock
Lewis, J.C.	Entertainment	12			25	Blues Drummer
Lewis, James	Entertainment	15	15	30	25	
Lewis, Jarma	Entertainment	5			12	Actress
Lewis, Jerry	Entertainment	5	6	15	25	
Lewis, Jerry Lee	Country Music	30			70	And Rock
Lewis, Joe E.	Entertainment	20	30	45	40	Nightclub Comedian
Lewis, John	Activist	5	15			Civil Rights Leader
Lewis, John L. 1880-1969	Labor	40	60	195	105	AFL-CIO Labor Leader

NAME	CATEGORY	SIG	LS/DS	ALS	SP	Comment
Lewis, Juliette	Entertainment	25			50	
Lewis, Kerrie McCarver	Entertainment	2			5	Mrs. Jerry Lewis
Lewis, Meriwether 1774-1809	Explorer	4500	5500	5725		Lewis & Clark Expedition
Lewis, Monica	Entertainment	5			10	Singer-Actress
Lewis, Morgan	Revolutionary War	50	70	110		Gen.Gates Chief of Staff. Gov.
Lewis, Ramsey	Entertainment	25			50	Pianist-Composer
Lewis, Richard	Entertainment	5			20	Stand-up Comic-Actor
Lewis, Shari	Entertainment	6	8	15	18	
Lewis, Sinclair 1885-1951	Author	100	325	750	300	1st Am. Awarded Nobel for Lit.
Lewis, Ted	Entertainment	20	25		75	
Lewis, Vera	Entertainment	50				Character Actress
Lewis, William Arthur, Sir	Science	20	25	40	25	Nobel Economics
Lewis, William H.	Aviation	10	22	40	28	ACE, WW II
Lewishon, Ludwig	Author	20		25		Ger.-Born Author of 31 Books
Lewisohn, Adolph	Business	20	45	65	25	Mining, Investment
Lewitt, Sal	Artist	25			100	
Ley, Bob	TV News	5			10	ESPN News
Ley, Willy	Science	25	75	145	35	Rocker Expert, Sci-Fi Writer
Libby, Willard F.	Science	20	35	55	25	Nobel Chemistry
Liberace	Entertainment	50	200		135	Sig/Piano Sketch $75
Liberace, George	Entertainment	6	8		10	
Liberman, Evsei, Prof.	Celebrity	15	35		20	
Lichtenberg, Byron, Dr.	Astronaut	7			20	
Lichtenstein, Roy	Artist	30	65	140	50	Repro S $175
Lichty, George 1905-83	Cartoonist			25		Grin and Bear It
Liddell, Henry George	Clergy	20	35	40	45	
Liddy, G. Gordon	Gov't Official	5	20	50	30	Lawyer, Watergate,Convicted
Lie, Jonas	Author	15	40	60		Nor. Novelist, Dramatist
Lie, Trygve 1896-1968	Head of State	42	148	250	175	1st Sec'y Gen'l United Nations
Lieber, Fritz	Entertainment	35			100	
Liebermann, Max 1847-1935	Artist			250		Ger. Impressionist
Liebig, Justus von, 1803-73	Science	195		1165		Ger. Chem. ALS/Content $1,750
Lienart, Archille, Cardinal	Clergy	30	40	50	40	
Liggett, Hunter	Military	15	45	60	35	Gen. WW I
Liggett, Louis Kroh	Business	85	170	350		Liggett's Drug Store Chain
Light, Enoch	Entertainment					Big Bandleader-Violinist
Light, Judith	Entertainment	12	15	25	30	
Lightner, Candy	Celebrity	12	30		20	1st Pres. MADD
Lightner, Winnie	Entertainment	19	25	45	45	
Ligi, Josella	Entertainment	5			25	Opera
Ligonier, John 1678-1770	Military	25				Br. Field Marshall of Queen Anne
Liles, Brooks	Aviation	8	20	38	22	ACE, WW II, USAAF Ace
Lilienthal, David E.	Business	15	30		20	Co-Fndr. I.J. Fox, Furriers
Lilienthal, Otto 1848-96	Inventor	150		2600		Aeronautical Eng'r , Author
Liliuokalani, Lydia K.	Royalty	140	460	955	475	Queen Hawaii
Lillie, Beatrice 1894-1989	Entertainment	25		65	35	Br. Comedienne. WW II Entertainer
Lillie, Gordon W. (Pawnee Bill)	Entertainment	100	795	435	400	Buffalo Bill Contemporary
Liman, Arthur	Celebrity	4	12		2000	
Limbaugh, Rush	Radio/TV	20			50	Radio/TV Commentator
Lin, Y. S. Maya	Artist	25	100			Designed Viet Nam Wall
Lincke, Paul	Composer	70	185	325		AMusQS $675, Glow Worm
Lincoln, Abraham (As President)	President	3583	7190	10821	24550	Brady SP $50,000. FF $6800. ALS $16,000
Lincoln, Abraham 1809-1865	President	3200	4325	8700		ALS '48 $101,500.ALS '64 $288,500
Lincoln, Benjamin (b.1700)	Justice of Peace	45	160			Father of Gen. Lincoln
Lincoln, Benjamin 1733-1810	Cabinet-Military	100	175	500		Gen. Rev. War.Sec'y War
Lincoln, Elmo	Entertainment	475			1500	

The Sanders Price Guide to Autographs

NAME	CATEGORY	SIG	LS/DS	ALS	SP	Comment
Lincoln, Evelyn	Gov't Official	15	25		35	JFK Presidential Sec'y
Lincoln, Joseph	Author	13	20	30		Writer of Cape Cod Stories
Lincoln, Levi	Cabinet	35	85	130		Memb. Continental Congr
Lincoln, Mary Todd	First Lady	300	985	9200	3000	FF on Mourning Env. $3,900
Lincoln, Robert Todd 1843-1926	Cabinet	80	232	325		Capt. CW. Content LS $750
Lincoln, Rufus	Revolutionary War		1650			Present at Burgoyne Surrender
Lind, Don L.	Astronaut	6			20	
Lind, Jenny (Goldschmidt)1820-87	Entertainment	65	125	272	882	Concert, Opera
Lindberg, Charles W.	Military	25	85		40	One of 6 Iwo Jimo Flag Raiser
Lindbergh, Anne Morrow	Author	15	45	150	30	Am. Writer-Poet.
Lindbergh, Charles A. 1902-74	Aviation	890	1932	3125	2935	ALS/Content $7,500
Linden, Hal	Entertainment	5			15	
Lindfors, Viveca	Entertainment	12			40	
Lindholm, Berit	Entertainment	10			25	Opera
Lindley, Audra	Entertainment	4			10	
Lindsay, E. Lin	Aviation	10	22	38	30	ACE, WW II, USAAF Ace
Lindsay, Howard	Entertainment	10	15	25	25	Theatrical Producer
Lindsay, John	Politician	4	8		10	Lawyer, Author, Mayor NYC
Lindsay, Margaret	Entertainment	15	25	45	50	Leading Lady. 30's-40's
Lindsay, Vachel	Author	50	185	575	125	Poet, Artist, Prairie Troubado
Lindsey, Ben B.	Law	15				Jurist
Lindsey, George	Entertainment	6	8	15	19	
Lindstrom, Pia	Entertainment	2			15	Actress. TV News.Daughter Ingrid Bergman
Liney, John*	Cartoonist				50	Henry
Linkletter, Art	Entertainment	7	25		15	Radio-TV MC.
Linn, Archibald L. 1802-57	Congress	10				Repr. NY, County Judge
Linn-Baker, Mark	Entertainment	5			15	
Linnaeus, Carolus von 1707-78	Science	925	7500			Carl vonLinne.Swe. Botanist.
Linville, Larry	Entertainment	10			25	
Liotta, Ray	Entertainment	25			50	
Lipchitz, Jacques	Artist	130	210	225		Pol.-Fr.-Am. Cubist Sculptor
Lipfert, Helmut	Aviation	35			70	#15 World Highest ACE. Ger.
Lipkovska, Lydia	Entertainment	75			325	Rus. Soprano
Lipman, Clara	Entertainment	12			20	Stage Actress
Lipmann, Fritz A.	Science	25	45	70	30	Nobel Medicine 1953
Lipovsek, Marjana	Entertainment	10			30	Opera
Lippman, Walter	Author	25	75		30	Journalist, Editor, Pulitzer
Lipscomb, William N., Dr.	Science	20	35		30	Nobel Chemistry
Lipsner, B.B.	Aviation	30	65		90	Pioneer Air Mail Pilot
Lipton, Peggy	Entertainment	4	4	9	15	
Lipton, Thomas, Sir 1850-1940	Business	100	440		330	Br. Tea Merchant-Yachtsman
Lisa, Manuel	Celebrity	763				
List, Emanuel	Entertainment	35			95	
Lister, Joseph, Lord 1827-1912	Science	225	420	698		Pioneer of Antiseptic Surgery
Liston, Robert 1794-1847	Science	15	30	50		Skilled Scottish Surgeon
Listowel, Earl of	Philosopher	20				Viscount Wm. Francis Hare
Liszt, Franz 1811-86	Composer	450	650	1350	1883	AMuQS $3,800,AMMsS $16,750
Litchfield, Grace D. 1849-1944	Author	5		25		
Litel, John 1892-1964	Entertainment	15	15	35	35	
Lithgow, John	Entertainment	5	6	15	20	Third Rock From the Sun
Litjens, Stefan	Aviation	7	15	25	20	
Little Richard (Penniman)	Entertainment	18	20	45	112	Rock
Little River Band	Entertainment	25			50	
Little, Cleavon	Entertainment	13			35	
Little, Little Jack	Entertainment	15			35	Big Band Leader
Little, Rich	Entertainment	3			10	

NAME	CATEGORY	SIG	LS/DS	ALS	SP	Comment
Little, Royal	Business	22		55		
Littlejohn, Abram N.	Clergy	10	20	35		
Littlejohn, Dewitt C.	Civil War	40	85	120		Union General
Litvak, Anatole	Entertainment	20			45	Film Director
Litvinov, Maksim M.	Diplomat	50		95	65	Soviet Foreign Minister
Liu-Li Pei	Entertainment	10			25	Chinese Opera Star
Livermore, Dan'l P.	Clergy	15	20	45		
Livermore, Mary A.	Reformer	60	75	125		Woman Suffrage, Temperance
Liverpool, 2nd Earl	Head of State	120	135	200		Robt. Banks Jenkinson, P.M.
Livingston, Alan	Composer	15	55			
Livingston, Edward	Cabinet	30	85	150		Sec'y of State 1831
Livingston, Henry B. (SC)	Supreme Court	100	310			
Livingston, Jay	Composer	15	40	85	40	AMusQS $35-$100-$300
Livingston, Margaret	Entertainment	10			25	
Livingston, Mary	Entertainment	15	25	45	40	
Livingston, Peter Van Brugh	Revolutionary War		275			Patriot, Merchant
Livingston, Philip 1716-1778	Revolutionary War	288	1080	1175		Signer Decl. of Indepen.
Livingston, Robert	Entertainment	20			85	Known for 30's-40's Western Roles
Livingston, Robert 1742-94	Revolutionary War	170	350	400		Dir. Bank of the U.S. (1792)
Livingston, Robert R. 1746-1813	Revolutionary War	195	440	1250		Continental Congress
Livingston, Robert R., Sr. 1718-75	Law		500			Att'y, Judge. Opposed Stamp Act.
Livingston, William 1723-90	Revolutionary War	300	888	1750		Continental Congr. Gov. NJ
Livingstone, David 1813-1873	Explorer-Clergy	225	885	1850		Missionary, Explorer of Africa
Llewellyn, Anthony	Astronaut	10			30	
Lloyd, Christopher	Entertainment	10	15	28	30	
Lloyd, Emily	Entertainment	10			40	
Lloyd, Frank AA	Entertainment	20	50			Film Director AA
Lloyd, Harold 1894-1971	Entertainment	212	225		300	Film Comedian-Actor
Lloyd, James 1769-1831	Senate/Congress	30	65	90		Senator MA 1808
Lloyd, Kathleen	Entertainment	4	4	9	15	
Lloyd, Norman	Entertainment	4	4	9	10	
Lloyd-George, David, 1863-1945	Head of State	60	240	425	262	Br. Prime Minister, 1st Earl
Lo Giudici, Franco	Entertainment	40			150	Opera
Loan, Nguyen Ngoc	Military	150			375	Gen. Viet Nam
Loasby, Arthur W.	Business	5	20			Wall Street Banker
LoBianco, Tony	Entertainment	6	8	15	19	
Locane, Amy	Entertainment				60	Actress. Melrose Place
Locke, D. R.	Journalist					SEE Nasby, Petroleum
Locke, John 1632-1704	Author	700	1950	5000		Br.Philosopher. LS/Cont.$12,500
Locke, Sandra	Entertainment	9	10	20	25	
Locke, William John	Author	20	35	75	30	Br. Novelist
Lockhart, Gene	Entertainment	18			50	
Lockhart, June	Entertainment	5	6	15	15	
Lockheed, Alan	Aviation	80	150	300	150	Pioneer Aviator, Plane Designer
Locklear, Heather	Entertainment	10	15	25	35	Pin-Up SP $45
Lockwood, Belva A. 1830-1917	Women's Rights	225	325	875		1st Woman to Practice Supr. Ct.
Lockwood, Chas.W, Capt	Civil War	95				1st MN to Enlist,Last Survivor
Lockwood, Margaret 1916-90	Entertainment	15	20	40	55	
Lockyer, Herbert	Clergy	25	35	45		
Lodge, Henry Cabot 1850-1924	Senate	40	160	200	95	MOC 1887, Senator MA 1893
Lodge, Henry Cabot, Jr.	Senate	20	60	95	25	Ambassador UN, Diplomat
Lodge, Oliver J., Sir 1851-1940	Science	90	130	225	250	Br. Physicist, Spiritualist
Loeb, William	Business	10	26	55	35	
Loesser, Frank	Composer	120				Broadway Composer
Loew, Marcus	Business	30	40	65	35	
Loewe, Frederick 1901-88	Composer	35	65	145	50	AMusQS $220-$895

NAME	CATEGORY	SIG	LS/DS	ALS	SP	Comment
Loewy, Raymond	Business	35	90	140	75	Designer
Lofting, Hugh 1886-1947	Author	95				& Illustrator of Dr. Dolittle Books
Loftus, Cissie	Entertainment	25	55			Br. Actress
Logan, Benjamin 1752-1802	Military	350	560	675		Pioneer Hero, Indian Fighter
Logan, Ella	Entertainment	5	9	20	15	
Logan, John A. (War Date)	Civil War	95		1192		Union Gen.
Logan, John A. 1826-86	Civil War	65	218	230		Union Gen.,Father Memorial Day
Logan, Josh(ua) 1908-88	Entertainment	25	40		45	Film & Stage Producer, Writer, Director
Logan, Olive	Author	25	35			
Logan, Thomas M.1840-1914	Civil War	80	225	408		CSA Gen.
Loggia, Robert	Entertainment	6	8	15	18	
Loggins and Messina	Entertainment	25			50	
Loggins, Kenny	Entertainment	10			25	
Loisy, Alfred	Clergy	20	25	35		
Lolobrigida, Gina	Entertainment	10	15	25	35	Pin-Up SP$30
Lom, Herbert	Entertainment	10			45	
Lomax, Lunsford Lindsey	Civil War	100	270	370		CSA General
Lombard, Carole	Entertainment	338	750	950	800	DS $750
Lombardo, Guy 1902-77	Entertainment	15	75	120	110	Big Band Leader. Royal Canadians
London, Charmian	Celebrity	40			175	2nd Wife of Jack London
London, George	Entertainment	35			70	Opera, Concert
London, Jack 1876-1916	Author	215	800	2300	1400	Am. Novelist, Adventurer
London, Julie	Entertainment	4	4	9	15	
London, Tom	Entertainment	50			100	
Long, Armistead L. 1825-91	Civil War	85	100	358		CSA Gen.
Long, Earl K.	Governor	20	30		25	Governor LA,
Long, Huey P.	Senate	85	175			Sen., Gov. LA. Assassinated
Long, John D.	Cabinet	12	30	40	20	Sec'y Navy, Governor MA
Long, Johnny	Bandleader	25			50	Big Band. Violinist
Long, Lotus	Entertainment	5			30	Actress-Oriental Dancer
Long, Pierse 1739-89	Revolutionary War	30	75	180		Continental Congress
Long, Richard	Entertainment	25			65	
Long, Russell	Senate/Congress	5	15		10	Senator LA
Long, Shelley	Entertainment	9	10	20	25	Pin-Up SP $25
Longacre, James B.1794-1869	Engraver	110		400		Chief Engraver of the U.S. Mint
Longet, Claudine	Entertainment	10	15	35	35	
Longfellow, Henry W.1807-82	Author	162	388	729	1093	Poet, Harvard Prof.AMsS $2295
Longfellow, Samuel	Clergy	40	50	75	55	
Longfellow, Stephen 1775-1849	Senate/Congress	20	50	145		MOC ME 1823
Longley, Charles T. 1794-1868	Clergy	25				Archbishop Canterbury
Longley, James B.	Governor	9	15			Governor ME
Longstreet, James (War Date)	Civil War	845		6433		CSA Gen.
Longstreet, James 1821-1904	Civil War	415	1250	1826	850	CSA General.Important ALS $7500
Longworth, Alice Roosevelt	Pres. Daughter	15	25	95	30	
Longworth, Nicholas	Congress	15	65	85		Speaker of the House, OH
Loo, Richard	Entertainment	20			55	
Loomis, Gustavus	Civil War	28	65	95		Union General
Loos, Anita	Author	17	35	70	30	Am. Novelist, Film Scripts
Loos, Walter	Aviation	10	20	35	25	
Loper, Don	Business	5	15	35	10	Fashion Designer
Lopez, Vincent	Entertainment	20			55	Big Band Leader-Pianist
Loraine, Robert	Aviation	15		55		
Lorca, Frederico Garcia	Author	435	1240	3125		Sp. Poet, Dramatist
Lord, Daniel, Rev.	Clergy	10			35	
Lord, E.J.	Congress	10		35		Senator CA
Lord, Herbert M.	Military		25			

NAME	CATEGORY	SIG	LS/DS	ALS	SP	Comment
Lord, Jack	Entertainment	6	8	15	15	
Lord, John Wesley, Bishop	Clergy	20	35	40	45	
Lord, Marjorie	Entertainment	6	12		25	Danny Thomas Show
Lord, Phillips H.	Entertainment	20				Writer-Producer
Lord, Walter	Author	3	5	10	5	
Lords, Traci	Entertainment	5	15	30	30	Pin-Up SP $65. Nude 130
Loren, Sophia	Entertainment	15			40	Pin-Up SP $50
Lorengar, Pilar	Entertainment	27			40	Opera
Lorillard, Peter	Business	125	260	475		Tobacco Industry
Lorimar, George C.	Clergy	20				Author
Loring, Gloria	Entertainment	5	8	15	18	
Loring, Israel	Clergy	25	75	125		
Loring, William Wing (War Date)	Civil War	180		745		CSA Gen.
Loring, Wm. Wing 1818-86	Civil War	120	255	315	425	CSA General
Lorne, Marlon	Entertainment	100			225	
Lorre, Peter	Entertainment	188			450	
Losey, Joseph	Entertainment	15			60	Film Director
Losigkeit, Fritz	Aviation	10	15	30	20	
Lossing, Benson	Author	15	30	50		Am.Historian, Engraver
Lott, Felicity	Entertainment	15			35	Opera
Lott, Trent	Congress	10			20	Republican Majority Leader
Loubet, Emile François 1838-1929	Head of State			125		Pres. France 1899-1906
Loughlin, Lori	Entertainment	5			55	
Louis II of Monaco 1870-1949	Royalty	30				Prince of Monaco
Louis Philippe (Fr)	Royalty	65	215	375		Citizen King Duc D'Orleans
Louis XII (Fr)	Royalty	800	1750	4200		King of France
Louis XIII (Fr)	Royalty	875	1475	3590		King of France
Louis XIV (Fr)	Royalty	450	1000	3750		The Sun King
Louis XV	Royalty	750	1595	5500		King of France
Louis XVI	Royalty	375	1305			King of France. Guillotined
Louis XVIII (Fr) 1755-1824	Royalty	205	475	1680		Louis Stanislas Xavier
Louise Caroline Alberta, Princess	Royalty	25		65	175	4th Daughter of Queen Victoria
Louise Vict.(Alex. Dagmar)	Royalty	15		105	195	Princess Royal
Louise, Anita	Entertainment	15			45	
Louise, Tina	Entertainment	9	10	20	25	Pin-Up SP $25
Lounge, John M.	Astronaut	10			20	
Lousma, Jack F.	Astronaut	10	20		35	
Love, Bessie	Entertainment	35			70	Vintage
Love, John A.	Governor	5	12		10	Governor CO
Love, Montagu	Entertainment	20			50	
Love, Mother	Entertainment	4			10	Comedienne
Lovecraft, H. P.	Author	165	290	475	425	Reclusive Horror Story Writer
Lovejoy, Frank	Entertainment	25			55	
Lovejoy, Owen	Clergy-Congress	15	30	45		MOC IL 1857-64
Lovelace, Linda	Entertainment	25			60	Porn Queen
Loveless, Patty	Entertainment	15			35	Singer
Lovell, Bernard Dr.	Science	15	25	40	20	
Lovell, James	Revolutionary War	75	195	450		Continental Congress
Lovell, James A. Jr. 1928-	Astronaut	15	102		123	Cmmdr. of Aborted Apollo 13.Cont. TLS $375
Lovell, Mansfield (War Date)	Civil War	185	560	849		CSA Gen.
Lovell, Mansfield 1822-84	Civil War	100	250	275		CSA Gen.
Loverboy	Entertainment	25			50	
Lovett, John 1761-1818	Senate/Congress	40		135		War 1812. ALS/Content $300
Lovett, Lyle	Country Music	25			75	
Lovett, Robert	Cabinet	5	10	25	10	Sec'y Defense
Lovkay, John	Business	3			7	CEO Hamilton Standard

NAME	CATEGORY	SIG	LS/DS	ALS	SP	Comment
Lovrenich, Rodger T.	Business	4	9	20	7	Inventor of electronic ignition
Low, David, Sir*	Cartoonist	15	45	110	140	NZ-Br Political.Colonel Blimp
Low, Frederick F.	Governor	45		175		Gov, MOC CA 1860, Diplomat
Low, G. David	Astronaut	5			15	
Low, Nicholas	Revolutionary War	90	245	450		Prominent NY, Backed Revolution
Low, Seth 1819-1916	Mayor NYC	10	35	45		Merchant, Pres. Columbia Univ.
Lowe, Ed	Inventor	20			45	Kitty Litter
Lowe, Edmund	Entertainment	25	30	60	45	
Lowe, Hudson, Sir	Military		1000	500		Last custodian of Napoleon
Lowe, Rob	Entertainment	20			45	
Lowe, Thaddeus S. C.	Civil War	195	325	500		Aeronaut,Inventor,CW Balloonist
Lowell, Amy	Author	35	125	250		Am. Poet,Critic.,Imagist School
Lowell, Carey	Entertainment	5			20	
Lowell, James Russell 1819-91	Author	45	145	233	350	Poet.Hall of Fame, Educator, Editor
Lowell, John H.	Aviation	12	25	40	32	ACE, WW II
Lowell, Joshua A. 1801-74	Congress	10				Repr. ME, Dem. Presidenial Elector
Lowell, Percival	Science	15	40	65		Am. Astronomer, Author
Lowell, Robert	Author	30	150			Pulitzer Poetry
Lowenstein, Allard	Congress	75			175	Dump Johnson Movement. Assassinated
Lowery, John	Senate/Congress	10	15		15	
Lowery, Robert	Entertainment	30			65	
Lowman, Seymour 1868-1940	Cabinet	5	10			Ass't Sec'y Treas., Lt. Gov. NY
Lown, Bert	Bandleader	10				Bye Bye Blues
Lowry, Robert	Governor	10	25			Governor MS
Loy, Myrna 1905-93	Entertainment	28	40	50	58	SP as Nora Charles (Thin Man) $100
Lubbers, Bob*	Cartoonist	10			70	Tarzan
Lubbock, Francis R.	Civil War	150	185	295	350	CSA Governor TX
Lubbock, Sir John 1834-1913	Statesman	10	15	35		Br. Banker.Author Science Books
Lubin, Arthur	Entertainment	25			65	Film Director
Lubin, Germaine	Entertainment				275	Opera. Legendary Fr. Soprano. RARE
Lubitsch, Ernst	Entertainment	55			120	Vintage Film Director
Lubke, Heinrich	Head of State	10		25		Pres. Ger. Fed. Repub.
Lucas, Clyde	Bandleader	15				
Lucas, Edward Verrall	Author	3	5	15	5	
Lucas, George	Entertainment	20	25	60	60	Film Director
Lucca, Pauline	Entertainment	30	70	102		Opera
Lucci, Susan	Entertainment	6	8	15	20	
Luccock, Halford E.	Clergy	20	35	50	40	
Luce, Clare Boothe	Author	30	100	175	40	Ambassador, Playwright
Luce, Cyrus G.	Governor	5	15	25		Governor MI
Luce, Henry R.	Publisher	40	115	205	50	Time, Life, Fortune, Sports Ill
Luce, Stephen Bleecker	Military	10	35	95	30	Adm. !st Pres. Naval War College
Lucid, Shannon W.	Astronaut	10			50	Set New Space Record
Luckinbill, Laurence	Entertainment	5			15	
Luckner, Felix, von 1881-1966	Military	195	205	280	92	The Sea Devil WW II
Luckner, Nicholas	Fr. Revolution	225	675			Marshal of Fr. Guillotined
Lucon, L. J., Cardinal	Clergy	45	55	75	60	
Ludde-Neurath, Walter	Military	15			45	Aide-de-camp to Donitz
Ludendorff, Erich von	Military	100	225	350	275	Ger. Gen. WW I, Politician
Ludin, Hanns	Military	130	350			Ger. Gen.-Storm Trooper WW II
Ludlington, Marshall I.	Civil War	65	135	195		Union General
Ludlum, Robert	Author	10	20	35	20	Super Spy novels
Ludwig I 1786-1868	Royalty	65	338	450		King of Bavaria
Ludwig II	Royalty	55	255	470		King of Bavaria
Ludwig, Emil	Authors	40	120	200		
Lufbery, Raoul	Aviation	125	350	590	400	ACE, WW I, Lafayette Escadrille

NAME	CATEGORY	SIG	LS/DS	ALS	SP	Comment
Luft, Lorna	Entertainment	5		10	10	Singer Sister of Liza Minelli
Lugar, Richard G.	Congress		25			Sen. IN
Lugosi, Bela 1882-1956	Entertainment	275	375	700	1415	
Luhan, Mabel Dodge	Author			225		
Lujan, Albert	Artist	20		45		
Lukas, Foss	Composer	20			75	Versatile Ger./Am./Composer/Conductor
Lukas, Paul	Entertainment	50			100	AA
Luke, Frank	Aviation	150	400	600	500	ACE, WW I, CMH, #3 U.S. Ace
Luke, Keye	Entertainment	15			50	'#1 Son' in Charlie Chan Films
Luks, George Benjamin 1867-1933	Artist	20	55	200		Member Ashcan Shool.
Lulu Belle (& Scotty)	Entertainment	10				C & W Music
Lum & Abner	Entertainment	25			65	
Lumet, Sidney	Entertainment	10			35	TV Director-Dramatist
Lumholtz, Carl	Celebrity	3	8	20		
Lumiere, Louis 162-1954	Inventor	175		565	375	Cinematographe Projector
Lumley, Joanna	Entertainment	5	6	15	15	
Luna, Barbara	Entertainment	4			10	
Lunceford, Jimmie	Entertainment	35			140	Big Band Leader-Arranger
Lund, John	Entertainment	5	6	15	15	
Lunden, Joan	TV Host	12			20	TV Host
Lundgren, Dolph	Entertainment	5			15	
Lundigan, William	Entertainment	15			30	
Lunn, George R. 1873-1948	Congress	4	15			Repr. NY
Lunney, G.	Astronaut	5			15	
Lunt, Alfred & Fontanne, Lynne	Entertainment	75			125	DS For Idiot's Delight $650
Lupino, Ida 18xx-1995	Entertainment	19	80	75	70	Actress, Director
Lupino, Stanley 1893-1942	Entertainment	15			35	Br. Comedian. Father of Ida
Lupton, John	Entertainment	10			20	
Luria, Salvador F.	Science	20	35	55	25	Nobel Medicine
Lurie, Bob	Business	10	25	45	15	
Luse, Harley	Country Music	10			20	
Luther, Hans	Head of State	40	55	85		Chancellor Ger., Ambass. US
Luther, Martin	Clergy	10000	30000	38375		LS/Extremely Rare $49,500
Lutyens, Edw. L.,Sir 1869-1944	Architect					Br.
Lutzi, Gertrude	Entertainment	15				Opera
Lutzow, Gunther	Aviation	175		445	450	
Lvov, Alexis	Composer			200		Rus.
Lyautey, Louis	Military	10	35	90	35	Marshal of Fr.,Statesman
Lyell, Charles, Sir	Science	95		425		Br. Founder of Modern Geology
Lyle, The Great	Entertainment	20			50	Vintage British Magician
Lyman, Abe	Bandleader	15			45	Big Band
Lyman, Charles Edwin	Clergy	15	25	50	30	
Lynch, David	Entertainment	20			50	TV Director Twin Peaks
Lynch, John R.	Congress		250			Former Slave. Repr. MS 1873-77, '82-'83
Lynch, Kelly	Entertainment	10			50	Pin-Up SP $75
Lynch, Thomas Jr.	Revolutionary War	5565				Rare Signer
Lynde, Paul	Entertainment	10	15	25	25	
Lynen, Feodor	Science	20	40		25	Nobel Medicine
Lynley, Carol	Entertainment	15	15	35	35	Pin-Up SP $40
Lynn, Porsche	Entertainment	5			20	Porn Queen
Lynn, Diana	Entertainment	15	15	35	30	
Lynn, Jeffrey	Entertainment	9	10	20	20	
Lynn, Loretta	Country Music	6			15	
Lynn, Vera, Dame	Entertainment	25			75	Br. WW II Singing Star
Lyon, Ben	Entertainment	15			35	
Lyon, Lucius 1800-51	Congress	12				Sen. & Repr. MI

The Sanders Price Guide to Autographs

NAME	CATEGORY	SIG	LS/DS	ALS	SP	Comment
Lyon, Mary Mason	Educator	55	165	340		
Lyon, Nathaniel 1818-61	Civil War	350		1892		Union Gen. KIA. RARE
Lyon, Sue	Entertainment	9	10	20	25	
Lyons, Lord, Adm.	Military	25		130		
Lyons, Richard B.P.,1st Earl Lyons	Diplomat	20		100		Br. Minister to US in Civil War
Lyons, William	Business	40	80	175		
Lytell, Bert	Entertainment	30	45	90	60	
Lytton, E. George Bulwer	Author	25	95	205		Novelist, Poet, Colonial Sec'y

NAME	CATEGORY	SIG	LS/DS	ALS	SP	Comment
Ma, Yo Yo	Entertainment	30			60	Cellist Superstar
Maas, Melvin G. 1898-1964	Congress	5				Repr. MN
Mabley, Jackie Moms	Entertainment	65			200	
MacArthur, Arthur	Military	45	90	125	70	CW Off'r, Sp.-Am. War. General
MacArthur, Charles	Author	15	30	350	25	Playwright Husband Helen Hayes
MacArthur, Douglas 1880-1964	Military	232	759	870	661	5 Star Gen. WW II.A.E.F. ID Card SP $8625
MacArthur, Douglas II	Military	10	15	20	15	
MacArthur, James	Entertainment	6	8	15	25	
MacArthur, Jean	Military	15	20	25	15	Mrs. Douglas MacArthur
Macartney, Clarence E.	Clergy	15	20	25	20	
Macartney, George	Head of State	10	35	85		
Macaulay, (Emilie) Rose, Dame	Author	10	20	35		Br. Novelist, Critic, Verse
Macaulay, Thos. B., Lord	Author	45	62	115		Historian & Poet. Politician
Macbeth, Florence	Entertainment	20			50	Am. Soprano
MacChesney, Nathan Wm.	Celebrity	10	20	85		
Macchio, Ralph	Entertainment	7			20	
MacCracken, Henry M.	Clergy	20	35	45	30	
MacDonald, Charles H.	Aviation	15	30	52	3	ACE, WW II
MacDonald, Cordelia H.	Entertainment	40	75	120		1st Eva in Uncle Tom's Cabin
MacDonald, George	Clergy	20	30	45		
MacDonald, George 1875-1961	Business	35				Public Utilities
MacDonald, J. Farrell	Entertainment	25			50	SP as Detective in Maltese Falcon $495
MacDonald, J. Ramsey 1866-1937	Head of State	45	130	170	255	Twice Br. Prime Minister
Macdonald, Jacques E.J.A 1765-1840.	Fr. Revolution	75	100	250		Marshal of Napoleon
MacDonald, Jeanette	Entertainment	62	188	275	175	
MacDonald, John Alexander	Head of State	35	90			Premier 1857, 1st P.M. Canada
MacDonald, Ross	Author	45	145	250		Mystery Writer
MacDonald, Torbet	Congress	10				MA. JFK Roommate & Lifelong Friend
Macdonogh, P. M. W.	Military	6	17	22		
MacDonough, Thomas 1783-1825	Military	95	290	700		Am. Naval Off'r. Tripoli, 1812
MacDougall, Clinton	Civil War	35	60			Union General
MacDowell, Andie	Entertainment	15			40	Col. Pin-Up 65
MacDowell, Edward 1861-1908	Composer	140	290	688	400	Songs, Concertos, Piano Pieces
MacDowell, Melbourne	Entertainment	15			40	Vintage Actor

NAME	CATEGORY	SIG	LS/DS	ALS	SP	Comment
Macfadden, Bernarr	Business	15	45	96	35	Physical Culturist, Publisher
Macfadyen, Dugald	Clergy	45	45	50	50	
MacGraw, Ali	Entertainment	8	9		20	Pin-Up SP $25
Machado, Anesia Pinheiro	Aviation	35	55	80	65	
Machiavelli, Niccolo 1469-1527	Author	500	1250	4500		
MacInnes, Helen	Author	5	15	20		Am Best Selling Novelist
Mack, Connie III	Senate	7	10		15	Senator FL
Mack, Helen	Entertainment	10			30	
Mack, Marion	Entertainment	10			35	
Mack, Ted	Entertainment	8			15	
Mackaill, Dorothy	Entertainment	20	30	70	65	Vintage Film Actress
MacKall, William W. (War Date)	Civil War	250		1250		CSA Gen.
MacKall, William W. 1917-91	Civil War	110	305			CSA General
MacKay, Charles	Clergy	20	25	35		
Mackay, John William	Business	40	100	215		Founder Postal Telegraph Co.
MacKaye, Percy 1875-1956	Author	40	90	150		Am. Poet, Dramatist
Mackensen, August von	Military	12	25	40	85	Ger. Gen. Fld. Marshal WW I. RK
MacKenzie, Gisele	Entertainment	3	5	6	15	
Mackenzie, Morell, Sir	Science	60	165	350		Larygologist. Misdiagnosed
Mackie, Bob	Business	5	10	25	15	Fashion Designer
MacLachlan, Kyle	Entertainment	10			30	Picket Fences
MacLagan, William D., Bishop	Clergy	15	25	35		
MacLaine, Shirley	Entertainment	15	25	35	40	Pin-Up SP $45
Maclane, Barton	Entertainment	50			125	Vint. Tough Guy. Maltese Falcon etc.
MacLaren, Donald M.	Military	25	40	95	75	
MacLean, Steve	Astronaut	7	15		16	
Macleay, Lachlan	Astronaut	5			15	
MacLeay, Lachlan	Astronaut	7			15	
MacLeish, Archibald 1892-1982	Author	30	115	135	40	Am. Poet, Lawyer. 3 Pulitzers
MacLeod, Gavin	Entertainment	6	8	15	20	
Macleod, George F.	Clergy	20	25	30		
MacMahon, Aline	Entertainment	20			60	
MacMahon, Marie E.P.	Head of State	35	110	225		Fr.Soldier, Politician, Marshal
Macmillan, Donald B. 1874-	Explorer	67	75	170		Am. with Peary at North Pole
MacMillan, Harold	Head of State	25	85	150	50	Br. P.M.
MacMurray, Fred 1908-91	Entertainment	20	95		50	
MacNee, Patrick	Entertainment	10			35	
MacNelly, Jeff*	Cartoonist	30			200	Shoe
Macnelly, Jeff*	Cartoonist	5			100	Shoe
MacNider, Hanford	Military	3	9	15		
Macomb, Alexander 1748-1832	Business		100	110		Fur & Shipping Merchant.
Macpherson, Elle	Cover Girl	10			25	Pin-Up SP $40
MacPherson, James B.	Civil War	117	240	335		Union General
MacRae, Gordon	Entertainment	15			30	
MacRae, Meredith	Entertainment	5			15	
MacRae, Sheila	Entertainment	3			12	
MacReady, George	Entertainment	20			40	
Macready, William C. 1793-1873	Entertainment	15		122		Foremost Br. Shakespearean Actor
MacVeagh, Franklin	Cabinet	10	25	60	20	Sec'y Treasury
MacVeagh, Wayne 1833-1917	Cabinet	65		98		Att'y Gen., Diplomat, CW Soldier
Macy, Bill	Entertainment	4			15	
Madden, Charles Edw.1919-	Military	45	120	215	100	Brit. Adm.
Maddox, Lester	Governor	25	40		30	Georgia Anti-Civil Rights Gov.
Madeira, Jean	Entertainment	15			40	Am. Contralto
Madigan, Amy	Entertainment	10			40	
Madison, Dolley Payne 1768-1849	First Lady	750	1792	3410		Free Frank $750-850-1,200

The Sanders Price Guide to Autographs

NAME	CATEGORY	SIG	LS/DS	ALS	SP	Comment
Madison, Guy	Entertainment	6			25	
Madison, James & Monroe, James	Presidents		2266			
Madison, James 1751-1836	President	325	2048	4383	2500	FF $925,Cont.ALS $7500
Madonna (Louise Veronica Cicone)	Entertainment	50	1250	1200	227	Currently, Top Pop Female Staar
Madriguera, Enric	Entertainment	15			30	Big Band Leader
Madsen, Chris	Pioneer Lawman		2250			Outlaw & Indian Fighter
Madsen, Virginia	Entertainment	10			25	Pin-Up SP $35
Maeterlinck, Maurice, Count	Author	35	115	205	425	Nobel Literature. Pelleas and Melisande
Maffett, Debbie Sue	Entertainment	4	5	9	9	
Magee, John A.	Senate/Congress	10		35		MOC NY 1827. Banker, RR
Magee, Patrick	Entertainment	10			35	
Magee, Walter W. 1861-1927	Congress	12	25			Repr. NY
Magg, Alois	Aviation	4	9	16	15	
Magilton, Jerry	Astronaut	4			12	
Magnani, Anna	Entertainment	300			650	
Magnus, Kurt	Science				50	Rocket Pioneer. Peenemuende Team/USSR
Magrath, Andrew G. 1813-93	Civil War	35	60	80		CSA Gov.SC. ALS '61 $150
Magritte, René 1898-1967	Artist	200	350	1181		Belg. Surrealist Painter.
Magruder, John B. 1807-71	Civil War	275	525	487		CSA Gen. Sig/Rank $450
Magsaysay, Ramon	Head of State	20	55	155	35	Pres. Philippines
Maguire, W.A. Cpt.	Military	25	50	75	60	
Mahan, Alfred Thayer	Military	50	75	100		US Navy Off'r-Historian. CW
Maharis, George	Entertainment	10	15	25	20	
Mahen, Robert A.	Business	15	30	70	40	
Mahendra Bir Bikram	Royalty	35	50	135	50	King, Leader Nepal
Mahler, Alma	Author	20		125		Author & Wife Gustav Mahler
Mahler, Gustav 1860-1911	Composer	550	1200	3500	24300	Austrian Composer
Mahone, William 1826-95	Civil War	120	252	365		CSA General, US Senator VA
Mahoney, Jock	Entertainment	20	35	55	45	
Mahurin, Walker M. Bud	Aviation	15	35	55	40	ACE, WW II, Legendary Ace
Maiakovski, Vladimir V.	Author	300	795	2200		
Maikl, George	Entertainment	5			20	Opera
Mailer, Norman	Author	25	125	200	75	S Oswald's Tale 75
Maillol, Aristide	Artist	200	460	800		Fr. Sculptor, Painter, Tapestry
Main, Majorie	Entertainment	105			250	
Maintenon, Francoise, Marquise de	Royalty			975		2nd Wife Louis XIV
Maison, Nicholas J. 1771-1840	Fr. Revolution	35	150	175		General under Napoleon
Maison, René	Entertainment	30			65	Opera
Maitland, Lester J.	Aviation	20		40		
Major, John	Head of State	5			20	Br. Prime Minister
Majorana, Gaetano (Caffarelli)	Entertainment			3200		Legendary Male Soprano (castrato)
Majors, Lee	Entertainment	5	6	15	15	
Makarios III, Mikhail, Archbishop	Clergy-Head State	50	65	140	75	Cyprus
Makarova, Natalia	Entertainment	10			15	Ballet
Mako	Entertainment	6			20	
Malamud, Bernard	Author	25	40	105	30	Am. Novelist, Pulitzer
Malcolm X (Little) 1925-65	Black Leader	200	3950	4565		TLS/Content $10,000-15,000
Malden, Karl	Entertainment	9			25	DS $250
Malenkov, Georgi M.	Head of State	175	350	800	250	Union Sov. Russia
Malet, C. Francois de	Fr. Revolution	120	240			Gen'l. Court-martialed, Shot
Malher, J.P.F.	Fr. Revolution	25	80			
Malik, Charles	Head of State	7	15	35	10	
Malipiero, Gian-Francesco	Composer					Important 20th Cent.Comp.AMuQs $225
Malis, David	Entertainment	10			25	Opera
Malko, Nicolai	Entertainment	75			225	Rus. Conductor
Malkovich, John	Entertainment	10			40	

NAME	CATEGORY	SIG	LS/DS	ALS	SP	Comment
Mallarmé, Stéphane 1842-98	Author	150		1100		Fr. Poet. Symbolist Movement
Malle, Louis 19xx-96	Entertainment	20		30	45	Fr. Film Director
Mallick, Don	Astronaut	5			15	
Mallory, Charles M.	Aviation	10	22	38	30	ACE, WW II
Mallory, Francis 1807-60	Congress	10				Repr. VA, Physician, RR Pres.
Mallory, Stephen R.	Civil War	125	225	240		CSA Sec'y of Navy.
Malmesbury, Ist Earl 1746-1820l	Br. Diplomat	15	30	45		James Harris. Minister, Ambass.
Malo, Gina	Entertainment	3	3	6	6	
Malodva, Milada	Entertainment	7	9	20	15	
Malone, Dorothy	Entertainment	40	75		65	
Malone, Dumas	Author	10	30	75	15	
Maloney, Francis T.1894-1945	Senate/Congress	10	20	40		Senator, MOC CT 1933-45
Malten, Therese	Entertainment	35			150	Opera
Malthus, Thomas Robert 1766-1834	Br. Economist	310	1100	1916		Educator, Author
Mamas and the Papas	Entertainment	350	900			(Four)
Mamas and the Papas, The (NEW)	Entertainment	10			20	(Four)
Mamet, David	Entertainment	10			25	Film Director
Mamoulian, Rouben	Entertainment	10	35		35	Film Director
Man Ray	Artist					SEE Ray, Man
Mana-Zucca (Zuckerman, Augusta)	Entertainment	20			100	Singer, Composer, Pianist
Manchester, Melissa	Entertainment	10			30	
Manchester, William	Author	5	10	20	15	
Mancini, Henry	Composer	20			70	Conductor-Pianist.AMusQS $85
Mandel, Howie	Entertainment	6	8	15	15	
Mandel, John	Entertainment	5	6	15	10	
Mandel, Marvin	Governor	10	15		22	Governor MD
Mandela, Nelson b.1918	Head of State	80	170		438	Leader African Nat'l Congress
Mandell, Howie	Entertainment	5	8	20	15	
Manderson, Charles	Civil War	70	105	150		Unlon Gen. , U.S. Sen. NE
Mandrell, Barbara	Country Music	6			20	
Manet, Edouard 1832-83	Artist	350	2198	2067		Impressionist School Founder
Maney, George E. 1826-1901	Civil War	145				CSA Gen. ALS '62 $760
Manfrini, Luigi	Entertainment	40			125	Opera
Mangano, Silvana	Entertainment	25	35	60	50	
Mangione, Chuck	Entertainment	5	6	15	15	
Manhattan Transfer	Entertainment	35			80	
Manigault, Arthur M. 1824-86	Civil War	105	288			CSA Gen. ALS '61 $1650
Manilow, Barry	Entertainment	15	45		70	Composer, Vocalist, Pianist
Manke, John	Astronaut	5			15	
Mankiewicz, Joseph L.	Entertainment	20		55	55	AA Film Director
Mankiller, Wilma	Author	5			20	
Manley, N. W.	Head of State	12		25	20	Prime Minister Jamaica
Mann, Daniel	Entertainment	10			35	
Mann, Delbert	Entertainment	20			45	Film Director
Mann, Hank	Entertainment	100				Keystone Kop. Caricature S 250
Mann, Heinrich	Author	35	145	275		Ger. Novelist. Exiled, Interned
Mann, Horace 1796-1859	Educator	35	135	250		Education Reformer, Abolitionist
Mann, Johnny	Bandleader	16				
Mann, Manfred (All)	Entertainment	125				
Mann, Orrin L.	Civil War	20	35	60		Union General
Mann, Thomas -1967	Aviation	12	25	48	35	ACE, WW II, Double Ace
Mann, Thomas 1875-1955	Author	125	415	1000	1080	Ger. Novelist, Nobel Prize
Mann, Thomas Clifton	Celebrity	3			10	
Manne, Shelly	Bandleader				45	Drummer
Mannerheim,c. Gustave, Baron	Head of State		290	850	775	Pres. Finland. Soldier, Patriot
Mannering, Mary	Entertainment	15			25	Vintage Stage Actress

The Sanders Price Guide to Autographs

NAME	CATEGORY	SIG	LS/DS	ALS	SP	Comment
Manners, David	Entertainment	10			35	
Manners-Sutton, Charles	Clergy	25	35	40		
Manning, Daniel	Cabinet	18	35	65		Sec'y Treasury
Manning, Henry E., Cardinal	Clergy	40	60	95	50	
Manning, Irene	Entertainment	6	8	15	10	
Manning, Stephen H.	Civil War	30	55	110		Union General
Manning, Timothy J., Cardinal	Clergy	35	40	50	45	
Manning, William T., Bishop	Clergy	20	35	75	25	
Manoff, Dinah	Entertainment	5			20	
Manone, Wingy	Entertainment	10			50	Jazz Trumpet-Vocalist
Mansfield, Jayne 1933-67	Entertainment	154			442	5x7 SP $375
Mansfield, Joseph K..F.(War Date)	Civil War	225		2865		Union Gen.KIA 1862
Mansfield, Joseph K.F.1803-62	Civil War	148	308	436		Union General
Mansfield, Katherine	Author		290			
Mansfield, Mike	Senate/Congress	10	25	40	15	MOC, Senator MT
Mansfield, Richard	Entertainment	50		175		Vintage Stage Actor
Manship, Paul Howard	Artist	40	275	450		Am. Sculptor Prometheus Fount.
Manson, Charles (Buglioni)	Criminal	75	215	455	175	Murderer, Cult Figure
Manstein, Erich von, General	Military	20	60	95	75	Planned Assault vs France WW II
Mantell, Gideon A 1790-1852.	Science	10	25	40		Paleontologist. 4 Dinosaurs
Mantell, Robert B.	Entertainment	12			25	Vintage Shakespearean Actor
Mantelli, Eugenia	Entertainment	25			60	Opera
Manteuffel, Edwin F. von 1897-1978	Military	75	595	420		Prussian Fld. Marshal WW II
Manteuffel, Hasso von	Military	40	295	190	90	Ger. Tank Commander
Mantovani	Entertainment	8	12		20	Conductor-Arranger
Manville, Tommy	Business	20		35		Much Married Asbestos Heir
Manzarek, Ray	Entertainment	15	25			The Doors, bassist
Mao Tse Tung	Head of State	3000				Chinese Communist Leader
Maphis, Joe and Rose Lee	Country Music	10			20	
Mapleson, James H.	Entertainment	75				Opera
Mara, Adele	Entertainment	5	8		10	
Maragliano, Luisa	Entertainment	5			15	
Marais, Jean 1913-19xx	Entertainment	10		30	45	Fr. Actor. Stage & Film
Marat, Jean-Paul	Fr. Revolution			4500		Leader-Doctor-Author.Murdered
Marbot, J.B.A.M.	Fr. Revolution	25	70	125		Napoleonic General
Marceau, Marcel	Entertainment	20	70		95	World Renown Mime
Marcellino, Muzzy	Entertainment	10	15	25	25	
March, Barbara	Entertainment	5			30	Star Trek
March, Fredric 1897-1975	Entertainment	35	80 .	95	80	AA
Marchesi, Mathilde	Entertainment	50		160	175	Ger. Mezzo-Sopr. Teacher
Marcinkus, Paul C., Archbishop	Clergy	45	65	100	50	
Marconi, Guglielmo 1874-1937	Science	200	712	2117	888	It. Physicist-Inventor. Nobel
Marcos, Ferdinand E.	Head of State	50	135		130	Pres. Philippines
Marcos, Imelda	Head of State	15	35		25	Phillipines
Marcovicci, Andrea	Entertainment	10			20	
Marcus, Jerry*	Cartoonist				35	Fatkat
Marcus, Rudolph A., Dr.	Science	20	35		30	Nobel Chemistry
Marcus, Stanley	Business	25	75	160	55	Merchant. Nieman-Marcus
Marcy, Randolph B. 1812-87	Civil War	30		180		Union Gen.
Marcy, Randolph G. (War Date)	Civil War	45	75	720		Union Gen.
Marcy, William L. 1786-1857	Cabinet	40	175	222		Sec'y War, State. Senator NY
Maren, Jerry	Entertainment	15			35	
Marescot, Armand S.	Fr. Revolution	30	80	170		
Maressyev, Alexei	Aviation	135				Rus. ACE & Soviet Hero
Maret, Hugues B., Duke 1763-1839	Fr. Revolution	75	210	375		Napoleon Confidential Advisor
Maret, Hugues B., Duke de	Napoleonic Wars	90	200			Diplomat-P.M.-Advisor Napoleon

NAME	CATEGORY	SIG	LS/DS	ALS	SP	Comment
Marey, Etienne	Science	50		700		Fr. Physiologist. Sphygmograph
Margaret of Austria 1522-86	Royalty		285			Duchess of Parma
Margie*	Cartoonist	20			250	Little Lulu
Margo (Mrs Ed Albert)	Entertainment	15	15	35	30	
Marguerite De Valois	Royalty		1750			Queen of Fr., 1st Wife of Henry of Navarre
Maria (Castile)	Royalty		2500			Queen of Alfonso V of Aragon
Maria Theresa 1717-80	Royalty	185	680	980		Archduchess, Qn Hung.-Bohemia
Marie Amelie (Queen of Fr.)	Royalty	170	240	538		Queen of Louis Phillippe I
Marie Antoinette (Fr)	Royalty	1200	4850			Queen of Louis XVI France
Marie of Modena (Queen Gr. Brit.)	Royalty	335	530			Queen of James II
Marie of Naples	Royalty	15		85		Queen of King Louis-Phillipe I
Marie of Romania	Royalty	85	115	240	100	
Marin, Cheech	Entertainment	5			20	
Marin, John	Artist	60	225	550		Am. Watercolorist, Etching
Marinaro, Ed	Entertainment	6	8	15	15	
Marion, Francis 1732-95	Rev. War		6500	8500		The Swamp Fox
Mariscal, Don Ignacio	Statesman	20	35	55		V.P. Mexico
Maritain, Jacques	Clergy	40	45	95	75	
Maritza, Sari	Entertainment	8	9		20	
Markham, Albert H., Sir	Celebrity	5	20	45		
Markham, Clements, Sir	Geographer	10	25	55		Historian,Pres.Royal Geogr.Soc.
Markham, Edwin	Author	30	125	140	65	The Man With The Hoe
Markham, William	Colonial America	135	450			Colonial Gov. PA
Markova, Alicia	Entertainment	20			50	Ballet
Markowitz, Harry M., Dr.	Economics	20	35	45		Nobel Economics
Marks, Johnny	Composer	35	90	125	50	AMusQS $175
Marks, William, Jr. 1778-1858	Senate	35	140			PA Senator, ALS/Content $400
Marlborough, Consuelo, Duchess	Royalty				920	1878-1964.Vanderbilt Heiress
Marlborough,John Churchill,1stDuke	Military	220	765			Br. General and Statesman
Marley, Bob	Entertainment	695			100	Rock HOF. Reggae King
Marlin, Mahlon F.	Business	40	115	225		Pres-Treas. Marlin Firearms Co.
Marlow, Lucy	Entertainment	5	6	15	15	
Marlowe, Hugh	Entertainment	25			50	
Marlowe, Julia	Entertainment	25	35	70	60	Major Stage Star/E.H. Sothern
Marly, Florence	Entertainment	4	4	9	9	
Marmaduke, John S. (War Date)	Civil War	167		2400		CSA Gen.
Marmaduke, John S.1833-87	Civil War	95	300			CSA Gen.
Marmont, A.F.L.V., Duke	Fr. Revolution	45	90			Marshal of Fr.,Napoleon A-D-C
Marney, Carlyle	Clergy	20	25	35	35	
Marquand, John P.	Author	40	120	165	45	Am. Novelist. Pulitzer
Marques, Antonio	Entertainnment	35			85	Opera
Marquez, Gabriel	Author				245	Nobel. One Hundred Year of Solitude
Marriott, J.	Business	20	35	70	30	Marriott Hotel Chain
Marryat, Frederick 1792-1848	Military-Author	30	100	225		Br. Naval Cmmdr. Novelist
Marsala, Joe	Entertainment	20			65	Clarinet, Sax, Composer
Marsalis, Branford	Entertainment	10			25	Conductor, Sax
Marsalis, Wynton	Entertainment	15			30	Trumpet Virtuoso. Classic-Jazz
Marsden, Jason	Entertainment	10			25	The Munsters
Marsh, Jean	Entertainment	7			20	
Marsh, Joan	Entertainment	15	20	40	35	
Marsh, Mae	Entertainment	30	40	75	40	
Marsh, Marion	Entertainment	15			40	
Marsh, Ngaio, Dame	Author	20	35	50	40	New Zealand Mystery Writer
Marshall, Catherine	Author	75	100	150	125	A Man Called Peter
Marshall, Cathy	TV News	7	20		10	CNN News
Marshall, Christopher	Revolutionary War	100				Am. Patriot & Diarist

 **The Sanders Price Guide to Autographs**

NAME	CATEGORY	SIG	LS/DS	ALS	SP	Comment
Marshall, E.G.	Entertainment	10			25	
Marshall, George C. 1880-1959	Military-Statesman	200	319	550	400	WW II Chief Staff. Nobel Peace
Marshall, George E.	Entertainment	35			75	Film Director. 400+ Films
Marshall, Herbert 1890-1966	Entertainment	10	75		65	Sophisticated Br. Actor
Marshall, Humphrey (War Date)	Civil War	270	512			CSA Gen.ALS/Cont $1825
Marshall, Humphrey 1812-72	Civil War	93	195			CSA General
Marshall, John (SC) 1755-1835	Supreme Court	435	1700	5000		Chief Justice
Marshall, John, Sir	Head of State	10	20	35	20	Prime Minister New Zealand
Marshall, Margaret	Entertainment	10			25	Opera
Marshall, Penny	Entertainment	8			20	And Film Director
Marshall, Peter	Clergy	75	95	100	125	Senate Chaplain
Marshall, Thomas R. (V)1854-1925	Vice President	75	175	400	175	Wilson VP
Marshall, Thurgood (SC)1908-93	Supreme Court	115	300	200	175	1st Afro-Am. Justice
Marshall, Tully	Entertainment	20			50	
Marshall, William	Civil War	25	40	75		Union Gen., Gov. MN
Marshall, William	Entertainment	15			25	Film Director
Marshall, William	Entertainment	8			25	Werewolf
Marshall. Catherine	Clergy	25	30	50	30	
Marston, Gilman 1811-90	Civil War	30	80			Union Gen. Leglslator. Sen.NH
Marterie, Ralph	Entertainment	10			20	Big Band Leader
Martin, Charles H.	Governor	10	25			Governor OR
Martin, Chris Pin	Entertainment	50			100	
Martin, Clarence D.	Governor	5	15		10	Governor WA
Martin, Dean & Lewis, Jerry	Entertainment	125			250	Comedy Team
Martin, Dean 1917-95	Entertainment	20		40	80	Actor-Singer-Comedian
Martin, Dean Vincent	Entertainment	5	6	15	15	
Martin, Dewey	Entertainment	9			25	Leading Man
Martin, Dick	Entertainment	6	8	15	20	
Martin, Frank 1890-1974	Composer	15			110	Prolific Swiss Composer.
Martin, Freddie	Entertainment	35			65	Big Band Leader-Pianist
Martin, Glenn L.	Aviation	75	170	265	250	Aeronautical Pioneer.
Martin, Hugh	Composer					AMusQS 45
Martin, James Green (War Date)	Civil War	182	663			CSA Gen.
Martin, James Green 1819-78	Civil War	95	225			CSA General
Martin, John A.	Governor	12		30		Governor KS
Martin, John C.	Senate/Congress	5	10			MOC IL
Martin, Joseph W. Jr. 1884-1968	Congress	20	35		25	Speaker of the House
Martin, Lori	Entertainment				25	Former Ingenue
Martin, Luther	Revolutionary War	70	175	360		Continental Congress
Martin, Mary	Entertainment	35	45		50	
Martin, Pamela Sue	Entertainment	6		15	15	Pin-Up SP $20
Martin, Ricardo	Entertainment	15			45	Opera
Martin, Ross	Entertainment	10	20	40	30	
Martin, Steve	Entertainment	5			30	
Martin, Struther	Entertainment	35			80	
Martin, Theodore, Sir	Author	5	15	25	10	
Martin, Thomas S.1847-1919	Congress	12	25			Senator VA 1893. CSA Army
Martin, Tony	Entertainment	10			25	
Martin, William C., Bishop	Clergy	15	25	30	35	
Martin, William T. (War Date)	Civil War	170	440	488		CSA Gen.
Martin, William T. 1823-1910	Civil War	112	295	400		CSA General
Martine, James E.	Congress	5	15		10	Senator NJ
Martineau, Harriet 1802-70	Author	15				Brit.
Martinelli, Giovanni	Entertainment	30	50		65	Opera. Dramatic Tenor
Martinez, Luis, Cardinal	Clergy	30	45	55	50	
Martini, Nino	Entertainment	15			45	Opera, Films. Handsome Tenor

The Sanders Price Guide to Autographs

NAME	CATEGORY	SIG	LS/DS	ALS	SP	Comment
Martini, Steve	Author	5	10		10	Novelist
Martino, Al	Entertainment	3	5		8	
Martino, Donald	Composer	20	35	90		Pulitzer, AMusQS $180
Martinu, Bronislaw	Composer					Czech. Composer AMusQS $900-1500
Martiny, Philip	Artist	25	40	80	30	
Marton, Eva	Entertainment	20			50	Opera
Marvel, Ik	Author	10		30		Pseud. Donald G. Mitchell
Marvin, Lee	Entertainment	85	175		200	
Marwood, William	Executioner	75		350		Br. Lord High Executioner
Marx Brothers (3)	Entertainment	750			1500	
Marx Brothers (4)	Entertainment	950			2650	
Marx, Arthur	Author	7	15		15	
Marx, Chico	Entertainment	125	170	325	325	
Marx, Groucho 1890-1977	Entertainment	248	509		333	Marx Bros. Leader
Marx, Harpo	Entertainment	400				
Marx, Karl 1818-83	Author	540	1500	14750	12650	Ger. Political Philosopher
Marx, Richard	Entertainment	20			50	Singer
Marx, Zeppo 1901-79	Entertainment	72	115		125	
Mary (of Teck) 1867-1953	Royalty	125	372	205	280	Queen of George V (Eng.)
Mary Adalaide (Dchs. Teck)	Royalty	25	70	150		
Mary I 1516-58	Royalty	900	3000	7500		Queen England, Bloody Mary
Mary II (Eng)	Royalty	370	1240	3100		Queen William II (NRPA)
Mary of Modena	Royalty					SEE Marie of Modena
Masaryk, Jan	Head of State	95	155	275	550	Pres. Czechoslavakia
Masaryk, Thomas G. 1850-1937	Head of State	100	250	625	600	Czech.Philosopher,1st President
Mascagni, Pietro 1863-1945	Composer	165	375	623	615	AMusQS $650-1250
Mascherini, Enzo	Entertainment	15			50	Opera
Masefield, John 1878-1967	Author	35	70	212	75	Br. Poet Laureate
Mash (Show-Cast of)	Entertainment				495	Eight Main Characters
Maslnl, Angelo	Entertainment				500	Opera. 19th Cent. Intern'l Star. RARE
Maskelyne, Nevil	Science	85	250	405		Br. Astronomer Royal. Inventor
Mason, Alfred Edw. W.	Author	10	30	45	15	Br. Novelist
Mason, George	Revolutionary War	1775	4500			Am. Planter & Rev. Statesman
Mason, Jackie	Entertainment	5			10	Comedian
Mason, James	Entertainment	20	45	65	60	Br. Actor-Film Director
Mason, James M.	Civil War	50	115	150		US Sen. VA, CSA Diplomat.Trent Affair
Mason, LeRoy	Entertainment	50			150	
Mason, Marsha	Entertainment	5	10		25	
Mason, Sully	Entertainment	5	6	15	10	
Mason, Walt	Author	5			20	Poet
Mason, William E. 1850-1921	Congress	12	20		15	MOC, Senator IL
Massen, Osa	Entertainment	4	6	10	10	
Massena, Andre, Duke 1758-1817	Fr. Revolution	95	375	450		Fr.Marshal.Greatest of Napoleon's Gen'ls
Massenet, Jules 1842-1912	Composer	65	145	255	295	AMusQS $475-$3500
Massey, Daniel	Entertainment	10			20	Actor
Massey, Gerald 1828-1907	Author	25	70	95		Br. Poet, Journalist, Editor
Massey, Illona	Entertainment	25		30	40	
Massey, Louise & Curt	Entertainment	25			45	Country Western
Massey, Raymond	Entertainment	20			55	Fine Vintage Canadian Actor
Massie, Paul	Entertainment	5	6	15	10	
Massie, Robert	Author		65			The Romanovs
Massine, Leonide	Entertainment	20			105	Ballet Dancer,Choreographer...
Masson, Andre	Artist	40	55	95		
Masters and Johnson	Sex Researchers	20			40	Wm. H. and Virginia
Masters, Edgar Lee 1869-1950	Author	50	150	250	65	Poet, Biographer. AMsS $600
Masters, Frankie	Entertainment	5			25	Big Band Leader

The Sanders Price Guide to Autographs

NAME	CATEGORY	SIG	LS/DS	ALS	SP	Comment
Masters, William H. & Virginia	Science	10			35	Sex Research Authors
Masterson, Mary Stuart	Entertainment	10			40	
Masterson, Wm. B. Bat 1853-1921	Lawman	4800		3850		Scout, Sheriff, Gambler
Mastroantonio, Mary Eliz.	Entertainment	10	15	25	40	
Mastroianni, Marcello	Entertainment	20			45	
Mata Hari (M.G. Zelle) 1876-1917	Spy	350	1100	4500	5290	Executed Secret Agent WW I
Mather, Cotton	Rev. War-Clergy	825	1950	3500		Author, Published 382 Books
Mathers, Jerry 'Beaver'	Entertainment	15			45	
Matheson, Tim	Entertainment	10			30	
Mathews, George 1739-1812	Revolutionary War	85	190			Statesman, General
Mathias, Bob	Senate/Congress	10	15		15	MOC CA
Mathis, Johnny	Entertainment	9	10	20	25	Alb. Cover S $55
Mathis, Samantha	Entertainment				80	Actress Broken Arrow
Mathiuci, Franca	Entertainment	5			15	
Matisse, Henri 1869-1954	Artist	700	800	2050	3220	Fr. Painter, Sculptor, Fauvist
Matlack, Timothy	Revolutionary War	85	275	450		Continental Congress
Matlin, Marlee	Entertainment	10		45	40	Pin-Up SP $100. AA
Matoni, Walter	Aviation	10			35	Ger. Ace WW II. RK
Matsushita, Konosuke	Business	25	65	145	40	Japanese Electronic Giant
Mattea, Kathy	Country Music	5			15	
Mattern, Jimmie	Aviation	15	25	60	35	
Matthau, Walter	Entertainment	5		15	25	AA
Matthews, DeLane	Entertainment	10			36	Actress Dave's World
Matthews, Frank Arnold	Clergy	20	25	35	25	
Matthews, Jessie	Entertainment	15			30	Br.Vintage Film Actress
Matthews, Stanley (SC)	Supreme Court	45	150	275		
Mattingly, Thos. Ken	Astronaut	15			115	
Mattson, Conrad	Aviation	8	15	28	22	ACE, WW II
Mature, Victor	Entertainment	9	10	20	40	
Matzky, Gerhard	Military	20	60			Nazi WW II Gen.
Maté, Rudy	Entertainment	15			55	Top Cinematographer
Maubourg, Lafayette	Celebrity	5	12	20		Nephew
Mauch, Billy	Entertainment	10	15	25	25	
Mauch, Bobby	Entertainment	30			65	
Maugham, W. Somerset 1874-1965	Author	68	412	323	397	Br. Novelist and Playwright
Mauldin, Bill*	Cartoonist	25			250	Willie & Joe
Maupassant, Guy de	Author	275	795	1185		Fr. Master of Short Story
Maura, Antonio	Head of State	110	165			Sp. P.M. Provoked Rif War
Maurey, Pierre	Clergy	10	15	30	25	Pres. Reform Church France
Mauro, Ermanno	Entertainment	15			40	Opera
Maurois, Andre (Emile Herzog)	Author	35	75	120		Fr. Biographer, Novelist
Maury, Dabney H. (War Date)	Civil War	142	280	1317	560	CSA General
Maury, Dabney H. 1822-1900	Civil War	85		350		CSA Gen.
Maury, Matthew F.1806-73	Civil War	98		672	1550	CSA Naval Cmdr., Hydrographer
Mawson, Douglas, Sir	Explorer	50	160	375		Australian Polar Explorer
Max, Peter	Artist	90	350			Am. Contemporary Art.
Maxey, Samuel Bell (War Date)	Civil War	245		2500		CSA Gen.
Maxey, Samuel Bell 1825-95	Civil War	127	225	234		CSA General, US Sen. TX
Maxey, Virginia	Entertainment	5			10	
Maxim, Hiram Percy 1896-1936	Science	40	265			Inventor Maxim Gun Silencer etc
Maxim, Hiram Stevens 1840-1916	Science	95	190	375	300	Inventor Maxim Machine Gun
Maxim, Hudson 1853-1927	Science	60	150	175	175	Inventor Smokeless Powder
Maximilian II (Bohemia-Hung.)	Royalty	110	415	770		Holy Roman Emperor
Maximilian, Ferdinand 1832-67	Royalty	310	675	1250		Emperor Mexico
Maxon, R.*	Cartoonist	20			100	Tarzan
Maxwell, Elsa	Columnist	8	25	35	15	Hostess & Professional Party

NAME	CATEGORY	SIG	LS/DS	ALS	SP	Comment
Maxwell, Lois	Entertainment	10			25	
Maxwell, Marilyn	Entertainment	8	10		35	
Maxwell, Robert	Aviation	12	25	28	22	ACE, WW II
Maxwell, Robert	Publisher	45			120	Died Mysteriously
Maxwell, William (Ld. Beaverbrook)	Publisher	25	110	180		Newspaper Proprietor, Statesman
May, Billy	Bandleader	10				Arranger
May, Edna	Entertainment	18		30	28	Vintage Stage & Film
Mayall, John	Entertainment	10			30	
Maybank, Burnet R.	Governor	10	18		15	Governor, Senator SC
Maye, Carolyn	Entertainment	10			25	
Mayer, Louis B.	Business	65	190	275	200	MGM Film Studio
Mayer, Maria, Dr.	Science	30	85		50	Nobel Physics
Mayfair, Mitzi	Entertainment	10			10	
Maynard, Ken	Entertainment	122		145	175	Western Film Hero
Maynor, Dorothy	Entertainment				275	30's-50's Concert & Recording Career
Mayo, 6th Earl(Rich.Bourke)	Head of State	10		30		Br. Politician.Viceroy of India
Mayo, Charles H., Dr. 1865-1939	Science	140	290	380	475	Co-Founder Mayo Foundation
Mayo, Charles W., Dr.1898-1968	Science	65	140	235	350	Surgeon Mayo Clinic.Prof. Surg.
Mayo, Frank 1839-96	Entertainment	12				Actor
Mayo, Henry Thomas	Military	15	40	75	40	Adm. Cmdr. Atlantic Fl. WW I
Mayo, Virginia	Entertainment	8			25	Pin-Up SP $40
Mayo, William J., Dr. 1861-1939	Science	105	290	380	475	Co-Founder Mayo Foundation
Mayron, Melanie	Entertainment	4			15	Actress 30 Something
Maytag, Frederick L.	Business	95	275	600	150	Maytag Electric Appliances
Mazurki, Mike	Entertainment	5	6	15	15	
Mazurski, Paul	Entertainment	5			20	Film Director
Mazzini, Joseph (Giuseppe)	Revolutionary	55	155	645		Italian Patriot.Unpublished ALS $2325
Mazzoleni, Ester	Entertainment	50			195	Opera. Dalmatian-Ital. Diva
McAdam, John	Inventor		850			McAdamized Roads
McAdoo, William G.	Cabinet	25	75	165	50	WIlson Sec'y Treasury
Mcaffee, Johnny	Entertainment	3	3	6	6	
McAllister, Lon	Entertainment	15			30	
McArdle, Andrea	Entertainment	5	6	15	15	
McArthur, John 1826-1906	Civil War	30			310	Union Gen.
McArthur, Kim	Playboy Bunny	4			8	Pin-Up SP $10
McArthur, William	Astronaut	7			15	
McAuliffe, Anthony A. 1898-1975	Military	85	175	175	395	WW II Gen'l. Replied Nuts
McAuliffe, Christa	Astronaut		1995			Died in Challenger Disaster
McAuliffe, S. Christa	Astronaut	450			650	
McAvoy, May	Entertainment	10			25	Vintage Film Actress
McBain, Diane	Entertainment	5	6	15	10	
McBain, Ed	Author	10	20	50	15	
McBride, George W. 1854-1911	Congress	5	15			Senator OR
McBride, Jon A.	Astronaut	5	15		30	
McCaffrey, Anne	Author	5			10	Novelist
McCain, John N.	Military	15	35			Admiral WW II
McCain, John S., Jr.(III)	Congress	5	30	45	40	Senator AZ, Vietnam war POW
McCall, Tom	Governor	5	10		15	Governor OR
McCalla, Irish	Entertainment	10		25	25	Pin-Up SP $35
McCallister, Lon	Entertainment	10			30	
McCallum, David	Entertainment	5	6	15	15	
McCambridge, Mercedes	Entertainment	40			75	
McCampbell, David S.	Aviation	15	25	45	75	ACE, WW II, Top Navy Ace, MOH
McCandless, Bruce II	Astronaut	10		90	24	
McCann, Chuck	Business	5	15	30	10	
McCarey, Leo	Entertainment	35			65	Academy Award Director, Prod.

NAME	CATEGORY	SIG	LS/DS	ALS	SP	Comment
McCarthy, Eugene J.	Congress	25	65		30	Senator MN. Pres. Candidate
McCarthy, Joe 1908-1957	Congress	35	150		95	Senator WI. McCarthyism
McCarthy, Kevin	Entertainment	10			25	
McCarthy, Mary	Author	45	135		50	Novelist
McCarthy, Michael W.	Business	3	5	10	5	
McCartney, Paul	Entertainment	100			486	Beatle SP 4x6 in. $295
McCaulay, Rose, Dame	Br. Author	20			45	
McCay, Peggy	Entertainment	10			35	Actress. Mayberry
McCay, Winsor*	Cartoonists	50			600	Little Nemo
McClanahan, Rue	Entertainment	10	10		25	
McClellan, George B.(War Date)	Civil War	340	485	1368		Union Gen.
McClellan, George B.1826-85	Civil War	241	250	500		Union Gen.ALS/Cont.'66 $2200
McClellan, John L. 1896-1977	Congress	10	20		25	Repr., Senator AR
McClernand, John A. (War Date)	Civil War	70	168	217		Union Gen.
McClernand, John A. 1812-1900	Civil War	45	110	175	600	
McClintic, James V.	Senate/Congress	5	10		7	MOC OK
McClintock, Francis Leopold	Explorer	45	115	200		Br. Adm., Arctic Navigator
McClintock, John	Astronaut	5	15		20	
McClinton, Delbert	Country Music	10			25	Singer-Musician. TX Blues Man
McCloskey, John, Cardinal	Clergy	95	125	250	100	
McCloskey, Lee	Entertainment	5	6	15	15	
McClosky, Pete	Senate/Congress	5	10		10	
McClung, J.T.M.	Senate/Congress	5	15		10	
McClure, Doug	Entertainment	5			30	
McClure, Samuel S.1887-1949	Editor	12				Publisher
McClurg, Alexander C.	Civil War	50	85			Union General
McColpin, Carroll W.	Military	25	45	75	50	ACE WW II, Maj. Gen.
McComb, William 1828-1918	Civil War	95	235	350		CSA Gen.
McConnell, Calvin D., Bishop	Clergy	20	25	30	30	
McConnell, Francis J., Bishop	Clergy	20	25	50	30	
McConnell, James, Bishop	Clergy	20	25	35	30	
McConnell, Joseph, Jr.	Aviation	75	140	175	150	ACE, Korea, Top Korea Ace
McCoo, Marilyn	Entertainment	5	6	15	15	
McCook, Alex. M. D.1831-1903	Civil War	35	70	115		Union Gen.
McCook, Alex. M.(War Date)	Civil War	45		195		Union Gen.
McCook, Anson	Civil War	30	55			Union Gen., MOC
McCook, Henry C.	Clergy	10	10	15		
McCormack, John	Entertainment	35	155	295	170	Famed Irish Tenor
McCormack, John W.	Speaker of House	10	25	80		Speaker of the House
McCormack, Patty	Entertainment	5	8	15	15	
McCormic, Mary	Entertainment	20				Opera
McCormick, Anne O'Hare	Author	30	45	110	35	1st Pulitzer Woman Journalist
McCormick, Cyrus H. 1809-84	Science-Business	225	900	1025		Invented the Reaper
McCormick, Myron	Entertainment	15	25	45	40	
McCormick, Nettie Fowler	Business	25		90		Mrs. Cyrus McCormick
McCormick, Robert R., Col.	Business	35	140	165	60	Editor Chicago Tribune
McCorvey, Norma	Celebrity		150			A.K.A. Jane Roe (Roe vs Wade)
McCown, John Porter (War Date)	Civil War	245	1095			CSA Gen.
McCown, John Porter 1815-79	Civil War	95	310			CSA Gen.
McCoy, Charles B.	Business	25		85	10	Pres. DuPont Co.
McCoy, Clyde	Entertainment	6	8	15	15	
McCoy, Tim	Entertainment	50			155	
McCoy, Wilson*	Cartoonist	15			75	Phantom
McCrea, Joel	Entertainment	15	95		40	
McCreery, Richard L., Sir	Military	30	75		40	Br. Gen. WW II/Montgomery. 8th Army
McCudden, James T.B.	Aviation	135	225	350	300	ACE, WW I, RAF

NAME	CATEGORY	SIG	LS/DS	ALS	SP	Comment
McCullers, Carson 1917-67	Author	60	195	508	75	Am. Novelist
McCulley, Michael J.	Astronaut	5			15	
McCulloch, Ben 1811-62	Civil War	155	470	565		CSA Gen. Morman War LS $2300
McCulloch, Henry E.	Civil War	145	350			CSA General
McCulloch, Hugh 1808-95	Cabinet	45	140	135		Lincoln, Johnson Sec'y Treas.
McCullough, Colleen	Author	35	105	225	40	Austr. Novelist.Thorn Birds
McCullough, John 1832-85	Entertainment	10			35	Vintage Stage Actor
McCullough, Julie	Entertainment	7			20	Pin-Up SP $35
McCutcheon, George Barr 1866-1928	Author	10				
McCutcheon, John T.*1870-1949	Cartoonist				30	Pulitzer.Political Cartoonist.Chicago Tribune
McDaniel, Hattie	Entertainment	750	1850	2100	2500	AA Gone With the Wind
McDermott, Dylan	Entertainment	15			35	
McDevitt, Ruth	Entertainment	10			20	
McDivitt, James A.	Astronaut	30			35	
McDonald, A. J. (Al)	Astronaut	20			30	NASA Whistleblower
McDonald, M. Nick	Celebrity	15	40		40	Captured Lee Harvey Oswald
McDonald, Marie	Entertainment	35	45	90	85	
McDonald, Richard J.	Business	90	225	450	175	MacDonald's
McDonald, Skeets	Country Music	10			20	
McDonnell, James S.	Business	20	45	95	35	Founder, McDonnell Aircraft
McDonnell, Mary	Entertainment	20			50	
McDougall, Alexander	Revolutionary War	90	200	415		Gen. Cont. Army,Cont. Congress
McDowell, Andre	Entertainment	5			30	
McDowell, Irvin (War Date)	Civil War	120	235	525	1250	Union Gen.Special DS $400
McDowell, Irvin 1818-85	Civil War	75		266		Union Gen.
McDowell, Malcolm	Entertainment	10			35	
McDowell, Roddy	Entertainment	15			25	
McDuffie, George 1790-1851	Congress	15				Sen. & Repr. SC
McElmurry, Thomas	Astronaut	5			20	
McElroy, Neil H.	Cabinet	15	35		25	Sec'y Defense. Pres. P & G
McEnery, S.D. 1837-1910	Congress	12	25			Governor LA and Senator
McEntire, Reba	Country Music	15			30	
McEntyre, Joe (New Kids)	Entertainment	10			45	
McFadden, Gates	Entertainment	5			15	Star Trek
McFadden, Obadiah B.	Senate/Congress	15	30	40		MOC WA 1873
McFarland, Spanky	Entertainment	15			45	Little Rascals Lobby Card S $195
McGarru. William D.	Aviation	15	30	45	40	ACE, WW II, Flying Tigers
McGavin, Darren	Entertainment	25			50	
McGee, Don	Aviation	25				WW II Am. Ace
McGee, Gale	Senate/Congress	5	15		10	Senator WY
McGill, John	Clergy	90		450		CW Bishop of Richmond
McGillis, Kelly	Entertainment	10		20	35	
McGinley, Phyllis	Author	10	30	45	20	Am Poet. Pulitzer
McGoohan, Patrick	Entertainment	20			45	
McGovern, Elizabeth	Entertainment	5			20	
McGovern, George	Senate	10	45		25	Senator SD, Pres. Hopeful
McGovern, John	Author	25	40			
McGranery, James P.	Cabinet	10	15	25		Att'y General
McGrath, J. Howard	Cabinet	5	20	35	15	Att'y General
McGuffy, William H.	Educator	95	475			McGuffy's Reader
McGugin, Harold C.1893-1946	Congress	10	25			Repr. KS
McGuigan, James, Cardinal	Clergy	5	10	15	12	
McGuire Sisters	Entertainment					Singing Group
McGuire, Barry	Entertainment	5	6		25	New Christy Minstrels
McGuire, Dorothy	Entertainment	15			30	
McGuire, Phyllis	Entertainment	4	15		10	McGuire Sisters

NAME	CATEGORY	SIG	LS/DS	ALS	SP	Comment
McGuire, Thomas B.	Aviation	150	300	650	450	ACE, WW II, #2 U.S. Ace
McHenry, James 1753-1816	Cabinet-Military	180	250	2800		Signer Constitution, Sec'y War
McHugh, Frank	Entertainment	20	25	65	60	
McHugh, Jimmy	Composer	25	75			AMusQS $825
McHugh, Joseph	Artist	5			10	
McIlvaine, Abraham R. 1804-63	Congress	10				Repr. PA, Whig Presidential Elector
McIntire, John	Entertainment	20			50	
McIntosh, Lachlan	Revolutionary War	550	855	1375		Killed Button Gwinnett. Duel
McIntyre, James F., Archbishop	Clergy	40	65	75	60	
McIntyre, Marvin H.	Cabinet	3	10	15		Sec'y to FDR
McIntyre, O. O.	Author	15	25	40	20	Journalist, Synd. Columnist
McKay, Douglas	Cabinet	15	25		20	Governor OR, Sec'y Interior
McKay, Gardner	Entertainment	6	8	15	20	
McKean, Thomas 1734-1817	Revolutionary War	250	449	853		Signer. ADS 1778 $2250
McKee, Thomas H.	Senate/Congress	10	20			
McKeever, Chauncey (War Date)	Civil War	40		175		Union Gen.
McKeldin, Theodore R.	Governor	5	17		10	Governor MD
McKellar, Kenneth D. 1869-1957	Congress	10	30			Senator TN
McKellen, Ian	Entertainment	16			35	Actor
McKenna, Joseph (SC)	Supreme Court	35	50	80	40	Att'y General
McKenna, Siobhan	Entertainment	15			35	
McKenzie, Fay	Entertainment	5		15	15	
McKeon, Nancy	Entertainment	4	6		30	
McKeon, Phillip	Entertainment	5			20	
McKern, Leo	Entertainment	15			40	Rumpole
McKinley, Ida S.	First Lady	400	625	975	450	
McKinley, Ray	Entertainment	20			65	Bandleader, Drummer
McKinley, William (As Pres.)	President	340	689	2525	1125	White House Card S $425
McKinley, William 1843-1901	President	248	694	965	1075	Assassinated by Anarchist
McKinly, John	Revolutionary War	65	180			First Gov. DE, Captured by Br.
McKone, John R.	Military	10	20	40	30	
McKuen, Rod	Author	20	25	35	50	Poet
McLaglin, Andrew V.	Entertainment	10		25		
McLaglin, Victor	Entertainment	150			275	AA
McLain, Raymond S.	Military	30			45	Gen. WW II
McLains, The	Country Music	20			45	
McLane, Louis	Business	35	150			Pres. Wells Fargo & Co.
McLane, Louis 1786-1857	Cabinet	15	45	60		Jackson Sec'y Treasury
McLane, Robert	Diplomat-Gov.	35	80	135		Gov. MD, U.S. Minister to Jap.
McLaughlin, E.A.	Business	10	35	45	20	
McLaughlin, James C.	Senate/Congress	10	15		15	MOC MI
McLaughlin, Kyle	Entertainment	20			75	
McLaws, Lafayette 1821-97	Civil War	165	347	412		CSA Gen. Sig/Rank $290
McLean, Don	Entertainment	20			45	Rock
McLean, George P.	Senate	10	15	25		Gov., Senator CT
McLean, John (SC) 1785-1861	Supreme Court	55	200	285		Dissented Dred Scott Opinion
McLean, Nathaniel C.	Civil War	60	80	170		Union General
McLeod, Archibald Norman	Fur Trader		2500			Hudson's Bay Co. vs NW Co.
McLeod, Catherine	Entertainment	6	9		15	
McLintock, Francis Sir	Celebrities	10	30	75		
McLuhan, Marshall	Author		37			
McMahon, Brien 1903-52	Congress	10	40		15	Senator CT
McMahon, Ed	Entertainment	5			15	
McMahon, Horace	Entertainment	20			50	
McManus, George*	Cartoonist	40			200	Bringing Up Father,Panel $1,500
McMichael, Morton	Journalist	45	95			1st Editor Saturday Eve'g Post

NAME	CATEGORY	SIG	LS/DS	ALS	SP	Comment
McMillan, Edwin M.	Science	20	35	69	30	Nobel Chemistry 1952
McMillan, James 1838-1902	Congress	12	20	35		Senator MI 1889
McMillan, James Winning	Civil War	40				Union General
McMillan, Kenneth	Entertainment	5	6	15	15	
McMillan, Terry	Entertainment	3	4	10	8	
McMonagle, Donald	Astronaut	4			12	
McMullen, Clements 1892-	Military	50	175			WW I Aviator, WW II General
McMullen, Richard C.	Governor	5	10			Governor DE
McNair, Howard	Entertainment	400				Actor. Andy Griffith Show
McNair, Leslie J.	Military	35	95	165	80	WW I, General, WW II KIA
McNair, Robert	Governor	5	15		10	Governor SC
McNair, Ronald E.	Astronaut	75			275	Died in Challenger Crash
McNally, Stephen	Entertainment	10			20	
McNally, W.	Entertainment	5	6	15	15	
McNamara, Robert S.	Cabinet	15	50		15	Sec'y Defense, Pres. World Bank
McNamara, William	Entertainment	5	8	25	25	
McNamee, Graham	Entertainment	20				Legendary Sports Announcer
McNarney, Joseph T.	Military	20	50			General WW II
McNary, Charles L. 1874-1944	Congress	15	35			Senator OR. McNary Dam
McNaughton, Kenneth	Military	4	9	15	10	
McNee, Patrick	Entertainment	10			25	
McNeil, Robert	Entertainment	5			30	Star Trek
McNeill, Don	Entertainment	10			20	
McNichol, Kristy	Entertainment	10			30	Pin-Up SP $35
McNutt, Paul V.	Governor	15	30			Governor IN
McPartland, Jimmy	Entertainment	30	55		85	Jazz Trumpet
McPhatter, Clyde	Entertainment	400		800		Classic Rocker
McPherson, Aimee Semple	Clergy	100	300	495	350	
McPherson, Craig	Artists					
McPherson, Isaac V.	Senate/Congress	5	15			MOC MO
McPherson, James B. (War Date)	Civil War	375		2286		Union General KIA 1864
McPherson, John R. 1833-97	Congress	12	20	30		Senator NJ
McQuade, James (War Date)	Civil War	45	85			Union Gen.
McQuade, James 1829-85	Civil War	25	70	178		Union General
McQueen, Butterfly	Entertainment	88	100		95	SP as Prissy (GWTW) $125
McQueen, Steve 1930-80	Entertainment	200	325	400	325	
McRaney, Gerald	Entertainment	5			25	
McReynolds, James C. (SC)	Supreme Court	30	125	145	100	Wilson Att'y Gen.
McShane, Ian	Entertainment	9	10	20	25	
McShann, Jay	Entertainment	50			125	Jazz Pianist,Vocalist, Bandlead
McWade, John	Entertainment	10				Character Actor
McWethy, John	Entertainment	4			20	ABC News
McWhorter, Hamilton	Aviation	12	25	45	35	ACE, WW II
McWilliams, Caroline	Entertainment	4	6	9	9	
Mead, Margaret 1901-78	Science	70	122	170	225	Anthropologist, Lecturer, Author
Meade, Carl J.	Astronaut	5			16	
Meade, George G. (War Date)	Civil War	692	945	2524	2500	Union Gen.
Meade, George G. 1815-72	Civil War	290	345	608	350	Union Gen. DS $1,750 War Dte
Meadowlarks	Entertainment	3			6	
Meadows, Audrey	Entertainment	15			40	Pin-Up SP $45
Meadows, Jayne	Entertainment	5			10	
Meagher, Thomas F. (War Date)	Civil War	122	685	1210		Union Gen.
Meagher, Thomas F. 1823-67	Civil War	45	180	240		Union Gen.
Meaney, Colm	Entertainment	15			30	Star Trek
Meany, George	Labor Leader	15	30		90	Pres. AFL-CIO
Meara, Anne	Entertainment	4	4		15	

NAME	CATEGORY	SIG	LS/DS	ALS	SP	Comment
Meat Loaf	Entertainment	5		25	45	Rock
Mecham, Edwin L.	Senate	5	15		12	Governor, Senator NM
Medawar, Peter B., Sir	Science	20	30	60	25	Nobel Medicine 1960
Medeiros, Humberto, Cardinal	Clergy	35	50	60	50	
Medici, Cosimo I, de 1519-74	Royalty	375	1320			The Great. Duke of Florence
Medici, Fernando de 1549-1609	Royalty	370	1250	3125		Son of Cosimo I. Gr. Duke
Medici, Leopoldo de, Cardinal	Clergy	300	385	550		Cardinal. Son of Cosimo II
Medicis, Catherine de	Royalty	270	800	5000		Queen of Henry II of France
Medicis, Francesco de	Royalty	100	200	500		NRPA
Medicis, Marie de 1573-1642	Royalty	350	950	2500		Queen of Henry IV (Fr)
Medill, Joseph	Journalist	125		250		A founder Repub. Party
Medill, William 1802-65	Congress	12				Repr. OH, Gov. OH
Medina, Harold R.	Jurist	10	25		15	
Medina, Patricia	Entertainment	4	5		15	
Medjugorje (Jugo) Children of	Religious	300				2 Who Saw Vision Virgin Mary
Medley, Bill	Country Music	6			20	
Meeker, Ralph	Entertainment	25			40	
Meese, Edwin III	Cabinet	5	20	35	25	Att'y General
Mehta, Zubin	Conductor	12			50	International Conductor
Mei-Figner, Medea 1859-1952	Entertainment				1200	Opera. It.-Russian Mezzo-Soprano
Meier, Waltraud	Entertainment	15			35	Opera
Meighan, James	Entertainment				20	Radio Actor. The Falcon
Meighan, Tom	Entertainment	35			85	
Meigs, Montgomery C.(War Date)	Civil War	45	250	255		Union Gen.
Meigs, Montgomery C.1816-92	Civil War	52	120	165	250	Union Quartermaster General
Meigs, Return J., Jr. 1764-1824	Military-Cabinet	80	205	360		Monroe P.M. General
Meiklejohn, G.D.	Cabinet	15	40			Ass't Sec'y War
Meinl, Tanaka	Entertainment	30			75	Opera
Meir, Golda 1898-1979	Head of State	128	275	605	345	TLS/Content $1,500-$2,500
Melachrino, George	Bandleader	14				Arranger
Melba, Nellie 1859-1931	Entertainment	75	135	205	467	Australian Operatic Soprano
Melbourne, Wm. Lamb, Lord	Head of State	40	70	150		Q.Victoria's 1st Prime Minister
Melchior, Lauritz 1890-1973	Entertainment	45	100		182	Opera Danish Tenor
Melis, Carmen	Entertainment	35			85	Opera, Teacher
Mellencamp, John	Entertainment	35			62	Rock. Album Cover S $60-$80
Mellnik, Steve	Military	5	25	35		
Mellon, Andrew 1855-1937	Business	188	556	410	275	Pittsburgh Millionaire Tycoon
Melnick, Bruce E.	Astronaut	5			16	
Melton, James	Entertainment	10			55	Am. Concert, Radio & Opera Tenor
Melvill, Thomas 1751-1832	Revolutionary War	90	250	550		Memb. Boston Tea Party
Melville, George W.	Military	40	105	170		Union Adm.
Melville, Herman 1819-91	Author	500	1820	9800		ALS's/Content $20,000-$40,000
Melville, Viscount 1771-1851	Royalty	55				
Memminger, Chris.G.(War Date)	Civil War	165	480	588		CSA Sec'y of Treasury
Mencken, Henry L. 1880-1956	Author	90	224	365	450	Satirist, Editor, Critic
Mendel, Gregor Johann	Science	400	850	2000		Laws of Biological Inheiritance
Mendeleyev, Dmitry 1834-1907	Science			1650		Rus. Chem. Developed Periodic Table
Mendelssohn-Bartholdy, F. 1809-47	Composer	600	1375	3238		ALS/Content $6,500
Mendes, Abraham Caulle	Author	15	35	100		Fr. Poet.Plays, Verses,Libretti
Mendez, Arnaldo Tamayo	Astronaut	6			15	
Mengelberg, Willem	Entertainment	75			210	Dutch Conductor
Menjou, Adolphe	Entertainment	20	25		75	
Menk, Louis W.	Business	5			10	CEO International Harvester
Menken, Helen	Entertainment	15	15	30	25	
Menkes, Sara	Entertainment	20			55	Opera
Mennin, Peter	Composer	10		65		AMusQS $75

The Sanders Price Guide to Autographs

NAME	CATEGORY	SIG	LS/DS	ALS	SP	Comment
Menninger, Karl 1893-1980	Science	35	90	120	75	Menninger Clinic & Foundation
Menninger, Roy	Science	10	25	55	30	
Menninger, William C., Dr.	Science	15	40	70	35	Psychiatrist, Pres. Foundation
Menocal, Mario G.	Head of State	25			40	Pres. Cuba 1913-21
Menon, V. Krisna	Diplomat	20		25		Ambassador Gr. Britain
Menotti, Gian Carlo	Composer	150	250	495	350	
Menuhin, Yehudi	Entertainment	40	55		134	Concert Violinist
Menzies, Robert, Sir	Head of State	15	55	125	25	Australian Prime Minister
Merbold, Ulf	Astronaut	10	25		25	
Mercadante, Saverio 1795-1870	Composer	150		450		Dir. Royal Conservatory, Naples
Mercer, Archibald	Revolutionary War					Patriot. Cont. ALS $750
Mercer, Frances	Entertainment	5	8		15	
Mercer, Hugh W.	Civil War	90	170			CSA General
Mercer, John Francis 1759-1821	Revolutionary War	70		125		Aide-de-Camp Gen Lee
Mercer, Johnny	Composer	50			135	Vocalist, Pianist
Mercer, Mable	Entertainer					Jazz Singer
Mercer, Marian	Entertainment	10			35	
Mercier, D. Joseph, Cardinal	Clergy	35	45	75		
Mercouri, Melina	Entertainment	25	30	45	65	
Mercury (6 Astronauts)	Astronaut				1100	No Virgil Grissom
Mercury (7 Astronauts)	Astronaut					All 7 Sigs $3795-$4000
Meredith, Burgess	Entertainment	10	15	25	30	As The Penguin $35
Meredith, Edwin T.	Cabinet	5	20	30	15	Sec'y Agriculture 1920
Meredith, James H.	Activist	35	90	185	60	Afro-Am. Activist
Meredith, Samuel 1740-1817	Cabinet	80	300	355		Rev. War Gen.,1st US Treasurer
Meredith, Solomon	Civil War	125		450		Union Gen. Iron Brig. of West
Meriam, Ebenezer	Science			225		Meteorologist
Merivale, Philip	Entertainment	7		25	25	Vintage Br.Actor
Meriwether, Lee	Entertainment	5	10	12	15	
Merkel, Una	Entertainment	10			25	
Merli, Francesco	Entertainment	25			75	Opera. Dramatic Tenor
Merli, Gino J.	Military	5	25			WW II Hero CMH
Merlin de Douai, P.A.	Fr. Revolution	40		200		Revolutionary. Min. of Justice
Merman, Ethel	Entertainment	25			50	
Merriam, Frank F.	Governor	5	15		10	Governor CA
Merrick, David	Entertainment	20	20	70	60	Theatrical Producer
Merrick, Samuel Vaughan	Business	40	175			Financier
Merrill, Dina	Entertainment	6	8	15	15	
Merrill, Frank D. 1903-55	Military	225	850	325		Gen.WW II.Merrill's Marauders
Merrill, Gary 1914-90	Entertainment	15	20	45	35	
Merrill, Henry T.	Aviation	30	45	100	100	
Merrill, Lewis	Civil War	60	175			Union General
Merrill, Richard Dick	Aviation	30	55	105	75	
Merrill, Robert	Entertainment	30			50	Metropolitan Opera Co. Baritone
Merrill, Stuart	Author	30		125		Am. Poet. Wrote in French
Merriman, Nan 1920-	Entertainment				58	Opera. U.S. Mezzo-Sop.
Merrimon, Augustus S. 1830-92	Congress	22	35			Senator NC
Merritt, Chris	Entertainment	10			30	Opera
Merritt, Wesley 1834-1910	Civil War	85	305	200		Union Gen., Indian Fighter
Merton, Thomas	Clergy	375	1135			Priest-Writer, Poet
Mesmer, F. Anton, Dr.1734-1815	Science	115	285	535		Ger. Dr.Mesmerise.DS $3750
Messerschmitt, Wilhelm	Aviation	125	275		395	Ger. Aircraft Designer-Mfg.
Messiaen, Olivier	Composer	70	200			Fr. Organist
Messick, Dale*	Cartoonist	15			105	Brenda Starr
Messick, Don	Entertainment	15			40	Voice of Scoobie Do
Messmer, Otto*	Cartoonist	55			400	Felix The Cat

The Sanders Price Guide to Autographs

NAME	CATEGORY	SIG	LS/DS	ALS	SP	Comment
Mesta, Perle	Business	25	30	70	35	Washington Hostess
Metallica (4)	Entertainment				90	Rock
Metcalf, Laurie	Entertainment	15			30	Actress. Roseanne
Metcalf, Victor H. 1853-1936	Cabinet	20	55	95		Sec'y Navy, Commerce, Labor
Metcalfe, Ralph H.	Senate/Congress	5	15		22	MOC IL
Metchnikoff, Elie	Science	60	95		150	Nobel Physiology 1908
Metternich, Prince Clemens W. von	Head of State	70	245	480		Austrian Statesman
Metzenbaum, Howard	Senate	10			20	Senator OH
Metzer, Joe	Artist	10				Illustrator. Origianal Sm. Sketch $45
Meusel, Lucille	Entertainment	10			25	Soprano
Mewman, Larry	Aviation	25			75	
Meyer, Albert G., Cardinal	Clergy	35	40	50	40	
Meyer, E. C.	Military	6	10	30	20	
Meyer, George von L.	Cabinet	15	20	35	20	P.M. General 1907
Meyerbeer, Giacomo	Composer	170	290	610	300	Ger. Composer of Fr. Operas
Mfume, Kweisi	Congress	10			40	Head of NAACP
Miaskovsky, Nikolai 1881-1950	Composer	125				27 Symphonies
Michael, George	Entertainment	20	30	95	100	
Michaels, Barbara	Author	5		25	15	
Michaels, Bret	Entertainment	10	20	50	45	
Michaels, Dolores	Entertaiment	10				Acctress
Michaels, Lorraine	Playboy Model	4			8	Pin-Up SP $10
Michaels, Marilyn	Entertainment	5		25	20	
Michel, Frank Curtis	Astronaut	5			15	
Michelangelo (Buonarroti)	Artist	2250	10000	25000		NRPA
Michele, Denise	Entertainment	3	3		8	
Michelet, Jules 1798-1874	Author			75		Great Historian of Romantic School
Michelson, Albert A.	Science	120		450		Nobel Physics 1907
Michelson, Charles	Political	12	15			Speech Writer New Deal
Michener, James A.	Author	30	265	340	115	Am. Novelist. Pulitzer
Middleton, Arthur	Revolutionary War	1100	3300	3850		Signer Decl. of Indepen.
Middleton, Charles	Entertainment	75			250	
Middleton, Charles, Sir 1726-1813	Military					Issued Orders for Victory at Trafalgar
Middleton, Henry 1717-84	Revolutionary War	3000	4500			Pres. of Congress. Special DS $9500
Middleton, Robert	Entertainment	50			150	
Middleton, Thomas Fanshaw	Clergy	30	50	80		
Middleton, Velma	Entertainment	30			70	Jazz Vocalist
Midler, Bette	Entertainment	15			45	Singer-Actress
Midori	Entertainment	15			50	
Mielziner, Jo	Entertainment	15		40	35	Film Director
Mifflin, Thomas 1744-1800	Revolutionary War	150	594			Gen. Pres. Continental Congr.
Mifune, Toshiro	Entertainment	15	25	65	40	
Migenes, Julia	Entertainment	15			35	Opera
Mihalovivi, Marcel	Composer	20			150	Rumanian
Miklas, Wilhelm 1872-1956	Head of State	35				Pres. Austria
Mikulski, Barbara	Congress	15			30	Democratic senator Maryland
Milano, Alyssa	Entertainment	20			45	
Milanov, Zinka	Entertainment	20			120	Metropolitan Opera
Milburn, William H. 1823-1903	Clergy	35				Blind Circuit Rider Minister
Milch, Erhard	Aviation	80	250	400	175	WW I, Insp. Gen.Luftwaffe WW II
Miles, Josephine	Author	7	15	25	10	
Miles, Nelson A. 1839-1925	Civil War	130	285	352		Union General, MOH
Miles, Sarah	Entertainment	9	10	25	25	Pin-Up SP $35
Miles, Sylvia	Entertainment	10	20	35	35	
Miles, Vera	Entertainment	6	8	15	20	Pin-Up SP $25
Milestone, Lewis	Entertainment	35			85	Film Director

NAME	CATEGORY	SIG	LS/DS	ALS	SP	Comment
Milhaud, Darius 1892-1974	Composer	185	250	315	450	AMusQS $500
Mill, James	Author	65	250	515		Scot.Philosopher,Historian,Econ
Mill, John Stuart	Author-Editor	150	400	850		Br. Economist, Philosopher
Mill, William Hodge	Clergy	20	25	30		
Millais, John Everett, Sir 1829-96	Artist	45	85	260		Pre-Raphaelite Painter
Milland, Ray	Entertainment	30	50		70	
Millay, Edna St. Vincent 1892-1950	Author	140	325	800	1265	Am. Poet, Dramatist. Pulitzer
Miller, Alice Duer	Author	15	25	45		Novelist, Poet
Miller, Ann	Entertainment	10			40	Pin-Up SP $30
Miller, Arjay R.	Business	3	10	25	5	
Miller, Arthur	Author	40	90	205	75	Playwright. Pulitzer.TMsS & AMsS $3,900
Miller, Caroline	Author	10	20			Pulitzer
Miller, Charles Henry 1842-1922	Artist	25			100	Landscape Painter
Miller, Denny	Entertainment	5			20	Character actor
Miller, Eddie	Entertainment	20			45	Big Band Tenor Saxophonist
Miller, Frederick C.	Business	12	32	64	25	Miller Beer
Miller, G. William	Cabinet	5	15	25	12	Sec'y Treasury
Miller, Glenn 1904-44	Entertainment	175	800	450	439	Big Band Leader-Trombonist
Miller, H.G.	Business	10			15	
Miller, Henry	Entertainment	30				Vintage Actor
Miller, Henry	Entertainment	35	40	75	70	Henry Miller Theatre
Miller, Henry V. 1891-1980	Author	85	160	368	150	Tropic of Cancer
Miller, Jacob W. 1800-1862	Congress	12				Sen. NJ
Miller, Joaquin	Author	50		125		Am. Poet, Journalist.Spec. TLS $3500
Miller, John F.	Civil War	35	50	60		Union Gen., U.S. Sen. CA
Miller, Ken	Entertainment	3			20	Child Actor
Miller, Leslie A.	Governor	10	20			Governor WY
Miller, Marilyn	Entertainment	72		240	215	Ziegfeld Follies Dancing Star
Miller, Marvin	Entertainment	10			25	
Miller, Mitch	Entertainment	5			15	Conductor, Arranger
Miller, Nathan L.	Governor	15	25		20	Governor NY
Miller, Patsy Ruth	Entertainment	25	35	55	45	
Miller, Penelope Ann	Entertainment	20			50	
Miller, Roger	Country Music	35			60	Composer
Miller, Samuel F. (SC)	Supreme Court	95	185	290		
Miller, Stanley	Science	15	35	65	20	
Miller, Stephen	Civil War	95	195	295		Union General
Miller, Taylor	Entertainment	4	4	9	10	
Miller, Warner 1838-1918	Congress	10	20	35		Repr., Senator NY
Miller, William H. H.	Cabinet	10	30	50	20	Att'y General 1889
Millerande, Alexandre 1859-1943	Head of State	40	45	60	35	Socialist Pres. France 1920-24
Milles, Carl	Artist	30	55	90		Am. Sculptor
Millet, Francis Davis 1846-1912	Artist	25	45	340		Am. Medal Winning Art. Journalist
Millet, Jean François 1814-75	Artist	200	450	2500		Fr.Religious,Classical,Peasant
Milligan, Edward	Business	5	15			Insurance Exec.
Millikan, John	Military	9	30	50	20	
Millikan, Robert A., Dr.1868-1953	Science	85	200	425	200	Nobel Physics,Educator,Author
Milliken, William G.	Governor	5	15		10	Governor MI
Millinder, Lucky	Entertainment	40			125	Bandleader
Millo, Aprile	Entertainment	10			35	Opera
Mills Brothers (4)	Entertainment	100			200	
Mills, Darius Ogden 1825-1910	Business	150	450			Merchant,Banker, Philan.
Mills, Donna	Entertainment	9	10		30	Producer. Pin-Up SP $25
Mills, Earle W.	Military	12	30			
Mills, Hayley	Entertainment	10	15	25	30	Pin-Up SP $28
Mills, John, Sir	Entertainment	20			35	

NAME	CATEGORY	SIG	LS/DS	ALS	SP	Comment
Mills, Juliette	Entertainment	10			20	
Mills, Madison	Civil War	35				Union Gen. Med.Off'r.. War Dte.ALS $275
Mills, Ogden L.	Cabinet	10	35	45	15	Sec'y Treasury 1932
Mills, Roger Q.	Civil War	25	35	50		CSA Colonel, MOC TX
Mills, Wilbur 1909-	Congress	25			35	Senator AR
Milne, A. A. 1882-1956	Author	215	450	1000	470	Winnie-the-Pooh. Playwright
Milner, Martin	Entertainment	4	6		15	
Milnes, Rich.M.(Baron of Houghton)	Celebrity	5	10	25	10	Man of Letters.Oxford Movement
Milnes, Sherrill	Entertainment	10			25	Opera. Am. Basso
Milosz, Czeslaw, Dr.	Author	45	125		50	Nobel Literature
Milroy, Robert H. 1816-90	Civil War	25	80			Union Gen. LS '61 $220
Milsap, Ronnie	Country Music	5	6	15	15	
Milstein, Nathan	Entertainment	38			75	Rus. Violinist
Miltonberger, Butler	Military	35	60			
Mimieux, Yvette	Entertainment	5	8		21	Pin-Up SP $25
Mincus, Leon	Composer	55			375	Austro-Rus. Many Ballets
Mindil, George W.	Civil War	35		210		Union Gen. MOH
Mindszenty, Jozef, Cardinal	Clergy	50	75	135	95	
Minelli, Liza	Entertainment	15	25		25	
Mineo, Sal 1939-76	Entertainment	200			450	Murdered at 37
Miner, Jan	Entertainment	5	6	15	10	
Mingus, Charlie	Entertainment					Jazz Musician-No Price Availabl
Minh, Duong Van Gen.	Military	15	40	75	40	
Minh, Ho Chi	Head of State	750	1500	2500	1500	Pres. & Founder N. Vietnam
Minich, Peter	Entertainment	5			20	Opera, Light Opera
Mink, Patsy T.	Senate/Congress	5	15		10	MOH HI
Minnelli, Liza	Entertainment	9	10	20	35	Pin-Up SP $35
Minnelli, Vincente	Entertainment	30			62	AA Film Director
Minor, Ruediger, Bishop	Clergy	25	40	45	50	
Minow, Newton N.	Law	12			15	Chairman FCC
Minter, Mary Miles	Entertainment	90	115	230	200	
Minton, Sherman (SC)	Supreme Court	40	165	250	100	
Minton, Yvonne	Entertainment	5			25	Opera
Minvielle, Gabriel	Fr. Revolution	850				NRPA
Miollis, S.A.F.	Fr. Revolution	100	215			
Mirabeau, Gabriel H.R 1749-91.	Fr. Revolution	95	275	575		Statesman, Diplomat,Politician
Mirabehin (M. Slade)	Celebrity	25		45		Companion-Follower of Gandhi
Miramon, Miguel (Mex)	Military	20	85	140		Cmdr. Army vs Juarez.
Miranda, Carmen 1913-55	Entertainment	125	185		395	Portuguese Singer-Movie Star
Miranda, Isa	Entertainment	35			85	Fr. Actress
Mirisch, Walter	Entertainment	6	8	15	20	Motion Picture Producer
Miro, Juan 1893-1983	Artist	200	575	700	310	Repro The Hare S $250,$325
Miroslava	Entertainment	25	30	70	65	
Mirren, Helen	Entertainment	10	20		65	Br. Actress
Mission Impossible (Cast)	Entertainment				195	4 Leads incl. Tom Cruise
Mister, Mister	Entertainment	15			55	
Mistinguett, Madamoiselle	Entertainment				250	Moulon Rouge Dancer-Actress
Mistral, Frederic	Author	30	75	130	50	Nobel Literature 1904
Mistral, Gabriela	Author	20	35	60	25	Nobel Lit.'43(Godoy Alcayaga)
Mitchel, Ormsby M.	Science-Civil War	125		475		Union Gen., Astronomy Prof.
Mitchell, Billy (William) 1879-1936	Aviation	200	900	975	1495	Gen. WW I. Pioneer Aerial Bombing
Mitchell, Cameron	Entertainment	15			40	
Mitchell, Charles E.	Business	20	35	65	25	Chmn. National City Bank
Mitchell, Edgar D.	Astronaut	10		148	85	Moonwalker. Apollo 14
Mitchell, Grant	Entertainment	35			80	
Mitchell, James P.	Cabinet	15	25	30		Sec'y Labor

NAME	CATEGORY	SIG	LS/DS	ALS	SP	Comment
Mitchell, John Grant	Civil War	30	50	140		Union General
Mitchell, John Inscho	Civil War	44	60			Union Gen., MOC PA
Mitchell, John N. 1913-88	Cabinet	25			275	Att'y General.TLS/Cont $200
Mitchell, John W.	Aviation	12	25	42	32	ACE, WW II
Mitchell, Joni	Entertainment	4			15	Singer
Mitchell, Maggie 1832-1918	Entertainment	50			20	Entertained 1st CSA Gov't & Troops
Mitchell, Margaret 1900-49	Author	550	2642	2900		Pulitzer.TLS/Content $15,000
Mitchell, Maria	Science	70	185	375		Astronomer, Mathematician
Mitchell, Martha	Celebrity	35	100		45	Wife Att'y Gen.-Watergate
Mitchell, Ormsby M. (War Date)	Civil War			957		Union Gen. Died 1862 RARE
Mitchell, Silas Weir	Science-Civil War	25	95			Civil War Surgeon
Mitchell, Stephen Mix 1743-1835	Revolutionary War	65	295			Cont'l Congr.Federalist Sen. PA
Mitchell, Thomas	Entertainment	225			550	GWTW
Mitchell, Thomas, Sir	Military	10				Lord Provost Aberdeen
Mitchell, William D.	Cabinet	5	25	30	10	Att'y General
Mitchelson, Marvin	Law	13	25		20	Trial Att'y. Specialty Divorce
Mitchum, Robert	Entertainment	10	10	20	30	
Mitford, Jessica	Author	18	25	20	20	
Mitropoulous, Dimitri	Composer	35	50	95	135	Greek Conductor
Mitscher, Marc A.	Military	375			450	Adm. WW II (RARE)
Mitterand, Francois	Head of State	15	25	40	20	Pres. France
Mittford, Mary Russell	Author	15	20	40		Br. Poet. Historical Drama
Mix, Tom 1880-1940	Entertainment	73		250	375	
Mix, Victoria	Entertainment	8	9	15	10	
Mizell, Wilmer D.	Senate/Congress	5	15			MOC KS, Prof. Baseball Pitcher
Mobley, Mary Ann	Entertainment	5	8	15	12	
Model, Walter	Military			500		NRPA
Modesti, Giuseppe	Entertainment	15			35	Opera
Modigliani, Amedeo	Artist	1200		4500		Content ALS $35,000
Modlne, Matthew	Entertainment	5			20	
Modjeske, Helena	Entertainment	15	25	35	30	
Moessbauer, Rudolf, Dr.	Science	20			55	Nobel
Moeur, Benjamin B.	Governor	12	15	25		Governor Arizona
Moffat, Robert	Clergy	50	90	100		
Moffett, W.A., Adm.	Military	15		50	55	MOH. With Adm. Dewey. FDC $90
Moffo, Anna	Entertainment	15			35	Opera, Concert
Mohler, A. L.	Business	8	20	40	15	
Mohnke,Wilhelm	Military	35			150	Ger. Gen. SS
Moholy-Nagy, Laszlo 1895-1946	Artist	80	255			Painter,Designer,Photographer
Mohr, Gerald	Entertainment	35			75	
Mohri, Momoru	Astronaut	12	25		25	
Mojica, Jose	Entertainment	60			225	Opera
Molders, Werner	Aviation	175	275	400	325	ACE, WW II, !st to 100 Kills
Molitor, Gabriel J.J. 1770-1849	Fr. Revolution	75	175	250		Napoleon Gen., Marshal of Fr.
Moll, Kurt	Entertainment	15			35	Opera
Moll, Richard	Entertainment	6	8	15	15	
Mollet, Guy	Head of State	20	40	65		Socialist Premier France
Molnar, Ferenc 1878-1952	Author	75	160	275		Playwright,Novelist, Journalist
Moltke, H. Johann L.von	Military	15	30	60	30	Nephew Helmuth.
Moltke, Helmuth von, Count	Military	100	220	400	295	Prussian Field Marshal
Moltmann, Jurgen	Clergy	50	75	100	80	
Momaday, N. Scott	Author	10	15	25	15	
Momo, Giuseppe	Entertainment	10			35	Opera
Monaghan, Tom	Business	10			20	Domino's Pizza
Moncada, Rivera y	Military		4500			1st Military Cmmdr.California
Moncey, Bon-Adrien J. de	Fr. Revolution	45	135	160		Marshal of France

NAME	CATEGORY	SIG	LS/DS	ALS	SP	Comment
Monck, George 1608-70	Military	95				1st Duke Albermarle.Restored Monarchy
Mondale, Walter (V)	Vice President	25	40		45	
Mondell, Franklin W.	Senate/Congress	10	15		15	MOC WY
Mondrian, Piet	Artist	225	675	1600		Dutch.Traditional-Cubism
Monet, Claude 1840-1926	Artist	300	1275	2650	1850	Fr. Impressionist
Money, Hernando De Soto	Senate/Congress	10	25	45		MOC, Senator MS. CSA Army
Money, Ken	Astronaut	5	15		15	
Monk, Thelonious	Entertainment	50			150	Jazz Musician
Monroe, Bill	Entertainment	45		150		Father of Blue Grass Music
Monroe, Elizabeth	First Lady					Rare 10-12 Known
Monroe, James & Adams, John Q.	President					SEE Adams, John Quincy
Monroe, James & Madison, James	President		3535			SEE Madison
Monroe, James 1758-1831	President	383	1412	3117		Free Frank $525. ANS $2000
Monroe, Marilyn (Norma Jean)	Entertainment			15000		Signed Norma Jean
Monroe, Marilyn 1926-1962	Entertainment	1758	2450	7500	6000	ALS/Cont. $15,000
Monroe, Vaughn	Entertainment	15	25		30	
Montagu, Charles 1661-1715	Politician		130			Wit, Author. Created Bank of England
Montagu, Edwin Samuel 1879-1924	Politician	15	50	80	35	Br. Statesman
Montagu, John (Earl of Sandwich)	Celebrity	65	205	450		Sandwich Named For Him
Montague, Andrew J.	Congress	5	15	35		Repr., Senator VA
Montal, Lisa	Entertainment	5			20	Actres, Vintage
Montalban, Ricardo	Entertainment	10	15	25	25	SP/Herve Villechaize & Montalban $50
Montalivet, J.P.B. Count	Fr. Revolution	35	100	225		
Montana, Bob*	Cartoonist	40			175	Archie
Montana, Bull	Entertainment	25			50	
Montana, Monte	Entertainment	5			15	
Montana, Patsy	Country Music	15			35	
Montand, Yves	Entertainment	10			35	
Montcalm, Louis J. Marquis de	Military	575	1765	3077		Cmdr. Fr.Troops in North Am.
Montefiore, Moses, Sir 1784-1885	Philanthropist	30	850	275		Br.-Jewish Philan.Sherrif of London
Montell, Lisa	Entertainment				15	Retired Actress-Heiress
Montenegro, Conchita	Entertainment	8	9	19	19	
Montessori, Maria 1870-1952	Educator	295		1050		1st Italian Woman Doctor
Monteux, Pierre	Entertainment	25	50		35	Conductor
Monteverde, Alfred de	Aviation	25	50	85	55	
Monteverde, George de	Aviation	25	50	85	55	
Montez, Lola	Adventuress	200		500		
Montez, Maria	Entertainment	50	55		100	
Montgolfier, Jacques-E.	Aviation			1800		With Joseph,1st hot air Balloon
Montgolfier, Joseph	Aviation					Special Content ALS $63,000
Montgomery, Bernard Law, Sir	Military	85	548		358	Special DS $2,500
Montgomery, Douglass	Entertainment	10	15	25	25	
Montgomery, Elizabeth	Entertainment	6	8		20	Pin-Up SP $25
Montgomery, George	Entertainment	6	8	15	20	
Montgomery, James 1771-1854	Composer	15				Scot. Poet-Hymnwriter
Montgomery, James Shera	Clergy	50	65	75		Chaplin U.S. Congress
Montgomery, M., Lady	Celebrity	5	10	20		Mother of Bernard L. Montgomery
Montgomery, Melba	Country Music	10			20	
Montgomery, Robert	Entertainment	15	30	60	25	
Monti, Carlotta	Entertainment	15		75	40	W.C. Fields Paramour
Monti, Nicola	Entertainment	35			85	Opera
Montoya, Carlos	Entertainment	10	10	25	25	Classical Guitarist
Moody Blues (All 5)	Entertainment	145			275	60's Rock Group
Moody, Dwight L.	Clergy	55	110	195	125	Evangelist, LS/Content $500
Moody, William H. (SC)	Supreme Court	45	125	175	50	
Moody, William V.	Author	30	85	125		Poet, Playwright

The Sanders Price Guide to Autographs

NAME	CATEGORY	SIG	LS/DS	ALS	SP	Comment
Moog, Bob	Science	50	70	110	65	Inventor. Synthesizer
Moon, Keith	Entertainment	175	280			Rock. The Who
Mooney, Art	Entertainment	10			20	Big Band Leader
Mooney, Edward, Cardinal	Clergy	30	40	50	40	
Mooney, Tom 1883-1942	Labor Activist	25	60	180	275	Bombed Parade. TLS/Cont.$550
Moore, Alfred	Supreme Court	3000				
Moore, Andrew B.1806-73	Civil War	45	105			CSA Gov. AL.ALS '61 $1485
Moore, Arch A. Jr.	Senate/Congress	5	15			Governor, MOC WV
Moore, Arthur J., Bishop	Clergy	20	25	40	40	
Moore, Barbara, Dr.	Celebrity	5		20		Br. Marathon Walker
Moore, Clayton	Entertainment	10			45	The Lone Ranger
Moore, Clement C.	Author	160	460	1100		'Twas the Night Before ....
Moore, Colleen 1900-88	Entertainment	8	25		35	Silent Screen Major Star
Moore, Constance	Entertainment	8			20	
Moore, Dan K.	Governor	5	15	30		Governor NC
Moore, Demi	Entertainment	20			92	
Moore, Dick	Entertainment	8			15	
Moore, Dudley	Entertainment	10			35	
Moore, Edward C.	Clergy	10	20	30		
Moore, Foster*	Cartoonist	15			50	Napoleon
Moore, Francis D., Dr.	Science	10	30	55	20	
Moore, Gary	Entertainment	12			25	
Moore, George	Author	45	150	125		Irish Novelist
Moore, Grace 1901-47	Entertainment	52	90		150	Opera. Films. Died in Plane Crash
Moore, Henry	Artist	50	210	550	105	Br. Sculptor. The Thinker
Moore, Jeremy, Sir	Military	5	15	25	15	General
Moore, Joanna	Entertainment	10			25	
Moore, John Bassett	Law-Jurist	65		250		International Lawyer
Moore, John, Sir 1761-1809	Military	60	225	350		Br. General vs Am.'til 1783. KIA 1809
Moore, Marianne C.	Author	60	185		75	Am. Poet. Pulitzer
Moore, Mary Tyler	Entertainment	10	32		25	Pin-Up SP $25
Moore, Mary Tyler (Show-Cast of)	Entertainment				425	Six Main Characters
Moore, Ray*	Cartoonist	25			190	Phantom
Moore, Rich'd Channing	Clergy			160		Episcopal Bishop 1814-41
Moore, Roger	Entertainment	10			65	
Moore, Roy D.	Business	10	25		20	Fndr. Newspaper-Radio Chain
Moore, Samuel P.	Civil War	595	725	800		Surgeon General CSA
Moore, Sara Jane	Radical	30	80	200		Attempted Assassination Ford
Moore, Sydenham	Congress-CW	40	55	90		MOC AL. CSA Officer
Moore, Terry	Entertainment	5	6	15	45	Pin-Up SP $20
Moore, Thomas 1779-1852	Author	45	105	475		Irish Poet.Tis The Last Rose of Summer
Moore, Thomas O.	Civil War		440			CSA Gen., CW Gov. LA
Moore, Victor	Entertainment	25			55	
Moore, William	Colonial	90	225			Colonial Am. Statseman-Jurist
Moorehead, Agnes	Entertainment	25			95	
Moorer, Thomas	Military	70	145		100	Adm. Survivor_Twice
Moores, Dick*	Cartoonists	10			30	Gasoline Alley
Morales, Ramon V.	Head of State	15	30			Ecuador
Moran, Lois	Entertainment	5	5	10	15	
Moran, Thomas	Artist	80	225	350		Specialized in American West
Moranis, Rick	Entertainment	5			25	
Moranville, H. Blake	Aviation	10	22	40	30	ACE, WW II, Navy Ace
More, Thomas, Sir	Author	19750				NRPA
Moreau, Jean-Victor	Fr. Revolution	90	275	300		Fr. General under Napoleon
Morehead, James B.	Aviation	10	22	38	28	ACE, WW II, USAAF Ace
Morehead, John M.	Governor	10	25			Governor NC

NAME	CATEGORY	SIG	LS/DS	ALS	SP	Comment
Morehouse, A.P.	Governor	10	20		25	Governor MO
Moreland, Mantan	Entertainment	100	125		200	
Morell, George W. (War Date)	Civil War	45	95	300		Union Gen.
Morell, George W. 1815-83	Civil War	30		80		Union Gen.
Moreno, Anthony	Entertainment	3	3	6	6	
Moreno, Bertha	Entertainment	20			95	Opera
Moreno, Buddy	Bandleader				45	
Moreno, Rita	Entertainment	9	10	25	20	Pin-Up SP $30. AA
Morgan, Barbara	Astronaut	5	35		15	
Morgan, Charles L.	Author	20	65	80		Br. Novelist, Drama Critic
Morgan, Dennis	Entertainment	8		15	15	
Morgan, Edward J.	Entertainment	10	12		25	
Morgan, Edwin Barber	Congress	40	75			NY, 1st Pres. Am.Expr.ALS $485-$985
Morgan, Edwin Denison, Jr.1811-83	Civil War	40	65	95		Union Gen.,CW Gov.,NY.ALS '62 $200
Morgan, F. Crossley	Clergy	10	15	15	15	
Morgan, Frank 1890-1949	Entertainment	400	600		650	Wizard of OZ
Morgan, G. Campbell	Clergy	20	30	45		
Morgan, George	Country Music	15			35	
Morgan, George 1743-1810	Revolutionary War	125	425	675		Indian Agent, Speculator
Morgan, George W. (War Date)	Civil War					Union Gen.ALS/Cont. $1650
Morgan, Harry	Entertainment	5	10	20	15	
Morgan, Helen 1900-1941	Entertainment	50	175		200	1st Julie in Show Boat
Morgan, J. Pierpont, Sr.1837-1913	Business	280	979	1500	950	Banker, Financier
Morgan, Jaye P.	Entertainment	5			15	
Morgan, John Hunt	Civil War	800	995	1750		CSA Gen. Wardte. DS $12,500
Morgan, John P., II 1867-1943	Business	275				Financier, Banker
Morgan, John Pierpont, Jr.	Business	85	185	280	95	Banker,Financier
Morgan, John Tyler (War Date)	Civil War	188		1600		CSA Gen.
Morgan, John Tyler 1825-1907	Civil War	125	198	350	240	CSA Gen., US Sen. AL.TLS/Cont. $1250
Morgan, Marion	Entertainment	6			14	Singer
Morgan, Michele	Entertainment	10			25	
Morgan, Ralph	Entertainment	35			65	
Morgan, Russ	Bandleader	20			65	Big Bandleader. Arranger
Morgan, Sydney, Lady	Author	15	35	60		Ir.Author.The Wild Irish Girl
Morgan, Thomas H.	Science	95	200	425	125	Nobel Medicine 1933
Morgan, Thos. Jeff.	Civil War	70	90	125		Union General
Morgan, Wm. H.	Civil War	25	55	75		
Morganna	Entertainment	5	8	20	15	Pin-Up SP $30
Morgenthau, Henry Jr.	Cabinet	35	75	145	60	FDR Sec'y Treasury
Moriarty, Michael	Entertainment	10			30	
Morini, Erica	Entertainment	20			50	Austrian-born Violinist
Morison, Patricia	Entertainment	15	15	30	25	
Morita, Pat	Entertainment	10		25	25	
Morland, Mantan	Entertainment	25			50	
Morley, Christopher	Author	38	90	145		Am. Writer, Editor
Morley, Robert 1908-92	Entertainment	25	65		65	Noted Br. Actor
Morphis, Joseph L. 1831-1913	Congress	10				Repr. MS, U.S. Marshal
Morrill, Justin Smith 1810-98	Congress	45	60	110		Repr., U.S. Senate VT 1855-98
Morrill, Lot M.	Cabinet	15	30	60		Sec'y Treas., Gov., Senator ME
Morris, Anita	Entertainment	6	8		20	
Morris, B. Wistar	Clergy	10		20		
Morris, Charles	Military	20	60			Commodore USN
Morris, Chester	Entertainment	45	40		75	
Morris, Clara 1846-1913	Entertainment	12				Vintage Actress
Morris, Edward Joy 1815-81	Congress	10				Repr. PA, Minister Turkey
Morris, Felix J.	Entertainment	15			40	Vintage Stage Actor

NAME	CATEGORY	SIG	LS/DS	ALS	SP	Comment
Morris, Gouverneur 1752-1816	Revolutionary War	190	585	625		Continental Congr., Diplomat
Morris, Harrison Smith	Publisher	30	55			Magazine Editor
Morris, Howard	Entertainment	3			15	Comedian-Actor
Morris, James	Entertainment	5			25	Opera
Morris, Lewis 1726-98	Revolutionary War	675	1025	1775		Signer Decl. of Indepen.
Morris, Lewis, Sir	Author	5	10	20		
Morris, Robert & J. Nicholson	Revolutionary War					Content DS $45,000
Morris, Robert 1734-1806	Revolutionary War	325	1146	1278		Signer.DS $13500-22,000
Morris, Robert Page W.	Senate/Congress	5	10			MOC MN
Morris, Thomas A. (War Date)	Civil War			3520		Union Gen.
Morris, Wayne	Entertainment	25			60	
Morris, William 1834-96	Artist	125	275	562		Br.Poet,Artist,Designer,Printer
Morris, William Walton 1801-65	Civil War	25	55	80		Union Gen. ALS '62 $160
Morrison, Harold	Country Music	10			20	
Morrison, Henry Clay	Clergy	25	35	50	40	
Morrison, Herb	Aviation	40	85	160	100	Announcer of Hindenburg Crash
Morrison, Jim 1943-71	Entertainment	650	2800		1375	Composer.Lead Singer The Doors
Morrison, Samuel E.	Author	12	20			Historian
Morrison, Toni	Author	35	35	130	25	Afro-Am. Nobel Literature
Morrison, Van	Entertainment	15			45	
Morrison, William Ralls	Civil War	25		80		Union Officer, MOC IL
Morrow, Buddy	Bandleader				45	
Morrow, Dwight W.	Diplomat	10	35			Lawyer, Banker, Amb. to Mex.
Morrow, Jeff	Entertainment	5	6	15	15	
Morrow, Rob	Entertainment	15			40	
Morrow, Vic 1932-82	Entertainment	100	120			Died in Tragic Helicopter Accident
Morse, Carleton E.	Writer-Producer	20	25		30	One Man's Family Vint. Radio
Morse, Jedediah 1761-1826	Science		75	125		Father of American Geography
Morse, Samuel F. B. 1791-1872	Science-Artist	375	1500	2100	4433	Telegraph, Pioneer Photographer
Morse, Wayne 1900-74	Congress	10	25		55	Senator OR
Mortier, Edouard A.C.J.	Fr. Revolution	35	115	230		Marshal of Fr., Statesman
Mortimer, Charles	Business	5	15	25	10	CEO General Foods
Morton, J. Sterling	Cabinet	25	50	145	75	Father Arbor Day, Sec'y Agri.
Morton, John 1724-77	Revolutionary War	448	1000	1100		Signer Decl. of Indepen.
Morton, Levi P. (V) 1824-1920	Vice President	60	85	240	240	Gov. NY
Morton, Oliver P.	Senate	10	25			Governor, Senator IN
Morton, Wm. Thos. Green	Science	170	450	825		1st To Us Ether as Anesthetic
Mosby, John S. (War Date)	Civil War		8500			Gray Ghost , Mosby's Rangers
Mosby, John S. 1833-1916	Civil War	438	1100	3019	2650	CSA Off., Content ALS $12,500
Moscona, Nicola	Entertainment	30			45	Opera
Moscone, George R.	Celebrity	80		95		
Mosel, Tad	Author	16	20	30	25	Am. Dramatist
Moseley, George Van Horn	Military		95			WW II.MacArthur's Dep. Chief of Staff
Moser, Edda	Entertainment	5			25	Opera
Moses, Anna Mary R. (Grandma)	Artist	175	500	860	612	1860-1961.ALS/Content $1,500
Moses, George H.	Senate/Congress	7	15	35		Senator NH. Diplomat
Moses, Robert 1888-1981	Public Official	15	35	65		Dominated NY Politics
Mosher, Terry	Celebrity	5		10		
Mosley, Jack*	Cartoonists	25			105	Smilin' Jack
Mosley, Oswald, Sir	Political	25	65	180	140	Founder Br. Union of Fascists
Moss, Kate	Model	4			25	Pin-Up SP 25, Nude 90
Moss, Ralph W.	Senate/Congress	10	15	25		MOC IN 1909
Mossadegh, Muhammad	Head of State	40	75	165		Premier Iran. Nationalized Oil
Mossbauer, Rudolf L.	Science	25	55	90	45	Nobel Physics
Mossdorf, Martin	Aviation				25	Ger. RK Winner. Stuka Pilot
Mostel, Zero 1915-77	Entertainment	25	225		175	Stage, Film Comedy Star

The Sanders Price Guide to Autographs

NAME	CATEGORY	SIG	LS/DS	ALS	SP	Comment
Moszkowski, Moritz	Composer	50		200		Ger. Pianist
Motherwell, Robert 1915-91	Artist	60	337	325		Am. Abstract Expressionist
Motley Crue (4)	Entertainment	30			95	Rock group
Motley, John Lothrop	Author	30	50	125		Historian,Diplomat,Hall of Fame
Mott, Charles S.	Business	25				Pioneer Auto.Exec. A Founder Gen'l Motors
Mott, Frank L.	Journalist	10		35	20	Educator, Pulitzer
Mott, Gershom (War Date)	Civil War	50	125			Union Gen.
Mott, Gershom 1822-84	Civil War	25		45		Union Gen.
Mott, John R.	Clergy	30	45	75	100	Nobel Peace Prize
Mott, Lucretia	Women's Rights	70	150	375	250	Reformer, Abolitionist
Mott, Neville F. Dr.	Science	20	35	50	25	Nobel Physics
Moulton, Louise Chandler	Author	25	70	125		1835-1908. Bed Time Stories
Moulton, Samuel W. 1821-1905	Congress	10				Repr. IL
Moulton, William	Revolutionary War	20	145			
Moultrie, William 1730-1805	Governor-Military	160	300			Revolutionary War Gen.
Mount, James A.	Governor	30	100			Gov. IN
Mountbatten, Edwina, Lady	Celebrity	10	35			Wife of Louis Mountbatten
Mountbatten, Louis, Lord 1900-79	Military	110	206	315	200	Of Burma. Adm. of Fleet
Mountevens,Baron (E Evans)	Military	20	45		335	Br. WW I Naval Hero
Moutrie, Alexander	Revolutionary War	35		200		
Mowbray, Alan	Entertainment	45			75	
Mowbray, H. Siddons	Artist	25	40	70		Murals. J.P. Morgan Library etc
Mower, Joseph A.	Civil War	35	95	115		Union General
Moyers, Bill	Author	5	15	45	15	TV Host
Moynihan, Daniel Patrick	Senate/Congress	10	20		20	Senator NY
Mozart, Wolfgang A.	Composer	2500	8000	30000		
Mubarak, M. Hosni	Head of State	60	110	275	80	President Egypt
Mucha, Alphonse	Artist	60		400		Czech Painter & Illustrator
Muck, Karl, Dr.	Conductor	10			50	
Mudd. Roger	News	5	10	30	15	Radio-TV News
Mueller, Frederick H.	Gov't Official	5	15	30		
Mueller, Reuben H., Bishop	Clergy	20	25	35	25	
Mueller-Stahl, Armin	Entertainment	4			10	
Muench, Aloisius J., Cardinal	Clergy	35	50	65	50	
Mugabe, Robert G.	Head of State	20	60	145	40	
Muggeridge, Malcolm	Clergy	30	40	50	40	
Muhammed, Elijah	Muslim Leader	115	375			
Muhlenberg, John Peter Gabriel	Revolutionary War	125	260	2400		Gen. Cont. Army.ALS/Cont. $2400
Muhlenberg, Peter S.	Rev. War		25			
Muhlenberg, W. Augustus	Clergy	25	40	60		
Muir, Jean	Entertainment	8	9		20	
Muir, John 1838-1914	Science	450	1450	1950	500	Scot.-Am. Naturalist, Explorer
Mukai, Chiaki	Astronaut	10	25		27	
Muldaur, Diana	Entertainment	6	8	15	20	
Muldaur, Maria	Entertainment	5			15	
Muldoon, Robert	Head of State	10	20	30	20	Prime Minister New Zealand
Mulgrew, Kate	Entertainment	5	6	15	15	As 'Janeway' from Voyager $55
Mulhare, Edward	Entertainment	15			40	
Mulheen, R.J.	Business	3	5		8	CEO Boston & Maine RR Corp.
Mull, Martin	Entertainment	5	6		20	
Mullane, Richard M.	Astronaut	5			10	
Muller, Herman J.	Science	20	35	75	25	Nobel Medicine 1946
Muller, Hermann 1876-1931	Statesman	45		200		Ger. Foreign Minister. Chancellor
Mullican, Moon	Country Music	10			20	
Mulligan, Gerry	Entertainment	12			25	Baritone Sax. Arranger-Composer
Mulligan, James A. 1830-1864	Civil War	225				Union Col. KIA Irish Brig.War Dte. $550

NAME	CATEGORY	SIG	LS/DS	ALS	SP	Comment
Mulligan, Richard	Entertainment	5	5		15	
Mulligan, Robert	Entertainment	5			20	
Mulliken, Robert S., Dr.	Science	30	185	65	35	Nobel Chemistry
Mullin, Willard	Cartoonist	10			30	Sports Cartoonist
Mullowney, Deborah	Entertainment	4	6	10	15	
Mumy, Bill	Entertainment	5	6	15	15	
Munch, Charles	Entertainment	10			35	Ger. Conductor
Munch, Edvard 1863-1944	Artist	55	350	1035		Nor.Painter-Printmaker
Mundelein, George Wm., Cardinal	Clergy	65	110	225	90	
Mundt, Karl E.	Senate	10	25		35	MOC, Senator SD, Educator
Munford, Thomas T. 1831-1918	Civil War	110		220		CSA Gen. Sig/Rank $310
Muni, Paul 1895-1965	Entertainment	75	95	120	205	AA
Munro, Caroline	Entertainment	5	6	15	15	
Munro, Janet	Entertainment	12			30	Br. Actress. Disney Charmer
Munro, Leslie K., Slr	Diplomat	10	15		25	Pres. UN Assembly
Munro, Peter Jay 1767-1833	Jurist	30	65	155		Nephew of John Jay.
Munsel, Patrice	Entertainment	10	20	50	50	Met. Debut at 18
Munsey, Frank A.	Editor	15		35		Muncey's Magazine
Munson, Ona	Entertainment	110			200	
Munster, Earl of	Military	10	25	40		
Munteanu, Petre	Entertainment	35	110	165		Opera
Muntz, Earl 'Madman'	Business	13	18	25	20	Pioneer TV Advertiser-Owner
Murat, Joachim 1767-1815	Fr. Revolution	135	675	590		Napoleon Marshal,Gov. Paris,King Naples
Murchison, Clint	Business	10	15	25	20	TX Oil Entrepreneur Millionaire
Murchison, Clint, Jr.	Business	5	10	20	12	
Murdoch, Rupert	Business	10	35	55	40	International Newspaper Publ.
Murphy Brown (Show-Cast of)	Enttertainment				273	Seven Main Characters
Murphy, Audie 1924-71	Military	70	175	325	400	CMH, Film Star
Murphy, Ben	Entertainment	5	6	15	15	
Murphy, Eddie	Entertainment	25			75	
Murphy, Edward, Jr.1836-1911	Congress	6	12			Senator NY
Murphy, Frank (SC) 1890-1949	Supreme Court	65	195	350	158	
Murphy, Franklin	Governor	5	10		10	Governor NJ
Murphy, George L. 1902-	Entertainment	12	20	25	25	And Senator from CA
Murphy, John Cullen*	Cartoonist	5			45	Big Ben Bolt & Prince Valiant
Murphy, Richard	Author	15		25		Screenwriter
Murphy, Turk	Entertainment	20	40		50	Bandleader, Composer, Trombone
Murphy, William P., Dr.	Science	30	75	120	35	Nobel Medicine 1934
Murray, Anne	Entertainment	5			20	
Murray, Arthur	Business	10	15	30	15	Ballroom Dance Studios
Murray, Bill	Entertainment	20			50	
Murray, Bob	Aviation	12	24	42	30	ACE, WW II
Murray, Don	Entertainment	5			15	
Murray, Eli	Civil War	30	65			Union Gen., Gov. UT Territory
Murray, George, Bishop	Clergy	25	40	50		
Murray, James A.H.. 1837-1915	Lexicographer			225		Oxford English Dictionary
Murray, Jan	Entertainment	4			10	
Murray, Jim	Journalist	5			20	Sports Writer, L.A. Times
Murray, John C., S.J.	Clergy	10	15	35	20	
Murray, Joseph E., Dr.	Science	20	30		25	Nobel Medicine
Murray, Ken	Entertainment	5	6	15	15	
Murray, Mae	Entertainment	30	35	70	60	
Murray, Philip	Labor Leader	35	45	70	50	Pres. CIO, United Steel Workers
Murray, Stuart S.	Military	25	75		45	
Murray, William Vans	Revolutionary War	25	40	90		Diplomat, Lawyer, MOC MD
Murrow, Edward R. 1908-65	Journalist	130	300		250	You Can Hear(See) It Now

NAME	CATEGORY	SIG	LS/DS	ALS	SP	Comment
Musante, Tony	Entertainment	4	4		15	
Musgrave, Story, Dr.	Astronaut	15			25	
Muskie, Edmund	Cabinet	10	20	40	20	Sec'y State
Mussolini, Benito 1883-1945	Head of State	390	783	3250	1428	Fascist Italian Dictator
Muybridge, Eadweard	Photographer	150		400		Br.-Am Pioneer Motion Pictures
Muzio, Claudia	Entertainment	200			640	
Myers, Carmel	Entertainment	10				Silent Screen Vamp
Myers, Mike and Dana Carvey	Entertainment				75	Wayne's World
Myers, Russell*	Cartoonist	10		25	70	Broom Hilda
Myerson, Bess	Celebrities	10	20		25	Miss America. NYC Official
Myrt and Marge	Entertainment	20			60	Vintage Radio Series

NAME	CATEGORY	SIG	LS/DS	ALS	SP	Comment
Nabokov, Vladimir	Author	325	1250		1095	Novelist, Critic, Researcher of Butterflies
Nabors, Jim	Entertainment	5	6	15	15	
Nache, Maria Luise	Entertainment	20			45	Opera
Nadar (F. Tournachon)1820-1910	Artist-Author	80	175	502		Fr. Caricaturist, Photographer
Nader, George	Entertainment	15		45	40	
Nadir Shah, Mohammed 1880-1933	Royalty	65				King Afghanistan. Assassinated
Nagaoka, Guishi, Gen.1858-1933	Military				975	Father of Japanese Aviation
Nagel, Anne 1912-66	Entertainment	25			50	Leading Lady 30's-40's
Nagel, Conrad	Entertainment	20	25	45	70	
Nagel, Steven R.	Astronaut	4			12	
Naglee, Henry M. 1815-86	Civil War	30	65			Union Gen.War Dte. DS $375
Nagy, Imre	Head of State	50	150			Premier Hungary. Executed
Naish, J. Carrol	Entertainment	25			85	
Nakasone, Y.	Head of State	25	35	85	35	Japan
Naldi, Nita	Entertainment	20			35	
Nansen, Fridtjof 1861-1930	Explorer	85	475	375	450	Nor. Zoologist, Statesman
Napavilova, Zofie	Entertainment	25			65	Opera
Napier, Alan	Entertainment	30			55	
Napier, Charles	Entertainment	4	4	9	9	
Napier, Chas. James, Sir	Military	15	30	80		Br. Gen. vs U.S. War 1812
Napier, McVey 1776-1847	Law	10	15	30		Editor 4-7th Encyclo.Britannica
Napier, Robert C., Sir 1810-90	Military	45	35	125		Field Marshal,Gov.Gen. India
Napier, Sir Wm. F.P.	Military	20	40	70		Br. General
Napoleon I (1769-1821)	Royalty	670	2370	15000		Important LS $7360
Napoleon II (Duke Reichstadt)	Head of State	260	800	2200		Francois-Charles-Jos. Bonaparte
Napoleon III, Emperor of France	Royalty	75	500	525		Louis Napoleon, Nephew of Nap.
Napoleon, Eugene L.J.J. 1856-79	Military				575	Son of Nap.III. KIA at 23
Nasby, Petroleum (D. Locke)	Author	50	75	145		Outstanding Humorist
Nash, Clarence	Entertainment	100			150	
Nash, Graham	Entertainment	10			25	Rock
Nash, Ogden	Author	45	65	150	35	Poet-Humorous, Unorthodox

NAME	CATEGORY	SIG	LS/DS	ALS	SP	Comment
Nash, Walter	Head of State	15	40	85	20	Prime Minister New Zealand
Nasir-edun Shah Qajar	Royalty	750		3500		King (Shah) Persia
Nasmyth, James 1808-90	Inventor	100		32		Machinist, Engineer. Inv. Steam Hammer
Nasser, Gamal Abdel	Head of State	75	400	350	275	President Egypt
Nast, Thomas* 1840-1902	Cartoonist	120	350		825	Political Cartoonist.CDV S $400
Nathan, George Jean	Author	10	15	35	15	Powerful Drama Critic, Editor
Nathans, Daniel, Dr.	Science	25	35	45	30	Nobel Medicine
Nation, Carry 1846-1911	Reformer	75	185	215	2185	Temperance Agitator
Natividad, Kitten	Entertainment				20	Model
Natta, Giulio	Science	25	35	80		Nobel Chemistry 1963
Natwick, Mildred	Entertainment	10			25	
Navon, Yitzhak	Head of State	20			50	Israel
Nazimova, Alla	Entertainment	68			100	Russian Stage & Screen Star
Ne'meth, Maria	Entertainment	20			60	Opera
Neagle, Anna, Dame 1904-86	Entertainment	10	15		30	Beautiful Br. Leading Lady
Neal, Bob	Aviation	15	35	45	40	ACE, WW II, Flying Tigers
Neal, Patricia	Entertainment	6	8		25	AA
Neal, Tom	Entertainment	10			20	
Neale, Bob	Aviation	20			70	Flying Tiger Ace. WW II
Nebel, Rudolf	Science	40	125			
Neblett, Carol	Entertainment	5			35	Opera. U.S. Soprano
Necker, Jacques	Fr. Revolution	125	350			Fr. Financier & Statesman
Needham, Hal	Entertainment	10			20	Film Director-Stunt
Neel, Louis Eugene Felix	Science	20	30	40	25	Nobel Physics
Neely, Thomas B., Bishop	Clergy	15	25	35		
Neeson, Liam	Entertainment	35			65	
Neff, Francine I.	Cabinet	4	10	25	10	
Neff, Hildegarde	Entertainment	20				40's Leading Lady
Neff, Pat Morris	Governor	10	15			Governor TX, Pres. of Baylor U.
Negley, James S.	Civil War	40	65	90		Union Gen., MOC
Negri, Pola	Entertainment	50	75		145	
Neher, Fred*	Cartoonist	10			95	
Nehring, Walter	Military		75			Ger. Gen. WW II/Rommel. RK
Nehru, B.K.	Diplomat	10	15		20	Ambassador
Nehru, Jawaharlal 1889-1964	Head of State	130	350	700	400	Assassinated Prime Minister India
Neidlinger, Gustav	Entertainment	15			40	Opera
Neil, Stephen, Bishop	Clergy	10	15	35	20	
Neil, Vince	Entertainment	20			50	Rock
Neill, James	Entertainment	15			35	Vintage Stage Actor
Neill, Noel	Entertainment	10			20	
Neill, Sam	Entertainment	15			45	
Neilson, Adelaide	Entertainment	20				Vintage Actress
Neiman, LeRoy	Artist	40	175	245	95	Repro Paintings S $125-$150
Nell, Stephen, Bishop	Clergy	10	15	35		
Nelligan, Kate	Entertainment	5	8	25	20	
Nelson, Bill	Astronaut	6			22	MOC FI
Nelson, Craig T.	Entertainment	10			30	Coach
Nelson, David	Entertainment	15				Ozzie & Harriett
Nelson, Ed	Entertainment	10			15	
Nelson, Gaylord	Senate	10	25	40		Gov., Senator WI
Nelson, Gene 1920-96	Entertainment	15			60	
Nelson, George D.	Astronaut	5			15	
Nelson, Harriet Hilliard	Entertainment	25			50	Band Singer-Actress
Nelson, Horatio 1758-1805	Military	813	3000	3920		Br. Admiral, Naval Hero
Nelson, Jimmy	Entertainment	3	3	6	6	
Nelson, John	Cabinet	20	50	95		Tyler Att'y General

The Sanders Price Guide to Autographs

NAME	CATEGORY	SIG	LS/DS	ALS	SP	Comment
Nelson, Knute 1843-1923	Senate	5	15		10	Senator MN
Nelson, Lori	Entertainment	5	6	15	15	Pin-Up SP $15
Nelson, Ozzie	Entertainment	35			75	Big Band Leader, Actor
Nelson, Ozzie & Nelson, Harriet	Entertainment		250			Contract Signed By Both
Nelson, Rick	Entertainment	100	425	475	275	Nelson Family Teen Idol
Nelson, Samuel (SC)	Supreme Court	50	150	250		
Nelson, Thomas Jr.	Revolutionary War	510	1550	3100		Signer.Important ALS $5900
Nelson, William L.	Senate/Congress	5	15			MOC MO
Nelson, Willie	Country Music	12			35	
Nelson, Wm. Rockhill 1841-1915	Author	10				Journalist
Nemerov, Howard	Author	10		35	25	3rd Poet Laureate US, Teacher
Nero, Peter	Entertainment	6	8	15	15	Jazz Pianist
Nesbit, Evelyn 1884-1967	Entertainment	50			1265	Girl in the Red Velvet Swing
Nesbit, Wilbur	Author		20	30		
Nesbitt, Cathleen	Entertainment	15			30	
Nesmith, Michael	Entertainment	20			45	Rock
Ness, Eliot	Law Enforcement	174	750		600	
Nethersole, Olga	Entertainment	15	40		45	Vintage Stage Actress
Nettleton, Lois	Entertainment	5	6	15	15	
Neubert, Frank	Aviation	25	75			Scored 1st Air Victory 9/1/39
Neumann, Theresa	Religious	65	175	395	150	Confirmed Stigmata Bearer
Neurath, Constantin von 1873-1956	Diplomat	45	80	150	115	Ger.Imprisoned For War Crimes
Nevelson, Louise	Artist	50	80	155	90	Am. Sculptor.Large Scale Pieces
Neville, Aaron	Entertainment	4			10	
Neville, Henry	Entertainment	4	4	9	10	
Nevin, Ethelbert	Composer	75	140	450	95	Short Piano Pieces & Songs
Nevins, Allan	Author	12	30			Am.Historian, Editor, Professor
New Kids on the Block	Entertainment	50			175	
New, Harry S. 1858-1937	Cabinet	15	30	50	20	PMG 1923. US Senn, IN
Newberry, Truman H.	Cabinet	15	20	35		Sec'y Navy 1908
Newcomb, Simon 1835-1909	Science	60	195	305		Am. Astronomer, Mathematician
Newell, Frederick B., Bishop	Clergy	20	25	50	30	
Newhart, Bob	Entertainment	6	8	12	15	
Newhouse, Samuel	Business	15	25	60	25	Newspaper-Radio-TV Empire
Newley, Anthony	Entertainment	5			15	
Newman, Barry	Entertainment	4	6		10	
Newman, Edwin	Celebrity	4	10	20	5	
Newman, John Henry, Card' 1801-90	Clergy	125	275	438	395	Leader Oxford Movement
Newman, Paul	Entertainment	80	150		175	
Newman, Randy	Entertainment	10			20	
Newmar, Julie	Entertainment	9	10	20	25	Pin-Up SP $30
Newsom, Tommy	Entertainment				15	Bandleader
Newsom, Tommy	Entertainment	5			20	Tonight Show Bandleader
Newton, Huey P.	Activist	100			350	Afro-Am. Activist
Newton, Isaac, Sir	Science	1100	7000	10000		LS/Cont. $16,500
Newton, John 1822-95	Civil War	30		375		Union General.Ware Dte/ALS 325
Newton, Juice	Entertainment	6	8	15	17	Rocker
Newton, Robert	Clergy	35	45	45	60	
Newton, Robert	Entertainment	50	65	90	75	Deceased British actor
Newton, Wayne	Entertainment	9	10		35	Singer
Newton-John, Olivia	Entertainment	15			50	Singer-Actress
Ney, Michael	Fr. Napoleon	125	295	650		Marshal of France
Ney, Richard	Entertainment	15			35	
Ngo Dinn Diem	Head of State	100				Pres. South Vietnam
Ngor, Haing S., Dr.19xx-1996	Entertainment	30		50	100	Murdered AA winner
Ni'matullah, Hajji	Author	4200		7200		Mystic Scholar. Clergy

The Sanders Price Guide to Autographs

NAME	CATEGORY	SIG	LS/DS	ALS	SP	Comment
Niarchos, Stavro	Business	45	110	190	75	Gr.Millionaire Shipping Magnate
Nicholas I 1796-1855	Royalty	175	1320			Czar of Russia
Nicholas II 1868-1918	Royalty		2071	9500		Last Czar of Russia. Executed
Nicholas, Denise	Entertainment	5	5		15	
Nicholas, Prince & King 1841-1921	Royalty	25	60	150		Greece
Nicholls, Francis R. T.1834-1912	Civil War	70	125	173		CSA General, Gov LA
Nichols, Barbara	Entertainment	10			25	
Nichols, Ebenezer B.	Business	35	195			Major Early TX Entrepreneur. Banker
Nichols, John Anthony	Senate/Congress	5		15		MOC NC
Nichols, Michelle	Entertainment	15			35	
Nichols, Mike	Entertainment	35			100	Film Director
Nichols, Red	Entertainment	35			60	Jazz Instrumentalist
Nichols, Ruth Roland	Aviation	125	295		250	Holder of Flying Records
Nichols, William A.	Civil War	25	80			General
Nicholson, Jack	Entertainment	15			52	SP as Joker $65
Nicholson, John 1783-1846	Military	30	75	190		Commodore U.S. Navy
Nicholson, Meredith	Author	20	50	125	30	
Nickerson, Francis Stillman	Civil War	25	50	65		Union General
Nicks, Stevie	Entertainment	20			50	
Nicol, Alex	Entertainment	10			25	Actor
Nicolai, Elena	Entertainment	30			65	Opera
Nicolay, John G.	Civil War	35	150	275		Lincoln Personal Sec'y. Author
Nicollet, Joseph N.	Explorer	105	225	345		1st Expedition Headwaters Miss.
Nicollier, Claude	Astronaut	15			30	
Niebuhr, H. Richard 1892-1971	Clergy	35	60	95	50	
Niebuhr, Reinhold	Clergy-Author	55	100	135	85	Am. Major Theologian
Nielsen, Alice 1876-1943	Entertainment	35			150	Opera-Operetta
Nielsen, Asta	Entertainment	20			50	Opera
Nielsen, Brigitte	Entertainment	5			20	Pin-Up SP $30
Nielsen, Carl	Composer	180	480	1100		Danish Composer, Conductor
Nielsen, Gertrude	Entertainment	10			25	
Nielsen, Terry	Entertainment	8	9		15	
Nielson, Leslie	Entertainment	10			25	
Niemack, Horst	Military	20			50	Ger. General Major
Niemoller, Martin 1892-1984	Clergy	60	175	410	200	In Concentration Camp WW II
Niesen, Gertrude	Entertainment	10			15	Singer
Nietzsche, Friedrich	Author	470	775	7765		Ger.Poet, Philosopher,Philology
Nigh, William	Entertainment	10			30	Actor-Director
Nightingale, Florence 1820-1910	Science	475	1350	1233		Br. Nurse, Hospital Reformer
Nijinsky, Vaslav 1890-1950	Entertainment	440			3250	Ballet
Nikisch, Artur	Conductor	25	65	85	375	Hung. Conductor.AMusQS $100
Nikolayev, Andryan G.	Astronaut	150			185	Russian Cosmonaut
Nillson, Christine	Entertainment	45		175		Opera
Nilssen, Anna Q.	Entertainment	15	20		45	
Nilsson, Birgit 1918-19??	Entertainment	15			35	Swe. Soprano, Opera
Nilsson, Harry	Entertainment	50			100	
Nimersheim, Jack	Author	5	8	20	20	Campbell Award nominee
Nimitz, Chester W. 1885-1966	Military	115	435	362	435	SP Japanese Surrender $1250
Nimoy, Leonard	Entertainment	35	62	75	72	Star Trek
Nin, Anais	Author	40	125	225	50	Content ALS $395
Nina	Model	4			15	Pin-Up SP $20
Nirenberg, Marshall W.	Science	15	25	45	20	Nobel Medicine 1968
Nirvana (3)	Entertainment				318	Rock
Nisbit, Eugenius Aristides	Senate/Congress	20	80	150		MOC GA 1839
Nissen, Greta	Entertainment	10			25	
Niven, David 1909-83	Entertainment	40	92	130	75	AA

NAME	CATEGORY	SIG	LS/DS	ALS	SP	Comment
Nivernais, Louis Mancini-. Duc de	Military			725		French Soldier-Diplomat
Nixon, John 1733-1808	Revolutionary War	125	320			Proclaimed Decl.Ind. 1st Time
Nixon, Marion	Entertainment	15			40	
Nixon, Marni	Entertainment	8			20	Sang for Audrey Hepburn, Susan Hayward
Nixon, Patricia 1912-92	First Lady	40	75	325	195	S WH Card $75-130
Nixon, Richard & Pat Nixon	President-1st Lady	300			595	
Nixon, Richard M. (As Pres.)	President	225	1317	5250	590	TLS/Cont. as VP $2000
Nixon, Richard M. 1913-94	President	225	592	6250	313	
Nizer, Louis	Law	25	75	215	35	Noted Trial Attorney
Nkomo, Joshua	Head of State	55	125	275	85	African Nationalist, Zimbabwe
Nobel, Alfred	Science	250	426	1180	450	ALS/Content $3,500
Nobile, Umberto 1885-1978	Aviation	65	195	335	175	It.Aeronautical Arctic Engineer
Noble, James	Entertainment	5	6	15	15	
Noble, John W. 1831-1912	Cabinet	35	50	120	95	Union Gen. CW. Sec'y Interior
Noble, Ray	Bandleader	25				British
Noe, Sydney P.	Numismatist	5	15			
Noel, Baptist W. 1798-1873	Clergy	20	35	38		Br. Evangelical Minister
Noel-Baker, Philip	Statesman	30	40	130	25	Nobel Peace Prize
Noguchi, Isamu	Artist	25		65		Am. Sculptor, Designer
Noguchi, Thomas T.	Celebrity	10	30		20	Coroner, Los Angeles
Nolan, Jeanette	Entertainment	5	6	15	15	
Nolan, Kathleen	Entertainment	8			15	
Nolan, Lloyd 1902-85	Entertainment	10	95		55	
Nolan, Mae E.	Congress	10	18			Repr.CA 1923
Nolte, Nick	Entertainment	10			40	
Nomura, Kichisaburo	Diplomat	275				Japanese Ambassador 12/7/41
Nono, Luigi 1924-90	Composer	115			175	Opera. Conductor
Noonan, Fred J. 1893-1937	Aviation					Guam-San Francisco Flight Cover S $995
Noonan, Peggy	White House	5	20			Reagan Speech Writer
Noone, Peter	Entertainment	20			50	
Noor, Queen	Head of State	15	40	125	70	Queen of Hussein (Jordan)
Norblad, Albin W.	Congress	15	30		20	Repr. OR.Intelligence Off'r WW II
Nordau, Simon Max 1849-1923	Science	50	105	357	60	Hung. Phys.-Writer,AMsS $1750
Nordenskjold, Nils Adolf E.	Explorer	200			340	Navigated North-East Passage
Nordenskjold, Nils Otto	Explorer	215			300	Led Antarctic Exped'n, Rescued
Nordhoff, Charles	Author	20	35	60		CollaboratorMutiny_ _Bounty
Nordhoff, Heinz, Dr.	Business	25			50	Auto Mfg.-VW
Nordica, Lillian 1859-1914	Entertainment	60			300	Am. Soprano
Nordsieck, Kenneth	Astronaut	6			16	
Norgay, Tenzing	Celebrity	40	110	255	50	Sherpa Guide. Mt. Everest
Noriega, Manuel A.	Head of State	100	100		50	Gen., Notorious Pres. Panama
Norman, Jessye	Entertainment	30			30	Opera. US Soprano
Normand, Mabel	Entertainment	150			475	
Norris, Chuck	Entertainment	8	10		40	
Norris, Frank 1870-1902	Author	125	275	525		Novelist, War Correspondent
Norris, George W.	Senate/Congress	15	30		40	MOC,Sen. NE. Fathered TVA
Norris, J. Frank Dr.	Clergy	5	15	25	10	Fundamentalist Baptist Pastor
Norris, Kathleen	Author	20	40	65	25	Prolific Am. Novelist
Norstad, Lauris	Military	20	50		40	Gen. WW II
North, Brownlow	Clergy	15	25	40		
North, Frederick, Lord 1732-92	Head of State	95	385	595		Br. P.M. During Am. Revolution
North, Jay	Entertainment	10			35	Child actor, Dennis the Menace
North, John Ringling	Business	30	70	135	70	Ringling Brothers Circus
North, Luther	Celebrity	28	83	225		NRPA
North, Oliver L.	Military	35	100	175	65	Col. Marine
North, Sheree	Entertainment	5	6	15	15	Pin-Up SP $20

NAME	CATEGORY	SIG	LS/DS	ALS	SP	Comment
North, William 1755-1836	Military	75	185	500		Gen. Cont. Army. US Senator NY
Northbrook,Lord (Thos. Baring)	Head of State	15	25	55		Br. Statesman, Gov.-Gen. India
Northrop, John K.	Business	45	125	275	95	Founder Northrup Aircraft
Northrup, John H.	Science	40	150		100	Nobel Chemistry 1946
Northumberland, 2nd Duke 1742-1817	Revolutionary War	50	145	250		Hugh Percy. Br. General vs Am.
Norton, Daniel Sheldon	Senate/Congress	7	10	25		Senator MN 1865
Norton, Mary Teresa	Senate/Congress	10	25		15	MOC NJ 1925-51
Norton, Oliver P.	Civil War	20	30	45		Civil War Gov. IN, U.S. Sen. IN
Norton-Taylor, Judy	Entertainment	10	15		20	Pin-Up SP $25
Norville, Deborah	TV News	8			15	TV News Anchor
Norvo, Red	Entertainment	15			40	Bandleader, Vibes, Xylophone
Norworth, Jack	Composer	130		295		Take Me Out to the Ball Game
Nott, Eliphalet 1773-1866	Clergy-Inventor	20	80			Pres. Union College 62 Years
Nouira, Hedi (Tunisia)	Head of State	7		15		
Nourse, Amos, Dr.	Senate/Congress	35	50			Senator ME 1/16-3/3/1857
Nourse, Joseph 1754-1841	Military	500	1250			DS/Content $2,000
Novak, Kim	Entertainment	8	11	15	80	Pin-Up SP $30
Novak, Michael	Clergy	15	20	35		
Novak, Vitezslav	Composer	40			150	Czech. Composer
Novarro, Ramon	Entertainment	35			95	Mexican Actor Murdered 1968
Novatna, Jarmila	Entertainment	15	45		35	Czech. Soprano
Novello, Ivor	Entertainment	25		80	75	Br.Actor, Composer, Film Star
Nowak, Max	Science	15			45	Rocket Pioneer/von Braun
Noyce, Phillip	Entertainment	10		25	20	Film Director
Noyes, Alfred	Author	15	40	55	30	Br. Poet, Poetic Plays, Stories
Noyes, Edward F.	Governor	10	20		15	Governor OH
Nugent, Elliott	Entertainment	6	10		15	Broadway & Film Actor
Nugent, Ted	Entertainment	15		35	35	
Nungesser, Charles	Aviation	135	225	290	300	
Nunn, Sam	Senate	15			40	Senator GA
Nureyev, Rudolf 1938-93	Entertainment	100	125	225	249	Kirov Ballet Dancer-Choreographer
Nurmella, Kari	Entertainment	15			30	Opera
Nutter, Mayf	Country Music	10			20	
Nuyen, France	Entertainment	5	8	15	15	
Nye, Bill (Edgar Wilson)	Author	15		100		Humorist
Nye, Gerald P.	Senate	10	35		15	Senator ND
Nye, James W.	Senate	75	140	175		Gov. Nevada Terr. 1861. Sen.'64
Nyerere, Julius	Head of State	10	25	65	30	Tanzania

O'Boyle, Patrick A., Cardinal	Clergy	30	45	75	50	
O'Brian, Hugh	Entertainment	5	6	15	15	
O'Brien, Conan	Entertainment	4			10	Late Night TV Host
O'Brien, Cubby	Entertainment	5			15	Mickey Mouse Club

NAME	CATEGORY	SIG	LS/DS	ALS	SP	Comment
O'Brien, Edmond	Entertainment	20	40		50	AA
O'Brien, George	Entertainment	20			40	
O'Brien, Hugh	Entertainment	6			20	TV Wyatt Earp
O'Brien, James	Business	5	10	15		
O'Brien, Lawrence F. 1917-1990	Cabinet	10	20	40	70	JFK Adviser-Strategist.P.M.Gen.
O'Brien, Margaret	Entertainment	15			35	Sig. As Child $50
O'Brien, Pat	Entertainment	45	150		100	
O'Brien, Virginia	Entertainment	5			10	Singer-Comedienne
O'Callaghan, Mike	Governor	5	15		10	Governor NV
O'Casey, Sean 1880-1964	Author	100	275	440	315	Irish Playwright. Abbey Theatre
O'Connell, Arthur	Entertainment	30			65	
O'Connell, Charles	Business	10	15	30	15	
O'Connell, Daniel 1775-1847	Statesman-Patriot	65	250	850		Irish Nationalist Leader
O'Connell, Helen	Entertainment	15			25	
O'Connell, William H., Cardinal	Clergy	50	65	75	65	
O'Conner, Flannery	Author	300	925			Am. Author. Died At Age 39
O'Connor, Basil	Celebrity	15	25		35	1st Pres.March Dimes Foundation
O'Connor, Bryan D.	Astronaut	5			15	
O'Connor, Carroll	Entertainment	6	8		20	Archie Bunker
O'Connor, Donald	Entertainment	5			20	
O'Connor, Glynnis	Entertainment	5			15	
O'Connor, Sandra Day (SC)	Supreme Court	35	160	200	35	Bush Appointee
O'Connor, Una	Entertainment	40			85	
O'Connor,Thos.P.(Tay Pay)	Author	60	100			Irish Journalist
O'Conor, Charles 1804-84	Law-Politician	60	75	385		1st Catholic Presidential Cand.
O'Conor, Herbert R.	Governor	5	10			Gov. MD
O'Daniel, W. Lee 'Pappy'	Senate/Congress	15	50		45	Governor, Senator TX
O'Day, Anita	Entertainment	20				Big Band-Jazz Vocalist
O'Dell, Doye	Entertainment	5			15	C & W Singer-Actor
O'Donald, Emmett	Aviation	15	30	50	35	
O'Donnell, Chris	Entertainment	10			65	'Robin' in Batman
O'Donnell, Chris & Val Kilmer	Entertainment					Batman SP 125
O'Donnell, Rosie	Entertainment	10			32	Comedienne
O'Driscoll, Martha	Entertainment	4			10	Pin-Up SP $20
O'Flaherty, Liam	Author	90	325			Ir. Novelist. The Informer
O'Grady, Gail	Entertainment	10				Actress NYPD...Pin-Up 60
O'Hair, Madalyn Murray	Celebrity	35				Atheist, Activist
O'Hanlon, George	Entertainmment	15				Actor-Comedian
O'Hara, Geoffrey	Composer	20	45		25	AMusQS $65
O'Hara, John	Author	160	500	660		Am. Novelist, Short Stories
O'Hara, John F., Cardinal	Clergy	50	85	100	75	
O'Hara, Mary (Alsop)	Author	20	50	75		Am. Novelist.My Friend Flicka
O'Hara, Maureen	Entertainment	12			20	
O'Herlihy, Dan	Entertainment	7			15	
O'Higgins, Bernardo	Head of State	750				Chile.Soldier,Statesmn,Dictator
O'Higgins, Harvey	Author	10	20	75	15	Am. Journalist, Novelist
O'Keefe, Dennis	Entertainment	5	6	15	15	
O'Keefe, Georgia	Artist	250	725	977	475	Scenes S.W. Desert.TLS/Cont.$3500
O'Keeffe, Adrian	Business	5	15		10	CEO First National Stores
O'Laughlin, Gerald S.	Entertainment	10			20	
O'Leary, Brian	Astronaut	5			15	
O'Mahoney, Joseph 1884-1962	Congress	10	35			Senator WY
O'Malley, J. Pat	Entertainment	25			50	
O'Neal, Frederick	Entertainment	5			15	Afro-Am. Actor
O'Neal, Ralph A.	Military	22	40	85	70	
O'Neal, Ryan	Entertainment	10			35	

NAME	CATEGORY	SIG	LS/DS	ALS	SP	Comment
O'Neal, Tatum	Entertainment	15			40	AA
O'Neil, Barbara	Entertainment	175			355	
O'Neill, Charles	Military	10	20	45		Adm. USN
O'Neill, Charles 1821-93	Congress	10		40		Repr. PA 1863
O'Neill, Eugene 1888-1953	Author	242	375	375	2185	Playwright. Nobel & 3 Pulitzers
O'Neill, Henry 1891-1964	Entertainment	10			50	Major Vint.. Character Actor
O'Neill, James	Entertainment	20	25	45	45	Vintage Actor
O'Neill, Jennifer	Entertainment	5	6	15	15	
O'Neill, Peggy	Entertainment	5	6	15	15	
O'Neill, Thomas 'Tip' 1912-94	Congress	15	30		45	Speaker of the House. MA
O'Shea, Michael	Entertainment	9			25	Late Actor-Spouse Virginia Mayo
O'Sullivan, Gilbert	Entertainment	25	75			
O'Sullivan, Maureen	Entertainment	15	25	35	30	
O'Toole, Annette	Entertainment	10			30	
O'Toole, Peter	Entertainment	25			98	
Oak Ridge Boys, The (4)	Country Music	10			25	Gospel
Oakes, Randi	Entertainment	5			15	
Oakie, Jack	Entertainment	20	95		50	
Oakley, Annie 1860-1926	Markswoman	2283		3400	6142	Am. Markswoman/Buffalo Bill
Oakley, Violet	Artist	35	95			Her The Tragic Muse Famous
Oates, Joyce Carol	Author	18	30	60	30	Am.Novelist,Critic,Poet,Teacher
Oates, Warren	Entertainment	25			50	
Ober, W.O. 'Willy'	Aviation	25		55		
Oberhardt, William	Artist	30	65	135		Portraits.Eisenhower,Hoover....
Oberon, Merle	Entertainment	45			90	
Oberth, Hermann, Dr.	Science	72	225		240	Early Rocket Pioneer. Taught von Braun
Oboler, Arch	Entertainment	12		35	25	Writer-Producer of Radio Dramas
Oboukhova, N.	Entertainment	35		400		Opera. Greatest Russ. Contralto of Century
Obratszova, Elena	Entertainment	10			40	Opera. Glamourous Rus. Mezzo
Ocasek, Ric	Entertainment	25			50	Rock
Ochles, Wubbo	Astronaut	10	25		25	
Ochoa, Ellen	Astronaut	5			20	
Ochoa, Severo, Dr.	Science	22	35	85	30	Nobel Physiology & Medicine
Ochs, Adolph S. 1858-1935	Business	150	165		65	Publisher-Founder NY Times
Odell, Benjamin Baker, Jr.	Senate/Congress	10	30	40		MOC 1895, Governor NY 1900
Odell, George C.D.	Author	5	15	30		Educator, Theatre Arts
Odell, Moses F. 1818-66	Congress	10	20	30		Repr. NY 1861
Odets, Clifford	Author	55	90	210	140	Playwright.Golden Boy, etc.
Oersted, Hans Christian 1777-1851	Science	2500	4750	750		Discovered Electromagnatism
Oesau, Walter 'Gulle'	Aviation	130		415	275	
Offenbach, Jacques 1819-80	Composer	145	240	500	275	ALS/Content 1,400
Offenhauser, Fred	Engineer	130	395			Automobile, Racing Engine Mfg.
Ogden, Aaron	Senator	35	110	225		Am. Rev. War Soldier, Gov. NJ
Ogden, Francis B.1783-1857	Military	10	45	80		Inventor. Steam Eng. Pioneer
Ogden, Thomas L.1773-1844	Law	20		45		Law Partner Alex. Hamilton
Ogle, Samuel	Colonial Am.	65	185			Colonial Gov. MD
Ogle, William	Celebrity	5	10	15	8	
Oglesby, Richard J. 1824-99	Civil War	40	80	105	150	Union Gen., Gov. IL, US Sen. IL
Oh, Soon-Teck	Entertainment	5			15	
Ohms, Elizabeth	Entertainment	35			150	Opera
Ohrbach, Jerry	Entertainment	8			20	
Oi, Narimoto	Military	40	125	195		
Oistrakh, David 1908-74	Music				150	Soviet Violinist, Conductor
Oland, Warner 1880-1938	Entertainment	150			275	Most Famous Charlie Chan
Olcott, Chauncey 1860-1932	Composer	65	90	150	90	My Wild Irish Rose etc.Noted Tenor
Oldenburg, Claes Thure 1929-	Artist	15	35	95	35	Swe. Sculptor. Soft Scuptures

NAME	CATEGORY	SIG	LS/DS	ALS	SP	Comment
Older, Charles H.	Aviation	12	30	45	32	ACE, WW II, Flying Tigers
Older, Charles S.	Civil War-Gov.	25	40	55		CW Gov. NJ
Oldman, Gary	Entertainment				40	Dracula
Olds, Ransom E. 1864-1950	Business	200	985			REO & Oldsmobile Motor Cars
Olds, Robin	Aviation	15	30	45	32	ACE, WW II, Korea, Nam
Olin, John M.	Business	6	12	20	12	Olin Industries
Olin, Ken	Entertainment	5			10	Actor
Olin, Lena	Entertainment	20			50	
Oliphant, Laurence	Author	10	25	60		Br. Writer. Cape Town, S.A.
Oliphant, Pat	Cartoonist	5			30	
Olitzka, Rosa	Entertainment	35			125	Pol./Ger. Mezzo
Oliver, Andrew	Revolutionary War	65	185	240		Am. Colonial Politician
Oliver, Edna May	Entertainment	45			120	
Oliver, Henry W., Jr.1840-1904	Business	45	60			Iron & Steel Tycoon
Oliver, Jane	Entertainment	6			15	
Oliver, Paul A.	Civil War	25	50	75		Credit For Inventing Dynamite
Oliver, Sy	Entertainment	30			75	Trumpet, Composer, Arranger
Olivero, Magda	Entertainment	20			60	Opera
Olivier, Laurence & Leigh, Vivien	Entertainment					SEE Leigh, Vivien
Olivier, Laurence, Sir 1907-69	Entertainment	58	185		184	Special DS $2,000. AA
Olliphant, Pat	Cartoonist	12			30	Political Cartoonist
Olmos, Edward James	Entertainment	5	6	15	15	
Olmstead, Frederick Law	Architect	80	175	340		Landscape Arch, NY Central Park
Olney, Richard	Cabinet	15	25	50	30	Att'y General
Olney, Thomas	Clergy	85	125	250		
Olsen & Johnson	Entertainment	35			75	Hellzapoppin
Olsen, George	Entertainment	25			120	Big band leader
Olsen, Merlin	Entertainment	9	10	20	25	
Olsen, Ole	Entertainment	25			50	
Olson, Nancy	Entertainment	6	8	15	15	
Onassis, Aristotle	Business	175	475		225	Gr.Millionaire Shipping Magnate
Onassis, Jacq. Kennedy	Celebrity	350	775	1250	1050	good content letter $10,000
Ondricek, Frantisek	Composer				950	Czech Violinist & Composer
Onizuka, Ellison S.	Astronaut	125			175	
Ono, Yoko	Entertainment	40		100	75	
Ontkean, Michael	Entertainment	5	6	15	15	
Opatoshu, David	Entertainment	6	8		20	
Opdyke, George 1805-80	Civil War					CW Mayor of NY.Chk.S '62 $900
Opp, Julie	Entertainment	12			25	Opera
Oppenheimer, Rob't, Dr.1904-67	Science	450	1150		1300	Exec. Dir. Manhattan Project
Opper, Frederick Burr*	Cartoonist	25		75	275	Happy Hooligan
Orbach, Jerry	Entertainment	10			35	Versatile Stage, Film, TV Actor
Orbison, Roy	Country Music	132			200	Blind Singer-Pianist
Orczy, Emmuska, Baroness	Author	35	55	105	145	Br. Novelist, Playwright
Ord, E.O.C. 1818-83	Civil War	50	145	375	750	Union Gen-Indian Fighter
Orenstein, Leo	Composer				100	Russ.-US Pianist-Composer
Orff, Carl 1895-1982	Composer	25			150	Ger. Carmina Burana
Orfila, Matthieu	Science			65		Founder of Toxicology
Orgonotzova, Ludmilla	Entertainment	5			25	Opera
Orient, John H., Bishop	Clergy	5	10	15		
Orita, Zenji	Military	50	160	255	100	
Orlando, Vittorio E.1860-1952	Head of State	65	135	275		It. Prime Minister, Pres. One of Big Four
Ormandy, Eugene	Conductor	25	45	90	80	Hung.-Am. Conductor
Ormond, Julia	Entertainment	25			75	Actress
Orpen, William, Sir 1878-1931	Artist	45	120	390	350	Portrait, Genre, War Painter
Orr, William T.	Entertainment	25				Film Director-Producer

NAME	CATEGORY	SIG	LS/DS	ALS	SP	Comment
Ortega, Katherine D.	Gov't Official	3	8		10	
Ory, Edward Kid	Entertainment	100			200	Dixieland Bandleader
Osborn, Joan	Entertainment	10			70	Singer
Osborn, Super Dave	Entertainment	12			20	Comic Daredevil
Osborne, Baby Marie	Entertainment	10			20	
Osborne, Henry Z.	Senate/Congress	10	20		15	MOC CA 1917
Osborne, John 1929-94	Author	10	20	40	20	Br. Playwright, Screenwriter
Osborne, Ozzy	Entertainment	20			35	
Osborne, Sidney P.	Governor	10	15		10	Governor AZ
Osborne, Thomas A.	Governor	10	15		10	Governor KS
Osborne, Will	Bandleader	20				1st Crooner
Oscar I, Joseph-Francois	Royalty	70	215	425		King Sweden & Norway
Oscar II	Royalty	25	70	145		King Sweden & Norway
Osgood, Charles	TV News	4			15	TV News, Host
Osgood, Samuel	Revolutionary War	125	385	535		Cont'l Congress,First P.M. Gen.
Osler, William, Dr. 1849-1951	Science	350	800	1500		Can. Phys., Medical Historian
Oslin, K.T.	Entertainment	5			20	
Osmena, Sergio	Head of State	65	200			Pres. Philippines 1944-46
Osmond Brothers (3)	Entertainment	10			30	
Osmond, Donny	Entertainment	5	8	15	15	
Osmond, Marie	Entertainment	5	15	20	22	
Osten, Hans Georg von der	Aviation				60	Ger. Ace WW I/Richthofen
Ostenso, Martha	Author	25	45	70		Am. Novelist, Poet
Osterhaus, Peter J.	Civil War	30	70	110		Union Gen.
Osterkamp, Theo	Aviation	35	60	130	70	
Osterman, Kathryn	Entertainment	20			50	Silent Films
Osvoth, Julia	Entertainment	20			45	Opera
Oswald, Lee Harvey 1939-63	Assassin	1950	7500	9800		Murdered John F. Kennedy
Oswald, Marina (now Porter)	Celebrity	50	125	150	55	Mrs. Lee Harvey Oswald
Oswald, Mark	Entertainment	10			25	Opera
Oswald, Steve	Astronaut	5			15	
Otis, Carre	Model	4				Mrs. Mickey Rourke.Pin-Up 60
Otis, Elita Proctor	Entertainment	10	15	25	25	
Otis, Elwell S.	Civil War	25	40	65		Union Gen.
Otis, Harrison Gray (War Date)	Civil War	50	175	295		Union Gen.,CW-Sp. Am. War
Otis, Harrison Gray 1765-1848	Congress	25	68	75		Repr. 1797, Sen. MA 1817 MA
Otis, James 1725-83	Revolutionary War	180	550	750		Statesman, Eloquent Lawyer
Otis, Johnny	Entertainment	25			40	R & R Producer, Director. HOF
Otis, Samuel A. 1740-1814	Revolutionary War		100			Continental Congr.
Otto I (Othon I) 1815-67	Royalty	105	365	225		Greece. King of the Hellenes
Otto I (The Great) 912-973	Royalty	2150				King of Germany, Holy Rom.Emp.
Oudinot,Charles N. Duc de	Napoleonic Wars	70	150			Marshal of Napoleon
Ouida (Louise de la Ramee)	Author	25	60	125		Br.Novelist.A Dog of Flanders
Ould, Robert 1820-82	Civil War	60	142			CSA Col. POW Exch.ALS '65 $690
Ouspenskaya, Maria	Entertainment	150			375	
Outcault, Richard*	Cartoonist	75			450	Yellow Kid, Buster Brown
Outlaw, Edward C.	Aviation	12	25	40	32	ACE, WW II, Ace in a Day
Overall, Park	Entertainment	5			20	
Overman, Lynn	Entertainment	15			45	30's-40's Film Character Actor
Overmyer, Robert (d. 1996)	Astronaut	5			95	2nd Space Shuttle Flight
Ovington, Earle	Aviation	45		245	180	Pilot 1st Air Mail Plane
Owanneco, Chief 1645-1710	Mohawk Chief		50000			Last of the Mohicans
Owen, David, Sir	Economist	10	25	40	15	Internat'l Planned Parenthood
Owen, John	Clergy	10	10	15	20	
Owen, Joshua T. (War Date)1	Civil War	70		225		Union Gen.
Owen, Joshua T. 1821-87	Civil War	32				Union Gen.

NAME	CATEGORY	SIG	LS/DS	ALS	SP	Comment
Owen, Reginald	Entertainment	25			35	
Owen, Robert 1771-1858	Political			250		Br. Utopian Socialist
Owen, Robert Dale 1801-77	Congress-Clergy	20		150		Scottish Born.Repr. IN. Reformer
Owen, Ruth Bryan (Rohde)	Diplomat	45	20		15	1st US Woman Diplomat-MOC FL
Owens, Buck	Aviation	12	28	45	30	ACE, WW II, Marine
Owens, Buck	Country Music	5			15	
Owens, Tex	Country Music	10			20	Wrote "Cattle Call"
Oxenberg, Catherine	Entertainment	25			40	
Oxnam, G. Bromley, Bishop	Clergy	35	50	95	45	
Oz, Frank	Entertainment	5	20		25	Self Caricature S $50

NAME	CATEGORY	SIG	LS/DS	ALS	SP	Comment
Paar, Jack	Entertainment	6	8	25	20	
Pabst, Fred	Business	150	395		225	Pabst Brewing Co.
Paca, William 1740-99	Revolutionary War	690	1500	2800		Signer.LS (War Date)$2750
Pacca, Bartolomeo, Cardinal	Clergy	45	300			Sec'y of State to Pope Pius VII
Pacetti, Iva	Entertainment	25			108	Opera
Pache, Jean Nicholas	Fr. Revolution	20	65	145		
Pacino, Al	Entertainment	10			50	
Pack, Denis, Sir	Military	25	80	125		
Packard, David	Business	20	45	90	25	Co-Founder Hewlett-Packard Co.
Packard, Vance	Author	10	20	45	15	Am. Nonfiction Writer
Packwood, Bob	Senate/Congress	10	25		35	Senator OR
Pacula, Joanna	Entertainment	9	10		25	
Paderewski, Ignace J. 1860-1941	Composer-Statesman	170	550	450	492	Pianist, AMusQS$550, $750
Padgett, Lemuel P.	Senate/Congress	5	15		10	MOC TN 1901-22
Paduca, Duke of	Country Music	20			40	
Paer, Ferdinando	Composer	40	110	200		Italian Opera Buffo
Paganini, Nicolo 1782-1840	Composer	300	4700	2100		Revolutionized Violin Technique
Page, Anita	Entertainment	8			15	
Page, Bettie	Celebrity				310	The Gibson Girl Model
Page, Carroll S.	Senate/Congress	10	25		20	Governor 1890, Senator VT 1908
Page, Geraldine	Entertainment	30			60	AA
Page, Joanne	Entertainment	5			15	
Page, John 1743-1808	Revolutionary War		275			Patriot,Activist, Gov. VA
Page, Patti	Entetainment	4			12	
Page, Richard Lucian 1807-1901	Civil War	100	190	542		CSA Gen. Sig/Rank $150
Page, Thomas Nelson	Author	10	20	40		Am. Novelist, Diplomat.
Page, William 1811-85	Artist	150		410		Am. Portr.Painter.ALS/Cont. $1150
Page, William Tyler	Congress	20				
Paget, Charles, Sir 1778-1839	Military	15				Brit. Adm. Napoleonic Wars
Paget, Debra	Entertainment	20			60	
Pagliughi, Lina	Entertainment	35			140	Opera
Pahlavi, Mohammed Reza	Head of State	135	200	375	375	Shah of Iran

NAME	CATEGORY	SIG	LS/DS	ALS	SP	Comment
Paige, Janis	Entertainment	10		15	15	
Paige, Mabel	Entertainment	10			25	Vintage Radio
Paine, John Knowles	Composer	15	40	50		Paine Hall at Harvard
Paine, Robert Treat 1731-1814	Revolutionary War	262	575	1148		Signer Decl. of Indepen.
Paine, Thomas	Revolutionary War	3200		13500		Am. Philosopher-Author
Pakula, Alan J.	Entertainment	5	10		15	Director
Pal, George	Entertainment	50			125	
Palacio, Ernesto	Entertainment	5			30	Opera
Palade, George E., Dr.	Science	20	35		25	Nobel Medicine 1974
Palance, Jack	Entertainment	15			60	AA
Palet, Jose	Entertainment	60			240	Opera
Paley, William S.	Business	15	30	65	25	Founded CBS in 1928
Palfrey, F.W.	Civil War	25		75		Union Gen.
Palfrey, John G.	Clergy	35	50	75		
Pallette, Eugene	Entertainment	60			85	Character actor
Palma, Tomas Estrada 1835-1908	Head of State	20	30	45		1st President Cuba
Palme, Olaf	Head of State	35	60	125	40	
Palmer, A. Mitchell	Cabinet	10	25	40	30	MOC PA. Att'y General
Palmer, Alice Freeman	Educator	15	35	50		Pres. Wellesley. Member HOF
Palmer, Betsy	Entertainment	4	4	9	9	
Palmer, Gregg	Entertainment	15			35	
Palmer, Innis N. 1824-1900	Civil War	45				Union Gen. Led Only Cavalry at Bull Run
Palmer, Jimmy	Entertainment	15			40	Bandleader
Palmer, John McCauley	Civil War	80	140	225		Union General
Palmer, Lilli	Entertainment	15	15		70	
Palmer, Potter	Business	35	65	110	50	Palmer House Hotel, Chicago
Palmer, Robert	Entertainment	20			35	
Palmerston, Henry J.T., Lord	Head of State	40	112	155		Prime Minister Eng.
Paluzzi, Luciana	Entertainment	5			15	Pin-Up SP $25
Pan, Hermes	Entertainment	30			65	Choreographer
Panerai, Rolando	Entertainment	5			25	Opera
Panetta, Leon	Congress	15			30	NY. White House Chief of Staff
Pangborn, Clyde	Aviation	75	140	250	250	Aviation Pioneer
Pangborn, Franklin 1894-1958	Entertainment	52			65	Comedic Character Actor
Pankhurst, E. Sylvia 1882-1960	Women's Rights	60	145	250	660	Br. Woman Suffrage Advocate
Pankhurst, Emmeline 1858-1928	Women's Rights	40	120	255	660	Br. Leader of Women's Suffrage
Pankhurst,Christabel,Dame	Women's Rights	25	65	160		Br. Woman Suffrage Advocate
Pannenberg, Wolfhart A.	Clergy	35	85	100	75	
Pantoliano, Joe	Entertainment	5			15	
Papen, Franz von	Military	40	185	230	150	Vice-Chancellor Under Hitler
Papp, Joseph	Entertainment	30	40		55	Major Producer, Theatre
Paquin, Anna	Entertainment	150				New Zealand Child Actress.
Paris, Joel B., III	Aviation	10	22	40	35	ACE, WW II
Park, Charles E.	Clergy	15	20	25		
Park, Frank	Senate/Congress	5	15	25		MOC GA 1913
Park, Roy H.	Business	10	25	55	20	Duncan Hines.Broadcast Stations
Parke, John Grubb 1827-1900	Civil War	45	155	150		Union General
Parker, Alton B.	Jurist-Pres.Cand.	15	35	75	20	Judge, Pres. Candidate 1904
Parker, Amelia, Mrs.	Celebrity	5	15	30		Alton B. Parker Wife
Parker, Charlie 1920-55	Entertainment	400	800		3450	Alto Sax Jazz Musician
Parker, David	Military	15	35	60		
Parker, Dorothy	Author	25	40	95	30	Critic, Poet, Humorist
Parker, Edward P.	Business	65	150			Parker Bros. Pen Co.
Parker, Eleanor	Entertainment	6	8	15	15	Pin-Up SP $20
Parker, Ely Samuel	Civil War	300	195			Seneca Indian Chief,Union Gen.
Parker, Fess	Entertainment	10	15	25	30	

NAME	CATEGORY	SIG	LS/DS	ALS	SP	Comment
Parker, Frank	Entertainment	10			35	Jack Benny's 1st Vocalist
Parker, Gilbert 1861-1921	Author	12				
Parker, Graham	Entertainment	20			35	
Parker, Isaac 1768-1830	Law	25		140		MOC MA 1796
Parker, Isaac C. 1838-1896	Law	195	798			Western Judge.The Hanging Judge
Parker, James 1768-1837	Congress	12				Repr. MA
Parker, James 1776-1868	Congress	12				Repr. NJ (Grandfather of Rich'd W. Parker)
Parker, Jameson	Entertainment	5			20	
Parker, Jean	Entertainment	15		30	30	
Parker, Joel 1816-1888	Governor-CW	15	30	75		Civil War Gov. NJ
Parker, John	Civil War		750			Captured by Commanches
Parker, Mary Louise	Entertainment	3			40	
Parker, Moses	Revolutionary War					POW ALS $625
Parker, Robert A.	Astronaut	6			20	
Parker, Roy, Jr.	Entertainment	5	6	15	15	
Parker, Sarah Jessica	Entertainment	20			40	Pin-Up SP $75
Parker, Suzy	Entertainment	6	8	15	15	
Parker, Theodore	Clergy	50	90	175		Abolitionist, Social Reformer
Parker, Thomas	Revolutionary War	55	90	145		Off'r Cont. Army. General
Parker, Tom, Colonel	Entertainment	10	125		40	Elvis Presley's Manager-Agent
Parker, Willard	Entertainment	10			25	Actor-Husband Virginia Field
Parkhurst, Charles H.	Clergy	25	30	60	30	Reformer. Anti Tammany Hall
Parkins, Barbara	Entertainment	6	8	15	20	Pin-Up SP $25
Parkinson, Dian	Playboy Cover	5			15	Pin-Up SP $25
Parkman, Francis	Author	25	70	150		Historian. The Oregon Trail
Parks, Bert	Entertainment	10			30	
Parks, Gordon	Author	20	50	70	40	Learning Tree. Photographer
Parks, Larry	Entertainment	20			50	
Parks, Rosa L.	Activist	100			125	Civil Rights, Bus Boycott
Parnell, Charles Stewart	Statesman	45	130	295		Ir.Nationalist.Home Rule Confed
Parr, Ralph	Aviation	12	28	42	32	ACE, Korea, Double Ace
Parran, Thomas	Senate/Congress	5	8	10		MOC MD
Parrish, Anne 1760-1800	Philanthropist					NRPA
Parrish, Anne 1888-1957	Author	15	20	30		Am. Novelist
Parrish, Helen	Entertainment	8			20	
Parrish, Julie	Entertainment	4	4	9	10	
Parrish, Maxfield 1870-1966	Artist	225	564	800	605	Repro S $600. TLS/Cont.$950
Parry, Charles Hubert H., Sir	Composer	10	25	50		Historian, Dir.Royal Coll.Music
Parry, William E., Sir 1790-1855	Explorer	40	85	210		Br.Adm. Arctic Explorer
Parseval, August von	Aviation	80				Ger. Aeronautical Engineer
Parsons, Albert Ross	Composer	5	10	15	5	
Parsons, Estelle	Entertainment	5	10		20	
Parsons, Louella O.	Entertainment	20	30	75	50	Hearst Entertainment Journalist
Parsons, Mosby M. 1822-65	Civil War	170				CSA Gen.ALS '65 $1650, Sig/Rank $250
Parsons, Samuel Holden 1737-89	Revolutionary War		325	475		Continental General
Parton, Dolly	Country Music	10			25	
Parton, James 1822-1891	Author	15				
Parton, Stella	Country Music	4			10	
Partridge, Bernard, Sir	Artist			45		Brit. Punch Cartoonist
Partridge, Wm. Ordway	Artist	10	20	50	30	Am.Sculptor. Portrait Busts
Parvis, Taurino	Entertainment	40			110	Opera
Pasch, Moritz	Science	60		95		Ger. Mathemat'n. Pasch's Axiom
Pasero, Tancredi	Entertainment	30			75	Opera
Paskalis, Kostas	Entertainment	15			45	Opera
Pasquarella, Gus	Photographer	55				Photo Hindenburg Burning $1500
Passman, Otto E.	Senate/Congress	5			10	MOC LA

NAME	CATEGORY	SIG	LS/DS	ALS	SP	Comment
Pasternak, Boris 1890-1960	Author	375	750	1850		Rus.Poet,Novelist.Dr. Zhivago
Pasternak, Joe	Entertainment	30	65	100	70	Film Director
Pasteur, Louis 1822-1895	Science	500	900	2087	3000	Pasteurization, Vaccines
Pastor, Tony	Entertainment	10			35	Big Bandleader
Pastore, John A.	Governor	5	10		15	Governor RI
Patat, Frederic	Astronaut	12	25		25	
Patch, Alexander M.	Military	85	225	395	205	Am. General WW II
Pate, MIchael	Entertainment	5			15	
Paterson, John 1744-1808	Revolutionary War	70	200	325		Berkshire Minute-Men. General
Paterson, William 1745-1806	Supreme Court					Continental Congress NRPA
Patey, Janet	Entertainment	25		80		
Patinkin, Mandy	Entertainment	20			60	Actor-Singer. Chicago Hope
Patman, J. Wm. Wright	Senate/Congress	5			10	MOC TX 1929
Paton, Alan	Author		150	400		S,Afr,Author,Political Activist
Patrick, Butch	Entertainment	10		25		
Patrick, Dennis	Entertainment	4			10	
Patrick, Gail	Entertainment	9	10	20	15	
Patrick, John	Author	4	15			
Patrick, Marsena R. (War Date)	Civil War	45	85	118		Union General
Patrick, Marsena R. 1811-88	Civil War	35	50	90		Union General
Patten, Gilbert (Burt Standish)	Author	30	70	160	50	Fictional Hero Frank Merriwell
Patten, Luana	Entertainment	15			25	
Patterson, Annie W.	Composer					S Bars of Music 50
Patterson, Basil	Celebrity	10			40	Vice-Chm. Dem. Committee
Patterson, Daniel Tod 1786-1839	Military	45	145	225		Navy Commandant vs Jean Lafitte
Patterson, John	Governor	12	25			Governor AL
Patterson, Paul L.	Governor	5	10		10	Governor OR
Patterson, Richard North	Author	5			10	Fiction
Patterson, Robert 1792-1881.	Civil War	25	55	80		Oldest Commissioned CW Maj.Gen.
Patterson, Robert P.	Cabinet	20	35	45	25	Sec'y War
Patterson, William Allan	Business	3	7	12	5	
Patti, Adelina (Niccolini) 1843-1919	Entertainment	140	180	370	425	Great Operatic Soprano
Patti, Amalia	Entertainment	40		135	150	Opera
Pattison, Robert T.	Governor	10	25		15	Governor PA
Patton, Francis L.	Clergy	15	20	25	20	
Patton, George S., III	Military	10	20	45	15	Son Of WW II General
Patton, George S., Jr.1885-1945	Military	1200	2465	7800	4633	Spec'l SIG $2,250
Paul I & Frederica	Royalty	250			250	King & Queen of Greece
Paul I, Pavel Petrovich	Royalty	230	750	1625		Emperor Russ.Son of Cath. Great
Paul II, Pope	Clergy		400			
Paul III, Pope	Clergy		1300			
Paul VI, Pope	Clergy	300	475	1100	600	Giovanni Battista Montini
Paul VI, Pope 1897-1978	Clergy		500		865	
Paul, Alexandra	Entertainment	4			15	Pin-Up SP $20
Paul, Arthur	Celebrity	3	7	12	15	
Paul, Les	Entertainment	25	35		75	And Manufacturer of Guitars
Paul, Wolfgang 1913-	Science		30		30	Nobel Physics 1989
Paulding, Hiram	Civil War	25	45	70		Commanded Navy Yard NY
Paulding, James Kirke 1778-1860	Cabinet-Author	30	85	155		Van Buren Sec'y Navy, War
Pauley, Jane	TV News	4	10	15	15	
Paulham, Louis	Aviation	40	75	135	80	
Pauling, Linus 1901-94	Science	60	292	545	105	Nobel in Chemistry, Nobel Peace
Paulsen, Valademar	Science	40	120			
Paulsson, Pat	Entertainment	5	6	15	15	
Paulter, Thomas C.	Celebrity	12	20			
Paulton, Harry	Entertainment	3	3	6	8	

NAME	CATEGORY	SIG	LS/DS	ALS	SP	Comment
Paulucci, Jeno F.	Business	15	25	35	20	
Pauly, Rose	Entertainment	20			60	Opera. Unequaled as Elektra
Pavarotti, Luciano	Entertainment	30	100	150	88	Opera, Concert
Pavie, Auguste-Jean-Marie	Diplomat	40	145	230		Fr. Explorer. Laos, Mekong
Pavlov, Ivan 1849-1936	Science			3900	7675	Rus. Physiologist.
Pavlova, Anna 1882-1931	Entertainment	350		450	565	Russian Ballerina
Pawnee Bill (Lillie,G.A.)	Entertainment					SEE Lillie, G.A.
Paxinou, Katina	Entertainment	150		300	275	
Paxton, Bill	Entertainment	10			45	Twister/Helen Hunt SP $130
Paxton, Elisha F. (War Date)	Civil War	638	2700			CSA Gen., Stonewall Brigade
Paycheck, Johnny	Country Music	8			25	
Payer, Julius von	Explorer-Artist	90	225		285	Austr-Hung. No.Polar Expedition
Payne, Cril	Celebrity	4	8	15	10	
Payne, Eugene B.	Civil War	25	45	65		Union General
Payne, Freda	Entertainment	4			10	
Payne, Henry C.	Cabinet	15	20	35		P.M. General 1902
Payne, John 1912-91	Entertainment	15	30	55	67	Film Actor
Payne, John Barton	Cabinet	7		15		
Payne, John Howard 1791-1852	Composer	90	250	525		Actor, Author.Home Sweet Home
Payne, T.H. (Act'g)	Cabinet	5	25			
Payne, William H. (War Date)	Civil War	170	390			CSA Gen.
Payne, William H. 1930-1904	Civil War	85		345		CSA Gen.
Payne, William W. 1807-1874	Congress	10				Repr. AL, Lawyer, Planter
Pays, Amanda	Entertainment	4			40	
Payton, Gary	Astronaut	8	20		15	
Peabody, Andrew Preston 1781-1883	Clergy	15	20	35	30	Unitarian Theologian, Author
Peabody, Charles, Dr.	Science	10	20	25		
Peabody, Eddie	Entertainment	15	15	35	30	
Peabody, Endicott	Clergy	35	45	60		Founder Of The Groton School
Peabody, Francis	Celebrity	10	25	85		
Peabody, Francis G.	Clergy	10	10	10	15	
Peabody, George 1795-1869	Business	50	140	475		Merchant, Financier
Peabody, George F. 1852-1938	Banker	35	90	385	150	Merchant,Financier,Philanthropy
Peale, Chas. Wilson 1741-1827	Artist-Rev. War	268	525	920		Officer. Portrait Painter, Engr.
Peale, Norman Vincent	Clergy	20	60	125	38	
Peale, Rembrandt 1778-1860	Artist	212	475	1725		Am.Portrait & Historical Artist
Peale, Titian 1799-1885	Artist		225	975		ALS/Content $695
Pearce, James Alfred	Senate/Congress	10	30	35		MOC, Senator MD 1835
Pearce, Richard	Entertainment	10	15		20	Film Director
Pearl Jam (Entire Group)	Entertainment	35			115	Rock, Alb. S $125
Pearl, Minnie	Country Music	10			35	Grand Ole Opry Star
Pearson, Lester B. 1897-1972	Head of State	35	90	175	45	P.M. Canada, Nobel Peace Pr.
Peary, Harold	Entertainment	20			45	
Peary, Robert E. 1856-1920	Military-Explorer	75	492	557	576	Adm. Arctic Explorer
Pease, Charles E.	Civil War	25				Carried Surrender Letter. ALS 1862 $225
Pease, Elisha M.	Governor		395			Comptroller Repub. TX. Gov. TX
Peck, Gregory	Entertainment	25	48	35	45	
Peck, Robert Newton	Author	10	15	25		Am. Novelist
Peckham, Rufus W. (SC)	Supreme Court	50	120	195	125	
Peckinpah, Sam	Entertainment	25			50	Director
Peddie, G.	Military	10	25			Gen. WW II
Pederson, Monte	Entertainment	10			30	Opera
Pederzini, Gianna	Entertainment	15			90	Opera
Pedro II	Royalty	80	240	305		Emperor Brazil
Peel, Robert, Sir 1788-1850	Head of State	45	115	150		Prime Minister Eng.Bobbies
Peeples, Nia	Entertainment	15			25	

NAME	CATEGORY	SIG	LS/DS	ALS	SP	Comment
Peerce, Jan 1904-84	Entertainment	30			75	Great Operatic Tenor
Pegler, Westbrook	Author	20	20	35	20	Am. Journalist, Columnist
Pegram, John (War Date)	Civil War	895	1795	6650		CSA Gen.
Pegram, John 1832-65	Civil War	650	838	445		CSA Gen.
Pei, I.M.	Architect	35	75	140		Internationally Recognized
Peirce, Benjamin 1809-80	Science	20	30	80		Mathematician, Astronomer
Pelham, Henry 1696-1754	Head of State	45	150	265		Prime Minister
Pelham-Holles,Thomas	Head of State	50	105	170		Brother of Henry. Prime Min.
Pell, John	Historian	10	25			Museum Director
Pell, Stephen H.P.	Historian	10	25			Curator
Pellegrini, Margaret	Entertainment	15	20		35	Munchkin, Wizard of Oz
Pellegrino, Francis	Aviation				112	Pilot 509th Bomb Gp. (Atomic Bomb)
Pelletier, St. Marie Euphraise 1796-1868	Clergy			2500		Saint Canonized 1940
Pelouze, Louis H.	Civil War		175	200		Union Gen. War Dte. DS $350
Pemberton, John C. (War Date)	Civil War	210	567	812		CSA Gen. Originator COCA COLA
Pemberton, John C. 1814-81	Civil War	85	408	312	400	CSA Gen.Originated COCA COLA
Pemsel, Max	Military				40	Nazi General
Pena, Elizabeth	Entertainment	10			20	
Pendarvis, Paul	Bandleader	10				
Pender, William Dorsey	Civil War	410				CSA Gen. War Dte. ALS $3,250
Penderecki, Krzysztof	Composer	20		90		Pol. Opera, Religious Music
Pendergast, Thomas J.	Political	17	50	105	35	KS Democratic Political Boss
Pendleton, Alex 'Sandie'	Civil War	205	525	475		CSA Staff Officer-T.J. Jackson
Pendleton, Edmund	Revolutionary War	350	680	975		Continental Congress
Pendleton, George Hunt 1825-89	Congress	20	35	75		Presidential Candidate. Sen. OH
Pendleton, Nat	Entertainment	30	45	60	45	
Pendleton, Nathanael G.1793-1861	Congress	10				Repr. OH, Father of G.H. Pendleton
Pendleton, William Nelson	Civil War	320		485	935	CSA Gen., Pre War Clergyman
Penn & Teller	Entertainment	10			25	
Penn, Arthur	Entertainment	10			20	
Penn, John	Revolutionary War	1525	2225	3712		Signer Decl. of Indepen.
Penn, Sean	Entertainment	5	15	30	35	
Penn, Thomas 1702-75	Colonial		150			Son of William. Proprietor of PA
Penn, William 1644-1718	Religious Reform	1500	4217	6700		AMsS $9,000. Founder PA
Pennell, Joseph	Artist	55	160	320		Am. Artist, Printmaker
Penner, Joe	Entertainment	20	25	45	45	
Penney, J. C. 18875-1971	Business	68	222	245	263	Founder of J.C. Penney
Penney, Joe	Entertainment	8		25	20	
Pennington, Ann	Entertainment	25	30	70	70	Ziegfield Star
Pennington, William 1796-1862	Congress	45	70			Gov. PA. Speaker of House
Pennoyer, Sylvester	Governor	10	15			Governor OR
Pennypacker, Galusha	Civil War	70	165	235		Union General
Pennypacker, Samuel W.	Governor	15	25		30	Jurist, Author, Gov. PA
Penrose, Boies 1860-1921	Congress	12	15			Senator PA. Pres. Pro Tempore
Penske, Thomas H.	Business	10	30		20	
Penzias, Arno, Dr.	Science	15	35	65	25	Nobel Physics
Peppard, George	Entertainment	6	8	15	25	
Pepper, Art	Entertainment	30			75	Bandleader
Pepper, Claude 1900-89	Congress	15	45		20	Champion of the Elderly Sen.FL
Pepper, George Wharton	Congress	5	15			Senator PA 1922
Pepperell, William, Sir	Military	95	550	375		Merchant.Gen. in Fr-Indian War
Pepys, Samuel	Author-Diarist	570	1990			Br. Sec'y of the Navy
Pequet, Henri	Aviation	16		37		
Perceval, Spencer	Head of State	120	250			Only Br. P. M. Assassinated
Percival, John 'Mad Jack'	Military	30	95	145		Am.Navy. War 1812 Exploits
Percy, Charles	Senate/Congress	10	15		25	Senator IL

NAME	CATEGORY	SIG	LS/DS	ALS	SP	Comment
Percy, Walker	Author-Doctor	60		235		Am. Novelist
Pereira, William L.	Architect	10	35	75	20	Internationally Recognized Arch
Perelman, S.J.	Author	45		160		Humorist, Film Scripts
Peres, Shimon (Isr)	Head of State	25	100		95	Israeli Statesman. Nobel Peace Prize
Perez, Mariano	Head of State	15	25	85	20	President Colombia
Perez, Rosie	Entertainment	10			45	Actress
Perez, Vincent	Entertainment	25			70	The Crow Star
Perier, Jean	Entertainment	25			75	Fr. Baritone. 45 Year Career
Perignon, D.C. Marquis de	Military	65	180	375		Marshal of Napoleon
Perkins, Anthony	Entertainment	25			75	
Perkins, Carl	Country Music	15			35	
Perkins, Frances	Cabinet	25	90	145	60	1st Woman Cabinet Member
Perkins, George C.1839-1923	Congress	14	20			Governor, Senator CA 1893
Perkins, Marlin	Zoo Director	12			20	Animal Expert
Perkins, Millie	Entertainment	10			30	
Perkins, Osgood	Entertainment	35			75	
Perkins, Thomas H.	Business	20	45	90		
Perkins, Tony	Entertainment	25			45	
Perlman, Itzhak	Entertainment	20			45	Am. Violinist
Perlman, Rhea	Entertainment	5	6	15	15	Cheers SP $45
Perlman, Ronuy	Entertainment	8	12	40	30	
Peron, Eva (Evita)	Head of State	1500	900			Argentina. Statesman
Peron, Juan & Peron, Eva	Heads of State		750			
Peron, Juan Domingo 1895-1974	Head of State	125	438	525	660	President Argentina
Perot, H. Ross	Business	30	55		100	Presidential Candidate
Perpich, Rudolph G.	Governor	10	15		15	Governor MN
Perrault, Charles 1628-1703	Author			2600		Fr. Poet. Fairy Tales. NRPA
Perrin, Jean 1870-1942	Science	75				Nobel Prize '26 Physics.TMsS $1,000
Perrine, Valerie	Entertainment	5	6	15	10	Pin-Up SP $30
Perris, Adriana	Entertainment	5			30	Opera
Perry, Alexander J.	Civil War			25		Union Brvt. Gen., Nephew Commodore Perrry
Perry, Antoinette	Entertainment			200		Tony Award
Perry, Lucas	Entertainment	20			75	
Perry, Madison S.	Governor	15	45			Governor FL
Perry, Matthew	Entertainment	4			55	Friends Actor
Perry, Matthew C.1794-1858	Military	398	775	1740		Opened Japan to World Trade
Perry, Nora	Author	3	10	20		Novelist
Perry, Oliver H.	Military	750	1000	1250		
Perry, Ralph Barton	Author	10	20	35		Philosopher, Pulitzer Prize
Perry, Susan	Entertainment	20				Actress
Perryman, Lloyd	Country Music	10			20	
Pershing, John J. 1860-1948	Military	60	270	295	675	Comm.-in-Chief AEF WW I
Persichetti, Vincent	Composer	10	25	60	15	
Persoff, Nehemiah	Entertainment	5	6	15	15	
Persons, Wilton B.	Gov't Official	5	15	25	10	Gen. Chief Ass't to Pres. DDE
Pertile, Aureliano	Entertainment	40			125	Opera
Perulli, Franco	Entertainment	20			50	Opera
Perutz, Max	Science	20	40	75	25	Nobel Chemistry 1962
Pesci, Joe	Entertainment	15			50	AA
Petain, Henri-Phillippe.	Head of State	35	105	265	50	Hero WW I. Treason WW II
Peter & Gordon (Both)	Entertainment	75			125	
Peter I	Royalty	90	225	400		King of Serbs, Croats, Slovenes
Peter I, The Great	Royalty	910	5000			Czar of Russia
Peter, Paul & Mary	Entertainment				35	SP All three/full name $35
Peters, Absalom	Clergy	15	20	35		
Peters, Bernadette	Entertainment	5	6	20	25	Pin-Up SP $35

NAME	CATEGORY	SIG	LS/DS	ALS	SP	Comment
Peters, Brock	Entertainment	5	6	15	15	
Peters, Jean	Entertainment	50	100	30	85	
Peters, Mike*	Cartoonist	5			45	Mother Grimm
Peters, Richard Jr.1744-1828	Revolutionary War	40	95	150		Soldier,Jurist,Continental Cong
Peters, Roberta	Entertainment	10			25	Opera, Concert
Peters, Susan	Entertainment	75	85	95	100	
Petersen, Paul	Entertainment	5			15	
Peterson, Bruce A.	Astronaut	5			15	
Peterson, Chesley	Aviation	15	30	55	40	ACE, WW II, Eagle Squadron
Peterson, Donald H.	Astronaut	5			15	
Peterson, Forrest (RADM)	Astronaut	5			15	
Peterson, Oscar	Entertainment	25			45	Jazz Pianist
Peterson, Roger Tory	Author	20	35		25	
Peterson, Rudolph A.	Business	4	6	15	10	
Petiet, Claude	Fr. Revolution	125	265			
Petion, Alexandre	Head of State	275	400			Haitian General, President
Petrella, Clara	Entertainment	20			50	Opera
Petrie, Wm. Matthew Flinders, Sir	Egyptologist	95	170			Pyramids At Giza
Petrillo, James C.	Labor	20	55			Czar of Musician's Union
Petroff, Paul	Entertainment	30			100	Am. Ballet Dancer-Teacher
Petrova, Olga	Entertainment	35			75	Silent Films
Pettet, Joanna	Entertainment	5	6	15	15	
Pettigrew, James J.1828-63	Civil War	148	518			CSA Gen.
Pettigrew, James, J. (War Date)	Civil War	375				CSA Gen. AES '61 $13,200
Pettit, Charles	Revolutionary War	70	185	315		Continental Congress
Pettus, Edmund W.	Civil War	85	170	360		CSA Gen.ALS War Dte $3500
Petty, Tom	Entertainment	35			95	
Peugeot, Eugene	Business	50	130	315		Fndr. Peugeot Automobile Co.
Pfeiffer, Michelle	Entertainment	30			85	Pln-Up SP $90.Batman SP $125
Pflug, Jo Ann	Entertainment	3	5	15	12	
Phelan, James D. 1864-1930	Congress	10	25	40		Senator CA 1915
Phelps, Austin	Clergy	20	30	40		
Phelps, John Smith	Civil War	25	65	100		Union General, Gov. MO
Phelps, John Wolcott	Military-CW	45	135	200		Raised 1st Negro Troops
Phelps, Noah 1740-1809	Military	50	165			Soldier, Patriot, Spy
Phelps, William Walter 1839-94	Congress	10		25		Repr. NJ
Philbin, Mary	Entertainment	25			55	
Philbin, Regis	TV Host	5			10	TV Host
Philbrick, Herbert A.	Celebrity	15	30	60	25	I Led Three Lives Agent
Philip (Duke Edinburgh)	Royalty	110	175	325	350	Prince Consort Elizabeth II
Philip II (Sp)	Royalty	245	1010			Special DS $2,350
Philip III (Sp) Philip II (Port)	Royalty	250	750			
Philip IV (Sp),III (Port)	Royalty	150	550	1250		
Philip V (Sp)	Royalty	150	395			Founder Bourbon Dynasty
Philippe II (Duc d'Orleans)	Royalty		500			Regent of Fr. for Louis XV
Philippi, Alfred	Military	5	15			Ger. Gen. WW II. RK
Phillip, Jack W.	Military	27	80			Captain USN
Phillips, Bill	Country Music	10			20	
Phillips, Chynna	Entertainment	30			75	Singer-Actress
Phillips, Irna	Entertainment	10			15	Actress. Today's Children
Phillips, J.B.	Clergy	35	50	95	50	
Phillips, John	Entertainment	15			35	Founder Mamas & the Papas
Phillips, Julianne	Entertainment	25			42	Pin-Up SP 72
Phillips, Lou Diamond	Entertainment	10	15	45	30	
Phillips, Mackenzie	Entertainment	10			35	
Phillips, Michelle	Entertainment	10			35	

NAME	CATEGORY	SIG	LS/DS	ALS	SP	Comment
Phillips, Phil	Composer	15			35	Singer-Songwriter
Phillips, Robert	Astronaut	6			16	
Phillips, Wendell 1811-84	Reformer	35	50	125	50	Abolitionist, Orator,Civ.Rights
Phillips, William	Revolutionary War	200	550	825		Br. Major General
Phillips, Wm.	Cabinet	4	15	20		
Phillpotts, Eden (Harrington Hext)	Author	10	35	55		Br.Novelist.Plays,Poems,Mystery
Phillpotts, Henry	Clergy	25	35	40		Under Sec'y
Phipps, Spencer	Colonial	55	175			Br. Colonial Gov. MA
Phoenix, River	Entertainment	100			200	Ill-fated actor
Piaf, Edith	Entertainment	150	385		262	Legendary Internat'l Chanteuse
Piaget, Jean 1896-1980	Science		375			Swiss Psychologist
Pianchettini, Pio 1799-1851	Composer					Pianist. ANS Framed/Portrait $3500
Piatigorsky, Gregor 1903-76	Entertainment	120	190	300	300	Rus./Am. Cellist
Piazza, Marguerite	Entertainment	10			30	Am. Met Sopr.
Picard, Emile	Science	70	215	475		Fr. Mathematician
Picasso, Pablo 1881-1973	Artist	900	1530	2325	1934	Signed sketch of fish $4,000
Picasso, Paloma	Artist	25		95		Artist-Designer. Daughter
Piccaluga, Nino	Entertainment	30			80	Opera
Piccard, Auguste	Science	35	115	180	110	Sw. Physicist. Bathyscaphe
Piccard, Jacques	Science	15	40	75	20	
Piccard, Jean-Felix	Science	65	195		125	Chemist, Aeronautical Eng.
Piccaver, Alfred	Entertainment	75			225	Br. Tenor, Opera
Piccolomini, Marietta	Entertainment	100	275		275	It. Soprano
Pichegru, Charles	Fr. Revolution	35	115	195		Fr. Gen. Strangled In Prison
Pick, Lewis A. 1890-	Military	35	125		40	Gen. WW II
Pickens, Francis W.	Civil War	35	80	140		CSA Gov SC
Pickens, Jane	Entertainment	25			50	(Pickens Sisters) & Actress/Singer
Pickens, Slim	Entertainment	100			200	
Pickens, T. Boone	Business	20	55		45	Corporate Raider. Controversial
Pickering, John 1737-1805	Congress	175	250			Impeached & Convicted by Congr.
Pickering, Thomas	Diplomat	10			20	Ambassador to Russia
Pickering, Timothy 1745-1829	Cabinet-Military	220	565	1851		Soldier, Politician, Rev. War
Pickering, William, Dr.	Science	15	35	60	25	Astronomer.Lowell Observatory
Pickett, Cindy	Entertainment	3	3	6	6	
Pickett, George Edward	Civil War	515	1250	2765		CSA Gen. Sig Offered @ $2,500
Pickford, Jack	Entertainment	50			150	
Pickford, Mary & Buddy Rogers	Entertainment				275	
Pickford, Mary 1893-1979	Entertainment	60	200		135	Co-Founder of United Artists
Picon, Molly	Entertainment	16	20		45	Yiddish Stage & Film Star
Pidgeon, Walter 1897-1984	Entertainment	20			75	
Pied Pipers, The (3)	Entertainment	20			45	Big Band Singing Group
Pierce, Benjamin	Revolutionary War	60	135	200		Father of Pres., Gov. NH
Pierce, Benjamin 1809-80	Science			67		Am. Math.& Astronomy.Harvard Prof.
Pierce, David Hyde	Entertainment	5			30	'Niles' in Frasier
Pierce, Franklin 1804-69	President	400	1069	1292		DS as Pres.$1800, FF $385-595
Pierce, James	Entertainment	25			45	Vintage Tarzan
Pierce, Jane M.	First Lady	215	500	1100		
Pierce, N. B.	Civil War	30	60	90		
Pierce, Walter M.	Senate/Congress	3	5	10		MOC OR
Pierce, Web	Country Music	4			10	
Pierne', H.C. Gabriel	Composer	15	50	125	225	Conductor. AMusQS $250
Pierrepont, Edwards	Cabinet	15	45	90		Att'y General 1875
Pierson, Roland	Aviation	10	25	35	30	
Pigni, Renzo	Entertainment	15			35	Opera
Pike, Albert 1809-91	Civil War	95	175	306		CSA Gen. Sig/Rank $180
Pike, Christopher	Author	4		15	10	Novelist

The Sanders Price Guide to Autographs

NAME	CATEGORY	SIG	LS/DS	ALS	SP	Comment
Pike, James A., Bishop	Clergy	85	185	320	125	
Pike, Zebulon 1751-1834	Revolutionary War	40	75	135		Officer Revolutionary Army
Pike, Zebulon M.1779-1813	Military	230	685	1250		General. Discovered Pike's Peak
Pilatre De Rozier, Jean Francois	Aeronaut	125		500		Pioneer Balloonist
Pillow, Gideon J. 1806-78	Civil War	115		505		CSA Gen.
Pillow, Gideon J.(War Date)	Civil War	168	440	500		CSA General.ALS/Cont. $3,750
Pillsbury, John S.	Business	30	45	70	35	Governor MN, Pillsbury Flour
Pillsbury, Parker	Reformer	15	25	60		
Pilsudski, Joseph Klemens	Military	115	320	550	275	Pol. Gen., Statesman,Dictator
Pinay, Antoine (Fr)	Head of State	15	35	50		Fr.
Pinchback, Pinckney	Senate	125	350	495		Early Black Elected Official
Pinchot, Bronson	Entertainment	5			15	
Pinchot, Gifford	Governor	35	95	120		Governor PA, Forester
Pinckney, Charles (1757-1824)	Revolutionary War	375		1500		Continental Congress,MOC,Sen.SC
Pinckney, Charles C. (1746-1825)	Revolutionary War	175	1200	725		General, Diplomat, XYZ Affair
Pinckney, Pauline	Author	5	10	20		
Pinckney, Thomas 1750-1828	Revolutionary War	200	458			Continental Army, Gov. SC
Pincus, Harry	Artist	10	30	60		
Pine, Phillip	Entertainment	3	3	6	8	
Pinero, Arthur Wing, Sir	Author	15	35	65	60	Br. Dramatist, Actor
Ping, Deng Xiao	Head of State	200		700		China. NRPA
Pingel, Rolf	Aviation	10	15	30	25	
Pingree, Hazen S.	Governor	10	15			Governor MI
Pink Floyd	Entertainment	75			140	
Pinkerton, Allan 1819-84	Am. Detective	225	676	1365	1150	Dir.Union Secret Service Bureau
Pinkerton, Robert A.	Business	35	105	220	75	CEO Pinkerton's Inc.Detectives
Pinkerton, William A.	Civil War	80	250			U.S. Army Secret Service 1861
Pinkney, William 1764-1822	Cabinet	90	185	200		MOC, Senator MD. Att'y Gen.1811
Pinochet, Augusto	Head of State	30	115	245	50	Chilean Mil. Leader
Pinza, Ezio	Entertainment	70			208	It.-Am. Basso, Opera, Films
Pioneers, Sons of the	Country Music	100			300	
Piper, William Thomasr.	Aviation	175	380			Founder Piper Aircraft Corp.
Pirandello, Luigi 1867-1936	Author	70	175	425	390	Nobel Lit. ALS/Content $2,400
Pirchoff, Nelly	Entertainment	10			30	Opera
Pire, Dominique George	Clergy	55		90	65	
Piscopo, Joe	Entertainment	10			35	
Pissarro, Camile 1830-1903	Artist	200	740	1660		Fr. Impressionist-Pointillist
Piston, Walter	Composer	75	225	470	95	Pulitzer Music 1947 & 1960
Pitkin, William 1694-1769	Colonial Am.		350			Soldier, Colonial Gov. CT
Pitney, Gene	Entertainment	5			25	
Pitney, Mahlon (SC)	Supreme Court	25	50	145	30	MOC NJ 1895
Pitt, Brad	Entertainment	20			55	
Pitt, Ingrid	Entertainment	3			10	Actress
Pitt, John, Sir 1756-1835	Military	45		95		Gen. Cmdr.Failed Walcheren Exp.
Pitt, William (Elder)1708-78	Head of State	110	225	1175		The Great Commoner
Pitt, William (Younger) 1759-1815	Head of State	115	250	540		England's Youngest Prime Min.
Pittenger, William 1840-	Clergy	15		25		Military (Civil War)
Pittner, William	Civil War-Clergy	15				
Pitts, Zazu	Entertainment	40			100	
Pius IX, G.M. Mastori	Clergy	175	250	400		G. M. Mastori
Pius IX, Pope	Clergy	40	150	275		
Pius VII, Pope	Clergy		1500			
Pius X, Pope 1835-1914	Clergy		700		5000	Giuseppe MelchiorreSarto
Pius XI, Pope	Clergy	350	950	3200	950	A.D. Achille Ratti
Pius XII, Pope	Clergy		1500		770	Eugenio Pacelli
Plainsmen, The	Country Music	25			50	

The Sanders Price Guide to Autographs

NAME	CATEGORY	SIG	LS/DS	ALS	SP	Comment
Planck, Max 1858-1947	Science	80	225	995	3750	Nobel Physics 1918
Plancon, Pol	Entertainment	125			400	Opera
Plant & Page (Both)	Enertainment				155	Rock
Plant, Robert	Entertainment	35			100	
Plato, Dana	Entertainment	5			15	
Platt, Ed	Entertainment	75			160	
Platt, Marc	Entertainment	5			35	Dancer-Choreographer
Platt, Orville H. 1827-1905	Congress	5	15			Senator CT
Platt, Thomas C 1833-1910	Congress	15		33	20	Senator NY
Platters, The (Group of 5)	Entertainment				250	Black Singing Group
Playfair, Lyon, 1st Baron	Science	10	25	40		Br. Chem. Modern Sanitation
Pleasant,Mary E.('Mammy')	Celebrity	400				
Pleasanton, Alfred (War Date)	Civil War	122	185	672		Union Gen. Sherman's Chief Cavalry
Pleasanton, Alfred 1824-97	Civil War	30		85		Union Gen.ALS War Dte $1,200
Pleasence, Donald	Entertainment	15			40	
Pleasonton, Alfred 1824-97	Civil War			200		Union Gen'l
Pleshette, Suzanne	Entertainment	6	8	15	15	
Plimpton, George	Author	7	20	25	17	
Plishka, Paul	Entertainment	5			25	Opera
Plitsetskaya, Maya	Entertainment	15			40	Ballet
Plowright, Joan	Entertainment	10			25	
Plummer, Amanda	Entertainment	16			25	Actress
Plummer, Christopher	Entertainment	6	8		25	
Plunkett, Edw. John	Author(SEE Dunsany)					Soldier,Traveler,Big Game Huntr
Pocahontas (Cast Of)	Entertainment				130	Mel Gibson & Two Others
Podmore, Thomas	Clergy	10	10	15	20	
Poe, Edgar Allan 1809-1849	Author	5200				AMsS $35,000
Pogany, Willy	Artist	70	190			Illustrator, Muralist,Designer
Poggi, Gianni	Entertainment	10			25	Opera
Pogue, William R.	Astronaut	6			20	
Poincaré, Raymond 1860-1934	Head of State	45	60	100	110	3 Times Prime Minister France
Poindexter, John	Military	40			150	US Adm. Iran-Contra
Poindexter, Joseph B.	Governor	10	15			Governor Hawii, Federal Judge
Poindexter, Miles	Congress	5	15		10	Repr., Senator WA 1909
Poinsett, Joel R. 1779-1851	Cabinet	70	460	375		Sec'y War. Poinsettia Flower
Pointer Sisters	Entertainment	30			60	
Poitier, Sidney	Entertainment	11			45	AA
Poland, Luke P.	Senate/Congress	10	15	30		MOC, Senator VT 1865
Polando, John	Aviation	30	60	110	75	
Polanski, Roman	Entertainment	20			125	Fugitive Director
Polaski, Deborah	Entertainment	5			25	Opera
Poli, Afro	Entertainment	10			45	Opera
Police, The	Entertainment	70			275	
Poling, Daniel A.	Clergy	20	30	60	35	
Polk, James K. & Buchanan, James	Presidents		2133			
Polk, James K. (As Pres.)	President		1710	3833		
Polk, James K. 1795-1849	President	475	1978	3660		FF $975.Political ALS $5250
Polk, Leonidas (War Date)	Civil War	500	685	3125		CSA General
Polk, Leonidas 1806-64	Civil War	338				CSA Gen. KIA
Polk, Sarah Childress	First Lady	400	600	1050	1200	
Pollack, Sidney	Entertainment	12	30	30	25	AA Director-Actor
Pollard, Snub	Entertainment	50			200	Keystone Cop
Pollen, Tracy	Entertainment	10			35	
Pollock, Channing	Author	30	55	145	45	Am. Playwright, Essayist
Pomeroy, Samuel Clarke 1816-91	Congress	12	20			Senator KS 1861
Pometti, Vincenzo	Entertainment	5			15	

The Sanders Price Guide to Autographs

NAME	CATEGORY	SIG	LS/DS	ALS	SP	Comment
Pompadour, Mme J. A,Duchess.	Royalty	135	470	1130		Louis VI Mistress
Pompidou, Georges	Head of State	10	25		20	Premier, President France
Ponchielli, Amilcare	Composer	175		1200		It. Opera. La Gioconda.Ballets
Pond, Enoch	Clergy	15	25	30		
Pond, Julian	Science	50		325		
Ponder, James	Governor	12	20			Governor DE
Poniatowski, Jozef A. Prince 1763-1813	Military	370	1750	2150		Rarest Napoleon Marsh'l
Pons, Juan	Entertainment	5			25	Opera
Pons, Lily	Entertainment	50			135	Coloratura Soprano Met. Star
Ponselle, Carmela	Entertainment	25				Mezzo Sister of Rosa
Ponselle, Rosa	Entertainment	25		75	305	Opera. SP in Opera Debut Role $475
Ponti, Carlo	Entertainment	15	20		30	It. Film Producer
Ponting, Herbert George	Celebrity	25	60	165		
Ponty, Jean-Luc	Entertainment	6	8	16	15	
Pool, Tilaman E.	Aviation	10	22	38	28	ACE, WW II, Navy Ace
Poor, Enoch	Revolutionary War	175	550	875		General. Patriot, Hero
Pope Pius X	Clergy	500			1975	Giuseppe Melchiorre Sarto
Pope, A.J.	Aviation	20	35			WW II Am. Ace
Pope, Alexander 1688-1744	Author	600	1850	2500	3500	Br. Poet, Satirist, Critic
Pope, Alexander 1849-1924	Artist	150	370	600		Am.NY Auction Still Life Sold $475,000 '82
Pope, Generoso Jr.	Business	10	40	50	25	It.-Born Publ. Il Progresso
Pope, James Pinckney 1884-1966	Congress	10	15		20	Senator ID. Dir. TVA
Pope, John 1822-92	Civil War	90	115	288	400	Union Genl. Cmdr. 2nd Bull Runn
Pope, John (War Date)	Civil War	155	442			Union Gen.
Popham, William 1752-1847	Revolutionary War			375		Aide-de-Camp to Gen. Clinton
Popkin, John S. 1771-185	Clergy		40	75		Greek Scholar & Harvard Prof. of Greek
Popovic, Cojetko	Celebrity	40		270		
Popovich, Pavel	Astronaut	45			175	Rus. Cosmonaut
Popp, Lucia	Entertainment	15			50	Opera
Porlzkova, Paulina	Entertainment	25			75	Model-Actress. Pin-Up SP $80
Porsche, Ferdinand, Dr.	Business	225	385		640	Inventor-Designer VW & Porsche
Portal, Charles	Aviation	20	40	80	50	
Porter, Cole 1891-1964	Composer	250	772	1135	1217	2¾x3¾ SPI $600
Porter, David 1780-1843	Military	45	145	250		Am.Naval Off. Fought 3 Wars
Porter, David Dixon 1813-91	Civil War	110	760	550		Union Adm., Mex. War,Civil War
Porter, Don	Entertainment	5	5	10	13	
Porter, Fitz-John 1822-1901	Civil War	40	100	400	750	Union Gen. Special ALS $825
Porter, Gene Stratton	Author	50	145	295	65	Am. Novelist. Freckles
Porter, George, Sir	Science	15	35	60	25	Nobel Chemistry 1967
Porter, Horace 1837-1921	Civil War	45	190	385		Union General-MOH.LS/Cont.$1750
Porter, James D.	Governor	5	20	35		Governor TN
Porter, James M. 1793-1844	Cabinet	20	77	120		Sec'y War 1843, Jurist, RR Pres.
Porter, Jane 1776-1850	Author	100		325		Br. Romance Novelist
Porter, Katherine Anne	Author	70	120	385	150	Am.Ship of Fools, Pulitzer
Porter, Noah	Clergy	30	65	100		Editor
Porter, Peter 1773-1844	Cabinet	65	145	180		Sec'y War J.Q.Adams
Porter, Quincy	Composer	17	45			Dean & Dir.New Eng.Conservatory
Porter, William Sidney (O.Henry)	Author	300	850	1717		Successful Short Story Writer
Portes-Gil, Emilio	Head of State	35		85		Pres. Mexico
Portland, 3rd Duke 1738-1809	Head of State	45	200			W.H.C.Bentinck, Prime Min.
Portman, Eric	Entertainment	35			95	
Portsmouth, Duchess (Chas II)	Royalty	65	270	550		Louise-Renee' Keroualle
Posey, Parker					60	
Poshetko, Joseph	Aviation	10	15	25	30	WW II Flying Tiger Ace
Possart, Ernst	Entertainment	15		55	50	Classical Musician
Post, Augustus	Aviation	25	45	55	50	Pioneer Aviator, Balloonist

The Sanders Price Guide to Autographs

NAME	CATEGORY	SIG	LS/DS	ALS	SP	Comment
Post, Emily 1873-1960	Author	95	50	125	35	US Etiquette Authority of Her Time
Post, Marjorie Merriweather	Business	15	35	70	25	Philanthropist, Postum Cereal
Post, Markie	Entertainment	6	8		20	Pin-Up SP $35-50
Post, Wiley 1900-35	Aviation	300	895	650	800	1st Solo Around the World
Poston, Tom	Entertainment	5			20	
Potter, Beatrix	Author	105	300	750	145	Illustr.Own Children's Books
Potter, Cora	Entertainment	10	15	30	25	
Potts, Annie	Entertainment	10			35	
Poulenc, Francis-Jean 1899-1963	Composer	130	375	600		Member Group of Six
Poulson, Norris	Mayor	4	30		10	Mayor L.A.
Poulter, Thomas C.	Explorer	20	40			2nd Arctic Expedition
Pound, Ezra 1885-1972	Author	200	808	1050		Poet, Editor, Critic, Translator
Poundstone, Paula	Entertainment	3			10	Standup Comedienne
Povey, Len	Aviation	5	10	25	20	
Povich, Maury	TV Host	10			20	TV Host
Powderly, Terence V.	Labor	45	95		50	Am. Labor Leader
Powell, Adam Clayton	Congress	30	40	55	35	MOC NY. Barred,Reelected
Powell, Colin L.	Military	35	117		100	Chmn. Joint Chiefs of Staff
Powell, Dick	Entertainment	35	30	60	65	SP 11x14 Bachrach $145
Powell, Eleanor	Entertainment	10	25		82	Popular Film Dancer
Powell, Jane	Entertainment	9	10	20	25	Pin-up SP $30
Powell, John Wesley	Explorer	250				Geologist.Pioneer Expl. West US
Powell, Lewis F.,Jr. (SC)	Supreme Court	25	100			In Robes-SP $950
Powell, Maud	Entertainment	20			90	Violinist
Powell, Max	Country Music	10			20	
Powell, Robert	Entertainment	4			10	Actor
Powell, Ross E.	Military	10	15	30		
Powell, Talmage	Author	10	20	45	15	Am. Novelist Mysteries
Powell, Teddy	Entertainment	20			70	Big band leader
Powell, William	Entertainment	30	50		95	
Power, Paul	Entertainment				20	Character Actor
Power, Tyrone	Entertainment	95	110		250	
Powers, Bert	Celebrity	4	10	15	10	White House Aide
Powers, Francis Gary	Aviation	80			100	U2 Downed Pilot Over USSR
Powers, Hiram	Artist	45	160	425	150	19th Cent. Major Sculptor
Powers, John 'Shorty' 1923-80	Celebrity	45	195		50	NASA Spokesman. A-OK
Powers, John Robert	Business	10	20	25	20	Fndr.One of 1st Modelling Agy.
Powers, Mala	Entertainment	5	7		15	
Powers, Preston	Artist	25	65	165		
Powers, Richard						SEE Tom Keene
Powers, Ridgely C.	Governor	10	15	30		Governor MS
Powers, Stephanie	Entertainment	9	10	20	25	Pin-Up SP $25
Pownall, Thomas	Colonial Am.	165	425	630		Lt. Gov. NJ, Gov. MA Bay, SC
Powter, Susan	Author	5			10	Non-Fiction
Powys, Llewelyn	Author	30	65	115	35	Essayist, Novelist
Powys, Theodore Francis 1875-1953	Author			350		Br. Allegorical Novels
Poynter, Edward John, Sir	Artist	10	35	75		Pres. Royal Academy
Pozzo de Borgo, Chas. A.	Corsican Diplomat	50		200		Opponent of Napoleon
Prado, Perez	Bandleader	25			85	
Pran, Dith	Celebrity	10	20	45	20	Cambodian photographer
Pratt, Francis & Whitney, Amos	Inventor		465			Pratt & Whitney Engine
Pratt, Ruth 1877-1965	Congress	10	30			Repr. NY 1929-33
Pratt, Thomas G.	Congress	5	20	25		Gov. 1845, Senator MD 1849
Preble, George H.	Civil War	20	60	85		Adm. USN.DS/Cont. $250
Precourt, Charlie	Astronaut	7			15	
Preddy. George E.	Aviation	10	30	45	30	

NAME	CATEGORY	SIG	LS/DS	ALS	SP	Comment
Preger, Kurt	Entertainment	5			20	Opera
Prelog, Vladimir	Science	20	30	45	25	Nobel Chemistry 1975
Preminger, Otto 1906-86	Entertainment	50			95	Important Film Director
Prentice, John*	Cartoonist	10			40	Rip Kirby
Prentiss, Paula	Entertainment	12			20	Pin-Up SP $25
Prescott, Oliver	Revolutionary War	70	175	465		Suppression of Shay's Rebellion
Prescott, Wm. Hickling	Author	30	60			
PRESIDENTIAL OATH	President		5500			FIVE PRES.(Printed Transcript)
PRESIDENTS	President				3250	FOUR PRESIDENTS
PRESIDENTS (5)	President				4900	Ford,Nixon,Bush,Reagan,Carter
Presley, Elvis 1935-77	Entertainment	619	953	2075	1160	AN/Content $10,000-$13,000
Presley, Priscilla	Entertainment	10		40	30	Pin-Up SP $35
Presley, Vernon	Celebrity	15			60	Father of Elvis Presley
Presser, Jackie	Celebrity	10	25		15	
Preston, Kelly	Entertainment	5			30	
Preston the Magician	Entertainment	4	6		8	
Preston, Robert	Entertainment	55			90	Actor Music Man
Preston, William (War Date)	Civil War	157	590	400		CSA Gen.
Preston, William 1816-87	Civil War	105	423			CSA Gen.
Preston, William Ballard	Cabinet	25	50	110		CSA Gov VA.Wardte SP $3,000
Preston, Wm. C. 1794-1860	Congress	15	35			Sen. SC
Pretenders	Entertainment	12			65	
Pretty Things, The	Entertainment				80	Br. Rock Group (All 5)
Preuss, Georg	Military	20		40		
Previn, Andre	Conductor-Comp.	20	40	80	75	
Previn, Dorey	Composer	5	10	20	10	
Prevost, Eugene-Marcel	Author	10	25	55		Fr. Moralist, Feminist Fiction
Prey, Hermann	Entertainment	10			30	Opera
Price, James H.	Governor	5	15			Governor VA
Price, Leontyne	Entertainment	25		45	55	Am. Soprano, Opera
Price, Margaret	Entertainment	15			45	Opera
Price, Ray	Entertainment	5			15	C & W
Price, Sterling (War Date)	Civil War	380		6900		CSA Gen. AES $575
Price, Sterling 1809-67	Civil War	218	345			CSA Gen.
Price, Vincent 1911-93	Entertainment	50	72	130	75	Self Sketch S $90. Egghead SP $125
Pride, Charley	Country Music	5			15	
Prien, Guenther	Military	300			750	
Priest, Ivy Baker	Cabinet	10	15	30	20	U.S. Treasurer
Priest, Royce W.	Aviation	10	22	35	30	ACE, WW II, USAAF Ace
Priestley, J. B. 1894-1984	Author	35	85	220	125	Playwright, Novelist, Playwright
Priestley, William O., Sir	Medical	50	120	200		Obstetric Physician
Priestly, Jason	Entertainment	20			50	
Priestly, Joseph 1783-1804	Science	350	1200	2200		Br. Clergyman, Chemist.
Prieur-Duvernois, Claude-A.,Count	Fr. Revolution	35	125			Fr. Revolutionary
Prigogine, Ilya	Science	20	30	45	25	Nobel Chemistry 1977
Prima, Louis	Entertainment	20			45	Big Band Leader-Trumpeter
Primrose, William	Entertainment	75			250	Great Violinist
Prince	Entertainment	110			200	
Prince, Harold 'Hal'	Entertainment	15	20	30	30	
Prince, Henry	Civil War	30	65	85		Union Gen.Pre War ALS $650
Prince, John Dyneley	Educator	10	25		15	Dean Graduate School NYU
Principal, Victoria	Entertainment	10	10	25	45	
Pringle, Aileen	Entertainment	15	15	35	30	
Prinz, Dianne	Astronaut	4			12	
Prinz, Rosemary	Entertainment	3	4		10	
Prinze, Freddie	Entertainment	45			85	

The Sanders Price Guide to Autographs

NAME	CATEGORY	SIG	LS/DS	ALS	SP	Comment
Pritchard, Jeter C. 1857-1921	Congress	10	15			Senator NC 1895
Pritchard, John, Sir	Conductor				45	Opera & Mozart Specialist
Procol Harum	Entertainment	35			65	
Proctor, Edna Dean 1838-	Author	35		80		Am. Poet, Magazine Writer
Proctor, Redfield 1831-1908	Cabinet	12	25	50	30	Gov, Senator VT, Sec'y War
Proctor, Richard Anthony	Science	5	15	35		Br. Astonomer, Science Writer
Profumo, John	Politician	40	65		100	Br.Traitor.Member of Parliament
Profumo, Valerie (Hobson)	Entertainment	10		25	25	Br. Film Star
Prokofieff, Serge 1891-1953	Composer	465	1412	1975	1022	AMusQS $2,900-$5,000
Prosky, Robert	Entertainment	5	6	15	15	
Protti, Aldo	Entertainment	5			20	Opera
Prouse, Juliet	Entertainment	10	8	15	40	Pin-Up SP $25-$45
Proust, Marcel 1871-1922	Author	500	875	2225	6000	ALS/Content $3,300, $3,500
Prouty, Jed	Entertainment	30			45	
Provine, Dorothy	Entertainment	5	6		10	
Provost, Jon	Entertainment	25			55	
Prowse, Dave	Entertainment	10			25	Darth Vadar $35
Proxmire, William	Senate/Congress	5	10		15	Senator WI
Pryor, David	Governor	5	15			Governor AR
Pryor, Richard	Entertainment	9	10	35	25	
Pryor, Roger	Entertainment	15	20		45	
Pryor, Roger A. (War Date)	Civil War	175		650		CSA Gen.
Pryor, Roger A. 1828-1919	Civil War	110	260	333		CSA Gen. US Repr. 1859-61
Pucci, Emilio	Business	10	25	40	15	It. Fashion Designer
Puccini, Giacomo 1858-1924	Composer	500	850	1472	1025	AMusQS $1,400-$4,000
Puck, Wolfgang	Business	5	10		15	Owner of Spago
Puelo, Johnny	Entertainment	10			25	
Puente, Tito	Bandleader	10			45	
Puett, Clay	Business	25	60		35	
Pulitzer, Joseph 1847-1911	Business	125	350	595		Pulitzer Pr. Editor-Publisher
Pulitzer, Joseph, Jr.	Business	15	25		20	Editor-Publisher
Pulitzer, Ralph 1879-1939	Business	65		250		Journalist, Publisher
Pulitzer, Roxanne	Celebrity	5	15	35	20	Pin-Up SP $25
Pullenberg, Albert	Science	20			60	Rocket Pioneer/von Braun
Pullman, Bill	Entertainment	12			45	Actor
Pullman, George M.	Business-Inventor	225	510	500	225	Pullman RR Car.DS/Cont.$1,200
Pullman, Hattie Sanger	Philantropist	15	25	30		Mrs. George M. Pullman
Puma, Salvatore	Entertainment	5			20	Opera
Punshon, W. Morley	Clergy	25	40	50		
Pupin, Michael, Dr.	Science	90	305	300	225	Physicist-Inventor-Author
Purcell, Edward M., Dr.	Science	20	30	45	25	Nobel Physics 1952
Purcell, Lee	Entertainment	4	5	12	10	
Purcell, Sarah	Entertainment	5	6	15	10	
Purdy, James	Author	15	50			
Purl, Linda	Entertainment	6	8	15	20	
Purvis, Melvin	Lawman	25	125	165	100	
Purvis, Robert	Anti-Slavery	15	40	85		Underground Railroad
Pusey, Edward B.	Clergy	25	35	95	30	
Pusey, Nathan M. 1907-	Educator	15	45	100	30	President Harvard
Pusey, Pennock	Political	10	15			Government Official
Pushkin, Alexander	Author	825	3250	16200		Rus. Poet, Dramatist,Novelist
Pusser, Buford	Lawman	50	150			Walking TallTennessee Sheriff
Putnam, George Haven 1844-1930	Business	9	480	50		Publishing House
Putnam, George Palmer	Business	15	40	75	30	Book Publisher, Author
Putnam, Israel 1718-90	Revolutionary War	195	2417	910		Don't Fire Till ...... War Dte. MsLS $3500
Putnam, Rufus	Revolutionary War	175	405	825		General. Ohio Pioneer

NAME	CATEGORY	SIG	LS/DS	ALS	SP	Comment
Putney, Mahlon	Celebrity	20	55			
Puzo, Mario	Author	20	75	100	45	Am. Novelist. The Godfather
Py, Gilbert	Entertainment	5			25	Opera
Pyle, Denver	Entertainment	4	6	10	20	
Pyle, Ernie	Author	250	400	485	350	Correspondent WWII, Pulitzer
Pyle, Howard	Artist	170	375			Am.Art Nouveau Illustrator-Auth
Pynchon, John 1621-1703	Colonial America			3750		Statesman, Soldier. NRPA

NAME	CATEGORY	SIG	LS/DS	ALS	SP	Comment
Qaddafi, Muammar el-(Alg)	Head of State	85	225	500	150	Chairman Libyan-Arab Republic
Quackenbush, Stephen P. (War Date)	Civil War	35		165		Union Adm.
Quaid, Dennis	Entertainment	20			50	
Quaid, Randy	Entertainment	6	48		20	
Quale, Anthony	Entertainment	20	25	55	45	
Qualen, John	Entertainment	10			20	
Quang, Thich Tri	Head of State	20	45	125	30	NRPA
Quant, Mary	Business	5	10	20	10	Br. Fashion Designer.
Quantrill, Wm. C.	Military	900	3000	4150		CSA Army Guerilla Leader
Quarles, William A.	Civil War	70	225			CSA General
Quarry, Robert	Entertainment	10			25	
Quasimodo, Salvatore	Author	25	40	55	30	Nobel Literature 1959
Quay, Matthew Stanley	Senate/Congress	12	25			Senator PA 1887
Quayle, Dan (V) 1947-	Vice President	48	200		45	Sen. IN
Quayle, Marilyn	2nd Lady	20			60	
Queen, Ellery	Author					SEE DANNAY
Queensberry, Wm. Douglas	Celebrity	15	40	95		
Quesada, E.R. 'Pete'	Military	15	35	55	25	
Quesada, Elwood R.	Aviation	16	30	45	30	
Questel, Mae	Entertainment	50				Original Voice of Betty Boop
Quie, Albert Harold	Senate/Congress	5			10	MOC MN
Quigg, Lemuel Ely	Senate/Congress	5	10			MOC NY 1894
Quillan, Eddie	Entertainment	20			45	
Quincy, Josiah 1772-1864	Congress	140	75	150		Repr. MA. Pres. Harvard
Quine, Richard	Entertainment	10			20	Actor turned Director
Quinn, Anthony	Entertainment	15	45		75	AA
Quinn, Carmel	Entertainment	5			15	
Quinn, Martha	Entertainment	4			10	MTV
Quinn, Robert E.	Governor	10	15			Governor RI
Quinn, William F.	Governor	5	10		15	Governor HI
Quintard, Charles Todd	Clergy	75	95	160		Served Confed. Army as Phys.
Quirk, Michael J.	Aviation	12	25	40	30	ACE, WW II
Quiros, Jean B.	Head of State	45	70			
Quisling, Vidkun	Military	115	220	475	450	Nor. Collaborator

The Sanders Price Guide to Autographs

NAME	CATEGORY	SIG	LS/DS	ALS	SP	Comment
Quitman, John A. 1799-1858	Millitary-Congr.-Gov.	25				General. Gov. & Sen. MS

NAME	CATEGORY	SIG	LS/DS	ALS	SP	Comment
Raab, Julius	Head of State	5	15	35	15	Chancellor Austria
Raabe, Meinhardt	Entertainment	25			50	
Rabaud, Henri 1873-1949	Composer	35			200	Fr. Composer-Conductor. Opera
Rabi, Isador I.	Science	35	55	80	40	Nobel Physics 1944
Rabin, Yitzhak	Head of State	210	540	775	775	PM Israel, Nobel. Assassinated '96
Rabinowitz, Solomon	Author					SEE Aleichem, S.(Pen Name)
Raboy, Mac*	Cartoonist	10			95	Flash Gordon
Rachin, Alan	Entertainment	5			15	
Rachmaninoff, Sergei 1873-1943	Composer	388	1105	1525	550	AMusQS $2,000, $3950, $4500
Racine, Jean 1639-99	Author	4500				Fr. Dramatist. NRPA
Rackham, Arthur	Artist	55	175	425		Illustrator Children's Books
Radford, William 1808-1890	Military		375			CW Naval Off'r. Adm. Mex. War
Radford, William 1814-1870	Congress	10	15	30		Repr. NY
Radhakrishnan, Sarvepalli	Head of State	65	180	380	75	Pres. India, Philosopher
Radner, Gilda	Entertainment	25			95	
Rae, Cassidy	Entertainment	5			40	Actress Models, Inc.
Rae, Charlotte	Entertainment	5			15	
Raeder. Erich	Military	65	195	550	125	Ger. Navy Cmdr., War Crimes
Raff, Joseph Joachim	Composer	25		150		Ger. Wide Variety Of Music
Rafferty, Frances	Entertainment	4			10	
Raffin, Deborah	Entertainment	6	8	15	15	
Rafko, Kaye Lani	Entertainment	8			15	Miss America 1988
Raft, George 1895-1980	Entertainment	40	105		145	11 x 14 Vintage SPI $200
Raglan, Fitzroy Somerset, Lord	Military	40	115	150		Crimean War. Raglan Sleeve
Ragsland, Rags	Entertainment	40			75	
Rahman, Abdul	Head of State	10	35	80	15	Malaysia. 1st Ambass. U.S.
Raimondi, Ruggero	Entertainment	20			50	Opera
Rain-in-the-Face	Indian Chief	13000			8260	
Rainer, Luise	Entertainment	15	20	40	45	
Raines, Ella	Entertainment	7			18	
Rainey, Ford	Entertainment	3	5		10	
Rainey, Henry Thomas	Senate/Congress	5	15			MOC IL 1903-21, Speaker
Rainger, Ralph	Composer	20			40	AMusQS $55, $85
Rainier III, Prince	Royalty	70	95	205	125	Monaco
Rains, Claude	Entertainment	90			100	
Rains, James E. (War Date)	Civil War		4850			CSA Gen.. KIA. RARE
Rainwater, Leo James	Science	20	30	45	25	Nobel Physics 1975
Rainwater, Marvin	Country Music	15			30	
Raisa, Rosa 1893-1963	Entertainment	30	45		60	Opera. Created Title Role in Turandot
Raitt, Bonnie	Entertainment	5			30	

NAME	CATEGORY	SIG	LS/DS	ALS	SP	Comment
Raitt, John	Entertainment	5	7	15	15	
Raksin, David	Composer					AMQS $75
Raleigh, Cecil	Entertainment	6	8		10	
Raleigh, Sara	Entertainment	6	8		10	
Rall, Guenther	Military-Aviation	30	75	150	90	#3 ACE, WW II, Ger./275 Kills.
Ralston, Esther	Entertainment	10	15	45	33	Am. Leading Lady 20's-30's
Ralston, Jobyna	Entertainment	25	35	65	50	
Ralston, Vera Hruba	Entertainment	7	15		25	
Ralston, William	Business	55	90	150		Founder Bank of California
Rama VI	Royalty	135				King Siam (Thailand)
Rambeau, Marjorie	Entertainment	20	25	45	45	
Rambo, Dack	Entertainment	15	20		50	
Rambo, Dirk	Entertainment	20			40	
Ramey, Samuel	Entertainment	10			35	Opera
Ramirez, Carlos	Entertainment	8			25	Baritone
Rampling, Charlotte	Entertainment	5			20	Pin-up SP $35
Ramsay, William, Sir 1852-1916	Science	150	410	650		Nobel Chemistry 1904
Ramseur, Stephen D.(War Date)	Civil War		13000			CSA Gen. RARE
Ramsey, Alexander	Cabinet	20	45	90		CW Gov. MN, Hayes Sec'y War
Ramsey, Michael, Archbishop	Clergy	35	45	50	45	
Ramsey, Norman F., Dr.	Science	15	25		20	Nobel Physics 1989
Rand, Ayn 1905-82	Author	500	1250		750	Objectivist Novels
Rand, Sally	Entertainment	25			55	Fan DancerPin-Up SP $60
Randall, James R.	Writer-Composer	70				Maryland, My..... MsS $1,900, AMsS $9,500
Randall, Samuel J.	Senate/Congress	7	20			MOC PA 1863-90
Randall, Tony	Entertainment	5	5	15	20	
Randell, Mike	Business	3			5	TV Exec.
Randolph, A. Philip 1889-1979	Labor	65				US Black Labor Leader.1925
Randolph, Beverly	Revolutionary War	100	325			Early Gov. Virginia 1788
Randolph, Boots	Entertainment	5			15	Country Rockabilly Saxaphonist
Randolph, Charles D.	Showman	75	210	315		Buckskin Bill Assoc./Wm. Cody
Randolph, Edmund J.1753-1813	Revolutionary War	200	665	625		Sec'y State,ADS/Cont.$1600
Randolph, Geo. Wythe 1818-67	Civil War	268	660	565		CSA Gen. ALS '62 $825
Randolph, John (of Roanoke)	Revolutionary War	85	265	485		MOC, Senator VA
Randolph, Joyce	Entertainment	4			15	
Randolph, Lillian	Entertainment	100			250	
Randolph, Peyton 1721-75	Am. Revolution	400	3000			1st Pres. Continental Congress
Randolph, Thos. Mann, Jr. 1768-1828	Congress	75	275			Repr. & Gov. VA. Special ALS $2800
Randy & the Rainbows (3)	Entertainment	20			40	Rock
Rangel, Charles B.	Senate/Congress	5			10	Congressman NY
Rank, J. Arthur, 1st Baron	Entertainment	25		75	55	Br.Industrialist, Film Magnate
Rank, Otto	Science	200		425		Austrian Psychoanalyst
Rankin, Jeannette 1880-1973	Congress	80	200			Voted against both World Wars
Rankin, Nell	Entertainment	10	20		25	Am. Contralto
Rankin, Robert J.	Aviation	12	25	42	35	ACE, WW II, Ace in a Day
Ransier, Alonzo Jacob	Senate/Congress	75				MOC SC
Ransom, John Crowe	Author	35	85	200		Am. Poet, Critic, Professor
Ransom, Matt W.	Civil War	80	285			CSA Gen.
Ransom, Robert, Jr.(War Date)	Civil War	220		2850		CSA Gen. (1828-92)
Rapaport, Lester	Artist	10	15	30	15	
Rapee, Erno	Conductor	15			45	Hung.-Am. Radio City Music Hall
Raphael	Artist	3500	9800	25000		
Raphael, Sally Jessy	TV Host	5			30	TV Talk Show Hostess
Rapper, Irving	Entertainment	15			35	40's Film Director
Rappold, Marie	Entertainment	30			95	Opera, Concert
Rashad, Phylicia	Entertainment	5			15	

NAME	CATEGORY	SIG	LS/DS	ALS	SP	Comment
Raskob, John J.	Business	10	20		15	CEO General Motors
Rasmussen, Knud J.V.	Explorer	200		325	150	Danish Arctic Explorer, Author
Rasputin, Gregori E.	Clergy	2000	4500	7500		Rus. Mystic. Assassinated
Rathbone, Basil 1892-1967	Entertainment	200	150	350	470	
Rathbone, Monroe J.	Business	4	8	15	10	Exxon.Important Oil Innovations
Ratner, Payne	Governor	5	15			Governor KS
Ratoff, Gregory	Entertainment	20	65		60	Film Director
Ratzenberger, John	Entertainment	5			15	Cheers SP $35
Raum, Green B.	Civil War	30	65			Union Gen., MOC
Ravel, Maurice 1875-1937	Composer	412	1495	1662	1695	AMusQS $1,675-$3,800-$4,800
Rawdon, Francis1732-97	Military			475		Br. Gen'l Rev. War.
Rawdon-Hastings, Francis, Lord	Revolutionary War	25	60	110		Br. Off'r. Bunker Hill
Rawlings, Edward V.	Military	10	20			
Rawlings, Marjorie Kinnan	Author	45	150			Am. Pulitzer. The Yearling
Rawlins, John A.	Civil War	75	160	245		Union Gen., Sec'y War 1869
Rawlinson, Herbert 1886-1853	Entertainment	15	20	45	65	Br. Actor. Starred in dozens of B Westerns,
Rawls, Lou	Entertainment	15	30		35	Singer
Rawson, Edward 1615-1693	Colonial America	125	350	685		Colonial Sec'y.ADS $1500
Ray, Aldo	Entertainment	4	5		15	
Ray, Charles	Entertainment	25	35	65	60	
Ray, Dixie Lee	Governor	15			40	Governor WA
Ray, James Earl	Assassin	55	150	275		Shot Martin Luther King, Jr.
Ray, Johnny	Entertainment				40	Singer-Actor
Ray, Leah	Entertainment	10			15	
Ray, Man (Rudnitsky) 1890-1976	Artist	262	575			Surrealist Painter,Photographer
Ray, Robert D.	Governor	5			10	Governor IA
Ray, Susan	Country Music	5			10	
Rayburn, Sam 1882-1961	Congress	35	50		75	Speaker of the House, TX
Raye, Cassidy	Entertainment				40	Models, Inc.
Raye, Collin	Country Music	10			25	
Raye, Martha	Entertainment	20	75		42	Pin-Up SP $35
Rayleigh, John W. S. 1842-1919	Science			402		Nobel Physics. 3rd Baron
Raymond, Alex*	Cartoonist	15			75	Rip Kirby, Secret Agent X-9
Raymond, Alex*	Cartoonist	60		95	55	Flash Gordon. Spec. Ltrhd. TLS $225
Raymond, Gene	Entertainment	10	15	25	25	
Raymond, Henry J.	Business	30	75	150		Fndr.New York Times, MOC NY
Raymond, Jim*	Cartoonist	15			75	Blondie
Raymond, John T. 1836-87	Entertainment	20				Vintage Actor
Raymond, Paula	Entertainment	5			15	
Razaf, Andy	Composer	45		225		Lyricist Ain't Misbehavin'
Re'jane, Gabrielle-Charlotte Re'ju	Entertainment	15	70	105		
Read, Albert Cushing	Aviation	40	85	180	115	Adm. Record Flight, WW I &II
Read, Dolly	Entertainment	5	6	15	15	Pin-Up SP $15
Read, George 1733-98	Revolutionary War	350	425	1265		Signer Decl. of Indepen.
Read, T. Buchanan	Artist	17	29	40		
Readdy, William F.	Astronaut	4			12	
Reade, Charles	Author	30	70	135		Br. Novelist, Dramatist
Reagan, John H.	Civil War	105	525	620		CSA Postmaster Gen.
Reagan, Maureen	Celebrity	5	15	30	15	Political Daughter of President
Reagan, Nancy	1st Lady		150	120	75	
Reagan, Ron,Jr.	Entertainment	4			30	Dancer
Reagan, Ronald (As Pres.)	President	220	848	3167	310	R. Reagan & Nancy SP $380
Reagan, Ronald 1911-	President	248	603	1420	358	Personal Paternal ALS $18,000
Real, Pierre F., Count	Fr. Revolution	15	35	80		
Reale, Antenore	Entertainment	20			55	Opera
Ream, Vinnie	Artist			450		Am. Sculptor

NAME	CATEGORY	SIG	LS/DS	ALS	SP	Comment
Reason, Rex	Entertainment	10			20	
Reasoner, Harry	TV News	15			40	60 Minutes
Rector, George	Business	20			35	World Famous Chef-Rector's NY
Rector, Henry M. 1816-18??	CSA Governor	190	650			CSA Gov. AR. War Dte.DS $875
Reddy, Helen	Entertainment	6		20	20	
Redenbacker, Orville 1907-95	Business	10	30	35	30	Popcorn King
Redfield, Billy	Entertainment	4	7		15	
Redfield, William C. 1889-1932	Cabinet	10	45	45	15	Sec'y Commerce 1913
Redford, Robert	Entertainment	40	225		88	
Redgrave, Lynn	Entertainment	7			25	
Redgrave, Michael, Sir	Entertainment	24		55	45	
Redgrave, Vanessa	Entertainment	20	30		65	
Redman, Don	Entertainment	20			45	Jazz Musician
Redmond, John E. 1856-1918	Politician	5	15	40	15	Ir. Leader of Home Rule
Redon, Odilon	Artist	70		450		Also Lithographer & Engraver
Redout,, Pierre Joseph	Artist	210	900	1450		Fr. Painter, Lithographer
Reed, Alan	Entertainment	25			50	
Reed, Carol, Sir 1906-76	Entertainment	45	500		150	Influential Br. Film Director
Reed, David H.C.	Clergy	20	25	35	30	
Reed, Donna 1921-86	Entertainment	40	50		208	Pin-Up SP $180
Reed, Erik	Entertainment	4			10	
Reed, Frances	Entertainment	10	12		20	
Reed, James Alexander	Senate/Congress	5	15		10	Senator MO 1910
Reed, James F.	Celebrity	1250				NRPA
Reed, Jerry	Entertainment	5			12	
Reed, John	Author	200	1200	1350	300	Radical Am.Journalist
Reed, Joseph 1741-85	Revolutionary War	75	200	550		PA Statesman, Continental Cong.
Reed, Lou	Entertainment	20			50	
Reed, Oliver	Entertainment	10			30	
Reed, Phillip	Entertainment	11	20	35	30	
Reed, Rex	Entertainment	5	6	16	16	
Reed, Robert	Entertainment	20	45		55	
Reed, Roland	Entertainment	15			35	Vintage Actor
Reed, Stanley (SC)1884-1980	Supreme Court	40	95	150		TDS $1500 (Opinion)
Reed, Thomas Brackett 1839-1902	Congress	15	35	45		Speaker of the House. ME
Reed, Walter	Entertainment	10			25	
Reed, Walter 1851-1902	Science	400	1050	5000	675	Proved Mosquito=Yellow Fever
Reedy, George	Cabinet	3			5	
Rees, Roger	Entertainment	4			10	
Rees, Thomas	Business	10	25	45	25	
Reese, Della	Entertainment	5			15	
Reeve, Christopher	Entertainment	50			130	
Reeves, George	Entertainment	1088	1200	1800	4250	
Reeves, Keanu	Entertainment	15			73	
Reeves, Martha	Composer	5			20	Composer-Entertainer
Reeves, Ronna	Entertainment	5			10	Singer
Reeves, Steve	Entertainment	20			50	
Reeves-Smith, Olive	Entertainment	5	7	15	15	
Refice, Licinio	Composer-Clergy	20				AMusQS $85
Regan, Donald	Cabinet	10	15		30	Sec'y Treasury
Regan, Phil	Entertainment	10	75		25	
Reger, Max	Composer	75	250	550		Ger. Composer
Reginald, Lionel	Entertainment	10			20	
Regnaud de Saint-Jean etc	Fr. Revolution	30		105		
Rehan, Ada	Entertainment	20			40	Fine Vintage Shakespearean Actr
Rehm, Dan	Aviation	12	25	45	30	ACE, WW II

The Sanders Price Guide to Autographs

NAME	CATEGORY	SIG	LS/DS	ALS	SP	Comment
Rehnquist, William H.(SC)	Supreme Court	50	160	185	100	Chief Justice
Reich, Wilhelm	Science	120	325	650		Austr. Psychoanalyst. Author
Reichers, Lou	Aviation	30	45	60	65	
Reid, Tim	Entertainment	5	6	15	15	
Reid, Wallace	Entertainment	180			650	
Reid, Whitelaw	Journalist	30	75		50	Correspondent, Ambassador
Reifel, Benjamin	Senate/Congress	5			10	MOC SD
Reightler, Ken	Astronaut	5			16	
Reik, Theodor 1888-1969	Science	105	285	475		Austrian Psychoanalyst
Reilly, Charles Nelson	Entertainment	5			10	
Reinburg, J. Hunter	Aviation	15	35	50	40	ACE. WW II, Marine Ace
Reinecke, Karl	Composer	55	145	225	250	Ger.Pianist, Conductor, Teacher
Reiner, Carl	Entertainment	10	30	30	25	
Reiner, Fritz	Entertainment	50	150		225	Hung. Conductor
Reiner, Rob	Entertainment	10			25	Film Director
Reinert, Ernst Wilhelm	Aviation				50	Ger. Ace. RK
Reinhardt, Max 1873-1943	Entertainment	110	175	470	275	Austrian Innovative Theatre Dir
Reinking, Ann	Entertainment	5	10	20	15	
Reisch, Walter	Entertainment	10			20	Director
Reischauer, Edwin O.	Celebrity	3	5	10	5	
Reiser, Paul	Entertainment	10			25	
Reiserer, Russell	Aviation	15		40		ACE WW II
Reitsch, Hanna	Aviation	65	165	270	185	Flew 1st Practical H'Copter.
Reitz, Francis W.	Head of State	50	135			South Africa
Reizen, Mark	Entertainment				750	Opera
Rejane, Gabrielle-Charlotte	Entertainment	35		78	90	Vintage Fr. Tragedienne
Remarque, Erich Maria 1898-1970	Author	40	150	375	50	All Quiet on the Western Front
Rembrandt van Rijn	Artist	2800		3600		Dutch Painter-Etcher
Remer, Otto	Military	20			70	SS Gen. WW II. RK
Remick, Lee	Entertainment	30			65	Pin-Up SP $65
Remington, Frederic 1861-1909	Artist	575	805	2938	1850	Sculptor,Writer,War Correspond.
Renaldo, Duncan 1904-80	Entertainment	25		100	225	Cisco Kid
Renaud, Maurice	Entertainment	35			175	Opera. Important Fr. Baritone
Renaud, Paul	Head of State	50			100	Premier France
Renault, Louis	Jurist	35	95	125		Nobel Peace Prize 1907
Renner, Karl, Dr.	Head of State	25	50	105	40	Fndr.,Pres.Austrian Republic
Rennie, John 1761-1821	Engineer			625		Br. Civ. Eng. Built Waterloo Bridge
Rennie, Michael 1909-71	Entertainment	95			188	
Reno, Marcus A.	Military	950	2750			Battle of Little Big Horn
Renoir, Jean	Entertainment	120	340			Fr. Inovative Film Maker
Renoir, Pierre-Auguste 1841-1909	Artist	250	700	2524	3500	Repro Artwork S $3,000-$5,000
Renquist, William	Supreme Court	75			150	Chief Justice
Renwick, Edward Sabine	Inventor	20	45	75		Father Modern Poultry Industry
REO Speedwagon	Entertainment	35			65	Rock
Repplier, Agnes	Author	5	15	35		Am.Dean of Essayists,Biographer
Requesens, Luis de Zunig	Military	750				NRPA
Resnick, Mike	Author	10	20	40	10	Hugo award winner
Resnick, Regina	Entertainment	15			60	Opera
Resnik, Judith	Astronaut	100	275		225	
Respighi, Ottorino	Composer	70	200	550		It.Opera, Orchestral,Choral
Reston, John 'Scotty'	Author	10	20	35	15	Journalist, Synd. Columnist
Rethberg, Elisabeth	Entertainment	40			155	Opera
Rethy, Ester	Entertainment	10	15	35	30	Opera, Operetta
Rettig, Tommy	Entertainment	10			25	
Reuter, Edzard	Business	35	60	250	150	
Reuther, Walter P.	Labor	25	40	95	30	Pres. UAW-CIO

NAME	CATEGORY	SIG	LS/DS	ALS	SP	Comment
Revelle, Hamilton	Entertainment	4	5	10	10	
Revels, Hiram Rhoades	Clergy-Civil War	500				1st Black U.S. Senator, MS
Revere, Anne	Entertainment	15			40	AA
Revere, Paul 1735-1818	Revolutionary War	1700	5400	9400		ALS $26000,DS Revere & J Hancock $95,000
Rexroth, Kenneth	Author	10	35	65	20	Am.Columnist, Poet, Avant-Garde
Rey, Alvino	Entertainment	10			75	Big Band Leader
Reybold, E.	Military	15	35	55		Gen. WW II. Engineer Corps.
Reymann, Hellmuth	Aviation	30		75		
Reynolds, A.W.	Civil War	65	145	190		CSA General
Reynolds, Albert	Head of State	15			25	P.M. Ireland
Reynolds, Burt	Entertainment	8			20	
Reynolds, Craig	Entertainment	10			25	
Reynolds, Daniel H. 1832-1902	Civil War	85		385		CSA Gen. Sig/Rank $115
Reynolds, Debbie	Entertainment	6			20	Pin-Up SP $25
Reynolds, Donn	Country Music	10			20	
Reynolds, Gene	Entertainment	5	6	15	15	
Reynolds, John Fulton	Civil War	350	1445			Union Gen. KIA Gettysburg
Reynolds, Joseph Jones	Civil War	45	110	190		Union General, Indian Fighter
Reynolds, Joshua, Sir	Artist	200	390	780		Br. Portraitist, Pres. R.A.
Reynolds, Marjorie	Entertainment	5	8	15	15	Pin-Up SP $15
Reynolds, R.J.	Business	225	750			Founder Tobacco Empire
Reynolds, Richard Samuel	Business	45	110	240	55	Reynolds Metal Co., Aluminum
Reynolds, William	Entertainment	6			12	TV FBI
Rhea	Entertainment	10	15	30	25	
Rhee, Syngman 1875-1965	Head of State	175	200	955	250	1st Pres. So. Korea
Rhett, Alicia	Entertainment	300				SP N/A
Rhett, Robert Barnwell	Civil War	140	285	610		CSA Gen. ALS/Content $2,500
Rhett, Robert G., Mrs.	Celebrity	3		10		Blanche Rhett
Rhodes, Billie	Entertainment	15			35	
Rhodes, Cecil John 1853-1902	Head of State	135	230	400	600	S.Afr. Fndr. Rhodes Scholarship Fund
Rhodes, Erik	Entertainment	20			45	
Rhodes, John J.	Senate/Congress	5	15		10	MOH AZ 1953-83
Rhys-Davies, John	Entertainment	4			20	Br. Actor
Ribbentrop, Joachim von	Military	160	525	645	325	Hitler Foreign Affairs Advisor
Ribbentrop, Rudolf von	Military	65	95	150		
Ribicoff, Abraham 1910-	Cabinet	10	15	35	25	Gov., Senator CT. Sec'y HEW
Ricci, Christina	Entertainment	20			67	Actress. Addams Family
Ricciarelli, Katia	Entertainment	5			25	Opera
Rice, Alexander H.1818-95	Congress-Gov.	10	15	20		Sen. & Gov.. MA
Rice, Alice C.	Author	65		220		Mrs. Wiggs of Cabbage Patch
Rice, Anne	Author	15			30	Novelist
Rice, Dan (Dan'l McLaren) 1823-1900	Business	50	100	558		Circus Clown & Owner
Rice, Donna	Model	15			30	Hart Stopper. Pin-Up SP $35
Rice, Elmer 1882-1967	Author	80	250		80	Pulitzer Prize. Playwright
Rice, Florence	Entertainment	5	9		15	
Rice, Grantland	Journalist	25			75	Sportswriter
Rice, Henry M.	Senate/Congress	5		15		Senator MN 1858-63
Rice, Merton S.	Clergy	20	20	40		
Rice, Tim	Composer	10	30	65	30	
Rice-Davies, Mandy	Celebrity	5	10	25	20	Involved In Br. Scandal
Rich, Buddy 1917-87	Entertainment	30			138	Big Bandleader-Drummer
Rich, Irene	Entertainment	5	8	15	15	
Richard, Cliff	Entertainment	15			40	Rock
Richard, Cyril	Entertainment	20				Brit. Actor
Richards, Ann	Governor	7			20	Governor TX
Richards, Dickinson W.	Science	25	35	70	30	Nobel Medicine 1956

NAME	CATEGORY	SIG	LS/DS	ALS	SP	Comment
Richards, J.K. (Act'g)	Cabinet	3	15	25		
Richards, Jeff	Entertainment	5			20	Was Young MGM Star
Richards, Keith	Entertainment	25			110	Rock
Richards, Richard N.	Astronaut	10			35	
Richards, William	Senate/Congress	15		50		Rep. NY 1871
Richardson, Dorothy	Author	35	110	285		Br. Introduced New Technique
Richardson, Elliot	Cabinet	7	25	45	15	Att'y Gen. Watergate Period
Richardson, Friend W.	Governor	5				Gov. CA 1923-27
Richardson, Ian	Entertainment	5	6		15	
Richardson, John P.	Governor	15	25			Governor SC 1840
Richardson, John, Sir	Science-Explorer	20	60	150		Surgeon-Naturalist Franklin Exp
Richardson, Michael	Entertainment	20			80	Kramer. Seinfeld
Richardson, Miranda	Entertainment	18			60	Br. Actress
Richardson, Natasha	Entertainment	15			50	
Richardson, Patricia	Entertainment	10			35	Tool Time
Richardson, Ralph, Sir	Entertainment	20	25	50	45	
Richardson, Robert Vinkler	Civil War	535	805			CSA General
Richardson, Tony	Entertainment	15			25	Film Director
Richardson, William A. 1821-96	Cabinet	18	48	95		Sec'y Treas.1873
Richardson, William Alex. 1811-75	Congress	10		20		Sen. IL
Richelieu,Armand E. du 1766-1822	Head of State	85	240	340		Military, Prime Minister France
Richelieu,Armand-Jean, Card'l	Head of State	245	890	2150		1585-1642.Special DS $3,450
Richey, Helen	Aviation	20	50		55	
Richey, Lawrence	Cabinet	3	10			
Richie, Lionel	Composer	10	70		40	Composer-Singer-Arranger
Richman, Charles	Entertainment	10	15	30	25	
Richman, Harry	Entertainment	15	50	35	35	Flew Lady Peace 1st R/T Atlantic Crosssing
Richter, Burton, Dr.	Science	20	45	70	35	Nobel Physics 1976
Richter, Charles, Dr. 1900-85	Science		175		65	Devised Richter Scale Earthquake Measure
Richter, Hans	Music	150		750		Ger. Conductor. AMusQS $350
Richters, Christine	Playboy Ctrfold	3			10	Pin-Up SP $15
Richthofen, Manfred von 1892-1918	Aviation	850	2750	5000	7733	ACE, WW I, The Red Baron
Rickard, George L. Tex	Business	350	950		675	Boxing Promoter DS $2,000
Rickenbacker, Edw V. 1890-1973	Aviation	112	262	585	280	ACE, WW I, TLS/Cont. $1500
Rickles, Don	Entertainment	5	6	15	15	
Rickover, Hyman G. 1900-	Military	100	308	570	325	Adm. Father of Atomic Sub.
Riddle, George	Country Music	10			20	
Ride, Sally K.	Astronaut	15	100		40	1st US Woman in Space
Riders in the Sky (3)	Entertainment	5			10	
Ridgway, Matthew B. 1895-1993	Military	90	195	175	125	Supreme Allied Cmdr. WW II
Riefenstahl, Leni	Photographer	25	45	80	70	Hitler's Photographer
Rieger, Vince	Aviation	12	25	40	30	ACE, WW II, Navy Ace
Riegger, Wallingford	Composer	20	65	125	35	Am. Orchestral, Choral, 12 Tone
Rigal, Delia	Entertainment	15			45	Opera
Rigg, Diana	Entertainment	15	20	45	45	
Riggs, Clinton E.	Inventor	27				Created Highway Yield Sign
Riggs, Tommy	Entertainment	5	8	15	15	
Righteous Brothers	Entertainment	45			110	
Riis, Jacob A. 1849-1914	Author-Reformer	15	50	90		Dan.-Am. Journalist. ALS/Cont. $350
Riley, James Whitcomb 1849-1916	Author	92	175	600	225	Prolific Am. Poet Little Orphan Annie
Riley, Jeannie C.	Country Music	5			15	
Riley, Larry	Entertainment	4			10	
Rilke, Rainer Maria	Author	140	345	1400		Ger. Lyric Poet
Rimsky-Korsakov, Nicolai 1844-1908	Composer	450	2250	3750	1500	Rus. AMusQS $6500
Rinehart, Mary Roberts	Author	20	80	125	25	Am. Novelist, Playwright
Ring, Blanche	Entertainment	15				Vintage Silent Star

NAME	CATEGORY	SIG	LS/DS	ALS	SP	Comment
Ringgold, George H.	Civil War	15	35	55		Union Paymaster
Ringling, Albert C. 1852-1916	Business-Circus	115	500			Ringling Bros.& Barnum & Bailey
Ringling, Charles 1863-1926	Business-Circus	115	435			Ringling Bros.& Barnum & Bailey
Ringling, Henry	Business-Circus	100	500		125	Special DS $1,250
Ringling, John 1866-1936	Business-Circus	125	617	615	700	Ringling Bros.& Barnum & Bailey
Ringling, Otto 1858-1911	Business-Circus	210	700			Ringling Bros.& Barnum & Bailey
Ringling, William	Business-Circus	100	325		125	2nd Generation Owners
Ringo, John	Outlaw	2000	6500			Cowboy Gunslinger
Ringwald, Molly	Entertainment	20		45	70	
Ripley, Eleazar W.1782-1839	Military	65		250		General War 1812
Ripley, George	Social Reformer	140	350	875		Critic,Editor,Unitarian Clergy
Ripley, James Wolfe	Civil War	55	185	210		Union General
Ripley, Robert* 1893-1949	Cartoonist	100	95		200	Believe It Or Not. SP $125
Ripley, Roswell 1823-87	Civil War	165	220	410		CSA Gen. Nephew of Union Gen.
Ripley, Roswell S. (War Date)	Civil War	228		1012		CSA Gen.
Risner, James R.	Military	10	25	35	20	
Ritchard, Cyril 1896-1977	Entertainment	15			50	Br. Dancer & Comedian
Ritchie, Adele	Entertainment	15		50	40	Vintage Musical Theater Star
Ritchie, Neil, Sir	Military	15	35	60	30	General
Ritchie, Steve	Aviation	12	35	45	40	ACE, Nam, Only AF Ace
Ritt, Martin	Entertainment	30			65	Film Director
Rittenhouse, David 1732-96	Science	850	1100	4500		Am Astronomer,1st US Telescope
Ritter, John	Entertainment	5	6	15	15	
Ritter, Tex	Country Music	100			250	
Ritter, Thelma	Entertainment	40			150	
Ritterscheim, Karl	Entertainment	5			20	Opera
Ritz Brothers, The (3)	Entertainment	75			150	Jimmy, Al, Harry
Ritz, Jimmy	Entertainment	15			40	
Rivera, Diego	Artist	295	620	1050	1500	Political-Social Muralist
Rivera, Geraldo	Entertainment	20	40		30	TV Host
Rivers, Joan	Entertainment	6	8	25	15	
Rivers, Larry 1923-	Artist	40	75	275		Forerunner Pop Art Movement
Rives, Amelie	Author	12		675		
Rivington, James 1724-1802	Revolutionary War	100	225			Journalist-Publisher-Spy
Rizzo, Frank L.	Political		20		25	Mayor Phila. Fmr. Chief of Police
Ro'Al, Zhang	Artist		700			
Roach, Hal, Jr.	Entertainment	5			15	
Roach, Hal, Sr.1892-1992	Entertainment	97	450		165	AA Film Pioneer. Our Gang Comedy
Roarke, Hayden	Entertainment	25			45	
Robards, Jason	Entertainment	15	15		30	AA
Robbins, Frederick C., Dr.	Science	20	30	45	25	Nobel Medicine 1954
Robbins, Gale	Entertainment	15	15	35	30	
Robbins, Harold	Author	20	100	150	35	Am.Novelist.The Carpetbaggers
Robbins, Jay T.	Aviation	10	25	40	35	ACE, WW II
Robbins, Jerome	Entertainment	40	75	125	68	Ballet Dancer, Choreographer
Robbins, John 1808-80	Congress	12				Repr. PA, Steel Mfg.
Robbins, Marty	Country Music	25			65	Country & Pop Singer
Robbins, Reg. L.	Aviation	25			60	Pioneer Aviator
Robbins, Tim	Entertainment	4			10	
Roberti, Margherita	Entertainment	15			30	Am. Soprano
Roberts, Barbara	Governor	7			20	Governor Or
Roberts, Cokie	Entertainment	10				TV-Radio Journalist
Roberts, David	Artist	40	90	175		Scottish Painter
Roberts, Doris	Entertainment	6	8	15	15	
Roberts, Eric	Entertainment	10			25	
Roberts, Frederick Sleigh, Earl	Military	40	55	85	100	Field Marshal, Kandahar

NAME	CATEGORY	SIG	LS/DS	ALS	SP	Comment
Roberts, Jack	Country Music	10			20	
Roberts, Jonathan 1771-1854	Senate	60		350		Introduced Important Legislatio
Roberts, Julia	Entertainment	30			100	
Roberts, Kenneth	Author	20	80	150		Am. Historical Novels
Roberts, Lee S.	Composer	30	65	150		AMusQS $285
Roberts, Oral	Clergy	20	90	50	25	Am. Evangelist
Roberts, Oran M.	Governor					Gov. TX 1879-83
Roberts, Owen J. (SC)	Supreme Court	50	150	220	100	
Roberts, Pat Hutchison	Author	5			10	cookbook author, editor
Roberts, Pernell	Entertainment	15	20		35	
Roberts, Ralph	Author	10	20	40	15	1st U.S. book on computer viruses
Roberts, Robin	TV News	4			10	ESPN News
Roberts, Roy	Entertainment	15			35	
Roberts, Tanya	Entertainment	10			25	Pin-Up SP $35
Roberts, Tony	Entertainment	5	6	15	15	
Roberts, William P.1841-1910	Civil War	85	800			CSA Gen.Youngest In CSA Service
Roberts, Xavier	Business	15	20	35	25	
Robertson, James 1720-88	Revolutionary War			975		Br. Gen. Fought in Rev. War
Robertson, Alice Mary	Senate/Congress	5		20	25	MOC OK,Self-Taught Creek Indian
Robertson, Beverly H.	Civil War	55	140			CSA General
Robertson, Cliff	Entertainment	5	6		25	AA
Robertson, Dale	Entertainment	10			35	
Robertson, Forbes 1853-1937	Entertainment					Vint. Theatre. SPc/Gertrude Elliott $125
Robertson, J. Forbes-, Sir 1853-1937	Entertainment	10			55	
Robertson, Morgan	Author	15		60		Sea Stories
Robertson, Pat, Rev.	Clergy	15	25	50	20	
Robertson, Willard	Entertainment	15				Actor
Robeson, George M.	Cabinet	20	50	95		Sec'y Navy 1869
Robeson, Paul 1898-1976	Entertainment	119	210	280	538	Am. Singer, Actor, Athlete, Activist
Robespierre, Maximilien 1758-94	Fr. Revolution	1150	3500	12500		Special DS $4,275
Robin, Mado	Entertainment	40			225	Opera. Coloratura.Young, Tragic Death
Robinson, Bill Bojangles1878-1949	Entertainment	75	190	450	458	Afro- American Dancer
Robinson, C. Roosevelt	Celebrity	5	15	20	5	
Robinson, Dwight P.	Business	5	15	25	15	
Robinson, Edward 1794-1863	Archaeologist		185	395		Biblical Scholar
Robinson, Edward A. 1869-1935	Author	55	125	217		Am. Poet, 3 Pulitzers
Robinson, Edward G. 1893-1973	Entertainment	50	125	100	183	Actor Famous for Gangster Roles
Robinson, George D.1834-96	Governor	10				Repr. & Gov. MA
Robinson, John 1761-1828	Revolutionary War	60	175	340		Soldier, Merchant
Robinson, John C.	Civil War	60	180	215		Union Gen., CMH Gettysburg
Robinson, Joseph T. 1872-1937	Congress	20				Sen. Arkansas
Robinson, Lucius	Governor	10	20	40		Governor NY 1876
Robinson, Smokey	Entertainment	25			45	Rock and roll
Robson, Flora, Dame	Entertainment	20	25	40	60	
Robson, May	Entertainment	35			75	
Robson, Stuart	Entertainment	20	25	45	45	Vintage Actor
Rochambeau, Count de 1725-1807	Revolutionary War	270	2500	825		Fr. Gen. in Am. Revolution
Rochan, Debbie	Entertainment	4				Actress. Pin-Up Col.45
Roche, James M. 1906-	Business	10	15	30	15	Pres. Ford Motor Co.,CEO Gen. Motors
Rochefort, Henri	Author	10	25	50		Fr.Journalist.Anti Napoleon III
Rochford, Leonard	Aviation	20	40			Br. Ace WW I
Rock, Blossom	Entertainment	200			45	
Rock, John	Science	25	80			
Rockefeller, Abby A.	Business	14	30	65	20	Socialite.Wife of John D., Jr.
Rockefeller, David	Business	20	55	75	25	Banker
Rockefeller, Happy	Business	5	15	25	10	Wife of Nelson Rockefeller

NAME	CATEGORY	SIG	LS/DS	ALS	SP	Comment
Rockefeller, John D. 1839-1937	Business	300	1671	1550	1495	Standard Oil. Philantropist
Rockefeller, John D., Jr. 1874-1960	Business	35	155	225	75	Rockefeller Ctr. Philanthropist
Rockefeller, Laurance	Business	5	15	25	10	Philanthropist
Rockefeller, Nelson A. 1908-79	Vice President	30	110		45	Governor NY
Rockerfeller, John (Jay) D., IV	Governor	5	15		10	Governor WV.Confidential Political ALS $450
Rockefeller, Winthrop	Governor	10	20		15	Governor AR
Rockwell, George Lincoln	Activist	50	100	200	95	Am. Nazi Party TLS $450. Assassinated
Rockwell, Norman* 1894-1978	Artist	100	293	575	434	Am. Illustrator-Artist
Rockwell, Robert	Entertainment	5	10		25	
Roddenberry, Gene 1931-91	Entertainment	160				Creator of Star Trek
Roddey, Philip D. (War Date)	Civil War	200	905	1992		CSA Gen.
Roddey, Philip D. 1826-97	Civil War	90	325	388		CSA Gen.
Roddy, Philip Dale	Civil War	110	285	425		CSA Gen.ALS War Dte $3,000+-
Roden, George	Civil War	30	55	85		
Rodenburg, Carl	Military	15			40	Ger. Gen. Stalingrad. WW II. RK
Roderick, Milton David	Business	5			10	CEO U.S. Steel
Rodes, Robert Emmett (War Date)	Civil War	750		8800		CSA Gen. RARE
Rodes, Robert Emmett 1829-64	Civil War	412		1050		CSA General KIA
Rodgers, Geo. Washington	Military	40	105	195		Naval Officer War !812
Rodgers, John	Aviation	55	125	240	135	
Rodgers, John 1771-1838	Military	80	425	100		Distinguished US Naval Officer
Rodgers, John 1812-82	ClvlI War	105	335	470		Un. Naval Commodore,-Explorer
Rodgers, Richard & Hammerstein	Composers	500				Oscar Hammerstein III
Rodgers, Richard & Hart, Lorenz	Composers	375	1350			
Rodgers, Richard 1902-79	Composer	93	340		151	Pulitzer. AMusQS $460
Rodin, Auguste 1840-1917	Artist	150	300	575	1150	SP of Sculpture $1250-1,700
Rodman, Hugh	Military	35				Adm. USN
Rodman, Judy	Entertainment	5	6	15	15	
Rodney, Caesar 1728-84	Rev. War-Cabinet	490	670	2075		Signer Decl. of Indepen.
Rodzinski, Artur	Conductor	30	75		75	Pol.-Am. Conductor
Roe, Edward Payson 1838-88	Author	15	25	35		Novelist, Clergy
Roe, Tommy	Entertainment	10	15		20	Singer
Roebling, John A.	Engineer	75	165	325		Designer of Brooklyn Bridge
Roebling, Washington A.	Science	100	225	450		Builder of Brooklyn Bridge
Roebuck, Alva Curtis	Business	65	215	320		Co-Fndr. Sears & Roebuck
Roederer, Pierre C., Count	Fr. Revolution	20	50	95		
Roehm, Ernest	Celebrity	200	540			
Roell, Werner	Aviation	5			20	Ger. RK Winning Stuka Pilot
Roentgen, Wilhelm 1845-1923	Science	512	1300	2517		1st Nobel in Physics
Roethke, Theodore	Author	35	135	275	40	Am. Poet. Pulitzer
Rogallo, Francis M.	Inventor	27				Invented Hang Glider.
Rogatchewsky, Joseph	Entertainment	20			85	Ukranian. Lyric/Dramatic Tenor
Roger, Gustav	Entertainment			158		Opera.Creator of Important Tenor Roles
Rogers, Andrew Jackson 1828-1900	Congress	10				Repr. NJ, Teacher, Lawyer
Rogers, Bernard W.	Military	10	25	50	40	
Rogers, Buddy	Entertainment	15	20	40	40	
Rogers, Carroll P.	Business	8	20	40	15	
Rogers, Fred	Entertainment	5	15		15	Mr. Rogers
Rogers, Ginger 1911-95	Entertainment	40	80		141	AA. Actress, Dancer
Rogers, Jean	Entertainment	25			65	
Rogers, Jimmy	Country Music	75			175	Vintage Entertainer
Rogers, John	Military		350	375		
Rogers, Joseph W.	Aviation	15	30	60	35	
Rogers, Kenny	Country Music	10			30	
Rogers, Marianne and Kenny	Country Music	10			35	
Rogers, Mimi	Entertainment	15			30	Actress

NAME	CATEGORY	SIG	LS/DS	ALS	SP	Comment
Rogers, Randolph 1825-92	Artist	18		30		Sculptor
Rogers, Robert	Revolutionary War	335	1195	3300		Frontier Soldier
Rogers, Roy	Entertainment	50			85	
Rogers, Samuel 1763-1855	Author	12	30	100		Br. Poet.Patron Of The Arts
Rogers, Wayne	Entertainment	20			35	
Rogers, Will 1879-1935	Entertainment	260	450	1030	922	America's Favorite Humorist
Rogers, Will Jr.	Senate/Congress	10			25	Congressman CA, Actor
Rogers, William F.	Civil War	15	25	35		Union General
Rogers, William Findlay	Senate/Congress	5		10		MOC NY, Soldier CW
Rogers, William P.	Cabinet	12	20	35	25	Sec'y State
Roget, Peter M., Dr.	Author	30	65	140		Br.Physician. Roget's Thesaurus
Rohmer, Eric	Entertainment	35	250			Fr. Director
Rohmer, Sax (A.S.Ward)	Author	75	240	250	100	Br. Mystery Novels. Fu Manchu
Rohrer, Henreich 1933	Science	20				Nobel Physics 1981
Rojo, Gustavo	Entertainment	10			30	On Screen from 1948
Roland de La Platiere,Jean	Fr. Revolution	30	95	185		Fr. Statesman. Suicide
Roland, Gilbert 1909-94	Entertainment	20	22		40	
Roland, Ruth	Entertainment	25	35		45	
Roldan, Salv. C.	Head of State	10	20	50	10	Columbia
Rolfe, William James	Author	5	10	20	5	
Rolland, Romain	Author	30	85	125	40	Nobel Lit. 1915, AMsS $2,000
Rolle, Esther	Entertainment	5			20	
Rolling Stones (All)	Entertainment	600			12000	
Rollins, Edward Henry	Senate	15	25	35		NH Railroad & Bank Executive
Rollins, Sonny	Entertainment	30			55	Jazz Tenor Sax
Rolls, Charles S.	Business	175	300	550		Roll-Royce Motors
Rolph, James	Governor	10		35	20	Governor CA
Roman, Ruth	Entertainment	10			25	
Romanoff, Michael, 'Prince'	Business	32	65	145	55	Romanoff's.Hollywood Restaurant
Romanov, Stephanie	Entertainment	10			40	Actress. Models, Inc.
Rombauer, Irma S.	Author	5	15	30	10	The Joy of Cooking
Romberg, Sigmund	Composer	142	250	385	225	AMusQS $650
Rome, Harold	Composer	15	50	105	30	AMusQS $125
Rome, Sydney	Entertainment	5	6	15	15	
Romero, Cesar 1907-93	Entertainment	25			70	
Romjue, Milton Andrew	Senate/Congress	5	12		10	Rep. MO 1917
Rommel, Erwin 1891-1944	Military	750	1850	3325	2808	Ger. Field Marshal WW II
Romnes, Haakon I.	Business	4	10		9	CEO A T & T
Romney, George 1734-1802	Artist	150	475	600		Signed Original Sketch $1,500
Romney, George W.	Business-Governor	15	30	55	20	Pres. American Motors. Gov. MI
Romulo, Carlos P.	Head of State	20	70	95	50	Philippines. Pres.UN, Pulitzer
Ronne, Edith M.	Explorer	20	30			Antarctic Land Named Edith Ronne Land
Ronne, Finn	Explorer	15		70		Proved Antarctic a Continent
Ronstadt, Linda	Entertainment	10	30	40	30	
Rooney, Mickey	Entertainment	15			35	
Roosa, Stuart R.	Astronaut	10			25	
Roosevelt, Alice (Longworth)	Pres. Daughter	35		275		
Roosevelt, Edith Kermit 1861-1948	First Lady	50	240	275	400	
Roosevelt, Eleanor (As First Lady)	First Lady		288	1400	805	White House Cd. S $90-$225
Roosevelt, Eleanor 1884-1962	First Lady	78	306	450	250	
Roosevelt, Franklin D.(As Pres.)	President	400	1625		981	WH Card $525.ALS/Cont $19,000
Roosevelt, Franklin D.1882-1945	President	300	938	1400	1012	
Roosevelt, Franklin Jr.	Senate/Congress	10			20	Rep.NY.Bussinessman-Farmer
Roosevelt, James	Senate/Congress	8	25	45	15	Rep. CA. General Marine Corps
Roosevelt, John A.	1st Family	20	35			FDR Son
Roosevelt, Nicholas J.	Revolutionary War	25	60	135		Inventor

NAME	CATEGORY	SIG	LS/DS	ALS	SP	Comment
Roosevelt, Quentin	Business	5	15	25	10	
Roosevelt, Sarah D. 1854-1941	Presidential	75	110	85	50	FDR Mother
Roosevelt, Theodore (As President)	President	700	1418	2000	2962	TLS/Cont.$12,000, WH Cd. $500
Roosevelt, Theodore 1858-1919	President	225	1317	1125	1185	TLS/Content $1,250-$9,000
Roosevelt, Theodore II	Celebrity	10	20	45	15	
Roosevelt, Theodore, Jr.1887-1944	Military-Author	20	50	100	40	WW I & II. Gov. Puerto Rico
Root, Elihu 1845-1937	Cabinet	65	140		140	Sec'y War, Sec'y State, Nobel
Root, George F. (G.Wurzel)	Composer	50	150	135		AMQS $895-$1,195
Root, Jesse	Revolutionary War	25	60	125		Continental Congress
Roper, Daniel	Cabinet	10	30	50	15	Sec'y Commerce 1933
Rops, Felicien 1833-98	Artist	55	165	455		Belg. Licentious Subjects
Rorem, Ned	Composer	15	45	110		Pulitzer, AMusQS $175
Rorke, Hayden	Entertainment	25			45	
Rosas, Juan M. de	Head of State	10	25	40		Argentina
Rose Marie	Entertainment	10			20	Dick VanDyke Show, Singer
Rose, Axl (Guns N' Roses)	Entertainment	20			40	Rock
Rose, Billy	Entertainment	25	90	35	55	Entrepreneur, Producer
Rose, David	Composer	10	20	35	20	
Rose, Fred	Country Music	30			60	Country Music Hall of Fame
Rose, Juanita	Country Music	10			20	
Rosebery, Archibald P., 5th Earl	Head of State	30	70	145		Prime Minister
Rosecrans, William S. 1819-98	Civil War	80	270	200		Union Gen.
Rosecrans, William S.(War Date)	Civil War	144		1192		Union Gen.
Rosellini, Albert D.	Governor	5	15		10	Governor WA
Rosenberg, Alfred	Military	175	340		450	Nazi Head of Foreign Policy
Rosenbloom, Slapsie Maxie	Entertainment	55			120	Heavyweight Boxer-Actor
Rosendahl, Charles E.	Aviation	75	170	225	200	Am. Adm.Premiere U.S. Dirigible Capt.
Rosenman, Samuel I.	Jurist	5	20	55	10	Confidant-Advisor to FDR
Rosenquist, James	Artist	20	60	150		Am. Pop Art. Huge Canvases
Rosenthal, Joe	Artist-Photographer	75	200	290	295	Iwo Jima Special 1st Day Issue $450
Rosenthal, Laurence	Composer	3	10	20	10	
Rosenthal, Moriz	Entertainment	75				Pol. Pianist
Rosenwald, Julius 1862-1932	Business	195	750			Bought out Roebuck (of Sears..)
Rosing, Bodil	Entertainment	10			30	
Ross, Charles J.	Entertainment	5	6	15	15	
Ross, Charlotte	Entertainment	4	6		10	
Ross, David 1755-1800	Revolutionary War			385		Cont'l Army & Congr.MD.
Ross, Dianna	Entertainment	35	70	165	88	
Ross, G.	Military	10	35	55		
Ross, George 1730-79	Revolutionary War	338	505	1319		Signer Decl. of Independ.
Ross, Jerry L.	Astronaut	5			15	
Ross, Joe E.	Entertainment	100			250	
Ross, John [Coowescoowe]	Am. Indian Chief	275	1365	1800		Chief Cherokee Nation
Ross, John, Sir 1777-1856	Explorer	40	180	275		Arctic Expeditions. Author
Ross, Katharine	Entertainment	15			40	
Ross, Lanny	Entertainment	20		25	25	Vintage Radio Tenor of 30's & 40's
Ross, Lawrence Sullivan	Civil War	165	600			CSA General, Texas Governor
Ross, Lewis W.	Senate/Congress	10	15	30		Rep. NY 1863
Ross, Marion	Entertainment	15			35	
Ross, Nellie Tayloe 1876-1977	Governor	35	75	145		1st Woman Governor in U.S., WY
Ross, Robert	Author	5	10	20	5	Mystery Writer. Poe Award
Ross, Ronald 1857-1932	Science		125	275		Br. Phys. Nobel for Studies in Malaria
Ross, Sobieski	Senate/Congress	10	15	25		Rep. PA 1873
Rosselini, Isabella	Entertainment	10			40	
Rosser, Thomas L. 1836-1910	Civil War	125	282	495	375	CSA Gen. Sig/Rank $170
Rossetti, Christina	Author	45	125	245		Br. Poet. Sister of Dante

NAME	CATEGORY	SIG	LS/DS	ALS	SP	Comment
Rossetti, Dante Gabriel 1828-82	Artist	180	220	640		Br. Poet & Painter
Rossetti, Wm. M. 1829-1919	Author	75		450		Pre-Raphelite Art Critic.AQS $300
Rossi, Dick	Aviation	10	25	45	32	ACE, WW II, Flying Tigers
Rossini, Gioacchino 1792-1868	Composer	500	1075	1933	3408	AMusMsS $3900. Spec,Engr.S $4500
Rossman, Edmond	Aviation	10	30	45	25	
Rossmann, Edmund	Aviation	15			50	Ger. Ace WW II. RK
Rostand, Edmond 1868-1918	Author	65	200	450	863	Fr. Playwright. Cyrano de....
Rostenkowski, Dan	Congress	15	10		40	Powerful Rep. IL, now in Federal prison
Rostropovich, Mstislav	Entertainment	25	75	100	68	Cello Virtuoso, Conductor
Rosza, Miklos b.1907	Composer			500		Hung. Known Best for Film Music AA
Roth, David Lee	Entertainment	30			75	
Roth, Lillian 1910-80	Entertainment	29	40	80	88	Tragic Vintage Vocal Star
Roth, Philip	Author	16	35	70	25	Novels. Portnoys' Complaint
Roth, Tim	Entertainment				45	Pulp Fiction
Rothafell, S. L. 'Roxy'	Entertainment	15	20	40	45	NY Entrepreneur,Theatre Owner
Rothenstein, William, Sir	Artist-Writer	20	45	75		Off'l Artist WW I & II
Rothschild, Alfred (b.1843)	Banker	35	90	150		Grandson of Nathan Mayer
Rothschild, Alix de	Banker	70	190	375		
Rothschild, Amschel Mayer 1773-1855	Banker		1000			Eldest Son of Mayer Amschel
Rothschild, Guy de	Banker	15	40	80	85	
Rothschild, Jakob 1792-1868	Banker	125	525			Founded Paris Branch
Rothschild, Leopold (b.1845)	Banker	35	75	150		Grandson of Nathan Mayer
Rothschild, Lionel Nathan (b.1808)	Banker	25	75	125	45	Son of Nathan Mayer
Rothschild, Mayer Amschel (b.1743)	Banker	135	400	550		Founder House of Rothschild
Rothschild, Nathan (b.1840)	Banker	50	150			Eldest son of Lionel
Rothschild, Nathan Meyer (b.1777)	Banker	262	900			Founder London Bank Branch
Rotia, Rocky	Business	5	15	30	25	
Rouault, Georges 1871-1958	Artist	200	475	822	1150	Landscapes,Religious,Clowns....
Rouget de Lisle, Claude-Joseph	Military,Composer	110	295	950		Composed La Marseillaise
Rountree, Richard	Entertainment	10			25	Opera, Concert
Rourke, Mickey	Entertainment	15			35	
Rous, F. Peyton, Dr,	Science	20	30	45	25	Nobel Medicine 1966
Roush, Clara	Author	10	15		15	
Rousseau, Jean-Jacques	Author	295	1050	2950		Fr. Philosopher, Political
Rousseau, Lovell H.1818-69	Civil War	45	80			Union Gen. Congress
Rousseau, Theodore	Artist	75	175	475		Fr. Leader of Barbizon School
Roussel, Albert 1869-1937	Composer			608		Leading Fr. Composer after WW I
Roux, Pierre Paul Emile	Science	20	45	90	40	Fr. Bacteriologist with Pasteur
Rovero, Ornella	Entertainment	15			45	Opera
Rowan, Andrew S.	Military	35	95	165	90	Delivered Message to Garcia
Rowan, Dan	Entertainment	10			35	
Rowan, John 1773-1853	Senate/Congress	90	250			Rep. 1807, Senator KY 1825
Rowan, Stephen C.1808-90	Civil War	25	60	150		Union Naval Commodore
Rowe, Leo S.	Cabinet	5	20	35	10	Ass't Sec'y
Rowe, Misty	Entertainment	6			20	Pin-Up SP $25
Rowland, David	Colonial America	40	150			Member Stamp Act Congress
Rowland, Gena	Entertainment	5	6	15	15	
Rowlandson, Thomas 1756-1827	Artist	250	625	900		Br. Caricaturist, Illustrator
Rowling, William E.	Head of State	10	15	20	20	New Zealand
Roxas, Manuel	Head of State	30	90	230	110	1st Pres. Philippines Republic
Roy and Siegfried	Entertainment				20	Animal Trainers
Roy, Maurice, Cardinal	Clergy	30	30	40	35	
Royce, F. Henry, Sir 1863-1933	Business	350	700	900		Founder Rolls-Royce, Ltd.
Roylance, Pamela	Entertainment	3	3	6	6	
Roze, Marie	Entertainment	40			145	Opera
Rozema, David Lee	Clergy	10	15	25	15	

NAME	CATEGORY	SIG	LS/DS	ALS	SP	Comment
Rubattel, Rudolph	Head of State	30	55			Switzerland
Rubens, Alma 1899-1931	Entertainment	65	85	165	175	Actress. Major Film Star Early 20th Cent.
Rubens, Paul A.	Composer	15		60		Br. Musical Comedy. AMusQS $75
Rubens, Peter Paul	Artist	2000	9250	21750		Flem.Baroque Landscapes, Portr.
Rubik, Erno	Science	35	65	85	45	Hung.Mathematician.Rubik's Cube
Rubin, Jerry	Celebrity	15		35	20	
Rubini, Jan	Entertainment	20			65	
Rubinoff, David	Entertainment	18			40	Rubinoff & His Violin
Rubinstein, Anton 1829-94	Composer	75	220	365	445	AMusQS $625-$1250 AMsS $4,750
Rubinstein, Artur 1887-1983	Entertainment	40	125	235	175	Pol./Am. Pianist,AMusQS $425
Rubinstein, Helena	Business	50	145	225	350	Invented the Cosmetics Industry
Rubinstein, Ida	Entertainment	125			500	Rus. Ballerina/Nijinsky
Rubinstein, John	Entertainment	5	6	15	15	
Rubio, P. Ortiz	Head of State	40				Pres. Mex. 1930-32
Ruby, Harry	Composer	30	90	200	50	AMusQS $265
Ruby, Jack 1911-67	Assassin	275	800	4950		Killed Lee Harvey Oswald
Rucker, Daniel H.	Civil War	25	65	80	120	Union Col., Bvt. General
Rudel, Hans-Ulrich	Aviation	85	295	700	345	Most Highly Decorated Ger. Ace
Rudman, Warren B.	Senator	10			20	Senator NY
Rudner, Rita	Entertainment	4			15	Actress-Comedienne
Rudolf I [Hapsburg (Aus)]	Royalty			750		
Rudorffer, Erich	Aviation	40			78	Ger. World's 7th Highest Ace
Ruehl, Mercedes	Entertainment	25			60	AA
Ruff, Charles F.	Civil War	20	45	60		Union General
Ruffo, Titta 1887-1953	Entertainment	75		765	410	It. Operatic Bariton
Ruge, Friedrich	Military	55			175	Ger. Vice Adm.
Ruger, Thomas H.	Civil War	30	50	75		Union General
Ruggles, Charles	Entertainment	40			75	
Ruggles, Daniel (War Date)	Civil War	155	735	1079		CSA General
Ruggles, Daniel 1810-97	Civil War	90	295	590		CSA Gen.
Ruggles, Wesley	Entertainment	20	25	45	45	Film Director
Ruick, Barbara	Entertainment	4	6	15	10	
Rukeyser, Louis	Business	4	15	25	15	Wall Street Week
Rulter, John (SC)	Supreme Court					No Entry
Rumpler, Edward	Aviation	20	40	75	50	
Rumsfeld, Donald	Cabinet	10	20	45	15	Sec'y Defense
Runcie, Robert A.K., Archbishop	Clergy	30	40	50	40	
Runco, Mario	Astronaut	8			16	
Rundstedt, Karl R. Gerd von	Military	225	415	370	275	Ger.Fld. Marshal.Pol.,Fr.,USSR
Runger, Gertrud	Entertainment	15			50	Opera
Runkel, Louis	Business	5	15		10	
Running Horse, Chief	Native American	5		30		
Running Water, Chief	Native American	75		275		Model For US Indian Head Nickel
Runyon, Damon 1884-1946	Author	160	415	500	195	Short Stories & Sports Writer
Ruppert, Jacob	Business	95	300	415	225	Founder Ruppert Brewing Co.
Rush, Barbara	Entertainment	5	6	15	15	Pin-Up SP $20
Rush, Benjamin	Revolutionary War	650		2250		Signer Decl. of Indepen.
Rush, Isadore	Entertainment	10			30	Stage
Rush, Richard 1780-1859	Cabinet	50	160	400		Att'y General 1814. Sec'y Treas.
Rusk, Dean	Cabinet	20	80		50	Sec'y State
Rusk, Jeremiah M.	Civil War-Cabinet	25	55	110		Union Gen.,Sec'y Agri. 1889
Rusk, Johnny	Country Music	4			12	
Rusk, Thos. Jefferson	Military	350	445	700		TX Provisional Gov., Sec'y War
Ruskin, John 1819-1900	Artist-Critic	50	130	345		Br. Painter, Critic, Author
Rusling, James F.	Civil War	15	30	40		Union Gen. Bvt.
Russell, Annie	Entertainment	10		25	20	Vintage Stage

The Sanders Price Guide to Autographs

NAME	CATEGORY	SIG	LS/DS	ALS	SP	Comment
Russell, Bertrand 1872-1970	Author	85	275	580	310	Philosophy, Math., Nobel Prize Lit.
Russell, Bruce*	Cartoonist	25			50	Political Cartoonist, Pulitzer
Russell, Charles	Governor	5	15			Governor NV
Russell, Charles M.	Artist	250	750	1650		Known For Cowboy-West Art
Russell, David Abel	Congress	10	20	35		Repr.NY 1835
Russell, David Allen	Civil War					Union Gen.-Killed at Gettysburg
Russell, Donald J. M.	Business	5	10	20	10	
Russell, Harold	Entertainment	5	10	20	25	Military Hero, Academy Award
Russell, Henry 1874-1936	Entertainment	10				Theatrical Mgr. & Singer
Russell, Jane	Entertainment	8	10	20	25	Pin-Up SP $35
Russell, John	Entertainment	20			45	
Russell, John, Lord, 1792-1818	Head of State	32	80	125		Br. Prime Minister, 1864-65
Russell, Johnny	Entertainment	5			13	Singer-Songwriter
Russell, Jonathan 1771-1832	Diplomat	390	800			Min. to Nor,Swe.Treaty of Ghent
Russell, Kurt	Entertainment	15			35	
Russell, Lillian 1861-1922	Entertainment	100	145	275	400	Vintage Musical, Operetta Star
Russell, Mark	Entertainment	4			10	
Russell, Richard B., Jr.1897-1971	Congress	20	35		35	Gov., Senator GA. Cont. TLS $300
Russell, Richard M.	Congress	5	10			Rep. MA
Russell, Rosalind	Entertainment	35	45		100	
Russell, Sol Smith	Entertainment	20			40	Vintage Comedian
Russell, Theresa	Entertainment	7	15	30	25	
Russell. George W.	Author	40	145		55	Leader Ir. Literary Renaissance
Russo, René	Entertainment	10			40	Actress, model "Ransom"
Rust, Albert 1818-70	Civil War	75	180	185		CSA Gen. AES '$155
Rustin, Bayard	Activist	15	35	70	25	Afro-Am Civil Rights Activist
Rutan, Dick	Aviation	15	70		30	
Rutan, Dick & Jeana Yeager	Aviation		75		125	Non-Stop Trans-World w.o. Refueling
Rutgers, Henry 1745-1830	Revolutionary War	95	295	345		Benfactor Rutgers University
Ruth, Babe 1895-1948	Entertainment	1050	1450	3500	4200	Baseball Immortal
Rutherford, Ann	Entertainment	10	15		52	Pin-Up SP $35. GWTW SP$50-75
Rutherford, Ernest 1871-1937	Science	155	495	925	225	NZ Born Physicist. Nobel Chem. 1908
Rutherford, Margaret, Dame	Entertainment	50		145	185	
Rutledge, Edward 1739-1800	Revolutionary War	220	500	1225		Signer.Important ALS $2400
Rutledge, John (SC)	Supreme Court	195	600	1775		Continental Congress
Rutledge, Wiley B. (SC)	Supreme Court	30	115	265	50	
Ruttan, Susan	Entertainment	5			15	
Ryan, Irene	Entertainment	75			250	
Ryan, James W. 1858-1907	Congress	12				Repr. PA
Ryan, Meg	Entertainment	20			55	
Ryan, Mitchell	Entertainment	5				Actor
Ryan, Peggy	Entertainment	10	15	35	30	
Ryan, Robert	Entertainment	20	30		60	
Ryan, Sheila	Entertainment	5	6	15	15	
Ryan, T. Claude	Aviation	85	300		225	Ryan Aircraft Mfg.-Designer
Rydell, Bobby	Entertainment	10			15	Rock
Ryder, Albert P. 1847-1917	Artist	90	250	560		Am. Landscapes,Marine,Portraits
Ryder, Wynona	Entertainment	25			80	
Ryle, Martin, Sir	Science	35	110	190	45	Nobel Physics 1974

NAME	CATEGORY	SIG	LS/DS	ALS	SP	Comment
Saarinen, G. Eliel	Architect	20	65	150	40	Am. Foremost Arch. Of His Day
Sabatier, Paul	Science	60		180		Fr. Chem. Nobel 1912
Sabatini, Rafael	Author	25	70	95		It. Historical Romance Novels
Sabin, Albert Bruce, Dr.	Science	25	90	150	120	Polio Vaccine
Sabin, Dwight May	Senate/Congress	5	10		10	Rep. MN 1883
Sabin, Florence R.,Dr. 1871-1953	Science	25		145		1st Woman Elected to Nat'l Acad.of Sciences
Sabine, Edward, Sir 1788-1883	Military	45		190		Br. Gen. With Ross & Parry on Arctic Exped.
Sablon, Jean	Entertainment	20	25	45	45	Vintage Fr. Romantic Singer
Sabu (Dastagir) 1924-63	Entertainment	50			150	Overnight Star in Elephant Boy
Sacco, Nicola	Political Radical			3700		With Vanzetti Convicted Murder
Sacher-Masoch, Leopold von	Author	130	275	420		Word Masochism Attributed
Sackett, Frederic 1868-1941	Congress	5	25			Sen. KY. Business. Ambass. Germany
Sackler, Howard	Author	5	15	25	10	
Sacks, Oliver, Dr.	Science	15	45		30	Awakenings. Neurologist
Sackville-West, Lionel, Sir	Diplomat	10	25	40		2nd Baron
Sackville-West, Victoria Mary	Author	100		415		Br. Poet and Novelist
Sackville-West, Vita 1892-1962 Member	Author		332	325		Br.Writer.Distinguished Aristocratic Family
Sadat, Anwar 1918-81	Head of State	50	145	325	600	Assassinated Pres.of Egypt
Sade	Entertainment	15			30	
Sade, Marquis de	Author	240	725	2050		Sadist, Sadistic Attributed
Safer, Morley	TV News	5	10		15	60 Minutes
Safire, William	Author	5			15	Journalist
Sagan, Carl, Dr.	Science	10	30	55	25	Am. Astronomer, Author.Pulitzer
Sage, Russell 1816-1906	Business	100	185	812	135	Financier, Speculator/J.Gould
Sagendorf, Bud* 1915-94	Cartoonist	45			250	Popeye after Segar
Sager, Carole Bayer	Composer	5	15	20	10	
Saget, Bob	TV Host	4			10	TV Host
Sahl, Mort	Entertainment	5	8	15	15	Political Humorist
Said, Nuri	Head of State	5	15	35	10	Pr. Minister Iraq
Saint Hilaire, L.V. Jos.	Fr. Revolution	30	75	155		
Saint James, Susan	Entertainment	10			20	
Saint Laurent, Yves	Business	20	35	75	45	Fashion Designer
Saint, Eva Marie	Entertainment	10	15		25	AA
Saint-Cyr, Gouvion	Military	50	175	190		Fr. Marshal, Minister of War
Saint-Exupery, Antoine de	Aviation	50	145	225	135	Fr. Aviator and Author
Saint-Gaudens, Augustus 1848-1907	Artist	100	335	2150	1150	Known For Monumental Projects
Saint-Just, Louis A.L. de	Fr. Revolution	375	1235			Guillotined Fr. Revolutionary
Saint-Saens, Camille 1835-1921	Composer	140	557	438	400	Opera, AMusQS $450-$650-$825
Saito, Hiroshi	Celebrity	5	15	35	20	
Saito, Makoto, Baron	Head of State	85	190	350		Prime Minister Japan
Sakai, Saburo	Aviation	35			85	3rd Highest Japanese Ace
Sakall, S.Z. Cuddles	Entertainment	150			350	Also: Szakall, Szôke

NAME	CATEGORY	SIG	LS/DS	ALS	SP	Comment
Sakharov, Andrei & Elena Bonner	Science	425				Nobel Phys.,Political Activists
Sakharov, Vladmir	Celebrity	20			40	Communist agent
Salalm, Abdus	Science	20	30	55	25	Nobel Physics 1979
Salan, Raoul	Military	20	55	95	50	
Salazar, Jose, Cardinal	Clergy	30	30	35		
Sale, Chic 1885-1937	Entertainment	25	35	65	95	Comedian-Actor
Sales, Soupy	Entertainment	5	8		15	
Saleza, Albert	Entertainment	15			45	Opera
Salinger, J[erome] D[avid]	Author	1575	5075	6500		Novelist "Catcher in the Rye"
Salinger, Pierre	Journalist-Author	40	45	40	20	Press Sec'y Pres. JFK
Salisbury, 3rd Marquis, Robert C.	Head of State	40	45	80		Prime Minister
Salisbury, Frank O. 1874-1962	Artist	25	70	125		Br. Portr. Painter of FDR as Pres., Geo. V, etc.
Salisbury, Harrison	Author	15			25	Pulitzer Journalist, Editor
Salk, Jonas, Dr. 1914-95	Science	50	150	300	225	Polio Vaccine Booklet S $200
Salling, John	Civil War	15	25	50		Union General
Salmi, Albert	Entertainment	25			40	
Salminen, Sally	Author	15	40	75		
Salt, Jennifer	Entertainment	3			10	
Salt, Titus, Sir 1803-76	Business	5	20	40		Pioneer Wool Industry.Inventor
Salten, Felix 1870-1946	Author	75	100	235		Austrian Author of Bambi
Saltonstall, Leverett 1892-1979	Congress	12	20		15	Senator MA
Salvini, Tomaso	Entertainment	45			175	Tragedian with Booth
Sam the Sham	Entertainment	10			20	Rock
Samaroff-Stokowski, Olga	Entertainment	20			88	Acclaimed Pianist,Teacher,Critic
Sambora, Richie	Entertainment	10			35	
Samms, Emma	Entertainment	6	8		20	Pin-Up SP $35
Sammt, Albert	Aviation	30			65	
Samples, Candy	Entertainment	25			60	
Sampson, Will	Entertainment	35	55	85	100	
Sampson, William T.	Military	30	80	135	75	Adm. Cmdr-in-Chief, Sp.-Am. War
Samuel, Herbert	Statesmand	25		150		1st Jew to Govern Palestine Since Romans
Samuelson, Paul A., Dr.	Economics	25	40		35	Nobel Economics
San Giacomo, Laura	Entertainment	15			40	
San Juan, Olga	Entertainment	5			10	
San Martin, Jose de 1778-1850	Head of State	500	800	2650		Soldier Hero of Argentina
Sanborn, Franklin B. 1831-	Author-Reformer	5	15	15	15	Journalist, Editor, Biographer
Sanborn, Katherine A.	Author	5	20	35		
Sand, George (Dudevant)1804-76	Author	100	200	548		Fr. Non—Conformist.ALS/Cont.$3500
Sandburg, Carl 1878-1967	Author-Poet	83	255	305	425	Orig. Pencil Portr. S $750
Sanders, George	Author	5			10	Autograph Price Guide author
Sanders, George	Entertainment	90			165	Laid Back Br. Actor. AA Award
Sanders, Gregg	Entertainment	10	12	25	20	Supporting Actor
Sanders, Harland	Business	25	75	150	90	KFC Colonel Sanders
Sanders, Helen	Author	5			10	Autograph Price Guide expert
Sanders, Horace T.	Civil War	20	35	60		Union General
Sanderson, Julia	Entertainment	10	20	30	30	Vintage Radio/Frank Crummit
Sandoz, Marie	Author	25	70	170	40	
Sands, Tommy	Entertainment	10			15	
Sandwich,4thEarl(Montagu)	Statesman	125	400	550		The Sandwich Attributed To Him
Sanford, Edw. Terry (SC)	Supreme Court	75	195			
Sanford, Isabel	Entertainment	5	7	15	15	
Sanger, Frederick	Science	20	35	60	25	Nobel Chemistry 1958
Sanger, Margaret 1883-1966	Reformer	65	210	350	105	Birth Control Advocate
Sangster, Margaret E.	Author	30	55	175		Journalist, Poet, Editor
Sangster, William E.	Clergy	25	40	55		Br. Meth. Minister-Author
Sankey, Ira D.	Clergy	75	95	150	100	

NAME	CATEGORY	SIG	LS/DS	ALS	SP	Comment
Sankford, Henry	Clergy	35	50	60		
Sano, Roy L., Bishop	Clergy	20	25	35	25	
Sansom, Art	Cartoonist	5			20	The Born Loser
Santa Anna, Antonio L. de 1794-1876	Head of State	235	1775	1570	585	General,Revolutionary,Pres.Mex.
Santa Cruz, Andres 1792-1865	Head of State	95	245			General. Pres.Bolivia. Exiled
Santa Rosa, Annibale S.,Count	Military	25	70	150		It.Piedmontese Insurgent
Santana	Entertainment	10			30	Singer-Musician
Santayana, George	Author	65	175	350		Poet, Philosopher, Critic
Santelmann, William H.	Entertainment		25			Marine Corps Bandmaster
Santley, Charles, Sir	Entertainment	40			175	Baritone. Debut/1857. Retired/1911
Santos, Joe	Entertainment	5	6	15	15	
Santos-Dumont, A.	Aviation	300	390	580	720	Brazil. Aeronaut. PioneerAirman
Santunione, Orianna	Entertainment	5			20	Opera
Saperstein, Abe	Business				150	Owner-Coach Harlem Globetrotters
Sara, Mia	Entertainment	15			50	Actress
Sarandon, Susan	Entertainment	9	15	150	40	Pin-Up SP $55, AA
Sarasate, Pablo de	Composer	100		250		Violin Virtuoso, AMusQS $275
Sardi, Vincent	Business	4	15	25	10	Fndr. Sardi's Restaurant NYC
Sardou, Victorien 1831-1908	Playwright	20	45	125	150	Fr. Librettist, Bourgeois Drama
Sarett, Lew	Author	75	100			
Sarfatti, Margherita	Author	10	30	50		
Sarg, Tony* 1882-1942	Artist	15			75	Illustrator-Marionette Maker
Sargent, Dick	Entertainment	7			20	
Sargent, John G.	Cabinet	15	30	60	25	Att'y General 1925
Sargent, John Singer 1856-1925	Artist	95	245	328		Am. World Famous Portraitist
Sargent, Kenny	Entertainment	20			45	Big Band Singer
Sargent, Winthrop	Revolutionary War	30	100	240		Cont'l Army, 1st Gov. MS Terr.
Sarnoff, David 1891-1971	Business	60	175	145	70	Broadcasting Pioneer
Sarocco, Suzanne	Entertainment	10			25	Opera
Saroyan, William	Author	60	225	285	80	Pulitzer The Time of Your Life
Sartain, John 1808-97	Artist-Engraver	25	85	100		Sartain's Union Magazine
Sarton, May	Author	5	15	40		
Sartre, Jean-Paul 1905-80	Author	100	325	500		Leader Existentialist Movement
Sassoon, Beverly	Entertainment	3	3	6	15	
Sassoon, Siegfried 1886-1967	Author	50	225	338		Br. Poet.Anti-War Verse
Sassoon, Vidal	Business	15	20	25	20	Hair Design & Products
Satie, Erik	Composer	210	825	1650		Eccentric, Avant Garde Music
Sato, Eisaku	Head of State	20	55	150	35	Premier Japan. Nobel Peace
Sauckel, Fritz	Military	50	200			Nazi War Criminal. Hanged
Sauer, Emil	Entertainment	15	15	75	30	
Sauguet, Henri	Composer	65		275	.	Fr. Opera, Ballet AMQS $250
Saulsbury, Grove	Governor	5	15	30		Governor DE
Saumarez, James, Sir, 1757-1836	Military	90	265	600		Br. Adm., Battle of the Nile
Saunders, Alvin	Senate/Congress	15	35	80		Sen.KY, CW Gov. Nebr.Territory
Saunders, Edward Watts	Senate/Congress	10	20			Rep. VA 1906
Saunders, Hugh W.	Aviation	5	10	20	15	
Saunders, John Monk	Entertainment	10	25			ANS 35, writer/director
Saunders, Lori	Entertainment	4			15	
Saunders, Stuart J.	Business	3	7	15	10	
Saunders, Stuart T. 1909-	Business	5			10	CEO Penn-Central RR
Savage, Ann	Entertainment	12	15		35	
Savage, Fred	Entertainment	7			20	
Savage, M. J.	Clergy	15	30	45		
Saval, Dany	Entertainment	5		25	20	Pin-Up SP $25. Fr. Actress
Savalas, George	Entertainment	15			40	
Savalas, Telly	Entertainment	15			40	

The Sanders Price Guide to Autographs

NAME	CATEGORY	SIG	LS/DS	ALS	SP	Comment
Savitch, Jessica	Journalist	20			95	TV-News.Died Young in Car Accident
Savitt, Jan	Bandleader	15			45	
Savles, Thomas F, Bishop	Clergy	30	40			
Savoia, Attilio	Artist	15	40	75		
Sawyer, Charles	Cabinet	5	25	30	10	Sec'y Commerce 1948
Sawyer, Diane	Journalist	5	20		25	TV Broadcast Journalist
Sawyer, Joe	Entertainment	75			200	
Sax, Adolphe	Science	55	180	375		Invented Saxophone & Others
Saxbe, William B.	Cabinet	8	12	20	15	Att'y General 1974
Saxe, John G.	Author	10	30	55	30	
Saxon, John	Entertainment	5			15	
Saxon, Rufus, Jr.	Civil War	25	55	70		Union General
Sayao, Bidu	Entertainment	15			75	Opera Soprano
Sayers, Dorothy 1893-1957	Author	200	425	575	125	Br. Mystery Novelist
Saylor, Anna, Mrs.	Socialite	5	10			
Scacchi, Greta	Entertainment	10			40	
Scaggs, Boz	Entertainment	15			35	
Scagliarini, Eleanora	Entertainment	10			40	Opera
Scalchi Lolly	Entertainment	35			75	
Scales, Alfred M.(War Date)	Civil War	165		342		CSA Gen. Sig $90-110
Scalia, Antonin (SC)	Supreme Court	30	90		55	
Scalia, Jack	Entertainment	10			25	
Scammell, Alexander 1746-81	Revolutionary War	350		1500		Officer. Wounded Died 1781
Scancarelli, Jim*	Cartoonist	10			45	Gasoline Alley
Scarborough, John	Clergy	10	15	20		
Scarlatti, Alessandro 1660-1725	Composer	725	4150	12000		115 Operas, Over 600 Cantatas
Scarwid, Diana	Entertainment	5		15	20	
Schaal, Richard	Entertainment	3	3	6	8	
Schaal, Wendy	Entertainment	3	3	6	6	
Schacht, Hjalmar	WWII	60	160	300		Nazi Minister WW II
Schafer, Natalie	Entertainment	20			35	
Schaff, Phillip	Clergy	40	55	75	50	
Schaffner, Franklin J.	Entertainment	30			75	
Schaffner, Hans	Head of State	10			20	Pres. Austria
Schall, Thomas D.	Senate/Congress	5	15			Rep., Senator MN 1915
Schallert, William	Entertainment	5	6	15	15	
Schally, Andrew V., Dr.	Science	22	30	45	30	Nobel Medicine 1977
Schanberg, Sydney, H.	Author	10	30	75	15	
Scharwenka, Franz Xavier	Composer	25		75	150	Pianist.Founder of Conservatory
Schary, Dore	Entertainment	15		25	30	Producer, Director, Writer
Schary, Emanuel	Artist	10	25	35		
Schawlow, Arthur L., Dr.	Science	22	30	35	25	Nobel Physics 1981
Scheer, Reinhard 1863-1928	Military	20	45	95	40	Ger. Adm. Battle of Jutland.
Scheff, Fritzi 1882-1954	Entertainment	20	15	30	25	Theatre & Silent Films
Scheidemann, Philippe	Head of State	10	20	50	40	1st Chancellor of Repub. 1919
Scheider, Roy	Entertainment	10			25	
Schell, Maria	Entertainment	5	7	20	15	
Schell, Maximillian	Entertainment	10	15	35	30	AA
Schenck, Robert C.	Civil War	35	45	70		Union Gen., Rep OH, Ambassador
Scherer, Paul	Clergy	20	25	40	30	
Schick, Bela, Dr.	Science	60	135	225	75	Schick Test for TB
Schiele, Egon	Artist		1400			Austrian Expressionist Painter
Schiff, Jacob H.	Business	15	40	65		
Schiffer, Claudia	Entertainment	20			45	Pin-Up SP $55
Schifrin, Lalo	Composer	5	15	25	25	AMusQS $40
Schildkraut, Joseph	Entertainment	75	150		150	Oscar winner

NAME	CATEGORY	SIG	LS/DS	ALS	SP	Comment
Schiller, Hans von	Aviation	20		45		
Schilling, David	Aviation	18	38	60	45	ACE, WW II
Schine, G. David	Business	20			40	Hotel Chain Owner
Schiotz, Fredrik A.	Clergy	20	25	35	30	
Schipa, Tito	Entertainment	45			142	Opera. Important Tenor
Schirach, Baldur Von	Ger. Politician	125	515			Nat'l Dir.Hitler Youth Movement
Schirra, Walter M.	Astronaut	20	75	168	75	Mercury 7 Astro.
Schlafly, Phyllis	Political	10	20	35	25	Activist, Feminist
Schlafly, Phyllis, Mrs.	Activist	10			35	
Schlesinger, Arthur Jr.	Author	10	30	50	15	
Schlesinger, James R.	Cabinet	5	10	25	15	Sec'y Defense 1973
Schlesinger, John	Entertainment	5			20	Film Director
Schley, Winfield Scott 1839-1909	Military	100	260	400	375	Arctic rescue of Greely
Schliemann, Heinrich 1822-90	Archaeologist	245		1780		ALS re Mycenae $5,000
Schmalz, Wilhelm	Military	15	40	75	30	
Schmidt, Friedrich	Astronaut	30				
Schmidt, Helmut	Head of State	15	25	40	20	Ger. Political Leader, Chanc.
Schmidt, Maarten, Dr.	Science	10	25	30	20	
Schmidtmer, Christiane	Entertainment	4			15	Ger. Actress. Pin-Up SP $25
Schmitt, Harrison H.	Astronaut	15		185	67	Apollo 17 Moonwalker
Schmitt-Walter, Karl	Entertainment	10			35	Opera. Baritone. Wide Repertoire
Schnabel, Artur	Entertainment	40	135	190		Austrian Pianist
Schnaut, Gabriella	Entertainment	5			25	Opera
Schneider, John	Entertainment	4	10		15	Singer-Actor
Schneider, Romy	Entertainment	75			130	
Schnelder,Wm. C.(SKYLAB)	Astronaut	6			20	
Schochet, Bob*	Cartoonist	5			35	
Schoenberg, Arnold 1874-1951	Composer	300	1133		675	AMusQS $2,250
Schoene, Heinrich	Military	125	450		195	Ger. Gen. Storm Trooper
Schoenebeck, Karl August	Aviation	30	65		75	
Schoenert, Rudolf	Aviation	10	20	40	25	
Schoepfel, Gerhard	Aviation	5	15	25	15	
Schofield, John Arthur	Civil War	98		185		Union General
Schofield, John M. (War Date)	Civil War	125	155	340		Union General, Sec'y War 1868
Schofield, John M.1831-1906	Civil War	45	80	160		Union Gen.
Schopenhauer, Arthur	Author	700	17500	5000		Ger. Philosopher
Schorner, Ferdinand	Military	40		120		
Schrader, Paul	Entertainment	5	15		20	Film Director
Schram, Emil	Business	3	10	20	5	
Schramm, Margit	Entertainment	5			15	Opera, Operetta
Schreiber, Avery	Entertainment	3	5	8	12	
Schricker, Henry F.	Governor	5	20		10	Governor IN
Schrieffer, John R.	Science	10	20	35	15	Nobel Physics 1972
Schriver, Edmund	Civil War	40	90	125		Union General
Schroder, Ricky	Entertainment	10			35	
Schroeder, Patricia	Senate/Congress	5	10		15	Rep. CO
Schroeder-Feinen, Ursula	Entertainment	5			30	Opera
Schroer, Werner	Aviation				65	Ger. Ace WW II. RK
Schroeteler, Heinrich	Military				60	Ger. Capt. U-667,U1023. RK
Schubert, Franz	Composer	2200	5400	10000		
Schuk, Walter	Aviation	25	45		85	Ger. 12th Highest ACE
Schulberg, Budd	Author	5	55		10	Novelist, Screenwriter
Schuller, Robert	Clergy	15	20		25	
Schultz, Theodore William	Agri-Science	10	15	25		Nobel Economics
Schulz, Charles	Cartoonist	85			268	
Schulz, Charles*	Cartoonist	100	175	680	395	Peanuts S Orig. Strip $1,500+-

The Sanders Price Guide to Autographs

NAME	CATEGORY	SIG	LS/DS	ALS	SP	Comment
Schulze, William	Science	15			45	Rocket Pioneer/von Braun
Schuman, William	Composer	10	30	75	60	
Schumann, Clara 1819-96	Pianist-Composer	60	165	385	920	ALS/Content $3,000
Schumann, Elizabeth	Entertainment	40			130	Opera
Schumann, Robert 1810-56	Composer	815	1100	4250	5000	Ger. Early 19th Cent, Romantic Music
Schumann-Heink, Ernestine	Entertainment	45		105	150	Opera, Concert. Contralto
Schurz, Carl 1829-1906	Civil War	45	102	150		Union Gen., U.S.Sen. MO
Schuschnigg, Kurt von	Head of State	50	85	220	75	Deposed Austrian Chancellor
Schuyler, Philip J. 1733-1804	Revolutionary War	200	568	922		Soldier, Statesman
Schwab, Charles M.1862-1939	Industrialist	30	65	105	100	Pres. Carnegie,US & Bethlehem
Schwab, Frank X.	Political	5	20			Mayor Buffalo, NY
Schwantner, Joseph	Composer	10		55	40	Pulitzer, AMusQS $95
Schwartz, Arthur	Composer					Dancing in the Dark AMQS on Ph. $410
Schwartz, Melvin, Dr 1932-	Science	24			30	Nobel Physics 1988
Schwarzenegger, Arnold	Entertainment	30	35	75	100	
Schwarzkopf, Elizabeth	Entertainment	15			50	Opera
Schwarzkopf, Norman	Military	30	125		90	Gen. Desert Storm
Schwatka, Frederick	Celebrity	10	20	55		
Schwedtman, Ferd. D.	Science	5	15		10	
Schweickart, Russell L.	Astronaut	7			25	
Schweiker, Richard S.	Senate/Congress	5	10		10	Rep., Senator PA 1961
Schweitzer, Albert, Dr. 1875-1965	Science-Music	162	560	995	789	Nobel. Clergy. 3x4 SP $650
Schwellenback, Lewis B.	Cabinet	10	35	70	15	Sec'y Labor 1945
Schwimmer, David	Entertainment	15			60	Actor. Friends
Schwinger, Julian, Dr.	Science	20	30	55	25	Nobel Physics 1965
Sciorra, Annabella	Entertainment	10			30	
Scobee, Dick	Astronaut		425		175	Challenger Victim
Scofield, Glenni W.	Senate/Congress	10	15	25		Rep. PA 1863
Scofield, Paul	Entertainment	10		150	35	AA
Scoggins, Tracy	Entertainment	5	8	25	20	Pin-Up SP $50
Scopes, John T. 1900-70	Educator	200	1800		1495	Defendant In Monkey Trial
Scorsese, Martin	Entertainment	20			47	Film Director
Scorupco, Izabella	Entertainment	5				Actress.Golden Eye Pin-Up 55
Scott, Blanch Stuart 1891-1970	Aviation				492	1st Fem. Pilot to Solo
Scott, Charles	Revolutionary War	90	195	350		General, Indian Fighter,Gov.KY
Scott, Charles Wm. A.	Aviation	25	50	80	50	Br. Won Harmon Trophy
Scott, Cyril Meir	Composer	15	50	105	20	Br. Orchestral, Piano, Chamber
Scott, David C.	Business	5	10		10	CEO Allis-Chalmers
Scott, David R.	Astronaut	10			295	Moonwalker
Scott, Eric	Entertainment	4	6		10	
Scott, Fred	Entertainment	20			55	Vintage Cowboy Actor
Scott, George C.	Entertainment	20			85	AA Patton
Scott, Gordon	Entertainment	15			35	
Scott, Gustavus	Revolutionary War	35	90	140		Lawyer, Patriot (MD)
Scott, Hazel	Entertainment	35	45		130	Piano-Organ
Scott, Hugh	Senate/Congress	5	15		25	Senator PA
Scott, Jack	Entertainment	10			25	Rock
Scott, Jerry*	Cartoonist	10			45	Nancy
Scott, John Morin	Revolutionary War	35	85	150		General, Patriot, Rep.NY
Scott, Lizabeth	Entertainment	8	10		20	Pin-Up SP $25
Scott, Martha	Entertainment	5			20	
Scott, Pippa	Entertainment	6			15	Actress
Scott, Randolph 1898-1987	Entertainment	40	50		85	
Scott, Raymond	Composer	25	40	65	50	Big Band Leader, Arranger
Scott, Robert Falcon	Explorer	90	255	500	195	Br. Arctic Expeditions
Scott, Robert Kingston	Civil War	55				Union Gen.,Scoundrel Gov. SC

NAME	CATEGORY	SIG	LS/DS	ALS	SP	Comment
Scott, Robert Lee, Jr.	Aviation	15	35	55	38	ACE, WW II, God's Co-Pilot
Scott, Thomas	Clergy	40	50	75		
Scott, W. Kerr	Senate	5			25	Gov. NC 1949, Senator NC 1954
Scott, Walter, Sir 1771-1832	Author	135	675	903		Poet, Novelist, Historian
Scott, Willard	Entertainment	4	4		10	
Scott, William R.	Business	5	15			RR Exec.
Scott, Winfield (War Date)	Civil War	175	490	682		Union General
Scott, Winfield 1786-1866	Civil War	125	338	622	450	Union Gen., Pres. Candidate
Scott, Zachary	Entertainment	25			50	
Scotti, Antonio	Entertainment	40			185	It. Baritone, Opera
Scotto, Renata	Entertainment	15			50	Opera
Scowcroft, Brent	Military	10	30		20	Gen., Statesman,Pres. Advisor
Scranton, Bill	Governor	5	15		15	Gov. PA. Pres. Candidate
Scriabin, Alexander 1872-1915	Composer	650	3500	5000	3200	Rus.Symphonies, etc.AMusQS $3500
Scribe, Eugene 1791-1861	Author	10	35	60		Fr. Librettist.Meyerbeer,Halevy
Scrimm, Angus	Entertainment	6			20	Actor
Scripps, William E.	Aviation	15	90		40	
Scudder, Horace E.1838-1902	Author	10	30	55		Ed.Atlantic Mnthly, Biographer
Scuderi, Sara	Entertainment	34			85	Opera
Scullin, James H. 1876-1953	Head of State	40				P.M. Australia
Scully, Thomas	Artist	190	375	650		
Scully-Power, Paul	Astronaut	25				
Seaborg, Glenn	Science	40	77	150	75	Chm. AEC. Nobel Chemistry 1951
Seaforth, Susan	Entertainment	5			20	Pin-Up SP $30
Seals, Dan	Country Music	5			15	
Searle, Ronald	Artist	10	35	80		
Sears, Edmund	Clergy	20	25	35		
Seaton, George	Entertainment	35			70	Film Director
Seawell, Molly Elliot	Author	5	15	35	10	
Seawell, William T.	Business	3	10	15	15	
Sebastini, H.F.B. 1772-1851	Fr. Military		80	150		Gen. under Napoleon, Marshal of Fr.
Seberg, Jean	Entertainment	75	75		155	Early Suicide
Sechelles, Marie-Jean Herault de	Fr. Revolution			895		Att'y to Louis XVI
Sedaka, Neil	Composer	5			25	And Entertainer
Seddon, James A. (War Date)	Civil War	170	550	2350		CSA Sec'y War Dte. DS $1,000
Seddon, Margaret R.	Astronaut	6			20	
Sedgewick, John	Civil War	135	350			Union General (Uncle John)
Sedgwick, Catherine M.1789-1867	Author	10	20	45		Am. Early Novelist. Moral Tales
Sedgwick, John 1813-64	Civil War	200	895			Union Gen. KIA. Twice Breveted
Sedgwick, Kyra	Entertainment	15			75	Actress
See, Elliot M. Jr.	Astronaut	225			250	
Seeburg, Justus Percival	Business	40	120	195		
Seeger, Pete	Composer	20	50	95	40	Folk Singer
Seeley, Blossom	Entertainment	5	6	15	15	
Seeley, Jeannie	Country Music	10			20	
Seelye, Julius Hawtry	Clergy	15	20	25		College Pres., Rep.MA
Segal, Erich	Author	20				Love Story
Segal, George	Artist	25		35		
Segal, George	Entertainment	5	8	15	25	
Segal, Steven	Entertainment	15			60	
Segar, Elzie C.*	Cartoonist	125			575	Popeye
Segar, Joseph E.	Senate/Congress	10	20			Rep. VA 1862
Seger, Bob	Entertainment	20			40	
Seger, C.B.	Business	15	45	85	40	
Segovia, Andres	Entertainment	120		475	140	Classical Guitar Virtuoso
Segre, Emilio, Dr.	Science	20	35	50	30	Nobel Physics 1959

NAME	CATEGORY	SIG	LS/DS	ALS	SP	Comment
Segura, Wiltz	Aviation	15	25	40	30	ACE, WW II, USAAF Ace
Segurola, Andres de	Entertainment	45			150	Sp. Bass
Seidel, Toscha	Entertainment	20			75	Noted Rus.-Am. Violinist
Seidelman, Susan	Entertainment	5	10		10	Film Director
Seignolle, Claude	Author	120	175	220		
Seinfeld (Cast)	Entertainment	150			337	Four Main Characters
Seinfeld (Show-Cast of)	Entertainment				345	Four Main Characters
Seinfeld, Jerry	Entertainment	15			40	
Seipel, Ignas Dr.	Head of State	10	30	80	40	Austrian Prelate & Chancellor
Seka	Entertainment	9	10	20	25	Pin-Up SP $35
Selassie, Haile 1891-1975	Head of State	200	380	740	900	Emperor of Ethiopia
Selfridge, Harry G.	Business	10	40	110	35	Founder Selfridge's, London
Selfridge, Thos. O.	Civil War	40	85	120		Union Naval Commander
Sellecca, Connie	Entertainment	10			30	
Selleck, Tom	Entertainment	10	15	25	30	
Sellers, David Foote	Military	20	55	95	50	
Sellers, Peter 1925-1980	Entertainment	95			150	British comic actor
Sellers, Winfield S.	Military	15	40	75	40	
Selman, John	Outlaw-Lawman	1200	3000			
Selznick, David O.	Business	108	400		150	Film Producer (GWTW)
Selznick, Irene	Entertainment	10	15		20	Film Executive
Sembrich, Marcella 1858-1935	Entertainment	85		300	228	Opera, Concert. Polish Soprano
Semenov, Nikolai	Science		95		75	Rus. Chem., Physicist. Nobel 1956
Semmelweis, Ignaz 1818-65	Science	500	1200	3200		Hung. Obstetrician.Antisepsis
Semmes, Paul J. 1815-63	Civil War	912	1372	900		CSA Gen. Sig/Rank $1450
Semmes, Raphael	Civil War	292	750	1525	1500	CSA Admiral Sig/Rank $475
Semple, James 1798-1866	Congress	15				Sen. IL, Elsa, IL Founder
Senechal, Michel	Entertainment	5			25	Opera
Senn, Nicholas	Civil War	35		140		Union Surgeon
Sennett, Mack 1880-1960	Entertainment	312	1012		550	Historic DS $4,500
Sergeant, John	Celebrity	10	20	35		
Sergeant, John 1779-1852	Congress	15	35	55		Rep.PA. ALS/Cont $1600
Sergievsky, Boris	Aviation	75			150	
Serkin, Rudolf	Entertainment	40		155	125	Piano Virtuoso, AMusQS $175
Serling, Rod	Author-Entertain.	125	260	375	340	
Serpico, Frank	Law	10	20	45	20	Undercover Detective-Hero
Serurier, Jean M.P., Count	Fr. Revolution	50	145	215		Marshal of Napoleon
Service, Robert W.	Author	75		260	400	Canadian Poet, Author
Sessions, Roger	Composer	15	45	165		Pulitzer, AMusQS $250
Sessions, William L.	Government	25	75		30	Dir. FBI
Seton, Ernest Thompson	Author	55	95	230	60	Help Found Boy Scouts of Am.
Seuss, Dr. (Theodore S. Geisel)*	Author	100	310		612	Orig. Sketch on FDC S $950
Severance, Joan	Entertainment	5			25	Nude Pin-UP S $85
Severeid, Eric	Journalist	10			25	TV-Radio Broadcast Journalist
Severeid, Susanne	Model	4			15	Pin-Up SP $20, Actress
Severinson, Doc	Entertainment	6	8	25	20	Trumpet, Big Band
Sevier, John 1745-1815	Revolutionary War	615	1875	750		Historical DS $3,750
Sewall, David	Revolutionary War	20	50	110		Jurist, Patriot, Justice Peace
Sewall, Samuel 1652-1730	Colonial America	275	1000	1300		Salem Witchcraft Trials
Sewall, Samuel 1757-1814	Senate/Congress	25		60		Rep. MA 1796.MA Chief Justice
Seward, Frederick Wm.(son of W.H.)	Cabinet	30	55	80		Ass't Sec'y State
Seward, William H. 1801-72	Cabinet	75	260	160	745	LS/Re Assassination $1,750
Sewell, William J. 1835-1901	Civil War	40	90	130		Union Gen., U.S. Sen. NJ
Sexton, Walton R.	Military	10	30	45	30	Adm. US Navy. WW II
Seymour, Anne	Entertainment	10			20	
Seymour, George F., Bishop	Clergy	25	25	40		

NAME	CATEGORY	SIG	LS/DS	ALS	SP	Comment
Seymour, Horatio 1810-1886	Governor	30	60	80		Civil War Gov. NY. Pres. Candidate
Seymour, Jane	Entertainment	10			30	Pin-Up SP $30
Seymour, Stephanie	Entertainment	20			45	Model-Actress
Seymour, Truman	Civil War	75	110	205		Union General
Shackelford, Ted	Entertainment	5			15	
Shackleton, Ernest H., Sir 1874-1922	Explorer	200	400	400	450	Br. Antarctic Explorer
Shaffer, Paul	Entertainment	5			15	
Shaffer, Peter L.	Author	10	20	35	15	
Shafter, William H. 1835-1906	Civil War	15	95	75	35	Union Gen. MOH. Indian Fighter
Shafter, William R.	Civil War	35	55	110	150	Union Gen.
Shaftesbury, A.A.C.7th Earl 1801-85	Reformer	25	75	160		Politician, M.P.
Shah, Zahir	Royalty	50				King Afghanistan
Shahn, Ben	Artist	55	150	240	145	Am.Painter-Graphic Artist
Shalamar	Entertainment	12	15	60	50	
Shaler, Alexander	Civil War	35	60	110		Union General
Shalikashvili, John	Military	10	25		20	Chm. Joint Chiefs of Staff
Shamir, Yitzhak	Head of State	20	30	55	70	Prime Minister Israel
Shamroy, Leon	Entertainment	20				Director, Cinematographer. AA
Shannon, Del	Entertainment	35			80	Country Music
Shannon, Wilson	Governor	25	65	100		Kansas Peacmaker 1870
Shapiro, Harry	Artist	10	25	45		
Shapiro, Karl	Author	10	30	70	20	
Shapiro, Robert	Law		125		37	O.J. Simpson Trial Attorney
Shapley, Alan	Military	10	35	50		
Shapley, Harlow 1885-1972	Science	35	275	150		Astronomer. Dlr.Harvard Observ.
Shapp, Milton J.	Governor	10	20			Governor PA
Sharan, Shri Chakradhar	Head of State	15	35		75	Pres. India
Sharett, Moshe (Shertok)	Head of State	45		275		Israeli Prime Minister
Sharif, Omar	Entertainment	20	25	65	75	
Sharkey, Ray	Entertainment	7			30	
Sharnova, Sonia	Entertainment	10			25	Am. Contralto
Sharon, Ariel	Military	20	50	90	45	Israeli General, Politician
Sharon, William	Senate-Business	45	110	200		Senator NV, Banker & Financier
Sharp, U. S. Grant	Military	10	25	35	15	
Sharp, William	Artist	15	40	105		
Sharpe, George H.	Civil War	20	45			Union Gen., Diplomat
Sharpe, Karen	Entertainment	4	6		8	
Sharpe, William, Dr.	Economist	22	30		25	Nobel Enconomics 1990
Shatner, William	Entertainment	12	15		50	Star Trek SP $75
Shaud, Grant	Entertainment	10			30	Murphy Brown
Shaunessy, Charles	Entertainment	5	6	15	15	
Shavelson, Melville	Entertainment	5	10		25	
Shaver, Helen	Entertainment	10			25	
Shaw, Anna Howard 1847-1919	Women's Rights	35	80	175		Physician, Suffragist, Clergy
Shaw, Artie	Entertainment	25			60	Big Band Leader-Clarinetist
Shaw, Bernard	Journalist	10			25	TV Broadcast Journalist
Shaw, Brewster H.	Astronaut	6			15	
Shaw, George Bernard 1856-1950	Author	283	1005	1392	1630	Ir. Playwright, Critic. Nobel
Shaw, Irwin	Author	25	70	170	40	Am.Novelist, Short Story Writer
Shaw, Lemuel	Revolutionary War	15	40	75		Chf.Justice MA Supreme Court
Shaw, Leslie M. 1848-1932	Cabinet	30	35	50		Sec'y Treasury 1902
Shaw, Robert	Entertainment	40			150	Conductor Robert Shaw Chorale
Shawn, Dick	Entertainment	40			100	
Shawn, Ted	Entertainment	45			100	Am. Dancer-Choreographer
Shay, John	Entertainment	4	6		10	
Shayne, Robert	Entertainment	10			30	

NAME	CATEGORY	SIG	LS/DS	ALS	SP	Comment
Shazar, Zalman	Head of State	20			60	Israel
Shea, George Beverly	Clergy	15	20	25	30	Singing Evangelist
Shea, John	Entertainment	4			15	Actor
Shea, William A.	Business	5	20	40	10	
Shear, Rhonda	Entertainment	4			10	TV Personality
Shearer, Moira	Entertainment	20		50	75	Ballet. Red Shoes
Shearer, Norma 1902-83	Entertainment	88	105		320	AA. Bull Orig. SP $650
Shearing, George	Entertainment	20			45	Jazz Pianist
Sheedy, Ally	Entertainment	6	15		30	
Sheehan, John	Entertainment	10				Character Actor
Sheen, Charlie	Entertainment	8	15		25	
Sheen, Fulton J.,	Clergy-TV Star	50		200	50	Archbishop Rochester, NY
Sheen, Martin	Entertainment	9	45		25	AA
Sheffer, Chris	Entertainment	6	8	15	15	
Sheffield, Johnny	Entertainment	10			25	
Shehan, Lawrence J., Cardinal	Clergy	35	45	50	60	
Shelby, Isaac 1750-1826	Revolutionary War	325	350	550		Officer VA Militia. 1st Gov. KY
Shelby, Joseph O. (War Date)	Civil War	450				CSA Gen.
Shelby, Joseph O. 1830-97	Civil War	280	1519	1250	1950	CSA General
Sheldon, Charles M.	Clergy	20	35	50	40	
Sheldon, Sidney	Author	5	15	25	15	Am. Novelist
Shelley, Mary Wollstonecraft	Author	475		1250		Frankenstein
Shelley, Percy Bysshe	Author	1060	2500	4375		ALS/Content $14,000
Shelton, Deborah	Entertainment	8	9		20	Pin-Up SP $30, Miss USA
Shepard, Alan B.	Astronaut	50	65	95	95	Mercury 7 Astro., Moonwalker
Shepherd, Cybill	Entertainment	15	25		50	Pin-Up SP $40
Shepherd, William M.	Astronaut	5			15	
Sheppard, Dick	Clergy	25	35	50	30	
Sheppard, Morris	Senator/Congress	10	20		15	Rep.,Sen. TX.Author 18th Amend.
Shera, Mark	Entertainment	5			20	
Sheridan, Ann	Entertainment	50			120	40's Oomph Girl
Sheridan, Nicollette	Entertainment	15			35	Pin-Up SP $60
Sheridan, Philip H. (War Date)	Civil War	295	1500	4500	2175	Union Gen.
Sheridan, Philip H. 1831-88	Civil War	213	580	598	1765	Union Cmdg. Gen.
Sheridan, Richard Brinsley	Author	65	120	325		Ir. Dramatist
Sherlock, Nancy	Astronaut	7			15	
Sherman, Forrest P.	Military	20	50	95	50	Adm.WW II.Ch. Naval Operationsl
Sherman, Frederick C.	Military	20	45	70	35	Adm. Cmdr Carrier Lexington
Sherman, George	Entertainment	10			25	
Sherman, James S. (V)	Vice President	75	225	325	230	
Sherman, John 1823-1900	Cabinet-Senate	95		95	85	Sherman Anti-Trust Act, OH
Sherman, Richard and Robert	Composer	40	60	100		AMusQS $150
Sherman, Roger 1721-93	Revolutionary War	212	665	975		Signed All 4 Major Fed. Papers
Sherman, Thomas West	Civil War	30	55	85		Union General
Sherman, William T. (War Date)	Civil War	435	1750	5950	2000	Content ALS's go up to & incl.$50,000+
Sherman, William T.1820-91	Civil War	388	575	1185	2000	Union Gen.War. Content ALS '74 $7500
Sherriff, Robert C. 1896-1975	Author	45		140	80	Playwright, Novelist, Screenwriter
Sherwood, (Mary) Martha 1775-1851	Author	10	15	35		Br. Author Juvenile Tales
Sherwood, Bobby	Entertainment	6	8	15	15	
Sherwood, Isaac R.	Senate/Congress	10	15		20	Rep. OH 1873
Sherwood, Percy	Composer	25			60	Ger. Pianist. AMusQS $75
Sherwood, Robert E. 1896-	Author-Cabinet	30	95	195	50	Am.Plays,Speeches FDR,Pulitzers
Sherwood, Samuel 1779-1862	Cogress	20	35	50		Rep. NY 1813
Shields, Arthur	Entertainment	10			25	Actor-Brother Barry Fitzgerald
Shields, Brooke	Entertainment	9	10	35	35	Pin-Up SP $36
Shields, James	Civil War	50	80	115		Union Gen., U.S Sen.IL,MN,MO

NAME	CATEGORY	SIG	LS/DS	ALS	SP	Comment
Shigeta, James	Entertainment	6	8	15	20	
Shillaber, Benjamin P.1814-90	Author		50	110		Humorist-Editor
Shimmerman, Armin	Entertainment	15			35	Star Trek
Shinn, Conrad S.	Aviation		35		25	Landed 1st Plane at So.Pole
Shipman, Nina	Entertainment	4			15	Hawaiian Leading Lady
Shippen, Edward	Revolutionary War	45	95	165		Ch. Justice PA, Statesman
Shipstad, Henrik 1881-1960	Congress	5	20		25	Senator MN 1922
Shiras, George, Jr. (SC)	Supreme Court	75	250	375		
Shire, David	Composer	15			30	Oscar winner
Shire, Talia	Entertainment	15			35	
Shirer, William L.	Author	15	40		20	News Commentator
Shirley, Anne	Entertainment	15	15	35	30	
Shirley, William 1693-1771	Colon'l Gov. MA	178	465	885		Cmdr.-in-Chief, Explorer, Author
Shivers, Allan	Governor	12			30	Governor TX
Shockley, William, Dr.	Science	35	100	150	100	Nobel Physics 1956
Shoemaker, Eugene M. & Carolyn	Science	45			75	Discovered Meteor Crater
Shoemaker, Lazarus D.	Senate/Congress	10	20		15	Rep. PA 1871
Shoemaker, William L.	Author	5	8	15		
Shoen, Sam	Business	5	15	35	25	
Shoma, William	Aviation	15	32	50	40	ACE, WW II, CMH
Shoop, Pamela Susan	Entertainment	5	6	15	15	
Shor, Bernard Toots	Business	30	45	75	35	NY Restaurateur.Celebrity Host
Shore, Dinah	Entertainment	20	58	100	50	Singer-Actress-TV Host
Short, Bobby	Entertainment	5			20	Nightclub Pianist-Vocalist
Short, Martin	Entertainment	15			50	
Shortridge, Samuel 1861-1952	Congress	10	20			Senator CA 1920
Shostakovich, Dmitri 1906-75	Composer	450	1050	1158	2000	ALS/Content $3,200, 4000
Shoumatoff, Elizabeth	Artist	25	45	60		FDR Portrait AT Time Of Death
Shoup, David M.	Military	15	40	75	35	
Shoup, Francis, A. 1834-96	Civil War	85		348		CSA Gen. Sig/Rank $120
Shoup, George L. 1836-1904	Congress	12	20	35		1st Gov. ID, Senator ID 1890
Showalter, Max	Entertainment	6	10	15	15	
Shower, Kathy	Entertainment	5				Actress-Model. Nude SP 60
Shrimpton, Jean	Entertainment	5	6	15	10	
Shriner, Herb	Entertainment	4	5		15	
Shriver, Edmund v1812-99	Civil War	20	40			Union Gen.
Shriver, Eunice Kennedy	Celebrity	15			35	Sister JFK,Wife Sargent Shriver
Shriver, Loren J.	Astronaut	5			15	
Shriver, Maria	Journalist	6			15	Broadcast Journalist
Shriver, Sargent	White House	4	10	25	20	Created Job Corps
Shroyer, Sonny	Entertainment	3			7	
Shrum, Cal	Entertainment	4			25	Cowboy Actor
Shubert, John	Entertainment	5	9		15	
Shubert, Lee 1873-1953	Business	20	70	85	40	Theatrical Mgr.-Producer
Shue, Elizabeth	Entertainment	10			35	Actress. Pin-Up S $60
Shugart, Alan	Inventor	10	20		20	Computer Disk Drive
Shulman, Ellen L.	Astronaut	6			20	
Shulman, Max	Writer	10			20	Creator Dobie Gillis
Shultz, George P.	Cabinet	15	25	55	50	Sec'y State, Labor, Treasury
Shuman, Charles B.	Celebrity	3	7	15	5	
Shuster, W. Morgan	Business	10	15	35	15	Chm.Appleton-Century-Crofts
Sibelius, Jan 1865-1957	Composer	397	950	1625	1085	Fin.Symph.AMusQS $1850-3500
Sibley, Henry H. 1816-86	Civil War	100	450	438		CSA Gen.,Pioneer, Indian Fighter. Gov MN
Sickles, Daniel E. 1819-1914	Civil War	110	225	200	175	Union General, CMH winner
Sickles, Noel*	Cartoonist	20			175	Scorchy
Siddons, F. Scott, Mrs.	Entertainment	25			50	Vintage Actress

NAME	CATEGORY	SIG	LS/DS	ALS	SP	Comment
Siddons, Sarah Kemble 1755-1831	Entertainment	215		860		Br. Tragedienne
Sidmouth, Viscount 1757-1844	Head of State	35	65	120		Henry Addington, Prime Minister
Sidney, George	Entertainment	15			35	Film Director
Sidney, Sylvia	Entertainment	10	15	25	25	
Siegbahn, Kai Manne	Science	30	55	100	90	Nobel Physics 1981
Siegbahn, Karl Manne G.	Science	35	65	130	100	Nobel Physics 1924
Siegel & Shuster*	Cartoonist	150			900	Superman
Siegel, Don	Entertainment	20	65		40	Film Director
Siegel, Franz	Civil War	40	85	200		Union General
Siegel, Jerry 1915-96	Entertainment	10	25		15	One of Creators. Superman
Siegel, Joel	Journalist	4			10	TV Film Reviewer
Siegfried & Roy	Entertainment	10			20	Animal Trainers
Siegmeister, Elie	Composer	25	85	175	40	
Siems, Margarethe	Entertainment	45			110	Opera
Sienkiewicz, Henryk 1846-1916	Author			350		Polish Writer. Nobel. Quo Vadis
Siepi, Cesare	Entertainment	10			80	Opera. Self-Taught Bass
Sierra, Gregory	Entertainment	4	4	9	9	
Sierra, Margarita	Entertainment	3	3	6	6	
Sigall, Joseph	Artist	100	190	385		Pres. Portraits & Eur. Royalty
Sigel, Franz 1824-1902	Civil War	75	115	200		Union General
Sighele, Mietta	Entertainment	10			30	Opera
Sigler, Kim	Governor	5	15		10	Governor MI
Signac, Paul	Artist	75	170	400		Watercolor Land & Seascapes
Signoret, Simone	Entertainment	65			150	Oscar winner
Sigsbee, Charles D.	Military	35	105	165	75	Capt. USN The Maine
Sihanouk, Norodom, Prince	Head of State	125	95	140	75	Cambodia
Sikes, Cynthia	Entertainment	5			15	Pin-up SP $25
Sikking, James B.	Entertainment	6	8	15	15	
Sikorsky, Igor I. 1889-1972	Aviation	85	308	350	367	Designed & Built 1st Helicopter
Silja, Anja	Entertainment	15			40	Opera
Silliman, Benjamin 1816-85	Science	30	65	125		Am.Chemist. Editor. Professor
Sills, Beverly	Entertainment	15		125	35	Am. Soprano
Sills, Milton 1882-1930	Entertainment	30	40	75	80	Leading Man of Silent Films
Silver, Abba Hillel	Zionist	15	50			Zionist Leader
Silver, Ron	Entertainment	15			40	Actor-Director
Silverheels, Jay	Entertainment	175			500	
Silverman, Fred	Business	3	9	20	10	Broadcasting Executive
Silverman, Jonathan	Entertainment	5			10	
Silverman, Robert	Entertainment	10	15		45	Contemporary Pianist
Silvers, Phil 1912-85	Entertainment	42	50		105	Am. Comedian-Actor
Silverstone, Alicia	Entertainment		35		52	Actress. Pin-Up SP $80
Sim, Alastair !900-76	Entertainment				150	Br. Actor
Simenon, Georges 1903-89	Author	65	125	275	125	Fr-Belg. Creator Insp. Maigret
Simeon II	Royalty	80				King of Bulgaria 1937
Simeon, Charles	Clergy	45		75		
Simmons, E.H.H.	Business	25	40			Pres. NY Stock Exchange
Simmons, Gene (Kiss)	Entertainment	9			30	
Simmons, Jean	Entertainment	8	10	20	20	
Simmons, Richard	Entertainment	15			40	Actor
Simmons, Richard	Entertainment	5			15	Diet & Aerobics
Simms, Ginny	Entertainment				22	Band Vocalist
Simms, William G.	Author	35	100	250		Lawyer, Pro-Slavery Editor
Simon and Garfunkel	Entertainment	40			100	LP S $110 (Both)
Simon, Carly	Entertainment	20			50	Singer-Composer
Simon, Claude	Author	150				Nobel Literature 1985
Simon, Herbert A.	Science	20	35	50	25	Nobel Economics

NAME	CATEGORY	SIG	LS/DS	ALS	SP	Comment
Simon, Neil	Author	45	75	150	75	Playwright, Screenwriter
Simon, Norton	Industrialist	15	35	65	25	Norton Simon, Inc.,Philanthropy
Simon, Paul	Composer	20			75	Entertainer
Simon, Paul Martin	Congress	5			10	Repr.,Senator IL
Simon, Simone	Entertainment	15			55	
Simon, William E.	Cabinet	5	15	25	20	Sec'y Treasury
Simoneau, Léopold	Entertainment	4			25	Opera
Simpson, Alan	Congress	5	10		15	Senator WY
Simpson, James H. 1813-83	Civil War	30	70			Union Gen.
Simpson, James Y., Sir	Science	25	90	195		Scot.1st Obstetric Ether Use
Simpson, Louis	Author	20			65	Am. Poet
Simpson, Matthew 1811-84	Clergy	90				Methodist Bishop. Lincoln Eulogy
Simpson, O.J.	Celebrity				150	Accused Murderer-Acquitted
Simpson, Russell	Entertainment	50			120	Grapes of Wrath, Meet John Doe
Simpson, Wallis Warfield	Head of State	110		675		Duchess of Windsor
Simpson, William H. 1888-	Military	25	150	400	75	Gen. WW II
Sims, William S. 1858-1936	Military	30	250	115	50	Adm. USN WW I, Pulitzer Author
Sinatra, Frank	Entertainment	193	300		355	MGM DS $375
Sinatra, Nancy	Entertainment	5	10	20	20	Pin-Up SP $25
Sinclair, Harry F.	Business	140	175	350	200	Teapot Dome
Sinclair, Upton	Author	40	75	145	125	Am. Writer-Socialist Politician
Sinding, Christian A.	Composer	45	120	210		Symphonies, Concertos, Sonatas
Singer, Isaac Bashevis 1904-91	Author	32		300	175	Nobel Literature 1978
Singer, Isaac M. 1811-75	Inventor	575		2500		Singer Sewing Machine
Singer, Marc	Entertainment	10	12		30	
Singlaub, John K.	Military	10	20	35	20	General WW II
Singleton, Penny	Entertainment	5	10	15	25	Blondie
Sinise, Gary	Entertainment	15	20	30	70	Oscar winner
Sinopoli, Giuseppe	Conductor	5			35	
Sioli, Franco	Entertainment	5			15	Opera
Siple, Paul A.	Aviation	22	45			Explorer, Geographer
Sirica, John J.	Jurist	20	35		50	Watergate Judge
Sirk, Don	Entertainment	65				Film Director
Siroky, William	Head of State	50				Premier Czech.
Sirtis, Marina	Entertainment	5			25	Actress. Star Trek
Siskel, Gene	Entertainment	5			15	Film Critic
Sisley, Alfred 1839-99	Artist	150	400	1865		Fr.Impressionist. Landscapes
Sissle, Noble	Entertainment	25			50	Big Band Leader-Arranger
Sitgreaves, John	Revolutionary War	30	75	145		Officer. Continental Congress
Sitting Bull (T. Iyotake)	Indian Leader	7175			15000	Sioux Indian Leader
Sitwell, Edith, Dame 1887-1964	Author	70	135	185	660	Br.Poet, Critic, Novelist
Sitwell, Osbert, Sir	Author	35	70	210		Playwright, Novelist
Sixty Minutes (all)	Entertainment	25			45	
Sizoo, Joseph R.	Clergy	20	25	35		
Skaggs, Ricky	Country Music	10			20	
Skala, Lilia	Entertainment	10	15	25	30	
Skelly, William Grove	Business	320				Founder Skelly Oil, Financier
Skelton, Red	Entertainment	15	20	40	40	
Skerrit, Tom	Entertainment	8	10	20	20	
Skinner, B. F.	Author	20	30	50	75	Behavioral Psychology-Theorist
Skinner, Cornelia Otis 1901-50	Entertainment-Author	10	40	50	25	Actress, Monologuist
Skinner, Cortlandt 1728-99	Military	40	85	155		Born NJ. Loyalist General
Skinner, Otis	Entertainment	32	40	70	65	Vintage Stage Star
Skinner, Samuel K.	Cabinet	10	20			Sec'y Transportation
Skinner, Stella	Artist	25	40	75		
Skipworth, Alison	Entertainment	15	15	30	25	

NAME	CATEGORY	SIG	LS/DS	ALS	SP	Comment
Skorzeny, Otto 1908-75	Military	245	225	540	500	Nazi SS Officer & Adventurer
Skouras, Spyros 1893-1971	Business	15			175	Fndr-Pres-Chm 20th Century Fox
Skovhus, Boje	Entertainment	10			25	Opera
Slack, Freddie	Bandleader				45	
Slade, William 1786-1859	Congress	12				Repr. VT, Gov. VT
Slater, Christian	Entertainment	10			40	
Slater, Helen	Entertainment	8	15	30	50	
Slaughter, Frank G.	Author	8	15	35	10	
Slayton, Donald K. Deke	Astronaut	35	95		122	Mercury 7 Astro (Deceased)
Sledd, Patsy	Country Music	4			12	Pin-Up SP $15
Slezak, Leo 1873-1946	Entertainment	45	60		125	Great Austrian Tenor, Opera
Slezak, Walter	Entertainment	15			35	
Slick, Grace	Entertainment	25			40	
Slidell, John 1793-1871	Civil War	75	450	195		Statesman, CSA Diplomat
Slim, Wm. Joseph, Sir	Military	30	75	120	60	Br. General WW II
Sliwa, Curtis	Celebrity	10			20	Founder of Guardians
Sliwa, Lisa	Celebrity	6	15		10	NY Street Protection Group
Sliwinski, Josef	Entertainment	20		100	75	Pol Pianist
Sloan, Alfred P. Jr.1875-1966	Business	45	45	90	50	Sloan-Kettering Inst. CEO GM
Sloan, John	Artist	85	275	550		Am.Painter,Etcher,Illustrator
Sloan, John 1779-1856	Cabinet	20	45	95		Fillmore Treasurer of U.S.
Sloane, Everett	Entertainment	30			55	
Sloat, John Drake	Civil War	45	95	130		Union Naval Officer
Slocum, Henry Warner 1827-94	Civil War	75	75	150		Union General, Rep. NY
Slough, John P. (War Date)	Civil War	160		950		Union Gen. Killed in Gunfight 1867
Small, John Humphrey	Senate/Congress	5		15		Rep. NC 1899
Smallens, Alexander	Conductor	20			50	World Premiere Porgy & Bess
Smallwood, Norma	Entertainment	20			50	Miss America 1926
Smart, Jean	Entertainment	5			15	
Smathers, George A.	Senate/Congress	5		25	15	Rep., Senator FL 1947
Smedley, Richard	Entertainment	3	3	6	8	
Smetana, Bedrich	Composer	1500		9000		Czech. Operas, Symphonies etc.
Smiley, Delores	Country Music	10			20	
Smirnoff, Yakov	Entertainment	8			15	
Smith, Adam 1723-1790	Economist	3000				Architect of Br. Political Econ
Smith, Addison T.	Senate/Congress	5	10	15		Rep. ID 1913
Smith, Al*	Cartoonists	15			60	Mutt & Jeff
Smith, Albert E. & Blackton, J. Stuart	SEE Blackton					
Smith, Alexis	Entertainment	15	45		35	Pin-Up SP $35
Smith, Alfred E.1873-1944	Governor	50	108	400	135	Presidential Candidate, Gov NY
Smith, Anna Nicole	Entertainment	10				Model-Actress. Nude Pin-up SP 95
Smith, Armistead B.	Aviation	10	22	38	28	ACE, WW II, Navy Ace
Smith, Ashbel	Civil War	140		615		TX Historical Politician, CSA
Smith, Bernie	Entertainment	6	8	15	15	
Smith, Betty	Author	50	110		65	
Smith, Buffalo Bob	Entertainment	10	15		30	Howdy Doody
Smith, C. Aubrey	Entertainment	35			80	
Smith, C.R.	Military	25	75			Adm. Flagship Fleet
Smith, Caleb 1808-64	Cabinet	40	200	365		Lincoln Attorney General
Smith, Carl	Country Music	5			12	
Smith, Charles E.	Cabinet	15		25	20	P.M. General 1898
Smith, Charles M.	Entertainment	10			25	
Smith, Charles M.	Governor	5	15			Governor VT
Smith, Connie	Country Music	5			12	
Smith, Edmund K. (War Date)	Civil War	390	975	1420		CSA Gen.
Smith, Edmund Kirby 1824-93	Civil War	308		580		CSA General

NAME	CATEGORY	SIG	LS/DS	ALS	SP	Comment
Smith, Elinor	Aviation	45	100	160	130	
Smith, Elizabeth Oakes	Reformer	90	205	385		Early Supporter Woman Suffrage
Smith, Ellison 1864-1944	Congress	5	25			Sen. SC
Smith, Elmo	Governor	10	25			Governor OR
Smith, Elton	Aviation	15	30			World Helicopter Record '52
Smith, Ely 1825-1911	Congress					Rep. NY, Mayor NYC
Smith, F. E.	Celebrity	36				
Smith, Francis Hopkinson 1838-	Artist	15	20	35		Am.Engineer-Artist-Illustrator
Smith, Francis M. Borax	Business	30	65	95		Founder U.S. Borax Co.
Smith, Frank, Bishop	Clergy	15	20	25	25	
Smith, Frederick W.	Business	15	30	55	20	Fndr., Chm. Federal Express
Smith, George Washington	Senate/Congress	5	15			Rep. IL 1889
Smith, Gerrit 1797-1874	Senate/Congress	50		483		Abolitionist, Reformer,Rep.NY
Smith, Gipsy	Clergy	25	45	75	35	
Smith, Green Clay	Civil War	50	65	140		Union Gen., Congress KY
Smith, Gustavus W.(War Date)	Civil War	120	330	929		CSA General. LS/Cont. $2500
Smith, H. Allen	Senate/Congress	5	10		10	Rep. CA 1957
Smith, Hamilton	Science	20	30	45	25	Nobel Medicine 1978
Smith, Harry	Journalist	4	10		10	Broadcast Journalist
Smith, Harsen	Business	3	10	25	10	
Smith, Hoke 1855-1931	Cabinet	10	35	70	30	Gov.,Sen. GA, Sec'y Int.1911
Smith, Holland M.Howlin Mad,Gen	Military					Iwo Jima Flag Raising FDC $550
Smith, Ian	Head of State	10	20	50	30	
Smith, Ida B. Wise	Reformer	30	55	95		Temperance Advocate, WCTU
Smith, J. Gregory	Governor	5	15		10	Governor VT
Smith, Jaclyn	Entertainment	6	8	20	20	Pin-Up SP $30
Smith, James 1719-1806	Revolutionary War	235	525	3750		Signer Decl. of Indepen.
Smith, James Y.	Governor	35	55			Civil War Gov. RI
Smith, James, Jr. 1851-1927	Congress	10	15			Senator NJ 1911
Smith, Joe	Entertainment	15			45	
Smith, John	Colonial Am.	2200	11500	29000		NRPA
Smith, John Pye	Clergy	20	25	35		
Smith, Joseph 1805-44	Religious Leader	775	1775			Founder Morman Church
Smith, Julia Holmes, Dr.	Science	90		425		1st Pres.Women's Med. Assoc.
Smith, Kate	Entertainment	45	195	175	103	Introduced God Bless America
Smith, Keely	Entertainment	10			30	Band Vocalist
Smith, Kent	Entertainment	6			15	
Smith, L. C.	Business	50	135	240		L.C.Smith Typewriters, etc.
Smith, Maggie	Entertainment	12	15	30	30	AA
Smith, Margaret Chase	Senate/Congress	6	20		15	Columnist, Rep., Sen. ME
Smith, Martha	Entertainment	5			15	
Smith, Martin Luther (War Date)	Civil War	110		375		CSA Gen. ALS/Cont.$2750
Smith, Martin Luther 1819-66	Civil War	75	135	240		CSA General
Smith, Matthew	Revolutionary War	25	75			
Smith, Melancton 1744-98	Revolutionary War	75	125			Continental Congress
Smith, Melancton 1810-93	Civil War	40	85	120		Un. Adm. Served Under Farragut
Smith, Michael J.	Astronaut	275			300	Died on Challenger
Smith, Nels H.F.	Governor	5	10		15	Governor WY
Smith, R.T.	Aviation	10	28	40	35	ACE, WW II, Flying Tigers
Smith, Richard	Revolutionary War	50	130	250		Continental Congress
Smith, Robert 1757-1842	Cabinet	55	170	290		Att'y Gen.,Sec'y Navy,Sec'y St.
Smith, Robert H. Snuffy	Aviation	15	30	50	35	ACE, WW II, Flying Tigers
Smith, Rodney Gipsy	Clergy	50	50	85	50	
Smith, Roger	Entertainment	5			20	
Smith, Roy L., Bishop	Clergy	20	30	45	30	
Smith, Samuel 1752-1839	Revolutionary War	55	165	225		General, Rep.,Senator MD

The Sanders Price Guide to Autographs

NAME	CATEGORY	SIG	LS/DS	ALS	SP	Comment
Smith, Samuel Francis 1808-95	Clergy-Poet	100	650	390		AQS America $500-$2,250
Smith, Shelley	Entertainment	4			10	Pin-Up SP $20
Smith, Stanley	Entertainment	9			25	Stage
Smith, Susan M.	Playboy Ctrfold	3			10	Pin-Up SP $15
Smith, Sydney*	Cartoonist	30			150	The Gumps
Smith, Thomas A.	Military	95	240			Fort Smith Arkansas. General
Smith, Thomas Church Haskell	Civil War	29	55	80		Union General
Smith, Tom E.	Business	10	20	30	25	Pres. Food Lion Grocery Chain
Smith, Truman 1791-1884	Senate-Cabinet	10	25	40		Rep., Sen. CT, Sec'y Interior
Smith, W. Angie, Bishop	Clergy	20	25	35	25	
Smith, W. Wallace	Clergy	40	45	60		
Smith, Walter Bedell	Military	35	50	95	45	Gen. WW II,Ambass.,Dir. CIA
Smith, William	Entertainment	5			10	Actor
Smith, William (War Date)	Civil War	188		3473		CSA Gen.
Smith, William 1797-1887	Civil War	118	250	284		CSA Gen., Congress, Gov. VA
Smith, William Farrar	Civil War	45		180		Union Gen.
Smith, William S.	Revolutionary War	35	95	185		Rev.Soldier.Pres.Soc.Cincinnati
Smith, William Sidney, Sir 1764-	Military	50		185		Br.Adm. Napoleonic War
Smith, Willie The Lion 1910-67	Entertainment	75			125	Jazz Alto-Baritone Sax,Clarinet
Smithers, Jan	Entertainment	6	8		15	
Smits, Jimmy	Entertainment	5			45	Actor. L..A.Law, NYPD Blue
Smoot, Reed 1862-1941	Congress	25	45			Senator UT. 1st Morman Sen.
Smothers Bros. (both)	Entertainment	10			25	Tommy and Dick
Smucker, Paul	Business	10			25	Smuckers Jams & Jellies
Smuts, Jan Christian 1870-1950	Head of State	45	130	425	250	Fld. Marshal. Pres. Un. So. Afr
Smythe, Reg*	Cartoonist	10	35		40	Andy Capp
Snead, Thomas L.	Civil War					
Snell, George D., Dr.	Science	15	30	45	45	Nobel Medicine 1980
Snipes, Wesley	Entertainment	15			70	
Snodgrass, W.D.	Author	25	75		65	
Snow, Charles Percy, Baron	Author	25	80	170	60	Br. Novelist, Physicist
Snow, Hank	Country Music	20			42	
Snyder, Howard	Military	10	25			
Snyder, John W.	Cabinet	15	30		25	Sec'y Treas.
Snyder, Simon	Governor	5	15	35		Governor PA
Soarez, Alana	Playboy Ctrfold	3	5	10	10	Pin-Up SP $15
Sockman, Ralph	Clergy	15	20	25		
Soddy, Frederick, Dr.	Science	60	160	275	125	Nobel Chemistry 1921
Soderstrom, Elisabeth	Entertainment				35	Opera
Soglow, Otto*	Cartoonist	20			100	The Little King
Sohn, Lee	Entertainment	4			20	Singer
Sokoloff, Vladimir	Entertainment	25			65	
Soles, P. J.	Entertainment	5			15	
Solow, Robert M., Dr.	Economics	22	30		25	Nobel Economics 1987
Solti, Georg, Sir	Entertainment	28	45		85	Conductor. Winner of most Grammys
Solzhenitsyn, Alex.	Author	100	350	495	185	Sov. Novelist. Nobel Lit. 1970
Somers, Suzanne	Entertainment	6			20	Pin-Up SP 60
Somerset, Lord Fitzroy	See Raglan					SEE RAGLAN
Somervell, Arthur, Sir	Composer	20	55	85		Br.Oratorios...AMusQS $150
Somervell, Brehon B. 1892-	Military	35	125			Gen. WW II
Sommer, Elke	Entertainment	9	10	20	25	Pin-Up SP $30
Sommers, Joannie	Entertainment	3	5		10	
Somoza, Anastasio	Head of State	20	95			Nicaragua
Sondergaard, Gale	Entertainment	40			75	AA
Sondheim, Stephen b.1930	Composer	25	80	135	125	AMusQS $275- $375
Sonny & Cher	Entertainment	30			100	

NAME	CATEGORY	SIG	LS/DS	ALS	SP	Comment
Sontag, Henrietta Rossi	Entertainment	70			375	Opera
Sontag, Susan	Author	10	25	45	20	
Soo, Jack	Entertainment	150			55	
Soong, T.V. (Tzu-wen)	Diplomat	35	50			Chinese Financier, Negotiator
Sooter, Rudy	Country Music	10			20	
Soper, Donald O.	Clergy	20	25	30	30	
Sopwith, Thos. O. M., Sir	Aviation	65	115	190	100	Br. Pioneer. ALS/Content $850
Sorenson, Ted	Author	6			15	JFK Aide
Sorkin, Arleen	Entertainment	4	5		10	Pin-Up SP $20
Sorma, Agnes	Entertainment	25				Opera
Sorrel, Gilbert M. (War Date)	Civil War	295	2175			CSA Gen.
Sorrel, Gilbert Moxley 1838-1901	Civil War	165	370	428		CSA General
Sorrvia, Agnes	Entertainment	20			45	Opera
Sorvino, Mira	Entertainment	15			80	AA 1996. Supporting Actress
Sorvino, Paul	Entertainment	15			35	
Sothern, Ann	Entertainment	12		35	58	
Sothern, E. A.	Entertainment	30	85	120		19th Century Romantic Idol
Soto, Talisa	Entertainment	10			40	Col. Pin-Up SP 60
Soucek, Appolo, Lt .	Aviation	15	25			World Altitude Records
Souez, Ina	Entertainment		50			Opera. Great Mozart Soprano
Soul Asylum	Entertainment					Rock. No Price Available
Soul, David	Entertainment	5	10	20	15	
Soule, Pierre	Civil War	75	170	285		Sessessionist. US Sen.LA., CSA Gen.
Soult, Nicolas Jean de Dieu, Duke	Fr. Military	105	325	388		Nap.Marshal of Fr.,Minister War
Sousa, John Philip 1854-1932	Composer	155	340	480	967	AMusQs$400-$690-$1250
Soustelle, Jacques	Head of State	5	15	40	15	
Souter, David H. (SC)	Supreme Court	40			55	
Southampton, 1st Earl of 1505-50	Royalty	75	215	450		Politician. Sec'y to Cromwell
Southcott, Joanna	Clergy	45	60	90		Br. Religious Fanatic
Southey, Robert 1774-1843	Author	95	280	450		Br. Poet Laureate 1813
Sovine, Red	Country Music	12			35	
Soyer, Raphael 1899-1987	Artist	20	50	130	100	Signed Repro. $200-$300
Soyinka, Wole (Akinwande O.)	Author	25	80			Nigerian. Nobel Literature 1986
Spaak, Paul-Henri	Head of State	15	30	50	25	Belg. Fndr. EEOC, NATO
Spaatz, Carl Tooey 1891-1974	Military-Aviation	55	141		120	Gen. WW II, AF Commander
Spacek, Sissy	Entertainment	10	15		40	AA
Spacey, Kevin	Entertainment	15			80	Actor. AA 1996 Supporting
Spaight, Richard Dobbs 1758-1802	Revolutionary War	115	325			Continental Congr.,Signer Constitution
Spain, Fay	Entertainment	10			30	
Spalding, Albert 1888-1953	Entertainment	35			75	Violinist, AMQS $85-$250
Spalding, J. Walter	Business	25	7	140	55	
Spallanzani, Lazzaro 1729-99	Science	120	400	700		It. Physiolog.Artificial Insem.
Sparkman, John 1899-1985	Congress	12			25	Senator AL. VP Candidate
Sparks, Chuncey	Governor	5	20			Governor AL
Sparks, Jared 1789-1866	Author	15	35	75		US Historian, Editor,Publisher
Sparks, Ned	Entertainment	25	30	60	70	
Sparks, William E.	Military	15	30	50		
Sparv, Camilla	Entertainment	8	9	25	20	
Spate, Wolfgang	Aviation			125		Ger. Ace WW II. Test Pilot
Spaulding, Albert	Composer	25	65			
Spaulding, R.Z.	Business	15	40	55	25	
Speakes, Larry	Cabinet	4	10	16	10	
Speaks, Oley	Composer	50	90	122		On The Road To Mandalay
Specter, Arlen	Congress	10			30	Sen. PA. Presidential Hopeful
Spector, Phil	Entertainment	75	95		82	Rock HOF
Speed, James 1812-87	Cabinet	45	80	135		Lincoln Att'y Gen. Cont. ALS $995

The Sanders Price Guide to Autographs

NAME	CATEGORY	SIG	LS/DS	ALS	SP	Comment
Speed, John Gilmer	Author	5	15	25		Journalist. Biographer
Speer, Albert 1905-1981	Military	45	245	275	170	Hitler's Architect & Nazi Leader
Speer, Robert Elliott	Clergy	15	20	25		
Speer, Robert Milton	Senate/Congress	5	10	20		Rep. PA 1871
Speidel, Hans	Military	35	90	165	75	Nazi Gen.,Rommel Chief-of Staff
Speight, J. J.	Senate/Congress	5	10			
Speir, Dona	Entertainment	5			15	Pin-Up SP $20. Playboy Ctrfold
Speke, John 1827-64	Explorer			2250		Found Lake Tanganyika/Rich. Burton
Spelling, Aaron	Entertainment	6	10		25	Film Producer, Writer
Spelling, Tori	Entertainment	5			65	Pin-up SP $40, Col.75
Spellman, Francis, Cardinal	Clergy	30	50	95	45	
Spelvin, Georgina	Entertainment	5			40	Porn Queen
Spencer, George Eliphaz	Civil War	35	80	145		Union General, Senator AL 1868
Spencer, Herbert, Sir 1820-1903	Author	50	120	225		Br. Philosopher
Spencer, John C.1788-1855	Cabinet	25	60	103		Tyler Sec'y War
Spencer, John P. 5th Earl	Politician	10	15	35		Liberal Leader House of Lords
Spencer, Susan	TV News	4			10	CBS News
Spender, Stephen 1909-95	Author	65	185	250	75	Br.Poet, Critic. Protest Poetry
Spenser, Tim	Country Music	15			25	Fndr. Sons of the Pioneers
Sperry, Elmer A.	Science	165	375	535	225	Inventor Gyroscope
Sperry, Roger W.	Science	22	30	35	25	Nobel Medicine 1981
Spielberg, David	Entertainment	5	6	15	200	
Spielberg, Steven	Entertainment	85			200	Producer-Director
Spillane, Mickey	Author	50	75	110	150	Am. Writer of Detective Fiction
Spiner, Brent	Entertainment	15			35	Star Trek
Spinner, Francis E. 1802-90	Cabinet	25	155	45		Treasurer for 4 Presidents
Spinner, Robert	Entertainment	4			25	Actor Star Trek
Spivak, Charlie	Entertainment	20			40	Big Band Leader-Trumpeter
Spock, Benjamin, Dr.	Science	35	75	115	50	Am. Pediatrician-Psychiatrist
Spofford, Harriet P. 1835-	Author	10	25	40		Am. Romantic Poet, Novelist
Spong, Hilda	Entertainment	15			40	
Spontini, Gaspare, Count de	Composer	95		385		It. Influenced Wagner Operas
Spooner, John C. 1843-1919	Congress	5	15		10	Senator WI 1885
Spooner, William A.	Clergy	25	35	45		Br. Creator Of The Spoonerism
Sprague, Charles A.	Governor	10	20		15	Governor OR
Sprague, Frank Julian	Science	55	100	165	115	Inventor Ass't To Thos. Edison
Sprague, William 1830-1915	Civil War	75	90	105		Union Gen., CW Gov. RI, Senate
Sprague, William Buell	Clergy	45	70	110		
Spreckels, Claus	Business	95	325		175	Am. Sugar Manufacturer
Spring, Gardiner	Clergy	25	35	45		
Spring, Samuel	Clergy	20	25	35		
Spring, Sherwood C.	Astronaut	6			15	
Springer, Robert C.	Astronaut	5			15	
Springfield, Rick	Entertainment	12	30		25	
Springfield, Sherry	Entertainment				50	Actress. E.R.
Springsteen, Bruce	Entertainment	50	75	150	175	
Sproul, William Henry 1867-1932	Congress	4	10			Repr. KS. Farmer. Oil & Gas Exploration
Spruance, Presley 1785-1863	Congress	12	20	40		Senator DE 1847
Spruance, Raymond A. 1886-1969	Military	25	125	130	60	Am. Adm. Victor at Midway WW II
Spurgeon, Charles H. 1834-1932	Clergy	75	105	242		Br. Evangelist & Baptist Minister
Squibb, Edward R.	Business	80	150	255		Pioneer Mfg. of Pharmaceuticals
Squier, Emma	Author	5	10	15		
Squier, George O.	Military	100				General. Inventor Radio Devices
St. Clair, Arthur 1734-1818	Military-Rev. War	135	315	931		Gen.,Pres. Continental Congr.
St. Cyr, Lili	Entertainment	10	15	30	25	Pin-Up SP $35
St. Denis, Ruth 1878-1968	Entertainment	50	140	250	310	Dancer, Choreographer

NAME	CATEGORY	SIG	LS/DS	ALS	SP	Comment
St. Jacques, Raymond	Entertainment	15			45	African-American actor
St. John, Al Fuzzy	Entertainment	150			350	
St. John, Isaac M. 1827-880	Civil War	85		330		CSA Gen. Sig/Rank $175
St. John, Jill	Entertainment	8	9	20	20	Pin-Up SP $30
St. Johns, Adela Rogers	Author	10	25	45	15	Star Hearst Reporter. Novelist
St. Laurent, Louis	Head of State	10			50	P. M. Canada
St. Vincent, John Jervis, Earl	Military	35	65	135		Br. Adm. 1735-1823
Stabile, Dick	Entertainment	20			40	Big Band Leader
Stacey Q	Entertainment	5			10	Rock
Stacey, John	Aviation	8	20	30	20	
Stack, Robert	Entertainment	10	20		35	AA
Stack, Rose Marie Bowe	Entertainment	4	5		9	
Stacpoole, Henry de Vere	Author	15	45	80		Writer, Publicist
Stadlman, Anthony	Aviation	10	20	30	20	
Stael, Anne-Louise, Mme. de1766-1817	Author	65	185	675		Fr. Writer. Exiled By Napoleon
Stafford, Jo	Entertainment	5			15	40's-50's Top Vocalist
Stafford, Robert T.	Governor	8	15	20		Governor VT
Stafford, Susan	Entertainment	10				Actress
Stafford, Thomas P.	Astronaut	15			80	
Stager, Anson	Civil War	20	60	110		Gen.Supt.Govt.Telegraphs
Stahl, Gerald	Aviation				233	Engineer 509th Bomb Gp. (Enola Gay)
Stahl, Leslie	Journalist	5	15		10	TV. 60 Minutes
Stainback, Ingram M.	Governor					Gov. HI 1942-51
Stalin, Joseph 1879-1953	Head of State	1290	4900	8600	2150	USSR
Stalin, Svetlana	Celebrity	35	105	250	45	Daughter of Stalin
Stallone, Sylvester	Entertainment	15	40	75	60	
Stamos, John	Entertainment	10			35	
Stamp, Terence	Entertainment	10			25	
Stanbery, Henry	Cabinet	10	20	45		Att'y General 1866
Stander, Lionel	Entertainment	10	15	25	25	
Standing, Guy, Sir	Entertainment	25			55	
Standish, Myles	Colonial America	1885	8800	26400		Mayflower Colonist. NRPA
Stanford, Leland 1824-93	Senate	115	1780	450	125	Railroad Pres.,Fndr. Stanford U., Gov.
Stanford, R. C.	Governor	6	15		10	Governor AZ
Stang, Arnold	Entertainment	5			15	
Stanhope, Edward	Military	10	20	30		
Stanhope, Hester, Lady 1776-1839	Non-Conformist	15	45	95		Adopted Eastern Ways.Prophetess
Stanhope, Phil. H., 5th Earl	Historian	10	20	25		Lord Mahon. M.P., Author
Stanhope, Phil.H., 7th Earl	Celebrity	7	20	45		
Stanhope, Philip D. 1694-1773	Author-Politician	125		625		4th Earl Chesterfield
Stanislavski, Konstantin 1863-1938	Entertainment	350			1433	Rus. Actor, Director, Producer
Stanislaw II Augustus Poniatowski	Royalty	95	375	730		Last King of Poland
Stanley, Arthur	Business	3	5		7	Pres. Stanley Works
Stanley, David Sloane	Civil War	25	65	90		Union Gen. Wardte ALS $750
Stanley, Freelan O.	Inventor	325		1400		Auto. Pioneer. Stanley Steamer
Stanley, Henry M.,Sir 1841-1904	Explorer-Civil War	275	350	570	792	Author, Journalist, CSA
Stanley, Henry, Capt.	Military	10	25	40		
Stanley, Reed (SC)	Supreme Court	25				
Stanley, Wendell M.	Science	20	25	90	30	Nobel Chemistry 1946
Stans, Maurice H.	Cabinet	25	35		40	Sec'y Commerce. Watergate
Stansbury, Howard 1806-63	Explorer	20	55	100		Surveyor, Military
Stanton, Benjamin	Senate/Congress	20	45	100		Rep. OH.ALS/Content $250
Stanton, Edwin M. 1814-69	Cabinet	150	274	525	150	ALS War Dte $1,495, Sec'y War
Stanton, Elizabeth Cady 1815-1902	Women's Suffrage	158	225	507		1st Pres.Nat'l Women's Suffrage
Stanton, Frank L.	Author	5	15	25		Am. Journalist, Poet, Publ.
Stanton, Frank, Dr.	Business	15	45	80	30	Pres. CBS

NAME	CATEGORY	SIG	LS/DS	ALS	SP	Comment
Stanton, Harry Dean	Entertainment	6	8	1	20	
Stanwyck, Barbara 1907-90	Entertainment	25	40		80	Pin-Up SP $95
Stapleton, Jean	Entertainment	5			20	
Stapleton, Maureen	Entertainment	8	10		25	
Stapp, John, Col.	Military	5	15	20	10	
Stapp, Olivia	Entertainment	10			35	Opera
Star Wars (Cast)	Entertainment				175	SP (7) $175
Stark, Benjamin 1820-98	Congress		30	70		Sen. OR, A Founder of Portland
Stark, Harold R.	Military	15	40	75	40	Adm.,Cmdr.Eur.Waters WW II
Stark, John	Revolutionary War	410	625	1565		Often Quoted General
Starker, Janos	Entertainment	6	8	15	15	
Starkey, Thomas A., Bishop	Clergy	20	35	40		
Starr, Belle	Outlaw	2000	6500			Early West Bandit Queen
Starr, Blaze	Entertainment	15			50	Pin-Up SP $50. Stripper
Starr, Dixie	Entertainment	20				Western Movies. Mrs. Jack Hovie
Starr, Kay	Entertainment	20			20	Big Band Singer. Vocalist
Starr, Leonard*	Cartoonist	25			160	Little Orphan Annie
Starr, Ringo	Entertainment	95	322		200	Beatles' Drummer.Endorsed Check $785
Starrett, Charles Durango1904-88	Entertainment	25	35		88	Early Cowboy Film Star
Starry, Donald A.	Military	5	6	15	10	
Starzl, Thomas E., Dr.	Science	15	25			Transplant Specialist
Stassen, Harold E.	Governor	10	15	35	20	Governor MN
Statler, Ellsworth M.	Business	75	205	375	150	Statler Hotel Chain
Statlers, The	Country Music	25			50	
Stead, Wm. Thomas 1849-1912	Journalist	20	60	140	45	Died On Titanic. AQS $95-$125
Stebbins, George C.	Clergy	45	70	95		
Steber, Eleanor	Entertainment	20			75	Opera, Concert
Stedman, Edmund C.	Author	20	35			Poet, NY Stock Broker, Publ.
Steel, Danielle	Author	10	20		25	Novelist
Steele, Barbara	Entertainment	20			35	
Steele, Bob	Entertainment	20	25	45	50	
Steele, Frederick	Civil War	45	95	185		Un.Gen. War Dte/Content $2500
Steele, Karen	Entertainment	4	5		10	
Steele, Richard, Sir 1672-1729	Author	200	600	1320		Essays, Drama. The Tatler
Steele, Tom	Entertainment	15		25	25	
Steely Dan	Entertainment	25			50	
Steenburgen, Mary	Entertainment	10			35	AA
Stefansson, Vilhjalmur	Explorer	65	155	250	295	Arctic Explorer, Ethnologist
Steffens, Lincoln 1866-1936	Author	85	100	175	25	Journalist. Leader Muckrakers
Steger, Will	Celebrity	35	90			Arctic explorer
Stegner, Wallace	Author	20		45		Am. Novelist. Pulitzer
Steichen, Edward J. 1879-1973	Artist	80	210	375	477	Pioneer Photgraphy as Art Form
Steig, William*	Cartoonist	20			100	New Yorker Cartoonist
Steiger, Rod	Entertainment	8			30	Oscar winner
Steimle, Edmund A.	Clergy	10	15	20		
Stein, Gertrude 1874-1946	Author	495	475	750	795	Expatriate Am. Writer
Stein, Jules	Humanitarian-Bus.	50	200			Founder MCA
Steinbeck, John 1902-68	Author	408	1983	2550	950	Pulitzer, Nobel Lit., DS $2,500
Steinem, Gloria	Feminist	15	25	45	25	Fndr.,Editor MsMagazine
Steinhoff, J. 'Mickey'	Aviation	15	25	50	30	
Steinlen, Theophile	Artist	35	105	250		Fr. Known For Posters, Lithogr.
Steinmetz, Charles P. 1865-1923	Science	60	150	425		Ger.-born Electrical Engineer
Steinway, Henry Z.	Business	20	55	85	30	Steinway Piano
Steinwehr, Baron Adolph von 1822-77	Civil War	85				Union Gen. Geographer, Cartographer
Steiwer, Frederick 1883-1939	Congress	5		15		Senator OR 1926
Stekel, Wilhelm	Science	60	275			Austrian Psychiatrist

NAME	CATEGORY	SIG	LS/DS	ALS	SP	Comment
Stella, Antonietta	Entertainment	25			55	Opera
Stempel, Robert	Business		60			Pres. & CEO of Gen. Motors
Stemple, Robert	Business	25				Pres. General Motors
Sten, Anna	Entertainment	15	15	30	35	
Stendhal (Marie H. Beyle)	Author	350	1020	2315		19th Cent. Fr. Novelist
Stengle, Charles I.	Senate/Congress	5	15	25		Rep. NY 1923
Stennis, John C.	Senate/Congress	10	15			Sen. MS 1947. Pres. Pro Tem.
Stephanie, Princess	Royalty	10			25	Princess of Monaco
Stephanopoulos, George	Government	10	20		25	White House Aide
Stephen, Adam 1730-1791	Revolutionary War	60	165	320		General. Trenton, Brandywine
Stephens, Alexander H.1812-83	Civil War	202	385	500		US Repr. & Gov. GA, VP CSA
Stephens, William D. 1859-1944	Congress	10	30			Governor CA, Senator CA
Stephenson, George 1781-1825	Science	275	425	875		Invented1st Practical Steam Locomotive
Stephenson, Henry	Entertainment	35			75	
Stephenson, Robert	Science	90	245	410		Br. Railroad Engineer-Designer
Stepp, Hans	Aviation	5	15	20	15	
Steppenwolf	Entertainment	75			150	
Sterling, Andrew B.	Composer	15	50	100		
Sterling, Robert	Entertainment	5			20	
Stern, Henry Aaron	Clergy	20	20	25		
Stern, Isaac	Entertainment	15	35	45	60	AMQS $80,ALS/Cont. $110
Sterne, Laurence 1713-68	Author	95	375			Br.Whimsical,Eccentric Humor
Sterrett, Cliff*	Cartoonist	35			300	Polly And Her Pals
Stettlnlus, Edward R.,Jr.1900-49	Cabinet	40	100	190	45	FDR, Truman, Sec'y State
Steuben, Friedrich von 1730-94	Revolutionary War	1200	3300			ALS/Content $9,750
Stevens, Albert W., Capt.	Aviation	25	35			Aviator-Balloonist.Record Holder
Stevens, Andrew	Entertainment	8	9	20	20	
Stevens, Brinke	Entertalnment	5			15	Pin-Up SP $20
Stevens, Cat	Entertainment	20			35	
Stevens, Clement H.(War Date)	Civil War	375	3740	2640		CSA Gen. 1821—64
Stevens, Connie	Entertainment	6	8	15	15	
Stevens, Craig	Entertainment	8	9	20	20	
Stevens, Ebenezer	Revolutionary War	65	195			Memb. Boston Tea Party
Stevens, George	Entertainment	30			60	Film Director
Stevens, Inger	Entertainment	75			150	
Stevens, James F. 1892-1971	Author	125	310			Paul Bunyan Stories
Stevens, John 1748-1838	Revolutionary War	20	45	90		Engineer Perfected Steam Engine
Stevens, John Paul, III (SC)	Supreme Court	40	90		150	
Stevens, K.T.	Entertainment	4	5		10	
Stevens, Onslow	Entertainment	30			65	
Stevens, Ray	Country Music	5			10	
Stevens, Rise	Entertainment	20	25		38	Opera, Concert, Films
Stevens, Robert T.	Cabinet	10	25		20	Sec'y Army
Stevens, Stella	Entertainment	6	8		20	Pin-Up SP $30.Topless $75
Stevens, Tabitha	Entertainment	10			25	
Stevens, Thaddeus	Senate/Congress	35	110	200		Rep. PA 1849-68, Abolitionist
Stevens, Wallace	Author	250	835		2000	Am. Poet, Pulitzer
Stevens, Wallace 1879-1955	Author	310	1000			Am. Writer-Poet
Stevens, Walter Husted	Civil War	250				CSA Gen.
Stevens, Warren	Entertainment	4	4	15	15	
Stevenson, Adlai E. 1835-1914	Vice President	55	200	305	160	Cleveland Vice Pres.
Stevenson, Adlai E. 1900-65	Governor	65	65	145	150	Gov. IL, Pres. Candidate
Stevenson, Adlai E., III	Governor	5	10		10	Gov. IL
Stevenson, Andrew	Senate/Congress	10	20	30		Rep. VA 1821
Stevenson, Carter L.	Civil War	95	205	500		CSA General
Stevenson, Coke	Governor	5	15			Governer TX

NAME	CATEGORY	SIG	LS/DS	ALS	SP	Comment
Stevenson, McLean	Entertainment	15	35		58	
Stevenson, R. H.	Civil War	10	20	30		
Stevenson, Robert Louis 1850-94	Author	335	1500	1785	4370	Novelist, Poet, Essayist
Stewart, Alexander P.(War Date)	Civil War	272		580		CSA Gen.
Stewart, Alexander P.1821-1908	Civil War	170	295	347		CSA Gen.
Stewart, Alexander T.	Business	10	25	40		Am. Merchant, Garden City, L.I.
Stewart, Catherine Mary	Entertainment	4			15	
Stewart, Charles	Military	95	275			Cmdr. USS Constitution
Stewart, Elaine	Entertainment	4			10	Pin-Up SP $15
Stewart, James (Jimmy)	Entertainment	40	145		140	S Harvey Original $300+
Stewart, James C.	Aviation	12	25	40	30	ACE, WW II
Stewart, James S.	Clergy	30	45	60	45	
Stewart, John A.	Business	3	10	25		
Stewart, Lisa	Entertainment	5			15	
Stewart, Martha	Author		10		30	Columnist
Stewart, Paul	Entertainment	10			30	
Stewart, Peggy	Entertainment	4			10	
Stewart, Potter (SC)	Supreme Court	35	110		95	
Stewart, Rex	Entertainment	75	95		150	Cornet
Stewart, Robert L.	Astronaut	5			20	
Stewart, Rod	Entertainment	10	15		65	Rock
Stewart, William	Senate	34	45	70		Drafted US Mining Law-1872 (NV)
Stewart, Wynn	Country Music	10			20	
Steyn, Martinus T. 1857-1916	Head of State	35				Last Pres. Orange Free State
Stiborik, Joe	Aviation	30			50	Enola Gay Radar Operator WW II
Stickney, Dorothy	Entertainment	5	7	20	25	
Stieglitz, Alfred 1864-1946	Artist-Photographer	200	675	812		Revolutionized Camera Technique
Stiers, David Ogden	Entertainment	30			150	
Stigler, George J.	Economist	20	25	40	25	Nobel Economics 1982
Stiles, William H. 1808-65	Congress	20				Repr. GA, CSA Colonel
Still, William Grant	Composer	120	265	385	250	1st Afro-Am. Symphony Conductor
Stills, Stephen	Entertainment	40			75	
Stilwell, Joseph W. 1883-1946	Military	165	200		450	Gen. WW II.Vinegar Joe
Stimson, Henry L. 1867-1950	Cabinet	40	125	195	50	Sec'y State 1929. Served Several Cabinet s
Sting	Entertainmebt	25			40	
Stirling, Linda	Entertainment	5			20	
Stirling, Wm. Alex., Lord 1726-83	Revolutionary War	385	950	1950		General Continental Army
Stock, Frederick A.	Composer	20	55	100	45	Dir. Chicago Symphony Orch.
Stock, Harold	Business	10	35	50	20	
Stockdale, James B.	Military	22	30		25	Adm. WW II. Perot Running Mate
Stockton, Frank R.	Author	25	125		35	Juvenile Fiction. Novels.Editor
Stockton, Richard 1730-81	Revolutionary War	500	1050	3500		Signer Decl. of Indepen.
Stockton, Richard 1764-1828	Senate/Congress	20	35	50		Rep., Senator NJ 1796
Stockton, Robert Field 1795-1866	Military	125	375	490		Sen. NJ, Stockton, CA Named
Stockwell, Dean	Entertainment	10			30	
Stockwell, Guy	Entertainment	10			30	
Stockwell, Harry	Entertainment	50			150	
Stoddard, Richard H.	Author	20	30	45		Poet, Writer, Literary Critic
Stoddart, James H.	Entertainment	20			40	Vintage Actor
Stoddert, Benjamin 1751-1813	Revolutionary War	95	270	430		1st Sec'y Navy 1798
Stoica, Chivu	Head of State	50				Premier Roumania
Stoker, Bram 1847-1912	Author	105	325	533		Ir. writer of Dracula
Stokes, Carl Burton	Political	5	15	35	10	Mayor Cleveland
Stokes, Louis 1925-	Congress	10	20		15	Afro-Am. Repr. OH
Stokes, William	Civil War	60				Union Gen., Rep. TN
Stokowski, Leopold 1882-1977	Entertainment	75	112	135	150	Conductor AMusQS $350

NAME	CATEGORY	SIG	LS/DS	ALS	SP	Comment
Stolle, Bruno	Aviation	5	15	20	15	
Stoloff, Morris	Entertainment	10			30	Conductor
Stoltz, Eric	Entertainment	9		10	20	25	
Stolz, Robert 1880-1975	Composer	20	75			Conductor. Composed 65 Operettas
Stolz, Teresa	Entertainment	40	75			ALS/Content $400
Stone Temple Pilots	Entertainment	25			75	Rock
Stone, Cliffie	Country Music	10			20	Singer, Songwriter, Record Exec
Stone, Ezra	Entertainment	25	35		50	Vintage Radio's Henry Aldrich
Stone, Fred	Entertainment	14		30	30	
Stone, George E.	Entertainment	20			45	
Stone, Harlan Fiske (SC)1872-1946	Supreme Court	70	225	300	225	Chief Justice
Stone, Harold J.	Entertainment	10			30	
Stone, Irving	Author	20	75	100	40	Historical Biographical Novels
Stone, John Samuel	Clergy	20		85		
Stone, Lewis	Entertainment	30	40	75	65	
Stone, Lucy (Blackwell)1818-93	Reformer	90	700	350		Suffragist, Women's Rights
Stone, Marcus	Artist		15	30		Illustrated for Chas. Dickens
Stone, Milburn	Entertainment	45	55	100	100	
Stone, Oliver	Entertainment	10			25	AA Film Director, Writer, Producer
Stone, Paula	Entertainment	25		10	40	Western Heroine
Stone, Sharon	Entertainment	15			50	Pin-Up SP $75
Stone, Thomas 1743-87	Revolutionary War	590	930	1750		Signer Decl. of Indepen.
Stoneman, George 1822-94	Civil War-Gov.	60	195	195		Union General, Gov. of CA
Stooges, The Three (3)	Entertainment	1500			3500	
Stoopnagle, Colonel Lemuel Q.	Entertainment	15	15	30	30	Vint.Radio (Fred. C. Taylor)
Stoppard, Tom	Author	30	80	155	35	Br. Plays of Verbal Brilliance
Storch, Larry	Entertainment	6	8	12	15	
Stordahl, Axel	Conductor-Arranger	25				
Storey, June	Entertainment	4				Actress. Westerns
Storm, Gale	Entertainment	7			20	Star of Early TV Series
Storm, Tempest	Entertainment	10	20	28	25	Pin-Up SP $35
Storms, Harrison A.	Business	9		25		
Storrs Richard Salter 1821-1900	Clergy	25	35	50		Congr. Minister-Scholar-Author
Story, Joseph (SC)	Supreme Court	75	150	300		ALS/Content $2,500
Stott, John	Clergy	15	25	30		
Stoughton, William 1632-1701	Colonial America	450	1200			Gov. MA, Stoughton Hall,Harvard
Stout, Rex 1886-1975	Author	35	110	215	40	Created Detective Nero Wolfe
Stowe, Harriet Beecher 1811-96	Author	250	320	725	1610	Anti-Slavery. AMsS $3,850
Stowe, Madeline	Entertainment	10			95	Pin-Up SP $30-90
Stracciari, Riccardo	Entertainment	50			375	Opera. Baritone/46 Year Career
Strachey, Lytton	Author	70	175	475		Br. Member of Bloomsbury Group
Stradlin, Izzy	Entertainment	15			40	Guns N' Roses
Straight, Beatrice	Entertainment	5	6	15	20	AA
Strait, Donald G.	Aviation	12	25	40	35	ACE, WW II
Strait, George	Country Music	10			30	
Strait, Horace Burton	Senate/Congress	10	15			Rep. MN 1873, Banker, Agri.
Stranahan, Robert A., Jr.	Business	5			10	CEO Champion Spark Plugs
Strand, Paul	Photographer	25	70	338		Am. Know for Photo Documentaries
Strange, Glenn	Entertainment	50			150	
Strasberg, Lee 1901-82	Entertainment	30	35	55	100	Drama Coach. Hd. Actor's Studio
Strasberg. Susan	Entertainment	12	15	35	20	Pin-Up SP $30
Stratas, Teresa	Entertainment	25			50	Opera
Stratemeyer, George F.	Military	30	40		50	
Stratten, Dorothy	Entertainment	100			250	
Stratton, Chas. S.	Entertainment	250		475	468	Barnum's General Tom Thumb
Stratton, Samuel S.	Senate/Congress	5	10		10	Rep. NY. Navy Intelligence

The Sanders Price Guide to Autographs

NAME	CATEGORY	SIG	LS/DS	ALS	SP	Comment
Stratton, William G.	Gov-Congress	4	10			Rep., Gov. IL
Straub, Robert W.	Governor	5	15			Gov. OR
Straus, Jack I.	Business	4	10	25	10	3rd Generation R.H.Macy Dept...
Straus, Nathan 1848-1931	Business	95	70		55	Owner R.H. Macy Co. Dept Store
Straus, Oscar 1870-1954	Composer	150	240	265	200	The Chocolate Soldier
Strause, Charles	Composer	8	15	30	25	
Strauss, Adolf	Military	10	15	35	15	
Strauss, Eduard	Composer	25				Younger Brother of Johann.AMusQS $150.
Strauss, Franz Josef	Head of State	15	45	125	35	
Strauss, Johann 1804-49	Composer	250	445	1775		Aus. Waltzes. Cond. Own Orchest
Strauss, Johann, Jr. 1825-99	Composer	450	1225	900	3950	The Waltz King
Strauss, Levi	Business					1850 Establ'd Levi Strauss & Co
Strauss, Peter	Entertainment	15			45	
Strauss, Richard 1864-1949	Composer	228	545	1077	710	AMusQS $700-$2,500
Strauss, Robert	Cabinet	4	12	20	10	
Strauss, Robert	Entertainment	25			45	
Stravinsky, Igor 1882-1971	Composer	325	612	925	808	AMusQS $975-$1,150-$1,750
Straw, Ezekiel A.	Governor	5	15			Governor NH
Strawbridge, James Dale	Senate/Congress	5	15			Rep. PA/. CW Brigade Surgeon
Stray Cats	Entertainment	35			100	Rock
Strayhorn, Billy	Entertainment					Jazz Musician-No Price Availabl
Streep, Meryl	Entertainment	20	30	45	50	AA
Street, Julian	Author	15			75	
Streett, St. Clair	Aviation	50	165			Alaskan Air Expedition
Streib, Werner	Aviation				60	Ger. Ace WW II. RK
Streich, Rita	Entertainment	10			25	Opera
Streicher, Julius	Journalist	50	170			Nazi Anti-Semetic, Hanged
Streight, Abel	Civil War	50	165			Union Gen. Escaped Libby Prison
Streisand, Barbra	Entertainment	150	700		258	AA. Pin-Up SP $275
Stribling, Thomas S.	Author	12	25	60		Am. Novlist. Pulitzer
Strindberg, August 1849-1912	Author	275		850	1093	Swe.ALS's/Cont. $1,400-$2,200
Stringfield, Sherry	Entertainment				40	Actress ER
Stringham, Silas Horton	Civil War	55	105			Union Adm.
Stritch, Samuel, Cardinal	Clergy	40	45	75	45	
Strode, Woody	Entertainment	50				Actor-Athlete
Stroheim, Eric von	Entertainment	160			490	Classic Film Director
Stromberg, Hunt	Entertainment	10	15		30	Film Producer, Director
Strong, Caleb 1745-1819	Revolutionary War	60	200	475		1st U.S. Senator & Gov. Mass.
Strong, George C. 1832-1863	Civil War	235	875			Union Gen.Mortally Wounded '63
Strong, Susan	Entertainment	12			20	Vintage Actress
Strong, William (SC)	Supreme Court	80	170	305		
Stroud Twins	Entertainment	18			40	
Stroud, Robert,Birdman of Alcatraz	Convict-Ornithologist			710		Remarkable 7 pp. ALS $15,000
Strouse, Charles	Composer	15			30	Annie AMusQS $120
Struck, Heinz	Science	10			35	Rocket Pioneer/von Braun/von Braun
Struthers, Sally	Entertainment	4		10	15	
Stryker (4)	Entertainment	10			20	Gospel Singers
Stuart, Alexander H. H.1807-91	Cabinet	25	60	95		Fillmore Sec'y Interior
Stuart, George R.	Clergy	10	15	20		
Stuart, Gilbert 1755-1828	Artist	200	500	850		Portraitist. Presidents-Royalty
Stuart, Gloria	Entertainment	5			15	
Stuart, J.E.B. (War Date)	Civil War	12500				CSA Gen.
Stuart, J.E.B. 1833-64	Civil War	3897	5775	12700		CSA Gen.,War Dte.ALS $19,000
Stuart, Leslie	Composer	20				Floradora AMusQS $200
Stuart, Marty	Country Music	10			25	
Stuart, Randy	Entertainment	3			10	

The Sanders Price Guide to Autographs

NAME	CATEGORY	SIG	LS/DS	ALS	SP	Comment
Studebaker, Clement	Business	200	500	765		Auto Pioneers.Studebaker Bros.
Studebaker, Jr., Clement	Business	40	105	195	75	Studebaker Bros. Mfg. Co.
Studer, Cheryl	Entertainment	10			35	Opera
Stultz, Wilmer	Aviation	50	135		150	Pioneer Aviator/A. Earhart
Stump, Felix B.	Military	25	80		50	Adm. Capt. Lexington WW II
Sturge, Joseph 1793-1859	Philanthropist	10	20	45		Pacifist,Reformer,Abolitionist
Sturgeon, Daniel	Senate-Cabinet	25	70	125		Sen. PA 1839, US Treasurer 1853
Sturges, John	Entertainment	5	6	15	15	
Sturges, Preston	Entertainment	20			50	Film Director, Producer, Writer
Sturgis, Samuel D.	Civil War	50	105			Union Gen.
Styne, Jule	Composers	25			60	AMusQS $180, $370
Styron, William	Author	15	35	80	75	Sophie's Choice MsS 1p $200
Styx	Entertainment	25			50	
Suchet, David	Entertainment	10			30	Br. Actor. Poirot
Suchet, Louis G.,Duc d'A	Napoleonic Wars	85	215	390		Marshal of Napoleon
Sucre, Antonio de	Military	295	1050			Liberator of Venezuela, General
Sudarmono, Pratiwi	Astronaut	12	25		25	
Suenens, Leo Joseph, Cardinal	Clergy	45	75	90	65	
Suharto, General	Head of State	15	30	75	35	Indonesia
Sul, Terra	Entertainment	4			10	
Sullavan, Margaret	Entertainment	60	65		149	Retired at 33. Suicide at 49
Sullivan, Anne (Annie)	Educator	100		425		TLS/Content $1,000
Sullivan, Arthur, Sir 1842-1900	Composer	175	400	650	1000	AMusQS $1,200
Sullivan, Barry	Entertainment	10	15		25	
Sullivan, Ed 1902-1974	Entertainment	25	35	60	118	Columnist, TV Host
Sullivan, Francis L.	Entertainment	10	20		25	
Sullivan, James	Revolutionary War	50	95	200		Continental Congress, Gov. MA
Sullivan, John1740-95	Revolutionary War	150	425	575		Continental Congress, General
Sullivan, Kathleen	Entertainment	10			20	TV Hostess
Sullivan, Kathryn D.	Aviation-Astro.	10	25	45	30	
Sullivan, Pat*	Cartoonist	50			400	Felix The Cat
Sullivan, Peter John	Civil War	55	105	160		Union General
Sullivan, Susan	Entertainment	5	6	20	15	
Sullivan, William 1774-1839	Author	20	40	95		Politician, Gen. Militia, Orato
Sully, Alfred	Civil War	35	80	110	150	Union General
Sully, Thomas 1783-1872	Artist	165	392	506		Lead Portrait Painter of His Day
Sully-Prudhomme, Ren, F.A	Author	40	135	225		Fr. Poet, 1st Nobel Literature
Sulzberger, Art Ochs, Jr.	Business	10	25	30	15	NY Times
Sulzer, William	Congress-Gov.	15	35		25	Rep.,Gov. NY, Impeached 1913
Sumi, Jo	Entertainment	5			35	Opera. Korean Coloratura
Summer, Donna	Entertainment	10	15		20	
Summerall, Charles Pelot	Military	10	20	35	25	Gen., Pres. Citadel 1931-53
Summerfield, Arthur E.	Cabinet	15	20	30	20	P.M. Genera, Modernized Systeml
Summersby, Kay	Military-WWII	95	325		125	D.D. Eisenhower's WW II Aide
Summerville, Slim	Entertainment	35			75	
Sumner, Charles 1811-74	Civil War	97	150	338		Abolitionist. Founder Rep.Party
Sumner, Increase 1746-99	Governor	65	175			Rev. War Jurist & Stateman
Sumner, John B. 1780-1862	Clergy	25				Archbishop Canterbury
Sumter, Thomas	Revolutionary War	375	1200			Soldier, Rep.,Sen., SC 1789
Sun Yat-Sen 1866-1975	Head of State	698	925	1550	2530	1st Pres. Chinese Republic
Sunday, William A. 'Billy'	Clergy	85	160	275	400	Early 19th Cent. Evangelist-Baseball Player
Sung, Kim Il	Head of State	50			150	North Viet Nam
Sununu, John	Cabinet	12	15	25	15	Chief of Staff White House
Supertramp	Entertainment	35			75	
Suppe', Franz von	Composer	110	225	450	395	Aus. Opera, Operetta,Choral
Susann, Jacqueline	Author	20	35	45	40	Valley of the Dolls etc.

PRICES 467

NAME	CATEGORY	SIG	LS/DS	ALS	SP	Comment
Sutherland, Donald	Entertainment	10	15	20	20	
Sutherland, George (SC)	Supreme Court	65	165	350	250	
Sutherland, Joan	Entertainment	15		35	35	Opera, Concert
Sutherland, Keifer	Entertainment	10			45	
Sutro, Adolph H. J.	Business-Engineer	35	90	185		Mining magnate. Sutro Tunnel
Sutter, John A. 1803-80	CA Pioneer	1190	3400	8875	1955	Sutter's Fort.ALS/Cont. $15,000
Sutton, Grady	Entertainment	8	10		15	
Sutton, John	Entertainment	5			25	Suave Br. Co-Star
Sutton, Willy	Criminal	45		290	75	Bank Robber. Prison Escapes
Svanholm, Set	Entertainment	15			45	Opera
Svenson, Bo	Entertainment	4	5	9	10	
Swaggart, Jimmy	Clergy	10	30	35	30	Evangelist
Swan, James	Revolutionary War	180	595	650		Finan'l Speculator.
Swann, Thomas	Senate/Congress	5	15			Senator,Gov, MD. Pres. B & O RR
Swanson, Claude A. 1862-1939	Cabinet	18	25	95	20	Sec'y Navy 1933 FDR
Swanson, Gloria 1897-1983	Entertainment	50	330		160	
Swanson, J.	Civil War	65	135	180		
Swanson, Kristy	Entertainment	15			70	Actress (See Zane, Billy)
Swart, Charles R. 1894-	Head of State	5		20	40	
Swarthout, Gladys	Entertainment	25	75		70	Opera and Film Star
Swasey, Ambrose	Business	40	90			
Swayne, Noah H. (SC)	Supreme Court	45	115	195		
Swayne, Wager	Civil War	25	45	105		Union General
Swayze, John Cameron	Entertainment	5			10	Radio, TV News & Commercials
Swayze, Patrick	Entertainment	25			35	
Swearingen, John	Business	10	25	40	15	CEO Continental Ill. Corp.
Sweat, Lorenzo DeMedici	Senate/Congress	10	15	25		Rep. ME 1863
Swedenborg, Emanuel 1688-1772	Science	3000				Swe.Science,Philosophy,Religion
Sweeney, Brian	Law Enforcement	4			10	Law Enforcement No. Ireland
Sweeney, Walter C.	Military	5	15	25	15	Gen. Tactical Air Cmd.
Sweet, Blanche	Entertainment	20		30	35	
Sweet, John H.	Business	5	15		10	CEO US News & World Report
Swenson, Ruth Ann	Entertainment	10			25	Opera
Swett, James E.	Aviation	15	30	50	42	ACE, WW II
Swift, Frederic W.	Civil War	55	135	195		Union General, MOH
Swift, George B.	Political	10	25			Mayor of Chicago
Swift, Harold Higgins	Business	20	50	95	35	Chm. Swift & Co., Meatpackers
Swift, John W. 1750-1819	Revolutionary War	65	180			Merchant. Soldier
Swift, Jonathan 1667-1745	Author	2500	7300	13230		Satirist,Poet,Clergy,Political
Swigert, John L. Jr.	Astronaut	40	75		125	
Swinburne, Algernon C.1837-1909	Author	185	295	617		Br. 19th Cent. Lyric Poet
Swing, Philip D. 1884-1963	Congress	5	25		15	Repr. CA
Swinnerton, Frank	Author	20	55	100		Br. Novelist, Critic
Swinnerton, James*	Cartoonist	35			180	Little Jimmy
Swinton, Ernest D.1868-1951	Military	45	110	310		British Inventor of Tank
Swit, Loretta	Entertainment	15			30	
Switzer, Carl Alfalfa	Entertainment	200			525	
Swope, Gerard	Business	60				CEO General Electric
Swope, Herbert Bayard 1882-1958	Author	10	125	75	20	Journalist, War Corresp.,Pulitz
Swope, James S.	Aviation	10	22	40	30	ACE, WW II
Sykes, Jerome H.	Entertainment	15			30	Light Opera
Sylva, Carmen (Queen of Romania)	Author	50	75			Elizabeth, Queen of Romania
Sylva, Marguerite	Entertainment	15			25	Vintage
Sylvia	Entertainment	5	6	15	15	
Symington, Stuart	Cabinet	5	15	35	20	Sen. MO, Sec'y Air Force
Symmes, John Cleves	Revolutionary War	110	375	550		Patriot. Continental Congress

NAME	CATEGORY	SIG	LS/DS	ALS	SP	Comment
Szell, George	Entertainment	10			65	Hung. Conductor
Szent-Gyorgyi, Albert	Science	40	65	125	50	Nobel Medicine 1937
Szigeti, Joseph	Entertainment	35			250	Violinist
Szilard, Leo 1898-1964	Science	25				Nuclear/Phys.TLS/Cont.$2500
Szold, Henrietta 1860-1945	Zionist Leader	140	475	600		Founder, Pres. Hadassah
Szymanowski, Karol M.	Composer	125		560		AMusMsS $1250

NAME	CATEGORY	SIG	LS/DS	ALS	SP	Comment
T Hooft, Visser	Celebrity	3	5	10	10	
T, Mr.	Entertainment	10			20	
Tabb, John Banister 1845-1909	Civil War Clergy	40		200		Rom.Cath. clergy, Poet.CSA
Taber, Robert	Entertainment	6	8	15	15	
Taft, Charles P.	Publisher	10	15	25	10	Owner-Ed. Cincinnati Times-Star
Taft, Helen Herron 1861-1943	First Lady	100	200	550	975	ALS White House $1,200
Taft, Helen Manning	First Lady	80	185	300	500	Daughter
Taft, Henry Wallace	Lawyer	3	7	15		Noted Brother Of Pres. Taft
Taft, Lorado 1860-1936	Artist	60	110	130		Influential Am. Sculptor-Author
Taft, Robert A. 1889-1953	Senate/Congress	20	30		25	SIGned caricature $75, OH
Taft, Robert, Jr. 1917-	Senate/Congress	7	15		10	Rep., Senator OH.
Taft, William Howard (As President	President	210	765	3000	542	
Taft, William Howard 1857-1930	President	175	476	848	400	ALS/Cont. As Chief Justice $2200-$4500
Tagliabue, Carlo	Entertainment	45			175	Opera
Tagliavini, Feruccio	Entertainment	35			95	Opera
Taglioni, Marie 1804-1884	Entertainment	300		935		It. Premier Ballerina
Tagore, Rabindranath, Sir	Author	105	265	388	350	Nobel Prize Lit., Indian Poet
Tait, A.C., Archbishop	Clergy	12	35	50		
Tait, Arthur Fitzwilliam	Artist	25	55	100		Landscape Artist
Taka, Miiko	Entertainment	15			25	Japanese Actress
Takahira, Kogoro, Baron 1854-1926	Diplomat	45				At Treaty Signing of Russo-Jap. War.
Takei, George	Entertainment	15			35	
Talbert, Melvin, Bishop	Clergy	20	25	30	35	
Talbot, Gloria	Entertainment	10			20	
Talbot, Helen	Entertainment	10			25	
Talbot, Lyle	Entertainment	5	10	15	15	
Talbot, Nita	Entertainment	4	6		20	
Talbot, Wm. Henry Fox 1800-77	Science	295		1250		Br.Inventor of Photogr. Process
Talbott, Harold D.	Cabinet	10	15			Sec'y AF
Talcott, Joseph 1669-1741	Colonial America	30	75	160		Colonial Governor CT
Talese, Gay	Author	10	550		25	Am. Novelist
Taliaferro, William B. (War Date)	Civil War	175	418			CSA Gen.
Taliaferro, William B. 1822-98	Civil War	90		361		CSA Gen.
Talking Heads	Entertainment	20			60	
Tallchief, Maria	Entertainment	15	20	35	30	Ballerina
Talley, Marion	Entertainment	15		45	50	Am. Soprano

The Sanders Price Guide to Autographs

NAME	CATEGORY	SIG	LS/DS	ALS	SP	Comment
Talleyrand, Charles Maurice de	Head of State	185	615	950		Grand Chancellor of Napoleon
Talmadge, Benjamin 1754-1835	Revolutionary War	220	465			Served Throughout War. Rep. NY
Talmadge, Constance	Entertainment	35			80	Silent Star. Intolerance
Talmadge, Eugene	Governor	20	60	95		Governor GA
Talmadge, Herman	Senate/Congress	10	20		15	Gov., Senator GA
Talmadge, Norma	Entertainment	50			175	
Talmage, T. Dewitt	Clergy	50	70	95		America Divine, Editor
Talman, William	Entertainment	50	70	150	125	Regular on Original Perry Mason
Talvela, Marti	Entertainment	30			75	Opera. Finnish Basso
Tamblyn, Russ	Entertainment	6	8		20	
Tambor, Jeffrey	Entertainment	6	8	15	15	
Tamiroff, Akim	Entertainment	30	40	75	70	
Tandy, Jessica 1904-94	Entertainment	20	35	45	65	AA
Taney, Roger B. (SC)1777-1864	Supreme Court	60	350	425		Chief Justice., Dred Scott Case
Tanner, Henry Ossawa	Artist	270		750		Religious Subjects,Realistic
Tanner, John Riley	Governor	12	20			Governor IL
Tanner, Richard, Dr.(Diamond Dick)	Old West	450				Companion to Wild Bill Hickok
Tansman, Alexandre	Composer	40	125		280	
Tappan, Arthur 1786-1865	Abolitionist	25	65	120		Merchant, Philanthropist
Tappan, James C.	Civil War	35	70	110		CSA General
Tarantino, Quentin	Entertainment				50	AA Pulp Fiction Writer-Director
Tarbell, Ida M. 1857-1944	Author	20	45	98	30	Muckraking Journalist re Std.Oil
Tarkington, Booth 1869-1946	Author	32	400	195	125	Playwright, Novelist. Pulitzer
Tarleton, Banastre, Sir	Revolutionary War	135	365	715		Barbaric Br.General. Am. Rev.
Tarnower, Herman Dr.	Medical	15	50	135	20	Diet Dr. Murdered
Tartakov, Joakim	Entertainment			450		Opera. Imperial Russ. Baritone Star
Tartikoff, Brandon	Business	10			30	TV executive
Tashlin, Frank	Entertainment	15			25	Director
Tashman, Lilyan	Entertainment	30	40	75	70	
Tassigny, J.M.G. de	Military	35	90	140		
Tate, Allen 1899-1979	Author	10	30	100		Am. Poet, Critic, Biographer
Tate, Henry, Sir, 1st Baronet	Business	40	95	240		Br. Philanthropist,Tate Gallery
Tate, Jackson R.	Military	5		30	25	Adm. WW II.
Tate, Sharon	Entertainment	200	300	500	550	Murdered By Manson Gang
Tattersall, Richard 1724-95	Business	20	45	100		Rendevous For Sporting-Betting
Tattnall, Joseph	Civil War			715		CSA Naval Capt.
Tatum, Edward L.	Science	45	70	125		Nobel Medicine 1958
Taube, Henry, Dr.	Science	22	35		25	Nobel Chemistry 1983
Tauber, Richard	Entertainment	50			150	Opera, Austrian Tenor
Taufflieb, Gen.	Military	45	120	215	100	
Taurog, Norman	Entertainment	50			150	Film Director
Taussig, Frank William 1859-1940	Economist	10	25			Author. Chm Tariff Bd.
Tawes, J. Millard	Governor	5	15			Governor MD
Tawney, James A.	Congress	5	15	25		Repr. MN 1893
Tayback, Vic	Entertainment	12			35	
Taylor, Thomas H. (War Date)	Civil War	120	210	550		CSA Gen.
Taylor, Bayard 1825-78	Author	20	70	135		Journalist, Traveller, Diplomat
Taylor, Charles H.	Congress	5	10		10	Congressman NC
Taylor, Deems	Composer	35	80	85	50	Musicologist, Critic, Author
Taylor, Don	Entertainment	5			20	Actor turned Director
Taylor, Dub	Entertainment	10			40	
Taylor, Elizabeth	Entertainment	181	275	275	362	AA
Taylor, Estelle	Entertainment	10	25	45	45	
Taylor, George 1716-81	Revolutionary War	1400	3575	7050		Signer. ALS $35,000
Taylor, Glen H. 1904-1984	Congress	10	25		25	Sen. ID, Actor, Singer
Taylor, Graham	Clergy	15	25	35		

NAME	CATEGORY	SIG	LS/DS	ALS	SP	Comment
Taylor, H. C.	Military	10	24	40		
Taylor, James	Composer	35	100	250	95	Singer-Guitarist
Taylor, James (Afro-Am.)	Entertainment	40			75	
Taylor, James Willis	Senate/Congress	4	10	20		Rep. TN 1919
Taylor, Joan	Entertainment	7			15	
Taylor, John	Celebrity	50	130			
Taylor, John W.	Senate/Congress	15		40		Early Rep. 1813, Speaker
Taylor, Joseph P. 1796-1864	Civil War	60	175			War 1812, Union Gen.
Taylor, Kent	Entertainment	5			15	
Taylor, Laurette	Entertainment	15	20	40	35	
Taylor, Margaret	First Lady					Only 1 Known. No Price Avail.
Taylor, Mary	Country Music	10			20	
Taylor, Maxwell D.	Military	25	75	110	65	Gen. WW II
Taylor, Meshach	Entertainment	5			20	Designing Women, Dave's World
Taylor, Niki	Model	20			75	
Taylor, Nikki	Entertainment				40	Actress-Model. Pin-Up $75
Taylor, Richard (War Date)	Civil War	390	1898			CSA Gen. Son of Pres. Taylor
Taylor, Richard 1826-79	Civil War	225	757			CSA Gen. Son of Pres. Taylor
Taylor, Richard E., Dr.	Science	20	50			Nobel Physics 1990
Taylor, Robert 1911-69	Entertainment	40	100	125	212	
Taylor, Robert L. 1850-1912	Congress	10	15		15	Gov., Rep. & Senator TN
Taylor, Rod	Entertainment	4	6		20	
Taylor, Thomas H. 1825-1901	Civil War	75	100	250		CSA General
Taylor, Vaughn	Entertainment	20			50	
Taylor, Walter H.	Civil War	40	90			CSA Col. Aide-de-camp R.E. Lee
Taylor, William, Bishop	Clergy		40	50	75	
Taylor, Wm. Levi (Buck)	Celebrity	175				NRPA
Taylor, Zachary (As Pres.)	President	1150	5900	6500		
Taylor, Zachary 1784-1850	President	750	2600	3525		
Taylor-Young, Leigh	Entertainment	5	8	15	15	
Tazewell, Littleton	Senate/Congress	45	135	250		Rep. 1800, Sen. 1824, Gov. VA
Tchaikovsky, Piotr I. 1840-93	Composer	2000	3450	6688	5000	Rus. Opera, Symphony, Ballet, Etc.
Tcherepnin, Alexander	Composer					AMusQS $350
Tchernihovsky, Saul	Author	175		550		Rus-Hebrew Dr., Poet, Translator
Te Kanawa, Kiri, Dame	Entertainment	25	55		75	Opera, Concert
Teagarden, Charlie	Entertainment	10			25	Jazz Trumpet
Teagarden, Jack	Entertainment	60	100		125	Big Band Leader-Trombonist
Teal, Ray	Entertainment	50			150	
Teale, Edwin W. 1899-1980	Nauralist			75	25	Photographer, Pulitzer Writer.
Tearle, Conway	Entertainment	15			40	Vintage Br. Actor
Tearle, Godfrey, Sir	Entertainment	20			50	Br. Actor. Vintage
Teasdale, Veree	Entertainment	20	25	45	45	
Tebaldi, Renata	Entertainment	20			48	Opera. Italian Soprano
Tedrow, Irene	Entertainment	3	4		16	
Teitjens, Therese	Entertainment	50			190	Opera
Telfair, Edward	Revolutionary War	30	95	150		Continental Congress from GA
Telford, Thomas 1757-1834	Engineer					Br. Roadbuilder
Teller, Edward, Dr. 1908-94	Science	45	130	210	95	Fermi Award
Teller, Henry M. 1830-1914	Cabinet	30	25	50	30	Sec'y Interior 1882, Arthur
Telva, Marion	Entertainment	15			40	Opera.. Noted Contralto
Temin, Howard M., Dr.	Science	20	35	55	25	Nobel Medicine 1975
Tempest, Marie	Entertainment	25	35	50	65	
Temple, Frederick 1821-1902	Clergy	22		90		Archbishop Canterbury, Educator, Author
Temple, Shirley (Agar)	Entertainment				385	
Temple, Shirley (as a child)	Entertainment	150			450	As Teenager SPI $250
Temple, Shirley (Black)	Entertainment	20	25	35	45	SP (Vintage Ph/'87 Sig.) $385

NAME	CATEGORY	SIG	LS/DS	ALS	SP	Comment
Temple, Wm.	Clergy	40	45	85	65	Archbishop Canterbury
Templeton, Alec	Entertainment	10			50	Br. Blind Jazz Pianist
Templeton, Ben	Cartoonist	5			20	Motley's Crew
Templeton, Faye	Entertainment	25	30	60	65	Musical Career For Over 50 Year
Temptations (All)	Entertainment	40			125	
Ten Broeck, Abraham 1734-1810	Revolutionary War	100	125	1025		Gen. Judge, Banker
Tennant, F.R.	Clergy	15	20	25		
Tennant, Veronica	Ballet	10			25	National Ballet of Canada
Tennant, Victoria	Entertainment	5	8	25	20	
Tenniel, John, Sir	Artist	70	110	260		Illustr. Alice in Wonderland
Tennille, Toni	Entertainment	5			15	Singer
Tennyson, Alfred, Lord 1809-92	Author	215	1038	795	1048	Br. Poet Laureate
Tennyson, Jean	Entertainment	10			20	Am. Soprano
Teresa, Mother 1910-	Clergy	125	254	350	250	Nobel Peace Prize
Tereshkova, Valentina	Cosmonaut	200	250		250	1st Woman in Outer Space
Terfel, Bryn	Entertainment	10			35	Welsh Operatic Baritone
Terhune, Alfred Payson 1872-1942	Author	25	75	110	50	Famous Writer of Dog Stories
Terhune, Max	Entertainment	100			250	
Terkel, Studs	Author	10	15	25	15	Columnist, Biographer, TV
Ternina, Milka	Entertainment	20		185		Opera. Croatian Soprano
Terrell, Bob	Author	10			25	author, newspaper columnist
Terriss, Ellaline	Entertainment				50	Br. Actress. 19th Century
Terry, Alfred Howe 1827-90	Civil War	100	475	590		Union Gen., Cmdr. Dakota Terr.
Terry, Clark	Entertainment	50				Trumpet, Fluegelhorn
Terry, Ellen, Dame 1848-1928	Entertainment	30	60	125	75	Br. Actress Partner of Henry Irving
Terry, Fred 1864-1933	Entertainment	10	15	25	25	Br. Stage & Film Star
Terry, Henry D.	Civil War	45	100	160		Union General
Terry, Luther, Dr.	Celebrity	3	5	10	5	
Terry, Paul*	Cartoonist	50			250	Animator-Mighty Mouse
Terry, Phillip	Entertainment	5	6	15	15	
Terry, William H. 1814-88	Civil War	73		255		CSA Gen. Sig/Rank $120
Terry, William Richard	Civil War	75	175	245		CSA General
Tesla, Nikola, Dr. 1856-1943	Science	470	950	1452	1150	Physicist, Electrical Genius
Tetard, J.	Aviation	45	60	170	100	
Tetrazzini, Luisa 1871-1940	Entertainment	75	115	200	233	Opera
Teyte, Maggie	Entertainment	35			130	Opera
Thacher, James, Dr. 1754-1844	Science-Author	40		300		Revolutionary War Surgeon
Thackeray, Wm. Makepeace 1811-63	Author	110	375	638		Br. Novelist Vanity Fair
Thaden, Louise McP.	Aviation		295			Altitude, Endurance, Speed Records
Thagard, Norman E.	Astronaut	10			25	
Thalberg, Irving	Entertainment	250	375	585	350	MGM's Boy Genius Producer
Thant, U 1909-74	Head of State	75	195	295	200	UN Sec'y General
Tharp, Sister Rosetta	Entertainment	65				Jazz Vocalist-Guitar
Tharp, Twyla	Entertainment	20	25		40	Dancer-Choreographer
Thatcher, Henry Knox	Civil War	50	95	140		Union Naval Commander
Thatcher, Margaret, Dame	Head of State	45	140	225	150	Prime Minister
Thatcher, Peter	Clergy	75	100	150		
Thaves, Bob	Cartoonist	5			20	Frank & Ernest
Thaw, Harry K.	Business	40	95	195	75	Playboy. Shot Sanford White
Thaw, Russell T.	Aviation	20				Racing Pilot
Thaxter, Celia	Entertainment	20	25	45	45	
Thaxter, Celia 1835-94	Author	20	45	95	150	Am. Poet
Thaxter, Phyllis	Entertainment				25	Stage & Film Leading Lady
Thayer, Abbott	Artist	15	35	70		Am. Ideal Figures, Landscapes
Thayer, Celia	Author	5	10	15		Am. Novelist, Screenwriter
Thayer, John Milton	Civil War	45	85	180		Union Gen., Gov. WY Terr.

NAME	CATEGORY	SIG	LS/DS	ALS	SP	Comment
Thayer, Silvanus 1785-1872	Military	60	140	245		Father of the Military Academy
Thebaw	Head of State	145				Burma
Thebom, Blanche	Entertainment	20	35		78	Am. Contralto, Opera, Concert
Theiss, Ursula	Entertainment	10	15	25	25	
Theissen, Tiffany Amber	Entertainment				75	
Thelen, Bob	Aviation	10	25	40	35	ACE, WW II, Blue Angels
Thesiger, Ernest	Entertainment	225			650	
Thicke, Alan	Entertainment	5			15	
Thielicke, Helmut	Clergy	20	50	65	60	Germ. Evangel. Theologian
Thiers, Louis-Adolphe	Fr. Revolution	30	65	155		1st Pres. 3rd Republic
Thiessen, Tiffany Amber	Entertainment	10			40	Actress. Pin-up $75
Thieu, Nguyen Van	Head of State	20	60	150	35	So. Viet Nam
Thinnis, Roy	Entertainment	5	6	20	15	
Thirsk, Bob	Astronaut	5	15		15	
Thomas, Ambroise 1811-1896	Composer			575		Fr. Romantic Comp.Mignon AMQS $525
Thomas, B.J.	Entertainment	4			10	
Thomas, Betty	Entertainment	5	6	15	10	
Thomas, C.-L.-Ambroise	Composer	70	105	275		Fr. Operas,etc. AMusQS $525
Thomas, Charles 1840-78	Military		800			45 Yrs. Service. Union Gen.
Thomas, Clarence (SC)	Supreme Court	25			40	
Thomas, Danny	Entertainment	20			45	
Thomas, Dave	Business	10	20		25	Founder of Wendy's
Thomas, Dylan 1914-53	Author	510		1550	1500	Welsh Poet,Playwright,Short Stories
Thomas, E. Donnall, Dr.	Science	15	25		30	Nobel Medicine 1990
Thomas, George Henry 1818-70	Civil War	118	395	595		Union Gen.Rock of Chickamauga
Thomas, Heather	Entertainment	10	10	30	25	
Thomas, Heck	Western Lawman					Special DS $2500
Thomas, Isaiah 1749-1831	Colonial Printer	135	380	1000		Publ. 1st Eng. Bible in America
Thomas, James, Bishop	Clergy	20	25	35	30	
Thomas, Jess	Entertainment	15			40	Opera
Thomas, John 1724-76	Revolutionary War	510	855	1750		Am. Physician & Gen. Cont.Army
Thomas, John Charles 1891-1960	Entertainment	20	55	45	45	Multi Media Am. Baritone
Thomas, Jonathan Taylor	Entertainment	10			70	Child Actor Home Improvement etc.
Thomas, Kurt	Entertainment	5	6	15	15	
Thomas, Lorenzo	Civil War	90	140	270		Union General
Thomas, Lowell	Entertainment	15		35	125	World Traveller, Top Radio News
Thomas, Marlo	Entertainment	4	6		15	
Thomas, Michael Tilson	Conductor	15			50	Am. Conductor
Thomas, Norman	Socialist Leader	35	115	215	55	6 Times Presidential Candidate
Thomas, Olive	Entertainment	65	70	150	150	Jack Pickford Wife.Suicide at36
Thomas, Philip Evan	Business	6	17	29		
Thomas, Richard	Entertainment	5	6	15	15	
Thomas, Robert Bailey	Author	20	45	105		Publ.,Editor Farmer's Almanac
Thomas, Samuel	Civil War	45				Union General
Thomas, Seth E.	Business	125	250	475		Founder Seth Thomas Clock Co.
Thomas, Seth E.,Jr.1816-88	Business	65	175	350		Cont'd Seth Thomas Clock Co.
Thomas, Terry	Entertainment	50		100	150	
Thomas, Theodore	Entertainment	15			30	Conductor. NY & Chic. Symph.
Thomasson, William P. 1797-1882	Congress	12				Repr. KY, Union Officer CW
Thomberg, Kerstin	Entertainment	15			35	
Thompson Twins	Entertainment	25			80	
Thompson, Benj. von Rumford	Revolutionary War	275	450	1600		Br.Physicist, Inventor,Loyalist
Thompson, Benjamin 1798-1852	Senate/Congress	5	10	25		Rep. MA 1845
Thompson, Denman	Entertainment	10			30	Vintage Stage Actor
Thompson, Dorothy 1894-1961	Author	35	55	110	85	Journalist,Correspondent,Column.
Thompson, Emma	Entertainment	20			50	Br. Actress-Playwright AA. Pin-Up SP $75

The Sanders Price Guide to Autographs

NAME	CATEGORY	SIG	LS/DS	ALS	SP	Comment
Thompson, Ernest Seton	Author	40	100	195		Wild Life Stories, Naturalist
Thompson, Gordon	Entertainment	8	9		20	
Thompson, Hank	Country Music	6			15	
Thompson, J. Walter	Business	25	70	130	50	J. Walter Thompson Adv. Agency
Thompson, Jacob 1810-85	Civil War-Cabinet	145	315	1380		Sec'y Interior, CSA Secret Agt.
Thompson, Jim	Governor	5	10		20	Governor IL
Thompson, John P.	Business	15	30	65	20	Pres. Southland Corp.
Thompson, John T. 1860-1940	Inventor-Military		300			USA Officer, Arms Inventor
Thompson, Lea	Entertainment	5	10		20	
Thompson, Linda	Entertainment	4			10	Pin-Up SP $20
Thompson, M.E.	Governor	5	15			Governor GA
Thompson, Marshall	Entertainment	15		25	35	
Thompson, Merriwether J.(War Date)	Civil War	185		3020		MO Militia General
Thompson, Merriwether J.1826-76	Civil War	135	425	465		CSA General
Thompson, Orlo and Marvis	Country Music	20			40	
Thompson, Richard W.	CabinetP	20	45	65		Sec'y Navy 1809
Thompson, Robert E.	Clergy	10	10	15		
Thompson, Ruth Plumly	Author	450				
Thompson, Smith (SC)	Supreme Court	75	150	185		
Thompson, Sue	Country Music	10			25	
Thompson, Wm. H. Big Bill 1869-1944	Mayor of Chicago	125				Gangster Era Mayor. Backed by Al Capone
Thomson, Andrew	Clergy	35	65	75		
Thomson, Charles 1729-1824	Revolutionary War	725	1480			LS As Sec'y Cont'l Congr.$1,750
Thomson, Elihu 1853-1937	Science	525	1250			Electrical Engineer-Inventor
Thomson, Geo. Paget, Sir 1892-1975	Science	52				Nobel Physics 1937
Thomson, Hugh	Br. Illustrator	25		100		
Thomson, James E.	Business	5	15	30	10	Pres. Merrill-Lynch.
Thomson, Virgil 1896-1989	Composer	40	85	150	125	& Music Critic, AMusQS $125
Thorborg, Kerstin	Entertainment	20			75	Opera
Thorburn, Grant	Colonial Am.	40	95			Grocery, Seed Merchant. Hero
Thoreau, Henry David	Author	1540	3000	7200		Am.Schoolmaster, Naturalist
Thorndike, Sybil, Dame	Entertainment	30	45		75	
Thorne, Chas. Rob't 1814-1893	Entertainment	65	80		120	
Thornhill, Claude	Bandleader	11			45	
Thornhill, F. D.	Military	15	25	40		
Thornton, Charles Tex	Business	5	15	25	15	
Thornton, Dan	Governor	5	15		10	Governor CO
Thornton, Dr. William E.	Astronaut	5			20	
Thornton, Kathryn	Astronaut	10			25	
Thornton, Matthew 1714-1803	Revolutionary War	625	1512	1925		Signer Decl. of Indepen.
Thornton, William	Astronaut	5			20	
Thornton, William 1759-1828	Revolutionary War	140	356			Am. Architect. Designed Capitol
Thornton, William A. 1803-66	Civil War	30				Union Gen. '62 DS $95
Thorpe, Jeremy	Politician	10	20	45	15	Br. Parliamentarian
Thorpe, Rose Hartwick	Author	10	20	35		Am. Curfew Must Not Ring.....
Thorson, Ralph'Papa'	Law	10	25	45	15	Bounty Hunter
Thorvaldsen, Bertel	Artist	105	325			Dan. Sculptor Lion of Lucerne
Three Stooges, The	Entertainment	1000			2200	With Moe, Curly and Larry
Three Suns, The	Entertainment	15			45	Jazz Musicians
Throop, Enos T.	Governor	25	55			Governor NY 1829
Thruston, Gates P.	Civil War	25	30	55		Union General
Thuot, Pierre	Astronaut	5			15	
Thurber, James 1894-1961	Author	105	750	505	110	Am. Humorist & Comic Artist
Thurber, James*	Cartoonist	105			500	New Yorker Illust. & Cartoonist
Thurman, Allen G.1813-95	Congress	10	30			Senator OH
Thurman, Howard	Clergy	35	40	50	50	

The Sanders Price Guide to Autographs

NAME	CATEGORY	SIG	LS/DS	ALS	SP	Comment
Thurman, Uma	Entertainment	15	30	65	50	Pin-Up SP $75
Thurmond, J. Strom	Senate/Congress	10	20		15	Senator, Governor SC
Thurston, Howard 1869-1936	Entertainment	60	212	250		Thurston The Magician
Thurston, John M. 1847-1916	Congress	15		30		Senator NE 1895
Thurston, Lorrin A. 1858-1931	Political	35		55		Pioneer Hawaiian Political Leader
Tibbatts, John W. 1802-52	Congress	10				Repr. KY, Officer Mexican War
Tibbett, Lawrence	Entertainment	50	125		123	Opera, Concert, Films
Tibbetts, Paul W.	Aviation	25	120	175	82	Pilot of Enola Gay
Tidball, John C.	Civil War	60	135	175		Union General Bvt.
Tiegs, Cheryl	Entertainment	8	9		20	Model. Pin-Up SP $25
Tierney, Gene	Entertainment	30	25	50	45	Pin-Up SP $50
Tierney, Harry	Composer	40	95	195		AMusQS $350
Tietjens, Therese	Entertainment	40			135	Ger. Soprano . Opera
Tiffany, Charles Lewis	Business	175	500		1500	Founder Tiffany and Co.
Tiffany, Louis Comfort	Artist-Business	175	500			Stained glass artist. Painter
Tiffin, Pamela	Entertainment	5	8	15	15	
Tilden, Samuel J.	Governor	75	160	250		Gov. NY, Presidential Cand.
Tilghman, James	Revolutionary War	25	70	165		Lawyer, Politician
Tilghman, Lloyd (War Date)	Civil War	235		1980		CSA Gen. KIA. AES $635
Tilghman, Lloyd 1816-63	Civil War	140	290	490		CSA General. NRPA. KIA
Tilghman, Matthew	Revolutionary War	200		950		Cont. Congress.ALS/Cont. $2,750
Tilghman, William M. 1755-1827	Law	200	850	1450		Early Western Sheriff
Tilkin-Servais, Ernest	Entertainment	25			85	Opera
Tillich, Paul	Clergy	70	95	125	100	
Tillinghast, Charles C. Jr.	Business	8	20	40	15	CEO TWA. Merrill-Lynch
Tillis, Mel	Country Music	5			15	
Tillman, Floyd	Country Music	10			20	
Tillman, Pitchfork Ben 1847-1918	Congress	25	40	55		Senator SC 1894
Tillotson, Johnny	Country Music	6			20	
Tillstrom, Burr	Entertainment	25			50	
Tilly, Jennifer	Entertainment	5		10	35	Pin-Up SP $35-60
Tilly, Meg	Entertainment	10	6	20	15	Pin-Up SP $35
Tilton, Charlene	Entertainment	25			40	
Tilton, Theodore 1835-1907	Journalist			88		Sued H.W.Beecher for Adultery
Tilton, Wm. Stowell	Civil War	45	100			
Timberlake, Bob	Artist					Litho S $600+
Timken, William Robert	Business	35	95	155	60	Fndr. Timken Roller Bearings
Ting, Samuel C. C., Dr.	Science	20	35	50	25	Nobel Physics 1976
Tingey, Thomas	Military	60	165	225		Continental Navy
Tingley, Clyde	Governor	12	20		15	Governor NM 1935
Tinker, Grant C.	Entertainment	8	9		20	TV Film Producer
Tiny Tim	Entertainment	25	35		40	
Tiny, Texas	Country Music	10			20	
Tiomkin, Dimitri 1894-1979	Composer	35		175	95	AMusQS $225-$675
Tippett, Michael Sir	Composer	40			150	
Tisch, Laurence A.	Business				45	CEO of CBS
Tisserant, Eugene, Cardinal	Clergy	35	45	50	40	
Tissot, James	Artist	75	170	230		Fr. Painter, Engraver, Enameler
Titchener, Paul	Business	10	35	45	20	
Titian (Vecelli, Tiziano)	Artist					It. NRPA
Tito, Marshal (Josip Broz)1892-1980	Head of State	80	205	280	250	Yugoslav Statesman. Communist
Titov, Gherman	Astronaut	40			135	
Tobey, Charles W.	Senate/Congress	5	15		10	Governor, Rep., Senator NH
Tobey, Ken	Entertainment	10			25	
Tobias, George	Entertainment	50			150	
Tobin, Genevieve	Entertainment	15		30	35	

NAME	CATEGORY	SIG	LS/DS	ALS	SP	Comment
Tobin, James, Dr.	Economist	22	30		25	Nobel Economics 1981
Tobin, Maurice	Cabinet	10	20	30	15	Sec'y Labor 1948, Gov. MA
Tocqueville, Alexis de	Author	45	140	350		Fr.Politician,Statesman,Writer
Tod, David	Governor	10	26			Governor OH
Today Show (Early)	Entertainment	35			75	
Todd, Alexander Robertus, Sir	Science	30	85		40	Nobel Chemistry 1957
Todd, Ann	Entertainment	20			40	
Todd, Charles Scott	Celebrity	5	15	40		
Todd, Richard	Entertainment	75			125	Portrayed Rev. Peter Marshall
Todd, Robert	Aviation	15	30	45	25	
Todd, Thelma 1905-35	Entertainment	200	195	350	550	Mysterious Death at 30
Tognini, Michel	Astronaut	15	25		25	
Togo, Heihachiro	Military	95	315	495	185	Jap. Adm. Sino-Jap. War
Togo, Shigenori	Diplomat	250			400	Jap. Foreign Minister-Statesman
Tojo, Hideki 1884-1948	Military	250	700	1500	1380	Jap. Adm. Pearl Harbor.Executed
Toklas, Alice B. 1877-1967	Author	30	95	895		Companion of Gertrude Stein
Tokody, Ilona	Entertainment	5			25	Opera
Tokyo Rose (Iva I. Toguri)	Military	225	330		250	WW II Radio Propagandist
Toledo, Francisco, Cardinal	Clergy	15000				
Toler, Sidney	Entertainment	150			425	Charlie Chan
Tolkien, John R.R. 1892-1973	Author	350	1705	1617		Br. Lord of the Rings
Tolstoy, Alexandra, Countess	Author	25				
Tolstoy, Leo, Count 1828-1910	Author	1200		2965	2165	Rus. Novelist
Tombaugh, Clyde W.	Science	25	135	270	135	Am. Astronomer, Proved Pluto
Tomei, Marissa	Entertainment	20			55	
Tomlin, Lily	Entertainment	5		15	25	
Tomlin, Pinky	Bandleader				36	Scat Singer
Tompkins, Angel	Entertainment	10	15	20	25	Pin-Up SP $35
Tompkins, Daniel (V) 1774-1825	Vice Pres.	85	200	150		Monroe VP, Governor NY
Tompson, Alexander K.	Clergy	15	25	35		
Tone, Franchot 1905-68	Entertainment	25		35	48	Am. Leading Man & Later Char. Actor
Toombs, Robert A. 1810-1885	Civil War	135	250	200		CSA General & Sec'y State
Toomey, Regis	Entertainment	15	20		45	
Toones, Fred Snowflake	Entertainment	150			300	
Toorop, Jan (Dutch)	Artist	20	100	210	125	Posters, Tiles, Stained Glass
Topal	Entertainment	10			30	
Topp, Erich	Military	35		175	95	Ger. U Boat Cmdr. WW II
Topping, Dan	Business	10	15	30	15	Millionaire Owner NY Yankees
Torisu, Kennosuke	Military	60		175	75	
Tork, Peter	Entertainment	10	35		20	Singer-Actor The Monkees
Torme, Mel	Entertainment	20			50	Vocalist, Composer
Torn, Rip	Entertainment	10			20	
Torrance, Ernest 1878-1933	Entertainment				150	Scot. Silent Films. Ex Opera
Torrence, Ridgely 1875-1950	Author	35	25	100	15	Am. Poet, Editor, Dramatist
Torres, Raquel	Entertainment	20			45	
Torrey, R.A.	Clergy	20	35	50		
Tors, Ivan	Entertainment	15			35	Producer-Director
Toscanini, Arturo 1867-1957	Conductor	300	635	967	715	AMusQS $750, AMusMs $3,750
Tosti, Paolo	Composer	25	60	155		It.
Toto	Entertainment	65			295	
Totten, Jos. G.	Civil War	15	35	70		Union Gen. Wardte DS $400
Totter, Audrey	Entertainment	5	15		15	Pin-Up SP $20
Toucey, Isaac 1792-1869	Cabinet	25	80	130		Att'y Gen. 1848, Sec'y Navy '57
Toulouse-Lautrec, Henri	Artist	1050	3200	5900		Fr. Parisian Nightlife. Lithogr
Toumanova, Tamara	Entertainment	30			110	Rus-Am Ballerina
Tourel, Jennie	Entertainment	20			50	Opera

The Sanders Price Guide to Autographs

NAME	CATEGORY	SIG	LS/DS	ALS	SP	Comment
Tourgee, Albion W. 1838-1905	Author	15	20	45		Lawyer, Judge, Diplomat
Tower, John	Senate/Congress	5	15		25	Senator TX
Tower, Zealous B.	Civil War	20	35	55		Union General
Towers, Constance	Entertainment	5	6	10	10	
Towl, E. Clinton	Business	20		55		
Townes, Charles Hanson	Science	25	35	65		Inventor. Nobel (Laser & Maser)
Townley, James	Clergy	35	50	75		
Townsand, Colleen (Evans)	Entertainment	5	9	20	15	
Townsend, Edward Davis	Civil War	30	55	60		Union General
Townsend, Francis Everett 1867-1960	Science	40			150	Social Reformer & Physician
Townsend, Frederick	Civil War	15	30	45		Union General
Townsend, George A. (Gath)	Author	15		40		War Correspondent
Townsend, Lynn	Business	10	20	35	15	CEO-Pres. Chrysler Corp.
Townsend, M. Clifford	Governor	10	15			Governor IN
Townsend, Pete	Entertainment	30			70	Lead Singer The Who
Townsend, Peter	Military	10	35	50	25	
Townsend, Robert	Entertainment	10	15		20	Film Director
Townsend, Washington	Senate/Congress	10	20			Rep. PA 1969
Toy Story (Cast Of)	Entertainment				275	Hanks, Varney, Potts, Rickles
Toynbee, Arnold 1852-83	Author	25	105	190	75	Br. Historian, Sociologist
Toynbee, Arnold Joseph	Author	20	45	120	30	Br.Historian, Prof.,Peace Conf.
Tozzi, Giorgio	Entertainment				40	Opera
Trachte, Don*	Cartoonist	25			75	Henry
Tracy, Edward Dorr (War Date)	Civil War		800			CSA Gen. KIA AES $1100
Tracy, Arthur	Entertainment	20			45	The Street Singer
Tracy, Benjamin F.	Cabinet	20	45	70		Sec'y Navy 1889
Tracy, Edward Dorr 1833-63	Civil War	155	500	838		CSA Gen., War Dte.DS $800
Tracy, Lee	Entertainment	10			25	
Tracy, Spencer 1900-67	Entertainment	175	300	375	388	50th Anniv.Movies/K.Hepburn $595
Train, Arthur	Author	10	15	35		
Trapier, James H. 1815-65	Civil War	130	310	375		CSA Gen. AES '61 $575
Trask, Diana	Country Music	10			20	
Traubel, Helen	Entertainment	50			100	Opera. Am. Soprano
Trautloft, Hannes	Aviation				50	Ger. Ace WW II RK
Travalena, Fred	Entertainment	5	8	15	15	
Travanti, Daniel J.	Entertainment	6	8	15	20	
Traven, Berwick (Torsvan)	Author	265	800	1765		Ger. Novelist, Actor, Pacifist
Travers, Henry	Entertainment	195			350	
Travers, Patricia	Entertainment	5		10	15	
Traverso, Giuseppe	Entertainment	15			45	Opera
Travis, Kylie	Entertainment	4			20	Actress. Models, Inc.Pin-Up SP 40
Travis, Merle	Country Music	20			40	
Travis, Nancy	Entertainment	20			81	Actress
Travis, Randy	Country Music	10			30	
Travis, Richard	Entertainment	5			20	Became Wealthy Hollyw'd Realtor
Travis, William Barret	Military		5000			Co-Cmdr. Alamo.Texas Frontier
Travolta, John	Entertainment	9	10	20	38	Get Shorty SP $50-80
Treacher, Arthur	Entertainment	25		40	40	Perrenial Br. Butler
Treadway, Allen Towner	Senate/Congress	4	15			Rep. MA 1913
Treadwell, John	Revolutionary War	25	60	95		Del. CT. Elected to Cont.Congr.
Treas, Terri	Entertainment	3	3	6	6	
Trebek, Alex	Entertainment	9	10	20	25	
Tree, Herbert Beerbohm, Sir	Entertainment	30	85	135	75	Br.Actor-Mgr.Fndr.Royal Academy
Treen, Mary	Entertainment	6	15	30	25	
Treilhard, Jean-Baptiste	Fr.Revolution	10	25	50		Fr. Politician
Trelawny, Edward 1792-1881	Author		445	750		Br.Author-Adventurer

The Sanders Price Guide to Autographs

NAME	CATEGORY	SIG	LS/DS	ALS	SP	Comment
Tremayne, Les	Entertainment	5			20	
Trench, Richard C., Archbishop	Clergy	45	60	95	65	
Trenholm, George A.	Civil War	95	170	450		CSA Sec'y Treasury
Trent, William	Celebrity		600			
Trettner, Henrich 'Heniz	Aviation	20	45		50	
Trevelyan, George Otto, Sir	Author	15	35	75		Br.Historian,Sec'y To Admiralty
Treves, Frederick, Dr.	Science	200		440		Dr. To Elephant Man
Trevor, Claire	Entertainment	15			30	AA
Trilling, Lionel	Author	10	25	55		Am. Lit. Critic. Professor
Trimble, Isaac R. (War Date)	Civil War	395		1575		CSA General
Trimble, Isaac Ridgeway 1802-88	Civil War	185	900	400		CSA General
Trinh, Eugene	Astronaut	5			15	
Tripler, Charles E.	Science	75	185			Inventor Liquid Air
Trippe, Juan T.	Aviation	30				Pan American Clipper Service
Tripplehorn, Jeanne	Entertainment	15			50	
Trist, Nicholas P.	Diplomat	75	225			Am.Negotiated Treaty Guadaloupe
Tritt, Travis	Country Music	15			40	
Tritton, William Ashbee, Sir	Science	25	70	125	40	Developed Military Tank
Trollope, Anthony 1815-82	Author	92	225	855		Br. Novelist. 50 Novels
Trollope, Frances	Author	30	115	225		Br. Novelist. Mother of Anthony
Trollope, Thomas A. 1810-92	Author		25	45		Novels, History. Tremendous Output
Trotsky, Leon 1879-1940	Head of State	950	2650	3200	1050	Communist leader-Assassinated
Trotter, James Monroe 1842-92	Civil War	45	235			
Trotter, Mark C.	Clergy	15		35		
Troubridge, Thomas, Sir	Military	75		250		Br. Admiral, Battle of the Nile
Troup, Bobby	Entertainment	10			20	Pianist, Composer, Vocalist
Trowbridge, John T. 1827-1916	Author	15				
Trower, Robin	Entertainment	15			30	
Troyanos, Tatiana	Entertainment	15			40	Opera
Truax, Ernest	Entertainment	10	20	40	30	
Trudeau, Gary*	Cartoonist	30			175	Doonesbury
Trudeau, Pierre	Head of State	25	65	90	80	Prime Minister Canada
Trueblood, D. Elton	Clergy	15	30	45	35	
Truett, George W.	Clergy	15	35	50	35	
Truffaut, François	Entertainment	55	400			Dir. & Critic, ALS/Content $800
Trujillo, Rafael 1891-1961	Head of State	35	950		325	Dominican Republic.Assassinated
Truly, Richard H.	Astronaut	20	75		40	
Truman, Benj. C. 1835-1916	Author	20				Soldier-Author
Truman, Bess W. 1885-1982	First Lady	70	120	250	175	S WH Card $85
Truman, Harry S. (As Pres.)	President	378	1813	4833	900	TLS/Cont. $4,750.DS as VP $1950
Truman, Harry S. 1884-1972	President	179	854	2633	431	ALS/Content $14,000
Truman, Margaret (Daniel)	First Family	25	65	80	30	Daughter Of Harry S. Truman
Truman,Harry (Mt.St.Helens)	Celebrity	5		25	25	Resident Volcano Eruption
Trumbo, Dalton	Author	50	200		75	Blacklisted Oscar Winner.
Trumbull, Annie E. 1858-1949	Author	15				
Trumbull, John 1750-1831	Author-Lawyer	75	230			CT Poet & Lawyer
Trumbull, John 1756-1843	Artist	90	295	858		ALS Content $8,000
Trumbull, Jonathan 1710-85	Revolutionary War	295	312	1200		Supplied Cont. Army,Bro. John
Trumbull, Jonathan 1740-09	Military-Senate	125	300	565		Sec'y Washington's Staff
Trumbull, Lyman	Senate	25	80	140	95	U.S. Senate IL 1855-1873
Trump, Donald J.	Business	10	60	75	50	Millionaire Entrepreneur
Trump, Ivana	Celebrity	10			40	Ex Mrs. Donald Trump
Trump, Marla Maples	Celebrity	15			40	Current Mrs. Donalt Trump
Truscott, L.K., Jr.	Military	15	40			
Truth, Sojourner	Abolitionist					RARE in any form. 3 Known
Truxton, Thomas	Revolutionary War	110	320	675		Cmdr. USS Constellation

NAME	CATEGORY	SIG	LS/DS	ALS	SP	Comment
Truxton, William Talbot	Civil War	20	45	75		Union Naval Officer. Adm. 1882
Tryggvason, Bjarni	Astronaut	5			16	
Tryon, Tom	Entertainment	10	20	25	20	Author-Actor
Tryon, William	Revolutionary War	145	375	770		Colon'l Gov. NC, NY
Tshombe, Moise	Head of State	40	75	145	90	Zaire(Congo Rep.)TLS/Cont. $795
Tsiolkovsky, Konstantin 1857-1935	Science			2500		Pioneer Rus. Space Program
Tsongas, Paul E.	Senator	15		25	20	Senator MA, Pres. Hopeful
Tubb, Ernest	Country Music	15			35	
Tubb, Justin	Country Music	5			10	
Tuchman, Barbara W.	Author	35	125	155	45	2 Time Pulitzer Pr., Historian
Tucker, Forrest	Entertainment	25	30	40	45	
Tucker, John R. (War Date)	Civil War	160	265			CSA Commdr. 1812-83
Tucker, Orrin	Entertainment	15			25	Big Band Leader
Tucker, Richard	Entertainment	30	25		120	Opera
Tucker, Samuel	Revolutionary War	125	325	675		Am. Naval Hero. Commodore
Tucker, Sophie	Entertainment	20		80	55	Burlesque,Vaudeville,Early Films
Tucker, Tanya	Entertainment	6	8		20	
Tucker, Thomas T. 1745-1848	Revolutionary War	45	185	175		Soldier, Statesman, Treasurer
Tucker, Tilghman M.	Senate/Congress	15	30	55		Senator 1838, Governor MS 1841
Tucker, Tommy	Bandleader				45	
Tudor, Anthony	Entertainment	35	45		100	Br. Dancer, Choreographer
Tuell, Jack M., Bishop	Clergy	20	25	35	30	
Tufts, Cotton 1734-1815	Revolutionary War	75	175	275		Highly Esteemed Physician. Patriot
Tufts, Sonny	Entertainment	20	25		35	
Tulford, Nellie Hughes	Astronaut	5			16	
Tully, Alice	Philanthropist	16	30		38	Lincoln Ctre. Tully Hall
Tully, Grace G.	White House	10	25	50	20	Sec'y to FDR
Tully, Tom	Cabinet	5	15	35	15	
Tully, Tom	Entertainment	25			45	
Tumulty, Joseph P.	White House	15	35	75	40	Aide to President Wilson
Tune, Tommy	Entertainment	6	8	15	20	Dancer, Choreographer
Tunnell, James M.	Senate/Congress	10	30		25	Senator DE 1940
Tunney, John V.	Senate/Congress	5	10		10	Rep., Senator CA
Tupper, Martin F. 1810-89	Inventor	25				Brit. Author-Inventor-Poet
Turgenev, Ivan 1818-33	Author	205	525	1100	1265	Russ. Novelist, Dramatist
Turkel, Ann	Entertainment	4	6		15	Pin-Up SP $20
Turkel, Studs	Author	10	20	35	20	Columnist. TV Commentator
Turlington, Christy	Entertainment	5			25	Model-Actress. Pin-up $50
Turner, Edward 1798-1837	Science	20		175		Scot. Chemist.Atomic Weights of Elements
Turner, Eva, Dame	Entertainment	40				Opera.Vocal Phenomenon
Turner, Frederick J.	Author			225		Pulitzer Prize. Historian
Turner, J. M. W. 1775-1851	Artist	225	605	1475		Br. Landscape Painter
Turner, Janine	Entertainment	20			60	Pin-Up SP $65
Turner, John Wesley	Civil War	100	125	300		Union General
Turner, Kathleen	Entertainment	10			40	Pin-Up SP $45
Turner, Lana	Entertainment	20			92	Pin-Up SP $50
Turner, Morrie	Cartoonist	5			20	Wee Pals
Turner, Philip	Revolutionary War	55	135	275		Unrivalled Sugeon During War
Turner, Roscoe, Col.	Aviation	75			100	Pioneer Aviator
Turner, Ted	Business	10	75		30	
Turner, Tina	Entertainment	15	20	40	45	
Turpie, David	Senator/Congress	15	25	35		Senator IN 1863
Turpin, Ben	Entertainment	195			450	
Turreau De Garambouville	Fr. Revolution	20		85		
Turtles	Entertainment	35			75	
Tusmayan, Barsag	Entertainment	5			25	Opera

The Sanders Price Guide to Autographs

NAME	CATEGORY	SIG	LS/DS	ALS	SP	Comment
Tuttle, Lurene	Entertainment	5	6	15	15	Radio Dramatic Star
Tuttle, Wes & Marilyn	Country Music	15			30	
Tutu, Desmond, Bishop	Clergy	65	100	225	75	Nobel Peace Prize
Tutwiler, Margaret D.	Cabinet	10	15		15	Ass'y Sec'y State
Tuve, Merle Antony 1901-82	Science	35	80	155	50	Neutron, Ionosphere, Radar
Twain, Mark (see Clemens)	Author					
Twain, Mark and Samuel Clemens	Author	1025				Both Signatures
Twain, Shania	Entertainment	10			70	Singer
Tweed, Shannon	Entertainment	6	10	20	25	Pin-Up SP $30, Nude SP 80
Tweed, William Marcy 'Boss'	Political Giant	120	230	385	980	Corrupt Tammany Hall Politician
Twiggs, David E. 1790-1862	Civil War & 1812	143	354	925		CSA General
Twiggy (Nee: Leslie Hornsby)	Entertainment	15	20	25	30	60's Brit. Fashion Model. Actress
Twining, Nathan F.	Aviation	45	135	185	65	Gen. WW II
Twiss, Peter	Aviation	7	15	30	20	
Twitty, Conway	Country Music	40	50		70	
Two Guns White Calf 1872-1934	Blackfoot Chief	350		4000	1910	Buffalo Nickel Model
Tydings, Millard E. 1890-1961	Congress	20	50		25	Rep., Senator MD, Author
Tyler, Asher 1798-1875	Congress	10				Repr. NY, Founder Elmira Rolling Mill
Tyler, Beverly	Entertainment	5			20	
Tyler, Bonnie	Entertainment	15			30	
Tyler, Daniel 1799-1882	Civil War		75	125		Union Gen.
Tyler, Edward Burnett, Sir	Science	15	30	50		!st Prof. Anthropology Oxford
Tyler, Gerald E.	Aviation	10	25	40	30	ACE, WW II
Tyler, John 1790-1862	President	417	1860	2679		As VP. ALS/Content $7,500
Tyler, Julia Gardiner	First Lady	195	545		650	Special DS $1,100
Tyler, Liv	Entertainment	10			45	Actress. Pin-Up $85
Tyler, Moses Coit	Author	5	15	25		Historian. Am. Historical Assoc
Tyler, Robert 1816-77	Military	105		250		President's Son. Mex War. CSA Register
Tyler, Robert C.	Civil War	220	580	850		CSA General
Tyler, Royall	Revolutionary War	20	50	120		Jurist, Author, Playwright
Tyler, T. Texas	Country Music	15			30	
Tyler, Tom	Entertainment	60			150	
Tyndale, Hector	Civil War	30	55	85	150	Union General
Tyndall, John 1820-93	Science	45	200	140		Irish Physicist, Philosopher
Tyner, James N.	Cabinet	10	40	75		P. M. General 1876
Tyner, McCoy	Entertainment	10	20		30	Jazz Pianist-Composer
Tyson, Cicely	Entertainment	5	10	20	15	
Tyson, Don	Business	18				Pres.,Founder,CEO Tyson's Chicken

NAME	CATEGORY	SIG	LS/DS	ALS	SP	Comment
U-2 (All)	Entertainment	185			300	Irish Rock Group
Ubico Casteneda, Jorge	Head of State	25	75			
Udall, Morris K.	Congress	4			10	Repr. AZ
Udet, Ernst 1896-1941	Aviation	225	375	700	500	ACE, WW I, German Ace

NAME	CATEGORY	SIG	LS/DS	ALS	SP	Comment
Ueberroth, Peter	Business	10	25	40	10	
Uecker, Bob	Entertainment	5	8	15	15	
Ufford, Edward S.	Clergy	40	50	70		
Uggams, Leslie	Entertainment	5	10	15	20	
Ullman, Liv	Entertainment	6	8	20	35	Sw. Film Actress
Ullman, Tracey	Entertainment	20			50	
Ulmanis, Karlis	Head of State	90				1st Pres. Latvia. Fate Unknown
Ulmar, Geraldine	Entertainment	6	8	15	15	
Umberto I (It)	Royalty	50	150	375		King Italy
Umeki, Miyoshi	Entertainment	235			450	
Umstead, William B.	Governor	5	15	20		Governor NC
Underwood, J. T.	Inventor	25	100	200		Underwood Typewriter
Underwood, Oscar W.	Senate/Congress	4	10		10	Rep., Senator AL
Undset, Sigrid 1882-1949	Author				325	Nor. Nobel Prize Winner
Unger, Jim	Cartoonlst	15	20		25	Henry
Ungher, Caroline 1803-77	Entertainment			150		Opera. Great Contralto
Unreal, Minerva	Entertainment	25			60	
Unruh, Howard B.	Celebrity	80				
Untermeyer, Louis	Author	20	55	90	25	Am. Poet,Critic,Satirist,Biogr.
Updike, John	Author	25	75	150	35	Am. Novelist,Poet,Short Story
Upjohn, E. Gifford, Dr.	Business	125	450			Founder Upjohn Pharmaceuticals
Upshaw, Dawn	Entertainment	10			25	Opera
Upshaw, William D.	Senate/Congress	5	15		10	Rep. GA 1919, Evangelist
Upshur, Abel Parker	Cabinet	25	65	80		Tyler Sec'y Navy
Upton, Emory	Civil War	25	55	85		Union Gen. Wardte DS $465
Urbanowicz, Witold A.	Aviatlon	35	70	125	60	Pol. ACE, WW II
Ure, Mary	Entertainment	5	10	20	20	
Urey, Harold C. 1893-1981	Science	60	550	550		Nobel in Chemistry 1934
Urich, Robert	Entertainment	10	15	25	30	
Uris, Leon	Author	20	75	125	65	Am. Novelist
Urso, Camilla	Entertainment	25			40	Fr. Violinist
Urvanowicz, Witold A.	Aviation	20	45	75	50	ACE, WW II, Polish Ace
Usher, John P.	Cabinet	40	110	195		Sec'y Interior 1863-65
Ustinov, Peter	Entertainment	25	125	60	75	And Playwright, Author, Actor. AA
Utrillo, Maurice 1833-1955	Artist	475	550	650	200	Fr. Montmartre, Paris Scenes

V

Vaccaro, Brenda	Entertainment	4	6	15	10	
Vaccaro, Tracy	Entertainment	5			15	Pin-Up SP $30
Vacio, Natividad	Entertainment	3	3	6	6	
Vadim, Roger	Entertainment	20			50	
Vague, Vera	Entertainment	25				SEE Barbara Jo Allen. Comedienne
Vai, Steve	Entertainment	15			35	Rock
Valdengo, Giuseppe	Entertainment	15			40	Opera

The Sanders Price Guide to Autographs

NAME	CATEGORY	SIG	LS/DS	ALS	SP	Comment
Vale, Virginia	Entertainment	15				Actress
Valens, Richie	Entertainment	500	600		1000	
Valenti, Jack	Entertainment	5	10		15	Pres. Moving Picture Assoc.
Valentine, Karen	Entertainment	4	6	10	15	
Valentine, Lewis	Law	35	105		50	Legend'y NY Police Commissioner
Valentino, Rudolph	Entertainment	1000		1550	2250	
Valery, Paul A. 1871-1945	Author	45	105	170		Fr. Noted Poet, Philosopher
Valette, A.J.M.	Fr. Revolution	15		75		
Valetti, Cesare	Entertainment	20			50	Opera
Vallandigham, Clement L.1820-71	Civil War	125		325		Civil War Copperhead
Vallee, Rudy	Entertainment	15	35	45	35	
Vallejo, Mariano Guadalupe	Military	140	450			Early CA Off'l & Military Leadr
Valli, Frankie	Entertainment	15			45	Singer
Valli, Virginia	Entertainment				40	Films From 1915-1931
Vallone, Raf	Entertainment	5	6	15	15	
Van Allan, Richard	Entertainment	5			25	Opera
Van Allen, James	Science	40	135	260	100	Nobel Physics
Van Ark, Joan	Entertainment	5	8	15	15	
Van Buren, Abigail	Journalist	10	18	30	20	Am. Syndicated Columnist
Van Buren, Angelica	First Lady					NRPA
Van Buren, Hannah	First Lady					No Known Examples
Van Buren, James D.	Gov't Official	5	15			Son of Pres. Van Buren
Van Buren, Martin (As Pres.)	President		1575			Free Frank $350-$475
Van Buren, Martin 1782-1862	President	335	1745	947		FF $450
Van Buren, Raeburn*	Cartoonist	10			50	Abbie & Slats
Van Cleef, Lee	Entertainment	25			45	
Van Dam, Rip 1662-1736+	Colonial America	60	175	360		Merchant,Politics,Col. Gov. NY
Van Damme, Jean-Claude	Entertainment	15			60	
Van Den Berg, Lodewik, Dr.	Astronaut	5			16	
Van Devanter, Willis (SC)	Supreme Court	40	125	200	75	
Van Dine, S.S. (W.H.Wright)	Author	45	100	190	225	Created Philo Vance
Van Dongen, Kees	Artist	30	45	120		Fauvist Painter, Portraitist
Van Doren, Carl	Author	15	45	60	20	Pulitzer in Biography
Van Doren, Mamie	Entertainment	10	15	25	25	Pin-Up SP $35
Van Doren, Mark 1894-1973	Author	10	50	58	25	Critic, Editor, Pulitzer Poetry
Van Dorn, Earl (War Date)	Civil War	350		5775		CSA Gen. Assassinated
Van Dorn, Earl 1820-63	Civil War	250		718		CSA Gen. Assassinated
Van Dresser, Marcia	Entertainment	15			40	Vintage Actress
Van Druten, John W.	Author	10	20	35	15	Playwright, Novelist
Van Dusen, Henry P.	Clergy	15	15	25	20	
Van Dyck, M. Ernest	Entertainment	15	25		40	Tenor
Van Dyke, Dick	Entertainment	8	8	15	35	
Van Dyke, Henry 1852-1933	Clergy-Author	20	55	100		Minister To Netherlands-Luxem.
Van Dyke, Jerry	Entertainment	5			20	
Van Dyke, Nicholas 1738-89	Revolutionary War	110	275	625		Statesman, Continental Congress
Van Fleet, James, Gen.	Military	20	75	95	45	Gen. WW II. US 8th Army, Korea
Van Fleet, Jo	Entertainment	15	20	45	40	AA
Van Halen (All)(4)	Entertainment	40			100	Rock LP Cover S $85
Van Halen (all-original)	Entertainment	80			170	Rock
Van Halen, Alex	Entertainment	20			50	
Van Halen, Eddie	Entertainment	25	30		50	Rock
Van Heusen, James (Jimmy)	Composer	60	90	175	75	AMusQS $250
Van Hoften, James D.	Astronaut	5			20	
Van Horn, Burt	Senate/Congress	10	20			Rep. NY 1861, Manufacturer
Van Horne, David	Revolutionary War	10		75		
Van Kirk, Theodore	Aviation	50	130		95	

NAME	CATEGORY	SIG	LS/DS	ALS	SP	Comment
Van Loon, Hendrik Willem	Author	15	30	75	40	Historian, Journalist, Lecturer
Van Loon, William	Journalist	10		50		Lecturer
Van Ness, Cornelius P.	Governor	15	35	60		Jurist, Gov. VT, Minister Sp.
Van Nuys, Frederick 1874-1944	Congress	10			25	Senator IN 1932
Van Patten, Dick	Entertainment	5	6	15	15	
Van Patten, Joyce	Entertainment	4	4	10	15	
Van Rensselaer, Henry	Civil War	225				Rep. NY 1841, Union General
Van Sloon, Edward	Entertainment	125			250	
Van Stade, Frederica	Entertainment	15			45	Opera
Van Sweringen, Otis P.	Business	15	40	90	35	RR Exec-Developer Shaker Height
Van Valkenburgh, Debbie	Entertainment	6	8	15	15	
Van Vechten, Carl	Author	40	80	220	45	Am. Novelist, Staff NY Times
Van Vleck, John H., Dr.	Science	30	45	75		Nobel Physics 1977
Van Vliet, Stewart 1815-1901	Civil War	45		295		Union Gen.,Indian Fighter
Van Vooren, Monique	Entertainment	4	6	10	15	Pin-Up SP $25
Van Wagoner, Murray D.	Governor	5	20		15	Governor MI
Van Wyck, Charles Henry	Civil War	40	70	90		Union General, Senator NE
Van Zandt, Philip	Entertainment	50			150	
Van Zant, Ronnie	Entertainment	25			100	
Van Zealand, Paul, Viscount	Head of State	15			35	Premier Belgium, Foreign Min.
Van, Bobby	Entertainment	5			12	
Van, Bobby	Entertainment	5			20	Dancer
Van, Gloria	Entertainment	5	6	15	15	
Van, Isabelle	Entertainment	5				Dancer
Van, Isabelle	Entertainment	5			10	Dancer
Van, Jackie	Entertainment	5			15	Dancer
Vance, A.T., Capt.	Aviation	15	25			Record Polar Flight
Vance, Cyrus	Cabinet	10	20	35	25	Sec'y State, Sec'y Army
Vance, Jack	Author	10	15	20	15	Hugo & Nebula winning SF writer
Vance, Louis Joseph	Author	15	35	90		Am. Novelist
Vance, Robert Brank 1828-99	Civil War	82	145	252		CSA Gen., Sig/Rank $145
Vance, Vivian	Entertainment	125	150		250	
Vance, Zebulon Baird	Civil War	175		650		CSA Gov. NC, Opposed J.Davis
Vandamme, Dominique Rene	Napoleonic Wars	50	150	210		Battle of Waterloo
Vandenberg, Arthur H. 1884-1951	Congress	20	70		25	Senator MI, Pres. Pro Tem.
Vandenberg, Hoyt S.	Military-Aviation	25	150		100	
Vander Pyl, Jean	Entertainment	10			15	Voice Wilma-Pebbles Flintstone
Vanderbilt, Alfred Gwynn	Business	15	35	65	25	
Vanderbilt, Amy	Author	10	25	40	35	Columnist, Authority on Manners
Vanderbilt, Cornelius 1794-1877	Business	412	1140	1100	2760	Commodore. Financier
Vanderbilt, Cornelius, Jr.1898-1974	Journalist	20	75	105	35	
Vanderbilt, George Washington	Business	200	145	270	100	Biltmore House
Vanderbilt, Gloria	Business	25	45	80	30	Fashion Designer
Vanderbilt, Harold S.1884-1970	Business	168				Philanthropist-Businessman
Vanderbilt, William H. 1821-85	Business	50	175	475	150	RR Exec., Philanthropist
Vanderbilt, William H., Jr.	Business	20	45	90	35	Governor RI
Vanderbilt, William K. 1849-1920	Business	55	220		125	RR Exec.,Financier-Yachtsman
Vandergrift, Alexander A.	Military	40	85	160	50	Marine Corps Gen. WW II
Vanderlyn, John 1775-1852	Artist	250	275	750		Am. Pres. Portraits, Capitol
Vane, John R., Dr.	Science	20	30	50	25	Nobel Medicine 1982
Vaness, Carol	Entertainment	10			35	Opera
Vanili, Milli	Entertainment	10			50	
Vanilla Ice	Entertainment	20			40	Rock
Vanity	Entertainment	4	7		15	Pin-Up SP $25
Vanzetti, Bartolomeo	Political Radical	600	1800	6500		Convicted Murderer,Electrocuted
Varese, Edgard	Composer	185	400	675		Fr.-Am. Music Pioneer

NAME	CATEGORY	SIG	LS/DS	ALS	SP	Comment
Varga, Francis	Celebrity	30				
Vargas, Alberto	Artist	135	345	575		Repro Varga Girl S $325-$450
Vargas, Getuilio	Head of State	50	150		75	Revolutionary Pres. Brazil.
Varick, Richard	Revolutionary War	75	200	290		Soldier, Washington's Sec'y
Varmus, Harold E., Dr.	Science	25	60		35	Nobel Medicine 1989
Varney, Astrid	Entertainment	5			25	Opera
Varney, Jim	Entertainment	7			20	
Vasarely, Victor	Artist	55	130			Op Art Repro S $150
Vasquez, Roberta	Playboy Ctrfold	4			10	Pin-Up SP $20. Actress
Vassar, Matthew	Business	45	105	210		Founder Vassar College
Vaubois, J.F.G.	Fr. Revolution	5	15	40		
Vaughan, Robert	Clergy	10	10	10		
Vaughn, Alfred J.,Jr..1830-99	Civil War	75		405		CSA Gen. Sig/Rank $150
Vaughn, George A.	Aviation	35	55	95	65	ACE, WW II
Vaughn, Herbert, Cardinal	Clergy	30	50	90	75	
Vaughn, John C. (War Date)	Civil War	195	325	2500		CSA Gen.
Vaughn, John C.1824-75	Civil War	90				CSA Gen. Wardte. DS $2,500
Vaughn, Robert	Entertainment	5	8	15	15	
Vaughn, Sarah	Entertainment	35	50	212	125	Jazz Vocalist-Pianist
Vaughn, William S.	Business	4	10		10	Pres. Eastman Kodak
Vaughn-Williams, Ralph, Sir 1872-1958	Composer	105	320	450	150	Established Br. Nat'l Musical Style
Vaux, Roberts 1786-1836	Philanthropist	110		522		Prison Reform, Houses of Refuge
Veach, Charles L.	Astronaut	5			15	
Vedder, Eddy	Entertainment	10			70	Rocker, Pearl Jam
Vedder, Elihu	Artist	50	135	225		Drew From Dreams & Fantasy
Vedral, Joyce L.	Author	5			10	Non-Fiction
Vedrines, Jules	Aviation	200	395	650	265	
Vee, Bobby	Entertainment	5			15	
Veidt, Conrad 1893-1950	Entertainment	85	90	130	310	
Veit, Stan	Author	5	10	20	20	Computer Shopper, PC historian
Velez, Lupe	Entertainment	85	95	175	200	
Veloz & Yolanda	Entertainment	15			35	30-40's Ballroom Dance Team
Venable, Evelyn	Entertainment	15	20	40	35	
Venable, William Webb	Senate/Congress	5	15		10	Rep. MS 1916, Judge
Vendela	Entertainment	20			45	Model-Actress
Vendome, L.J., Duke de 1654-1712	Fr. Military	150	450			Marshal of France
Ventura, Charlie	Entertainment	40			150	Am. Bandleader-Saxophonist
Venuta, Benay	Entertainment	7			15	
Vera Ellen	Entertainment	20			45	Dancer, Films. Pin-Up SP $50
Verdi, Giuseppe 1813-1901	Composer	1100	1750	2472	5690	AMusQS $5,000, $5,700, $7,500
Verdin, James, Lt.Cdr.	Aviation	10	25			US Navy Pilot. Record Holder
Verdon, Gwen	Entertainment	5	6	15	15	
Verdugo, Elena	Entertainment	10			15	Actress
Verdy, Violette	Entertainment	10			30	Opera
Vereen, Ben	Entertainment	5			20	
Vereshchagin, Vassili V.1842-1904	Artist	35		150		Paintings of Russian Wars
Vergennes, Chas. G.,Le Comte de	Statesman	175	375			Fr. Ambass. Supported Am. Rev.
Verlaine, Paul 1844-96	Author	175	490	850		Fr. Symbolist Poet
Vermehren, Werner	Aviation	14	35	55	58	Ger. Capt. WW I Zepps..
Verne, Jules 1828-1905	Authors	185	655	1120	1725	Fr. Sci-Fi Novelist
Vernier, Theodore, Count	Fr. Revolution	30	100			
Vessey, John W.	Military	10			30	
Vetch, Samuel 1668-1732	Colonial America	80	225	450		Colonial Governor
Vetri, Victoria	Entertainment	4			10	Pin-Up SP $20
Veverka, Jaroslav	Entertainment	20			45	Opera
Vezzani, Cesare	Entertainment	45			150	Opera. Corsican Dramatic Tenor

NAME	CATEGORY	SIG	LS/DS	ALS	SP	Comment
Viardot, Pauline	Entertainment	30		150	100	
Vickers, Jon	Entertainment	15			55	Opera. Dramatic Tenor
Vickers, Martha	Entertainment	3	3	6	6	
Victor Emmanuel I, 1759-1824	Royalty		275			King of Sardinia
Victor Emmanuel II (It)	Royalty	70	250	475	100	
Victor Emmanuel III & B.Mussolini	Royalty, Hd of St					Fine DS by both $850-$1050
Victor Emmanuel III 1869-1947	Royalty	25				King Italy 1900-46
Victor, Claude Perrin 1766-1841	Fr. Military	150	75	135		Marshal of Napoleon
Victoria, Duchess of Kent	Royalty			125		Mother of Queen Victoria
Victoria, Empress (Fred. III, Ger)	Royalty	30		125		Eldest Daughter Queen Victoria
Victoria, Mary Louisa	Royalty	40	110	175		Mother of Q. Victoria
Victoria, Queen 1819-1902	Royalty	178	524	800	1385	Great Britain etc.
Victors, Henry	Entertainment	65			200	
Vidal, Gore	Author	10	20	30	15	Am. Novelist,Playwright,Critic
Vidor, Florence	Entertainment	40	35	65	60	
Vidor, King 1894-1982	Entertainment	25			102	AA Film Director. LS/Cont. $250
Vieira, Meredith	TV News	4			15	Commentator
Viele, Egbert L.	Civil War	25	40	55	85	Union General, Engineer
Vigneaud, Vincent du	Science	10	25	45	15	
Vigran, Herb	Entertainment	10	15		20	
Vila, Bob	Entertainment	4			15	TV Tool Show
Vila, George R.	Business	7	20	40	15	CEO Uniroyal Tire
Vilas, Jack	Aviation	6	16			
Vilas, William F.	Cabinet	15	30	45	35	P.M. Gen., Sec'y Interior 1888
Viljoen, Benjamin	Celebrity	5	15	40	10	
Viljoenk, B.J.	Military	35		145		
Villa, Francesco (Pancho)1878-1923	Military	550	1500	3050	3680	Guerilla Leader, Revolutionary
Villa-Lobos, Heitor 1887-1959	Composer	100	225	525	262	AMusQS $500,AMusMsS $1,000
Villalpando, Catalina Vasquez	Cabinet	15			30	US Treasurer
Villechalze, Herve	Entertainment	15	25		40	
Villepique, John B. 1830-62	Civil War	250		690		CSA Gen.Sig/Rank $350
Villiers, Alan J.	Author	10		20		Australian. Maritime, Adventure, History
Villiers, Frederic	Artist	10	20	50	25	
Vinay, Ramon	Entertainment				200	Opera. Sang Otello Internationally
Vincent, Gene	Entertainment	175			295	Rock
Vincent, Jan-Michael	Entertainment	10		15	20	
Vincent, June	Entertainment				25	
Vincent, Romo	Entertainment	5	10	20	15	
Vincent, Stenio J.i	Head of State	125				Pres. Haiti. Lawyer, Diplomat
Vincent, Thomas M.	Civil War	30	55	100		Union General, Bvt.
Vinci, Leonardo da	Artist	5100	13000	34000		NRPA
Vinson, Carl 1883-1991	Congress	20	40		70	Rep. GA 1914
Vinson, Frederick M. (SC) 1890-1953	Supreme Court	95	235	425	322	Chief Justice, Cabinet, Rep. KY
Vinson, Helen	Entertainment	15	20	40	35	
Vinton, Bobby	Composer	5			15	AMusQS $40
Vinton, David	Civil War	125	325			Union Gen., 1st P.O.W.
Vinton, Will	Celebrity	12	25			
Virchow, Rudolf 1821-1902	Science	175		1188		Founder Cellular Pathology
Virtanen, A. I.	Science	30	85	140	50	Nobel Chemistry 1945
Vishinsky, Andrei	Head of State	70	230	580	120	Rus.1st Deputy Foreign Minister
Visitor, Nana	Entertainment	15			35	Star Trek
Vittor, Frank	Artist	40		165		
Vivian, Richard H. Sir	Revolutionary War	45	125	255		
Vlaminck, Maurice de 18876-1958	Artist	125	235	625	325	Fr. Fauvist Painter
Voelker, John D.	Author	5	10	15	15	
Voight, Deborah	Entertainment	5			25	Opera

NAME	CATEGORY	SIG	LS/DS	ALS	SP	Comment
Voight, Jon	Entertainment	5		20	25	AA
Voisin, Gabriel	Aviation	65	135	225	125	Fr. Airplane Mfg. Pioneer
Vokes, Christopher	Military	15	30	40	25	
Vokes, Rosina	Entertainment	10	8	20	15	
Volcker, Paul A.	Cabinet	5		10	10	Chm. Federal Reserve
Voliva, Wilbur G. 1870-1942	Clergy	30		50		
Volk, Leonard W. 1828-95	Artist	50	350			Sculptor
Volkov, Vladislav	Cosmonaut	75			160	
Voll, John J.	Aviation	18	40	65	45	ACE, WW II
Volstead, Andrew J. 1860-1947	Congress	70	210	250		Rep. MN 1903. Volstead Act
Volta, Alessandro	Science	400	2500	2500		Volt, Electrical Unit, For Him
Voltaire, François M. 1694-1778	Author	400	1400	3500		Fr. Writer-Philosopher-Satirist
Volz, Nedra	Entertainment	4			10	
Von Behr, Henrich, Baron	Military	10			30	
von Braun, Magnus	Science	15			40	Rocket Pioneer/Brother Wernher
Von Braun, Wernher 1912-77	Science	165	540	600	372	Ger-Am Rocket Pioneer
Von Bulow, Claus	Celebrity	15	25		20	Danish Count. Accused Murderer
Von Bulow, H.	Entertainment	15		120		Germ. Pianist
Von D„niken, Erich	Author	10	30	75	20	Sci-Fi
Von Debizka, Hedwig	Entertainment	40			150	Opera
Von der Chevaerie, Kurt	Military	10			40	
Von Edelsheim, Macmilian	Military	20			45	Panzer General
Von Gazen, Waldemar	Military	20			50	Panzer General
Von Gronau, Wolfgang	Aviation	165			500	Ger. ACE, WW I
Von Gronau, Wolfgang	Aviation	40			175	
Von Hesse-Nassau, Adolph	Royalty	100	300			1st Duke of Luxembourg
Von Kleist, Paul	Military	50	85		100	Ger. WW II Tank Commander
Von Kretchmer, Otto	Military	35	90			Top Ger. U Boat Cmdr. WW II
Von Oy, Jenna	Entertainment	5			15	Blossom
Von Papen, Franz	Military	95	200	395	175	Ger.Acquitted Major War Crimes
Von Paulus, Friedrich	Military	165	600			Ger. WW II Field Marshal
Von Sauken, Dietrich	Military	25			75	Panzer General
Von Sternberg, Joseph	Entertainment	30	100		45	Film Director
Von Stroheim, Erich 1885-1957	Entertainment	150			595	Vintage Film Director
Von Sydow, Max	Entertainment	10		15	20	
Von Tilzer, Albert	Composer	30	110	200	45	Founder ASCAP
Von Trapp, Maria, Baroness	Celebrity	35	150	250	75	Sound of Music Fame
Von Zell, Harry	Entertainment	10	15	25	25	Radio Announcer-Comedian
Vonnegut, Kurt, Jr.	Author	20	90	105	50	Am. Black-Humor Novels.
Voorhees, Daniel W.	Senate/Congress	15	40			Rep., Senator IN 1861
Voronoff, Serge 1866-1951	Science	25				Rus.Phys.Animanl Glands for Rejuvenation
Vorster, Balthazar J	Head of State	25	70	165	50	Prime Minister South Afr.
Voss, James	Astronaut	5			14	
Voss, Janet	Astronaut	5			10	
Vosseller, Aurelius B.	Military	35	95			
Voysey, Charles	Clergy	35	50	75		
Vraciu, Alex	Aviation	15	25	50	35	ACE, WW II
Vuillard, Edouard 1868-1949	Artist	140	290	500		Fr.Painter,Printmaker, Illustr.

NAME	CATEGORY	SIG	LS/DS	ALS	SP	Comment
Wachtel. Theodor	Entertainment			195		Opera. 19th Cent. Ger. Tenor
Wade, Benjamin Franklin 1800-1878	Congress	40	95	160		Senator OH 1851-69
Wade, Leigh	Aviation	30	100	100	45	Pilot '24 Round The World
Wadopian, Eliot	Entertainment	10			25	Bassist. Paul Winter Consort
Wadsworth, James S.	Civil War	50	95	185		Union Gen.
Wadsworth, James W., Jr.1877-1952	Congress	12	30			Senator NY
Wadsworth, Jeremiah 1743-1804	Revolutionary War	145	490	585		Army Officer. Rep. CT. Merchant
Wadsworth, Peleg	Revolutionary War	105	315			General, Aide Artemas Ward
Waesche, R.R.	Military	20	50			US Coast Guard Commandant
Wagener, David D. 1792-1860	Congress	12				Repr. PA, Founder Easton Bank
Waggin, Patti	Entertainment	3	3	6	6	
Wagner, Cosima 1837-1930	Celebrity			450		Wife of Richard. Daughter of Liszt
Wagner, Jane	Author	10	15		20	Playwright. Emmy & Peabody
Wagner, Lindsay	Entertainment	6	8	15	20	Six Million Dollar Woman
Wagner, Richard 1813-83	Composer	1300	1865	3236	3150	ALS/Content $5,000, $5,500
Wagner, Robert	Entertainment	15	15	25	30	
Wagner, Robert F. 1877-1953	Senate/Congress	30	120	225	40	Senate NY 1926, Wagner Act
Wagoner, Porter	Country Music	5			20	
Waigel, Theo, Dr.	Ger. Government	4	10		12	Ger. Government Official
Wainwright, James	Entertainment	4			15	Actor
Wainwright, Jonathan 1883-1953	Military	112	275	315	225	Gen. WW II. MOH
Waite, H. Roy	Aviation	15	25	40		
Waite, Morrison R. (SC)1816-88	Supreme Court	40	95	435	60	Chief Justice Supreme Court
Waite, Ralph	Entertainment	5	6	15	15	
Waite, Terry	Hostage	30		40	35	Also Hostage Negotiator
Wakely, Jimmy	Country Music	30			100	
Wakeman, Rick	Entertainment	15			30	
Waksman, Selman A. 1888-1978	Science	45	75	95	60	Nobel Medicine 1952
Walburn, Raymond	Entertainment	10	15	45	35	Vintage
Walcott, Charlels F. 1836-87	Civil War	15		45		Union Gen. Final Campaign
Walcott, Fred C. 1869-1949	Congress	10	30			Senator CT 1929. Mfg., Banker
Walcutt, Charles C.	Civil War	30	65	85		Union General
Wald, George	Science	15	30	50	25	Nobel Medicine 1967
Wald, Jerry	Bandleader	10				
Wald, Lillian D. 1867-1940	Reformer	30	90	175	50	1st City School Nurse Service
Waldheim, Kurt	Head of State	15	65	150	40	Prime Minister Austria
Waldo, Anna Lee	Author	15			20	
Waldo, Janet	Entertainment	4			15	Major Radio Actress. Judy Jetson Voice
Waldron, Hicks B.	Business	5			10	CEO Heublein Inc.
Walesa, Lech	Head of State	25	65		110	Nobel Peace Pr., Pres. Poland
Walgreen, Charles Rudolph	Business	35	60	145		Pharmacist Fndr. Walgreen Drugs
Walken, Christopher	Entertainment	15		45	35	
Walker, Alice	Author	30			45	Color Purple

The Sanders Price Guide to Autographs

NAME	CATEGORY	SIG	LS/DS	ALS	SP	Comment
Walker, Benjamin	Revolutionary War	105	315			Rev. Army Officer. Rep. NY
Walker, Bree	TV News	5			10	TV News
Walker, Charles	Astronaut	5			14	
Walker, Clint	Entertainment	60	50	100	125	
Walker, David M.	Astronaut	5			30	
Walker, Francis Amasa	Civil War	45	105	145		Union Gen. Rose From Private
Walker, Frank C.	Cabinet	5	15		10	P.M. General 1940
Walker, Fred L.	Military	10	35	50		
Walker, Gilbert C.	Governor	12	20	25		Gov. VA 1869, Rep. VA 1875
Walker, James 1794-1874	Clergy	15	20	42		Pres. Harvard
Walker, James J.	Politician	25	70	155	40	Mayor NYC. Corruption Charges
Walker, Jerry Jeff	Entertainment	10	15	30	35	
Walker, Jimmy	Entertainment	5			15	
Walker, John Brisben	Journalist	10	30			Editor Cosmopolitan Magazine
Walker, John George	Civil War	75	170	255		CSA General
Walker, Leroy Pope (War Date)	Civil War	250	400	640		CSA Gen.-1st CS Sec'y of War
Walker, Mary E. 1832-1919	Civil War	295		575	4370	Union Nurse & Surgeon, CMH
Walker, Mort*	Cartoonist	15			75	Beetle Bailey
Walker, Nancy	Entertainment	20			40	
Walker, Percy 1812-80	Congress	15	35			Repr. AL, Medicine, Soldier
Walker, Reuben L. 1827-90	Civil War	80		285		CSA Gen.
Walker, Robert J.	Cabinet	25	75	175		Polk Sec'y Treasury
Walker, Robert Jarvis C.	Senate/Congress	12	20			Rep. PA. 1881.
Walker, Robert, Jr.	Entertainment	10			25	Actor son of Rob't Walker
Walker, Robert, Sr.	Entertainment	50		150	155	
Walker, T. Bone	Entertainment	30			85	Jazz Guitar-Vocalist
Walker, Walton H.	Military	30	55	95	50	General. Killed in Korea 1950
Walker, William	Military					
Walker, William S. 1822-99	Civil War	85		305		CSA Gen. Sig/Rank $150
Walker, Wm Henry T.1816-64	Civil War	138	350	520		CSA Gen. KIA
Walker, Wm. Henry T.(War Date)	Civil War	195	1350	1742		CSA Gen.
Wallace, Alfred R. 1823-1913	Science	75	160	505		Developed Theory of Evolution
Wallace, Dee	Entertainment	5	6	15	15	
Wallace, Dewitt	Publisher	30				Founder Readers Digest
Wallace, Dillon	Author	5	15	30	10	
Wallace, Edgar 1875-1932	Author	75	270	345	369	Popular Thriller Writer
Wallace, George C.	Governor	10			20	Governor AL
Wallace, Henry A. (VP)1888-1965	Vice President	45	140	275	100	FDR V.P.
Wallace, Henry C.	Cabinet	10	25	50	20	Sec'y Agriculture 1921
Wallace, Irving	Author	20	125	200	75	Am. Novelist
Wallace, Jean	Entertainment	10	15	20	25	
Wallace, John	Civil War	100	300			Black Leader 1860's
Wallace, Lewis Lew 1827-1904	Civil War, Author	148	300	493		Union Gen.-Statesman-Author
Wallace, Lila Acheson	Business	10	25	35	20	
Wallace, Lurleen B.	Governor	20	75		25	Governor AL
Wallace, Marjorie	Entertainment	4			20	Miss USA, Actress
Wallace, Mike	Journalist	5	10	15	15	News Journalist. 60 Minutes
Wallace, William H.	Civil War	85	258			CSA (Prices Courtesy Seagrave)
Wallach, Eli	Entertainment	5	6	15	15	
Wallburg, Donnie	Entertainment	10			45	
Wallenberg, Knut	Financier	60	155			Swe. Enskilda Bank, Statesman
Wallenda, Debbie	Entertainment	20				Flying Wallendas
Wallenda, Karl 1905-1978	Entertainment				450	Flying Wallendas Circus Legends
Wallenstein, Alfred, Dr.	Conductor	20			75	Am. Cellist/Conductor
Waller, Littleton	Military	100				Marine General 1880-1920
Waller, Robert James	Author	5			10	Novelist

NAME	CATEGORY	SIG	LS/DS	ALS	SP	Comment
Waller, Thomas Fats 1904-43	Composer	300	425	775	555	Jazz Pianist. AMusQS $900
Waller, Thomas M.	Governor	15	25	40		Governor CT 1883
Walley, Deborah	Entertainment	5	6	15	30	Actress
Wallis, Barnes, Sir	Aviation	30	75			Br. Aircraft Designer. Inventor
Wallis, Hal	Entertainment	15			40	Major Film Producer
Wallis, Ruth	Entertainment	10			25	
Wallis, Shani	Entertainment	4	5	8	6	
Wallmann, Jeff	Author	5	10	15	5	
Walmsley, John	Entertainment	5				Actor
Walpole, Horace 1717-97	Author	150	450	1160		Br.Wit, Letter Writer, Novelist
Walpole, Hugh Seymour, Sir	Author	30	105	120		Novelist, Playwright,Biographer
Walpole, Robert, Sir 1676-1745	Head of State	85	250	575		Prime Minister. 1st Earl Orford
Walpole, Spencer H.	Celebrity	5	15	25		
Walsh, Blanche	Entertainment	15			35	Vintage Actress
Walsh, David I. 1872-1947	Congress	10	15			Governor MA 1914, Senator 1919
Walsh, John	Entertainment	4	5		10	Fox TV Host
Walsh, Kenneth	Aviation	15	25	50	35	ACE, WW II, CMH
Walsh, M. Emmet	Entertainment	5	6	15	15	
Walsh, Raoul	Entertainment	35			75	Film Director
Walsh, Thomas J. 1859-1933	Cabinet	15	40		20	Senator MT 1912. FDR Att'y Gen.
Walston, Ray	Entertainment	8	9	15	20	
Walter, Bruno	Conductor	60		150	375	Ger. Conductor. AmusQS $200
Walter, Jessica	Entertainment	6	8	15	15	
Walters, Barbara	Entertainment	10	10	20	20	TV Anchor, Specials Hostess
Walters, Julie	Entertainment	5	6	15	15	
Walters, Vernon A.	Military	5		10		
Walthall, Edward C. (War Date)	Civil War	185	975			CSA Gen.
Walthall, Edward C. 1831-98	Civil War	95	210	292		CSA Gen.
Walthall, Henry B.	Entertainment	25		55	65	
Walton, Ernest T.S.,Dr.	Science	75				Nobel Physics 1951
Walton, George 1740-1804	Revolutionary War	388	1048	1285		Signer. ADS/Content $2,500
Walton, Gladys	Entertainment	5	6	15	15	
Walton, Jayne	Entertainment	5	6	15	10	
Walton, Sam M.	Business	70	145		80	Founder Walmark
Walton, William, Sir 1902-83	Composer	75	90	195	150	AMusQS $375-$700
Wambaugh, Joseph	Author	10	20	35	15	Am. Novelist re Law Enforcement
Wanamaker, John 1838-1922	Business-Cabinet	45	60	165	100	Dept. Store Pioneer, P.M. Gen.
Wang, Cheng-T'ing	Diplomat	20	60	90		Chin. Political Leader, Ambass.
Wang, Taylor	Astronaut	7			20	
Wanger, Walter 1894-1968	Entertainment	30	150			Am. Film Producer
Wapner, Jos. A., Judge	Jurist	4			12	TV Judge
War	Entertainment	15			35	Rock
Warburton, Irvine Cotton	Entertainment	30		45		AA Film Editor,Football Star
Ward, Aaron	Senate/Congress	15	35	50		General, War 1812, Rep. NY 1825
Ward, Artemas (pseud of C.Browne)	Author	15	35	60	20	Humorist
Ward, Artemas 1727-1800	Revolutionary War	350	1500			Revolutionary War Commander
Ward, Burt	Entertainment	15			30	Bat Man
Ward, David	Entertainment	10			35	Opera
Ward, Genevieve	Entertainment	3	5		8	
Ward, Henry 1732-97	Revolutionary War	150	430	870		Colon'l Cong.Pro Independence
Ward, Henry A.1835-	Merchant	40		150		1st White Child Born on Site of Chicago
Ward, J.H. Hobart	Civil War	35	60	75		Union General
Ward, John Q. Adams 1830-1910	Artist	25	80	118	40	Am. Sculptor
Ward, Joseph, Sir	Head of State	15	25	60		PM New Zealand
Ward, Marcus L.	Congress	15	25			Repr. NJ 1873
Ward, Mary A. (Mrs. Humphrey)	Author	10	30	60		Br. Moral, Reforming Novels

NAME	CATEGORY	SIG	LS/DS	ALS	SP	Comment
Ward, Rachel	Entertainment	9	10	20	25	Pin-Up SP $30
Ward, Richard 1689-1763	Colonial Am.	20	35			Colon'l Gov. RI
Ward, Samuel 1725-1776	Am. Revolution		625	775		Patriot,Farmer,Merchant,Colon'l Legislator
Ward, Sela	Entertainment	12			30	
Warden, Jack	Entertainment	6	8	15	15	
Wardlaw, Ralph W.	Clergy	30	35	45		
Ware, Eugene F.1841-1911	Author-Lawyer	15	30			
Ware, Henry 1764-1845	Clergy	15	25	55	30	Led Separation Unitarian
Ware, Linda	Entertainment	3	5		15	40's Teen Singing Star in Films
Warfield, David 1866-	Entertainment	35	40	75	75	Am. Stage Actor for Belasco Prod.
Warfield, Marsha	Entertainment	5			20	
Warfield, William	Entertainment	6	8	20	42	Ol' Man River Baritone
Warhol, Andy 1930-87	Artist	150	320	575	275	Celebrity Repros S $450-$2,000
Waring, Fred	Entertainment	15	45	50	25	Big,Big Band & Chorus. Waring Blender
Warner, A.P.(Borg-Warner)	Business	45	145		75	Fndr.Stewart-Warner.Speedometer
Warner, Adoniram J.	Civil War	25		115		Union Gen., Rep. OH 1879
Warner, Charles Dudley 1829-1911	Author	18	65	115		Am. Man of Letters, Essays
Warner, H.B.	Entertainment	25			65	
Warner, Harry M.	Business	95	285	395	150	Fndr. Warner Bros.(One oF Four)
Warner, Jack L.	Business	80	175	300	150	Fndr. Warner Bros.(One of Four)
Warner, James	Aviation	25		40		
Warner, John W.	Senate-Cabinet	10	15		10	Sec'y Navy 1972,Senator VA
Warner, Malcolm Jamal	Entertainment	10	30		25	
Warner, Seth 1743-84	Revolutionary War	200		1200		Officer.Leader With Ethan Allen
Warnow, Mark	Entertainment	10			25	Big Band Leader
Warrant	Entertainment	25			50	Rock
Warren Commission	Kennedy Assass.				975	Photograph of Entire Comm.
Warren, Chas. Marquis	Author	5	15	25	10	
Warren, Earl (SC) 1891-1974	Supreme Court	75	248	215	250	Chief Justice, Governor CA
Warren, Earl.(Entire Court)	Supreme Court				5175	All Nine
Warren, Francis 1844-1929	Congress	80	100	150		CW CMH, Gov.,Senator WY
Warren, Gouverneur (War Date)	Civil War	175	512			Union General
Warren, Gouverneur K. 1830-82	Civil War	88	190	350		Union Gen., ALS/Cont. $1,250
Warren, Harry	Composer	30	100		40	AMusQS $450
Warren, James 1726-1808	Revolutionary War	110	275	540		Patriot, Mercant, Colon'l Assembly
Warren, Jennifer	Entertainment	4		10	15	
Warren, Joseph 1741-1775	Revolutionary War	6875				Physician, Patriot. NRPA
Warren, Joseph, Sr.	Colonial America	45	135	175		
Warren, Lavinia	Entertainment	45			295	Mrs.Tom Thumb, Charles Stratton
Warren, Leonard	Entertainment	75			275	Opera. Am. Baritone
Warren, Leslie Ann	Entertainment	5	6	15	20	
Warren, Michael	Entertainment	3	3	10	15	
Warren, Robert Penn	Author	30	100	125	75	Am. Poet, Novelist. Pulitzers
Warren, Russell 1783-1860	Architect	25		165		RI Designer of Many Early Banks, Churches
Warren, William 1812-88	Entertainment	5		25		Am. Character Actor
Warrick, Ruth	Entertainment	9	10	20	25	
Warsitz, Erich	Aviation	15	35	65	40	
Warwick, Countess Evelyn F.	Celebrity	35	125			Mistress of Edward VII
Washburn, Bryant	Entertainment	5	9	20	20	
Washburn, Cadwallader C.	Civil War	45	75		85	Union Gen., Gov. WI 1855
Washburn, Israel, Jr.	Governor	30	80	135		Civil War Gov. ME
Washburn, W. D.	Senate/Congress	4	15			Rep. MN 1879, Senator 1889
Washburne, Elihu B. 1816-87	Cabinet	20	40	75		Sec'y State 1869, Minister Fr.
Washington, Booker T.1856-1915	Author-Educator	412	744	762	1495	Afro-Am.Built Tuskegee into Great Institution
Washington, Bushrod (SC)	Supreme Court	115	340	795		
Washington, Denzel	Entertainment	15	20		50	AA

The Sanders Price Guide to Autographs

NAME	CATEGORY	SIG	LS/DS	ALS	SP	Comment
Washington, Dinah	Entertainment	125			200	Vocalist
Washington, George 1732-99	President	4750	11980	19750		G.Washington&T.Jefferson DS $20,000
Washington, George Augustine	Presidential Relative			900		
Washington, George C.	Senate/Congress	15	35	55		Rep. MD 1827
Washington, Harold	Senate/Congress	4	15	35	15	Rep. IL 1981,Mayor Chicago 1983
Washington, John A.	Civil War	125		590		CSA Lt.Col.,Gen. R.E.
Washington, Martha	First Lady					RARE. Sig. $8500
Washington, Ned	Composer	45			100	
Washington, William 1752-1810	Military	65	165	315		Patriot. General
Wassel, Corydon M., Dr.	Military	45	85	150	50	Med.Missionary China.WW II Hero
Wasserman, Dale	Composer	15		35	30	Man of LaMancha
Watanabe, Gedde	Entertainment	9	10	20	25	
Waterhouse, Benjamin 1754-1846	Science	255	765	2750		Pioneer in Small Pox Vaccination
Waterhouse, J. W.	Artist	10		50		
Waterhouse, Richard	Civil War	150	320	550		CSA General
Waterloo, Stanley	Author	10	20	35		
Waterman, F.D.	Business	75	195			Waterman Pen
Waterman, W.	Aviation	15		25		
Waters, Ethel 1896-1977	Entertainment	40	115	130	188	Prominent Black Actress-Singer.
Waters, Muddy	Entertainment	20	100		50	Jazz Musician
Waterston, Robert Classie	Clergy	10	15	30		
Waterston, Sam	Entertainment	6	8	15	20	Law & Order
Watkins, Henry George Gino	Explorer	125		450		Youngest Arctic Expl.Died at 25
Watkinson, William L.	Clergy	15	20	35		
Watson, Harold F.	Aviation	10	30	45	25	
Watson, J. Crittenden	Civil War	25	60	105		Union Commodore
Watson, James D., Dr.	Science	28	35	55	30	Nobel Medicine 1962
Watson, James E. 1863-1948	Congress				195	Senator IN. Majority Leader
Watson, John 1850-1907	Clergy	15		35		Presbyterian Minister-Author
Watson, Minor	Entertainment	5	8		15	Fine Stage-Film Character Actor
Watson, R.J. Doc	Aviation	10	22	38	28	ACE, WW II, USAAF Ace
Watson, Thomas A. 1854-1934	Science	65	275	315	1840	Ass't To A.G.Bell.Teleph. Pioneer
Watson, Thomas E. 1856-1922	Congress	15	35			US Sen. GA, 1904 President'l Cand.
Watson, Thomas J., Jr.	Business	10	20	50	75	Chmn. IBM in Productive Years
Watson, Thomas J., Sr.1874-1956	Business	65	145		125	Founder IBM
Watt, James	Cabinet	7	10	20	25	Controversial Sec'y Interior 1981
Watt, James 1736-1819	Science	400	895	1850		Inventor. Steam Engine
Watt, James, Jr. (1769-1848)	Science	40	85	185		Marine Engineer.Son of Inventor
Watterson, Bill*	Cartoonists	25			180	Calvin & Hobbes
Watterson, Henry 1840-1921	Journalist-Congress	15	50	90	95	CSA Army. Editor, Pulitzer
Watts, George Frederick 1817-1904	Artist	75	150	350		Br. Painter & Sculptor
Watts, Thomas H. 1819-92	Civil War	45		460		CSA Att'y Gen.,Gov. AL
Waugh, Evelyn 1903-66	Author	45	195	325	50	Brideshead Revisited.ALS/Cont.$1350
Wavell, Archibald, Sir 1883-1950	Military	50	235	175	60	Br. Field Marshal,Viceroy India
Wayans, Keenen Ivory	Entertainment	4			25	Actor. In Living Color
Wayne, Anthony 1745-96	Rev. War Military	625	1750	3000		Mad Anthony ...ADS $4500
Wayne, Carol	Entertainment		55	130	150	
Wayne, David	Entertainment	7	6	15	25	
Wayne, Henry C. (War Date)	Civil War	175	270			CSA Gen.
Wayne, Henry C. 1815-83	Civil War	95	200	325	250	CSA General
Wayne, James M. (SC)	Supreme Court	75	200	350		
Wayne, John 1907-79	Entertainment	422	618	750	866	DS Wayne & John Ford $1,500
Wayne, Pat	Entertainment	10			20	
Wazniak, Steve	Business	15			70	Cofounder of Apple Computer
Weare, Meshech 1713-86	Revolutionary War		100			Pres. of New Hampshire
Weatherhead, Leslie D.	Clergy	30	35	60	40	

The Sanders Price Guide to Autographs

NAME	CATEGORY	SIG	LS/DS	ALS	SP	Comment
Weathers, Carl	Entertainment	6	8	15	20	
Weaver, Dennis	Entertainment	6	8	15	25	
Weaver, Doodles	Entertainment	20			30	
Weaver, James B.	Civil War	30		140		Union Gen., Pres. Candidate
Weaver, Robert C.	Cabinet	25	45		30	1st Afro-Am. Cabinet. Sec'y HUD
Weaver, Sigourney	Entertainment	10			40	Pin-Up SP $45
Webb, Alexander S.1835-1911	Civil War	20	150	55		Union General
Webb, Beatrice Potter 1858-	Reformer		125			Member Fabian Society
Webb, Charles Henry	Author	5	15	30		
Webb, Clifton	Entertainment	35			65	
Webb, Del	Business	5	15	20	30	Desert Inn Casino
Webb, Jack	Entertainment	40	45	110	125	
Webb, James E.	Astronaut	10			25	Admiral
Webb, Jimmy	Composer	20	35		65	
Webb, Richard	Entertainment	15			35	Capt. Midnight
Webb, Samuel B.	Revolutionary War	105	400	645		Fndr. Soc. of Cincinnati
Webb, Sidney	Statesman	15		75	175	Br Economist, Founder Fabian Society
Webb, U.S.	Political	6		25		California Official
Webb, W.R. Spider	Aviation	15	30	45	35	ACE, WW II, Ace in a Day
Webber, Andrew Lloyd 1948-	Composer	100	250		325	Br. Musical Theatre
Webber, Robert	Entertainment	15	20		35	
Weber (Joe)and Fields (Lew)	Entertainment	85			175	Pioneer Vaudeville Comedians
Weber, Joe 1867-1942	Entertainment	20	35	45	45	Vintage Comedian/Lew Fields
Weber, Karl Maria von	Composer	375	1035	1320		
Webster, Ben	Entertainment	125				Tenor Sax-Arranger
Webster, Daniel 1782-1852	Cabinet-Senate	112	483	467	538	NH Statesman,LS/Cont.$1750
Webster, H.T.*	Cartoonist	20	45		125	The Timid Soul. Caspar Milquetoast
Webster, Jean	Author	15	45	135		Am. Novelist.Daddy-Long-Legs
Webster, Noah 1758-1843	Author	500	795	1580		Am.Lexicographer,Editor etc.
Webster, Paul Francis	Composer	20	50	70	45	
Webster, William	Celebrity	10			40	Director FBI
Wedell, Jimmie	Aviation	10	30	40	35	
Wedemeyer, Albert C. 1897-	Military	25	200		150	Gen. WW II
Wedgwood, John H., Sir	Business	10	20	35	15	
Weed, Marian	Entertainment	15			50	Opera
Weed, Thurlow	Politician	15	30	50		Political Leader NY, Journalist
Weede, Robert	Entertainment	10			35	Opera, Concert, Operetta
Weeks, Anson	Entertainment	15			45	Dancin' with Anson
Weeks, John W.	Cabinet	15	35	70		Sec'y War 1921
Weeks, Sinclair	Cabinet	5	15	35	15	Sec'y Commerce 1953
Weems, Ted	Bandleader	20	20	70	45	Big Band Leader-Trombone
Weicker, Lowell Jr.	Congress	10	10		15	Repr.CT 1969, Senator 1971
Weidler, Virginia	Entertainment	7	9	20	15	
Weidman, Jerome	Author	5	10	20	5	
Weikl, Bernd	Entertainment	5			20	Opera
Weill, Kurt	Composer	250	778	1200	375	Opera, Ballet, Musical Comedy
Weinberg, Steven, Dr.	Science	25	35		30	Nobel Physics 1979
Weinberger, Casper	Cabinet	5	10	25	50	Sec'y HEW, Sec'y Defense
Weingartner, Felix von	Composer	40		250	150	Austrian Conductor
Weir, Benjamin M.	Celebrity	12	15	25	15	
Weir, Julian Alden	Artist	40	135	250		Early Am. Impressionist
Weir, Robert Walter	Artist	50	140	265		Prof. Drawing. Taught R.E. Lee
Weisbart, David	Entertainment	15				Director-Producer
Weiser, Jan Conrad	Fr. Revolution	290	950	1600		
Weisiger, David A. 1818-99	Civil War	80	265			CSA Gen. ALS/Cont. $1045
Weiss, John 1818-79	Clergy	10	15	28		Unitarian Author, Abolitionist

NAME	CATEGORY	SIG	LS/DS	ALS	SP	Comment
Weissmuller, Johnny 1904-84	Entertainment	95	200		325	SPI As Tarzan $695
Weitz, Paul J.	Astronaut	8			25	
Weitzel, Godfrey (War Date)	Civil War	35	90	192		Union Gen.
Weizman, Vera	First Lady	25	80		35	Widow of 1st Pres. Israel
Weizmann, Chaim 1874-1952	Head of State	445	1350	2335	875	1st Pres. Israel
Weizmann, Ezer	Head of State	25	65			Israeli AF Gen. Pres. of Israel
Welby, Amelia	Author	450		2900		Poet. Appreciated by E.A.Poe
Welch Herbert, Bishop	Clergy	15	25	30	35	
Welch, Raquel	Entertainment	10	15	20	25	Pin-Up SP $30
Welch, Robert A.	Business	25	40	90	30	Batchelor Oil Multi-Millionaire
Weld, Tuesday	Entertainment	10	15	30	25	
Welden, Ben	Entertainment	10			25	
Weldon, Felix de	Artist	60				Iwo Jima Memorial Statue
Welensky, Roy, Sir	Head of State	15	55	115		
Welk, Lawrence	Entertainment	10	50	35	25	
Weller, Peter	Entertainment	10	15	25	35	
Weller, Thomas H., Dr.	Science	25	35	50	30	Nobel Medicine 1954
Welles, Gideon 1802-78	Cabinet-CW	100	248	300	675	Sec'y of Navy, LS Wardte $775
Welles, Orson 1915-85	Entertainment	85	462		444	AA. Special DS $650
Welles, Sumner 1892-1961	Diplomat	25	75	150	55	State Dept.,Ambassador
Wellington, 1st Duke of 1769-1852	Head of State	185	250	390		Arthur Wellesley,Prime Minister
Wellington, George Louis 1852-1927	Congress	12	20			Rep. 1895, Senator MD
Wellman, Manly Wade	Author	35	100		60	North Carolina Literary Figure
Wellman, Walter	Aviation	60	145	230	75	Aviator-Explorer-Writer
Wells, Carolyn	Author	10	25	40	15	Sketches, Parodies,Detective
Wells, Carveth	Author	20	45	110	25	Explorer, Author, Lecturer
Wells, Dawn	Entertainment	5	6	15	20	Pin-Up $35
Wells, H.G. 1866-1946	Author	150	295	415	1035	Br. Sci-Fi Novelist, ALS/Cont.$6000
Wells, Henry & Fargo, James	Business	850	1375			Wells-Fargo, American Express
Wells, Henry & Fargo, William G.	Business		1477			Wells-Fargo, American Express
Wells, Henry 1805-78	Business	285	750	1500		Wells-Fargo, Founder American Express
Wells, James M.	Governor	15	40			Governor LA 1865
Wells, Junior	Entertainment	4			10	
Wells, Kitty	Country Music	5			15	
Welty, Eudora	Author	35	100	225	100	Am.Short Stories, Novelist
Wenck, Walter	Military	25	60	120	55	
Wendelin, Rudolph*	Cartoonist	20			125	Smokey the Bear
Wendorf, E.G. Wendy	Aviation	10	25	40	30	ACE, WW II, Navy Ace
Wendt, George	Entertainment	5			30	
Wenrich, Percy	Composer	55	125			AMusQS $175, $350
Wentworth, Benning 1696-1770	Colonial America	95	270	550		Col. Gov. NH. Bennington, VT
Wentworth, John 1737-1820	Revolutionary War	80	250	340		
Wermuth, Arthur W.	Military	15	35	50	25	WW II Hero
Werner, Oskar	Entertainment	20		45	50	
Werrenrath, Reinald 1883-	Opera	15		25	50	Am. Baritone. Met.Début 1919
Wert, Richard L.	Military	5	15	25	15	
Wesley, Charles	Clergy	150				
Wesley, John	Clergy	375	650	1500		Methodist Fndr, ALS/Cont.$3000
Wessell, Vivian	Entertainment	10		40	35	
Wesselowsky, Alessandro	Entertainment	40			160	Opera
Wesson, Daniel B.	Inventor	425				Gunsmith (Smith & Wesson)
West, Adam	Entertainment	10	25		30	Batman
West, Benjamin 1738-1820	Artist	160	838	1750		Am. Historical Painter
West, Dottie	Country Music	10			40	
West, F.H.	Civil War	40	110			Union Gen. War Dte LS $250
West, Jessamyn	Author	12	30	35	15	Popular Novelist

The Sanders Price Guide to Autographs

NAME	CATEGORY	SIG	LS/DS	ALS	SP	Comment
West, Joseph R. 1822-98	Civil War	38	80			Union Gen.
West, Mae 1892-1980	Entertainment	65	135		246	Provocative Seductress
West, Morris L.	Author	15	45	80	30	Shoes Of The Fisherman
West, Rebecca, Dame 1892-1983	Author	15	45	90		Br. Novelist, Critic, Historian
West, Richard L.	Aviation	10			30	ACE WW II
West, Roy O.	Cabinet	25	40			Sec'y Interior 1928
Westall, William	Artist	15	40	95		
Westheimer, Ruth, Dr.	Medical	4	15	25	15	Sex Therapist
Westinghouse, George	Business	125	720	835	350	Inventor. Fndr. Westinghouse Co
Westman, Nidia	Entertainment	15	15	35	30	
Westminster, 2nd Earl	Royalty	15	50			Robert Grosvenor
Westmore, Wally	Entertainment	15			50	Hollywood Makeup Director
Westmoreland, Wm. C. 1914-93	Military	20	77	75	65	Gen. Korea, Viet Nam
Weston, Agnes, Dame	Celebrity	6	20	40	25	
Weston, Edward 1850-1936	Business	40	125	315	70	Weston Electrical Instruments
Weston, Edward 1886-1958	Artist	35		600		Am. Western Photographer
Weston, Paul	Bandleader	16				Arranger
Westover, Russ* 1887-1966	Cartoonist	15		35	75	Tillie The Toiler
Wetherbee, James D.	Astronaut	5			15	
Weyer, Kurt	Military	15			60	
Weygand, Maxime	Military	40	75	150	125	Fr. Gen.,Foch's Chief of Staff
Weyman, Stanley J.	Author	15	35	75		Brit. Novelist
Whalen, Grover	NYC Official	10	30		15	Merchant-NYC Official Greeter
Whalen, Michael	Entertainment	15	15	35	30	
Wharton, Edith N. 1862-1937	Author	190	475	1250		Pulitzer, Age of Innocence,Ethan Frome
Wharton, Gabriel C. 1824-1906	Civil War	80		185		CSA Gen. DS '64 $470
Wharton, John A. 1828-65	Civil War	150	450	1100		CSA Gen. ALS Wardte $1,950
Wharton, Thomas 1735-1778	Revolutionary War	115	385	565		Gov. PA, Patriot. Pres. PA 1777
Wheatley, Melvin E., Bishop	Clergy	20	25	35	30	
Wheaton, Nathaniel S. 1792-1862	Clergy			52		Founder Trinity College, Hartford
Wheaton, Will	Entertainment	15			35	Star Trek
Wheatstone, Charles, Sir	Science	100	320	565		Br. Physicist, Inventor
Wheeler, Bert	Entertainment	25			75	Comedy Team Wheeler & Woolsey
Wheeler, Burton K. 1882-1975	Congress	25	70		35	Senator MT 1922
Wheeler, Earle G.	Military	10			50	
Wheeler, Ellie	Entertainment	10	15	25	25	
Wheeler, Joseph (War Date)	Civil War	285	1350	1745		CSA Gen.
Wheeler, Joseph 1836-1906	Civil War	118	298	316	950	CSA Gen.
Wheeler, Lyle	Entertainment	15				Film Art Director
Wheeler, William A. (V)1819-87	Vice President	75	225			Hayes VP
Whelan, Arleen	Entertainment	10		25	20	
Whelchel, Lisa	Entertainment	5			10	
Whipple, Abraham 1733-1819	Revolutionary War	250	750			Fired 1st Gun of Rev. on Water
Whipple, Amiel Weeks 1818-1863	Civil War	115	235	350		Astronomer, Surveyor, Union Gen
Whipple, Edwin Percy 1819-86	Author	15		30		Essayist, Critic, Lecturer
Whipple, Fred L. 1906-	Author-Science	10	25		15	Astronomer. Rocket Research
Whipple, George H.	Science	45	75	150		Nobel Medicine !934
Whipple, Henry B.	Clergy	50	100	200		
Whipple, William 1730-85	Revolutionary War	645	900	4200		Signer Decl. of Ind.
Whipple, William D.	Civil War	25	40	50		Union General
Whirry, Shannon	Entertainment	5			25	Actress Exit
Whisner, William T.	Aviation	20	45	75	50	ACE, WW II
Whistler, James McNeill 1834-1903	Artist	300	575	759		Am.Painter,Etcher. Lived Abroad
Whitaker, Johnnie	Entertainment	10			25	
White, Alice	Entertainment	25	45		75	Vintage Actress
White, Andrew Dickson 1832-1918	Educator-Diplomat	20	72	70	50	Co-Fndr. Cornell University

NAME	CATEGORY	SIG	LS/DS	ALS	SP	Comment
White, Anthony Walton 1750-1803	Revolutionary War	55	165	250		Washington Aide de Camp. Genera
White, Betty	Entertainment	9	10	20	25	
White, Byron R. (SC)	Supreme Court	55	125	170	55	
White, E.B.	Author	30	110			Charlotte's Web
White, E.H. & McDivitt, J.	Astronauts				1200	SP After Pickup Gem. 4. $595
White, Edward D. (SC)	Supreme Court	50	190	225	135	
White, Edward H. II 1930-67	Astronaut	200	325	585	688	1st Am. To Walk In Space
White, George	Entertainment	60	70	575	100	Producer George White's Scandals
White, George Stuart 1835-1912	Military	40		65		Br.Fld.Marshal. Ladysmith Seige
White, Horace 1865-1943	Governor	10	25			Gov. NY
White, Hugh	Governor	5	20		15	Governor MS 1936
White, I.D.	Military	10			25	
White, Jacqueline	Entertainment	4			15	
White, Jesse	Entertainment	10			20	
White, Jim	Explorer	40		175		Discover Carlsbad Caverns
White, Josh	Entertainment	55			225	Am. Folk Singer
White, Julius	Civil War	25	55	120		Union General
White, Lee Lasses	Entertainment	25				Minstrel
White, Paul Dudley, Dr.	Science	45	125		80	Heart Specialist
White, Pearl	Entertainment	150		320	300	Queen of the Silent Serials
White, Robert, Maj.	Aviation	10	25		30	'60 Speed & Altitude Records
White, Sanford	Architect	100	305	790	150	TLS/Content $1,600-5,500
White, Stewart E.	Author	10	20	40	15	Am. Western Adventure Stories
White, Theodore	Author	8	15	25	10	Detailed Presidential Campaigns
White, Vanna	Entertainment	5			15	Pin-Up SP $25
White, Vanna & Pat Sajak	Entertainment	10			25	Wheel of Fortune
White, Wallace H., Jr. 1877-1952	Congress	10	15			Rep. ME 1917, Senator 1930
White, William 1748-1836	Clergy	130	265	250		1st P.E. Bishop
White, William Allen 1868-1944	Author	20	120	85	65	Pulitzer Journalist Sage of Emporia
White, Windsor T.	Business	110		550		Pioneer Auto-Truck Mfg.
Whitelaw, Billie	Entertainment	15			30	
Whiteman, Paul 1890-1967	Entertainment	55	140	170	225	King of Jazz.Intro Gershwin
Whitestone, Heather	Entertainment	10			40	Miss America 1995. Hearing impaired
Whiting, Jack	Entertainment	6	8	15	15	
Whiting, John D.	Diplomat	4		20		Jerusalem
Whiting, Margaret	Entertainment	15			15	Vocalist
Whiting, Richard	Composer	50		135	100	AMusQS $150
Whiting, William Henry 1824-65	Civil War	200				CSA General ALS '65 $935-1500
Whitlam, Gough	Head of State	10			25	Prime Minister Australia
Whitley, Ray	Country Music	10			35	Cowboy Movies
Whitman, Charles S.	Governor	10	30		15	Governor NY 1915
Whitman, Slim	Country Music	5			15	
Whitman, Walt 1819-92	Author	955	2500	2900	3073	Controversial Am. Poet
Whitmore, James	Entertainment	5		10	15	
Whitney, Adeline D.1824-1906	Author	20				
Whitney, Asa 1797-1872	Merchant	25		100		Promoter of Transcontinental RR
Whitney, C.V.	Business	15	35	70	25	
Whitney, Casper	Publisher	10	25	35		Publisher
Whitney, Courtney	Military	15	40	75	35	General WW II. MacArthur Aide
Whitney, Eli 1765-1825	Science	650	2375	3900		Am. Inventor Cotton Gin
Whitney, Grace Lee	Entertainment	15	30	40	35	Star Trek
Whitney, Josiah D. 1819-96	Science	65		292		CA State Geologist. Mt. Whitney
Whitney, Richard	Business	35	50			Pres. NY Stock Exchange
Whitney, William Collins 1841-1904	Cabinet	25	45	65	25	Financier, Cleveland Sec'y Navy
Whittaker, Charles E.(SC)	Supreme Court	50	75	165	85	
Whitten-Brown, Arthur, Sir	Aviation	250	375			Pioneer Aviator/John Alcock

The Sanders Price Guide to Autographs

NAME	CATEGORY	SIG	LS/DS	ALS	SP	Comment
Whittier, John Greenleaf 1807-92	Author	53	350	525		Quaker Poet.Abolitionist
Whittle, Frank, Sir	Aviation	15	50		45	Invented jet engine
Whittle, Josephine	Entertainment	5	6	15	15	
Whittlesey, Elisha 1783-1863	Statesman	10		45		Founder of Whig Party
Whitty, Dame May	Entertainment	35	45	85	75	
Who, The (All 4)	Entertainment	450	2050		750	Rock
Wickard, Claude	Cabinet	15	25			Sec'y Agriculture 1940
Wicke, Lloyd C., Bishop	Clergy	15	25	35	30	
Wicker, Irene	Entertainment	10			25	Vintage Radio's Singing Lady
Wickersham, George W.1858-1936	Cabinet	15	45	75	45	Taft Att'y Gen. 1909
Wickes, Mary	Entertainment	15			30	
Wickham, William C. (War Date)	Civil War	140	390			CSA Gen.
Wickham, William C.1820-88	Civil War	80	250			CSA Gen.
Wickliffe, Charles A.	Cabinet	30	65	95		P.M. Gen. 1841
Widmark, Richard	Entertainment	9	10	20	25	
Widor, Charles Marie	Composer			165		Fr. Organist, Teacher
Wieck, Dorothea	Entertainment	15	15	35	30	
Wieghorst, Olaf	Artist	60	225	350	180	Dean of Western Art
Wiemann, Ernst	Entertainment	5			20	Opera
Wien, Noel	Aviation	25	55	105	65	
Wiere Brothers	Entertainment	15			25	
Wiesel, Elie	Author	20	45	55	25	Nobel Peace Prize 1986
Wiesel, Torsten S., Dr.	Science	22	30	45	25	Nobel Medicine 1981
Wiesenthal, Simon	Activist	20	45	90	35	Famed Nazi Hunter
Wiest, Diane	Entertainment	10			45	AA
Wigfall, Louis T. 1816-74	Civil War	140	250			CSA Gen. CSA Senator
Wiggin, Kate Douglas 1856-1923	Author	125		190	95	
Wigglesworth, Frank	Composer					AMusQS $100
Wigglesworth, Richard B	Congress	5	10			Repr. MA 1928, Diplomat
Wigner, Eugene P. Dr.	Science	15	25	50	20	Nobel Physics 1963
Wihan, Hanus	Entertainment	30		120		Czech Viol-Cellist.AMusQs $85
Wilberforce, Samuel, Bishop	Clergy	30	45	60		
Wilberforce, William 1759-1833	Abolitionist	50	145	350		Br. Anti-Slavery Politician
Wilbur, Curtis D.	Cabinet	10	25	35	15	Sec'y Navy 1924
Wilbur, Ray Lyman	Cabinet	20	25	55	20	Sec'y Interior 1929
Wilbur, Richard	Author	5	135	35	10	U.S. Poet Laureate. Pulitzer
Wilbur, W.H.	Military	5	15	25	10	
Wilcott, Terry	Astronaut	5			10	
Wilcox, Cadmus M. (War Date)	Civil War	175	400			CSA Gen.
Wilcox, Cadmus M. 1824-90	Civil War	90	190	310		CSA Gen.
Wilcox, Ella Wheeler 1850-1919	Author	20	35	100		Journalist, Poet, Essayist
Wilcoxon, Henry	Entertainment	20		35	45	
Wild Choir	Entertainment	5			10	Rock
Wild, Edward A.	Civil War	70	150	210		Union General
Wilde, Cornel	Entertainment	15	25	40	32	
Wilde, Oscar 1856-1900	Author	800	1550	2662	2215	Ir. Poet, Playwright, Wit
Wilde, Percival	Author	20	55	120		Playwright, Novelist
Wilder, Billy	Entertainment	15			50	Multiple AA Film Dir. DS $285
Wilder, Gene	Entertainment	10	25		25	
Wilder, Marshall P.	Entertainment	12	20	30	35	Reciter, Imitator. Vintage
Wilder, Thornton 1897-1975	Author	70	176	408	200	Pulitzer, ALS/Content $675
Wilding, Michael	Entertainment	30			55	
Wilentz, David T.	Celebrity	25				
Wiley, Alexander 1884-1967	Congress	15	40			Senator WI 1938
Wiley, Harvey W., Dr.	Science	80	195			Created FDA
Wilhelm I (Ger) 1797-1888	Royalty	75	350	435		King of Prussia, Emperor Ger.

NAME	CATEGORY	SIG	LS/DS	ALS	SP	Comment
Wilhelm II (Kaiser)(Ger) 1859-1941	Royalty	170	438	525	288	Official DS $8500
Wilhelm, August	Military	120			500	Ger. Gen. Storm Trooper
Wilhelmj, August	Entertainment	25			75	Ger. Violinist
Wilke, Robert J.	Entertainment	10			25	
Wilkerson, Guy	Entertainment	25			65	
Wilkes, Charles	Civil War	50	105	200		Union Adm., Explorer
Wilkes, Earle	Military	10			50	
Wilkie, David, Sir 1785-1841	Artist	35	80	142		Br.Genre Paintings, Portraits
Wilkins, Geo. Hubert,Sir 1888-1958	Explorer	30	50	115	55	Led Arctic & Antarctic Exped.
Wilkins, Hans	Aviation	10	25	45	30	
Wilkins, Roy	Activist	15	35	85	20	Sr. Statesman of Civil Rights
Wilkins, T. H.	Science	15	25	40	20	
Wilkinson, Geoffrey	Science	15	25	40	20	Nobel Chemistry 1985
Wilkinson, James	Revolutionary War	120	390	485		General
Wilkinson, June	Entertainment	6	8	15	25	Pln-Up SP $30
Wilks, Matthew	Clergy	15		25	50	
Willard, Charles	Aviation	15			35	
Willard, Edward S.	Entertainment	15		35	30	Vintage
Willard, Frances E.	Temperance	40	70	160		Pres. W.C.T.U.
Willard, Frank*	Cartoonist	35			190	Moon Mullins
Willard, Fred	Entertainment	4	6	10	15	
Willard, John	Entertainment	10			25	Playwright
Willcox, Orlando B.1823-1907	Civil War	40	85	153		Union Gen.
Willebrands, John, Cardinal	Clergy	30	45	65	40	
Willem VI & I, 1772-1848	Royalty		735			Prince of Orange, King Netherlands
Willett, Marinus 1740-1830	Revolutionary War	75	150	250		Officer Cont. Army.Mayor NYC
William III (Eng)	Royalty	560	1685	2500		
William IV (Eng) 1765-1837	Royalty	65	269	358		The Sailor King, DS $575
William, 4th Duke of Devonshire	Head of State	75	185	355		Prime Minister 1756
William, Warren	Entertainment	10	15	40	45	Am. Film Leading Man & Character Actor
Williams, Andy	Entertainment	20			45	
Williams, Barry	Entertainment	4	6	10	15	
Williams, Bart	Entertainment	5			20	
Williams, Ben Ames	Author	15	25	40	20	Am. Novelist
Williams, Bill	Entertainment	10	15		25	
Williams, Billy Dee	Entertainment	10	15		25	
Williams, Cindy	Entertainment	4	6	15	15	
Williams, Clifton C.	Astronaut	6			25	
Williams, Donald E.	Astronaut	5			15	
Williams, Edward B.	Law	5	15	40	10	Top Criminal Lawyer
Williams, Edward M.	Business	35	90	155		
Williams, Edy	Entertainment	5			20	Pin-Up SP $30
Williams, Eleazer 1787-1858	Clergy	45	115	1600		Missionary.Louis XVII Lost Dauphin??
Williams, Esther	Entertainment	8	10	20	20	Pin-Up SP $20
Williams, Geoffrey	Science	10	20	35	20	
Williams, George H.	Cabinet	10	25	40		Att'y Gen. 1872, Senator OR 186
Williams, Gluyas* 1888-19xx	Cartoonist	10		45	75	New Yorker Cartoonist
Williams, Grant	Entertainment	45			125	
Williams, Griff	Bandleader	26				
Williams, Guinn Big Boy	Entertainment	75			150	
Williams, Gus	Entertainment	12			25	Showman
Williams, Guy 1924-89	Entertainment	100	125		265	SP as Zorro $695
Williams, Hal	Entertainment	4			12	Afro-Am Actor
Williams, Hank	Country Music	775	1200		1250	
Williams, Hank Jr.	Country Music	20			40	
Williams, Harrison A., Jr.1919-	Congress	15	35		20	Rep. 1953, Senator NJ

NAME	CATEGORY	SIG	LS/DS	ALS	SP	Comment
Williams, J.R.*	Cartoonist	20	25		100	Way Out West
Williams, JoBeth	Entertainment	10			25	
Williams, Joe	Entertainment	15			40	Jazz Vocalist
Williams, John	Composer	20	65	75	75	Conductor.AMusQS $225
Williams, John Sharp	Congress	10	20		20	Repr. MS 1893, Senator 1910
Williams, Jonathan	Author	5	15	25		
Williams, Jr., Alford J.	Aviation	30	45	95	125	
Williams, Mary Alice	Journalist	10			20	TV News Journalist
Williams, Mason	Composer	10			20	Guitar Soloist
Williams, Otho 1749-1800	Revolutionary War	140	400	735		Officer. Fought/Gates & Greene
Williams, Paul	Composer	5	7	15	15	
Williams, Robin	Entertainment	5	15	30	35	Actor-Comedian
Williams, Roger	Entertainment	4		10	35	Pianist-Arranger
Williams, Seth 1822-66	Civil War	30	65	85		Union Gen. War Dte. LS $175
Williams, Tennessee (Thomas L.)	Author	150	375	650	395	Pulitzer. Cat on a Hot Tin Roof & Streetcar....
Williams, Tex	Country Music	10			20	Big Band
Williams, Treat	Entertainment	5	15	25	20	
Williams, Van	Entertainment	38			75	TV's Green Hornet
Williams, Vanessa	Entertainment	18			50	Miss America, Pin-Up SP $ 55
Williams, William 1731-1811	Revolutionary War	300	596	705		Signer Decl. of Indepen.
Williams, William Carlos 1883-1963	Author	275	375		300	Am. Poet, Novelist, Physician
Williams, Willie, Chief	Law Enforcement				25	Los Angeles Chief of Police
Williamson, Fred	Entertainment	8			20	Afro-Am. Actor
Williamson, Hugh	Revolutionary War					Continental Congress
Williamson, James A.1829-1902	Law	5				
Williamson, Marianne	Author	5			10	Non-Fiction
Williiams, Roger Q.	Aviation	10				'29 Record Non-Stop Flight
Willing, Foy	Country Music	10			20	(Riders of the Purple Sage)
Willing, Thomas	Revolutionary War	75	250			Banker,Continental Congress
Willis, Bruce	Entertainment	20			50	
Willis, Nathaniel P. 1806-67	Author	20	40	125		Major Editor Poetry Mags.
Willis, Richard S.	Clergy	20	25	35		
Willkie, Wendell	Politician	25	75		125	Pres. Candidate
Wills, Bob	Country Music	75			200	
Wills, Chill	Entertainment	52			85	
Willson, Meredith	Composer	25	80	225	80	The Music Man
Willys, John North	Business	60	110	245	90	Auto Pioneer, Diplomat
Wilmer, Richard Hooker, Bishop	Clergy	8	25	40		
Wilmot, David 1814-68	Congress	85	230			Repr. & Senator PA. Wilmot Proviso
Wilson, August	Author	10	30	45	20	Dramatist, Dir., Pulitzer,Tony
Wilson, Brian	Entertainment	200	250		550	Beach Boys
Wilson, Bridget	Entertainment	5				Actress. Mortal Combat. Pin-Up 45
Wilson, Charles E.	Business-Cabinet	20	35	70	30	Pres. GM., Sec'y Defense 1953
Wilson, Charles Edward	Business	20	75			Pres. General Electric
Wilson, Demond	Entertainment	10			25	
Wilson, Dennis	Entertainment	95			190	
Wilson, Don	Entertainment	5				Jack Benny Announcer
Wilson, Dooley	Entertainment	350			900	Supporting Player Casablanca
Wilson, E. Willis	Governor	12	25			Governor WV 1885
Wilson, Earl	Journalist	10	15	30	15	Powerful Synd. Columnist
Wilson, Edith Bolling 1872-1961	First Lady	80	220	250	200	ALS as 1st Lady $500-750
Wilson, Edmund	Author	25	90	165		Am. Critic.ALS/Content $650
Wilson, Edmund Beecher	Author-Science	350	450			Am. Biologist
Wilson, Ellen Louise	First Lady	100	365	600		1st Wife - Pres. Wilson
Wilson, Flip	Entertainment	10			25	
Wilson, Francis 1854-1935	Entertainment	12		15	25	Vintage Actor

NAME	CATEGORY	SIG	LS/DS	ALS	SP	Comment
Wilson, Gahan*	Cartoonist	10		75	50	Mag. Cartoonist
Wilson, George W. Lt.	Celebrity	15	35	120		
Wilson, Harold, Sir 1916-95	Head of State	40	105	148	55	Br. Prime Minister
Wilson, Henry (VP) 1812-75	Vice President	85	150	85		Grant VP
Wilson, Jackie	Entertainment	15			40	
Wilson, James (SC) 1742-98	Supreme Court	725	1062	1600		Signer. ALS/Content $4,000
Wilson, James 1835-1920	Cabinet	15	50	95		Sec'y Agriculture 1897
Wilson, James G. 1833-1914	Civil War	60		275		Union Gen. Colored Cavalry
Wilson, James H. 1837-1925	Civil War	85	180	395		Union Gen. Cavalry
Wilson, John Lockwood 1850-1912	Congress	15	30	40		Rep. 1889, Senator WA 1895
Wilson, Joseph R.	Celebrity	40		175		Father of Woodrow Wilson
Wilson, Julie	Entertainment	10			35	
Wilson, Kemmons	Business	15	75	80	50	Founder Holiday Inn
Wilson, Lois	Entertainment	15	15	35	40	
Wilson, Marie	Entertainment	25	35	65	60	My Friend Irma Early TV
Wilson, Mary	Entertainment	10			20	Rock, The Supremes
Wilson, Pete	Governor	10	20		20	Governor CA
Wilson, Robert, Dr.	Science	15	25	35	20	Nobel Physics 1978
Wilson, Sloan	Author	15	35	75	20	Man in the Grey Flannel Suit
Wilson, Teddy 1912-86	Entertainment	40		75	90	Pianist-Arranger
Wilson, Tom*	Cartoonist	10			30	Ziggy
Wilson, William B.	Cabinet	10	25	50	15	Sec'y Labor 1913
Wilson, Woodrow & Roosevelt, F.D.	Presidents		1500			DS
Wilson, Woodrow (As Pres.)	President	375	1090		810	
Wilson, Woodrow 1856-1924	President	177	774	1633	760	
Wiman, Dwight Deere	Business	5	20			John Deere Farm Implements
Winans, Ross	Inventor	85	250			Railroad Equipment
Winchell, Paul	Entertainment	10	20	35	30	Talented Ventriloquist
Winchell, Walter 1897-1972	Journalist	35	42	45	35	Powerful Radio-Newspaper Columnist
Winchester, Oliver F.	Inventor	250	2980	1100		Winchester Repeating Arms, Inc.
Winchester, Wm.P.Sir,1st Marquis	Elizabethan					Lord Treasurer Eng. 1485-1572
Winder, Charles S.(War Date)	Civil War			6335		CSA Gen. 1829-62 KIA
Winder, John Henry (War Date)	Civil War	135	769	450		CSA Gen.
Winder, Levin	Rev. War-Gov.			58		Gov. MD 1812
Windgassen, Wolfgang	Entertainment	15			45	Opera
Windom, William	Cabinet	25	35	70	40	Sec'y Treasury 1881
Windom, William	Entertainment	4	6	10	15	
Windsor, Claire	Entertainment	10	15		25	
Windsor, Duke & Duchess of	Royalty	491			650	Edward & Wallis
Windsor, Marie	Entertainment	5	8	15	15	Pin-Up SP $20
Windsor, Wallis, Duchess of	Royalty	130	265	550	175	Content ALS $775
Winfield, Paul	Entertainment	5	6	15	15	Afr.-Am. Actor
Winfrey, Oprah	Entertainment	18			50	
Wing, Toby	Entertainment	10	15	25	25	
Wingate, Francis R., Sir	Military	30	75	155	75	Gen. Succeeded Kitchener
Winger, Debra	Entertainment	10	15	30	35	Pin-Up SP $40
Winkler, Betty	Entertainment	5	6	15	15	
Winkler, Henry	Entertainment	5	8	15	20	
Winkler, K.C.	Entertainment	4			10	Pin-Up SP $20
Winner, Septimus	Composer	85	205	350		AMusQS $495-$1,000
Winninger, Charles	Entertainment	25		50	60	
Winningham, Mare	Entertainment	10			30	Actress
Winslow, Edward 1699-1753	Colonial America	225	675			Silversmith.Government Official
Winslow, Edward 1714-84	Revolutionary War	20	50	90		Loyalist.Port Plym'th Collector
Winslow, John 1753-1819	Revolutionary War	20	55	95		Soldier, Hero, Patriot, General
Winslow, John Ancrum	Military	95	275	385		Union Naval Officer

NAME	CATEGORY	SIG	LS/DS	ALS	SP	Comment
Winslow, John F.	Civil War	55	150	225		Builder of the Monitor
Winsor, Kathleen	Author	15	35	90	25	Novelist Forever Amber
Winter Consort, Paul	Entertainment	50			125	Enviromental Music, Grammy
Winter, William 1836-1913	Author	20	30	42		Drama Critic, Poet, Biographer
Winters, Jonathan	Entertainment	9	10	20	25	
Winters, Roland	Entertainment	30	45	85	75	
Winters, Shelley	Entertainment	6		20	25	Pin-Up SP $30
Winthrop, John 1714-1779	Revolutionary War	200	685			Physicist-Astron.Science Leader
Winthrop, John, The Younger	Colonial America	800	1900	4750		Col. Gov. CT. NRPA
Winthrop, Robert C.1809-94	Congress	15	30	25		Repr. 1840, Senator MA
Winthrop, Thomas L. 1760-1841	Revolutionary War	25	50	95		Merchant. Widely Esteemed
Winwood, Estelle	Entertainment	25	35		45	
Wire, Calvin C.	Aviation	8	15	28	20	ACE, WW II
Wirt, William 1772-1834	Cabinet	35	100	165		Att'y General 1817. Author
Wirtz, Willard	Cabinet	5	10	20	10	Sec'y Labor 1962
Wirz, Henry Hartmann	Civil War	450	3850	4950		CSA Gen., Comd. Andersonville
Wisch, Theodor	Military	110		65		NRPA
Wise, Henry A. (War Date)	Civil War	188		245		CSA Gen.
Wise, Henry A.1806-76	Civil War	93	195	258		CSA General. Gov.,Senator VA
Wise, Robert	Entertainment	10	40		25	Film Director
Wise, Stephen	Clergy	30	50	110	35	
Wiseman, L.H.	Clergy	10	15	25	15	
Wiseman, Nicholas 1802-65l	Clergy	25	45	88		Br. Cardinal
Wisliceny, Gunther-Ehrhardt	Military				55	Ger. SS-Panzer Div. RK
Wister, Owen 1860-1938	Author	50	145	215	75	Am. Novelist, The Virginian
Withers, Jane	Entertainment	5	10	20	20	Shirley Temple Sidekick
Withers, Robert E.	Civil War	25	40	75		CSA Colonel, US Sen. VA
Witherspoon, Jimmy	Entertainment	8			30	Jazz Musician
Witherspoon, John 1723-94	Rev. War-Clergy	675	2235	6500		Signer Decl. of Indepen.
Wittber, Bill	Aviation	20	50	75	80	
Witte, Serge (1st Prem Rus)	Head of State	20	50	95		1st Constitutional Russian Prem
Wittig, Georg F.K.	Science	25	50		40	Nobel Chemistry 1979
Wixell, Ingvar	Entertainment	20			45	Opera
Wodehouse, P. G. 1881-1875	Author	160	782	292	550	Br. Novelist Creator of Jeeves
Woggon, Elmer	Cartoonist	5			20	Big Chief Wahoo
Woidick, Franz	Aviation	15	25	45	30	
Wolcott, Derek	Author	15	20		25	Poet. Nobel Literature
Wolcott, Edward O. 1848-1905	Congress	15	25			Senator CO 1889
Wolcott, Oliver 1726-97	Revolutionary War	140	638	1350		Signer Decl. of Ind.
Wolcott, Oliver, Jr. 1760-1833	Cabinet	55	257	355		Washington Sec'y Treasury
Wolf, Gary	Entertainment	5			15	Voice of Roger Rabbitt
Wolf, George (Wolfe)1777-1840	Governor	35	90	185		Gov. PA 1829, Statesman
Wolf, Hugo 1860-1903	Composer	172		1500		Austrian.RARE ALS/Cont.$3500
Wolfe, Ian	Entertainment	10			25	
Wolfe, James 1727-59	Military	1550		8250		Br. Gen. French & Indian War
Wolfe, Thomas 1900-38	Author	425	2000	2800		Early Death For Gifted Writer
Wolfe, Tom	Author	15	40	75	30	Am. Novelist
Wolfe-Barry, John, Sir 1836-1918	Civil Engineer	10	25	45		London Electr.RR, Docks,Bridges
Wolff, Amalie	Entertainment	15	15	30	25	
Wolff, Joseph	Clergy	35	40	50		
Wolff, Karl	Military	175	550			Ger. Gen. SS
Woll, Matthew	Labor	10	30	80		Lux.-Am. Labor Leader
Wolper, David	Entertainment	5	6	15	15	
Wolseley, Garnet J.,Viscount	Military	25	100	108	35	Br.Field Marshal; Crimean War
Wolsey, Thomas 1475?-1530	Statesman		7800			Influential Cardinal, Statesman
Wonder, George*	Cartoonist	10			75	Terry & The Pirates

NAME	CATEGORY	SIG	LS/DS	ALS	SP	Comment
Wonder, Stevie	Entertainment	5	6		15	
Wonders, Whitney	Entertainment				34	Porn Queen
Wong, Anna May 1907-61	Entertainment	87	150	160	200	1st Major Chinese Film Star
Wood, Edward F.L. 1881-1959	Statesman	15	35	50	25	Diplomat, Ambassador to U.S.
Wood, Evelyn, Sir.	Military	15		55		Br.Fld.Marshal (Boer War)
Wood, F. Derwent	Artist	10	25	60		
Wood, Fernando 1812-81	Civil War	20	60	90		Civil War Mayor NYC
Wood, Garfield 'Gar'	Science	60		80	75	Boat Designer, Builder, Racer
Wood, Grant	Artist	150	372	575		American Gothic
Wood, Haydn	Composer	20	55	85	30	AMusQS $150
Wood, Henry J.	Composer					Br. Conductor
Wood, James 1750-1813	Revolutionary War	50	75	120		House of Burgesses; Gov. VA
Wood, Lana	Entertainment	4	50	10	15	Pin-Up SP $30
Wood, Leonard, Dr.	Military	25	45	70	250	T. Roosevelt'sRough Riders
Wood, Murray	Entertainment		125			Munchkin Wizard of OZ
Wood, Natalie 1938-81	Entertainment	140			200	SP/R. Wagner $210
Wood, Nigel	Astronaut	7			24	
Wood, Peggy	Entertainment	20			35	Theatre & TV Award Winner
Wood, Robert	Astronaut	5			16	
Wood, Robert E.	Military	20	75			Business (Sears), Gen. WW II
Wood, Robert W.	Science	10	25		15	Physicist. Manhattan Project
Wood, Sam	Entertainment	40			90	Film Director-Producer Westerns
Wood, Sterling Alexander M.	Civil War	95	280	305		CSA General
Wood, Thomas J. 1823-1906	Civil War	45	105	95		Union Gen.
Wood, Thomas Waterman 1823	Artist	10	20	55		Pres. Am. Water-Color Society
Woodbury, Levi (SC)1789-1851	Supreme Court	55	171	250		Gov., Sen., Sec'y Navy & Treas.
Woodcock, Amos Walter, Gen.	Military	10	20		20	War Crimes Prosecution Staff
Woodfill, Samuel	Military	10	30	50	25	Major WW I CMH Winner
Woodford, Stewart L. 1835-1913	Civil War	30	100	225		Union Gen., Gov. NY
Woodhouse, Henry	Financier-Explorer	65	265			Turned Forger
Woodhull, Victoria C.	Reformer	115	240	510		1870's Feminist
Woodring, Henry H. 1890-1967	Cabinet	20	45	70	30	FDR Sec'y War. Content TLS $300
Woodruff, Wilford	Religion	25	65	130		Am. Morman Religious Leader
Woods, Charles Robert	Civil War	30	55	85		Union General
Woods, Donald	Entertainment	15	20	35	35	
Woods, James	Entertainment	15	15	25	40	Actor
Woods, Phil	Entertainment	15			45	Jazz Alto Sax-Clarinet
Woods, Rose Mary	White House	15		30		Nixon Sec'y. Watergate
Woods, William B. (SC)	Supreme Court	40	85	190	125	
Woodward, Bob	Author	10	20	35	25	Uncovered Watergate/C.Bernstein
Woodward, Edward	Entertainment	10	15	25	20	
Woodward, George W. 1809-75	Congress	10				Repr. PA, Attorney, Judge
Woodward, Joanne	Entertainment	15	65		30	
Woodward, Marjorie	Entertainment	4	6	10	15	
Woodward, Robert Burns	Science	20	40	85	25	Nobel Chemistry 1965
Woodworth, Samuel	Author	45	140	350		Wrote The Old Oaken Bucket
Wool, John E. 1789-1869	Civil War	100	210	375		Union Gen.,Vet. of 1812. ALS '65 $950
Wooley, Mary E.	Celebrity	30	90	215		
Wooley, Monty	Entertainment	25	35		45	
Wooley, Sheb	Country Music	5			15	
Woolf, Virginia 1882-1944	Author	330	1250	2200	4500	Br. Novelist, Essayist
Woolley, Mary E. 1863-1947	Educator	20	70			1st Woman Grad. Brown U. Pres. Mt. Holyoke
Woolrich, Cornell	Author	150	550			Am. Writer of Detective Fiction
Woolsey, Theodore D. 1801-89	Educator		50	75		Pres. Yale
Woolworth, Charles S.	Business	40	110	205		F.W. Woolworth Co.
Woolworth, Frank W.	Business	295	1090	1550		Fndr. F.W. Woolworth Co.

The Sanders Price Guide to Autographs

NAME	CATEGORY	SIG	LS/DS	ALS	SP	Comment
Woorinen, Charles	Composer	10	25	40		Pulitzer, AMusQS $100
Wooster, David 1710-77	Revolutionary War	235	875	2638		General; Continental Army
Wopat, Tom	Entertainment	6	8	15	15	
Worden, Al M.	Astronaut	15			30	
Worden, Hank	Entertainment	15			35	
Worden, John L.	Civil War	125	185	385		Union Navy, Comdr. Monitor
Wordsworth, Christopher	Clergy	20	30	35	35	
Wordsworth, William 1770-1850	Author	225	1137	2012		Br. Romantic Poet Laureate
Work, Hubert	Cabinet	20	45	110	30	Sec'y Interior 1923
Worley, Jo Ann	Entertainment	5				Laugh In
Worth, Irene	Entertainment	10			25	
Worth, William J. 1794-1849	Military	30	75	125		General; Mexican War
Wouk, Herman	Author	30	100	175	125	Am. Novelist; Caine Mutiny
Woulfe, Michael	Fashion Designer				30	Film
Wray, Fay	Entertainment	45			100	1st King Kong Heroine
Wren, Christopher	Architect-Science	1550	5600	4500		St. Paul's Cathedral, London
Wright, Bobby	Country Music	7			15	
Wright, C.S.	Celebrity	15	35			
Wright, Cobina Sr. & Jr.	Entertainment	5			10	Socialite-Actresses of the 40's
Wright, Edyth	Entertainment	15				Band Vocalist
Wright, Frank Lloyd 1867-1959	Architect	900	1725	4350	2070	ALS/Content $4,000, $4,750
Wright, Harold Bell	Author	10	20	35	15	Am. Novelist.
Wright, Henry C. 1797-1870	Reformer	10	20	35		Anti-Slavery Reformer-Lecturer
Wright, Horatio G. 1820-99	Civil War	40	175	200		Union General
Wright, Jerauld	Military	10	35		20	
Wright, Jim (James Claude)	Senate/Congress	10	30		15	Rep. TX 1955, Speaker
Wright, John J., Cardinal	Clergy	40	75	95	70	
Wright, Luke E. 1846-922	Cabinet	15	45	90	35	Sec'y War 1908, Ambass. Japan
Wright, Marcus J. 1831-1922	Civil War	125	160	160		CSA Gen. Sig/Rank $175
Wright, Orville & Wright, Wilbur	Aviation				12500	First Flight Pioneers
Wright, Orville 1871-1948	Aviation	614	1576	1750	2255	TLS/Historical Content $15,000
Wright, Richard	Author	70	225		375	Afro-Am. Suffering, Prejudice
Wright, Robin	Entertainment	10			35	
Wright, Silas, Jr. 1795-1847	Senate/Congress	20		75		Gen'l,Statesman, Gov. & Sen. NY
Wright, Teresa	Entertainment	30			60	AA
Wright, Turbutt 1741-1783	Revolutionary War	25	60	95		Continental Congress
Wright, Wilbur 1867-1912	Aviation	875	2595	8583	5950	Historic SP $12,500,TLS $15,000
Wrigley, Philip K.	Business	75	145	200	125	Wrigley Gum; Chicago Cubs
Wrigley, William, Jr.1861-1932	Business	165	350	285	145	Founder Wrigley Gum Mfg.
Wunderlich, Fritz	Entertainment	75			500	Opera
Wunsche, Max	Military	50			125	Hitler's Adj. WW II
Wyant, Alexander Helwig	Artist	85		350		ALS/Cont.$750
Wyatt, Jane	Entertainment	5			15	
Wyatt, Wendell	Congress	5	10		12	Rep. OR 1964
Wyeth, Andrew 1917-	Artist	225	450	919	1025	Eminent Am. Painter
Wyeth, Henriette	Artist	75	225			
Wyeth, Jamie	Artist	145	540	400	325	Orig. Ink Sketch Pig $550-$950
Wyeth, John A.	Medical Author	65		250		Noted Surgeon
Wyeth, N. C. 1882-1945	Artist	140	435	1338	850	Am. Illustrator & Painter
Wyler, Gretchen	Entertainment	5	6	15	15	
Wyler, William	Entertainment	30			97	3 Best Picture Acad. Awards
Wylie, Elinor	Author	60	95	285		Am. Poet, Novelist
Wylie, Philip	Author	15	30	95	25	Iconoclastic Author.
Wylie, Robert 1839-1877	Artist	45	150			
Wyllys, Samuel 1739-1823	Revolutionary War		28	43		Military. Sec'y State of CT
Wyman, Bill	Entertainment			495		Rolling Stones Bass Guiitar

The Sanders Price Guide to Autographs

NAME	CATEGORY	SIG	LS/DS	ALS	SP	Comment
Wyman, Jane	Entertainment	18	100	125	80	Pin-up S $40+
Wyman, Willard G.	Military	15	25	40	25	4 Star General WW II
Wymore, Patrice	Entertainment	6	9	15	15	
Wyndham, Charles, Sir 1837-1919	Entertainment	15	35	45	60	Br. Actor-Mgr, Physician Civil War
Wyndham, Mary, Lady	Entertainment	4	6	10	18	
Wynette, Tammy	Country Music	5			20	
Wynn, Ed	Entertainment	50	65	100	138	Special DS $350
Wynn, Keenan	Entertainment	25	30		45	
Wynter, Dana	Entertainment	6			15	
Wynyard, Dianna	Entertainment	5	6	15	25	Br. Leading Lady 30's-40's
Wysong, Forrest R.	Aviation	10	15	30	20	
Wyszynski, Stefan, Cardinal	Clergy	50	65	95	75	
Wythe, George 1726-1806	Revolutionary War	500	1238	3075		Signer. ALS/Cont.War dte. $7,500

Xenia, Alexandrova	Head of State	65		300		Russia

Yadin, Yigael	Science		55		85	War Hero.World Famous Archaelogist
Yalow, Rosalyn S.	Science	15	25	40	20	Nobel Medicine 1972
Yamaer, George	Celebrity	10	20	80	15	
Yamamoto, Isoroku, Adm.	Military	150	295	625	475	Pearl Harbor Attack, 12/7/1941
Yamanashi, Hanzo	Military	95	265			
Yamasaki, Minoru	Celebrity	10	25	60	20	
Yamashiro, Katsumari	Military	100			300	
Yamashita, Tomoyuki	Military	115	275	500	275	Jap. General. Hanged
Yang, Chen N.	Science	15	20	35	20	Nobel Physics 1957
Yang, Y. C.	Diplomat	10			20	Ambassador to Republic of Korea
Yankovic, Frank	Entertainment	4	4	9	10	
Yardbirds	Entertainment	325				The Set
Yarnell, Harry E.	Military	15	35		20	Adm. Fleet Commander
Yarnell, Lorine	Entertainment	3	3	6	6	Shields & Yarnell

The Sanders Price Guide to Autographs

NAME	CATEGORY	SIG	LS/DS	ALS	SP	Comment
Yarrow, Ernest A.	Clergy	15	20	25		
Yates, Edmund 1831-94	Author	4	10	25		Br. Journalist-Novelist
Yates, Peter W. 1747-1826	Revolutionary War	30	120	175		Continental Congress
Yates, Richard 1815-73	Civil War	40	120	200		Civil War Governor IL 1861
Yaw, Ellen Beach	Entertainment	30			200	Am. Soprano
Yeager, Chuck 1923-	Aviation	45	45	85	92	Ace, WW II, Pioneer, Test Pilot, Broke Sound
Yeager, Jeana	Aviation	15	65		35	
Yeager, Jeana & Dick Rutan	Aviaton	75	75		125	Voyager
Yearwood, Trisha	Country Music	10			25	Singer
Yeates, Jasper 1745-1817	Revolutionary War	15	35	60		Jurist
Yeats, Jack Butler	Artist	25	60	150		Brother of Wm. Butler Yeats
Yeats, Wm. Butler 1865-1939	Author	200	600	908		Nobel Poet, Dramatist;Abbey Theatre
Yeltsin, Boris	Head of State	750	1350			Russia
Yen, C.K.	Head of State	50	175			Pres. Republic China
Yerby, Frank G.	Author	35	80	165	40	Afro-Am. Novelist
Yerkes, Charles T.	Business	35	100			Capitalist. TLS/Content $450
Yes	Entertainment	40			80	
Yo Yo Ma	Entertainment	20			125	Concert Cellist
Yogananda, Paramhansa	Religious (Yoga)			495		
Yokum, Dwight	Country Music	10			25	
Yon, Pietro A. 1886-1943	Composer					Ital-Am. Gesu Bambino AMusQS $195
Yorgesson, Yogi	Country Music	10			20	
York, Alvin, Sgt. 1887-1964	Military	275	340	700	425	MOH WW I
York, Dick	Entertainment	25			50	
York, Michael	Entertainment	8	10	20	20	
York, Susanna	Entertainment	6	8	15	20	
Yorty, Sam	Political	5	10		10	Rep. CA, Mayor L.A.
Youmans, Vincent	Composer	55	165	255	150	Tea for Two. MusMsS $800
Young, Alan	Entertainment	6	8	15	15	
Young, Andrew	Political	10	20	35	25	Afro-Am. Mayor Atlanta
Young, Ann Elizabeth	Celebrity	125				One of Brigham Young's Plural Wives
Young, Art*	Cartoonist	20			125	Political Cartoonist
Young, Brigham 1801-1877	Clergy	495	1775	4450	2778	Morman Leader. Rare DS $8500
Young, Burt	Entertainment	6			20	
Young, Charles Augustus	Science	35	140	225		Am. Astronomer, Author
Young, Chic* 1901-73	Cartoonist	35	60		200	Blondie
Young, Clara Kimball	Entertainment	40			75	Vintage Stage Actress
Young, Coleman	Political	5	15		20	Afro-Am. Mayor of Detroit
Young, David H.	Aviation	10	25		30	
Young, Dean	Cartoonist	25				Dagwood. Orig. Strip $275
Young, Faron	Country Music	10			30	deceased
Young, Gig	Entertainment	30	50	70	50	
Young, Henry E.	Civil War	25	45	70		CSA Major, Judge Advocate
Young, John	Astronaut	30			118	Moonwalker. Apollo 16, Shuttle Cmdr.
Young, John	Senate/Congress	15	25	45		Rep. NY 1836
Young, Lester	Entertainment	70	75	145	150	Jazz, Tenor Saxophone
Young, Loretta	Entertainment	20	15	25	81	
Young, Lyman*	Cartoonist	10			50	Tim Tyler's Luck
Young, Neil	Entertainment	15			45	Rolling Stones
Young, Owen D. 1874-1962	Business	15	25	50	20	CEO Gen. Electr.,Financier, Law
Young, Pierce M.B.1836-96	Civil War	80		300		CSA Gen.
Young, Robert	Entertainment	15	25	45	45	
Young, Roland	Entertainment	20			50	
Young, Samuel B.M.	Civil War	30	55	80		Union General Bvt.
Young, Sean	Entertainment	15			40	Pin-Up SP $35-70
Young, Thomas L. 1832-88	Congress	35				General, Gov OH

NAME	CATEGORY	SIG	LS/DS	ALS	SP	Comment
Young, Trummy	Entertainment	15			45	Jazz Musician
Young, Whitney	Activist	5	20	45	15	Am. Civil Rights Leader. Author
Youngdahl, Luther	Governor	5	15		10	Governor MN 1947
Younger, Bob	Outlaw	2500				Fought/Quantrill. Died in Prison
Younger, Cole (Thomas Coleman)	Civil War	2000	3350	4200		Served/Quantrill; Bank Robber
Youngman, Henny	Entertainment	6	8	15	15	
Ysaye, Eugene	Composer	30			225	Belg. Violin Virtuoso,Conductor
Yudenich, Nikolay N.	Military	95			175	Rus. Gen. Russo-Jap.& WW I
Yukawa, Hideki	Science	35	45	70		Nobel Physics 1949
Yulee, David Levy 1810-1886	Civil War	45		140		CSA Congress
Yun, Isang 1917-	Composer		80		150	Korean Born. Kidnapped by S. Korean Agents
Yung, Carl Gustav	Science	375	1710			Swiss Founder Analytical Psych.
Yung, Victor Sen	Entertainment	35			65	
Yunge, Traudl	Military	15			55	Hitler's Pers'l Sec'y End of WW II
Yurka, Blanche 1886-1974	Entertainment	30		75	45	Hamlet/Barrymore
Yutang, Lin (Lin Yutang)	Author	50	165			Chin. Novels,Philosophy,Plays

Zabach, Florian	Entertainment	5			20	
Zablocki, Clement John	Senate/Congress	5			20	Rep. WI 1949
Zabriskie, Andrew C.	Business	35		140		Capitalist, Financier
Zackerly	Entertainment	3			10	TV Horror Host
Zadora, Pia	Entertainment	5			15	Pin-Up SP $20
Zaharoff, Basil 1850-1936	Manufacturer				1495	Mystery Munitions Mfg. A Cause of WW I
Zahn, Timothy	Author	10			35	Star Wars Trilogy
Zais, Melvin	Military	10	20	35	15	
Zajic, Dolora	Entertainment	5			25	Opera
Zancanaro, Giorgio	Entertainment	10			30	Opera
Zandonai, Riccardo 1883-1944	Composer		60		195	Opera
Zane, Billy	Entertainment					Phantom Cast of $100+
Zangwill, Israel 1864-1926	Author	35	110	125	55	Br. Playwright, Novelist, Poet
Zanuck, Darryl F. 1902-79	Entertainment	50	300		75	Producer. Co-Founder 20th Century Fox
Zanuck, Richard Darryl	Entertainment	6	8	15	15	Film Producer, Exec.
Zapata, Emiliano 1879-1919	Revolutionary	500	1600	1625		Mex. Guerilla Leader
Zappa, Frank 1940-93	Entertainment	25			195	Composer, Guitarist
Zapruder, Abraham	Celebrity	40				Filmed JFK Assassination
Zavodszky, Zoltan	Entertainment	30			85	Opera
Zeani, Virginia	Entertainment	15			45	Opera
Zeeman, Pieter 1865-1943	Science			1000		Nobel for Physics
Zefferelli, Franco	Entertainment	10			25	Film Director
Zelenski, Wladyslaw	Composer	50		150		Polish Music Teacher
Zellerbach, James D	Business	15	40	85	35	US Ambassador, Industrialist
Zeman, Jacklyn	Author-Actress	5	8	15	10	Pin-Up $20
Zemekis, Robert	Entertainment	5	15		20	Film Director

NAME	CATEGORY	SIG	LS/DS	ALS	SP	Comment
Zemke, Hubert Hub	Aviation	15	35	65	40	ACE, WW II, Triple Ace
Zemlinsky, Alexander	Composer	90	265			Aus. Conductor
Zenatello, Giovanni	Entertainment	45			125	Opera
Zeppelin, Ferdinand von, Graf	Aviation	275	1098	1500	1035	Inventor Dirigible Air Ship
Zerbe, Anthony	Entertainment	10		25	25	
Zetland, 2nd Earl, Thos. Lawrence	Freemason					Master of the Freemasons NRPA
Zetterling, Mai	Entertainment	15			35	
Zhukov, Georgi K.	Military	80	200	500	325	Rus. Marshal. Soviet Hero WW II
Ziegfeld, Florenz 1869-1931	Entertainment	245	350	575	525	ALS/Content $950
Ziegler, George M.	Civil War	40	55	75		Union General, Bvt.
Ziegler, Karl	Science	45	85	170	55	Nobel Chemistry 1969
Ziegler, Ronald L.	White House	5	95	25	15	White House Aide. Nixon Press Sec'y
Ziegler, Vincent C.	Business	5			10	CEO Gillette Safety Razor Co.
Ziering, Ian	Entertainment				25	Actor. Beverly Hills 90210
Zimbalist, Efrem, Jr.	Entertainment	5	8		20	
Zimbalist, Efrem, Sr.	Entertainment	45			295	Violinist, Composer
Zimbalist, Stephanie	Entertainment	6	8	15	20	Pin-Up SP $30
Zimmer, Norma	Entertainment	3	5		15	
Zindel, Paul	Author	10	20		30	Playwright
Zinnemann, Fred	Entertainment	20		35	58	AA Film Director
Ziolkowski, Korczak	Artist	20	35	65	40	
Zmed, Adrian	Entertainment	5	6	15	15	
Zog I	Royalty	40			85	King Albania
Zola, Emile 1840-1902	Author	165	350	819	2070	Fr. Novelist & Social Reformer
Zollicoffer, Felix K. (War Date)	Civil War	575	1750			CSA Gen. KIA
Zollicoffer, Felix K.1812-62	Civil War	300	350	845		CSA General
Zorina, Vera	Entertainment	20			35	Ballerina, Films, Stage
Zuazo, Hernan Siles	Head of State	10	15	25	15	
Zucco, George	Entertainment	85			250	
Zukoffsky, Louis	Author	25		80	50	Am. Poet
Zukor, Adolph 1873-1976	Entertainment	50	145	200	120	Founder Paramount.Pioneer Film Producer
Zuloaga, Ignacio	Artist	25	75			Sp. Painter
Zumwalt, Elmo R., Jr.1920-	Military	15	125	125	55	Adm. WW II
Zweig, Arnold	Author	25	65		50	Ger. Novelist, Playwright
Zweig, Stefan	Author	30	90	195	45	Aus. Psychoanalytical Biogr.
Zweigert, Eugen, Lt.	Aviation	100			300	Ger. ACE WW II
Zwicky, Fritz	Science	20	35		45	Am. Astronomer. Jet Propulsion
Zworykin, Vladimir	Science	55	120	230	75	Am. Inventor TV System
ZZ Top	Entertainment	35			70	Rock group

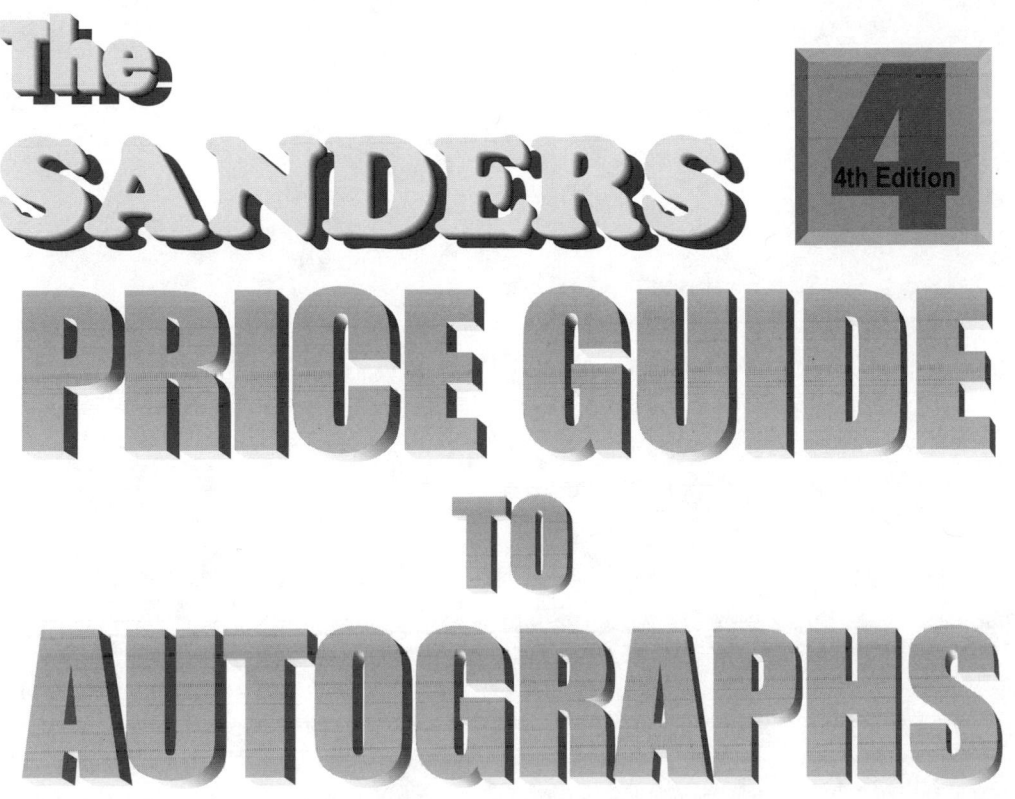

THE WORLD'S LEADING AUTOGRAPH PRICING AUTHORITY

Section III:
FACSIMILES

FACSIMILES

Anyone can sign John Wayne's name, and many do! A person of low morals might invest $2 in an 8x10 glossy of Wayne, sign it as Wayne, and sell it at a collectibles show for $35 or $40. If this unprincipled thief got a good deal on an assortment of Hollywood stars, he might come away with several hundred dollars from the pockets of unsuspecting autograph collectors. The trash they've bought is, of course, worthless!

Our best advice is to buy autographs only from reputable dealers (such as the ones advertising in this book). Yet, we all dream of finding that signed Greta Garbo photograph at the flea market for $5. It's good to dream but, how do you know what's authentic and what's just so much ink on paper? The answer is having known authentic examples of signatures available. These are called *facsimile signatures*. They are simply copies of real signatures of the celebrity. Compare your "find" to a known good sig and, if it matches, you're much more likely to have an authentic autograph!

The following pages are a good start to developing your own reference library of facsimiles. This book presents you with several thousand facsimiles known to be good. While our attorney screams if we try to say anything absolute (i.e. we make no warranties either express or implied), the sigs in this book are good to the best of our knowledge.

Use this book as a start in amassing a reference library of facsimiles. Enlarge the library with other facsimile books (we have a few of those in the works ourselves) and by keeping (*never* throwing away!) all the dealer catalogs you can find. Please write the dealers advertising in these pages, many of them put out most useful and interesting catalogs, chock full of facsimiles. Then when you

come across a questionable signature, a few minutes of browsing through your facsimile library can answer the question of authenticity by simple comparison with a known good example.

Which is not to say all of this is easy. Over the course of years, a person's signature changes with age and through other factors such as injury or just the technology of writing instruments. You'll want to accumulate, wherever possible, the facsimiles of an individual's autograph at differing ages.

There is no such thing as having too many facsimiles!

We hope these that follow prove helpful.

We were all young once! Here a 31-year-old Angela Lansbury(long before "Murder She Wrote") autographed a special copy of the movie premiere program of Paramount's "High Society" during George Sanders's 1956 broadcast around the world on the Armed Forces Television and Radio Network from Hollywood. George's long stint in broadcasting and the entertainment business means that he was able to meet and personally obtain the autographs of thousands of celebrities. This "in-person" knowledge is the basis of the authentic facsimiles in this book.

A

Bud Abbott

Red Adair

Ansel Adams

President John Adams

President John Quincy Adams

Maude Adams

Charles Addams

Jane Addams

Richard Adler

Louis Agassiz

Vice President Spiro T. Agnew

Edward Albee

Jack Albertson

Buzz Aldrin

Horatio Alger

Fred Allen

Roald Amundsen

Wally "Famous" Amos

General Robert Anderson

Jack Anderson

Marian Anderson

Maxwell Anderson

Maxine & Patty Andrews

Norman Angell

Walter H. Annenberg

Roscoe "Fatty" Arbuckle

Sir William Armstrong

President Chester A. Arthur

Isaac Asimov

Nils Asther

Lady Astor

Waldorf Astor

William Backhouse Astor

President David R. Atchison

Clement Attlee

Jacqueline Auriol

Gene Autry

B

Leo Hendriik Baekeland

F. Lee Bailey

Theodorus Bailey

Bernt Balchen

James Baldwin

Stanley Baldwin

Tallulah Bankhead

Michael A. Banks

John Bardeen

Vice President Alben William Barkley

Christian Barnard

P. T. Barnum

J. M. Barrie

Mona Barrie

Ethel Barrymore

Lionel Barrymore

Frederic Auguste Bartholdi

Freddie Bartholomew

Clara Barton

Bernard M. Baruch

P. G. T. Beauregard

Noah N. Beery

Menachem Begin

S. N. Behrman

Alexander Graham Bell

Ralph Bellamy

Saul Bellow

Peter Benchley

Your obedient servant,

Stephen Vincent Benet

Joan Bennett

Jack Benny

Ezra Taft Benson

Most sincerely,

Gertrude Berg

Gertrude Berg

Elizabeth Bergner

Irving Berlin

Sarah Bernhardt

Father Daniel Berrigan

Ken Berry

Josh Billings

Clarence Birdeye

Jussi Bjoerling

Hugo L. Black

Patrick M. S. Blackett

Harry A. Blackmun

Bud Blake

Eubie Blake

Mel Blanc

Major General Zenas Bliss

Herb Block

Guion S. Bluford Jr.

Eleanor Boardman

Niels Bohr

Ray Bolger

Louis Napoleon Bonaparte

Julian Bond

Pat Boone

Edwin Booth

Evangeline Booth

Norman E. Borlaug

Frank Borman

[signature]

Major Edward Bowes

[signature]

Bill "Hopalong Cassidy" Boyd

[signature]

Ray Bradbury

[signature]
General of the Army

Omar Bradley

[signature]

Louis D. Brandeis

[signature]

Dan Brandenstein

[signature]

Willy Brandt

[signature]

Karl Branting

[signature]

Bertolt Brecht

[signature]

John Cabell Breckinridge

[signature]

Justice William J. Brennan, Jr.

[signature]

Leonid I. Brezhnev

[signature]

David Brinkley

[signature]

W. E. Brock

[signature]

Clive Brook

[signature]

Rand Brooks

Joe E. Brown

Johnny Mack Brown

Dik Browne

Robert Browning

President James Buchanan

Pearl S. Buck

General D. C. Buell

David D. Buick

Ned Buntline

Luther Burbank

Justice Warren E. Burger

Billie Burke

William John Burns

General Ambrose E. Burnside

David Burpee

Aaron Burr

President George Bush

Vannever Bush

Francis Bushman

Major General Benjamin F. Butler

C

James Branch Cabell

James Cagney

Sammy Cahn

Erskine Caldwell

John Caldwell Calhoun

Melvin Calvin

Rod Cameron

Albert Camus

Milton Caniff

Yakima Canutt

Truman Capote

Al Capp

Mary Carlisle

King Juan Carlos

Hoagy Carmichael

Andrew Carnegie

Dale Carnegie

Scott Carpenter

John Carradine

Dr. Alexis Carrel

Sunset Carson

President Jimmy Carter

Enrico Caruso

George Washington Carver

Pablo Casals

Kellye Cash

Catherine II (The Great)

Bruce Catton

Whittaker Chambers

Coco Chanel

John Charles XIV

Cesar Chavez

Paddy Chayefsky

Gilbert Keith Chesterton

Maurice Chevalier

Walter P. Chrysler

Lady Clementine Churchill

Andre Citroen

Joe Clark

Mae Clarke

President Grover Cleveland

President Bill Clinton

Dewitt Clinton

Irvin S. Cobb

Major General Howell Cobb

Jacqueline Cochran

William F. "Buffalo Bill" Cody

Ronald Coleman

Vice President Schuyler Colfax

P.F. Collier

Jerry Colonna

Jackie Coogan

President Calvin Coolidge

Peter Cooper

General Samuel Cooper

Aaron Copeland

Jean Baptiste Camille Coret

"Wrong Way" Corrigan

Jacques Cousteau

(signature)

Joan Crawford

(signature)

Michael Crichton

(signature)

Dr. A. J. Cronin

(signature)

Bing Crosby

(signature)

E. E. Cummings

(signature)

Sir Samuel Cunard

(signature)

Charles Curtis

(signature)

Harvey W. Cushing

(signature)

Richard Cardinal Cushing

D

(signature)

Idi Amin Dada

(signature)

Richard J. Daley

(signature)

Vice President George M. Dallas

(signature)

Charles Darwin

(signature)

Marion Davies

(signature)

Richard Harding Davis

(signature)

Sir Humphry Davy

Charles G. Dawes

Dr. Lee de Forest

Charles de Gaulle

Geoffrey de Havilland

Alexander P. de Seversky

Dr. William DeVries

Dr. Michael DeBakey

John Deere

Delores Del Rio

Cecil B. de Mille

Thomas Dewey

Charles Dickens

Benjamin Disraeli

Dorothea Dix

James D. Dole

Abner Doubleday

Cordially yours,

Donald W. Douglas

Lloyd C. Douglas

William O. Douglas

Sir Arthur Conan Doyle

W. E. B. DuBois

Pierre S. Du Pont

Pierre S. Du Pont

Love 'n kisses,

JIMMY DURANTE
JD/lt

Jimmy Durante

E

Amelia Earhart

Jubal Early

George Eastman

Kevin Eastman

Abba Eban

Hugo Eckener

[signature]

Mary Baker Eddy

[signature]

Sir Anthony Eden

[signature]

Thomas A. Edison

[signature]

Albert Einstein

[signature]

Dwight D. Eisenhower

[signature]

Julie Nixon Eisenhower

[signature]

Mamie Doud Eisenhower

[signature]

T. S. Eliot

Queen Elizabeth II

[signature]

Ralph Waldo Emerson

[signature]

Charles Evers

 **F**

[signature]

John Eberhard Faber

[signature]

Vice President Charles Fairbanks

[signature]

Michael Faraday

[signature]

Diane Feinstein

[signature]
Edna Ferber

[signature]
Cyrus W. Field

[signature]
Eugene Field

[signature]
Marshall Field, Jr.

[signature]
President Millard Fillmore

[signature]
James Montgomery Flagg

[signature]
Father Flanagan

[signature]
Sir Alexander Fleming

[signature]
Errol Flynn

[signature]
Anthony Fokker

[signature]
Henry Fonda

[signature]
Malcolm Forbes

[signature]
Benson Ford

[signature]
Edsel B. Ford

[signature]
President Gerald R. Ford

[signature]
Henry Ford II

Henry Ford

E. M. Forster

Justice Felix Frankfurter

King Frederick VII

John Charles Fremont

Milton Friedman

David Frost

G

R. Buckminster Fuller

John Galsworthy

Indira Gandhi

Mahatma Gandhi

Greta Garbo

Ava Gardner

Erle Stanley Gardner

President James A. Garfield

Guiseppe Garibaldi

Vice President John Nance Garner

William Lloyd Garrison

Richard Gatling

King George I

Henry George

Elbridge Gerry

Ira Gershwin

J. Paul Getty

Charles Dana Gibson

A. C. Gilbert

John Gilbert

Allen Ginsberg

Lillian Gish

John A. Glenn, Jr.

Paulette Goddard

Arthur Godfrey

George W. Goethals

William Golding

Samuel Goldwyn

Samuel Gompers

Benny Goodman

Charles Goodyear, Jr.

Mikhail S. Gorbachev

Chester Gould

Betty Grable

Cary Grant

Ulysses S. Grant

Dave Graue

Horace Greeley

John Green

Zane Grey

Zane Grey

issued by the METROPOLITAN LIFE INSU
David Wark Griffith

David W. Griffith

Gus Grissom

Gus Grissom

Gilbert Grosvenor

Gilbert Grosvenor

Edgar Guest

Edgar Guest

Very sincerely yours,
Daniel Guggenheim

Daniel Guggenheim

Peggy Guggenheim

Paggy Guggenheim

Charles Guiteau

Charles Guiteau

H

H. Rider Haggard

Josephine Hall

Josephine Hall

Dr. Armand Hammer

Dr. Armand Hammer

Sincerely,
Oscar Hammerstein

Oscar Hammerstein

E. Y. Harburg

E. Y. "Yip" Harburg

Warren G. Harding Defendant

President Warren G. Harding

Oliver Hardy

Oliver Hardy

Thomas Hardy

Thomas Hardy

W. Averell Harriman

Joel Chandler Harris

President Benjamin Harrison

President William Henry Harrison

Johnny Hart

Moss Hart

William S. Harts

Paul Harvey

Prince Hassam

Brig General Joseph R. Hawley

Helen Hayes

President Rutherford B. Hayes

Susan Hayward

William Randolph Hearst

Edward Heath

Christie Hefner

Joseph Heller

Lillian Hellman

Henry III (old age)

Henry III (young)

Katharine Hepburn

Frank Herbert

Victor Herbert

Thor Heyerdahl

Sir Edmund Hillary

Alfred Hitchcock

Vice president Garret A. Hobart

William Holder

Oliver Wendell Holmes

Winslow Homer

Herbert Hoover

J. Edgar Hoover

Hedda Hopper

Harry Houdini

Major General Oliver Otis Howard

Julia Ward Howe

Victor Hugo

Hubert H. Humphrey

King Hussein

Will Hutchins

Aldous Huxley

I

Lee Iacocca

Henrik Ibsen

James B. Irwin

J

Andrew Jackson

Jesse Jackson [signature]

Jesse Jackson

Andrew Johnson [signature]

Andrew Johnson

Lyndon B. Johnson [signature]

Lyndon Baines Johnson

Richard Mentor Johnson [signature]

Richard Mentor Johnson

Quincy Jones [signature]

Quincy Jones

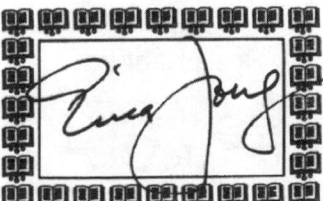

Erica Jong

Janis Joplin [signature]

Janis Joplin

Fibber McGee [signature]

Jim Jordan "Fibber McGee"

C. G. Jung. [signature]

C. G. Jung

K

Sincerely,

Henry J. Kaiser [signature]

Henry J. Kaiser

Henry J. Kaiser

Chiang Kai-Shek [signature]

Chiang Kai-Shek

Madame Chiang Kai-Shek [signature]

Madame Chiang Kai-Shek

Bob Kane

Boris Karloff

Bill Keane

Major General Philip Kearny

Buster Keaton

Carolyn Keene

Helen Keller

W. K. Kellogg

Emmett Kelly, Sr.

Grace Kelly

Arthur Kennedy

Ethel Kennedy

Sincerely yours,

John F. Kennedy

Joseph P. Kennedy

Rose Kennedy

Hank Ketcham

Cammie King

Coretta Scott King

Coretta Scott King

William R. King

William R. King

Lane Kirkland

Lane Kirkland

Sincerely, Calvin Klein

Calvin Klein

Werner Klemperer

Werner Klemperer

Evel Knievel

Evel Knievel

Henry Thatcher Knox

Henry Thatcher Knox

Ed Koch

Edward I Koch

Christopher C. Kraft

Christopher Kraft

Eugene Kranz

Eugene Kranz

Paul Kruger

Paul Kruger

Charles Kuralt

Charles Kuralt

L

Alan Ladd

Alan Ladd

Fiorello LaGuardia

Fiorello LaGuardia

Simon Lake

Simon Lake

Veronica Lake

Dorothy Lamour

Louis L'Amour

Bert Lance

Edwin Land

Ann Landers

Carole Landis

Alf Landon

Samuel Pierpont Langley

Lillie Langtry

Walter Lantz

Ring Lardner

Lash LaRue

Stan Laurel

Yves Saint Laurent

Ernest Lawrence

Gertrude Lawrence

Mary D. Leakey

Norman Lear

John leCarre

Anna Lee

Gypsy Rose Lee

Robert E. Lee

Dr. Willy Ley

Liberace

Trygve Lie

Beatrice Lillie

Abraham Lincoln

Robert Todd Lincoln

Jenny Lind

Charles Lindbergh

Joseph Lister

Franz Liszt

David Livingstone

Harold Lloyd

David Lloyd-George

Allan Lockheed

Gina Lollobrigida

Alice Roosevelt Longworth

King Louis VIII

King Louis Philippe

Bernard Lovell

James Russell Lowell

Clare Booth Luce

Henry R. Luce

Allen Ludden

Robert Ludlum

M

Marion Mack

Ted Mack

Archibald MacLeish

Dolley Madison

President James Madison

Ramon Magaysay

Norman Mailer

Bernard Malamud

Henry Mancini

Edouard Manet

Horace Mann

Thomas Mann

Mantovani

Gugelielmo Marconi

Ferdinand Marcos

Johnny Marks

Justice Thurgood Marshall

Hiram Percy Maxim

Glenn L. Martin

Louis B. Mayer

Groucho Marx

Dr. Charles W. Mayo

Harpo Marx

Dr. William Mayo

Zeppo Marx

Frederick L. Maytag

Raymond Massy

General George McClellan

Henri Matisse

Cyrus McCormick

W. Somerset Maugham

Colonel Tim McCoy

President William McKinley

Ray Milland

Aimee Semple McPherson

Arthur Miller

Margaret Mead

Henry Miller

General George Meade

Newton Minow

George Meany

Ed Mitchell

Adolphe Menjou

Tom Mix

Burgess Meredith

Walter F. Mondale

Ethel Merman

President James Monroe

Robert Moog

Russell Myers

Christopher Morley

N

Samuel F. B. Morse

Napoleon

Major John "the Gray Ghost" Mosby

Ogden Nash

Grandma Moses

Poli Neri

R.G. Mugabe

Edwin Newman

Rupert Murdock

Brigitte Nielsen

Edward R. Murrow

Story Musgrove

President Richard Nixon

John Ringling North

Lord North

Alfred Noyes

O

Hermann Oberth

Edmond O'Brien

Sandra Day O'Connor

Clifford Odets

Ransom E. Olds

Eugene O'Neill

Robert Oppenheimer

Baroness Orczy

P

David Packard

William S. Paley

John Dos Passos

Lester B. Pearson

Sir Robert Peel

J.C. Penney

George Plimpton

Svetlana Peters

President James K. Polk

Eugene Peugeot

Lily Pons

Slim Pickens

Admiral David Porter

Mary Pickford

Cole Porter

President Franklin Pierce

Katherine Anne Porter

J.S. Pillsbury

Marina Oswald Porter

Zasu Pitts

Emily Post

Ezra Pound

Dick Powell

Lewis Powell

Tyrone Power

Francis Gary Powers

Otto Preminger

Jackie Presser

Robert Preston

Andre Previn

John Profumo

Joseph Pulitzer

Melvin Purvis

Mario Puzo

Ernie Pyle

Howard Pyle

Q

Sally Rand

Col. Muammar el-Qaddfi

James Earl Ray

Dan Quayle

Ronald Reagan

Ellery Queen

William Rehnquist

Vidkun Quisling

Renek

R

Duncan Renaldo

Pierre Auguste Renoir

Prince Ranier

Judith A. Resnick

James B. Reston

Robert Reud

Walter Reuther

Richard Reynolds

Captain Eddie Rickenbacker

Leni Riefenstahl

James Whitcomb Riley

Robert Ripley

Jason Robards

Kenneth Roberts

Oral Roberts

Ralph Roberts

Happy Rockefeller

John D. Rockefeller, Jr.

Nelson Aldritch Rockefeller

Norman Rockwell

Richard Rodgers

Richard Rodgers

August Rodin

August Rodin

Ginger Rogers

Ginger Rogers

Charles S. Rolls

Charles S. Rolls

Sigmund Romberg

Sigmund Romberg

Stu Roosa

Stu Roosa

Franklin Roosevelt

Franklin Roosevelt

Theodore Roosevelt

Theodore Roosevelt

General William S. Rosecrans

General William S. Rosecrans

Jerry Rubin

Jerry Rubin

Arthur Rubenstein

Arthur Rubenstein

Sincerely yours,
Helena Rubenstein

Helena Rubenstein

CHARLIE RUGGLES

Charlie Ruggles

Damon Runyon

Damon Runyon

Bertrand Russell

Bertrand Russell

Lillian Russell

Lillian Russell

Dick Rutan

S

Rafael Sabatini

Dr. Albert B. Sabin

Pierre Salinger

Dr. Jonas Salk

George Sand

Carl Sandberg

David Sarnoff

Vidal Sassoon

Arthur Schlesinger

Charles Schulz

Charles Schwab

Randolph Scott

Sir Walter Scott

General Winfield Scott

Glenn Seaborg

Jean Seberg

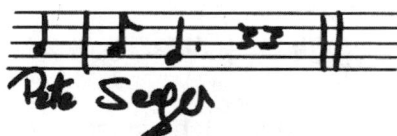

Pete Seeger

Andres Segovia

David O. Selznick

Mack Sennett

Rod Serling

Dr. Seuss

Sir Ernest Shackleton

George Bernard Shaw

Alan B. Shepard Jr.

Ann Sheridan

General Philip Sheridan

General W. T. Sherman

William Shockley

Maria Shriver

Phil Silvers

Georges Simenon

Neil Simon

Frank Sinatra

Harry F. Sinclair

Upton Sinclair

Isaac B. Singer

B. F. Skinner

Alfred P. Sloan

Alfred Smith

Kate Smith

Sir Charles Kingsford-Smith

Sir Thomas Sopwith

Ann Sothern

John Philip Sousa

F. Cardinal Spellman

Francis Cardinal Spellman

Elmer A. Sperry

Elmer A. Sperry

Mickey Spillane

Mickey Spillane

Ben Spock

Dr. Benjamin Spock

Edward R. Squibb

Edward Robinson Squibb

Lili St. Cyr

Lili St. Cyr

Henry M. Stanley

Sir Henry Stanley

Frank Stanton

Frank Stanton

Harold E. Stassen

Harold Stassen

John Steinbeck

John Steinbeck

Charles P. Steinmetz

Charles P. Steinmetz

Inger Stevens

Inger Stevens

Adlai E. Stevenson

Adlai E. Stevenson

James Stewart

James Stewart

Jimmy Stewart

Jimmy Stewart

Tempest Storm

Tempest Storm

Sincerely

Rex Stout

Igor Stravinsky

Ed Sullivan

Arthur Sullivan

T

William Howard Taft

Booth Tarkington

Zachary Taylor

Edward Teller

God bless you

Mother Teresa

Valentina Tereshkova

Studs Terkel

Nikola Tesla

Margaret Thatcher

Jeremy Thorpe

Etrangères
Yougoslavie,

Tito

Arnold J. Toynbee

George A. Trenholm

Gary Trudeau

Pierre Trudeau

Harry S. Truman

Donald Trump

Forest Tucker

Ted Turner

U

John Updike

Leon Uris

V

Rudy Vallee

James Van Allen

Martin Van Buren

S. S. Van Dine

Carl Van Doren

Mark Van Doren

Amy Vanderbilt

W

Cornelius Vanderbilt

George W. Vanderbilt

Jules Verne

Queen Victoria

Wernher von Braun

Erich Von Daniken

Alexander von Humboldt

Maria Von Trapp

Terry Walte

Kurt Waldheim

Lech Walesa

Agard Henry Wallace

Irving Wallace

Barbara Walters

Andy Warhol

Robert Penn Warren

Jessamyn West

George Washington

George Westinghouse

Harold Washington

James McNeil Whistler

Thomas Watson

Byron White

James Watt

Edward H. White

John Wayne

Theodore H. White

Charlie Weaver "Cliff Arquette"

Walt Whitman

Daniel Webster

Eli Whitney

Charles E. Whitaker

John Greenleaf Whittaker

Oscar Wilde

Thornton Wilder

Sincerely yours,

Wendell Wilkie

King WIlliam IV

Ben AMes Williams

Esther WIlliams

John Williams

Mason Williams

Paul Williams

Tennessee Williams

Meredith Willson

Henry Wilson

Woodrow Wilson

Walter Winchell

Owen Wister

Thomas Wolfe

Grant Wood

Natalie Wood

Orville Wright

Andrew Wyeth

Y

Charles E. "Chuck" Yeager

Jeana Yeager

Frank Yerby

Sgt. Alvin E. York

Brigham Young

Z

Ferdinand von Zeppelin

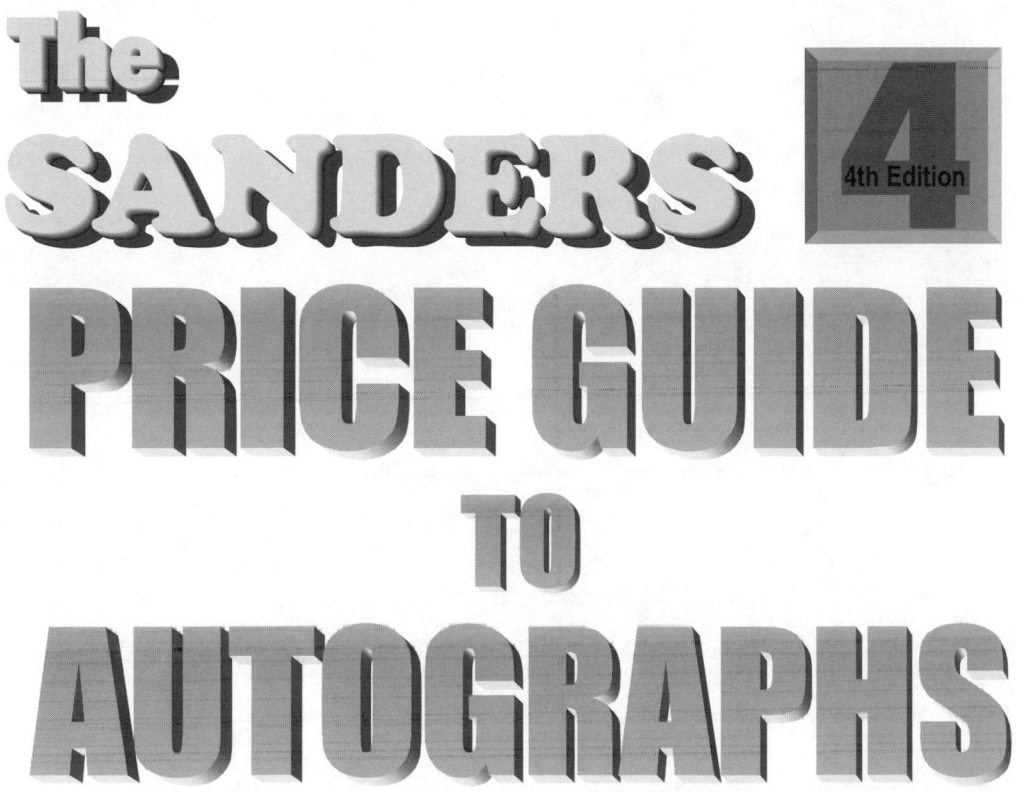

THE WORLD'S LEADING AUTOGRAPH PRICING AUTHORITY

Section IV:
BIBLIOGRAPHY

BIBLIOGRAPHY

I n the firm knowledge that you can never have *too much knowledge*, we offer you a list of recommeded reference sources. The more you know about autographs, the more fun this wondrous hobby returns to you!

Benjamin, Mary A. Autographs: A Key to Collecting, Privately Printed, 1963.

Berkley, Edmund Jr. Autographs and Manuscripts, Scribner's.

Burford, Thomas Celebrity Access - The Directory, 1996, Celebrity Access Publications

Cahoon, Herbert with Thomas V. Lange and Charles Ryskamp American Literary Autographs, 1977, Dover Publications.

Carr, Paul The Universal Autograph Collectors Club's Study of Machine Signed Signatures, UACC, 1989.

Hamilton, Charles American Autographs, U. of Oklahoma Press, 1983.

Hamilton, Charles Signatures of America, Harper & Row, 1977.

Hamilton, Charles, Collecting Autographs and Manuscripst, 1993, Modoc, Inc. Santa Monica, CA

Koschal, Stephen Collecting Books and Pamphlets Signed by the Presidents of the United States, Patriotic Publishers, 1982

Koschal, Stephen, The American Antiquarian, 1992, Compiled and Reprinted by Stephen Koschal

 **The Sanders Price Guide to Autographs**

Mashburn, J.L. The Artist-Signed Postcard Price Guide, 1993, WorldComm

Mashburn, J.L. The Postcard Price Guide (2nd Ed.), 1996, Colonial House

Patterson, Jerry E. Autographs: A Collectors Guide, Crown, 1973.

Raab, Susan and Steven Movie Star Autographs of the Golden Era, 1994, Steven S. Raab Autographs

Rawlins, Ray The Stein and Day Book of World Autographs, 1978.

Reese, Michael Autographs of the Confederacy, Cohasco Publishing, 1981.

Sanders, Sanders, & Roberts The Collector's Guide to Autographs, Wallace-Homestead, 1988.

Sullivan, George Making Money in Autographs, Coward, McCann & Geoghegan Inc., New York, 1977.

Taylor, John M. From the White House Inkwell, 1968, Charles E. Tuttle, Rutland, Vermont. (just reissued)

Vrzalik, Larry F. and Michael Minor, From the President's Pen, An Illustrated Guide to Presidential Autographs, State House Press 1990, $15.95.

Wittnebert, Al, Signatures of the Stars, 1988, UACC

Wittnebert, Al, The Study of Star Trek Autographs (2nd Ed.), 1994, UACC

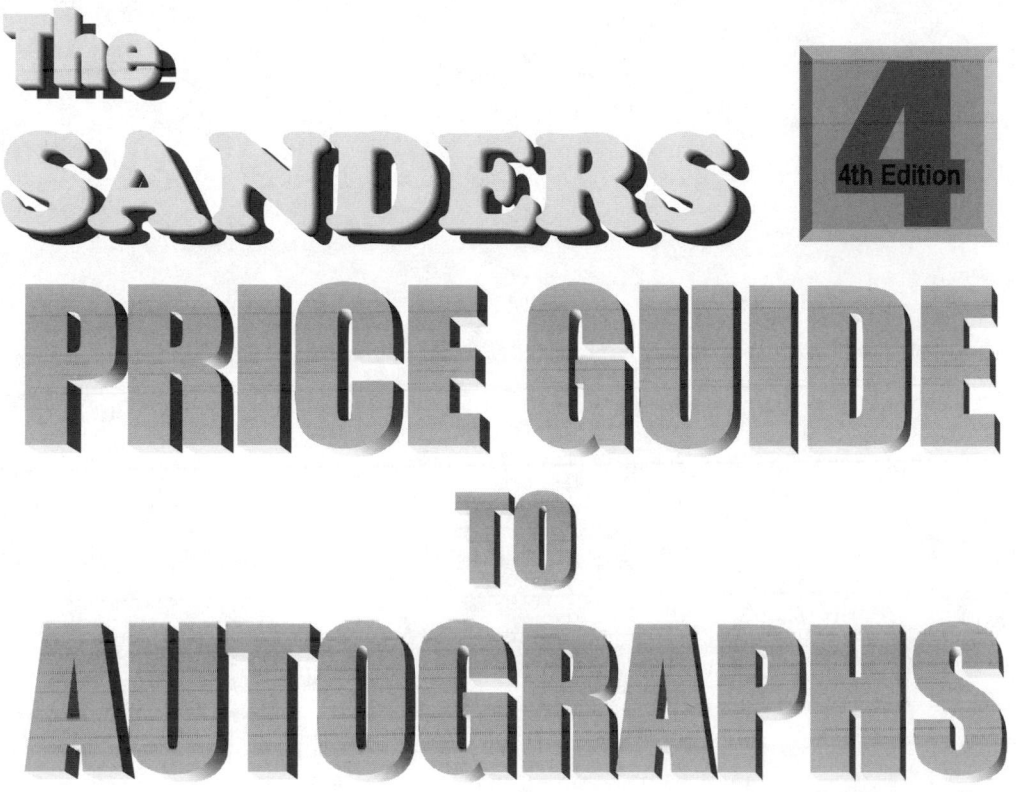

The SANDERS 4 4th Edition
PRICE GUIDE
TO
AUTOGRAPHS

THE WORLD'S LEADING AUTOGRAPH PRICING AUTHORITY

Section V:
DEALERS

DEALERS

This section contains an extensive Buyer's Guide representing many of the major dealers in the autograph world. While inclusion here does not per se mean we endorse a particular dealer over one not participating in this guide, it does mean we believe the dealers here to be reputable experts in their various areas of expertise. And—on the other hand—just because a dealer elected not to participate does not necessarily mean that he or she should be avoided. While we did refuse ads to a few unscrupulous rascals best avoided by the honest, we certainly make no blanket statement about those not advertising in this book.

However, we hasten to point out that the kind folks who *are* in this book deserve a great vote of thanks (and even a little business, perhaps) from all of us, authors and readers alike. They made this huge book practical and allowed us to both add much more than otherwise would have been possible, and to keep the retail price down to a most reasonable $24.95. Believe us, the printing bill on this tome is immense, please at least say "thank you" to our wonderful advertisers.

Index to Dealers

Visit us on the web at **http://www.autograph-book.com**

TODD MUELLER AUTOGRAPHS

Specializing in everything from Abraham Lincoln to Brad Pitt. Over 40,000 items in inventory. I am a member of the Manuscript Society, Creator of the "Golf's Greatest" Card set, and author of "Addresses of the Famous and More".

To order my latest edition of "Addresses of the Famous and More" which contains over 11,000 addresses send; $26.95 + $3.00 for P/H

Get on my mailing list for only $5.00 and you will get my next 4 catalog's and be aware of my monthly auctions, quarterly catalog's and be informed on all the exclusive private signings I am involved in from Rosa Parks to Bettie Page.

Bettie Page 8X10 B&W Photos signed $95.00
Bettie Page 11X14 Nude Bunny Yeager photographs signed exclusively for me $150.00

TODD MUELLER AUTOGRAPHS
P.O. BOX 701182
DALLAS, TX 75370-1182
(214) 385-0055

AUTOGRAPH OUTLET

Plug in to Electrifying Values

Susan Sanders
Wadopian
3 Ellenwood Drive
Asheville, NC 28804
(704) 253-5202

For free catalog,
send SASE

*Autograph Letters · Manuscripts · Historical Documents
Purchased and Sold · Major Auctions*

J.A.STARGARDT

Established 1830 in Berlin
Since 1885 property of the Mecklenburg family

At our special autograph sales, held once a year, we offer about 1700 lots from
the fields of Literature, Science, Fine Arts, Music, Theatre, and History.
Please write or call for our illustrated auction and stock catalogs.

J.A.STARGARDT · Clausewitzstrasse 4 · D-10629 Berlin
Tel +49 30-882 25 42 · Fax +49 30-882 24 66

RICHARD GALASSO
APPRAISER
DOCUMENT EXAMINER

Richard Galasso is one of the nation's leading appraisers of American manuscripts. He is widely regarded as the country's premier Board Certified Forensic Examiner of American autographs.

Mr. Galasso's services are utilized by law enforcement officials, major auction houses, forensic examiners and thousands of discriminating dealers and collectors of North America. Frequently he is interviewed and quoted by the New York Times, the New York Daily News and the Boston Globe.

Forgers and proxy signers have become prolific. Whether it is a George Washington autographed letter, a Babe Ruth autographed photograph or an entire manuscript collection, acquire the documentation that will stand the test of time.

CALL FOR A FREE CONSULTATION

RICHARD GALASSO, BCFE
273 Pascack Rd., Suite 484. Washington Township, NJ 07675
201-358-1670 ◆ Fax 201-358-2338

SAFKA & BAREIS AUTOGRAPHS
The leading dealers in performing arts

Finest quality autographed photos, letters, documents, programs, & signatures in all categories, specializing in movies, music, opera, ballet, & theater. Signed and unsigned photos by Bull, Hurrell, Willinger, Mishkin, Dupont, Nadar, Falk, & Sarony. Affordable prices. Call or write for catalogue. We buy single items or whole collections.

P.O. Box 886 Forest Hills, NY 11375
Phone & Fax (718) 263-2276

Member: Antiquarian Booksellers' Association of America; Professional Autograph Dealers' Association; Manuscript Society; UACC.

SEAPORT AUTOGRAPHS
6 BRANDON LANE
MYSTIC, CONNECTICUT 06355
(860) 572-8441
WE ARE THE OLDEST AND LARGEST DEALER IN CONNECTICUT
****

Historical autographs including Colonial America, Civil War, American Revolution, artists, authors, presidents, statesmen, musicians, religious leaders, other distinguished Americans and well as foreign dignitaries.
****

FREE CATALOGUES ISSUED
****

We are always interested in buying fine material.

Member: Professional Autograph Dealers Association, Manuscript Society, UACC

MAX RAMBOD
Your Expert Source
for Autographs

Your expert source for autographs, documents and signed photos of: *U.S. Presidents, Civil War , Entertainers, Authors, Aviators, Scientists, Artists, Military, Astronauts and Historical Figures* from all around the world.

We offer you a lifetime guarantee of authenticity on all your purchases. Let us help you find the autographs you want from our large selection. We are always interested in purchasing *your* quality autographs. Please contact us for a premium price. **Call us for an illustrated catalog**.

MAX RAMBOD Autographs
9903 Santa Monica Blvd, Ste. 371
Beverly Hills, CA. 90212
Phone: 310-475-4535 Fax: 310-475-9484

Member: UACC
The Manuscript Society

CATHERINE BARNES
Autographs & Signed Books

Fine Autographs in American & European History, Science, Finance, & the Arts

I BUY AUTOGRAPHS,
ranging from single items to partial or whole collections.
Please call or write for a prompt and fair offer!

AUTOGRAPHS FOR SALE
Sample catalogue sent on request

2031 Walnut Street, Suite 305, Philadelphia, PA 19103
Mailing Address: P.O. Box 30117-G, Philadelphia, PA 19103

Tel: 215-854-0175   Fax: 215-854-0831

Established 1985

Member: Professional Autograph Dealers Association;
Antiquarian Booksellers Association of America; Manuscript Society; UACC

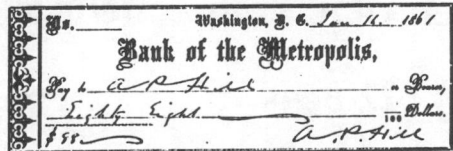

Bring Your Valuable
Autographs, Letters & Documents
to the
Marketplace

Signature House

Find out what your autograph will bring in our auctions. You will get a "square deal" at *Signature House*. Write, phone or fax for details.

Consignments are accepted in all fields. At no charge to you, we will tell you what you can expect, when you can expect it and give you information on how to do it. Bidders at our auctions get a free catalog. We also buy your autographs, letters, documents and entire collections. Call us to discuss what is best for you.

Gil & Karen Griggs

2212 Corbett Road, Monkton, MD 21111

Phone: 410-472-3448   Fax: 410-472-2580

Call Today!

"In the Beginning Was the Word..."

DAVID SCHULSON
AUTOGRAPHS

HISTORICAL AUTOGRAPHS
Letters
Documents
Manuscripts & Photographs

Specializing in fine quality American and European science, art, literature, music, cinema, photography, and history.

We are always interested in purchasing autographs from single items to collections.

**DAVID SCHULSON
AUTOGRAPHS
11 East 68th Street
New York, New York 10021
(212) 517-8300
(212) 517-2014 (fax)**

Catalogs Issued Regularly

for Your Postcard Library

Soft Cover - $19.95
6 x 9 - 352 pages
ISBN 1-885940-02-5

Soft Cover - $16.95
6 x 9 - 464 pages
ISBN 1-885940-00-9

Soft Cover - $19.95
6 x 9 - 352 pages
ISBN 1-885940-01-7

Available at Bookstores and Book Wholesalers.

When ordering from Colonial House, add $2.50 P&H for first book; $1.50 for each additional.

COLONIAL HOUSE PUBLISHERS

P. O. Box 609, Enka, North Carolina 28728 U.S.A.
Phone: (704) 667-1427 • Fax: (704) 667-1111

Email: JMashb0135@aol.com • Web Site: http://www.postcard-books.com

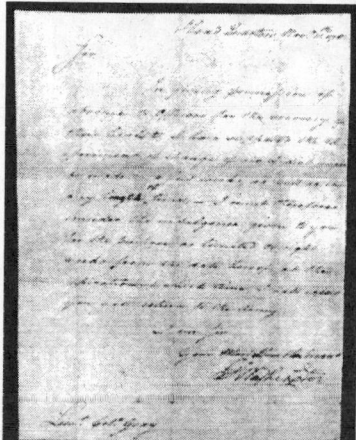

George Washington

Babe Ruth

Irving Berlin

What do these people have in common?

John F Kennedy

George Bernard Shaw

596

602

ADS AUTOGRAPHS

AUTHORS - ARTISTS - SCIENTISTS
COMPOSERS - U.S. HISTORICAL

Member

Free catalogs issued

Established 1983

Joseph R. Sakmyster   P.O. Box 8006
Webster, New York 14580-8006
Tel: (716) 671-2651
Fax: (716) 671-2651

PROFESSIONAL AUTOGRAPH DEALERS ASSOCIATION, INC.

Founded in 1995 by many of the nation's leading dealers, PADA is now the largest organization of sellers of historical material. All members provide a lifetime guarantee of authenticity and are bound by a strict code of professional ethics. For a free directory of PADA members and an informational brochure on collecting historical autographs, please write:

PADA, P.O. Box 1729, Murray Hill Station, NY 10156
or call toll free: 888 338–4338
Visit our web site at: http://www.padaweb.org

PADA

For the only guarantee you will ever need, look for our logo

605

607

ALEXANDER Books

Founded 332 B.C.

a division of Creativity, Inc.

65 Macedonia Road
Alexander, NC 28701 USA
(704) 255-8719

Founded in 332 B.C. by world conqueror Alexander the Great, the city of Alexandria was for hundreds of years the world's foremost repository of knowledge. The lighthouse of Pharos—one of the Seven Wonders of the Ancient World—was a symbol of this citadel of learning; its beacon light could be seen for 40 miles out across the Mediterranean sea.

The lighthouse—over 440 feet or 36 stories high—stood for some 1600 years. It was the first of its kind and furnished the model for the earliest church spires and also for the minarets of the Mohammedan mosques. It fell in 1326 A.D.

But the true eternal monument of Alexandria was the fabulous Alexandrian Library. Although there had been libraries before in the world, this one far surpassed all others, eventually housing over 700,000 volumes. The art of cataloging and managing such a huge collection was new. The first Chief Librarian was Zenodotus of Ephesus, but the first catalogue of the library was done by the poet and philosopher Callimachus. He listed all the known books of value—by titles and by authors. This first great book catalogue filled over 120 books itself.

Alexander Books of Alexander, North Carolina, is a continuation of the *spirit* of the Alexandrian Library. The thirst for the collection and dissemination of knowledge that guided Zenodotus of Ephesus and the other Chief Librarians is also ours. We exist to publish worthwhile and interesting books in the heritage of our founders circa 332 B.C.

We are always looking for good books. Send us yours!

ALEXANDER BOOKS, 65 Macedonia Road, Alexander, NC 28701
(704) 252-9515, fax (704) 255-8719

600